Lust Unearthed

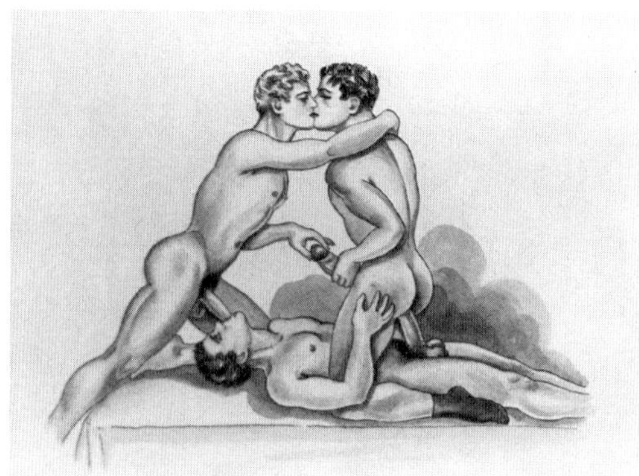

LUST UNEARTHED

Vintage Gay Graphics From the DuBek Collecton

By

THOMAS WAUGH

WITH WILLIE WALKER

ARSENAL PULP PRESS

VANCOUVER

2nd printing: 2009

ARSENAL PULP PRESS
Suite 200, 341 Water Street
Vancouver, BC
V6B 1B8
arsenalpulp.com

The publisher gratefully acknowledges the support of the Canada Council for the Arts and the British Columbia Arts Council for its publishing program, and the Government of Canada through the Book Publishing Industry Development Program for its publishing activities.

Design by Robert Ballantyne
Cover illustration by "Bellhops"
Printed and bound in Canada

Library and Archives Canada Cataloguing in Publication

Waugh, Thomas, 1948-

Lust Unearthed: Vintage Gay Graphics from the DuBek Collection / Thomas Waugh ; with Willie Walker.
Over 200 images from the collection of Ambrose DuBek, which was donated to the Gay, Lesbian, Bisexual, Transgender Historical Society.

Includes index.

ISBN 978-1-55152-165-7
1. Gay erotic art. 2. Gay men in art. 3. Erotic drawing. 4. DuBek, Ambrose—Art collections. I. Walker, Willie II. DuBek, Ambrose III. Gay, Lesbian, Bisexual and Transgender Historical Society IV. Title.

N8217.H67W375 2004 743'.928 C2004-902950-9

Frontispiece illustration: Jean Vincent, date unknown.
Page 319 illustration: Unknown artist, c. 1960.

CONTENTS

FOR WALKER, IN LOVING MEMORY

Acknowledgments

The artists, living and dead, anonymous and known, are above all responsible for this book, and Walker and I would like to acknowledge our great indebtedness to their lust and the raw beauty of their work.

Also to Ambrose DuBek's loyal and unforgetting friends and associates, who were unstinting of their logistical assistance, memories, vision, and generosity, Anddrew B. Alder, Gus Head, Ned Kell, Buddy McCarthy, executor David Schlemmel and facilitator Bud Flounders, as well as DuBek's surviving partner, who has requested that his identity be withheld.

To the Social Science and Humanities Research Council of Canada as well as Concordia University for their longstanding support of my research in sexual representation.

For their sharp eyes, solid shoulders and open hearts, to my Montreal and Concordia pals Sarah and Cris Brunetti, Jason Garrison, Marcus Skidley Greatheart, Ross Higgins, Steve Kokker, Simon Laroche, and my research assistant Tim Lawrence.

To pioneer artists and facilitators Felix Lance Falkon, David Lehman, and Charles Renslow for their gracious input.

Also to San Francisco stalwarts John Fagundes, Bob Mainardi, and Trent Dunphy for their friendship, support and expertise.

For their knowledge generously shared, to experts Nicole Canet of "Galerie Au Bonheur du Jour," Paris (*www.curiositel.com/aubonheurdujour/default.htm*); "Drummer;" Louis Godbout; Paul Jackson; Gayle Rubin; Justin Spring; and Jonathan Weinberg.

To the Gay Lesbian Bisexual Transgender Historical Society (San Francisco) for their generous institutional support to this initiative to share their treasure; to its individual officers Daniel Bao, Kim Klausner, Jacob Richards, and Susan Stryker for their indispensable contribution to getting this project off the road and seeing it through to fruition; and to sharp-eyed Gerard Koskovich for help with filling in gaps and suggesting corrections for the second printing.

To Robert Ballantyne, Brian Lam, scanner David Clausen, and the entire Arsenal Pulp family for their commitment and miracles.

Above all, to Willie Walker indefatigable archivist, collector, cataloguer, and visionary, as well as champion of the right to desire.

T.W.

Introduction: The Pleasures and Politics of *Lust*

Unearthing *Lust*

Where on earth did this lustful volume devoted to the treasure trove of explicit underground graphics from before Stonewall, collected by New York film and television art designer and gay bon vivant Ambrose DuBek (1916-2002), come from?

My last book, *Out/Lines: Underground Gay Graphics from Before Stonewall*, brought out by my friends at Arsenal Pulp in 2002, was the most "successful" I've ever written. It surpassed by far, in terms of copies printed and sold and modest income generated, the other three books that I'd written since the 1980s for scholarly presses. Nominated for a Lambda Literary Award in Visual Arts, I was even a little more gratified by an Honorable Mention citation for the Gustavus Myers Book Awards, from the Center for the Study of Bigotry and Human Rights (Boston), an organization I'd been unaware of. And, as I write this at the end of a sultry July 2004, *Out/Lines* had an Amazon.com sales rank of 261,741, whatever that means. I am humbled by this success, since I know that it was not my pontifical musings, but rather those naughty drawings that sold the book, despite—or perhaps even *because* of—their often misty reproduction from ragged and thumbworn duplicates. I wish I could thank those artists, mostly dead and unknown, for the immense satisfaction that I experienced in birthing that collection of their work and pushing it out into the world. But there is enough of the Protestant work ethic and attendant sexual guilt in me to be also a little embarrassed that the book which was the easiest, fastest, and most fun to write should have been the most "successful," and that those earlier ones which emerged from so much blood, sweat, and tears should have been less "successful" than the one which emerged from, well, other bodily fluids.

Success, of course, is relative. Like many authors, especially other academics who never expect to make a profit from their research—let alone break even—I value reader and critic response as much as I do sales figures. Immensely important are the verdicts from critics, both scholarly and community-based, whether I have indeed contributed to knowledge or history or community, and the sense from readers that something, sometimes inarticulate, has moved them. On that latter score, I will never forget the little envelope I received from a

West Coast woman (transgendered, if I am reading between the lines correctly), who enclosed several of her own lovely "post-coital" "romantic" drawings, as well as an invitation to sample some of her wares at her chocolate boutique the next time I'm in town.

But a letter that touched me even more was the one written in a slightly shaky seventy-something hand that claimed authorship of perhaps the most intriguing series of anonymous pictures in *Out/Lines*. Figures 140-143 of that book were a selection taken from a larger cluster of images delineating a rough S/M scene. A sweating and hunky blond sailor is being given the works—including titclamps, ballweights, a wooden paddle, a collarstrap, plus a good piss dousing—by a rather nasty-looking gang of leather and denim tops, two white men and one black man with dynamite abs and a particularly fierce grimace. "Small world!" David wrote, adding that he had produced the pictures in 1964 at the tender age of thirty-three, that he hadn't seen them since, that they were hard to recognize I'd reduced the scale so much, and that, by the way, they were not his best work. But the palpable feeling of recognition, surprise, pride, and pleasure in his letter made the whole enterprise worthwhile and constituted for me the real meaning of success as a writer and cultural historian. I will maintain my correspondent David's confidentiality here, though when I subsequently telephoned and got through to the mid-Atlantic interior decorator (not without some kibitzing from his ribald lover in the background), he authorized me to reveal his identity in the upcoming reissue of *Out/Lines*.

My publisher and editor, Brian and Robert, shared these small joys with me, but they of course have other, slightly different, definitions of success as well. When another reader informed me that pirate copies of *Out/Lines* illustrations were everywhere on the net, I was secretly gratified. Though my publishers must have seen dollar bills flying away, my head was temporarily distracted by theoretical thoughts comparing the gay photo print underground of the forties and fifties with the transgressive queer cyber underground of the new century. In any case, my publishers, like all non-academic and commercial publishers, no doubt have many criteria for "success" other than a certain bottom line of the sales figures necessary for staying afloat—from awards recognition to local community political impact (for example, on Vancouver's lively anti-censorship fronts). One of these must have kicked in, for their proposition to me was, How about a sequel? Well, like David's sweaty blond sailor, I am a glutton for punishment (as well as a serious workaholic) and needed another book project like that sailor needed another paddle whack and immediately said yes. Instantly in the back of my mind a follow-up project crystallized.

One of my major collaborators for *Out/Lines* had been Willie Walker, the San Francisco archivist who in 1986 had been one of the founders of the queer community archives that is one of the richest in the world (though not in the cash flow sense): San Francisco's Gay Lesbian Bisexual Transgender Historical Society. The GLBTHS had been a major institutional source for my *Out/Lines* pictures—almost twenty of them—and Walker had been my major local contact person as well as host, inspiration, and co-conspirator. He was struggling with a life-threatening illness throughout the preparation of the book, but all the same never knew when to take a breather. His enthusiasm and humor, despite his evident pain, as well as his frustration with both his body and the U.S. medical system (neither of which would cooperate) was such an inspiration to me that I dedicated *Out/Lines* to him and to "archivists, collectors, fanatics, and lechers everywhere."

Well enough, but Walker was also causing a lot of trouble. Even as the book went to press, new e-mails were coming in daily from this incorrigible aficionado of both history and smut, suggesting this or that addition or replacement. One startling piece of news was that a humungous new collection of materials had just come into the archives; worse, there was the growing intimation that this new acquisition was chockful of images that were part of my pre-Stonewall underground filthy graphics corpus; worse still, they were in much better condition in many cases than the fragmentary and blurred treasures that I was reprinting for posterity at that very moment, and often in complete sets. This new bequest had belonged to one Ambrose DuBek, just dead at the age of eighty-six (see Walker's biography of this great humanist collector queen below), and as if to torture and titillate me even more, we were able to cajole one beautiful treasure out of that collection for the book even as the bequest was being catalogued (a strict no-no in archive-land): the quietly enigmatic, apparently Japanese drawing of an impassive threesome and an unfulfilled bottom waiting for his turn, his ass in the air, in that book's Figure 154.

So when Arsenal Pulp suggested the sequel, I knew what it had to be: visions danced through my head of the ravishing and sharp treasures of the DuBek collection spread out on facing pages of a fine book. Walker agreed to be intermediary with the Archives and collaborator, and although his health continued to decline, things went into motion, with the final result being the book you are holding in your hands. Walker helped me with the selection via e-mail and a whirlwind on-site visit in the fall of 2003. He had been doggedly determined to be present for the launch of the book that in many ways started as his persistent harassment and the gleam in his sharp, concupiscent eye. But a few days before we went to press in September 2004, Walker pulled another fast one and opted for another launch, the big one.

COLLECTING *LUST*

Walker had already eagerly taken on the job of cataloguing the DuBek collection for the GLBTHS, and this was a monumental accomplishment, finally completed in August 2003. Donated by DuBek's executor Steve Schlemmel with the help of fellow Phoenixite Bud Flounders and with the authorization of DuBek's surviving partner, the collection was housed in almost fifty large document boxes that took up over twenty linear feet on the Archives' metal shelves. (How this truckload ever fit into DuBek's two-bedroom retirement apartment is one of the great wonders of the queer world that his executor Steve Schemmel has still not figured out.) Entirely focused on erotica, mostly gay male but also including minor elements devoted to heterosexual and "bisexual" eroticism, the materials were organized into five series: Original Art, Photographs, Magazines, Books, and Moving Images. The selection for *Lust Unearthed* comes wholly from the first two series. The "Original Art" choices consist entirely of drawings by Dom Orejudos ("Etienne," Figures 63, 180-198), while the remaining 220 or so items in the present selection come from the series "Photographs," gathered largely over forty years between the 1930s and the 1970s. These items are technically photographs because, as discussed in *Out/Lines*, most of the "obscene" artwork circulating in the pre-Stonewall underground did so as small photographic copies of original drawings, paintings or graphics, for technological, logistical, and economic reasons—but also out of strategic and political necessity. In addition to the mammoth collection of hundreds of these small erotic photographs of graphics, the series also includes more documentary photos of sexual activities among men in leather, mostly bondage and S/M. Because of our choice to focus entirely on graphics, only two glimpses of this documentary material are included in *Lust Unearthed*, namely, Figures 65-66, photographs (perhaps by DuBek himself?) of a large mural (graphics, after all . . .) that apparently adorned a leather hangout, probably in Manhattan, in the early 1950s.

The "Magazines" series, gathered by the collector between 1937 and the 1990s, consisted of eighty-five volumes, which DuBek regularly had fastidiously bound for safekeeping over those years. Most of the magazines come from the 1960s and early 1970s, the period of the large-scale emergence of gay male erotic culture above ground. Each volume holds up to fourteen titles, but they are apparently organized in order of acquisition rather than more standard principles of cataloguing, so a given volume might contain ten different magazines received roughly at the same time. Volume 1, for example, contains an issue each of the following specialized, um, "scholarly" periodicals from the 1960s: *American Male Showcase, Beach Adonis, Boys, Continentals, Demi-Gods, Jr Special, Modern Male, Muscle Teens, Muscleboy, Teen Torso, Tomorrow's Man, Young Guys,* and *Young Physique.* In general, the magazines range from the discreet and closety physique magazines originating in the early 1950s, like *Tomorrow's Man,* to the rather more forthright and, er, specialized magazines of a later post-Stonewall age and sensibility, such as *Crisco Kids.*

The "Books" series, eight large cartons which include volumes dating as early as 1932 and accumulating until the 1990s, emphasizes what might now be called "coffee table books," tony or pseudo-tony tomes on the nude and eroticism, mostly male but also hetero, bi, and lesbian in orientation. These range from *On Going Naked,* by "Jan Gay" (Garden City Publishing, Garden City, NY, 1932) to *The Private Erotic Art of Duncan Grant, 1885-1978* (London: Gay Men's Press, 1989). The fifth and final series, "Moving Images," comprises six boxes of films, containing over 120 8mm reels, ranging from early 1940s stags and 1950s Scandinavian treats to 1960s American pseudo-nudist pseudo-documentaries and minor 1970s hardcore treasures such as *Cadets on a Waterbed.* There are also three boxes containing almost thirty video cassettes of a predictable content, all acquired in the 1980s, with titles like *Surfer Sex* (1983).

No doubt the DuBek collection is typical of a score of other large personal gay collections that have come to light over the last generation and have come to rest in community or public archives. Such collections reflect the personal tastes, eccentricities, and obsessions of the collectors, their individual resources and situations as well as their geographical and cultural contexts (See "Ambrose DuBek, the Man," page 33). Stamped all over the DuBek collection is the collector's positioning within the ghetto-like networks of the cultural industries and gay artistic circles of the American metropolis in the postwar period—his collection somehow has that distinctive Manhattan style—as well as his personal wealth and mobility (he made frequent visits to Europe over his career, had a special fondness for Amsterdam, and obviously made many purchases on the Continent). From his World War II military connections to his personal charm and sociability, his personal history and disposition are all palpable in the collection as well as in the samples of personal photos assembled as Figures 1, 2, and 3.

The collection also reflects a certain contradictory negotiation of public and private domains in DuBek's life, an even schizophrenic status as legally closeted in the era of both the criminalization of sodomy and McCarthyism. DuBek's employer was the television network CBS, which was redbaited by the anti-Communist witchhunters in the early 1950s and pushed into damage control mode when two of its biggest stars, Lucille Ball and Ed Sullivan, were briefly scraped by the mounting hysteria; as a result, it required all its employees to sign a loyalty oath and became the most compliant and "most easily intimidated of all networks" (Kanfer 1973, 122, 232). Even though he was well protected by his friendship with the boss, DuBek, like all homosexuals employed high up in the media, public service, and educational institutions, must have watched carefully as queers got caught up in the security panic and lost their livelihoods (D'Emilio and Freedman, 1988, 292-94). At the same time, DuBek was selectively but flamboyantly "out" in his arts-related vocation and among upper-class gays who were largely insulated from social stigma and legal persecution by their status (volleyball with Noel Coward on Fire Island, anyone?). As with many necessarily secret collectors of risky materials, DuBek's collecting was neither shaped by professional archival or curatorial training, nor sanctioned by public prestige (no TV crews were led on a tour of his Tom of Finland collection for a 1960s version of *Lifestyles of the Rich and Famous*). His acquisitions were both discriminating and indiscriminate at the same time, reckless and coy, cultivated and deliciously crass, helter-skelter and fastidious (he continued his indulgent and expensive habit of binding magazines the old-fashioned way as he moved past his 1986 retirement into the digital age).

In some ways, DuBek's collection reminds me of Andy Warhol's legendary collection that became public after the artist's death in 1987. I don't think DuBek's comparatively modest resources allowed him to amass anything approaching Warhol's stupendous assortment of Art Deco objects, American Indian art, vintage furniture, jewelry, and a wide range of "collectibles"—10,000 individual objects that earned $30 million on the auction market in the famous buying frenzy after his death. But DuBek's indiscriminate and profligate accumulation of "valueless" and "ephemeral" erotic materials from magazines to porno pictures over more than forty years, and his apparent inclination to keep *everything*, resembles at least in part the drive of his fellow Upper East Side resident (Warhol was twelve years DuBek's junior) to accumulate everyday objects alongside his more traditional antique "bargain shopping." Warhol's collecting included a legendary assortment of pornography, a focused piling-up of thousands of Polaroids of the genitals of men who visited his "Factory," and an accumulation of 600 "Time Capsules," cartons in which porno magazines would join theater tickets, newspapers, movie memorabilia, and personal ephemera—and even, it is said, half-eaten pizza—and be sealed away for posterity (Smith 2002, 38-39). There is no space here to enter in much detail into the art historians' debates that the Warhol legacy has sparked: about theories of collecting and (post-)modernity, and about Warhol's packrat manias and their links to queer culture in general. (Michael Lobel [1996, 44] cites Wayne Koestenbaum [1993, 62] to the effect that "collecting is a code for homosexual activity and identity," and his analysis of the uneasy interface of private and public in the gay collector's "closet" is certainly a trigger for further reflection—as well as for nervous glances around my own cluttered house.)

Despite obvious differences, the parallels and echoes between the accumulations on East 66th Steet (Warhol) and East 61st Steet (DuBek) are suggestive, and it is fascinating to think how DuBek's fanatically bound skin magazines and well-preserved stashes of hardcore graphics operate as their own kind of Time Capsules, not only as records of one man's lust but also as archives of communal desire within a particular time and cultural space. Unlike Warhol's cartons, DuBek's time capsules were not sealed and secreted away for posterity: every evidence suggests that the collection continued to be kept accessible, treasured, and consulted as DuBek aged and eventually retired. Did the binding of *Teen Torso* and *Crisco Kids* simply facilitate continued "use" (as masturbation aids? as "trade-breakers"?[1] as conversation starters and shared ritual relics among DuBek and his inner circle?), or just make these stroke materials look more respectable in front of the cleaning lady, friends, and CBS visitors?

There is no mention of books in the literature on the Warhol collection, nor any evidence to my knowledge that he actually read books, but DuBek certainly did so alongside his picture collecting. His massive book collection was no doubt more respectable than the erotica, at least according to the pre-Stonewall mentality, and certainly more functional, not as stroke material, but in terms of his livelihood in television art design. This extensive research library of 3,000 books pertaining to design history, costumes, and decoration was unsurprisingly treated by the estate as a separate category from the erotica and left to the Phoenix Art Reference Library. Still other components of DuBek's collection were also dealt with differently, distributed among friends or sold after his death, most notably the hoard of original art that ranged from Salvador Dalí to Tom of Finland (an original commissioned Tom that hung above the jacuzzi in his Phoenix retirement apartment showed a single male nude amid a pyramidal assemblage of thirteen of "Tom's Men," all clothed). Many queer erotica collections go the way of all flesh upon the death of their owner and similar collections of "non-original" art items and "specialized books" are dumped on uninterested dealers for a minuscule fraction of their worth, while the "decent" books and original art having any value are carefully preserved for resale. In DuBek's case, the GLBTHS was most fortunate to have received the erotica collection intact, uncensored, and in excellent condition, and with the support and sympathy of an enlightened estate. And DuBek himself was fortunate to have such loyal and respectful trustees. Although the exact relation of the GLBTHS cataloguing structure to the way DuBek himself stored and used the collection remains to be clarified, the collection is a very exciting introit to a period, a subculture, and a personal sensibility that might otherwise have vanished.

1. Underground artist Blade's term for porno pictures used as ammunition to "break" wavering potential tricks who were "straight."

SELECTING AND ORGANIZING *LUST*

Perhaps some day, another "coffee table book" will document DuBek's whole mind-blowing assortment of typographic and visual erotic materials in its entirety, from every rung of the ladder of cultural status, but *Lust Unearthed* cannot do that. Instead, following the *Out/Lines* model, we decided to be very selective and provide a coherent glimpse of just one of the several specialized holdings that DuBek treasured, that assortment of photographed and original gay male "obscene" graphics that he may well have been most secretive about. (Not only is he extremely unlikely to have shown it to his friends Franklin and Eleanor, but several of his closest surviving friends from the 1950s and 1960s weren't aware of this stash nor his skin magazine obsession and remember him only as a dedicated careerist and *bon vivant* . . .)

As I argued in *Out/Lines*, explicit and illicit homoerotic materials in the pre-Stonewall twentieth century "belonged to the secret realm of the damned," and justify a "fetishistic and exclusive focus" as we attempt to appreciate and make sense of them. Their anonymous abjection, the "ephemerality, stigma and chaos of the 'obscene' underground" (Waugh 2002, 14, 16) as reflected in DuBek's lustful hoarding, can benefit only so much from traditional art historical perspectives. Instead, a respectful and even loving encounter with these pictures on their own terms, as well as an outsider's viewpoint from another century and another worldview, can hopefully make them come alive. This is the dual meaning of *Lust Unearthed*, the sibilant title that I chose for this collection. Lust, that most debased emotion that is also a Deadly Sin, and the artifacts of lust must be validated on their own terms. Unearthing these artifacts, digging them up and exposing them to life is an archeological undertaking that aims for both the historicization and the reclamation (re-use in book form and over the uncontrolled cybersphere) of images buried by shame, censorship, and the passage of time. Perhaps we can help these pictures point us towards an understanding and even fulfillment of the utopian promises of sexuality that DuBek's generation yearned for but seldom expected to see in their lifetimes (he was fifty-three years of age in the year of Stonewall, sixty-five at the time of the discovery of AIDS). Perhaps by touching this filth and letting its shame touch us, we, his heirs, can see, as I put it inspired by Foucault, the "possibilities of an art where truth is truly drawn from pleasure" (Waugh 2002, 90).

Great hopes for a large smut collection! In fact, the collection was so large that immediate practical concerns displaced the utopian musings. We had to impose a very strict selection upon the collection, using Walker's resourceful and reliable catalogue as a departure point, in order to produce a manageable book-sized selection from it. Of DuBek's almost 2,300 explicit images bequeathed to the GLBTHS, we had the space in this book to use only about one in ten. This, however, may have been less challenging than with *Out/Lines*. The earlier book's materials came from a dozen different sources and collections, and were ultimately more diverse than DuBek's collection in terms both of cultural, ethnic, and racial diversity and of sexual/gender diversity (biological female, sexworker, intersex, and transgender bodies and identities are less visible in *Lust Unearthed* than in *Out/Lines*). I am not sure exactly why, since it was not only his personal erotic taste that dictated his acquisitions. Perhaps DuBek had neither the political imperatives nor the research networks and resources that we take for granted in the twenty-first century.

Meanwhile, as the selection proceeded, categories and boundaries were narrowed or re-aligned radically, and certain eliminations imposed themselves almost from the start. Spoiled by the quality of most items, we set aside low quality works that would not effectively communicate their original impact. As well, some artists well covered in *Out/Lines* and for whom DuBek's sampling was not particularly distinctive were passed over (for example, DuBek's friend and fellow Manhattanite "Blade": see Figure 54 for his sole fleeting appearance). Another artist, namely Tom of Finland, whose work DuBek collected passionately, having even visited him in Helsinki in the early 1950s, was also passed over since his momentous oeuvre has become extremely well known thanks to the work of the foundation named after him and many publications.

Several artists discovered in *Out/Lines* are more fully fleshed out here thanks to DuBek's high quality representation of their work. These include not only

1. the mysterious author of the Japanese "Yokohama" series (98-103), now identifiable as Frenchman "Paul Smara"; but also
2. the pseudonymous German-speaking romantic "Jean Vincent" (4-17, 78-83, 209, 219, 236);
3. the Frenchman really named Rolland Caillaux (18-26, 168-69, 199; a.k.a. Caillaud, active in the 1940s, died around 1975), whose passionate, Genet-inspired idyls in Parisian garrets and street corners bedazzled *Out/Lines* readers;
4. another Frenchman, Tola Soungouroff, whose pouty anonymous postcards

graced the cover of *Out/Lines* along with Figs. 50-53, but who can now be identified thanks to French vintage erotic picture specialist Nicole Canet (Figs. 33 to 37); of Russian origin, Soungouroff (born around 1920 and died in poverty around 1987) was based in Cannes and well known for his decorations of the waterfront bar "Zanzibar"; his licit paintings of sailors, soldiers and gypsies, exhibited in Paris and Cannes galleries, were paralleled by his unsigned porno works, including an pseudonymous 1947 book of explicit lithographs, *Jours sans dimanche*, about a procuress and her horny male clients;

5. the unnamed jolly Britons, poets of promiscuity that I named "Happyface" (43-51, 94) in *Out/Lines* and "Bellhops" (111-15, 157-60, 200-05, 213-15) in this volume respectively. And of course, as I have already mentioned,
6. the American Dom Orejudos (Etienne), a personal friend of DuBek's from whom he acquired almost 150 original sketches and finished drawings and almost double that number of copies, is well represented in *Lust Unearthed* (63, 180-198), an index of that artist's importance for his kindred spirit and excellent customer.
7. Another of DuBek's acquaintances, this time from New York, also makes an appearance: Paul Cadmus, whose rare and often rumored explicit drawings from the 1930s were only acknowledged in passing by the artist before his death (Spring 2002, 32-33). This work had popped up fleetingly and unacknowledged in *Out/Lines*, but Cadmus has now been tentatively identified as the author of several sketch pages and more finished drawings, duplicated in DuBek's collection (163-65, 217-18; at least one of the originals is in the archives of the Kinsey Institute, according to Spring, and the whereabouts of the others is a topic for further research). More of Cadmus later.

Finally, a few artists not present in *Out/Lines* appear here, including;

8. the anonymous French pencil conjuror of lanky, horny sailors, possibly an amateur, whom I call "El Greco" (27-32, 119-120);
9. the licentious British amateur whom I have labelled "Lipstick" (52-53), and whom I was prevented from representing more (see below); and most importantly,
10. the French poet of scarred and blank-eyed machismo Paul Smara (pseud. E. Paul Dubois, died around 1980; Figures 98-110), around whom attributions in *Out/Lines* were impulsive and misleading, but have been corrected in the second printing; Canet concurs with me (correspondence August 2004) that Smara is without a doubt the "Yokohama artist" who appeared so intriguingly as the sole "Asian" representative in *Out/Lines* (154).

Despite this rhapsodic evocation of those artists who have moved on or have come back to haunt us in fuller form, or have just appeared for the first time, the *Lust Unearthed* selection is not organized around individual artist names (as *Out/Lines* was, to no small extent). Instead, the almost 240 images are organized under several other helpful rubrics, truer perhaps to the sensibility of the collector. This organization is certainly truer to the anonymous energy of the underground, with its cumulative genius of what I called in the previous book (citing André Bazin) its anonymous 'common fund,' and tradition, characterized by vigour, richness, spontaneity, and 'harmony with its public'" (2002, 52). I argued there that a "genre" analysis was often more suitable for making sense of explicit erotic images—that is, comparing pictures that form a narrative sequence, tell the same stories or evoke the same cultural flavor, or else deploy the same settings, character or body types, fetishes, or sexual specialities—rather than those that are by the same hand. Certainly we can speculate confidently that the original audience for this corpus would have related to the images on this general level—except for the most sophisticated collectors—rather than assembling them in terms of authorial groupings. Would the typical consumer not keep, for example, his five favorite French sailor pictures or the ones that remind him of his college roommate together in the same wornout envelope? With this in mind, I have tried out such groupings in a more focused way in *Lust Unearthed*, and discovered interesting connections, rhymes, and underlying qualities.

First, I introduce four sets of national mythologies from the four principal porno-producing cultures that dominated the underground: German-speaking Europe, France, Britain, and the U.S.A. Obscene erotic mythologies, whether oral, typographic or visual, have always been spiced with the shorthand of national, ethnic, and racial stereotypes, but then so have respectable theories about national sexual characteristics or sensibilities as well. When gay playwright Joe Orton heard in 1967 about a Swedish agent thinking of acquiring his play *Loot*, his diary tirade about various national sexualities says more about a certain British resentment of the Continent than about real Swedes, French, and Americans, and certainly lots about mythologies, types and caricatures absorbed from movies:

> The Swedes, like the French have a strange reputation for broadmindedness and unshockability. On the strength, I suppose, of a few films in which "free love," "lesbianism," and "nude bathing" are indulged in.
>
> And Paris has been living on a reputation of "naughtiness" for a century or more by the expedient of pretending that "adultery" and "little women down the road" are the height of rudery and licence.
>
> America the same. All of them like fifty-year-old virgins talking about the pleasures of sexual intercourse and knowing nothing about the subject—except in theory. (Orton 1986, 117).

All this is to say that launching *Lust Unearthed* with four self-serious clusters of erotic images under the rubric "National Dreams" must necessarily be self-reflexively superficial, a willfully tongue-in-cheek exercise in unmasking stereotypes and playing with caricatures as much as in acceding to socio-cultural truths. When so much about the *materiality* of the production, distribution, and reception of these images is entirely missing, this may be the best we can do. The queer artists and images representing these four national and linguistic entities are for the most part anonymous, with the exception of several Frenchmen, and in many cases not verifiably linked to a specific setting—I have a recurring nightmare that I'll get a letter from Denmark claiming authorship for the ploughboy image, Figure 56, thereby sabotaging my profound hypotheses about its American-ness. Such anonymous authorial ciphers could thus never really be definitively shown to represent national cultural characteristics around (homo-)sexuality. All the more so, since to generalize around collective national cultures without taking into account intra-national dynamics of class, gender, ethnicity, or raciality is a very risky activity indeed.

The remaining nine clusters all derive from generic categories, groups of images organized according to the visual motifs, erotic themes, or narrative formulae of the operative fantasy: phallic, "classical," uniforms, "Boys in the Sand" (beaches), S/M, couples, trios, groups, and "softcore" (the latter of course being a market category as well as a genre, tied into narrative and iconographical features of an image). In doing so, I have enjoyed bringing out tensions or similarities or "conversations" among pictures that may well be from different historical or geographical zones and voices: for example, in the "Fantasies: Classical" section, a confrontation on facing pages between interwar German and postwar American fantasies of ancient military homoeroticism (83-84), or, in my "Fantasies: Uniforms" section, a confrontation between a British fantasy about a bobby in full regalia fucking-in-the-park and an American fantasy about an army staff sergeant receiving a little head with his liquor handy and his fully displayed uniform barely opened (94-95).

The national and generic organization of the selection also helps me to avoid a trap that I was vigilant about both in *Out/Lines* and here. Cadmus offers the book's only temptation of the high art legitimation (his erstwhile lover Jared French also enters and appropriates the final frame, 237), which I rejected quite self-righteously in *Out/Lines* and hereby maintain: "leaving out all of the bountiful eligible work that continues to surface by bearers of high cultural status, such artists as Aubrey Beardsley, Sergei Eisenstein, Duncan Grant, Jean Cocteau, Charles Demuth, Donald Friend, Pavel Tchelitchev, Andy Warhol, and others. . . . I bracket these modernist queer rebels partly because I like the idea of reclaiming the 'low' and 'unclaimed.' I refuse to legitimize the 'abject' through connections to high culture canons. . . ." (Waugh 2002, 15).

My resolve has been reinforced and my indignation further inflamed by a recent Cocteau exhibition at Montreal's Musée des beaux-arts, "Jean Cocteau. L'enfant terrible" (6 May to 29 August, 2004). The multidisciplinary artist's erotic drawings were first of all ghettoized, restricted to a little tongue-in-cheek "red light zone" from which children and families were warned away. The drawings' nature was also completely falsified: a small selection of the homoerotic images were balanced with equal number of uninspired heterosexual drawings, mechanically based on partouze photos and scrounged up god knows where, as if they were somehow commensurate to the literally thousands of brilliant and delightfully obscene sailor scrawls, doodles, and arabesques for which Cocteau is so famous among his brethren (Cocteau 1999). The squeamishness, distortion, and cultural apartheid of this exercise in pseudo-hip, Miss Grundy curating, far from elevating the obscene through a "high art" alibi, effected a symptomatic reverse process, cleansing a canonical "high art" *enfant pas très terrible* of his association with the queer and the obscene, a cleansing process that has been imposed on all of the names listed above at various points of their careers and thereafter.

Inspired perhaps by Cocteau—who was both a writer and a visual artist who provided both words and pictures in *Le livre blanc* (Cocteau [1928] 1990)—I have also played with words and pictures: to heighten the cross-historical conversations among pictures that I am aiming for, I have also experimented with captions. In *Out/Lines,* I attempted to provide whatever basic contextual information that was available, plus the occasional insight or wry exclamation mark. In *Lust,* I used snippets from an assortment of cross-cultural pre-Stonewall literature, mostly canonical but also some pulp, mostly fiction but also poetry, a diary, and a memoir, mainly from the five host cultures to this corpus (German-language, French, British, American, Japanese), plus a bit of proudly Canadian content to reflect my host culture and city. My intention is certainly not to heighten the cultural status of this filthy smut with the aura of high literature and humanist values, far from it;[2] rather, I felt the impulse simply to thicken our sense of sexual representation, both fantasy and lived experience, by gay men in other media at the same time as the pictures were being made. I wanted to counterbalance visual

2. I rediscovered, as I was finishing my literary captions, that I was following in the footsteps of Cécile Beurdeley in her brilliant and pioneering *L'Amour Bleu* (1978), which also juxtaposes literary passages with artistic images from the history of the representation of/by male homosexuals through the ages. Beurdeley's intent was more general and more ambitious than my specific focus on the abject genre of explicit eroticism in graphic media within the narrow historical framework of the pre-Stonewall twentieth century. However meticulous, enterprising, and ultimately indispensable Beurdeley's magnificent book is, the author-compiler occasionally yields to the temptation of the high cultural alibi, whipping up status for her once-stigmatized visual repertory through their association with Shakespeare and Appollinaire, etc. Furthermore, although Beurdeley includes, in small format glimpses, a sprinkling of "hardcore" images in the book—amazingly and to her credit—they all benefit from the "high art" benediction, and she was thus ultimately not able to rise above the squeamishness that no doubt prevailed in Rizzoli's high end "coffee table book" sector in the late 1970s.

desire with written desire in its contemporaneous format, trying to think about the translation of gesture, act, expression, and feeling to words and images, however much the materialist historian in me worries about the ahistoricity of bringing in a Japanese author discovering an erotics of pain in 1949 to comment on an American S/M fantasy from almost two decades later (Figure 145). I decided to throw caution to the winds and hope that this gamble would succeed in deepening the historicity of images, not only by highlighting the essential sameness of arousals and identities across cultures and generations, but also by suggesting their specificity. It's not that the pictures need words or that the words need pictures, but that the two of them can work together. I hope thereby I have been able to anchor DuBek's fantasies in their material status as pictures, to harness their visual pleasure to real-world experience, true to the spirit of good ol' straight Walter Benjamin:

> What we must demand from the photographer is the ability to put such a caption beneath his picture as will rescue it from the ravages of modishness and confer upon it a revolutionary use-value. (Benjamin, ([1934] 1973, 95).

POLITICIZING *LUST*

Benjamin was not interested in transcultural arousal (as far as we know), rather in international revolution. So much the better, for it's impossible to produce a book like this without constantly being reminded of its inescapable political implications. *Out/Lines* appeared in a very volatile political environment, in both Canada and the U.S. Everywhere was the shadow of groundbreaking jurisprudence: on same-sex marriage in both countries, and on the decriminalization of sodomy south of the border; and also, in both countries—and more relevant to this corpus of graphic fantasies—on so-called "child pornography," on community values, and on the criminal obscenity of fantasies and the legal difference between ideas and actions (Waugh 2002, 21-27). Furthermore, as we went to press with *Out/Lines,* there was no resolution in sight for litigation brought forward by Vancouver's brave little queer bookstore Little Sister's against the Canadian government. Little Sister's challenged the constitutionality of the obscenity provisions of the criminal code as well as the policy of Canada Customs whereby the American S/M comics *Meatmen* had been impounded at the border (Leyland 1996, 2000). As I write this in August 2004, this case has amazingly still not been resolved, but progress has been made—the courts have formally accepted the constitutional relevance of the challenge and required the Crown to provide legal costs for the bookstore.[1] This judicial struggle over S/M and the right to minority lust—and especially to minority-within-a-minority lust—is even more relevant to *Lust Unearthed* since DuBek's collection of S/M images is proportionally even louder and prouder than in *Out/Lines.* Various shades along the explicit S/M spectrum constitute about 15 percent of our overall selection from his hoard. The challenge to a criminal code whose provisions against the "harm" and "degradation" allegedly inherent in obscene images have systematically served to scapegoat queer erotic imagery and culture could not be more important. The atmosphere is all the more fraught since legislative trial balloons floated before and after the June 2004 election of the precarious Liberal minority government threaten to withdraw the "artistic defense" that has been the lynchpin of civil liberties for sexual minorities (and majorities) in Canada since at least the Omnibus

1 2009 update: Little Sister's valiant struggle of more than twelve years finally came to an end with the January 2007 Supreme Court of Canada judgment that, in the absence of a compelling public stake in the bookstore's litigation, Little Sister's was not eligible for advance legal costs from the state. As this second printing goes to press, Little Sister's is for sale.

de-criminalization act of 1969, the same year as Stonewall.

Interestingly, however, it's not S/M that has drawn out the radical political stakes in the actual production of *Lust Unearthed*, but rather intergenerational desire. Well into the writing of *Lust*, my publishers regretfully decreed that seven already scanned and selected images from the DuBek collection were *verboten*. What the problematical images had in common might be called their ephebophile eroticism: they explicitly depicted sexual relations among post-pubescent males or between adult males and pubescent or post-pubescent males. I agree with Robert and Brian that these images might be susceptible of misinterpretation as constituting that amorphous, absorbent, and panic-inducing "crime" of "child pornography," either by booksellers, who must usually be cautious and cannot be expected to foot the bill for challenging unfair legislative and marketing policy any more than poverty row publishers can, or by the law enforcers, who are rather persuasive in their power to harass even when they do not eventually convict. A few other pictures seemed potentially to be on the line as well. A compiler develops a neurotic personal attachments to images, and furthermore I have a history of responding rather dramatically to being censored (Waugh 2000, 272-296). However, I did not even try to argue that all seven doomed images were 1) produced in Europe (except one), and therefore outside of U.S. or Canadian jurisdiction, 2) produced no less than forty or fifty years ago, and lay sort of beyond the moral statute of limitations, 3) were indexical fantasy images (not related to real world people or events), the very issue that had just been decided in our favor by appellate courts in both countries (Waugh 2002, 21-22), and 4) were being published as archival evidence in a scholarly historical study of gay visual art, in demonstrably good faith, and were thus incontrovertibly covered by the artistic and scientific defense allowed by both American and Canadian law. Instead, I negotiated (i.e. horsetraded), persuading Arsenal Pulp to allow me to run three of the suspect pictures, openly cropped in a self-reflexive manner (Figures 6, 21, and 211), provided I deleted the remaining four.

The four deleted images were: two French images from the late 1940s, respectively Soungouroff's postcard of a nasty monk masturbating a compliant but uneasy pubescent youth (cf. 33-37), and Cheekbones's drawing of a smoking toughie preparing to anally penetrate a bound and gagged supine youth (cf. 38-42); two British ink drawings from the 1950s, following Figure 52, in which the background figure, clearly an effeminate young adult, engages with the sailor and the Scots guard (who don't look so macho themselves) in two successive sandwich positions (the amateur draughtsman has trouble with scale and renders the pansy's body smaller than appropriate and might be misinterpreted if the image is viewed away from the context of the three-item series).

We apparently have no choice in the current political climate but to cave in to the attenuation of the artistic and scientific (scholarly) defense and to the disregard of context and community standards (despite their enshrinement in the Criminal Code). This is a grave strategic compromise whose repercussions will resonate for decades to come, especially if the 2004 U.S. election goes in a certain way, and if a certain Canadian election, bound to happen before the term of the Liberal minority government plays out, follows in step.

The reader must have noticed that I have thus far avoided pronouncing personally on intergenerational desire, one situation as with S/M where I suppose the personal may not be terribly political. All I will say is that my first response to the three pictures before their cropping is, like most other gay men that I know in my situation, to project onto the teenage figure the fond wish that I had once been in their situation instead of waiting to become sexually active after I had moved beyond my teens. Beyond this authorial statement of fantasy and regret, I cannot avoid pointing to the outrageous hypocrisy of the current political climate around this issue. In this climate, equally liable to prosecution are 1) fantasies of today *and* fantasies our great uncles entertained generations ago, 2) representations of legal activities (for example, two teenagers beyond the age of consent but conceivably below the age of eighteen having sex, such as in Figure 6) *and* representations of illegal activities, and 3) archives holding "suspect" images as part of a historical collection *and* producers of "suspect" images in a current context. The law is an ass, of course, but even more so the cultural climate of cowardice, wilful distortion, hypocrisy, mendacity, and mediocrity, perpetrated by media, demagogues, and pundits as well as by upholders of the law.

Some excellent recent scholarly literature—two articles and a book, all from 2004—exploring all of these contradictions correctly fall back upon the even broader context of youth sexual agency and representation, and do so in a calm and reasoned manner within the disciplinary frameworks of the social sciences, the history of sexuality, and my own field of queer cultural studies. This convergence of British and American scholarship may hopefully presage a turning of the tide in an otherwise very ominous conjuncture indeed: Steven Angelides's "Feminism, Child Sexual Abuse, and the Erasure of Child Sexuality"; Rachel Thomson's "'An Adult Thing?': Young People's Perspectives on the Heterosexual Age of Consent"; and Steven Bruhm and Natasha Hurley's anthology *Curiouser: On the Queerness of Children*. Angelides hits the nail on the head, and I hope his parting shot, along with DuBek's three defaced and four "disappeared" treasures, will provoke a much needed debate:

> What is the relationship between consent, power, and age-stratified concepts of subject formation? To engage these kinds of questions, we ought to follow psychoanalytic and poststructuralist insights and examine child, adolescent, and adult subjectivities and sexualities not as fields of autonomous meaning but as mutually constitutive domains of meaning, both experientially and epistemologically, spatially and temporally. Only then will it be possible to begin to theorize the inevitably continuous relations structuring age—and gender, sexuality, and other factors—and thus attend to the fluid and overlapping boundaries assumed to demarcate the categories of childhood, adolescence, and adulthood. **In a contemporary context of escalating**

anxiety and panic surrounding pedophilia and child sexual abuse, it is increasingly difficult, and perhaps for this reason all the more imperative, for queer studies to problematize the cultural and relational construction of age, child sexuality, and subjectivity. (2004, 167-68, my emphasis)

LUST, THE SEQUEL

I have discovered, in this summer of *Spiderman 2,* that sequel writing is not as obvious a skill as those of us who once cast scorn on *Rocky V* and *Scary Movie VIII* might have assumed. The challenge is always to build on the original without repeating it, and at the same time to create a new work that adds to it without being dependent on it. Possible, but not easy: both *The Godfather* and *The Godfather Part II* got the Oscar, but interestingly only the third installment of the *Lord of the Rings* cycle did. Will cool blue *Lust* build on its red hot precursor and at the same time establish its own integrity? While it will be up to the reader to determine if *Lust* adds something distinct to *Out/Lines,* perhaps a few provisional comments will be useful here.

First of all, the promise that DuBek would add quality and completeness to the fleeting and blurred images of *Out/Lines* has by and large been fulfilled with his beautiful objects. We have, I believe, returned honorably into circulation the dense fantasy data in the lines and strokes of the images that he acquired with both his unerring eye and indiscriminate compulsion, preserved so carefully. Otherwise, does *Lust* contain any new historical discoveries about this corpus, its context and the deeper meanings of this fascinating underground traffic in photographed/graphic queer filth? There has been slight progress in the attributions department, especially with the Europeans, not only the addition of the name Soungouroff and the greatly advanced clarity around the name Smara. But even where the names are absent, a substantial fleshing out of a few distinctive pictures to build up a more coherent oeuvre than was available before represents an important stride toward identification in the case of several artists, and more importantly toward understanding. For example, this has now happened with the intriguing figure of Bellhops, represented here by the bountiful harvest of Figures 111-115, 157-160, 200-205—a brilliantly charming celebration of smiling sexual spontaneity and willowy corporal grace, in harmony with the natural kingdom of anal-fixated seagulls and dachshunds. And hopefully a new David will come forward this time claiming the authorship, perhaps, of the superb ink-and-pen draftsman of raunchy coupledom, American this time I think, of Figures 118, 144-145, 175-76, 208.

A further small step forward came with another reader's letter to me in response to *Out/Lines.* This one, from an anonymous e-mail correspondent with the pseudonym of "Drummer," gave me a well deserved tonguelashing for an "egregious omission" in my discussion of Etienne's work. I quote it at length with his permission:

> The lacuna I find is that you make no mention whatsoever of "Etienne's" enormous interest and fetish for male feet, socks, and footwear, particularly in feet that smell. Although his works treating this particular aspect of "power fantasies" were not widely disseminated, they constitute a fairly large and important portion of his work. I even own cassette tapes of the artist himself reading short stories of forced "foot worship" that he wrote himself—and occasionally illustrated. I realize that your work focuses on "gay" sensibilities in general, but, because of his work as a dancer and choreographer, and the obvious sensual delight that the male foot gave him, as an artist, whether the theme of his illustrations or paintings had to do with foot-fetishism or not, makes it a feature that should at least be MENTIONED, I think, in any serious discussion of this important figure in American homosexual erotic art. Indeed, I think it is the artist's loving and careful depiction of his characters' feet that makes it possible to identify images of otherwise doubtful origin! It is by no means a minor or incidental aspect of his work, and is of particular interest, I think, because this sort of interest made him a minority within a minority—it is an interest which men like him often hide, even today, from other "gay" men. The artist corresponded with others who shared his enjoyment, circulated drawings among them (indeed, one can often find "pairs" of drawings by him, one having a foot-worship theme, and the other "converted" to a more conventional male sex scene for publication), and took commissions from Doug Gaines, who ran a sort of club for male foot-fetishists called "The Foot Fraternity," which are among some of his most intensely erotic works.

Flushed and chastened, I tore open the book to find Etienne's work exactly as Drummer had described it. It is indeed no less pronounced in its graphic fetishism than the twenty works by Etienne in *Lust* (63,180-198), whose dynamic foreground depictions of white wool and argyle socks (with suggestive holes worn by those wriggly and odorous toes), Wellingtons, and penny-loafers, one pair of ladies' pumps and, of course, several pairs of naked lumpy feet (which no doubt smell . . .) all leap off the page. How could I have missed this in *Out/Lines*? Several lessons emerge from this polite scolding, not the least of which is the urgency of looking itself, piercing the invisibility of difference, looking for the complexities of visual language and the polyvocality of iconography, and looking again, *really* looking and *seeing*. It's about uncovering intensities within the prosaic and the everyday, and of course affirming the diverse spectrum of desire within queer and not-so-queer communities. Etienne's surviving partner had never mentioned his foot fetish to me, and his friend and collaborator Felix Lance Falkon who had published his work in *Gay Art*, his pioneering collection of gay erotic work in 1972, was completely unaware of it—even though that sampling had included the same explicit master-slave boot-licking image as I was to reprint in *Out/Lines* thirty years later (Falkon 1972,

Fig. 60; Waugh 2002, Fig. 98)! This discovery of a truth so obvious and so invisible was a timely reminder for all queer historical researchers to keep on their toes. . . .

Coming out of this correspondence, there is also an amplification of our sense of how the underground actually worked, with its layers of visibility and invisibility, minorities within minorities. Most specifically interesting to me is the sense of an active relationship between consumer and artist that disappeared within so many levels of post-Stonewall commodification. The commissioning of works from artists by consumers seems to have been much more important than I understood, based on the evidence regarding both the "Foot Fraternity" and DuBek. David's letter also indicated that his rough sailor titclamp series had also been commissioned for one "Mr. Hoag" in New Jersey. I had wondered for a moment whether Mr. Hoag might have been a mafioso porno distributor in the burgeoning marketplace of the 1960s, but on reflection I'm pretty sure he was just a horny specialist with the money to invest in pictures of exactly what his turn-on was. The biographical material we have about Tom of Finland also points to the importance of commissioning in the pre-Stonewall erotica underground (Hooven 1993). In a research field where so little is known, a few anecdotes of this nature about commissioning constitute fairly conclusion evidence. We must qualify any sense we have of a pre-Stonewall subculture overdetermined by the chaos of anonymity and arbitrary and haphazard distribution-in fact where one-way circulation based on a producer throwing his picture out into a universe with which he otherwise did not interact is assumed to have prevailed. Instead, the underground seems to have more often been characterized by relations of active engagement and exchange. Consider:

- the richness of the amateur contributions to the network (e.g. Figs. 52-53, 93, 177);
- the dazzling contributions by autodidacts like Etienne and Blade;
- the busy activities of the tracers of earlier photos and drawings (220) and the appropriators or transformers (54, 135, 139 vs 152);
- the hobbyist re-photographers (those ruler edges holding down the drawings being copied tell all, 133-36);
- the iconoclasts whose flirtation with taboos not only meant serious risks to life and livelihood for themselves and their correspondents and friends in the pre-Stonewall period, but also censorship half a century later;
- the compulsive archivists who saw a mural so bold that they knew it would disappear very soon but must not be forgotten (65-66).

All of these imprints on the images of *Lust Unearthed*, these personal traces of active and interactive networks seeking, creating, and sharing the pleasures of lust throughout those generations of illegitimacy and invisibility—we must continue to unearth them and celebrate them, we must learn from them as well.

Please, master reader, I know you have already looked at DuBek's beautiful pictures instead of dutifully first reading this introductory essay. That is all right, for this book is all about not feeling guilty, as the amazing collector Ambrose DuBek apparently never did. We have designed this book to enable you to flip back and forth and to start at the end and finish at the beginning with impunity. I have tried in this introduction to show how reproducing an archival collection of erotic images is not only a dry albeit spicy scholarly exercise, but also a process, a personal voyage of discovery of another milieu and period, an exploration in the interface between knowledge and desire, an exercise in extending friendship and exploring and affirming community, a interpersonal process in which you are the final link.

Ambrose DuBek: The Man

by Willie Walker with Thomas Waugh

Ambrose M. DuBek, born in Plainfield, New Jersey in 1916, was the only son of the former Countess Maria Luckal Von Hapsburg. His father, a high-ranking Austrian Officer, sent Maria to the United States at the beginning of the slaughter that would become known as World War I. There is talk among DuBek's friends about a sister, but it is unclear whether she was older or younger, and whether she came with her mother to America, or stayed in Austria under the guardianship of her father. One story has DuBek traveling much later to Austria to look for her but finding no trace.

Maria and her baby Ambrose settled onto a sprawling farm, Long Brook, near Plainfield in rural New Jersey. The farm was located not far from a rural retreat owned by Franklin Delano Roosevelt and his wife, Eleanor. Mrs. Roosevelt would frequently stop at Long Brook for fresh water on her way into the city. Ambrose's memory was that they had chickens, pigs, a milk cow, and raised a good deal of produce. He apparently went to high school in the area.

After graduating, DuBek studied design, for which he must have demonstrated enough talent that when, as a very young man, he moved to Hollywood in the late 1930s and he secured an apprenticeship with the famed gay costume designer Adrian. During his comparatively brief stint in Hollywood, he met and got to know many well-known actors and actresses, and apparently began his collecting of gay books, pictures, and magazines at that time. Over time he created costumes and set designs for both Paramount and Columbia Pictures; some of his most admired work includes gowns and other smart outfits worn by the panoply of great leading ladies who strutted through George Cukor's *The Women* (MGM, 1939—Adrian got the official credit).

DuBek joined the United States Army some three months prior to Pearl Harbor and, trained as a surgical nurse, was personally commissioned by Roosevelt right after the U.S. entry into the War to set up the nursing unit at the Victorville, CA, military hospital, serving there for the duration. Also with Roosevelt's personal support, DuBek set up a scheme to provide entertainment to hospitalized G.I.s, hospital staff, and returning veterans which became the "Hospital Special Services." He arranged shows and visits from film stars and entertainers, and coordinated short term visits for service men and women to the homes of Hollywood personalities, including Tyrone Power and Edward G. Robinson, and worked closely with the Beverly Hills USO.

In the postwar years, DuBek continued to work in the design and performance world. After his discharge, he was invited by William S. Paley, head of the newly created CBS Television, to become the Chief Set Designer and Decorator for CBS's New York Studios, a position he held until his retirement in 1986. DuBek was best known for the design for the news show *60 Minutes* during the peak of his career, but he also had a hand in ballet specials. DuBek was an intimate family friend of Paley and his wife, the renowned socialite and high fashion diva, Babe Paley, whose homes he decorated. Settled into his rent-controlled sixth-floor apartment on Manhattan's Upper East Side (East 61st Street at Third Avenue), he was neighbors with Eleanor Roosevelt and Montgomery Clift, but it is not known if one or the other attended his legendary well-run orgies his friends have described. Renowned for pursuing his desires, DuBek was able to preside "flamboyantly" (a word many of his surviving friends use admiringly) over both intellectual salons and Fire Island summers alike, scarves and curly blond-gray locks aflutter. The degree to which his social, intellectual, and sexual worlds overlapped is unclear.

DuBek was an inveterate advocate and patron of the arts. Even before his departure to Hollywood, he had befriended two queer arts pioneers, dancer Ted Shawn and photographer John Lindquist. The latter had captured the beginning and rise of the "Jacob's Pillow" all-male dance troupe and the community it nurtured from its earliest days, and would later do portraits of DuBek (see Figs. 1, 3d, 3f). (DuBek himself also tried his hand at photography from time to time, and his nude studies often used his latest ballet star protégé as model.) Other friends included Noel Coward and Leonard Bernstein, with whom he traveled at least once. DuBek helped launch the careers of numerous artists in many fields, and bought art from many graphic artists, including erotic art from Paul Cadmus, Jean Boullet, and Jean Cocteau. His erotica collection was principally gay male in focus, but also contained bisexual and heterosexual imagery as well as a wealth of S/M materials, all gathered more out of intellectual curiosity than personal sexual interest, according to those who were close to him. Known in the worlds of theater, dance, music, film, radio and television, ballet, and opera, DuBek was admired for his keen intelligence and perception, his personal honesty and integrity, and his consistent adherence to a belief in people's right to keep their personal lives private.

DuBek was a personal friend to such people as Kneeland Bate (Blade), Touko Laaksonen (Tom of Finland), and Dom Orejudos (Etienne), all skilled draftsmen prominent within the canon of twentieth-century homoerotic art. As early as the 1950s, DuBek had visited Laaksonen in Finland, where he purchased some of his original artwork. He also bought many pieces from Orejudos, with whom he stayed when in Chicago. He enjoyed such images without furtiveness; at various points in his life he openly displayed homoerotic works in his home, even if he did not always share the most explicit materials or his hundreds of skin magazines with his friends. Otherwise, DuBek felt that life and the body were to be celebrated; he had no patience for other people's guilt or attempts to make him feel guilty for his attractions and desires. Needless to say, throughout his life DuBek was adamantly opposed to censorship of any form.

After his retirement in 1986, DuBek, who had always been single, went on vacation and met a young sculptor, almost forty years his junior. They spent the last sixteen years of DuBek's life together in Phoenix, where he died of post-polio syndrome in 2002 at the age of eighty-six.

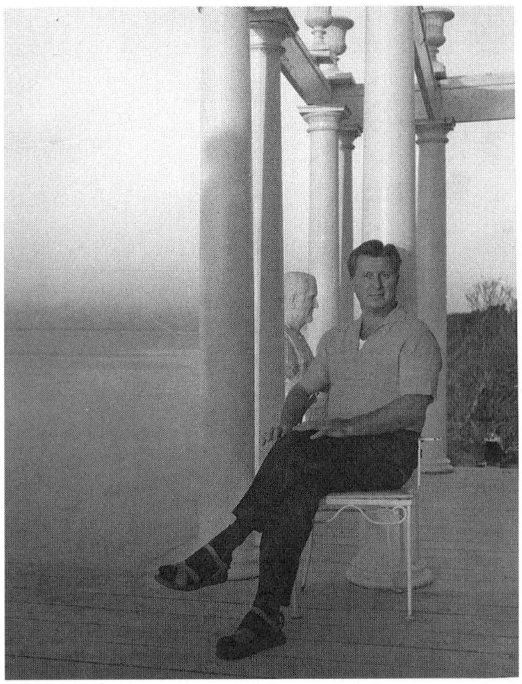

Ambrose's class.
Photo: John Lindquist

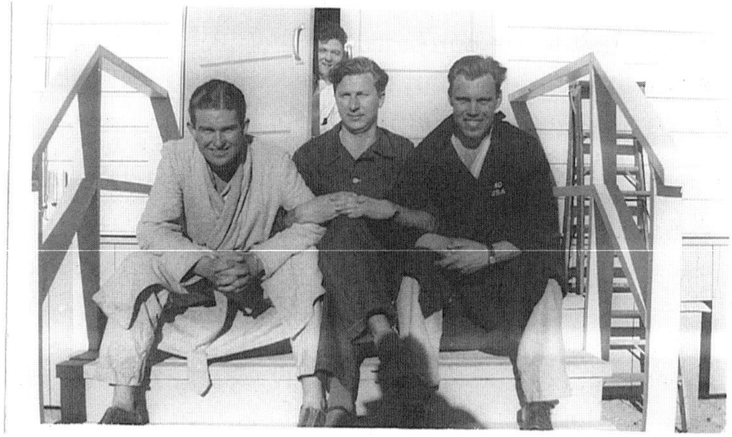

DuBek (center), flanked by two of his patients, c. 1942, was proud to have been personally commissioned by Present Roosevelt to set up the surgical service of the Victorville, California military hospital. Fresh from his apprenticeship in Hollywood with costume designer Adrian, he used his Hollywood connections to entertain the troops.

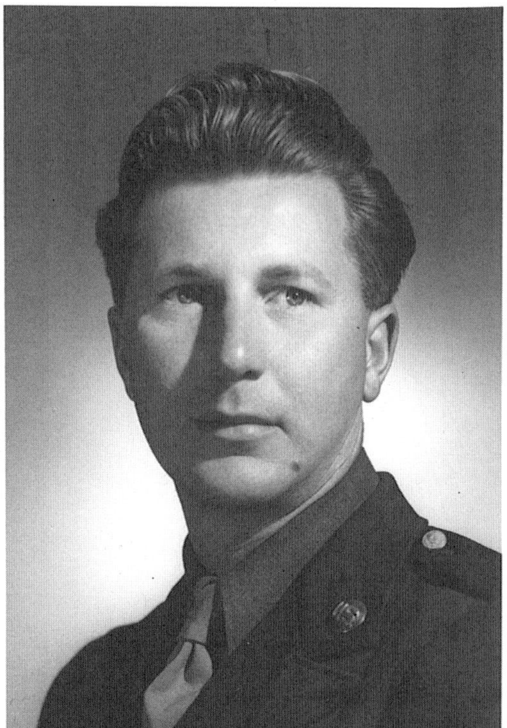

Formal portrait, World War II.

2 a,b

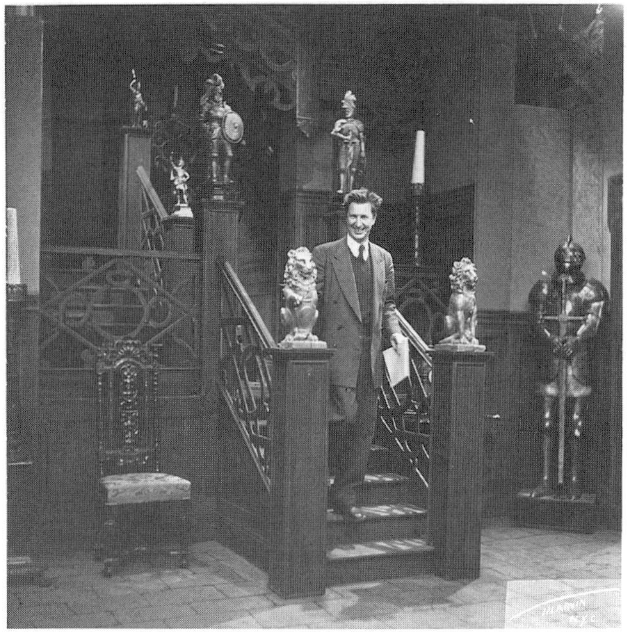

Established after World War II as CBS's head designer and decorator for its New York studios, DuBek is seen among his statuary on set.

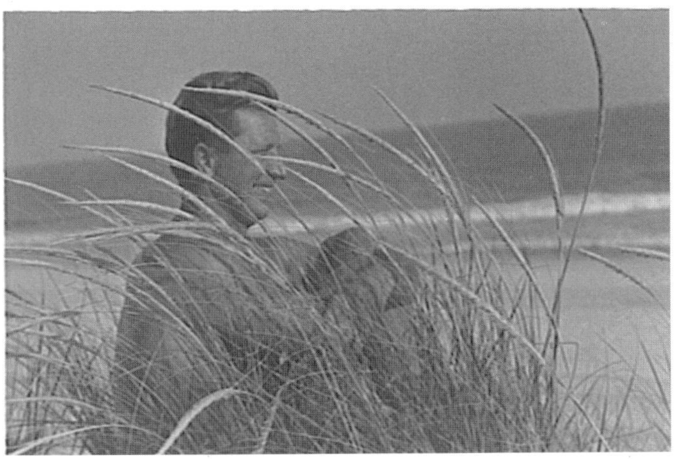

Happy gaze, Fire Island

3 a,b

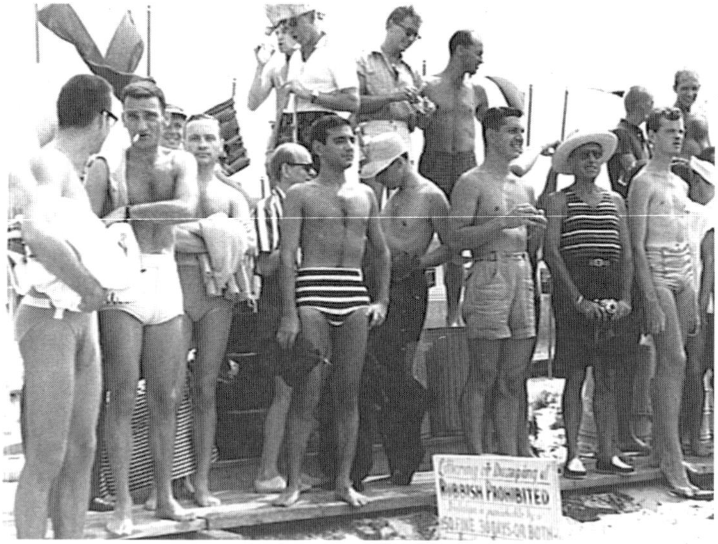

Fire Island, 1955.

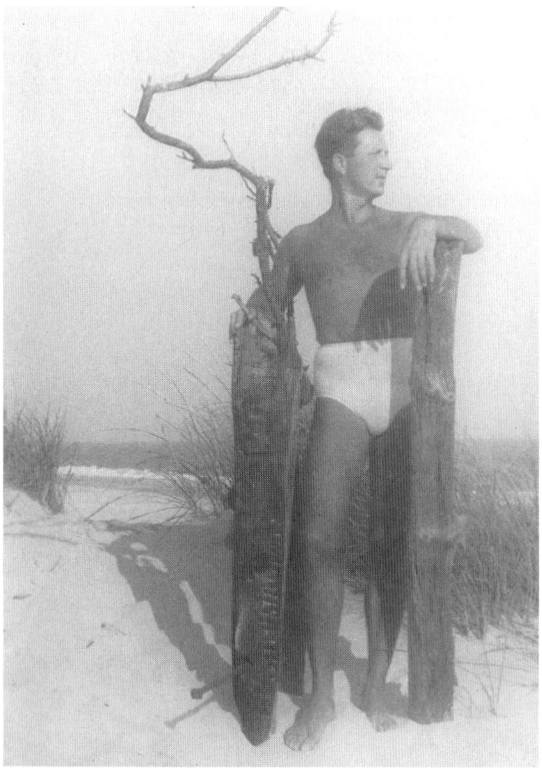

DuBek, settled in Manhattan's tony upper East Side, started summering at Fire Island in the late 1940s.
Photo: John Lindquist

3 c,d

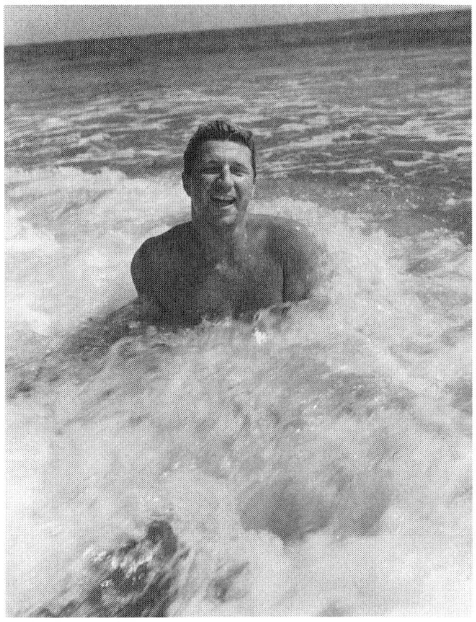

Fire Island, circa early 1950s.

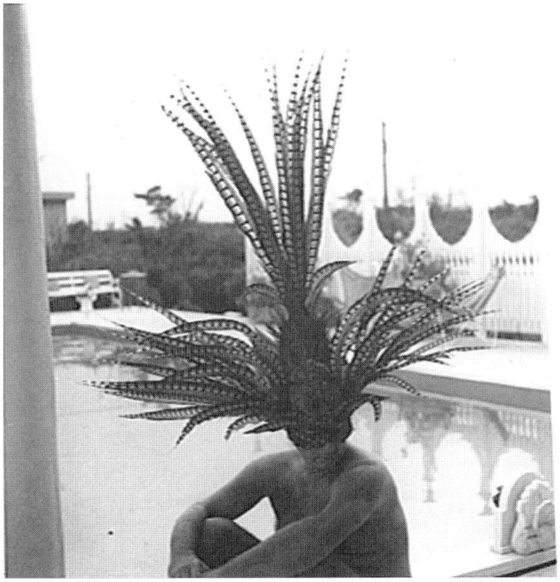

DuBek showing off his design skills in his own self-expressive getup, date unknown.
Photo: John Lindquist

3 e,f

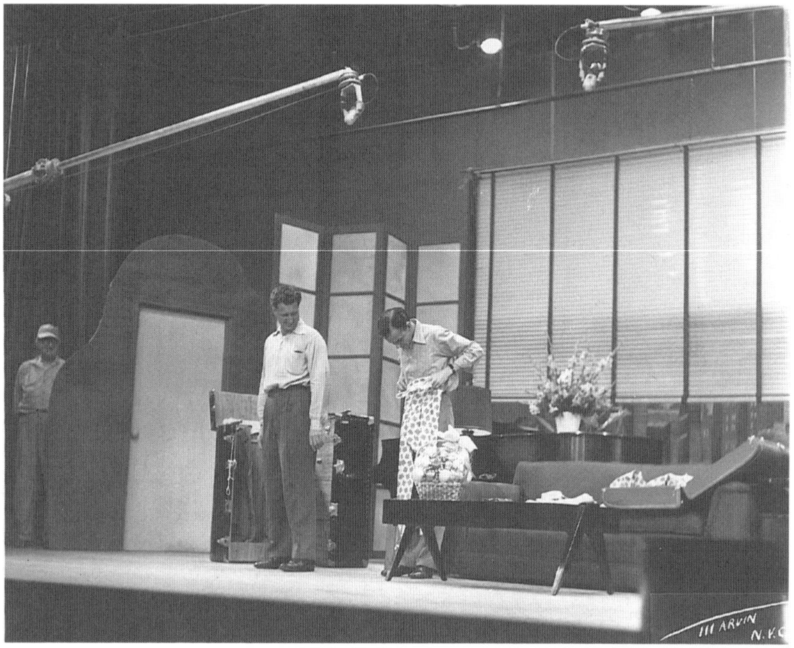

At the CBS studios, DuBek, (center), tries to persuade Frank Sinatra to try on some tasteful pyjamas, c. 1950s.

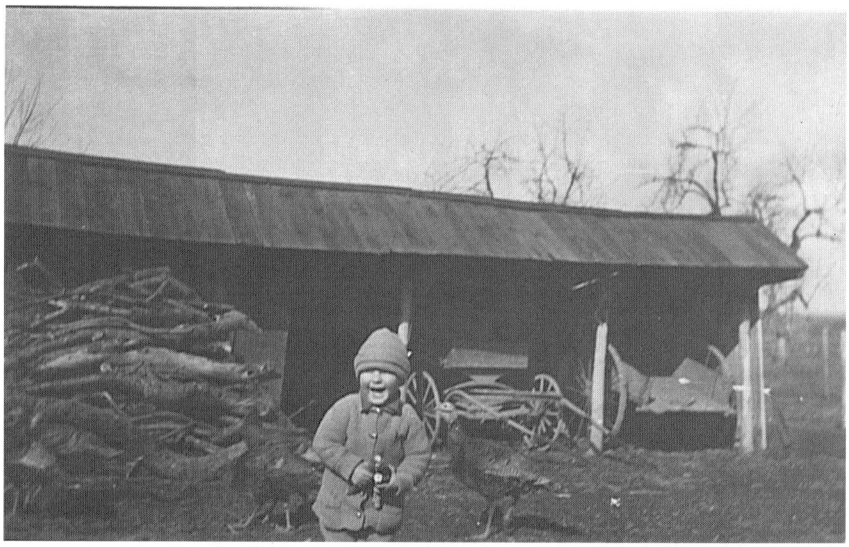

Young Ambrose on the New Jersey chicken farm, c. 1920.

3 g,h

National Dreams:
teutonic plates

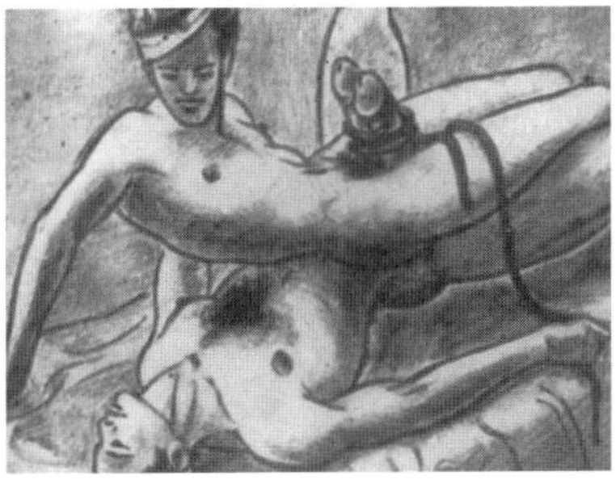

This "Germanic" cluster of fourteen images are in all likelihood the work of a single artist, of which we know almost nothing except the period and the language in which he started working. "Jean Vincent" probably became active in the 1930s and worked in German but with a French pseudonym and an iconography that was largely Anglo-Saxon and Macedonian(!). Based on the single shred of information *possibly* linking him to a publication site, the 1937 Viennese porno magazine *Gelbe Rose*, Jean Vincent may well have been Austrian. His pseudonym appears only once, and his initials a few other times, in the examples of his work sprinkled throughout this volume; otherwise, his oeuvre is linked only in terms of his evolving, distinctive way of rendering youthful male bodies and their sexual activities. Based on internal evidence in four of the Jean Vincent groupings ("Schoolboy *Wandervögel*," fig. 4-7; "Friar and Shepherd," 8-11; "On Board 'The Priates,'" 12-17; "Alexander the Great," 78-83), his

National Dreams: Teutonic Plates

original audience probably extended through all the German-speaking lands of Europe. No doubt archives will yield other hardcore graphic artists working within the bustling scene of sexual culture, consumerism, and revolt that existed between the wars in Weimar Germany, and even connections to "high art" artists producing erotic work in the same milieu at the same time, such as Christian Schad and Otto Schoff (as Gerard Koskovich has reminded us). But for now Jean Vincent is all we have, and let's not let this puzzle prevent us from having fun hypothetically wondering about Germanic mythologies of gay sexuality in these pictures and stories.

Here is one observation, intended as a question for further research. German gay literature of the first half of the twentieth century, from the canonical novelists Robert Musil and Thomas Mann to the unremembered contributors of the fiction and poetry that came out in the gay magazines of Berlin and later Zürich, was full of narratives of coming of age, mentorship, initiation, and institutions of male (homo-)socialization. Jean Vincent's fantasies of young men in hiker shorts, kindly friars, intergenerational orgy cruises, and ancient military subcultures are fully in step. Yet his work was clearly not addressed to Magnus Hirschfeld's vanguard constituency of "third sex" liberation, rather to its more conservative masculinist counterpart. Grouped around the *Gemeinschaft der Eigenen* (Community of the Self-Owned, founded in 1902), this tendency stood for an "'anti-modernist backlash' . . . traditional models of masculinity and gender politics (if not male supremacy), homosocial institutions and Socratic mentorship, *Lieblingminne* (Chivalric love) and *Freundesliebe* (love of friends)" (Waugh 1996, 402), and was not inconsistent with the growing militarism of 1930s German culture and politics. The introduction to the orgy-yacht epic "Priates" (a combination of "Priapus" with "nates," British slang for "buttocks"), regardless of how tongue-in-cheek it probably was, unfortunately says it all:

> The following pictures of the voyage of eight youths may offer the reader not only bodily joy and stimulation; they should also act as an antidote to the feminization of our age. Manly strength and beauty celebrates its resurrection in the visible sexual arousal of the young man in his godly nakedness, wild with desire. . . .

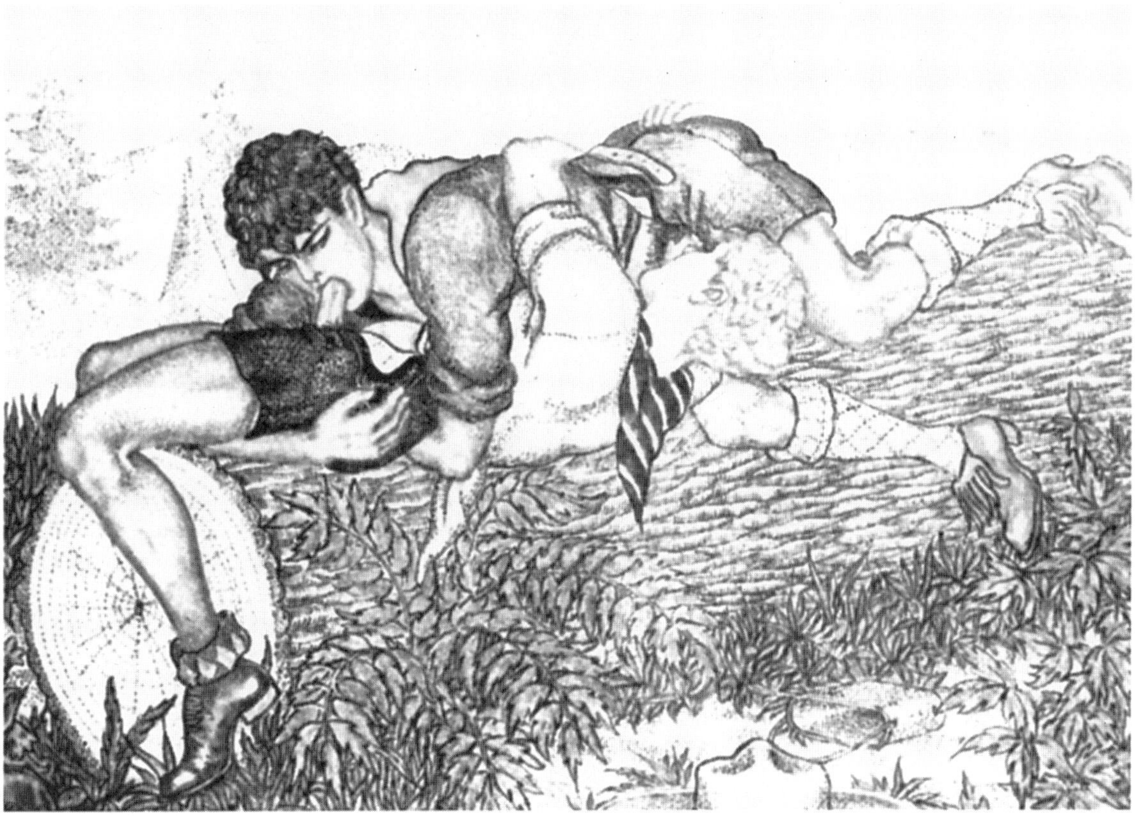

DuBek owned twelve panels from this daring series from the interwar period. Dapper, curly-haired youths
frolic amid nature in costumes that combine over-the-top private-school chic with the outdoorsy fashions of the
notorious Germanic homosocial youth movement the *Wandervögel* (roaming birds), which had affinities with
both German proto-queer and Nazi youth culture. Jean Vincent may well have been the author (Figures 9-17,
78-83, 210, 219, 236): his other work has a similar sense of the body, minus the eye makeup and Fauntleroy 4
fabrics!

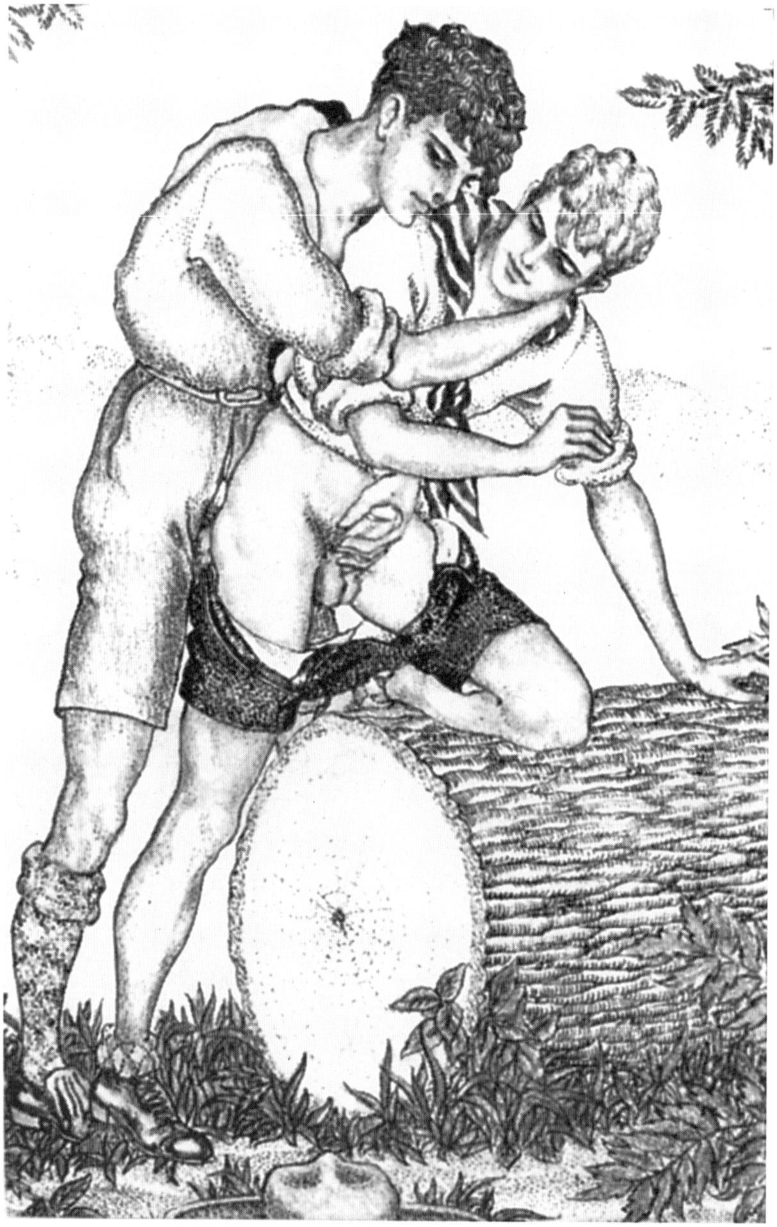

Apparently this anonymous series was the only material that DuBek had acquired that may have originated in his ancestral homeland, Austria. At least one item from this series about teenage hiker dandies in heat was published in *Gelbe Rose* ("pink yolk"), the Vienna porno magazine that had been launched secretly around 1927-28 but functioned increasingly openly in the 1930s, flirting with taboos other than intergenerational eros as
5 well (Hohmann 1980, 224). Another similar magazine called *El Dorado* also circulated at that time, for some of
Berlin's decadent sexual underground apparently relocated to Vienna after Hitler's rise to power—temporarily.

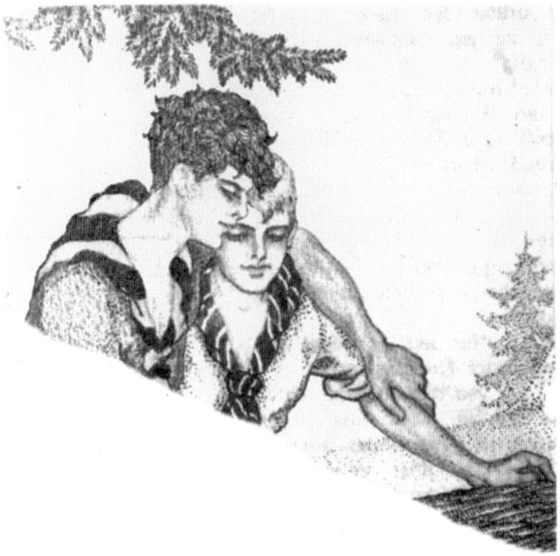

This image of mutual masturbation has been cropped by the publisher because of the current volatility of the legal climate as well as of bookstore practice. I regret any moratorium on historical research into the representation of legal sexual activity among teenagers (over the current age of consent in most jurisdictions) in the first half of the twentieth century. Archives are also at risk in this climate, since most holdings discreetly
include visual materials produced before the current panic, and in some jurisdictions such as the Netherlands 6
irreplaceable historical research collections have already been destroyed.

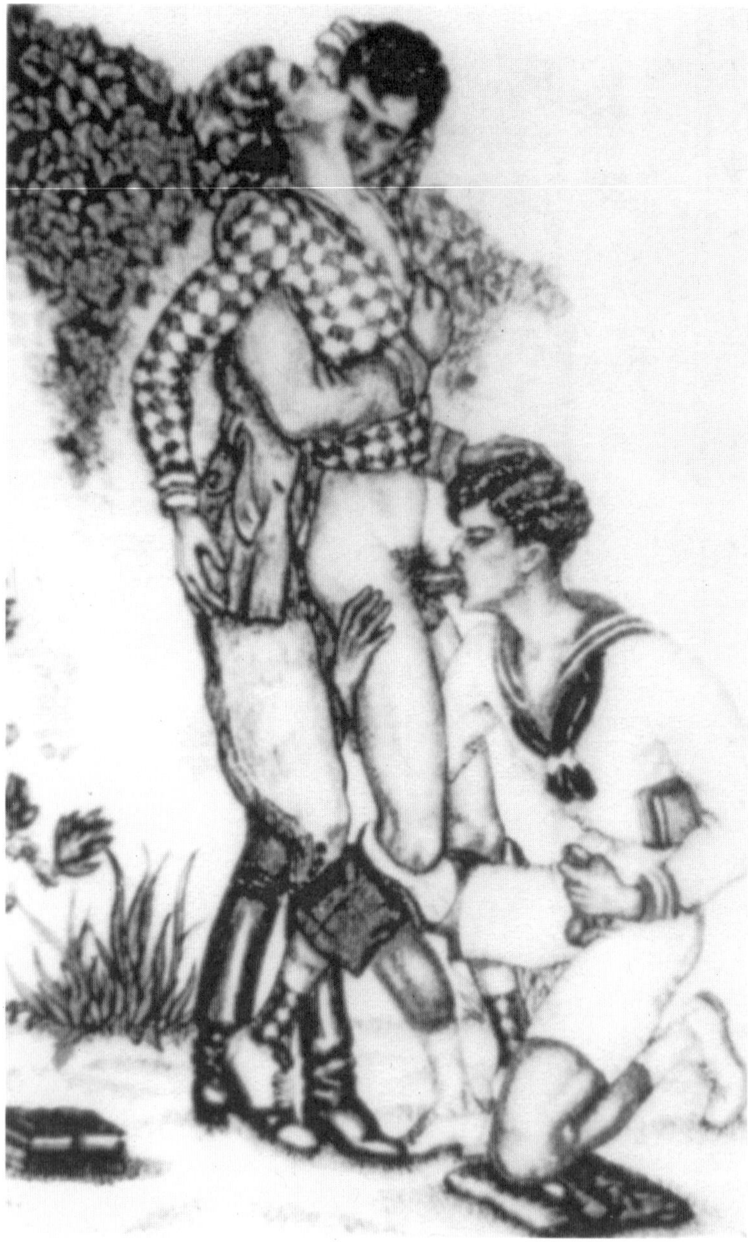

Reminiscent of children's illustrations from the period, these images are clearly more interested in their fey figures' getups than the mechanics of their get-downs. Nevertheless, elsewhere in the series, these forthright young men get even more adventurous and fuck a goat. One panel shows one of the young men engaged in auto-fellatio beside a classical priapic statue, while one of the items from *Gelbe Rose* shows a four-man daisy
7 chain in an indoors setting, still in fastidious *Wandervögel* outfits. Unfortunately, DuBek's copies were dupes and badly out of focus.

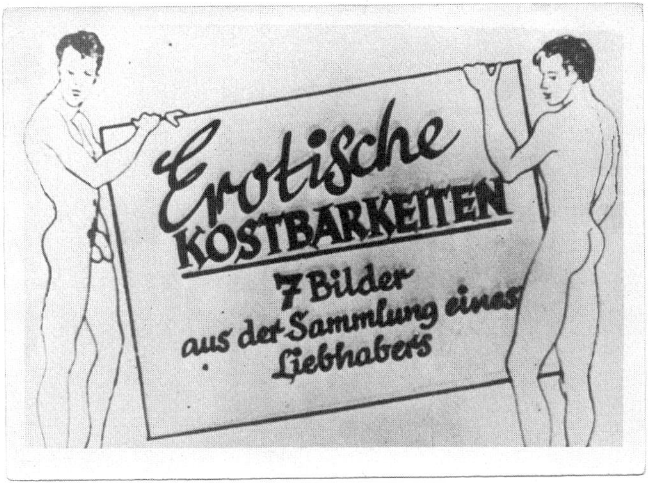

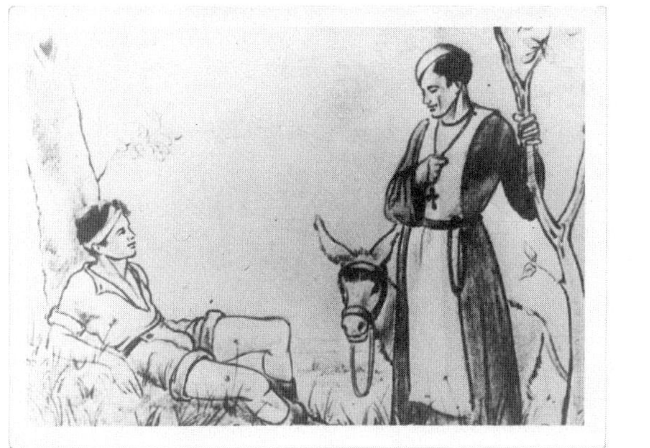

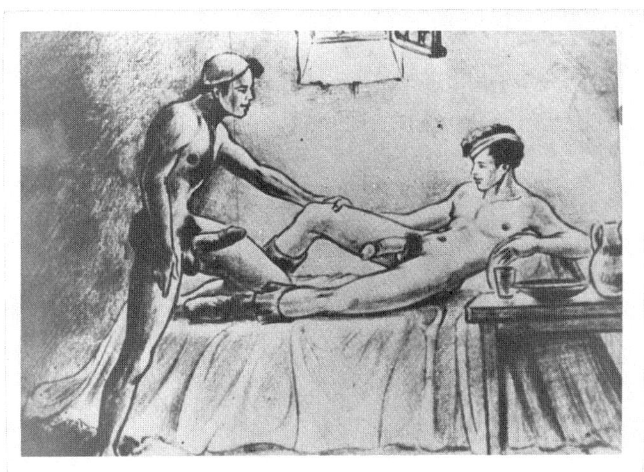

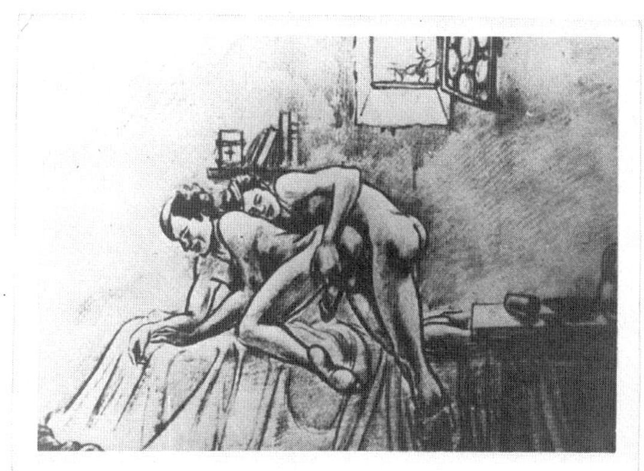

Only these four images from this legendary pre-war series appeared in *Out/Lines* because of a space shortage. DuBek's holdings from this series were of better quality than my foggy dupes, so the series can be fleshed out, as it were, in this volume. It is not absolutely certain that the title "Erotic Treasures: 7 Pictures from the Collection of a Lover" belongs to the friar and shepherd story, but the fact that exactly seven frames showing the tender lovers have surfaced suggests that this is the case. 8

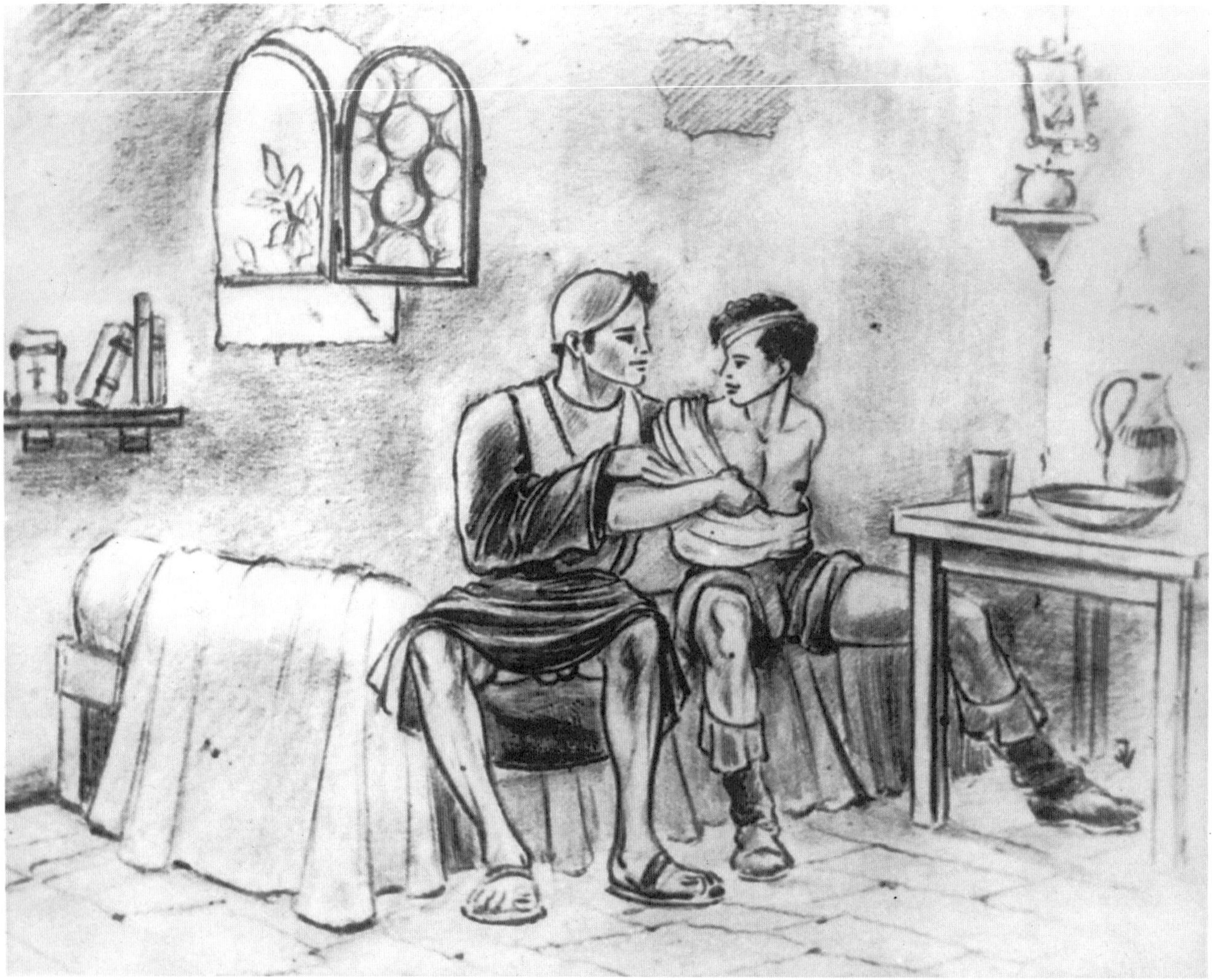

The friar plies his wounded protegé with nourishment and comfort, and wants to offer more, judging from
the stirrings under his cassock. The chicken scratch in the lower right corner of this and the next two frames
seems to be "J.V." I don't remember why I concluded that the youth looks after ruminants—no doubt a long-
9 buried fantasy from a childhood that began with *Heidi* stories and ended with the "Lonely Goatherd" song from
The Sound of Music. Judging from the leather shorts and boots, he could also be a solitary *Wandervögel* (for
other interest in alpine shorts, see Figures 231-232).

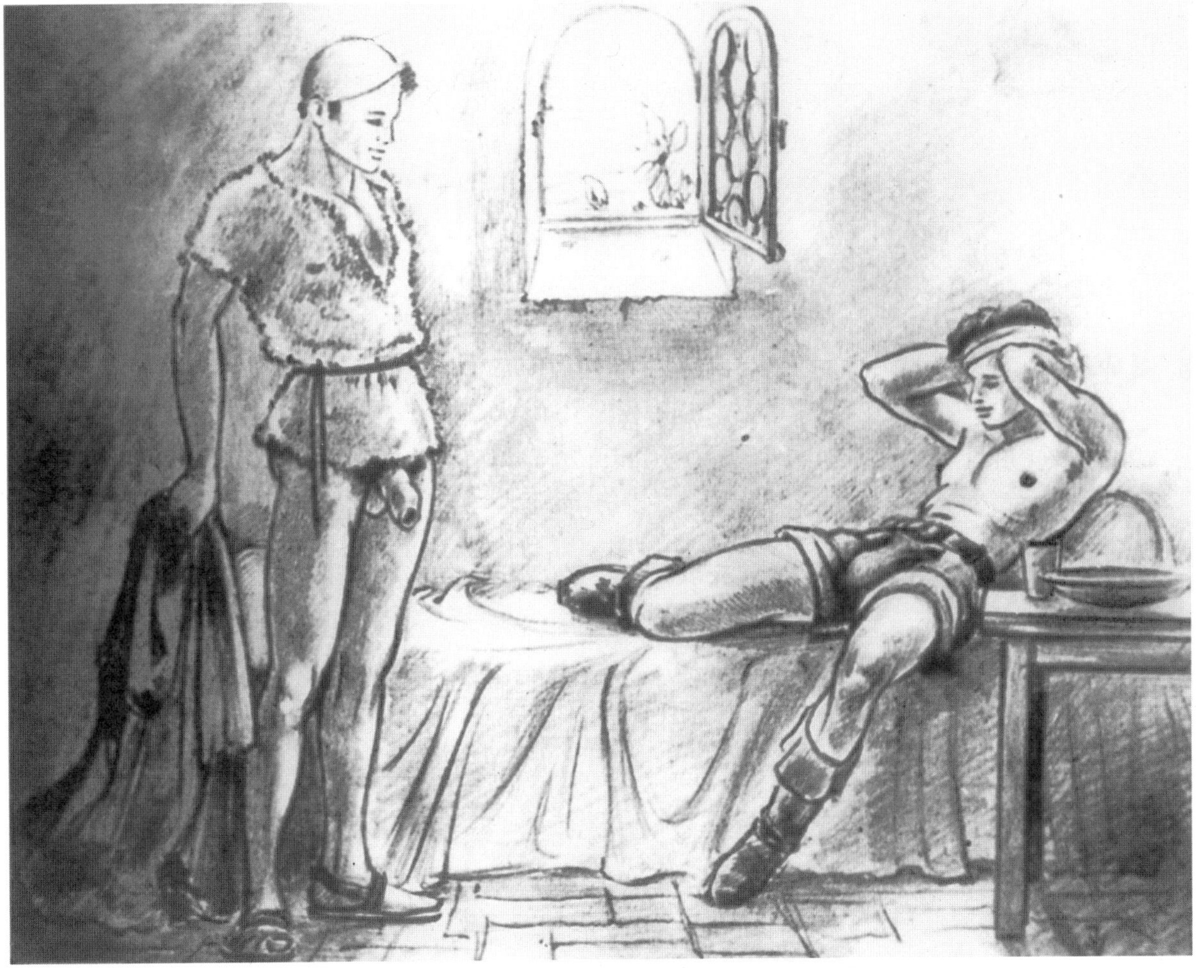

Like any good pornographer, Jean Vincent accords the narrative buildup and the graceful rituals of seduction, disrobing, and self-offering as much weight as the actual fucking. This seems to be the third image in the sequence, after the title card. Next came the moment from *Out/Lines* where the partners, erections proudly bared, establish touch with their fingers joining on the shepherd's knee. Needless to say, the friar keeps on his skullcap, and the shepherd his boots, throughout. **10**

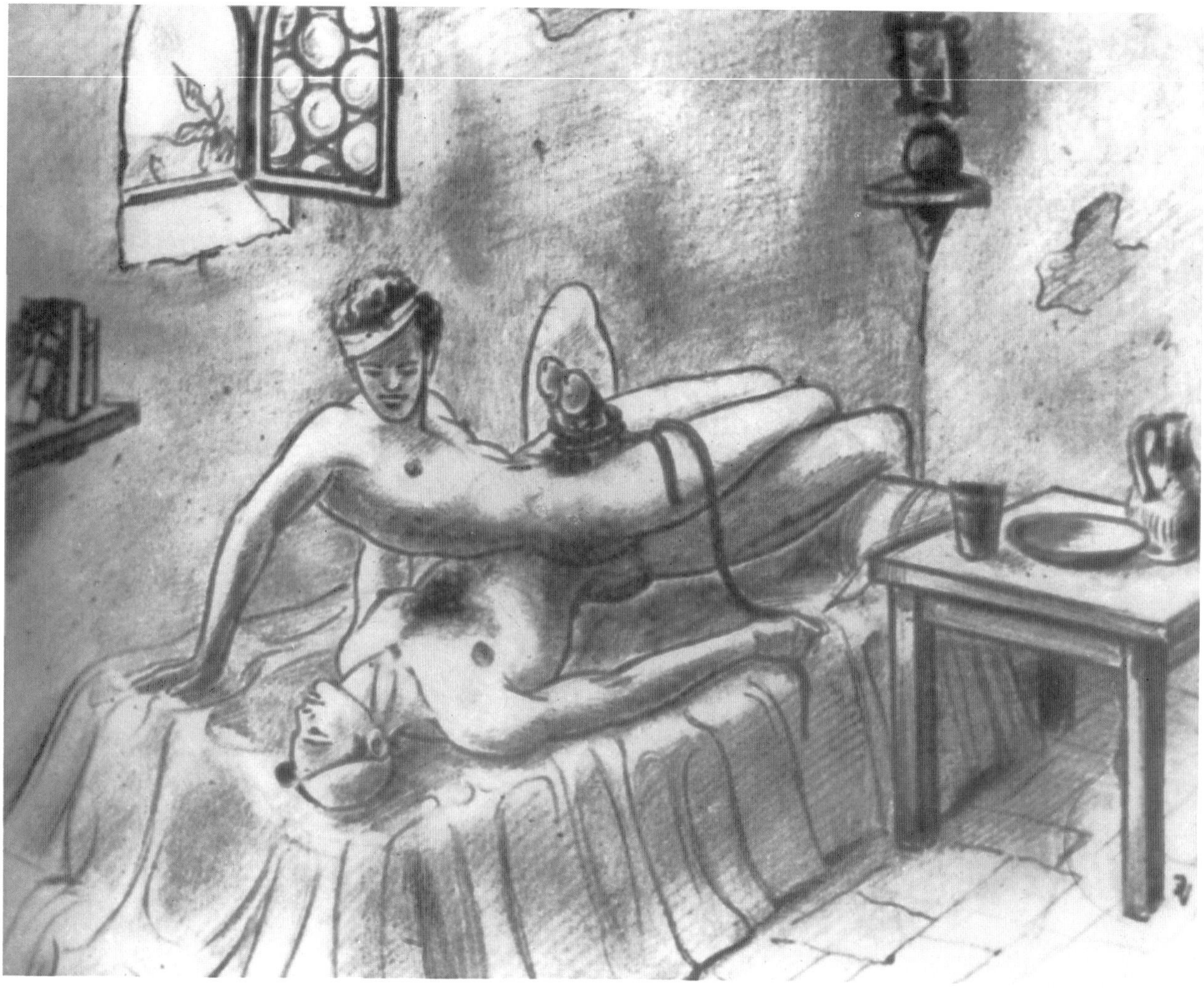

This panel probably comes next, and it's a sexual position that is unique to both *Out/Lines* and Lust Unearthed—"intracrural," as they say in Latin. At first I didn't notice that the partners' cocks were bound together by more than lust: using the friar's waistcord in this ways gives the eroticism an unexpected twist. . . . The series presumably ends with the image from *Out/Lines* of goblet symbolically overturned, the grazer taking
11 his turn as ploughboy. Sort of a capsule history of civilization, isn't it?

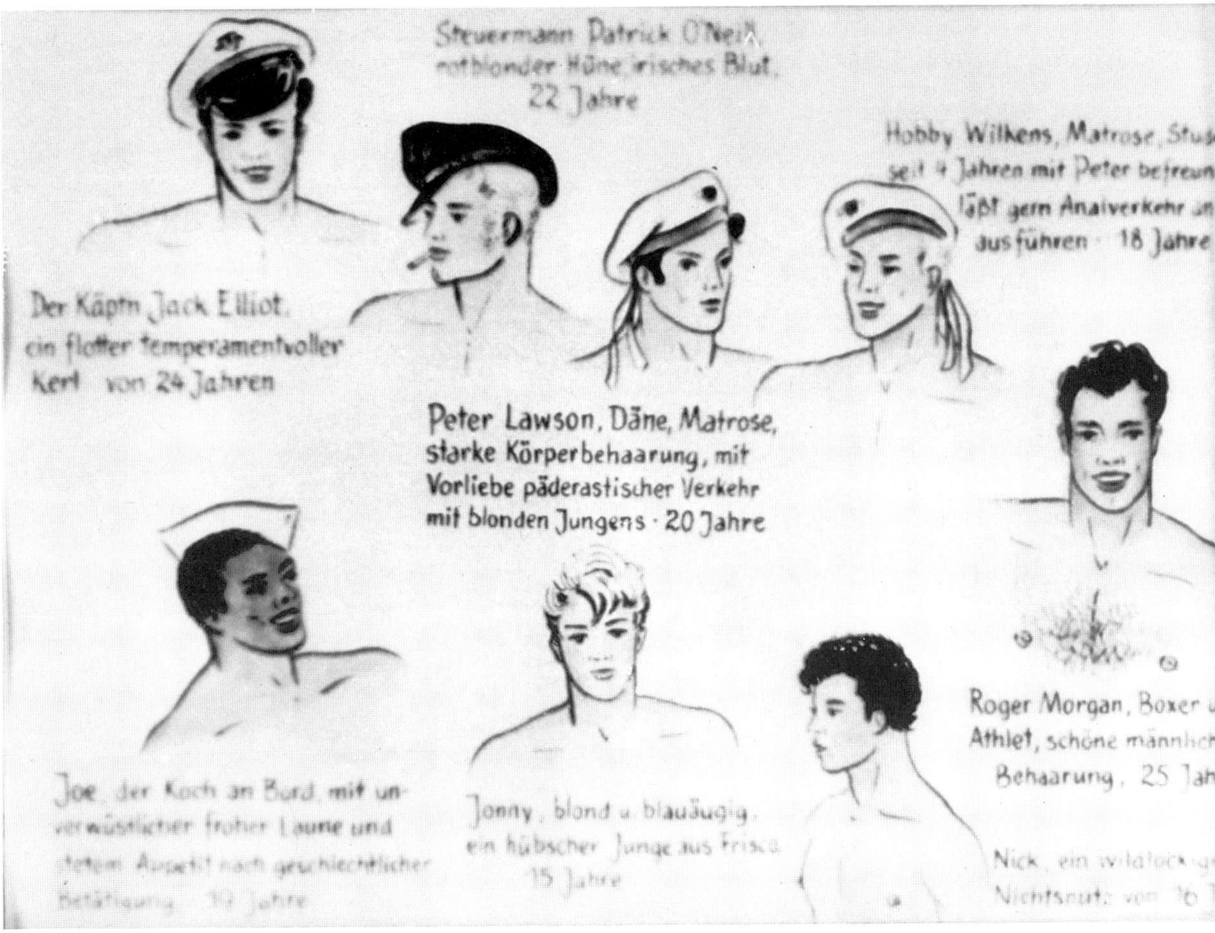

"Captain Jack Elliot, a lively, temperamental guy of 24 years. Helmsman Patrick O'Neill, a reddish-blond giant with Irish blood, 22. Peter Lawson, Danish, a seaman, with thick body hair and a predilection for pederastic intercourse with blond boys, 20. Hobby Wilkens, a seaman and student who for the last four years has been Peter's friend, gladly allows anal interference, 18. Roger Morgan, boxer and athlete, with beautiful, manly body hair, 25. Nick, a wild curly-haired good-for-nothing, 16. Jonny, blond and blue-eyed, a pretty boy from Frisco, 15. Joe, the cook on board, with indestructible good spirits and a steady appetite for sexual activity, 19."

12

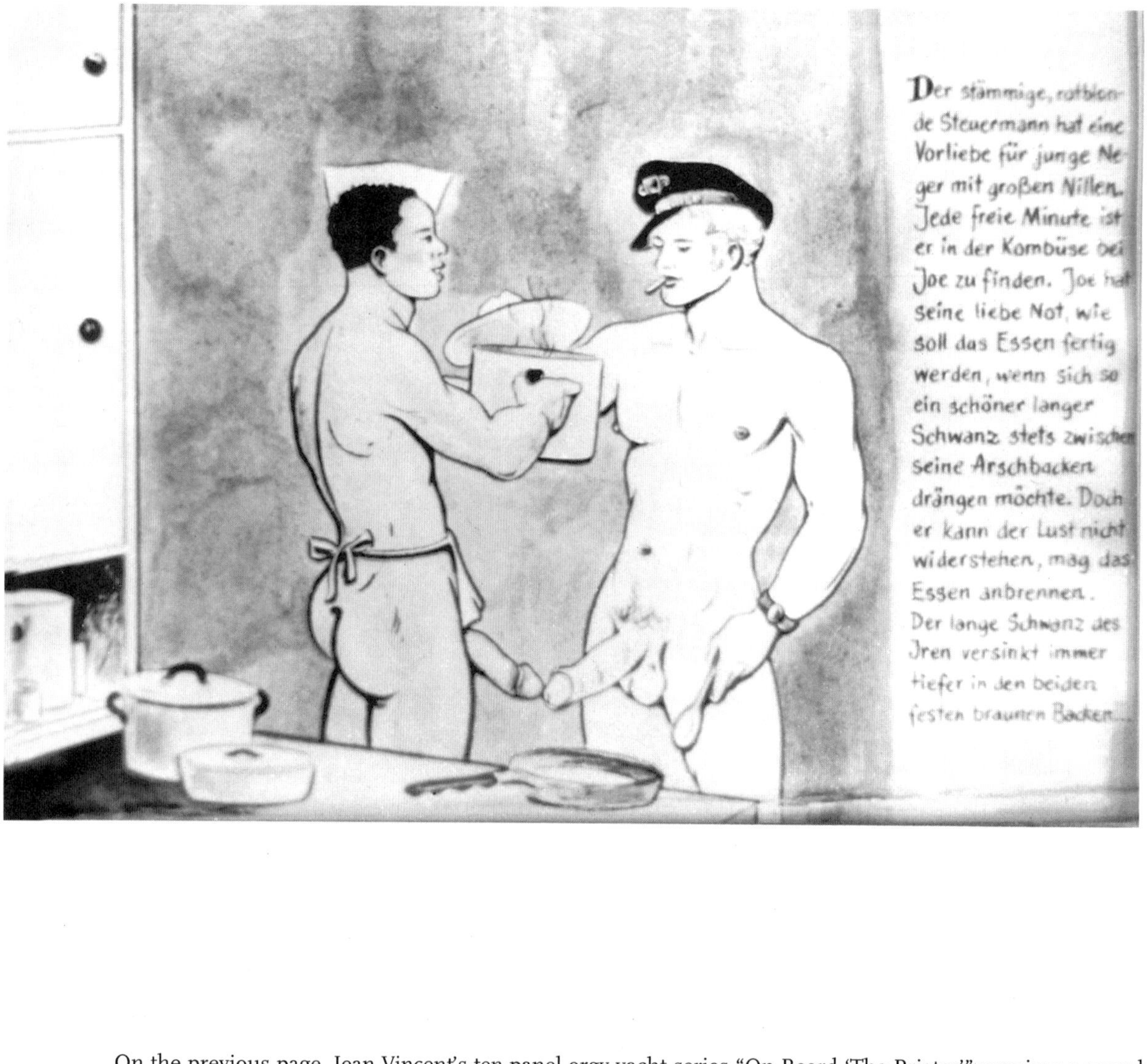

13 On the previous page, Jean Vincent's ten-panel orgy yacht series "On Board 'The Priates'" requires a complex setup. Complete with racial stereotypes, the *dramatis personae* (clockwise from upper left) could belong to a porno film a half-century later. Here, contrary to the German caption, Patrick hits on Joe's stew more than his buns . . . : "The sturdy, reddish-blond helmsman has a predilection for young black men with big cocks. Every free minute, he can be found in the galley with Joe. Joe was worried: how to get the meal with a beautiful long cock always pushing between his cheeks? But he can't withstand his desire, even if the dinner burns. The Irishman's long cock sinks deeper and deeper between his solid brown buttocks. . . ."

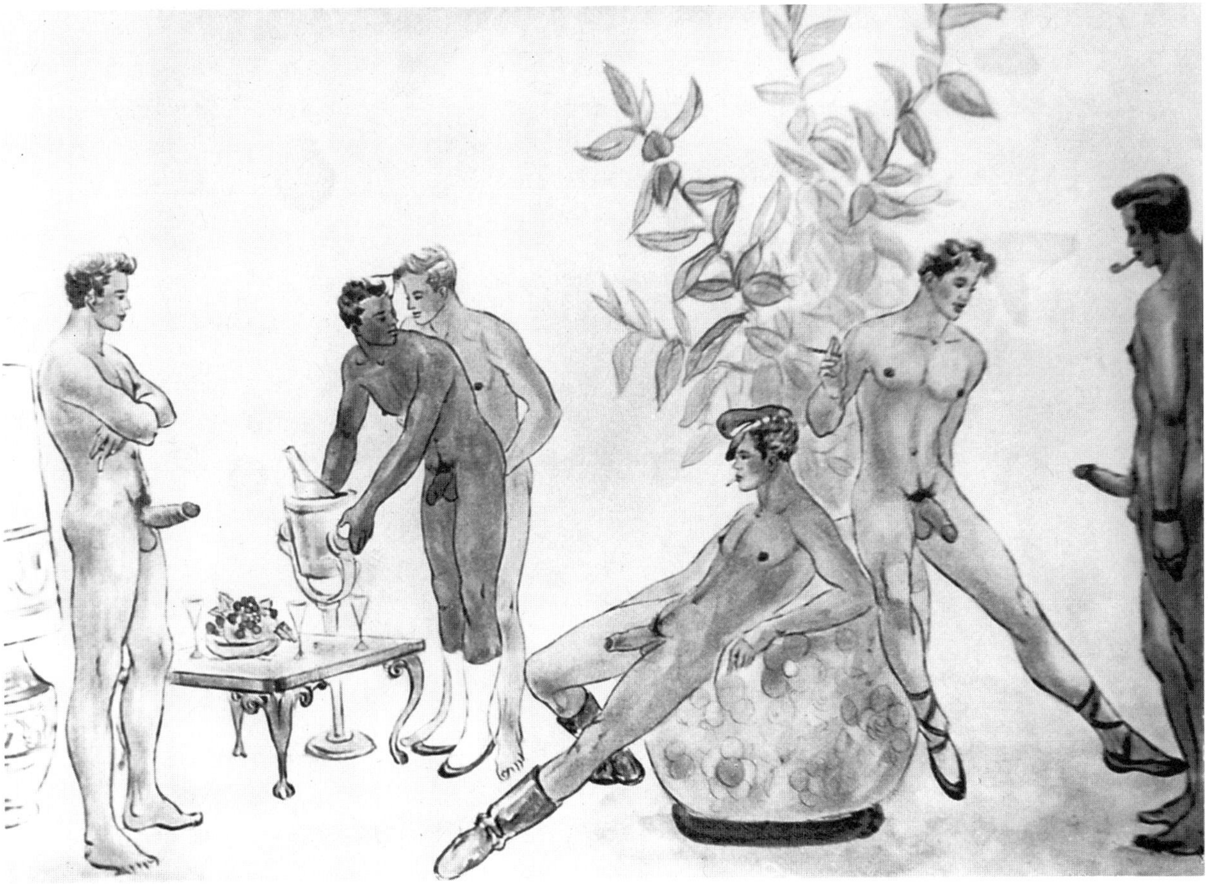

Only seven of the yacht's passengers are present in this lounging scene that preludes the orgy. I confess I can't really tell who is who, especially since there now seem to be two men of color in the party, and the figure second from the right (Hobby?) seems to have veered somewhat swishward and developed an interest in ballet.

14

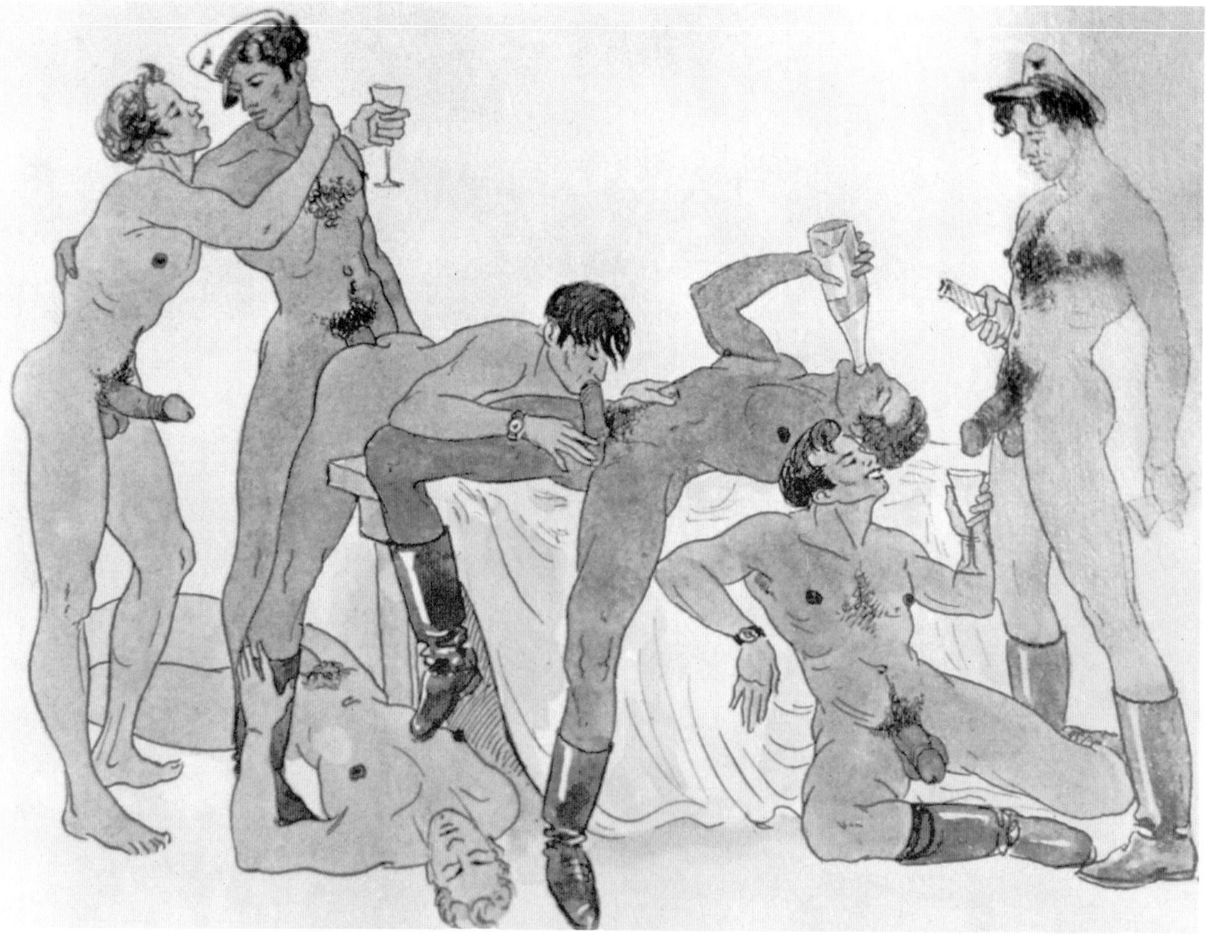

The seven-some in full orgy mode, but the continuity errors abound since Joe seems to have suddenly headed back to the galley and three of the sailors have donned riding boots, the blond has swooned from either drunkenness or bottomish ecstasy, and all participants seem to be getting thirsty—and not only for wine!

15

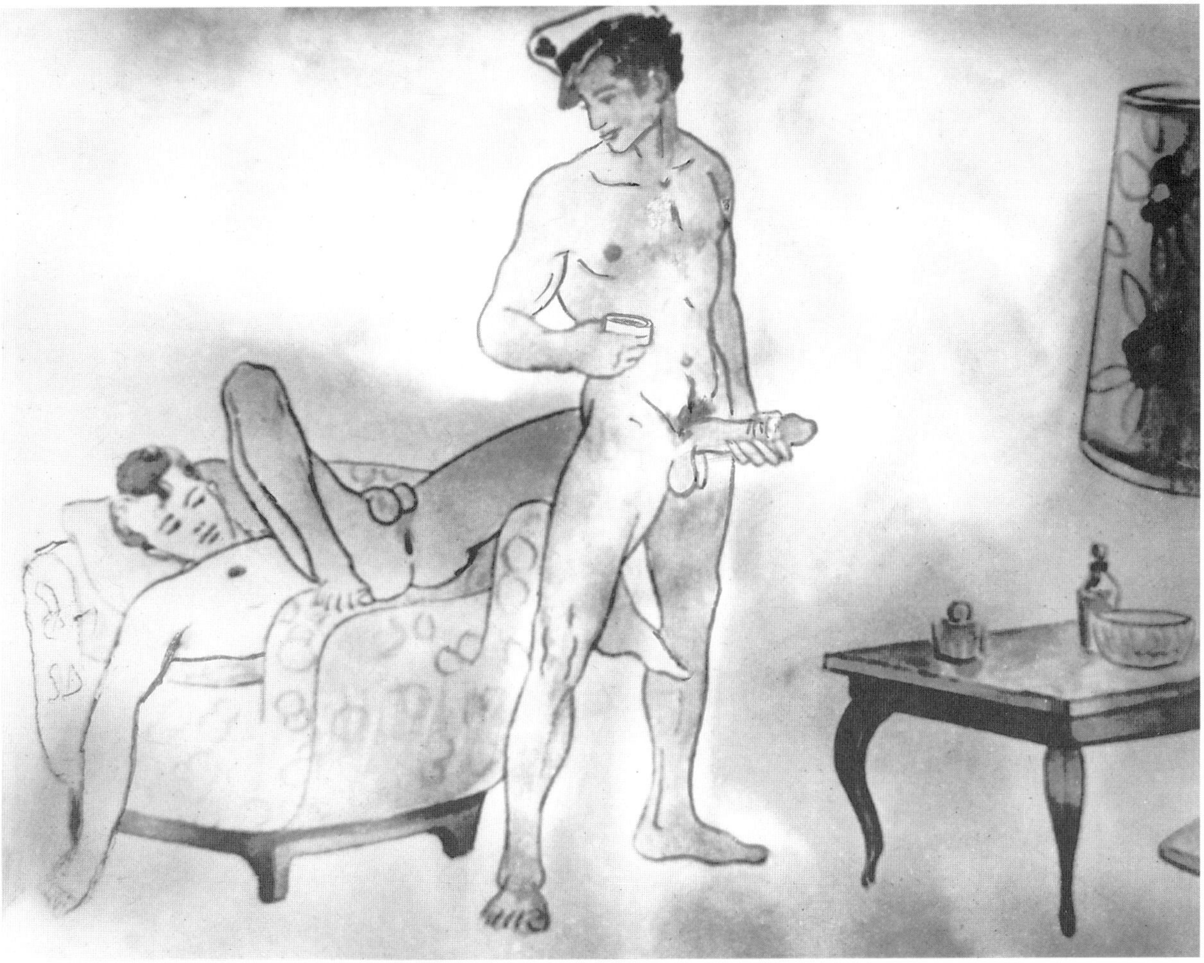

The title card for the yacht series shows a sailing vessel with a long bowsprit and introduces the adventures of the eight youths onboard, explaining that the pictures should elicit not only bodily pleasure, but also an antidote to the feminization of our era. The resurrection of manly strength and beauty were to be celebrated in the open nakedness on board and the love of boys, described in its original Greek as "*Paidon eros.*" Here, Jonny is eager as the Captain applies vaseline. Despite the democratic ambience, the "Priates" maintains an ancient **16** Greek sense of sex role hierarchy around age.

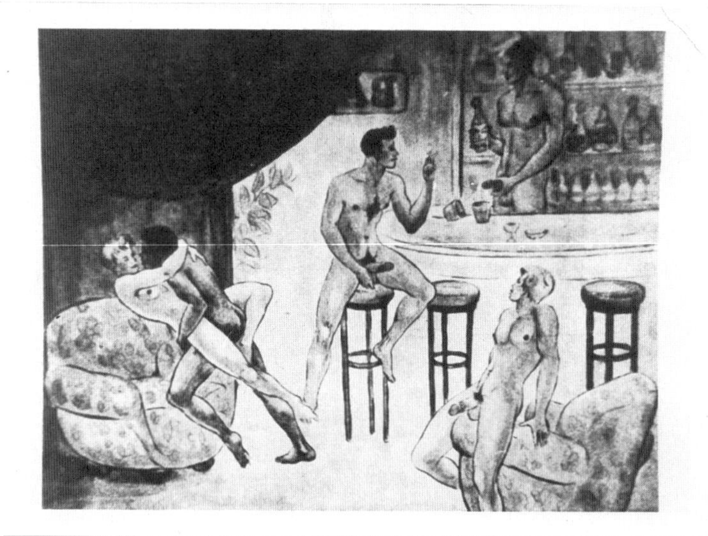

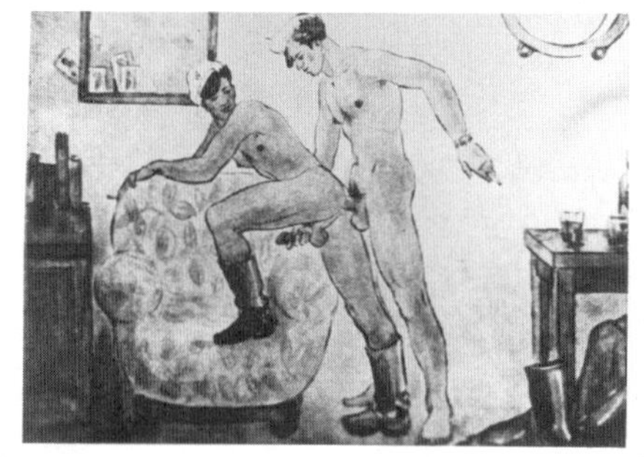

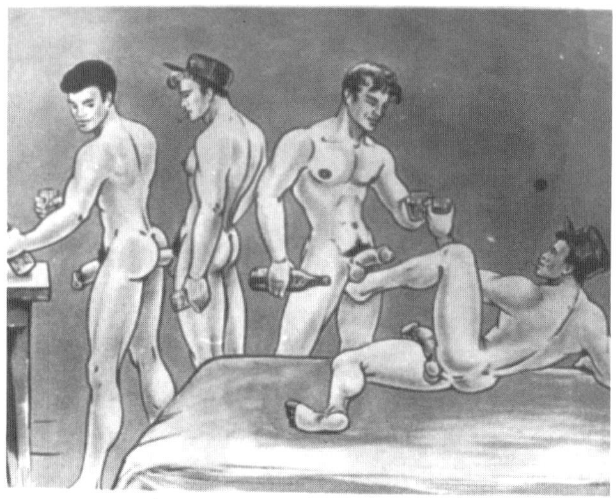

The panels from "Priates" published in *Out/Lines* located the stuffed chairs (with a testicular motif?) in the onboard bar, complete with portholes, where Joe serves as bartender in addition to all his other duties. The third panel may not really belong to the series since the headgear has been switched and the style of outlining the figures has evolved (but the narrative universe of free-flowing erotic energy has not).

17

National Dreams:
french active

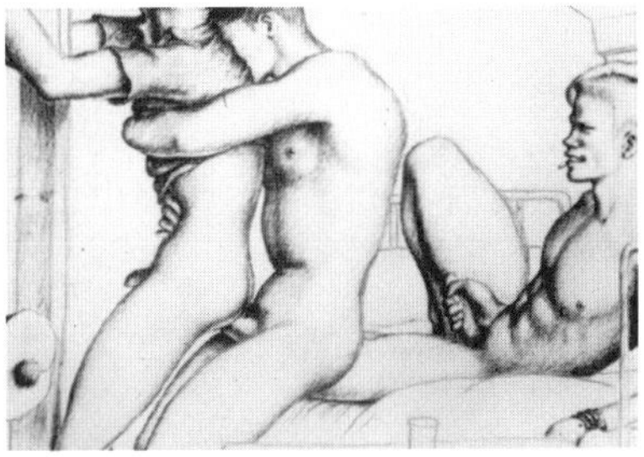

If the Germans seemed somewhat systematic in their fornications, pursuing them as if studying for a physics exam, their Gallic neighbors imagined themselves going at it drenched in attitude—namely, existential angst. The French artists included here—Roland Caillaux (fig. 18-26, 199, perhaps 167-168), "El Greco" (fig. 27-32, 119-120), Tola Soungouroff (fig. 33-37), and "Cheekbones" (fig. 38-42), as well as Paul Smara (fig. 104-110)—all fit this pattern. They epitomize for me the tendency of French gay pornographers of mid-century to somehow invest sex and the body with the grand weight of being itself, as if in anticipation of Jean-Paul Sartre's existentialist reading of Genet, *Saint Genet; comédien et martyr* (1952).

National Dreams: French Active

One of DuBek's images by Soungouroff, unfortunately not included in this book, pertains to another specifically historical French iconographic tradition. The 1940s postcard, part of DuBek's series that often made their trans-Atlantic way in American suitcases, shows a rather unhappy looking monk masturbating a similarly unhappy pubescent youth (and uncannily couldn't refer with more relevance to North America of the 2000s). It is part of the continuous stream of anti-clericalist obscene images, unmasking the sexual hypocrisy of the Church, that go back to the pre-Revolutionary period. It also refers to a more recent and less historically momentous motif popular in French stag movies from the turn of the twentieth century, complete with rutting priests and ribald nuns. Soungouroff's vignette of a man of the cloth is decidedly dour compared to the gentle German romance already encountered in Figures 8 to 11.

Key to our *feelthy* French pictures is this tradition of political porn, as well of course as Paris's centuries-long heritage of *littérature maudite*, writing of sexual dissidence whose queer vector extends from the Marquis de Sade through nineteeth-century poet Arthur Rimbaud to twentieth-century novelists André Gide, Marcel Proust, Jean Cocteau, and Jean Genet. As we shall see, the latter two are contemporaraneous to, acquaintances of, and a strong influence on most if not all of the French artists represented here (in their sailor iconography if nothing else, whether ember-eyed à la Caillaux or blank-eyed à la Smara). In this context, the French underground has a cultural respectability that none of the other national traditions have, and in fact was not even very *under*ground, considering that France had a culture of sexual representation and sociality that was largely tolerated and licit in a de facto way. DuBek's French images stand out from the rest of his collection in the way they reflect this socio-political legitimacy and intersection with high cultural artistic forms. No wonder there's room for all that angst—or should I say *angoisse*?

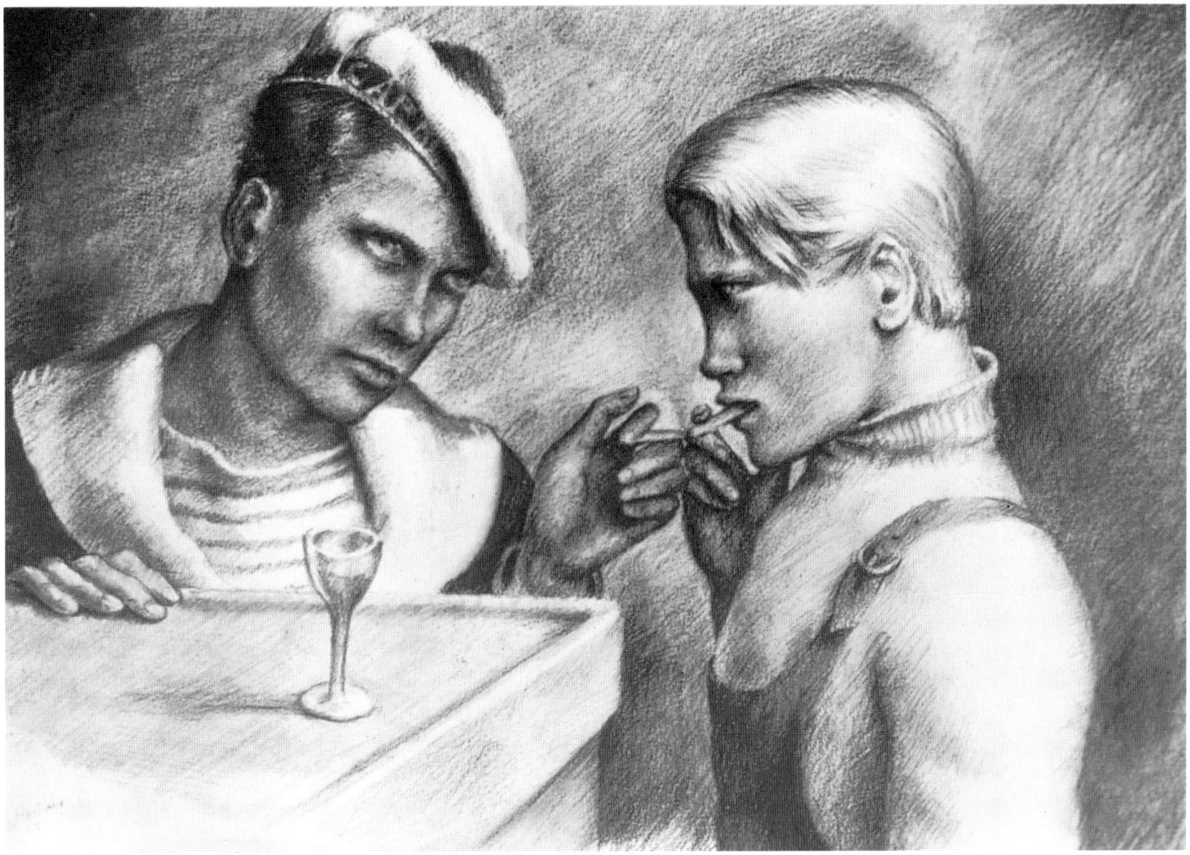

If the exquisite 1945 illustrations by Roland Caillaux for Jean Genet's *Notre-Dame des Fleurs (Our Lady of the Flowers)* were one of the revelations of *Out/Lines,* it was a major coup when Caillaux pictures reportedly produced for Genet's 1947 novel *Querelle de Brest* turned up in the DuBek collection. This frame in particular feels very Genet, with its intense sharing of a light between a fully costumed sailor and civilian in a waterfront bar. The subsequent genitally-explicit illustrations were hard put to rise to this level of drama.

18

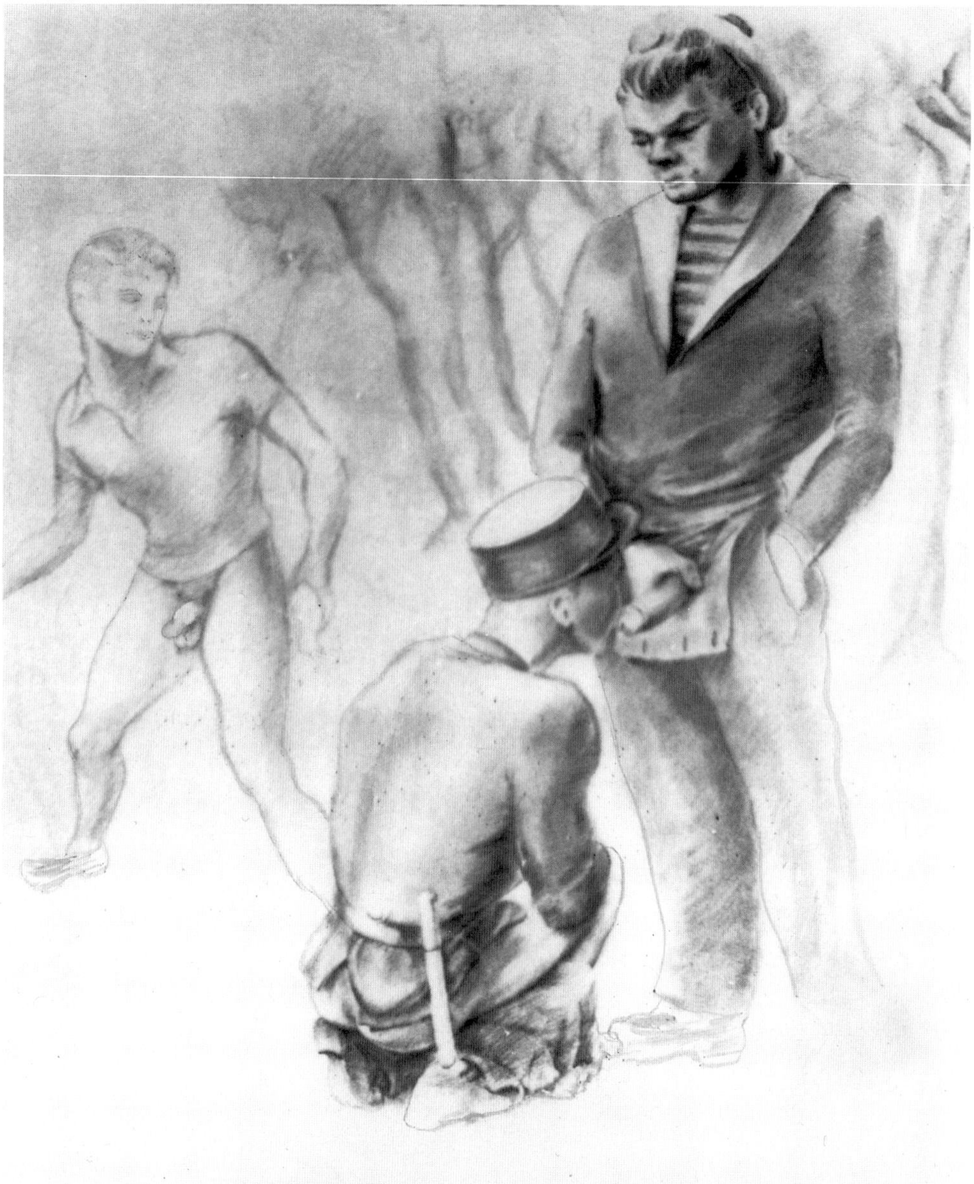

This panel may seem to be the most literal reference to the plot of *Querelle* with its dalliance between cop and
sailor, witnessed by a horny eighteen-year-old civilian. However, in the novel, it is Querelle the sailor/murderer
who sucks and is fucked by Mario the detective, rather than the other way around. Never mind; the ambience
of *Querelle's* wooded cruising ground on the edge of the seaport is vivid and true. If this is *Querelle*, it's clearly
19 the loose Hollywood-esque adaptation credit "inspired by," rather than a faithful transcription of the novel, that
applies.

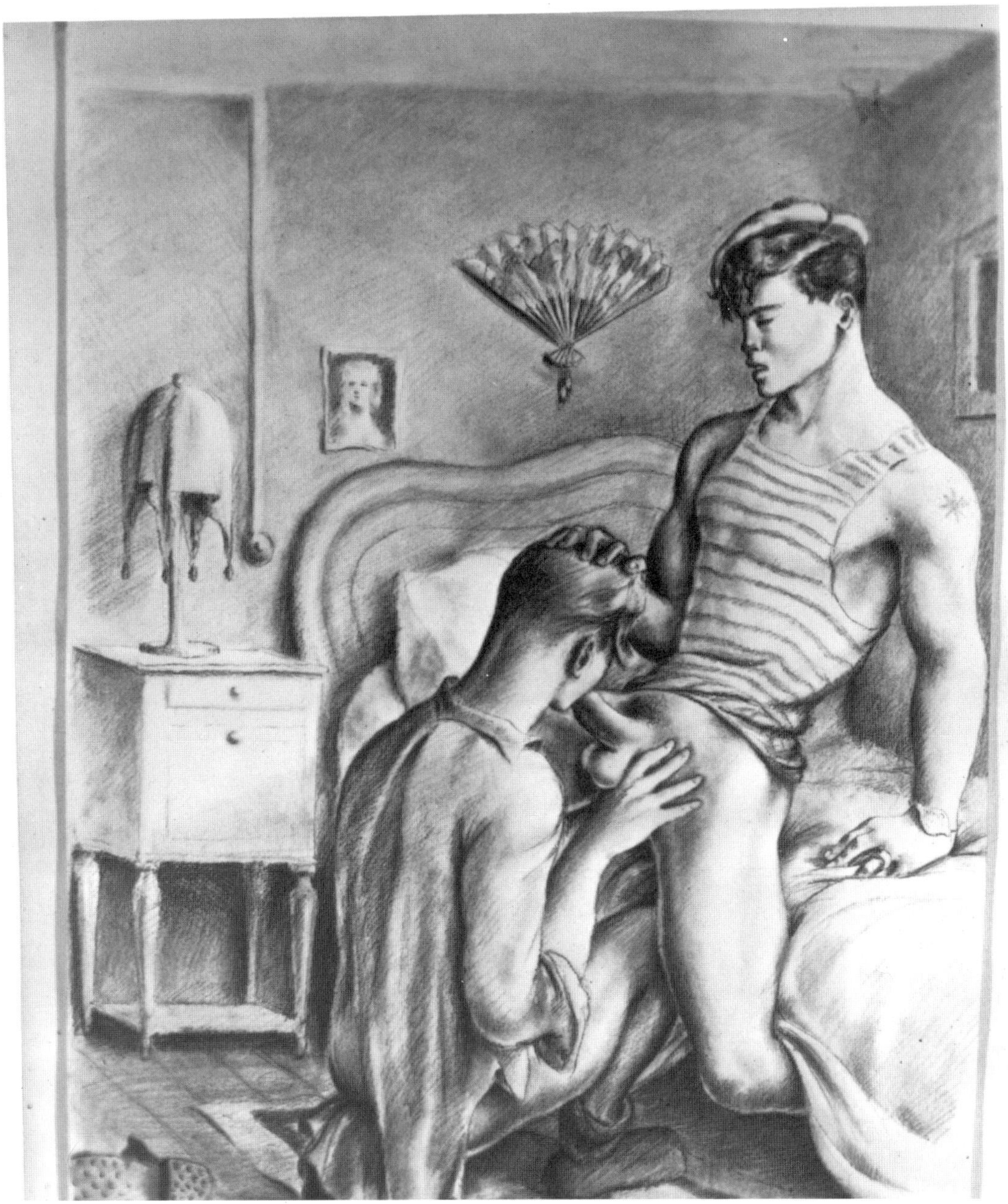

Caillaux's friend Jean Cocteau also produced a series of illustrations for *Querelle* in 1947 and DuBek may have confused the two not dissimilar French artists (he owned a set of Cocteau originals). Among other discrepancies, Caillaux seems decidedly more "French passive" in his fantasy world than "Greek passive" Genet. Nevertheless, Caillaux offered a cast of macho types and a seedy, cobwebbed environment (is this the room above Madame Lysiane's bar?) that rings authentic even if it is not a literal narration of *Querelle's* plot. **20**

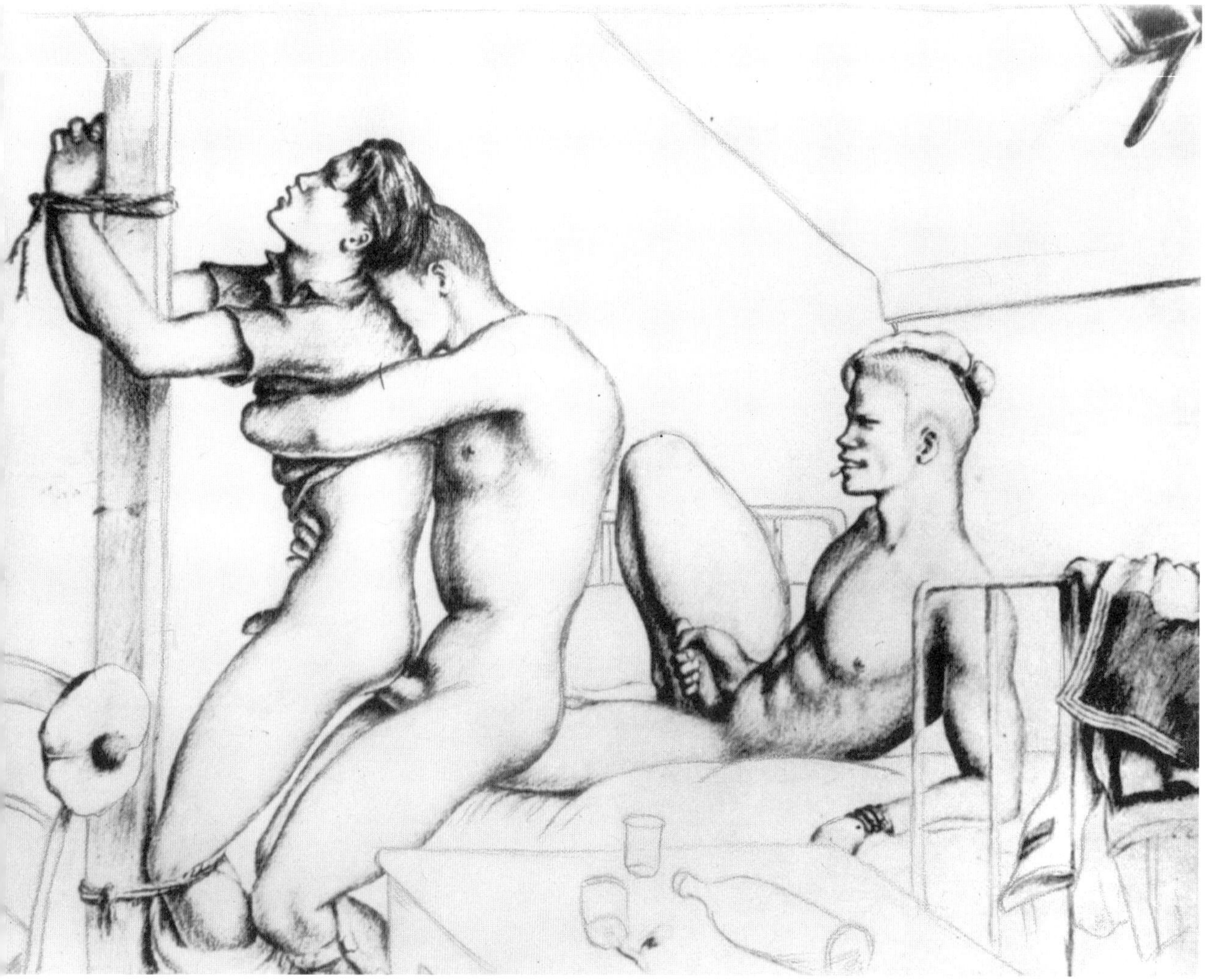

Here, as well as in his images for *Notre-Dame des Fleurs,* Caillaux loves these attic rooms with their sloping ceilings, skylights, and handy pillars. This odd three-way setup, a couple watched by an aroused voyeur (or sometimes two), occurs more than thirty times in this selection. What does *that* mean? Something about
21 the centrality of the participatory outsider within gay male erotic imagination?

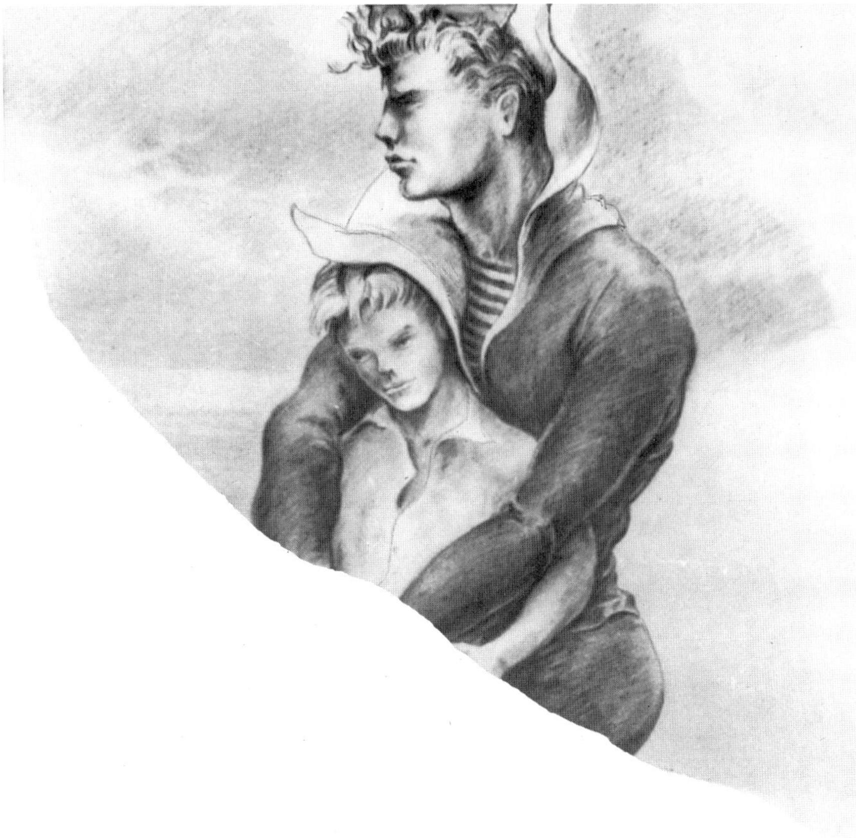

This image of intergenerational sexuality has been cropped due to sensitivities in the current legal climate, wherein the threat to remove the "artistic defense" for so-called "obscenity" is always on the horizon, and literary descriptions of sexual activity within the literary canon are less threatening than their visual depiction. In fact, no teenager jerks off a sailor (literally) in *Querelle de Brest*, but this illustration evokes Genet's teenaged initiates/go-betweens/informers Roger and Dédé, who are onshore onlookers implicated in the erotic drama, each with a "full-fledged man within him, still slumbering and germinating there." Jean Genet, *Querelle de Brest* ([1947; 1953] 1974, 120) **22**

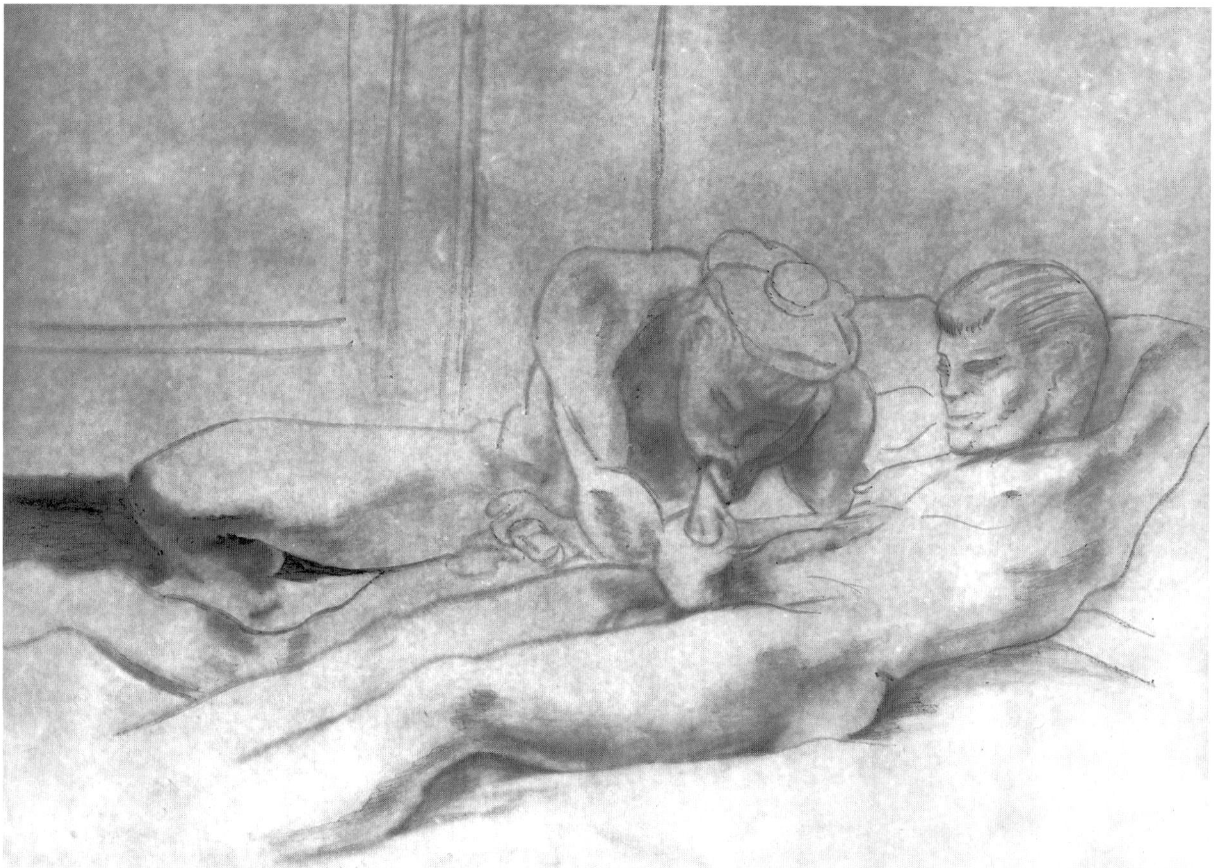

23

This apparently unfinished image resembles in style two other apparent sketches (Figures 165 and 166) but DuBek had not grouped them together. If the three belong together and to Caillaux's hand, they suggest his working method, a kind of instinctual simultaneous development of slender outline and rich shading. Again this is not an incident literally from *Querelle*, but a very Genet encounter of a sailor who explores submission and a supine toughie "*qui fait la planche*" ("who makes like a board," as we say in another French-language seaport—Montreal).

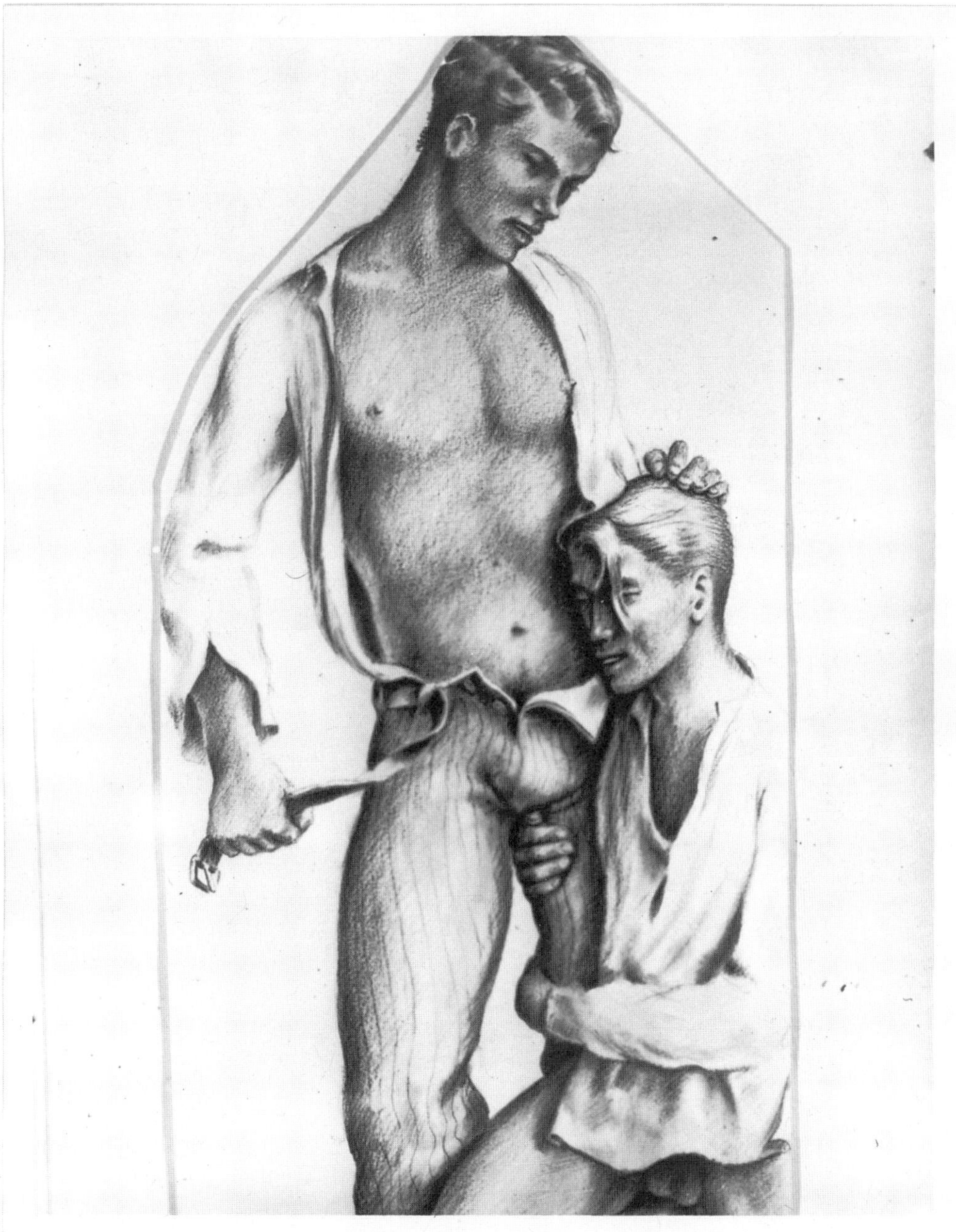

There is much talk of belts in *Querelle*, and Querelle holds onto his during the entire scene where he is fucked by Nono. Though this image is different and these men are apparently in civvies, Genet's sense of ritual around the strip of leather at the waist is still evident. Aside from the unusual framing that gives the composition a saint-like aura, readers will also notice the tracings of the two men's erections beneath the fabric, a favorite Genet motif. And the very tumescent nipples—which is not. **24**

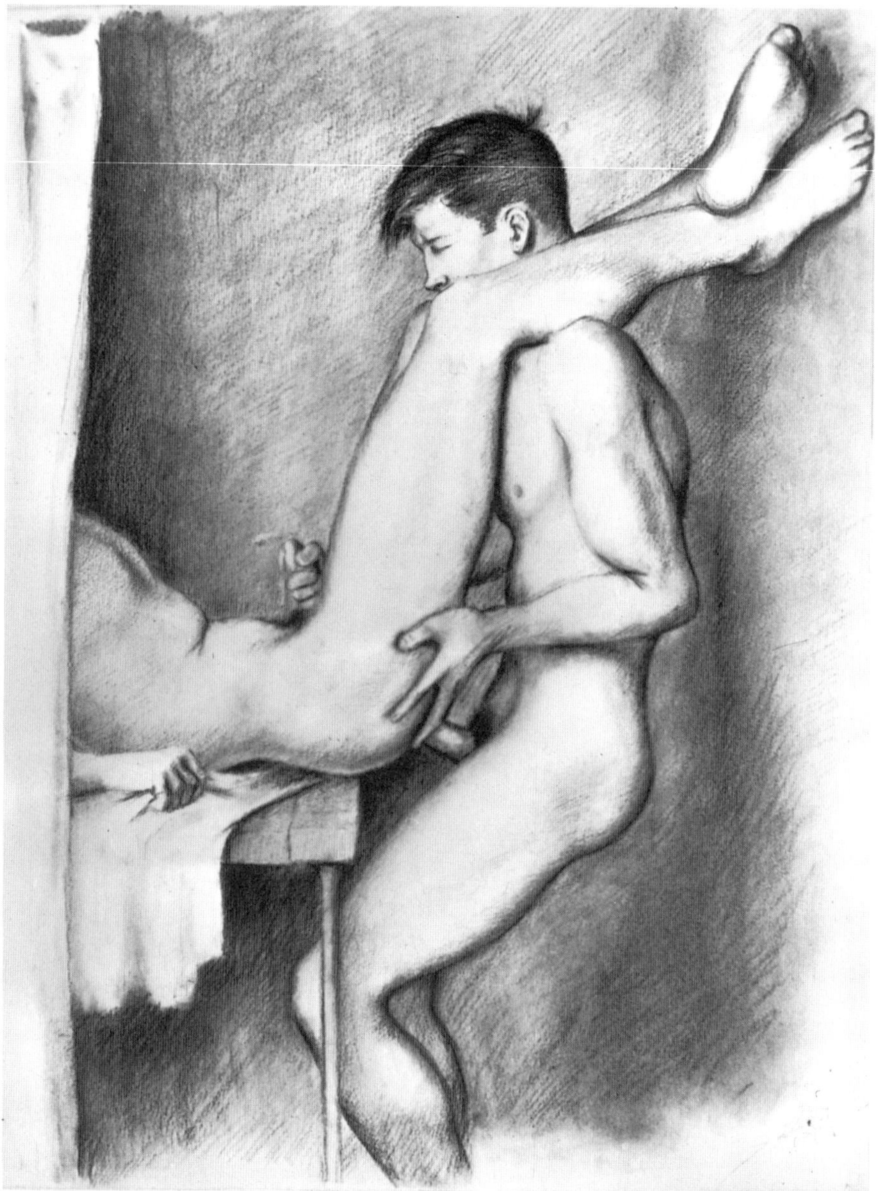

These two images were apparently not considered part of the *Querelle* group by DuBek; and neither fucking missionary-position nor coming while being fucked were a big part of Genet's repertory. In any case, these are two of Caillaux's most beautiful drawings and choreographies . . .

25

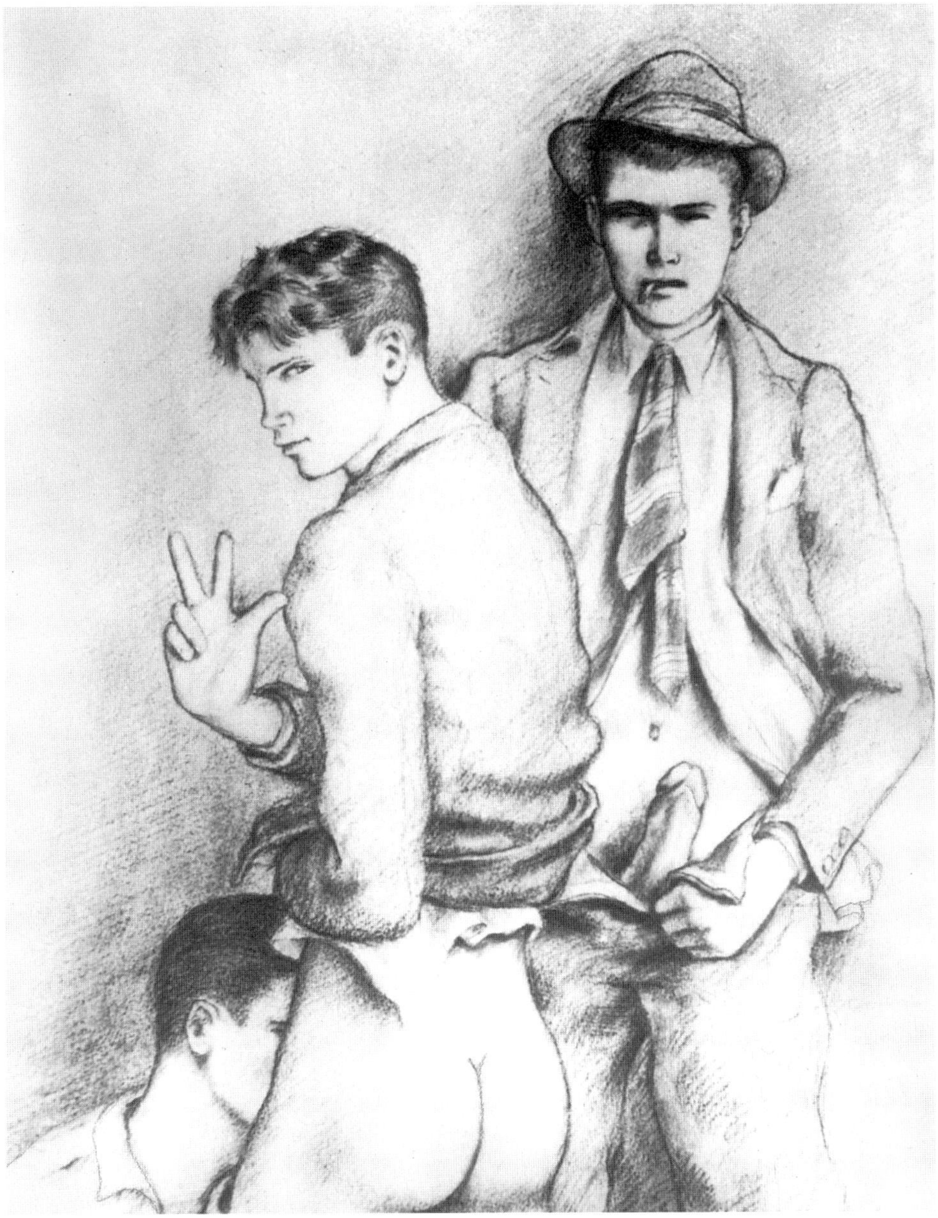

. . . and this one, with its unusual look and enigmatic signal flashed at the viewer (accomplice?), is spellbinding. (Gerard Koskovich suggests that the digital three signal is a "sly reference to the fact that a three-way is in progress . . . and may even hint that the boy could invite an additional participant by raising the next finger on his hand" . . . perhaps even the viewer, whom Caillaux is so adept at engaging "as an acknowledged participant in the narrative.") After all, civilians and street clothes can be almost as erotic as sailors and uniforms. 26

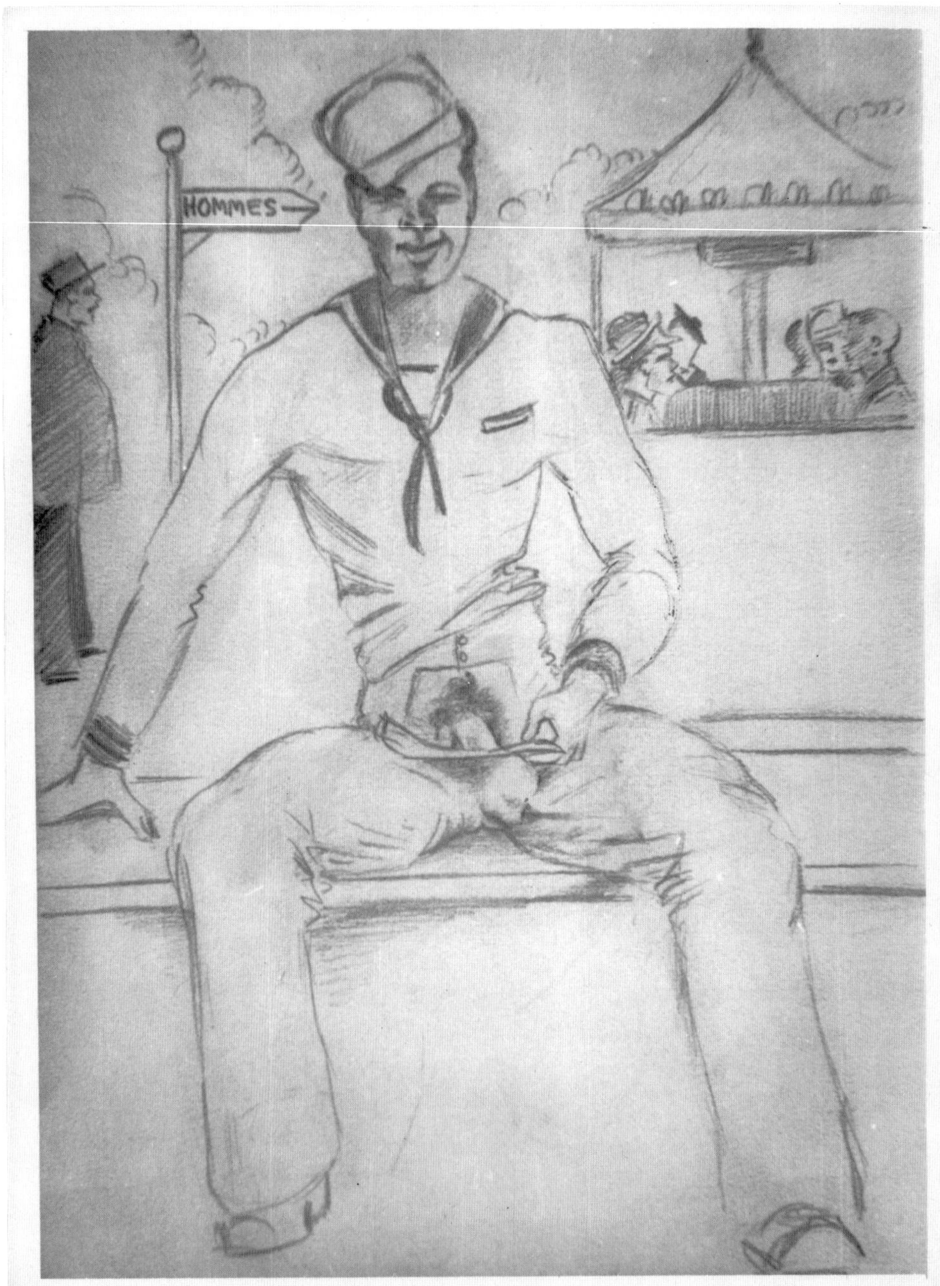

This artist was equally interested in the armed forces but less taken up with existentialism, more inclined toward the smirk than expressions of saint-like intensity.

27

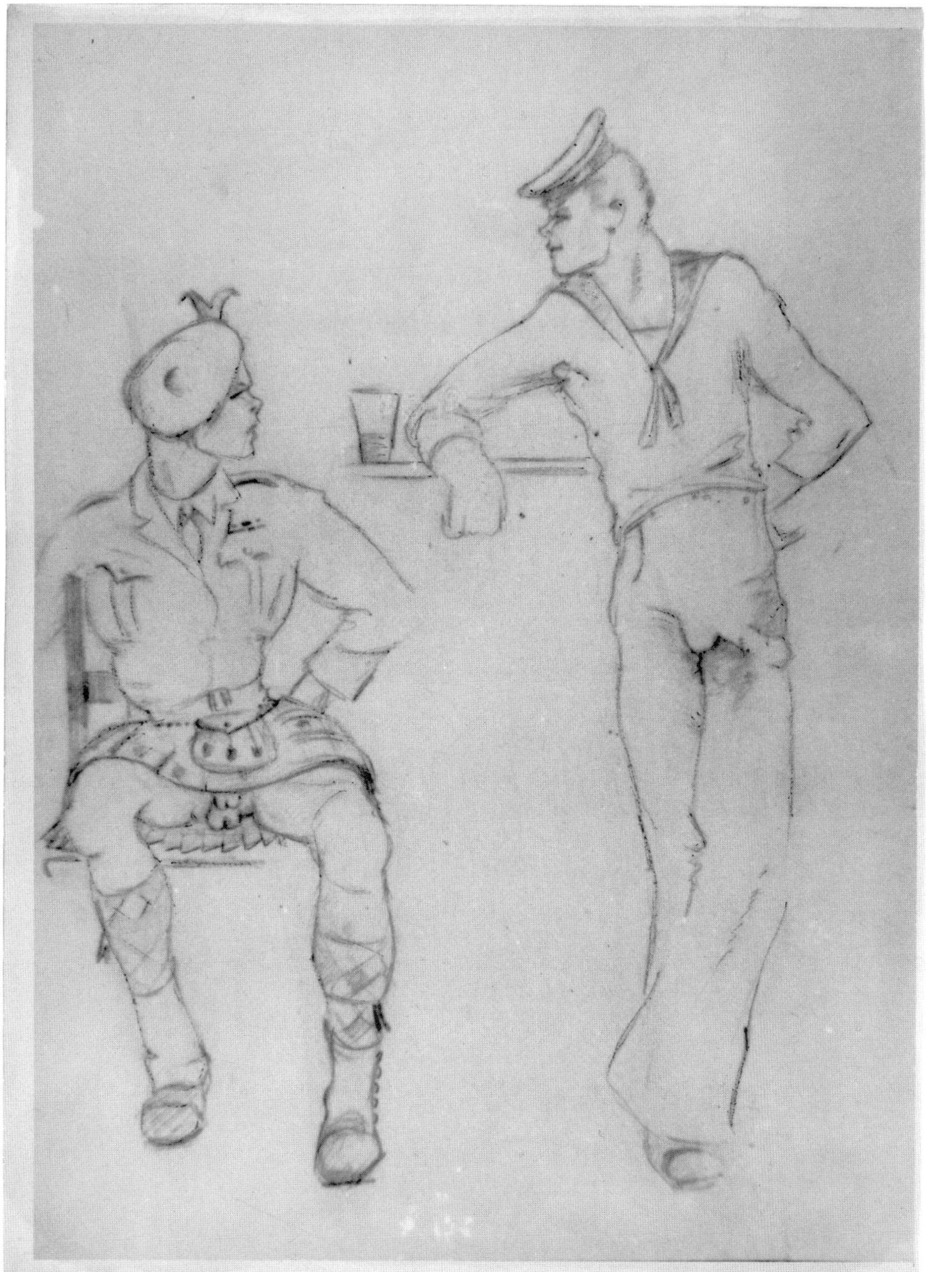

This anonymous French penciller, no doubt a contemporary to Caillaux and perhaps an amateur, might be called "El Greco" in honour of his predilection for elongated and standing male bodies. Kilt aficionados should also refer to Figure 52 and to *Out/Lines* 130-131.

28

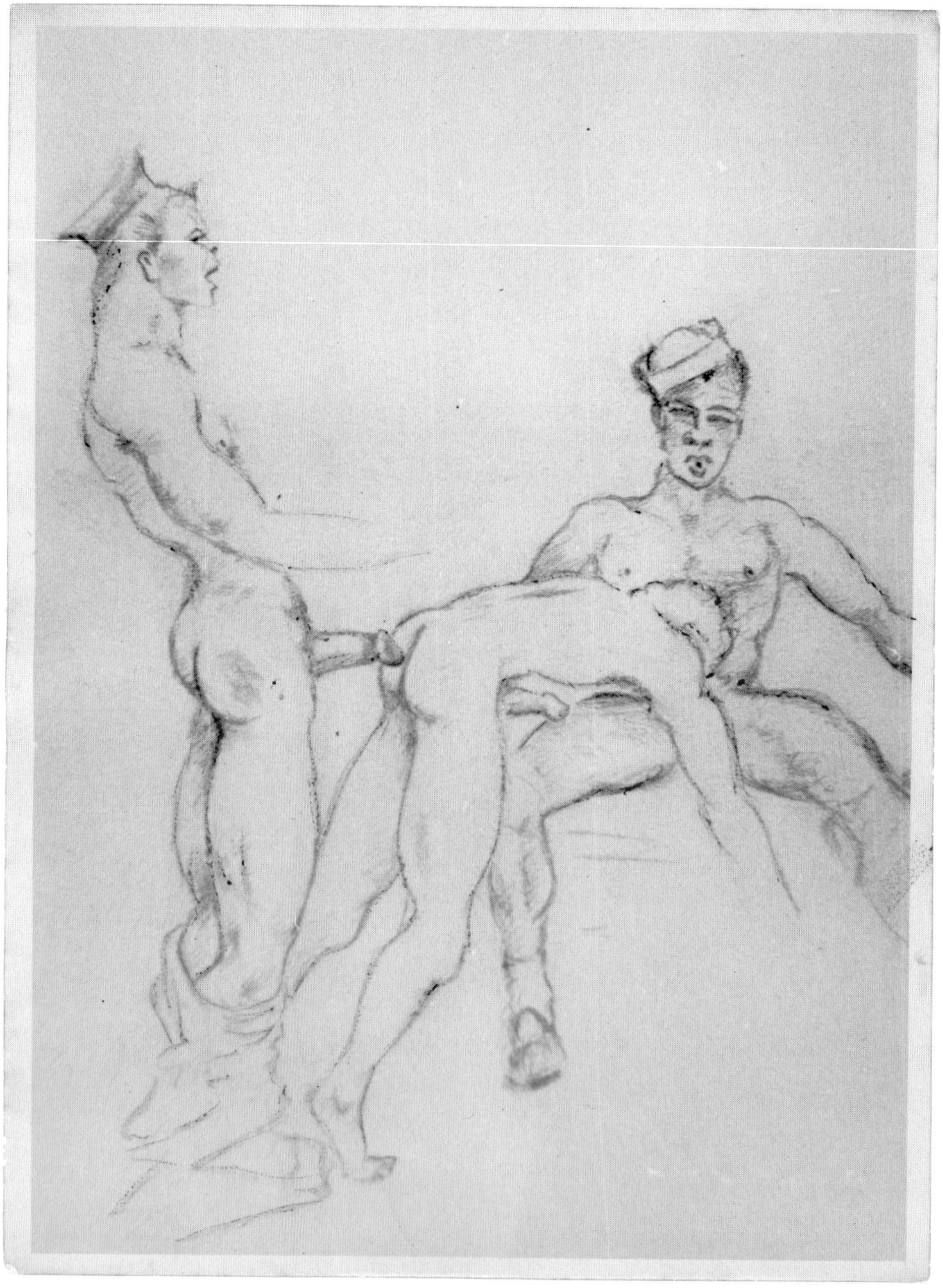

Several of El Greco's drawings had not made the final cut for *Out/Lines*, so if he is still alive, he will be relieved that DuBek appreciated him despite his not always accurate sense of body proportion and facial symmetry. In addition to these six, see also Figures 119-120.

29

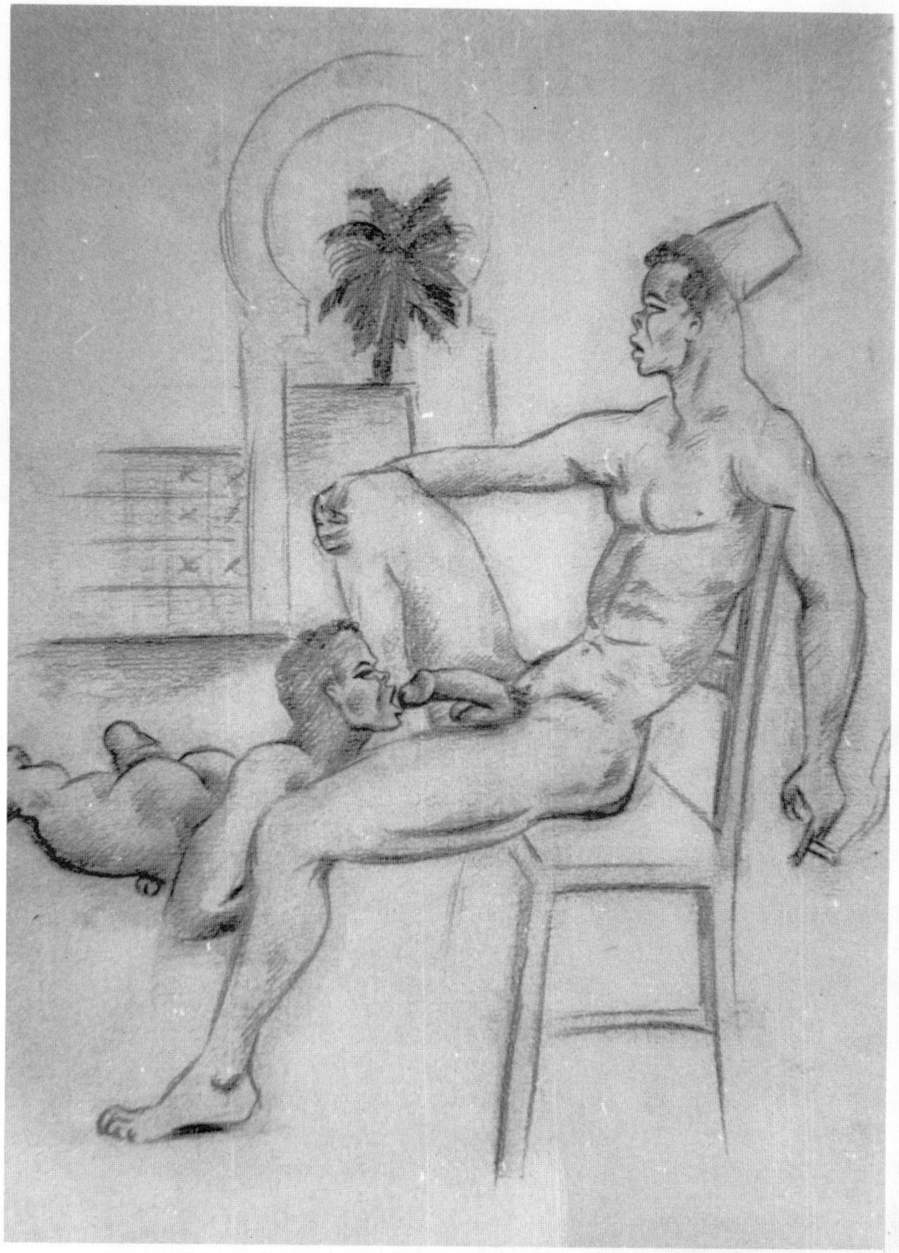

The metropolitan French tendency to eroticize the colonial army surfaced also in *Out/Lines* (Figures 36-37). "El Greco" shares the taste for African soldiers, whom he renders, in their tropical settings, no less statuesque than his white figures (see also Figure 120).

30

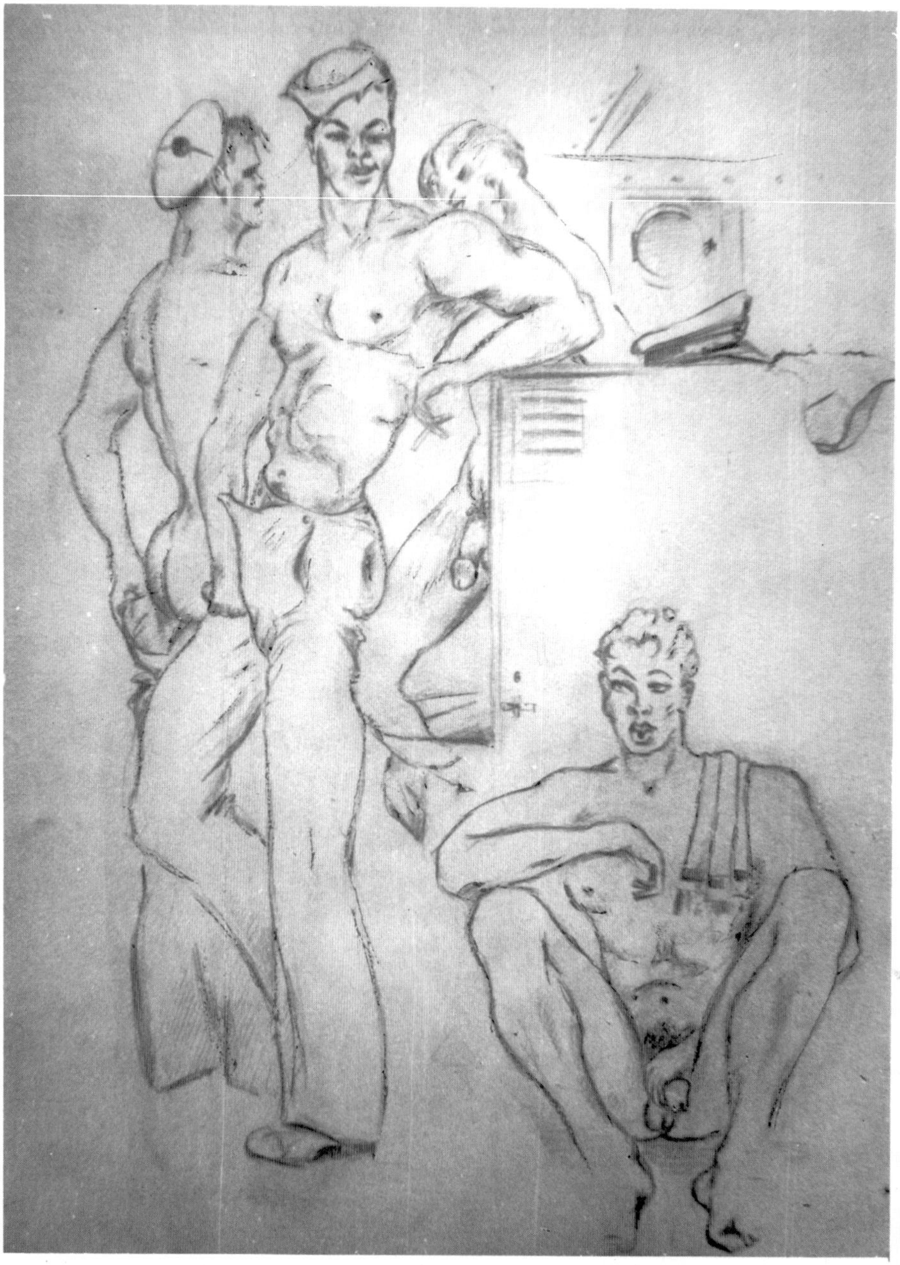

"There was a sailor, dressed all in white, coming across the boulevard, walking with that funny roll sailors have and with that aura, hopeful and hard, of having to make a great deal happen in a hurry. I was staring at him, though I did not know it, and wishing I were he. He seemed—somehow—younger than I had ever been, and blonder and more beautiful, and he wore his masculinity as unequivocally as he wore his skin." James
31 Baldwin, *Giovanni's Room* ([1956] 1988, 121)

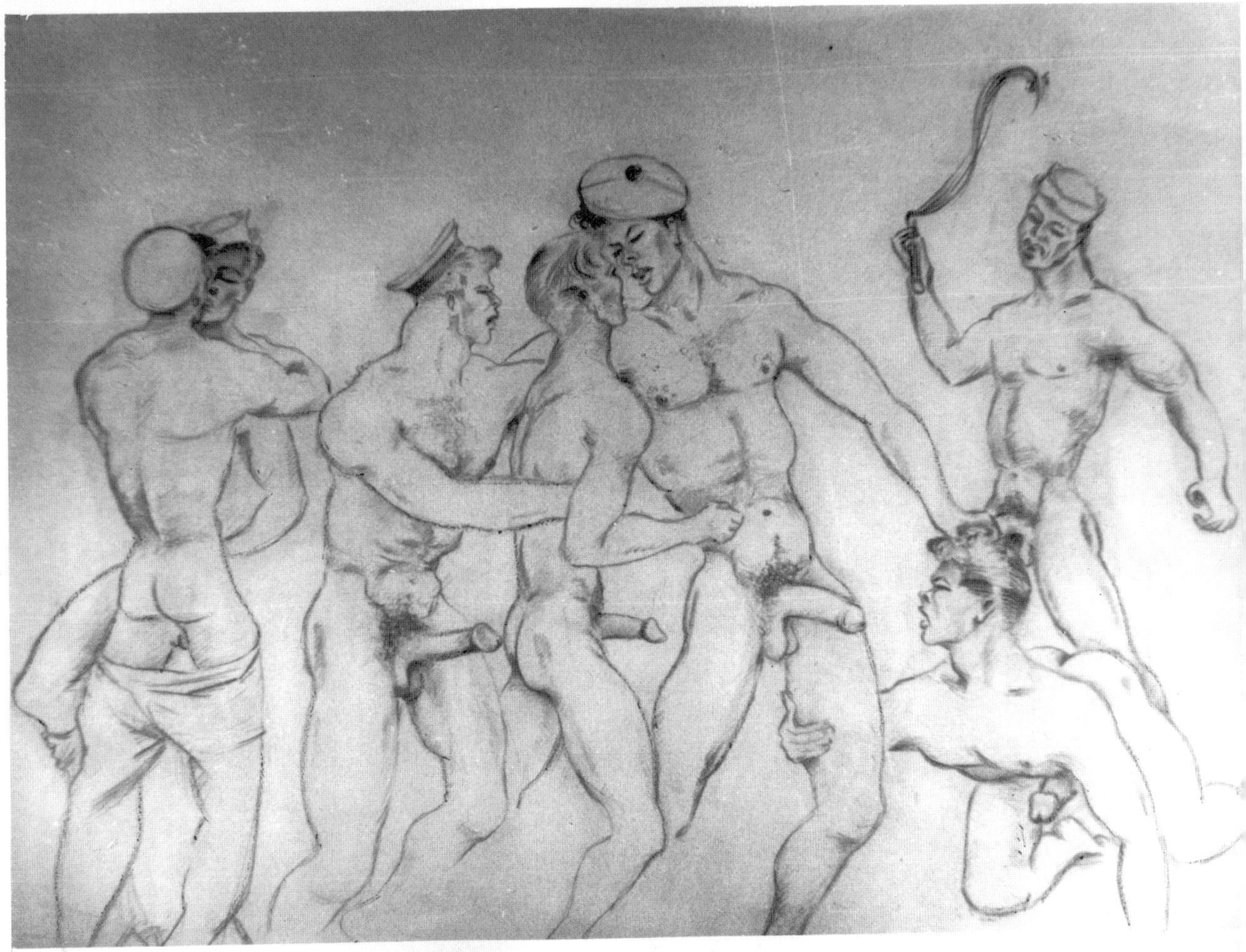

These infernally-tinted orgiasts with their frenzy (unfulfilled?) remind me of backup dancers for a Madonna video, those early 1990s Voguers. Or are they more like Lorca's 1930s Manhattanites?: ". . . they dive /on your chaste and numinous beard,/ blonds from the north, negroes from the sands, / multitudes shouting, gesticulating / like cats, like snakes, / the faggots, Walt Whitman, the faggots, / turbulent with weeping, with flesh for whipping, / for the boot or the bite of the butch." Federico Garcia Lorca, "Ode to Walt Whitman" ([1934] 1983, 32
310)

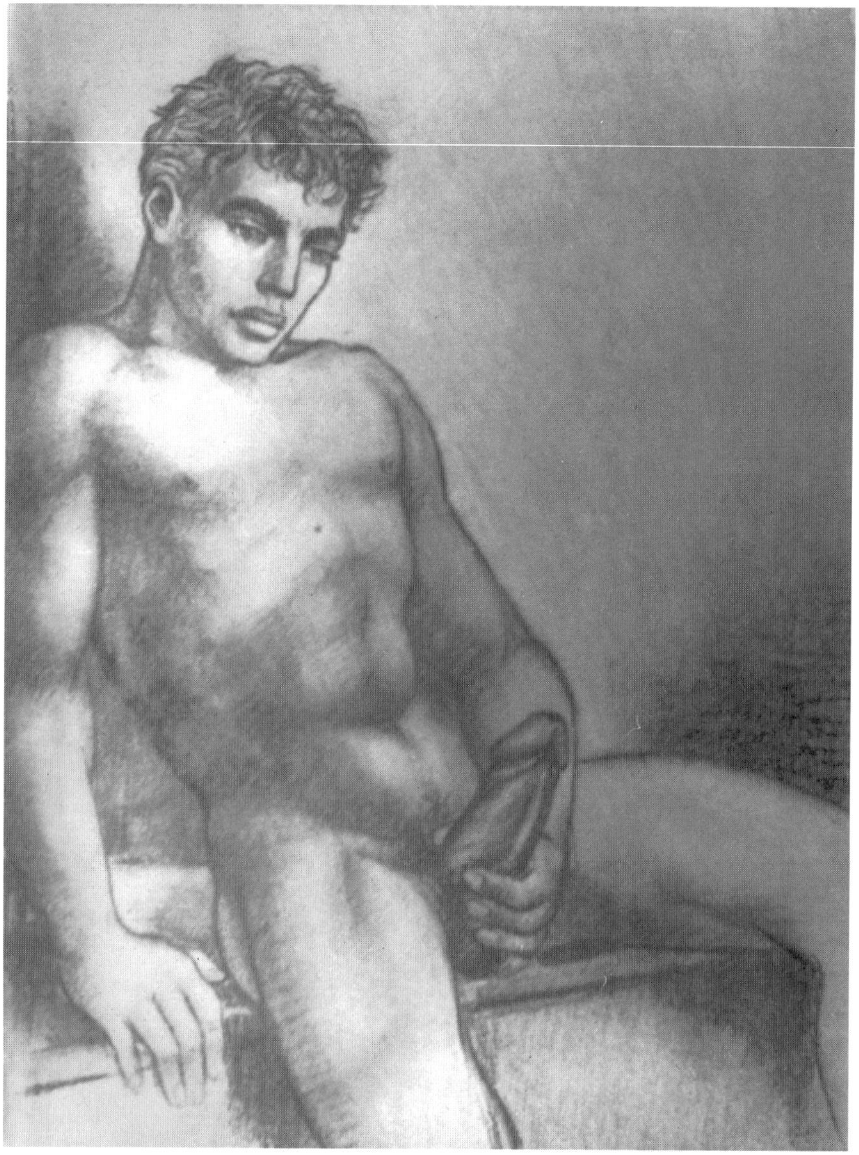

33

"I was failing to take into account one of the clearest evidences there is of sexual love—the phenomenon of erection. Over a truly long period of time I had my erections, and also indulged in that 'bad habit' which incited them whenever I was alone, without ever becoming aware of the significance of my actions. . . ." Yukio Mishima, *Confessions of a Mask* ([1949] 1958, 80). This set of commercial French postcards by Yola Soungouroff, dating from as early as 1940 or even earlier, were popular with tourists (cf. *Out/Lines*, Figures 50-53).

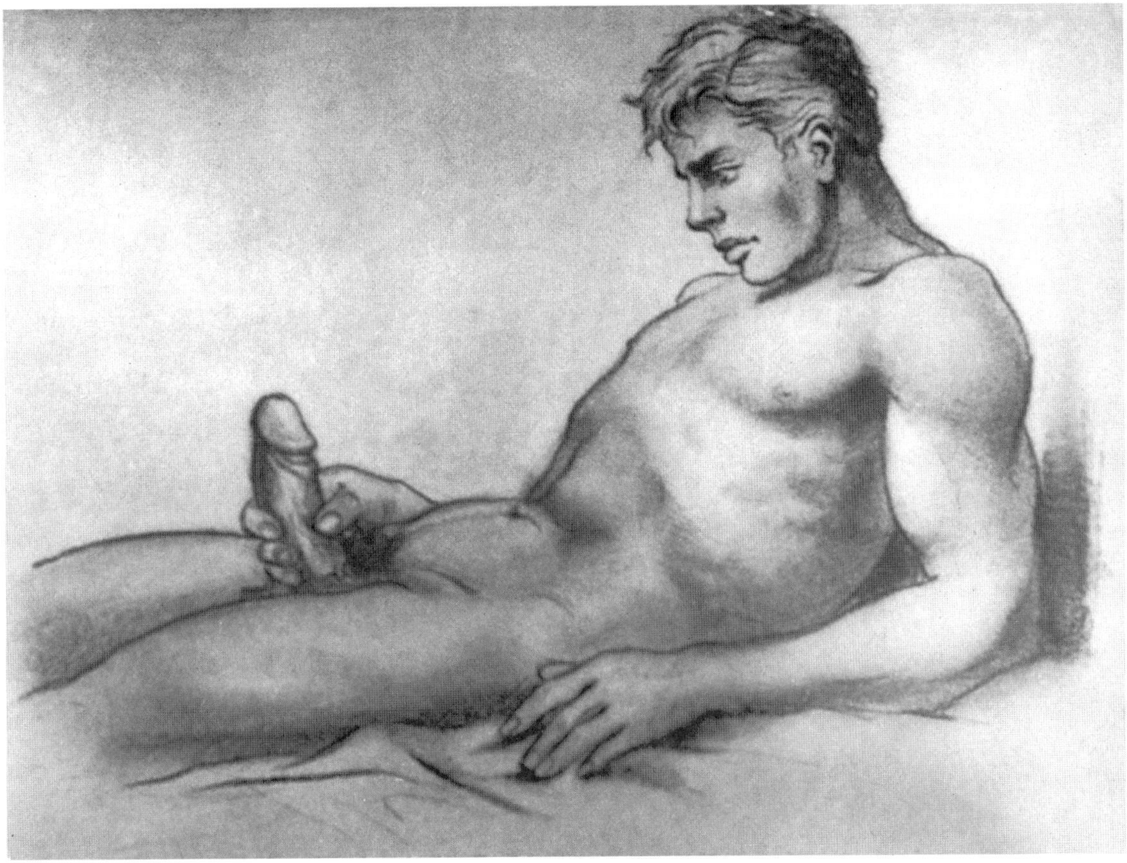

"Standing up in the bath, they would look at themselves (and me) and begin by a Parisian grimace that bares the gums. Then they would rub one shoulder, pick up the soap and make it lather. The soaping turned into a caress. Suddenly their eyes left the world, their head would fall back and their body spit like a furious animal. [. . .] . . .the youngest ones were distinguishable because they climbed out of the bath and wiped from the tiles the sap that their blind stems had hurled distantly, madly, towards love." Jean Cocteau, *Le Livre blanc* ([1928] 34
1990, 53)

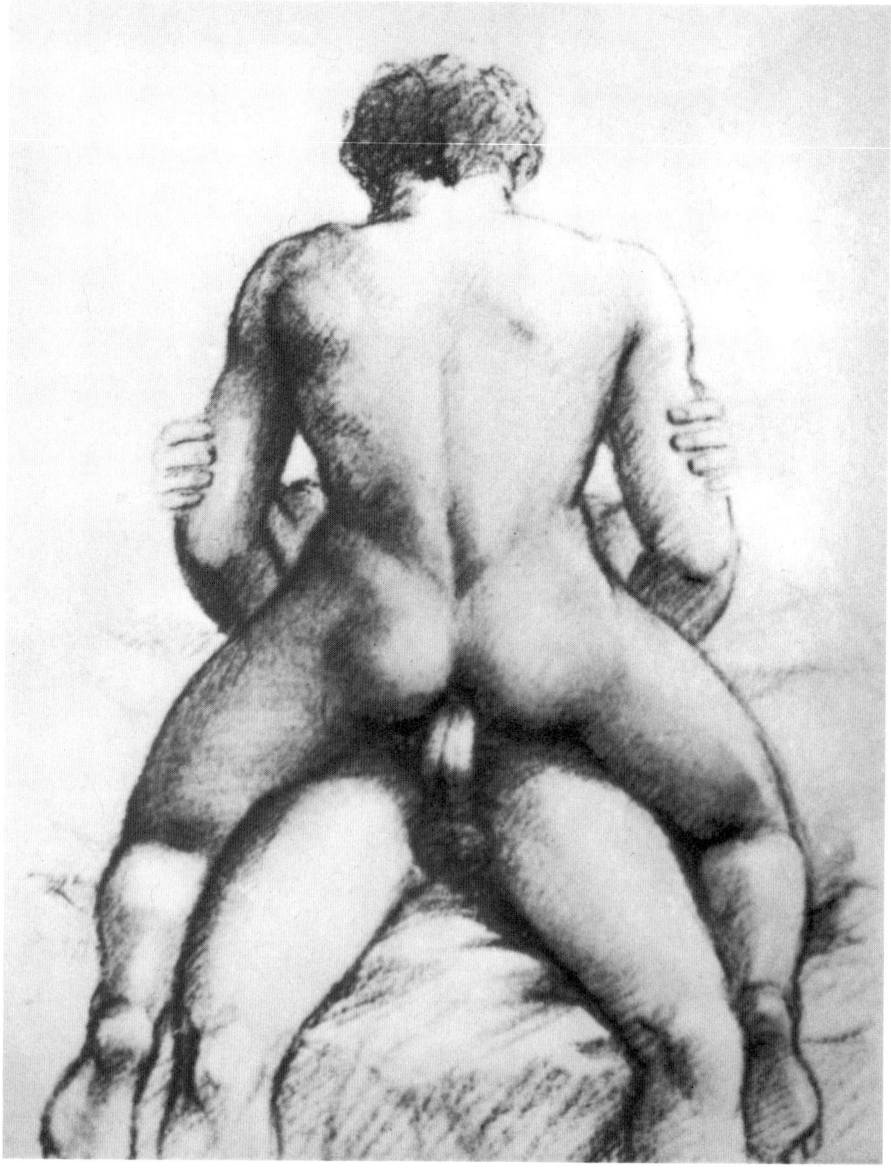

Definitely not Genet, who focused almost exclusively on the more manly doggie-style. A tentative identification for the postcards is now possible: a minor French artist of Russian origin named Tola Soungouroff, active from around 1940 to the 1980s. These five images from DuBek, plus the one self-censored intergenerational image mentioned in my introduction above, may well fill out the set since ten seems a likely total number.

35

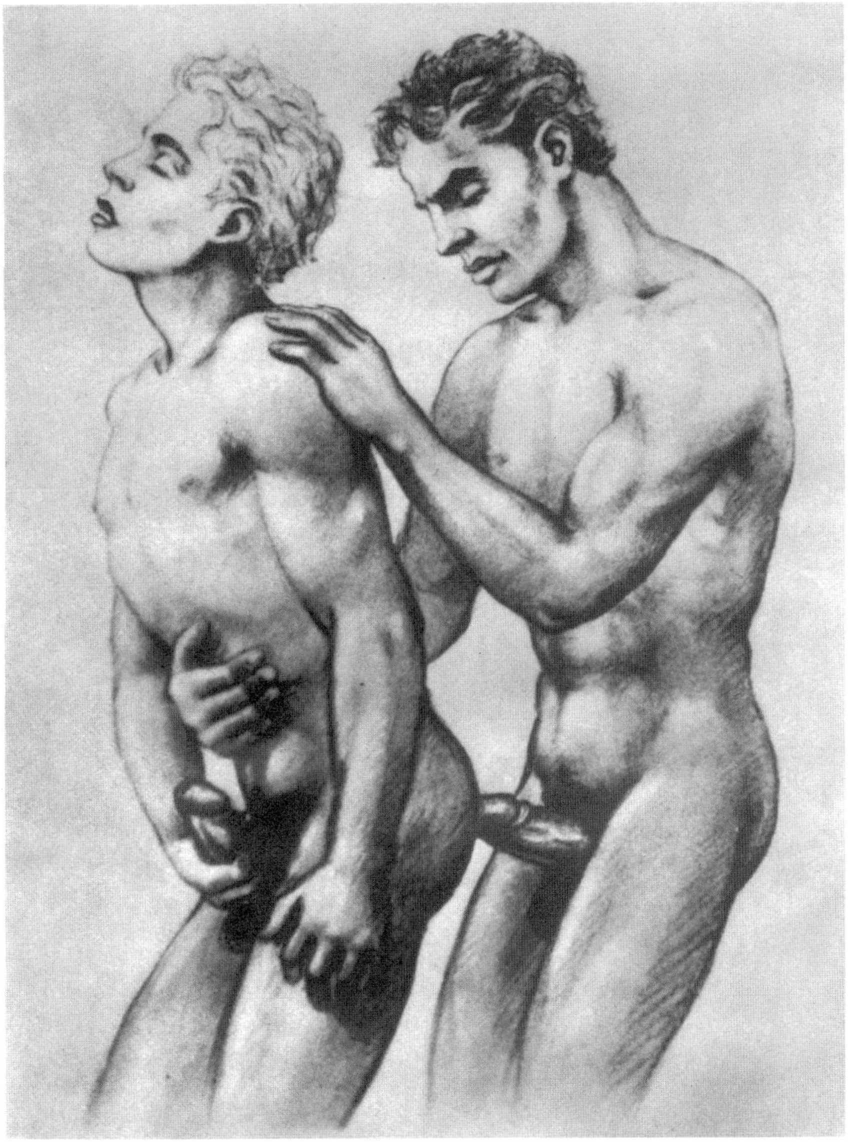

"André winch sideways, snubbed cocknosing out from under his acquiescing belly—Holy Hermaphrodisiac . . . and I manhandle his gift . . . right hand on his bedded shoulder for leverage, left hand plying him as I steepen into nave [. . .] André thrusts assoul onto my rootle, generous bequest as I ride acceptance down into his shunt." Scott Symons, *Place d'Armes* ([1967] 1978, 225)

36

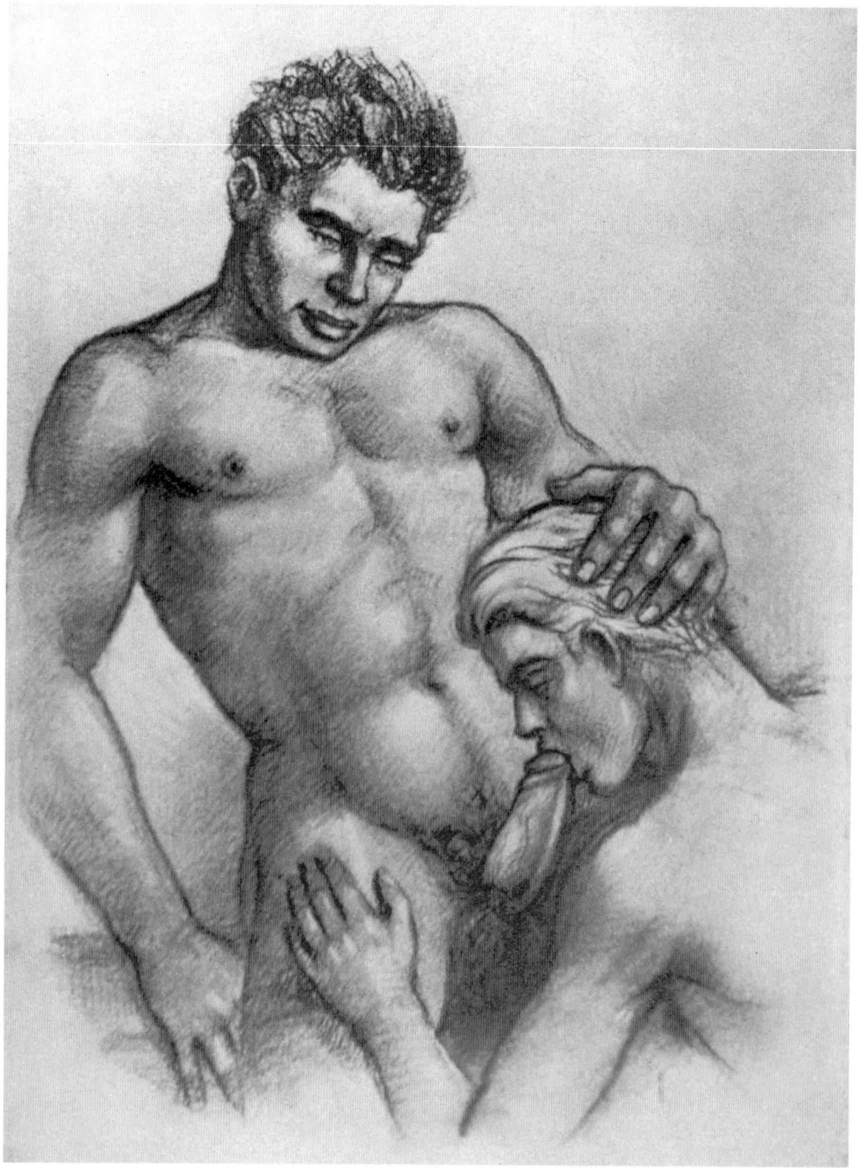

Soungouroff's dreamy young men with sculptured cheekbones and Jeanne Moreau lips stare at each other and their bodies with a mixture of disbelief and self-doubt: they are worthy new entries into Richard Dyer's inventory of "sad young men" infected with "delicious melancholy" throughout the pre-Stonewall period in fiction and films (Dyer 1993, 90).

37

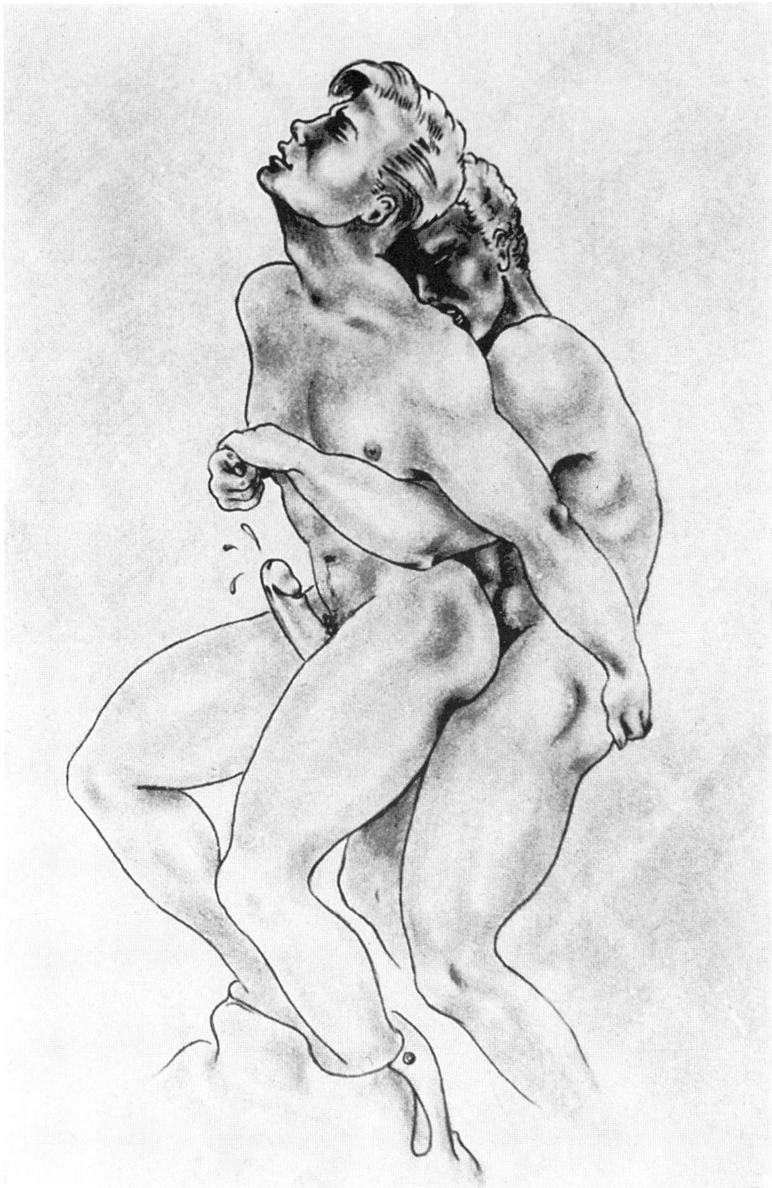

I wondered in *Out/Lines* (Figures 144-145) whether this artist might be the same Paul Smara who had apparently also done Figures 187-188 in the same book (images dated c. 1945). But the jury is out again, and now I am skeptical. Postwar Paris was full of horny imitators and tracers, as well as a slew of original artists, from the prolific Jean Cocteau on down the cultural hierarchy.

38

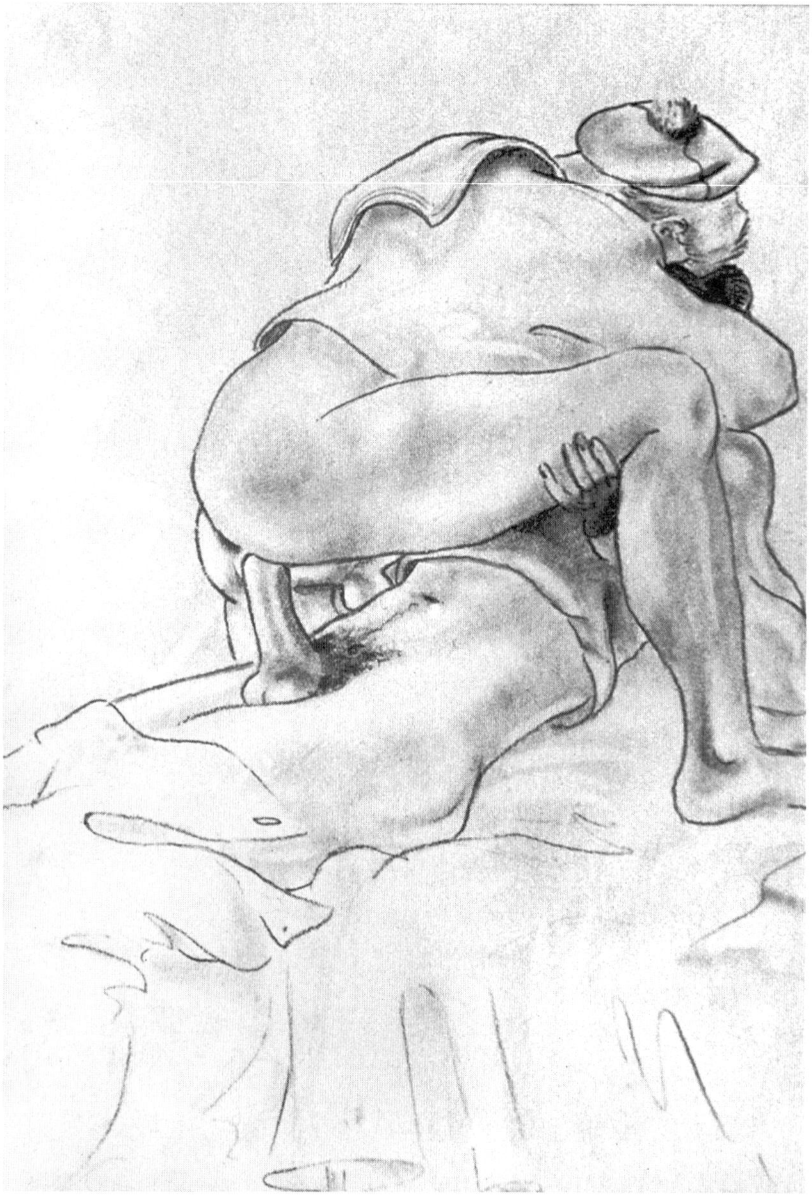

And all them apparently hobnobbed in the same *Rive gauche* bistros and shared major fixations on sailors, trade, attitude . . .

39

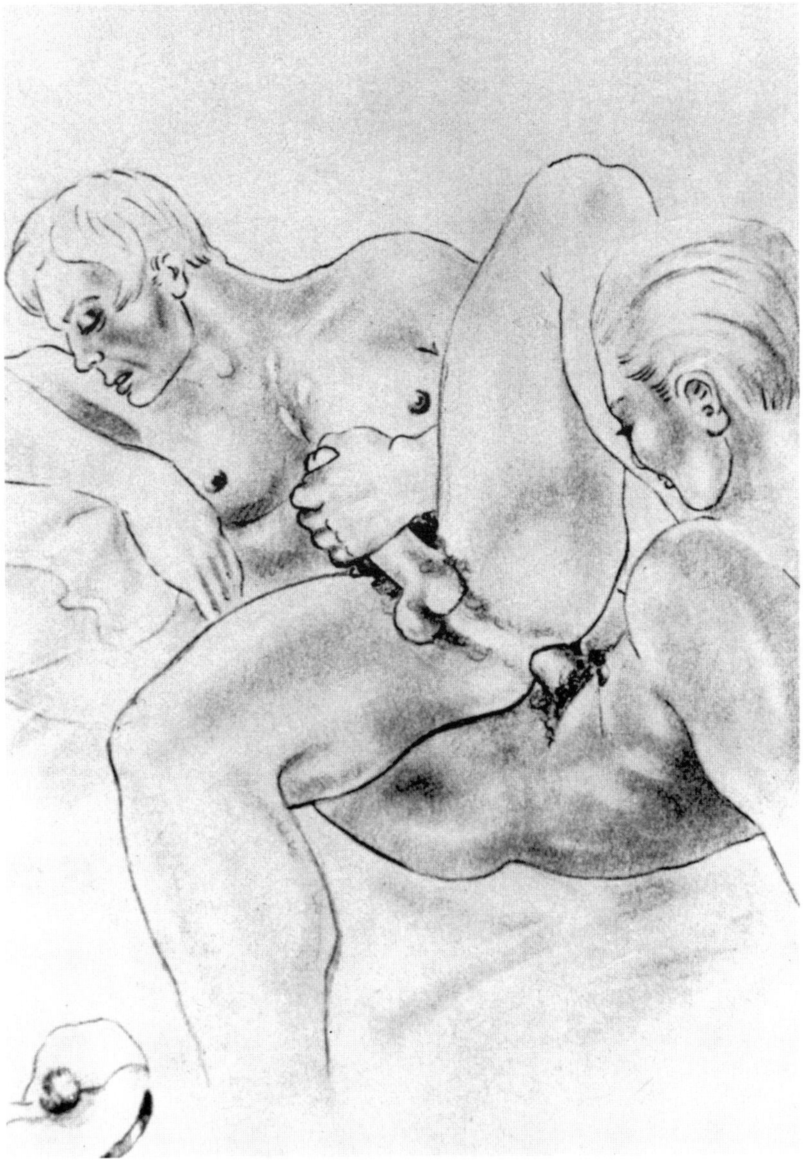

. . . and cheekbones. So let's call this particular anonymous artist-who-is-not-Smara "Cheekbones."

40

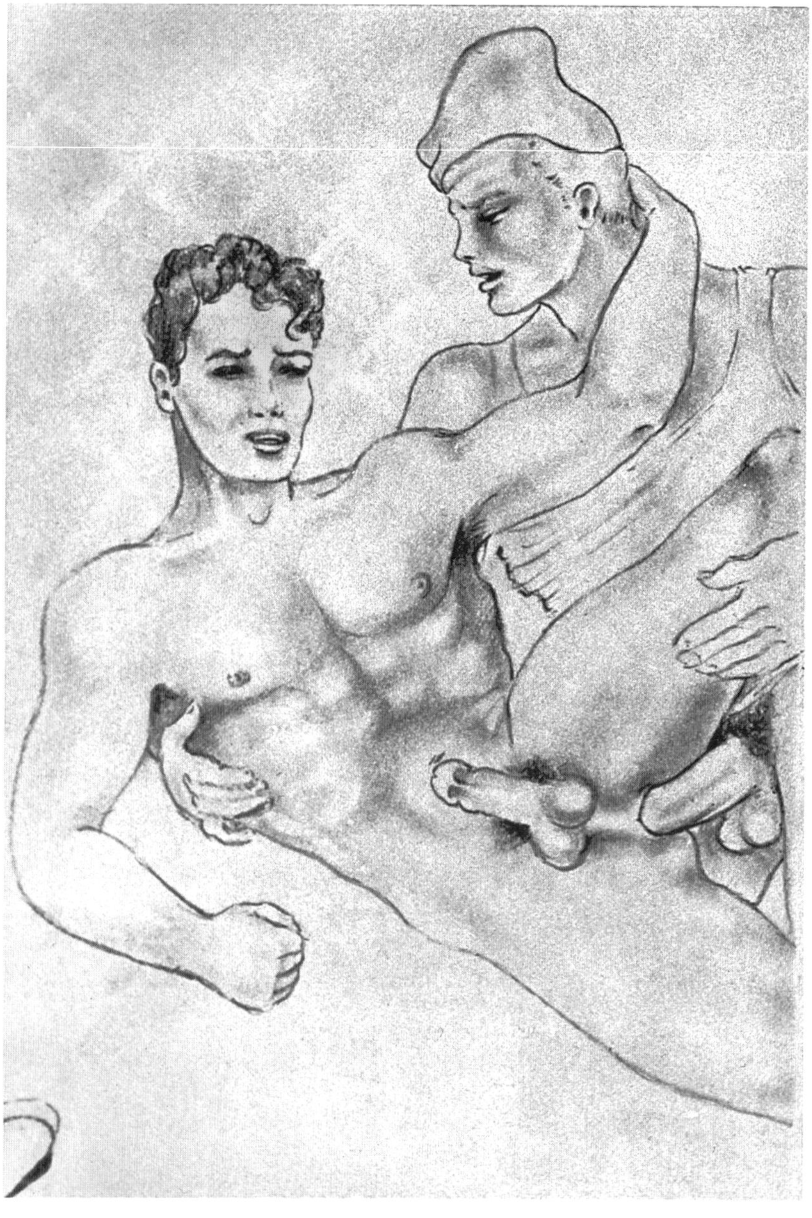

Did Cheekbones keep reworking this face, making it worse and worse so that it ended up looking like an addition by a later hand? Or is that in fact what this smiling imposter mask is?

41

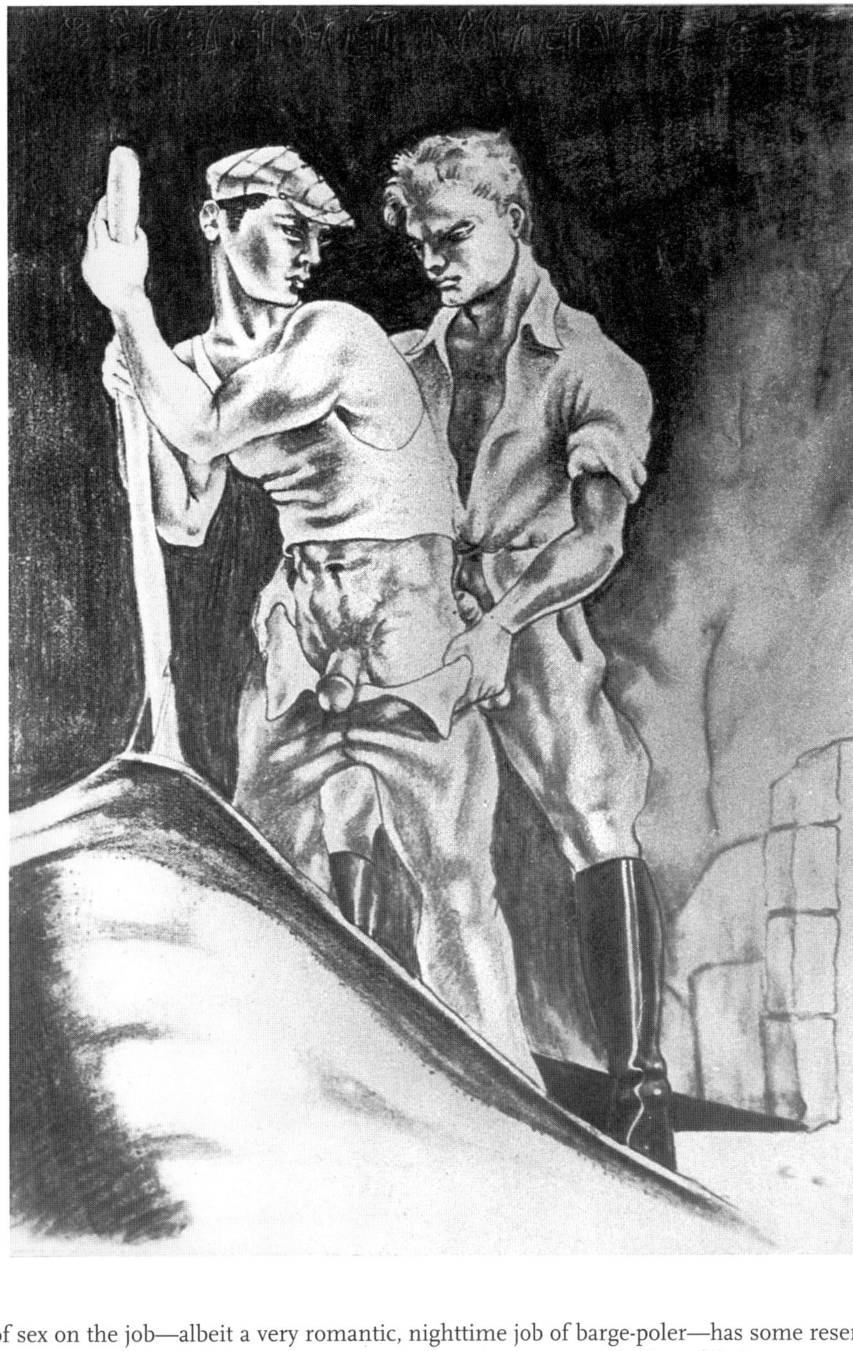

This unique fantasy of sex on the job—albeit a very romantic, nighttime job of barge-poler—has some resemblances to Cheekbones's other drawings in terms of body rendering, despite its anomalous filled-in setting and gleaming boots. And it certainly fits in with a certain French *je-ne-sais-quoi*.

42

National Dreams:
carry on britannia

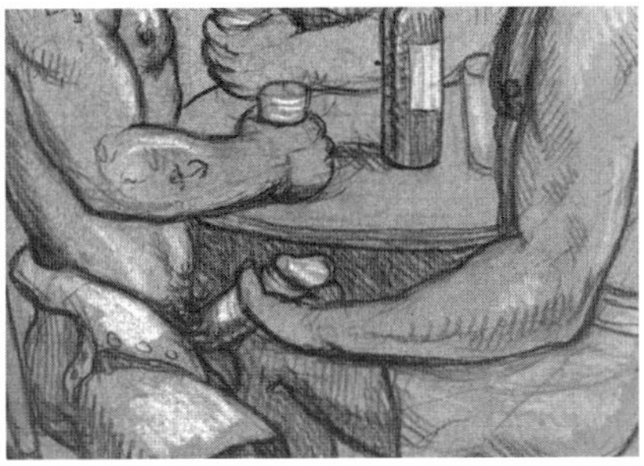

More than anything else, the discovery of the anonymous British artist I call "Happyface," whose work was distributed out of London in the 1950s and early 1960s (figs. 43-51, 98, 131-132), drove me to produce *Out/Lines.* One might think that his edgier contemporary "Lowenhaupt" would epitomize the postwar queer Britain of Francis Bacon and Joe Orton

NATIONAL DREAMS: CARRY ON BRITANNIA

better than Happyface with his "world of cynical flesh-merchants and class conflict" (Waugh 2002, figs. 58-64). But DuBek unfortunately had only a few, not very sharp, examples of Lowenhaupt, and Happyface, for all his irreverent insouciance, does indeed point to certain mythologies of English gay male culture just on the brink of 1960s Swinging London. Also included in the present British national team is the amateur I call "Lipstick" (figs. 52-53); two other Lipstick images are self-censored from this selection because the clumsily out-of-scale body of his "pansy" (fig. 51) playing sandwich between a kilt and a sailor suit could be interpreted as juvenile by those who are not up on British iconography of the "sad young man" (Dyer 1993). See also later on in the selection the marvelously prolific "Bellhops" (figs. 111-115, 157-160, 200-205, 213-215), and no doubt a few unrecognized other subjects of Her Majesty hiding elsewhere in the book.

It would be hard to see in Happyface echoes of the "kitchen sink" tendencies within British theatre and film of the 1950s, since his jolly proletarians aren't exactly angry young men (well, perhaps his rather gritty fucking-in-the-pit fantasy fits, [fig. 49], and maybe his wanking rugby player, [fig. 47], is a refugee from that communal bath for battered jocks in queer Lindsay Anderson's morbid film *This Sporting Life*, 1963). One more significant cinematic connection does occur to me: Happyface enthusiastically recruits for his omnisexual universe the cast of types familiar from British farce—the Ealing comedies, for example, and the endless "carry on" cycle: *Carry on Doctor*, *Carry on Constable*, and the like. His men seem at home in, and rather proud of, their caricatural uniforms as they play the spectrum of white working-class masculinity: bobbies, sailors, guardsmen, kilt-wearing Scots, miners, athletes, even boy scouts—plus the occasional figure of African descent who was increasingly popular in 1950s British physique photography, seen here mostly *without* uniforms. Lipstick and Bellhops are less vanilla than Happyface, but both share his celebration of uniformed social types, especially military specimens. Taken together, do the pulsating frescos of all three artists reflect a society stereotyped by both insiders and outsiders for its inextinguishable class hierarchy, its thriving sexwork industry, its Protestant delight at scandal, legendary taste for bondage and discipline (fig. 114-115), and the criminalization of sodomy that was one of its major gifts to civilization? No doubt. Stiff upper lip, stiff prick, as Queen Victoria no doubt once said to her kilted groom.

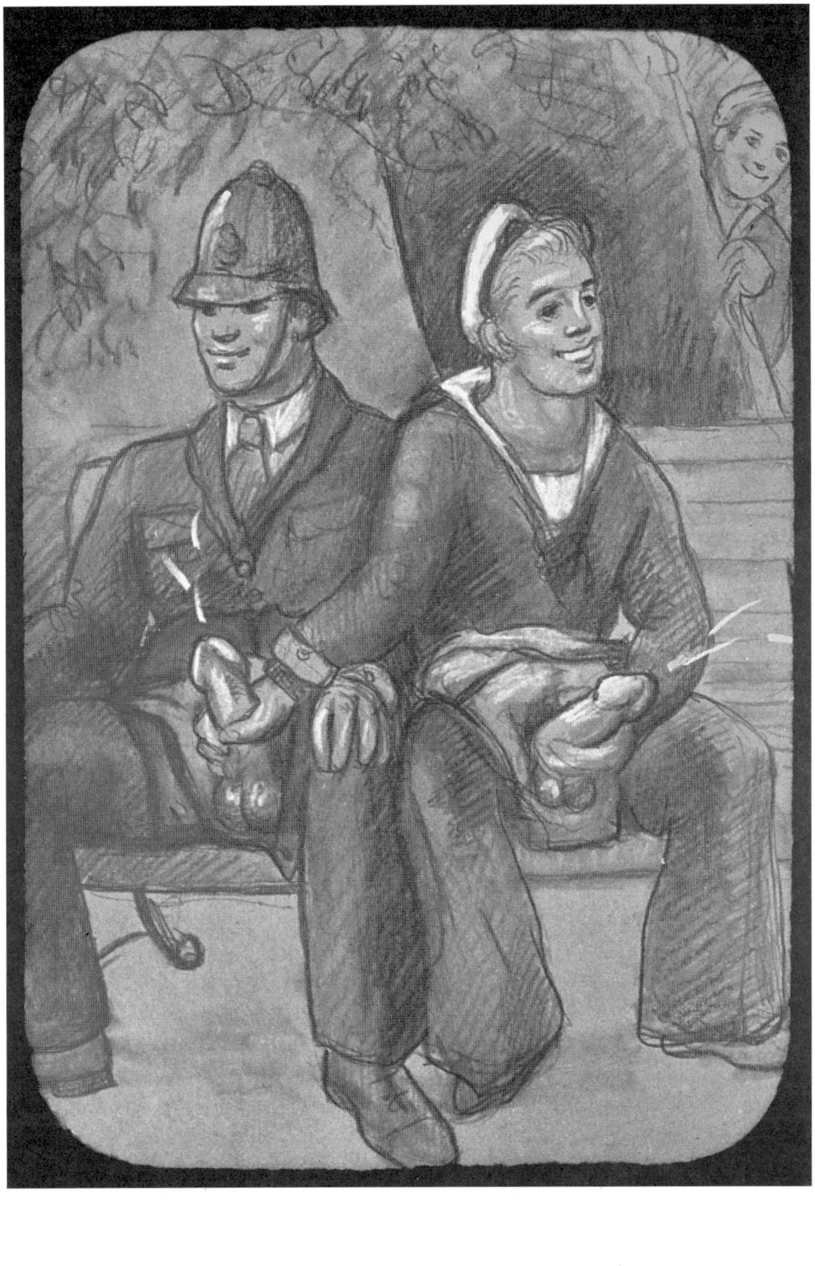

DuBek clearly adored Happyface, the chronicler of happy-go-lucky coupling in every corner of every park, beach, tavern, and alleyway on the sceptred isle—and always a happy voyeur on hand. What could better celebrate the new spirit of postwar reconstruction than"twin jets"—fireworks with which to celebrate the Coronation?

43

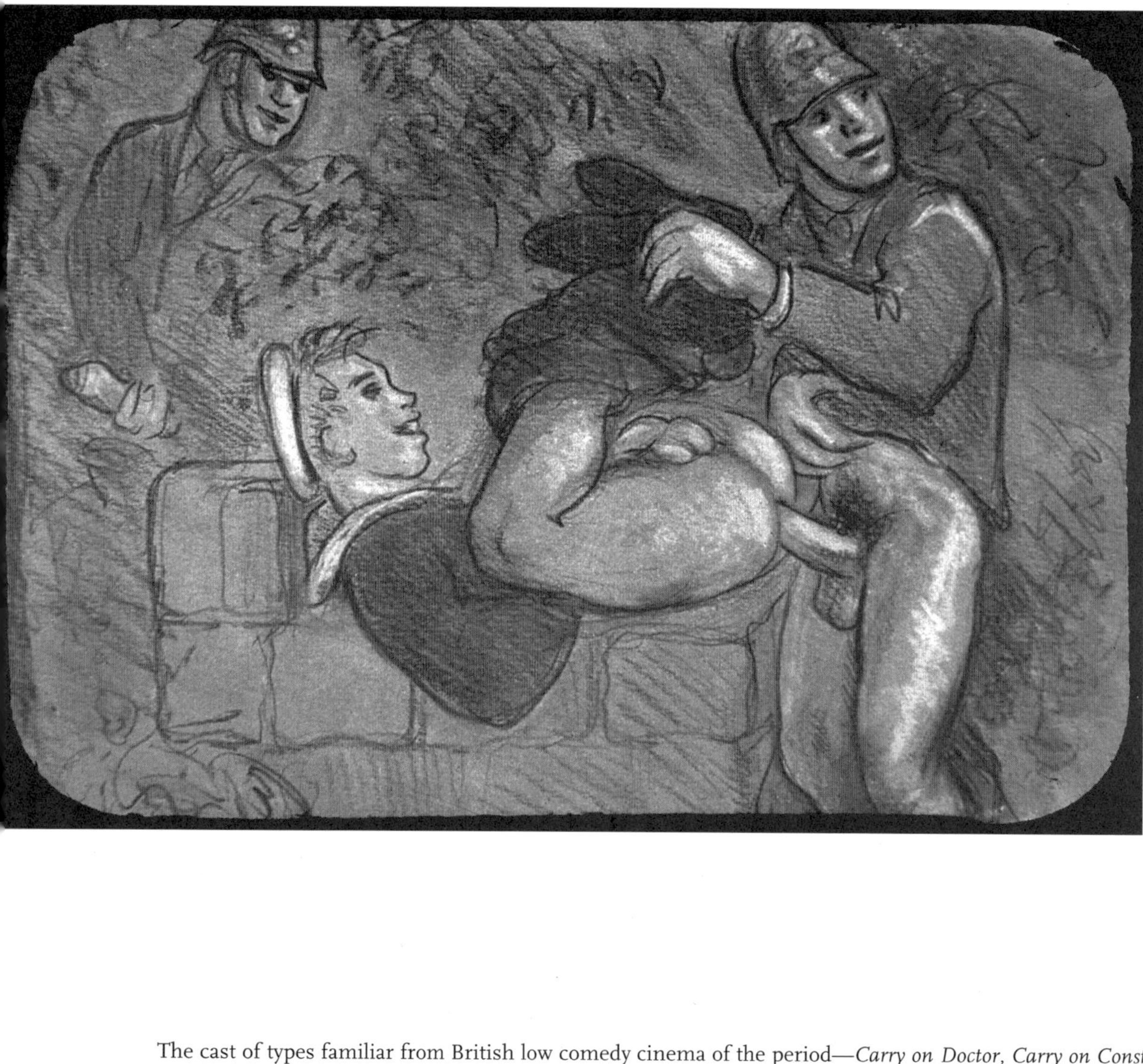

The cast of types familiar from British low comedy cinema of the period—*Carry on Doctor, Carry on Constable* and the like—are all recruited in their caricatural uniforms to play the spectrum of working-class masculinity: bobbies, sailors, guardsmen, Scots, miners, athletes, even boy scouts—plus the occasional representative of the new Caribbean immigration to the cities.

44

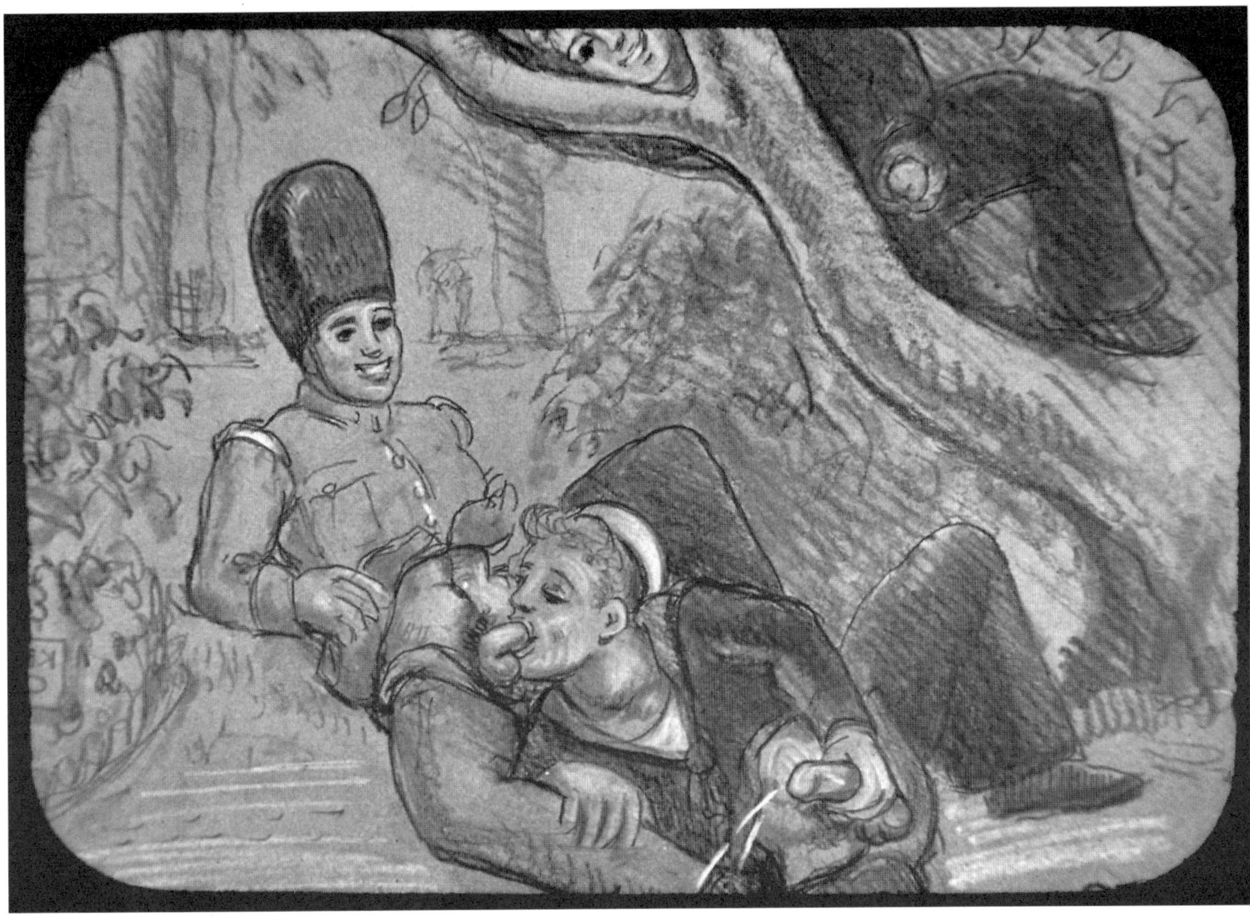

Happyface's sense of geography is very public and always bursting with queer potential. It includes these paradisiac versions of nighttime urban parks, where stone walls are exactly the right height for fucking and include a stone pillow, and every spot has an overhanging tree ideal for voyeur wankers.

45

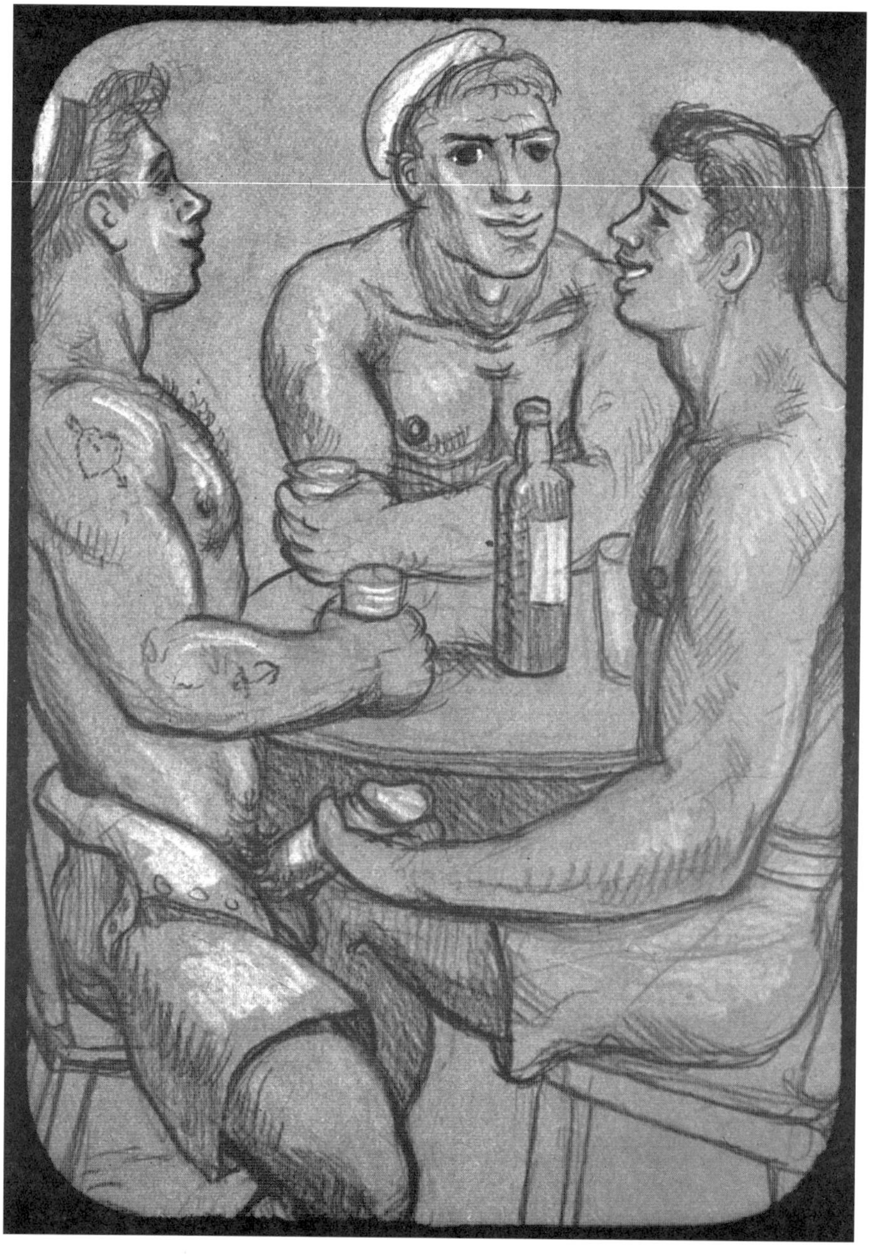

But the Happyface territory includes other public spaces of workaday and playaday Britain, from tavern to sportsfield to public toilet to mineshaft to harbor. Is this bar, with its particular dress code, aboard a frigate steaming through a hot tropical night towards Suez?

46

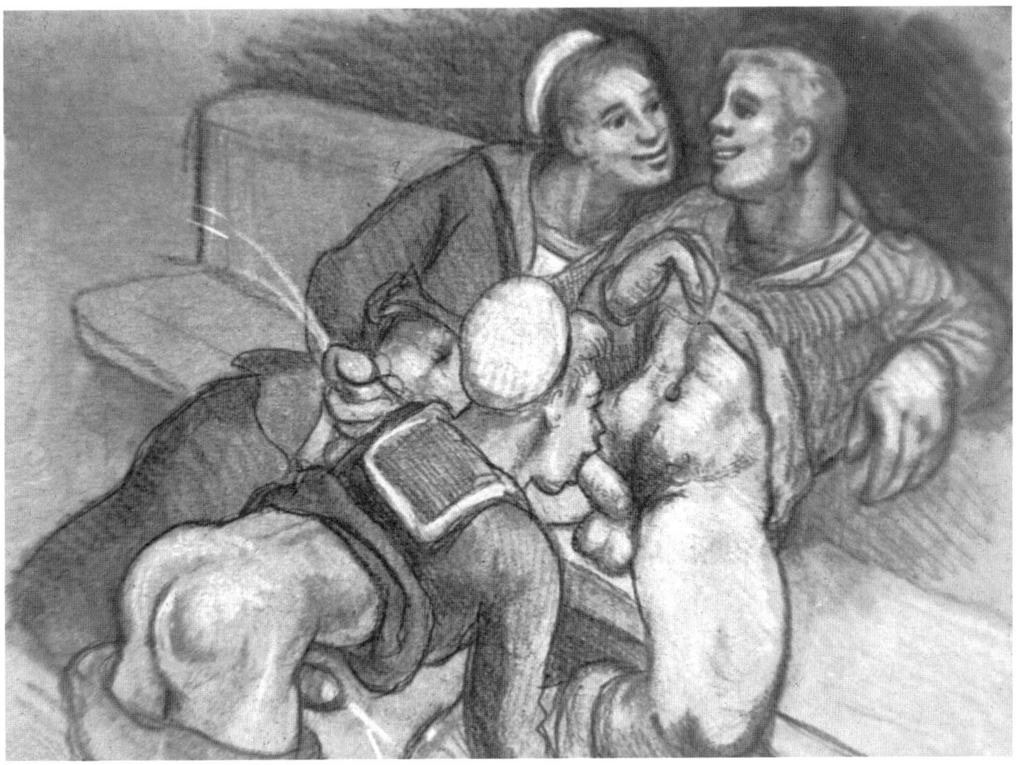

I am not sure what sport this rugged chap plays other than trade: rugger? soccer? His uniform is rather clean, indicating that the match hasn't yet begun, so he shouldn't wear himself out.

47

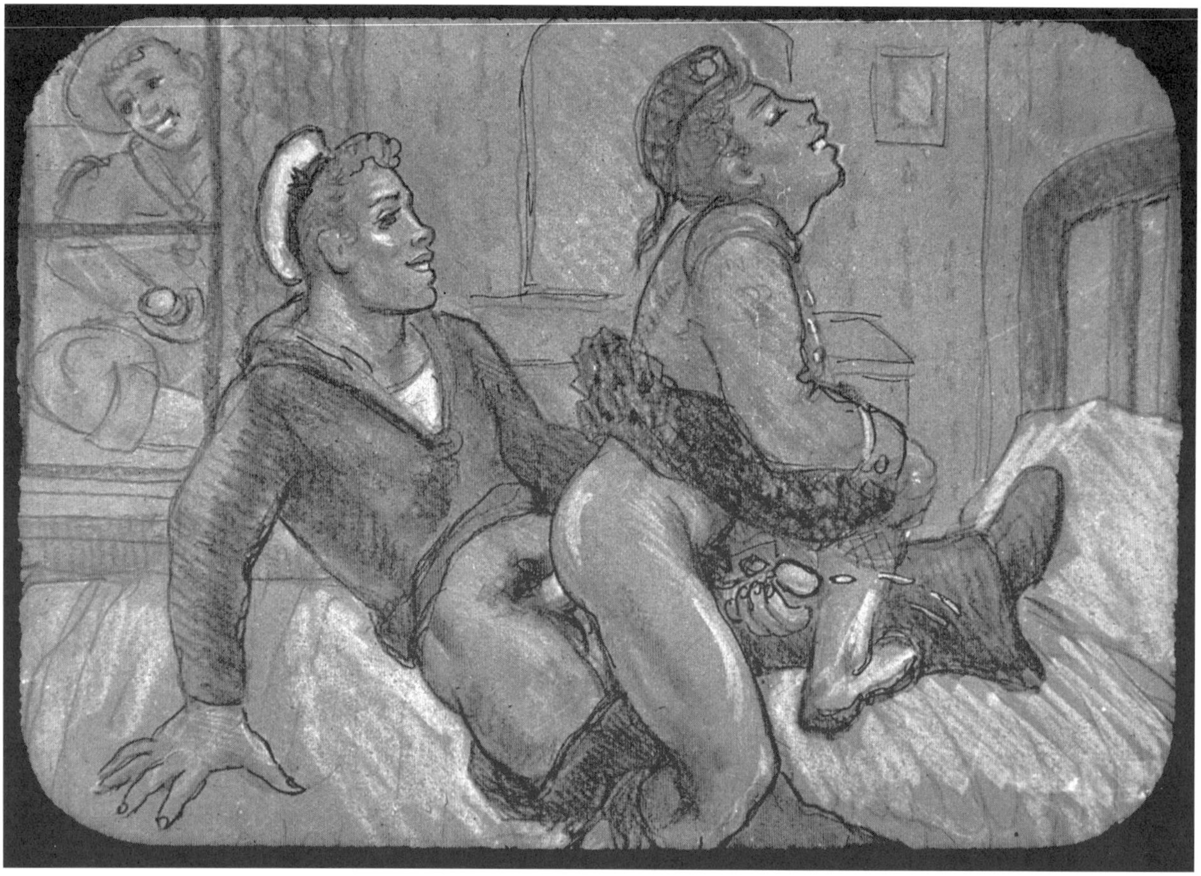

Happyface's sailors are usually contented bottoms, but this one is versatile, a fact much appreciated by the voyeur boy scout. "On the way home I met an ugly Scotsman who said he liked being fucked. He took me somewhere in his car and I fucked him up against a wall. The sleeve of my rainmac is covered in whitewash from the wall. It won't come off. I hate Christmas." Joe Orton, *The Orton Diaries* ([1966] 1986, 38)

48

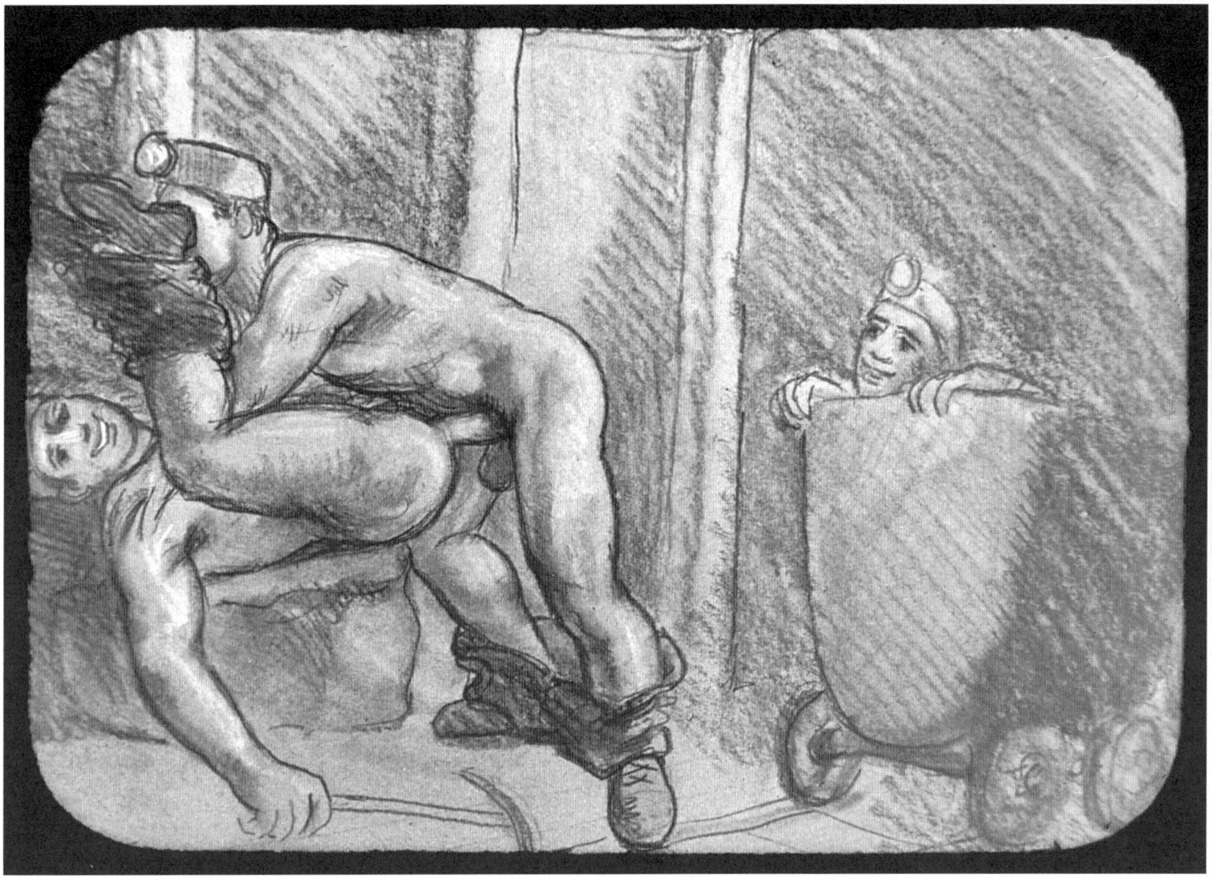

The tea break put to good use far down the shaft. . . . Happyface seems something of an insider in his comfort with these horny proletarians (as opposed to the slumming Joe Orton, who lied to one of his tricks that his tan was due to being just back from a working class resort in Spain rather than the more bourgeois holiday spot, Morocco, as described in *The Orton Diaries*).

49

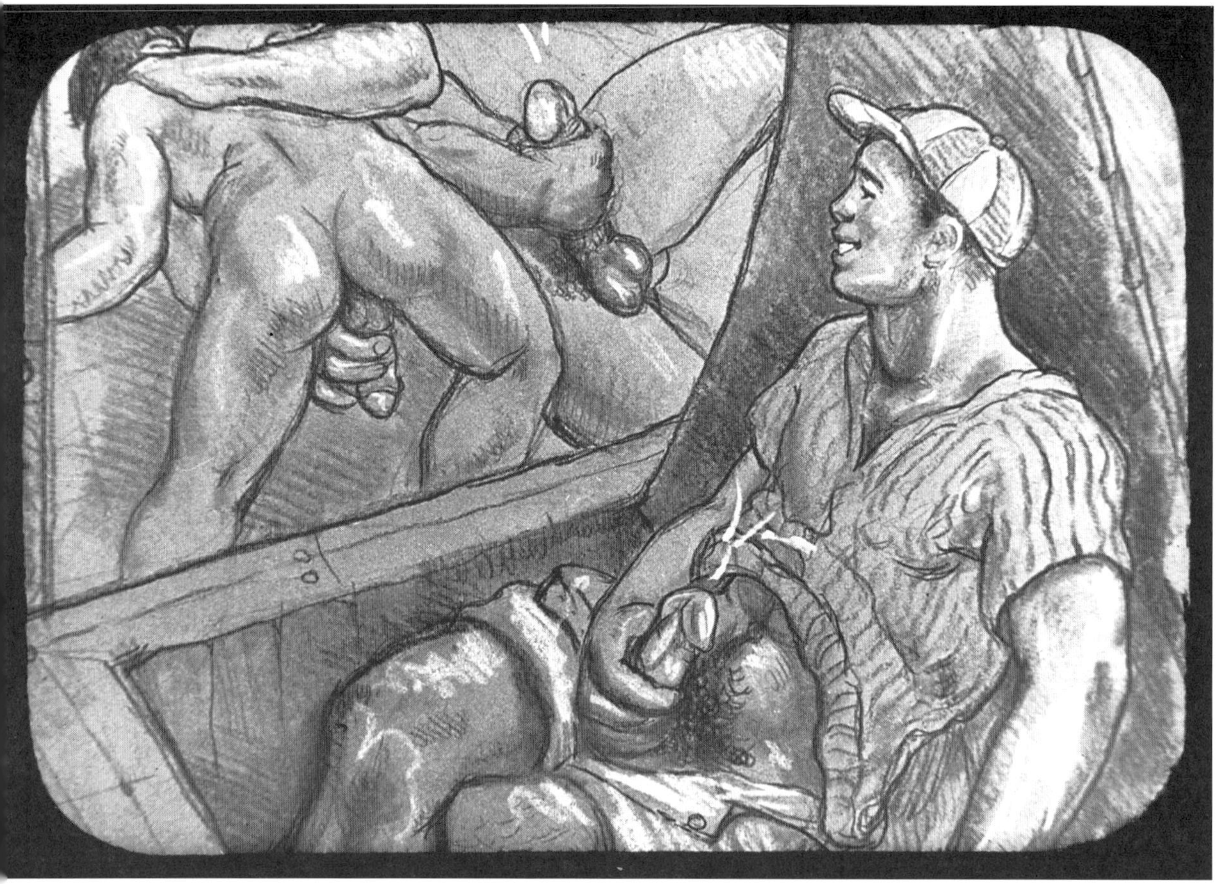

"... whether we ever repeated these pleasures during the night (we slept in one bed) I don't recall; I doubt it; since he was an athlete, always boxing or training for it, I expect it was tacitly understood that he should conserve his strength." J.R. Ackerley, *My Father & Myself* (1968, 128). (Readers who decipher the nature of this happy footballer's location—a dugout? a dhow?—please rush me the answer!)

50

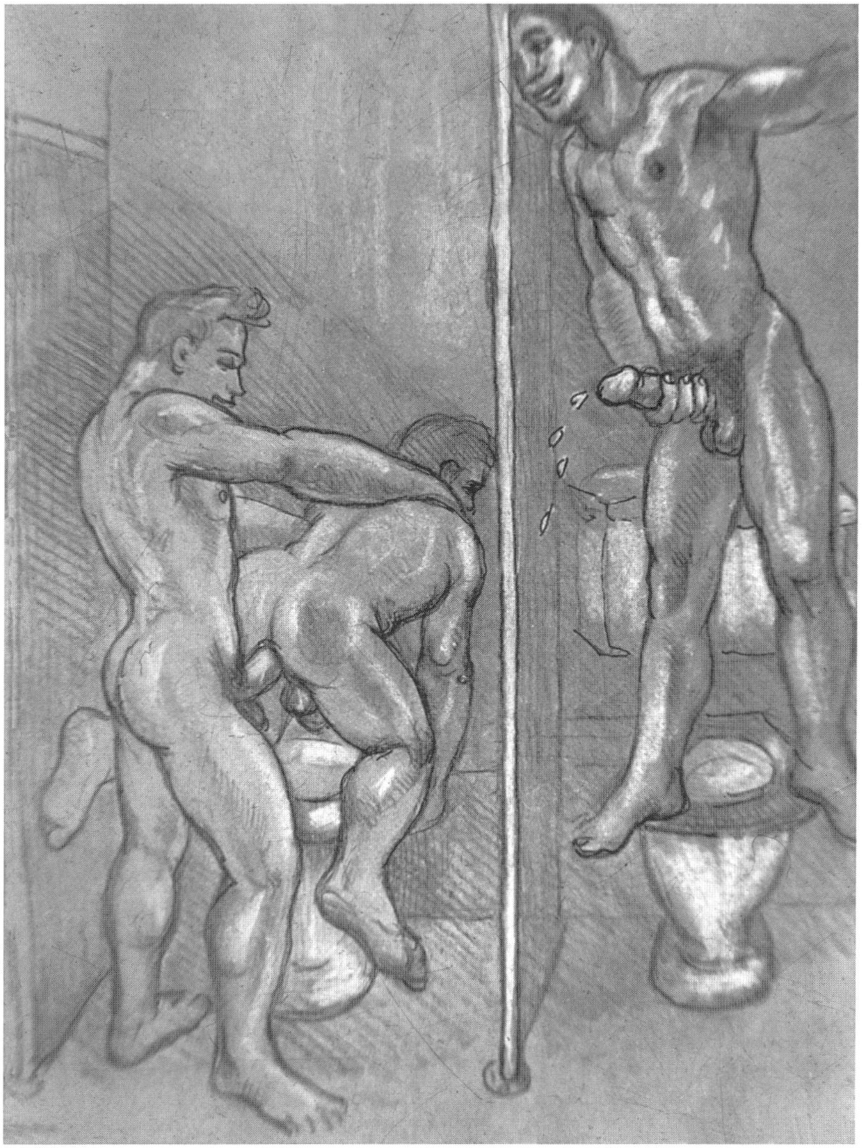

"I took the Piccadilly line to Holloway Road and popped into a little pissoir. . . . For some moments nothing happened. Then an eighth man, bearded and stocky, came in. He pushed the sixth man roughly away from the fair-haired man and quickly sucked the fair-haired man off. The man beside me had pulled my jeans down over my buttocks and was trying to push his prick between my legs. . . ." Joe Orton, *The Orton Diaries* ([1967] 1986, 105-06) **51**

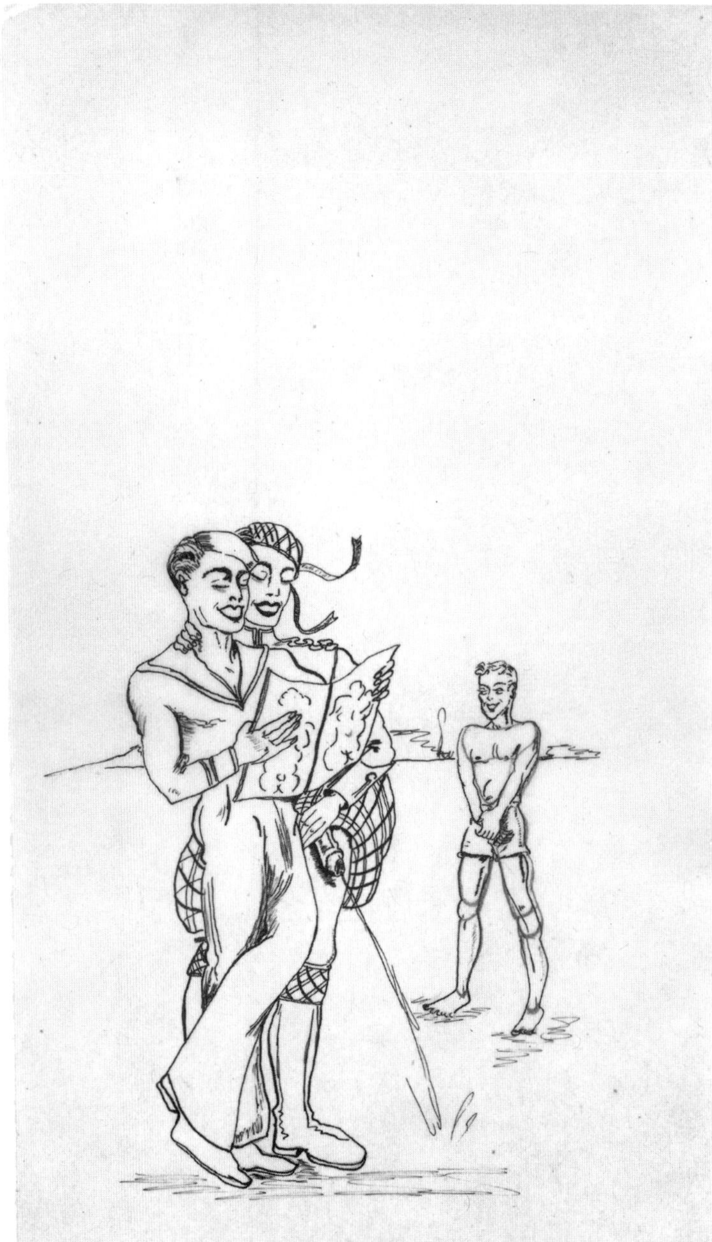

52 This compatriot is a little less accomplished as a draughtsman, a little more edgy, than the wholesome Happyface, but still struts out the same menagerie of uniformed types, with freshly applied lipstick and mascara. In his world, however, the uniforms are sharply differentiated from the civilian pansy bottom, who is introduced on a deserted beach getting all excited looking at two military types getting all excited looking at porn—so excited that the Scots grenadier needs unaccountably to piss on the sand and fortunately is wearing no underwear to get in the way. c. 1950s.

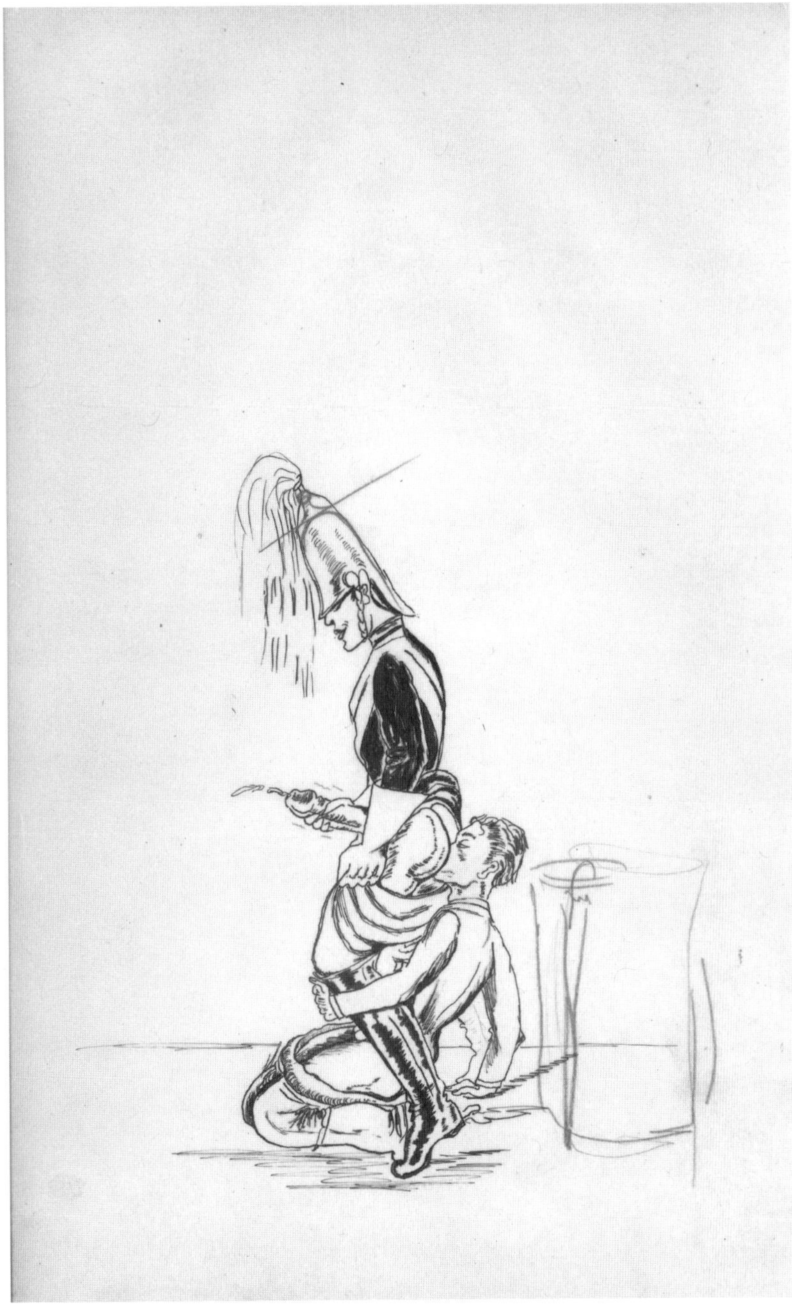

Let's call this anonymous artist "Lipstick" though by all evidence his characters certainly risked getting their lipstick smeared. "Prying the buttocks aside, I nosed my way in / Down the shaggy slopes. I came to the puckered goal. / It was quick to my licking. He pressed his crotch to my chin. / His thighs squirmed as my tongue wormed in his hole." "The Platonic Blow," attrib. W. H. Auden (c. 1930s)

53

National Dreams:
HOMO ON THE AMERICAN RANGE

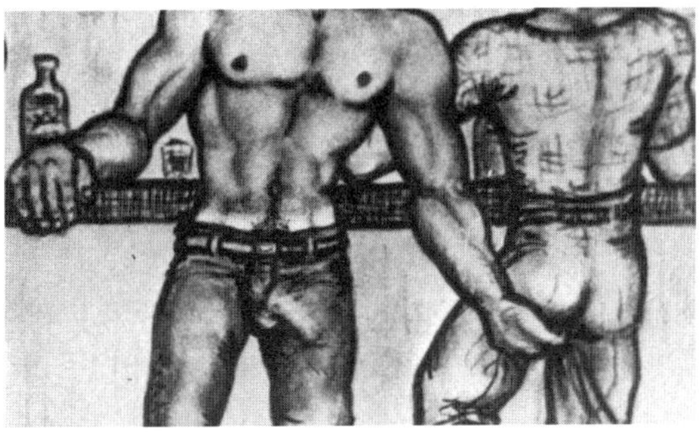

. . . he said that he could not endure being surrounded by so many Americans. He said they all looked alike—as I am sure they did, to him. But they didn't look alike to me. I was aware that they all had in common something that made them Americans, but I could never put my finger on what it was. I knew that whatever this common quality was, I shared it. And I knew that Giovanni had been attracted to me partly because of it. . . .

—James Baldwin, *Giovanni's Room* (1956)

National Dreams:
HOMO ON THE AMERICAN RANGE

It took an African American adrift in Europe during the 1950s to develop the sensitivity to others' stereotypes of Americans evidenced in this citation, and to the erotic dimensions of those stereotypes. I don't think Baldwin had cowboys in mind, but surely they epitomize the archetype of American masculinity as a sexual fantasy in a way similar to the German *Wandervögel* or the French and British sailor. The American erotic artist Blade understood this when he defaced *Life Magazine* in 1951, and cowboys are among the most popular icons of pre-Stonewall gay erotic fantasy, as the bestselling pulp novel *Song of the Loon* (1966) summed up for a whole generation. Cowboys by "Red Riding Wolf" (fig. 55) and Etienne (63) complete the picture, but they're connected to larger agrarian mythologies about real men's relation to to the land as a fantasy of freedom and mastery. I think that's what the farmboys in figures 56-62, ploughing their pals against the limitless open pastoral horizons, are about, and that's what's going on even in the parodic picture of the midnight cowboy lost on the beach with his big big fish (fig. 136), or the backdrop of ye olde haymow in (figs. 139 and 226). What did Rodgers and Hammerstein really mean in *Oklahoma!* (1943) when they sang "The Cowboy and the Farmer Should Be Friends"?

The plurality of the images in this book are American in provenance, and they may feel too close and too invisible for us to identify further national mythologies. In parting, however, let's just throw out two others for rumination.

1) "Supersize me" did not originate with fast food or documentaries in 2004. Most of the national clusters take account of cock size of course (though not all). But could the incredible hulk bursting out of Etienne's jock strap in figure 63, or the detached allegorical monsters in figures 66-72, or the coach's patriarchal training prong in 234-235 come from anywhere else but the land of the Cadillac, the Whopper with Cheese, and the Empire State Building?

2) The British mixed sex and moralism, granted, but the ex-colonials are out of control. "Red Riding Wolf" unsurprisingly sees sexual exchange as a matter of innocence seduced, as trickery, exploitation, and coercion (figs. 55, 95-97, 171-174), while Etienne (figs. 180-198) and Spartacus (figs. 230-235) add violence and ultimate anal punishment to the same mix. The most interesting anal chastisement takes place in the inner sanctum of the American ideology, the single-family-dwelling (fig. 64), complete with a sanctimonious wall plaque, "Home Sweet Home." Isn't that a phrase from "America the Beautiful?" Did this artist knowingly prophesy the political issue of 2004, gay marriage?

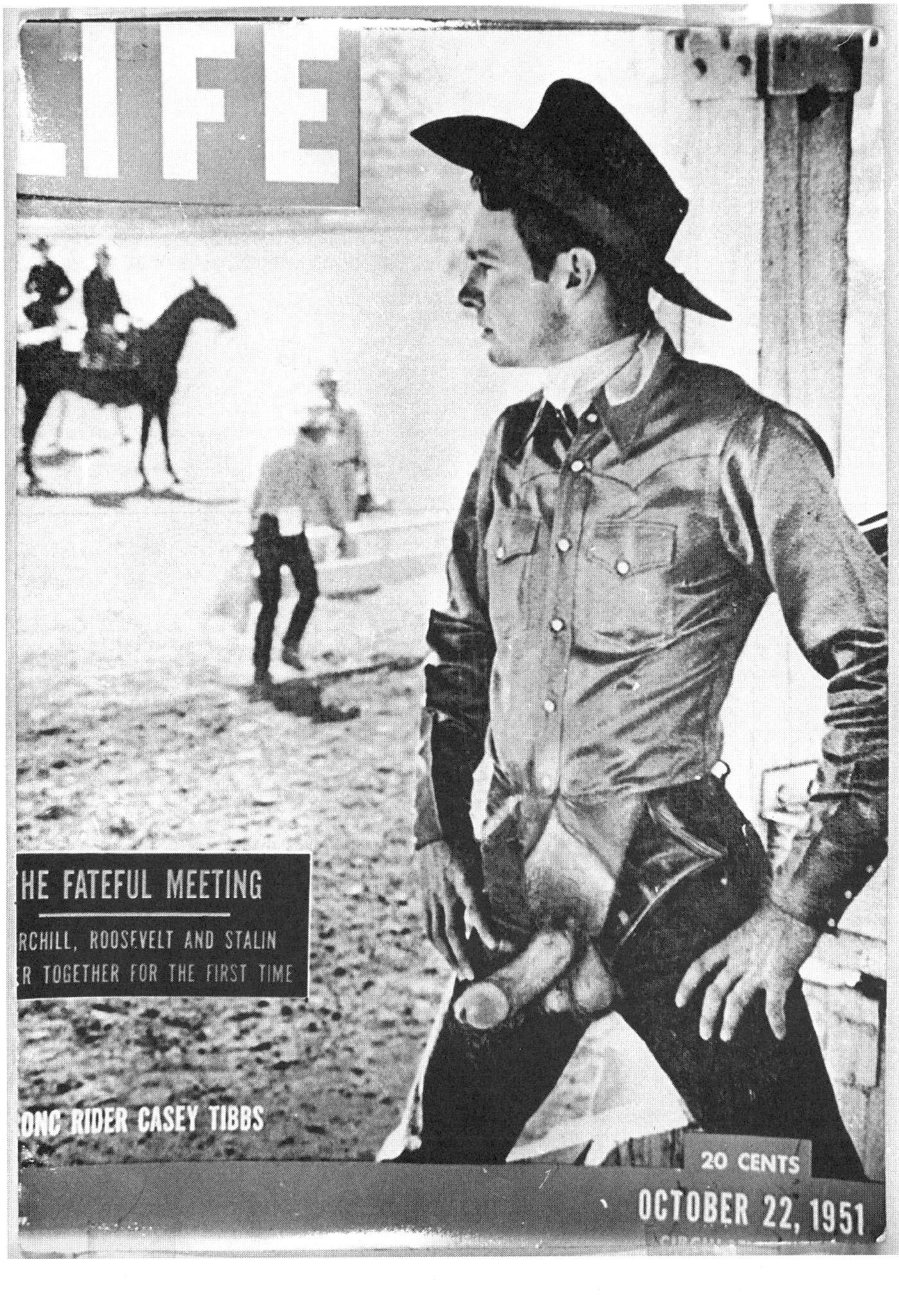

Life Magazine and a real-life cowboy whose phallic iconicity has been subversively pointed out by the ex-sailor rebel nicknamed Blade. Kneeland Bate (1916-1989), a friend of DuBek's, was one of the stars of *Out/Lines*, the self-taught virtuoso storyteller whose horny slim-waisted, big-pronged young men epitomized for me "the volatile intensity of erotic hunger." (Waugh 2002, 75) DuBek's samples of his famous horny pinups are so dim that none is included here, but his irreverent collage is the ideal synthesis of the erotic mythologies of the Land of 54
the Free.

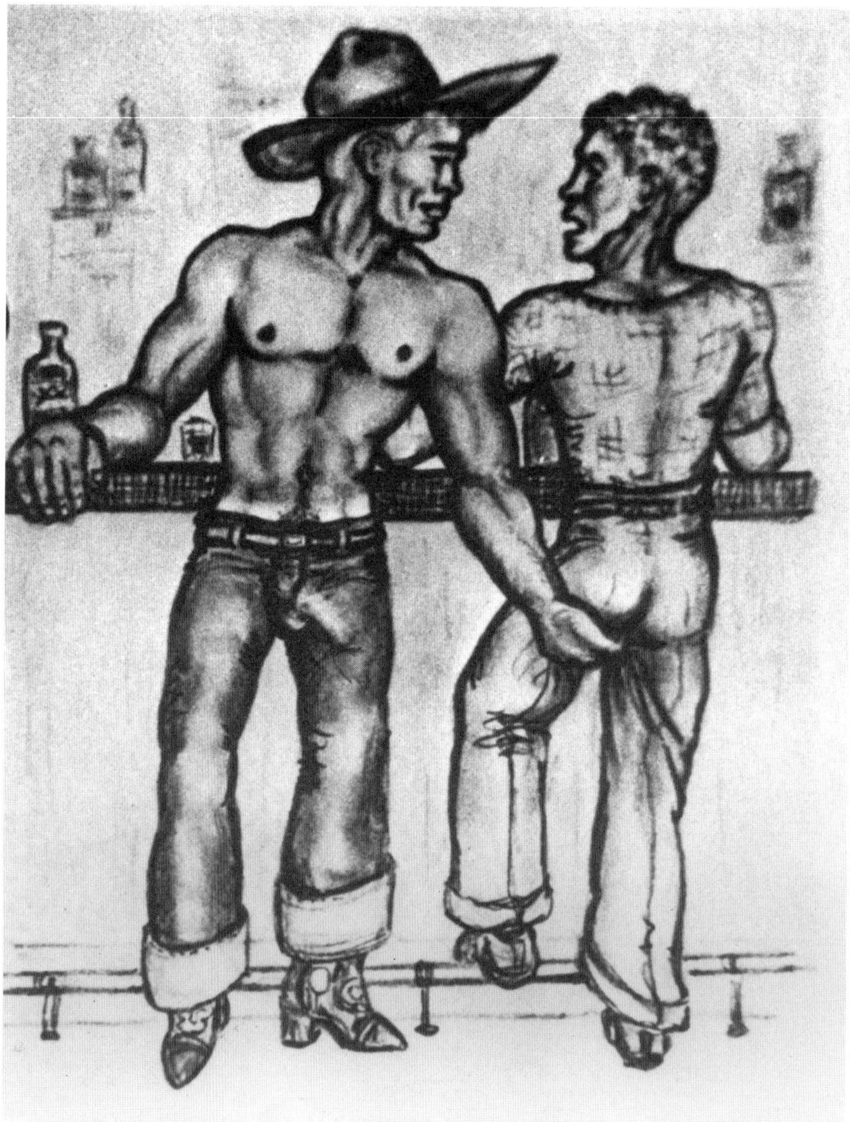

55 This anonymous artist (I have a hunch he's from California . . .) we can call "Red Riding Wolf," after his cynical tale printed in *Out/Lines* (Figures 158-163) of a hardened sailor having his way with a slim young pickup in bellbottoms (see also Figures 95-97, 171-74). Why do I think that the formula of innocence seduced is as much a part of the American ethos as the cowboy, and his buddies, the sailor and farmer? Is it something about a never-overcome frontier moralism that sophisticated Europeans never had to deal with?

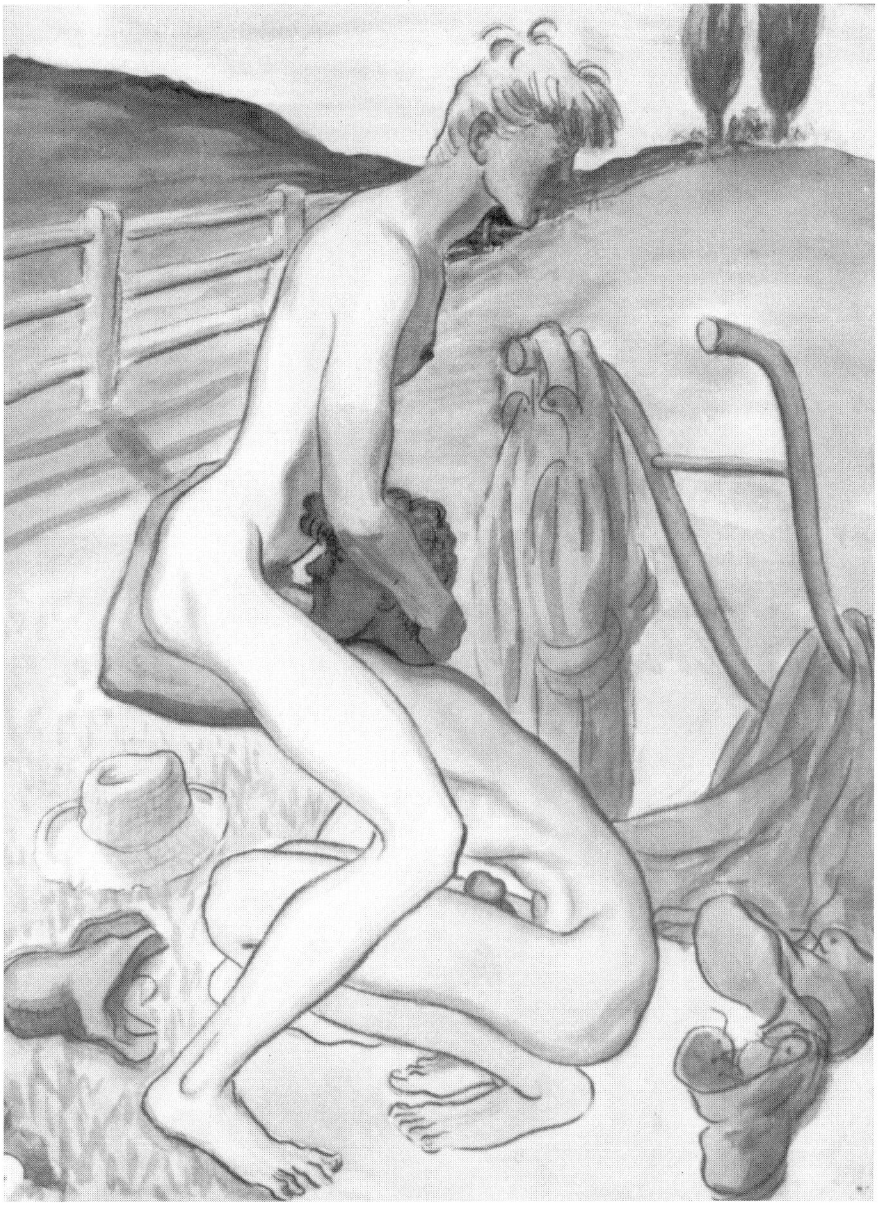

Something also about territory, wide open spaces and skies, whereunder the horny farmboy can have lunch with his cousin with relative impunity. A masterful one-of-a-kind by an artist that DuBek seemingly never encountered again. U.S.A., c. 1960.

56

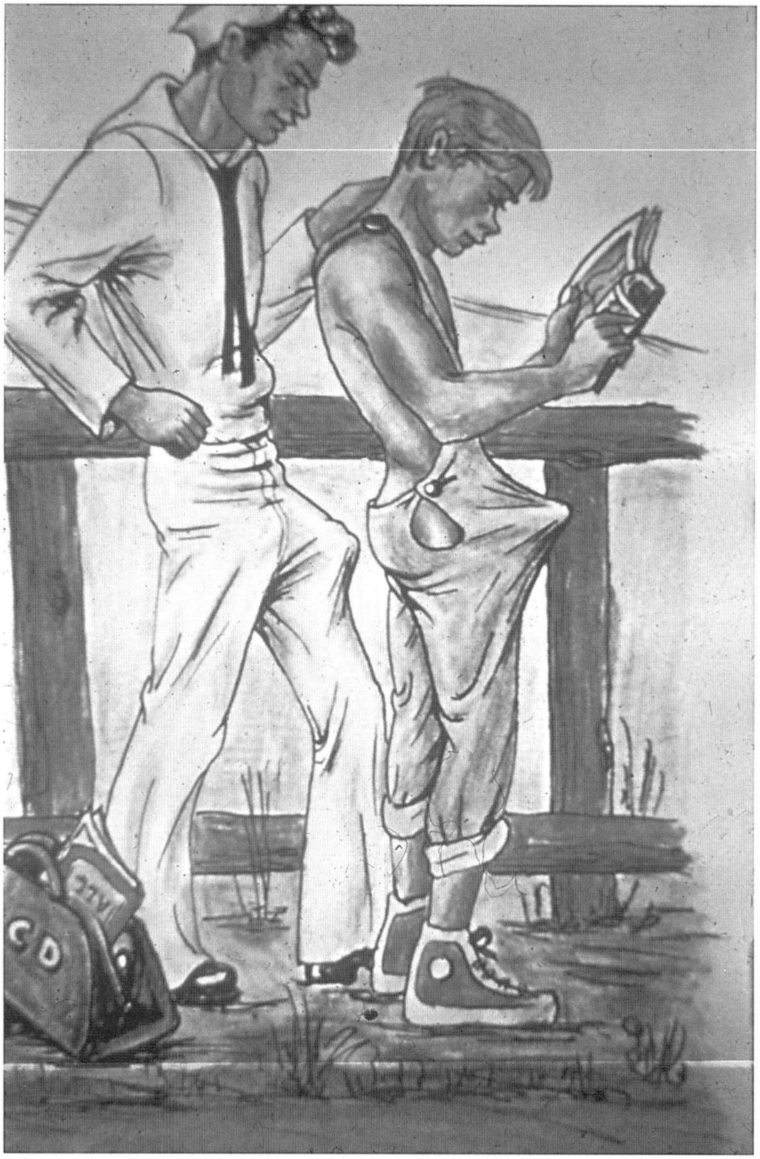

Another encounter of innocence and experience under the prairie sky, but almost free of the cynical moralism of Red Riding Wolf. Artist unknown, U.S.A., c. 1960.

57

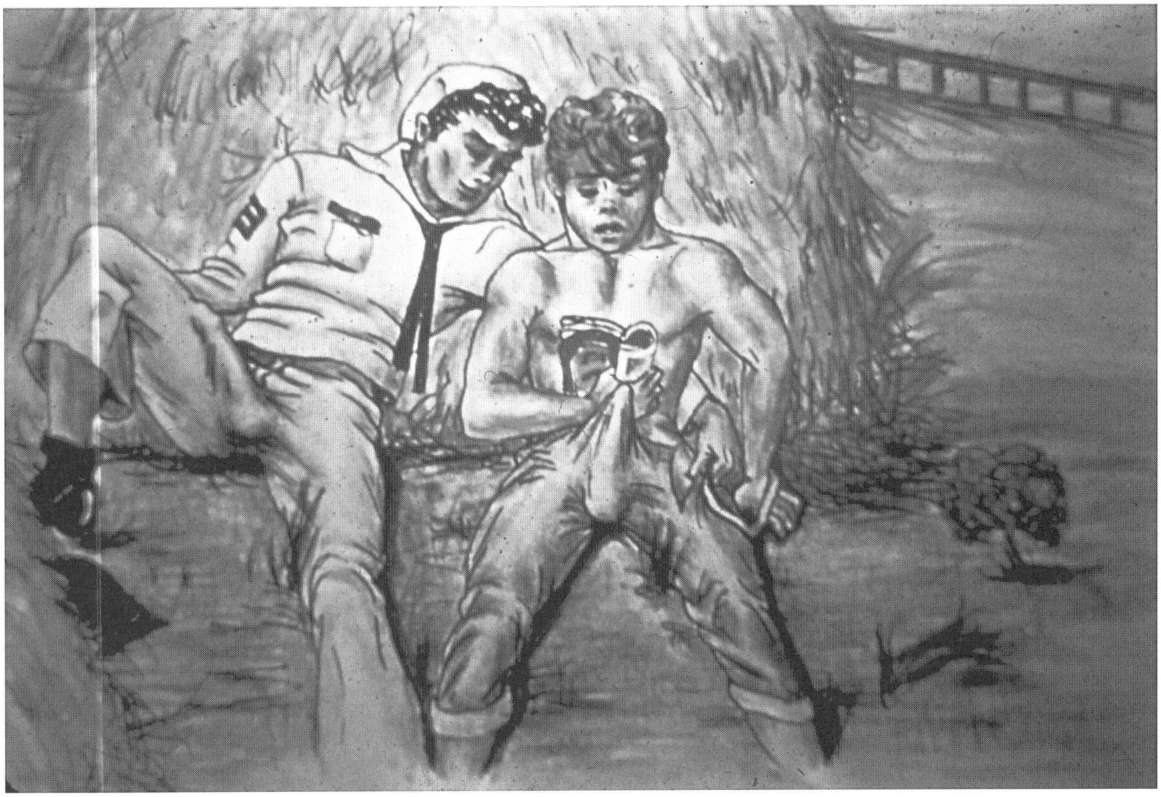

Yes, porn is the corrupter of youth, but it didn't take much. "Blade" and others loved their stories about using images to break down barriers, "breaking trade" as he called it, and ye olde haystack is just the place.

58

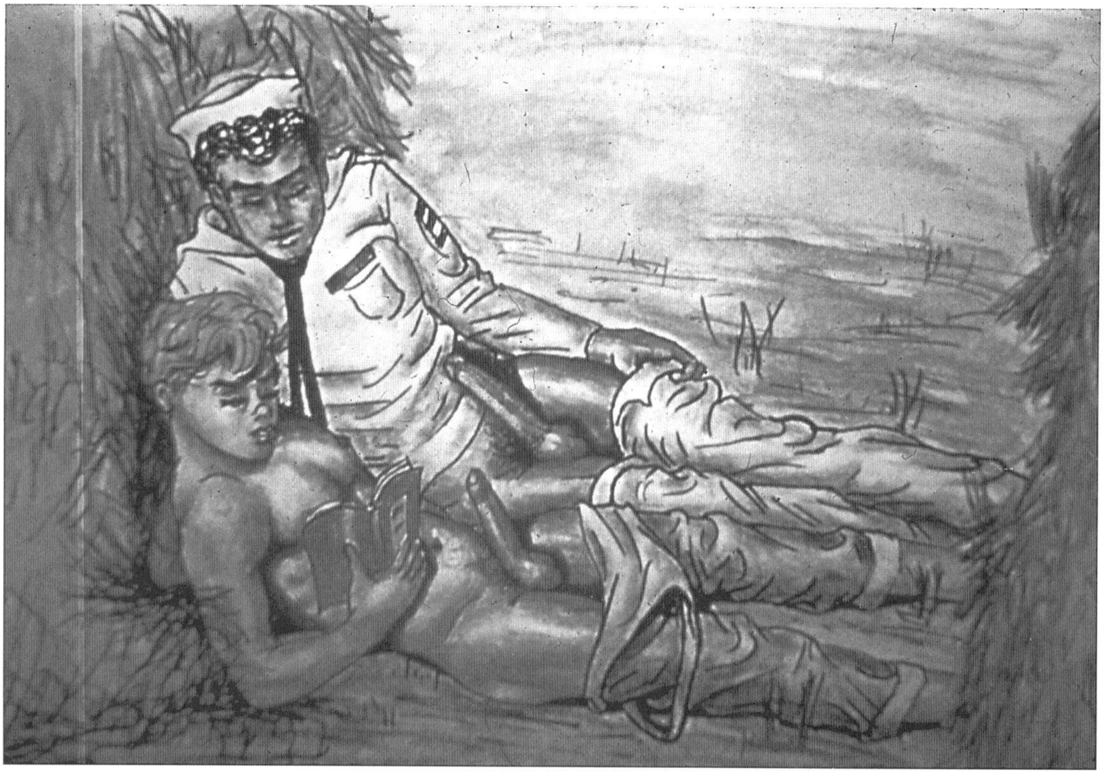

"Youre too old for me anyway,' he said. 'I prefer them very young and very, *very* dumb, dear,' he went on cuttingly. . . .

59

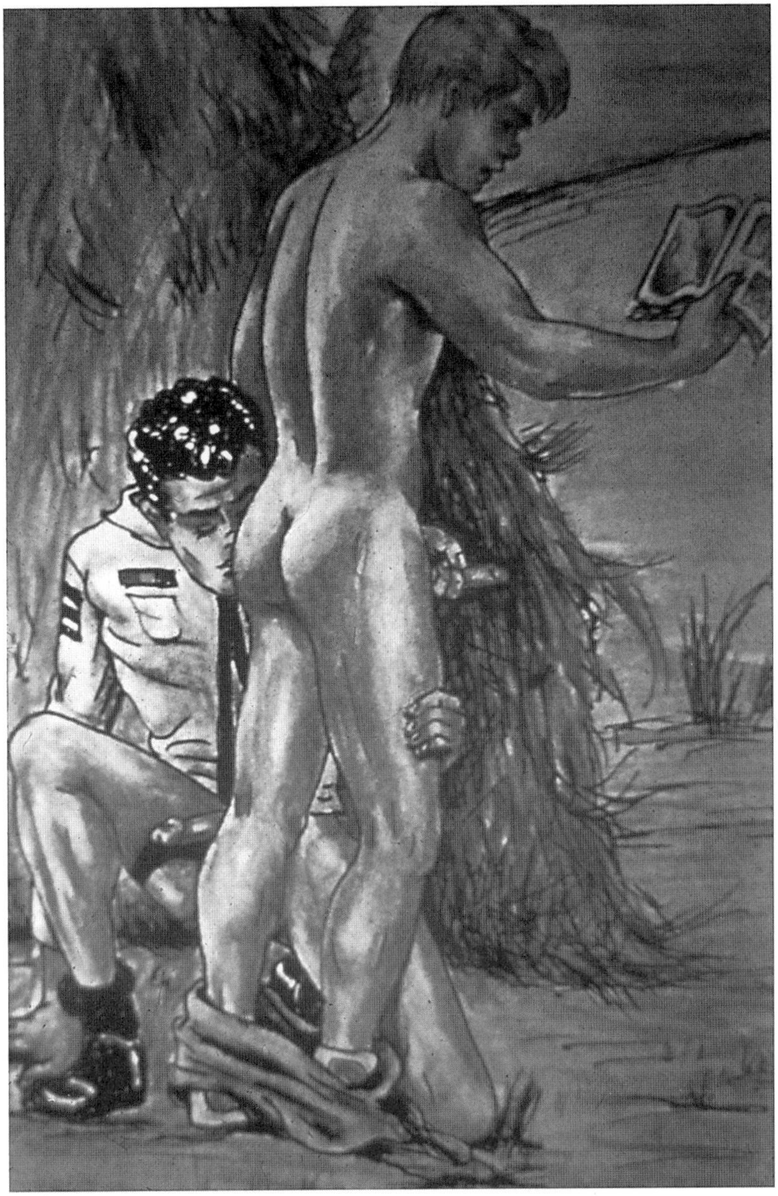

. . . In their 20s, theyve already been had too often—and in too many ways. I like the little boys who can still get aroused by dirty pictures. I like to watch the naughtiness awaken. . . ." John Rechy, *City of Night* (1963, 214)

60

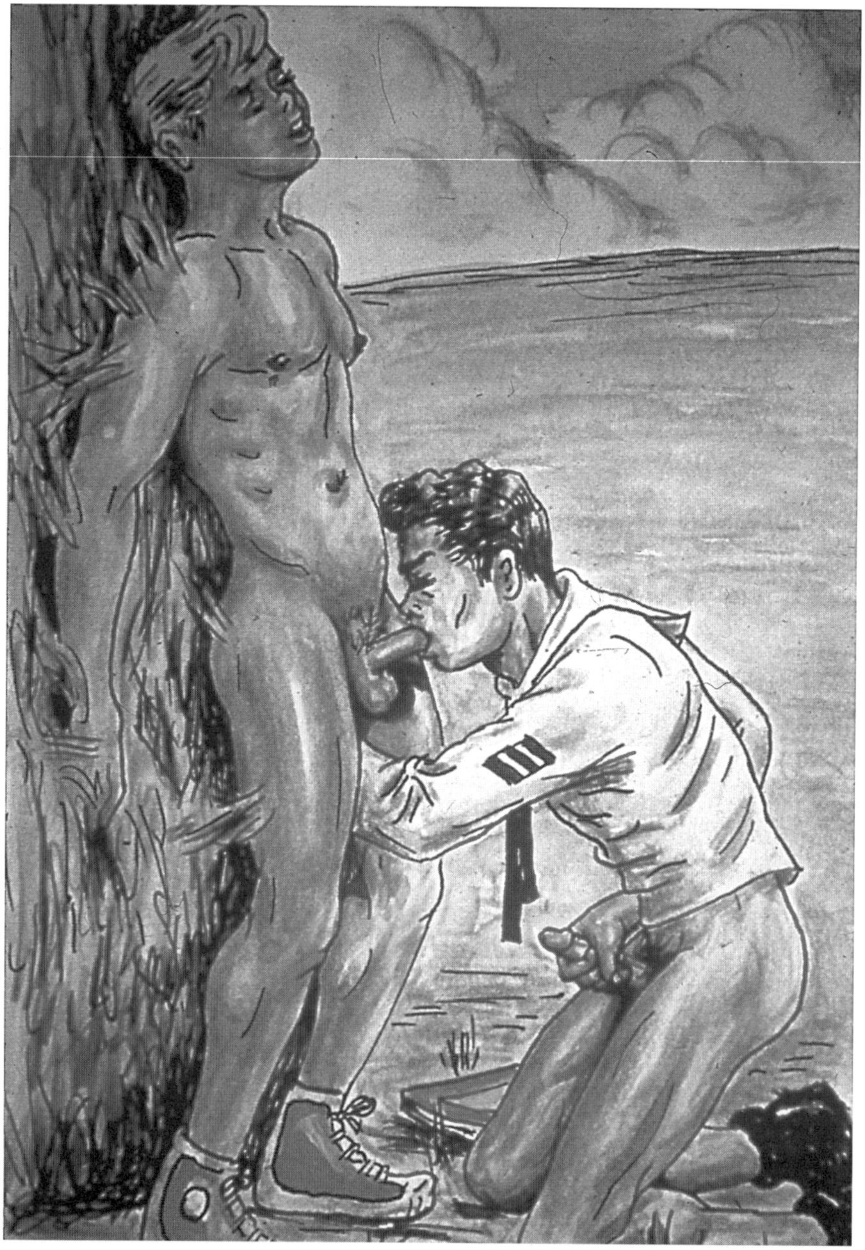

“Thus, when confronting those possessors of sheer animal flesh unspoiled by intellect—young toughs, sailors, soldiers, fishermen— . . .

61

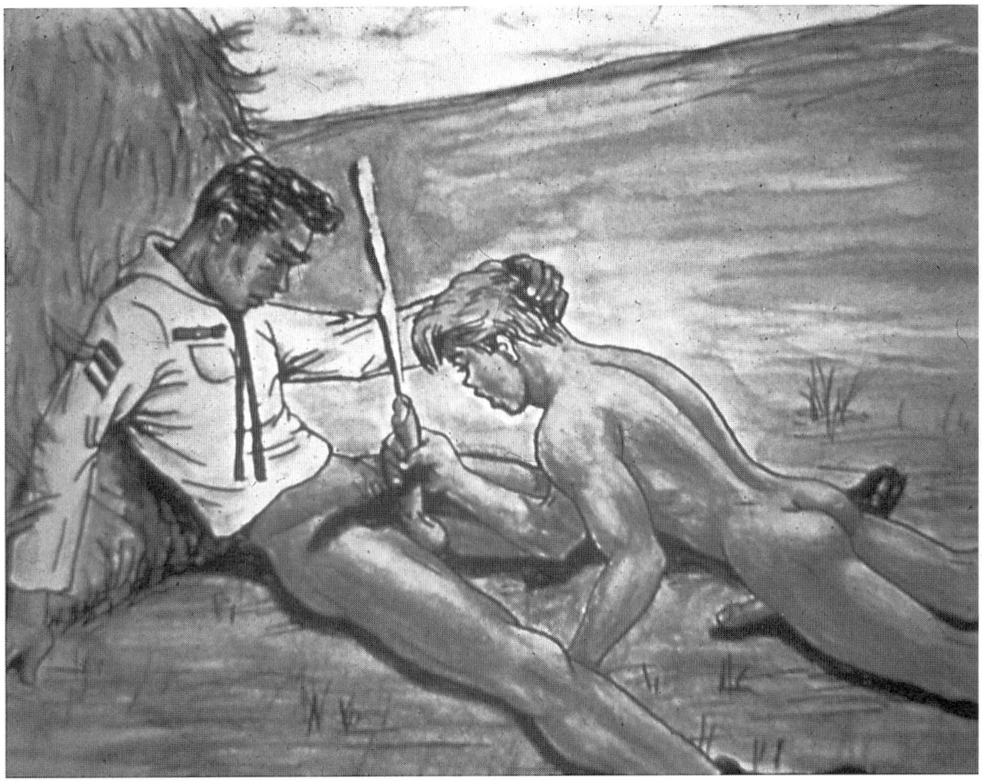

. . . there was nothing for me to do but be forever watching them from afar with impassioned indifference, being careful never to exchange words with them." Yukio Mishima, *Confessions of a Mask* ([1949] 1958, 65)

2

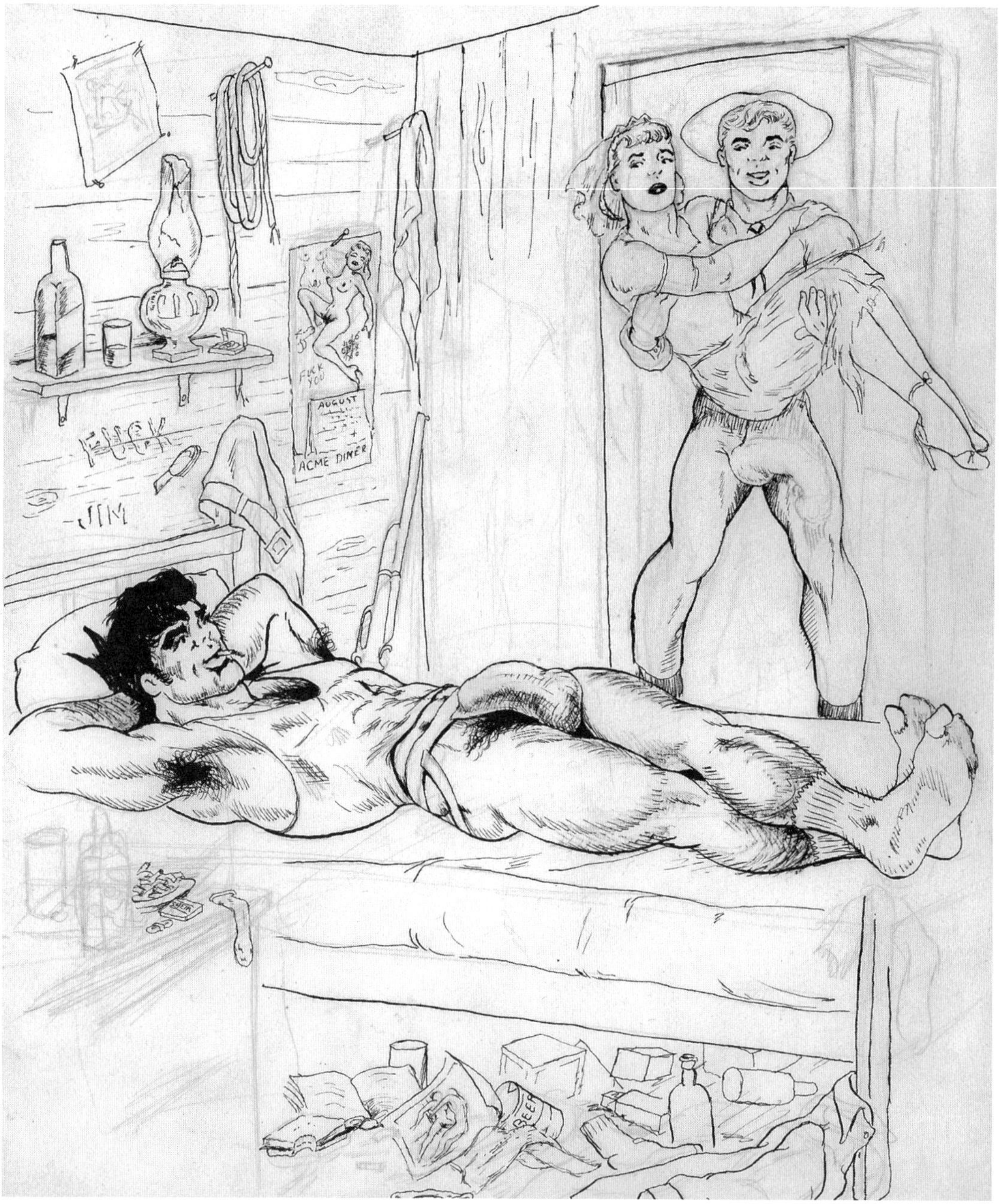

Etienne (Dom Orejudos, 1933-1991) is perhaps the best-known of American gay erotic artists of the postwar period, along with Blade. This raunchy series, another of his classic triangle narratives, sets up a caricaturally American sense of male desire disguised as rivalry and class tension. See Figures 180-198. See also two nice sets of footwear.

63

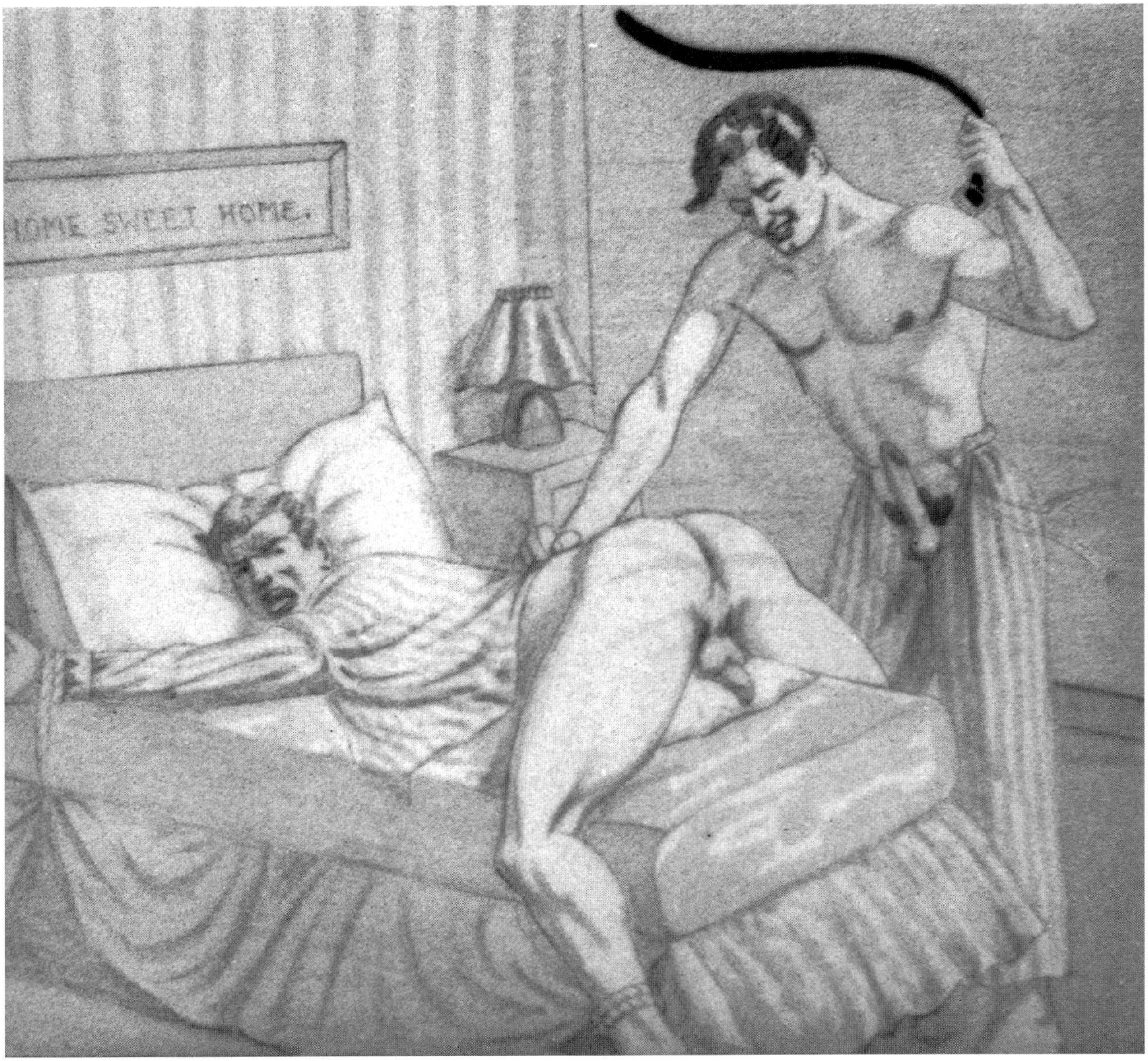

The sanctimoniousness of the American mythology of the home sweet "nuclear family" home, complete with twin bed, flared bedspread—plus ideal couple wearing matching pyjama top and bottom just like Doris Day and John Raitt in *The Pajama Game* (1957)—is lacerated with so much relish here. This unknown S/M dream-catcher is also responsible for Figures 145-149.

64

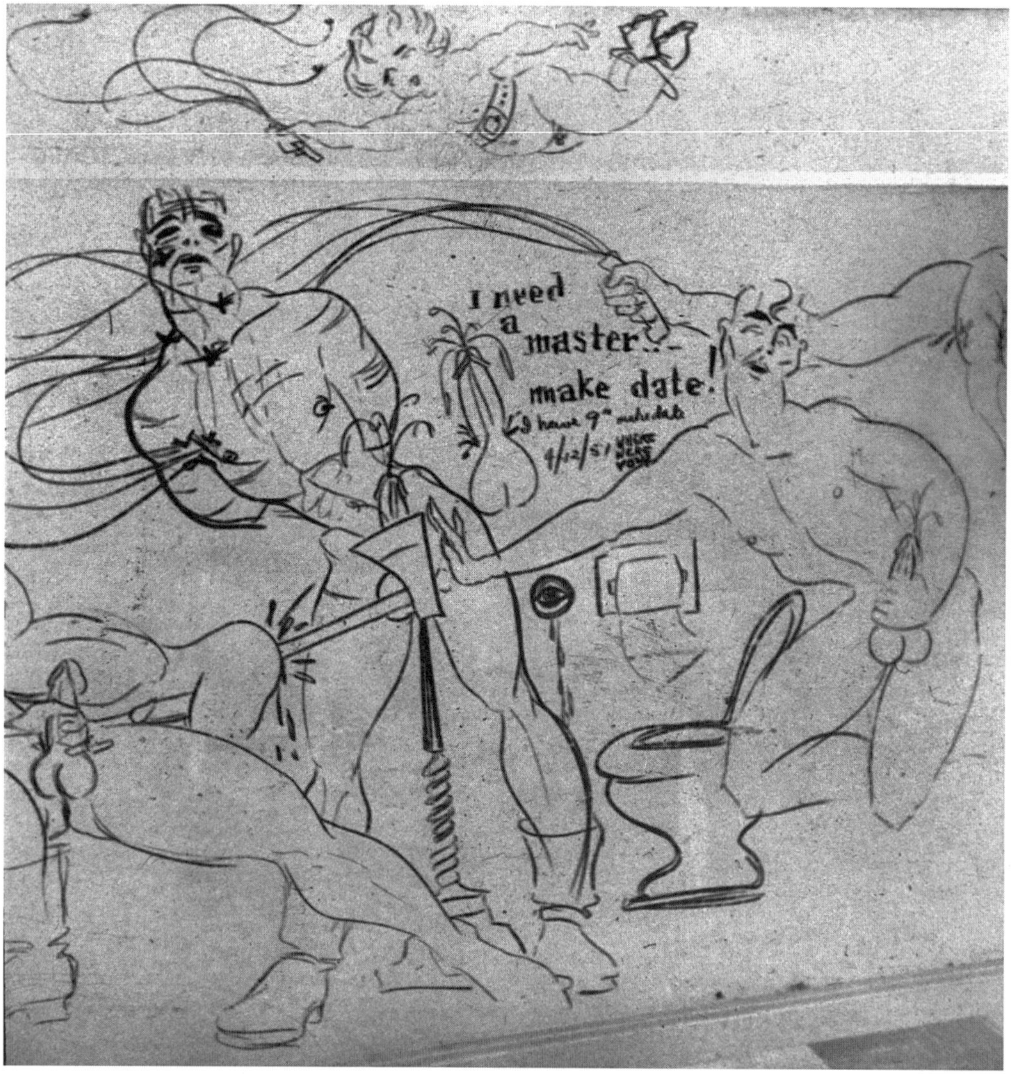

Real spaces are as much a part of national mythologies as the foregoing fantasies. DuBek prized these photos of a grand mural depicting a toilet bondage epic that apparently decorated a specialty site, presumably in New York City, in 1951 (if the inscription is to be believed). Hard to believe that it could have been a public bar, no doubt rather a clandestine and probably ephemeral club.

65

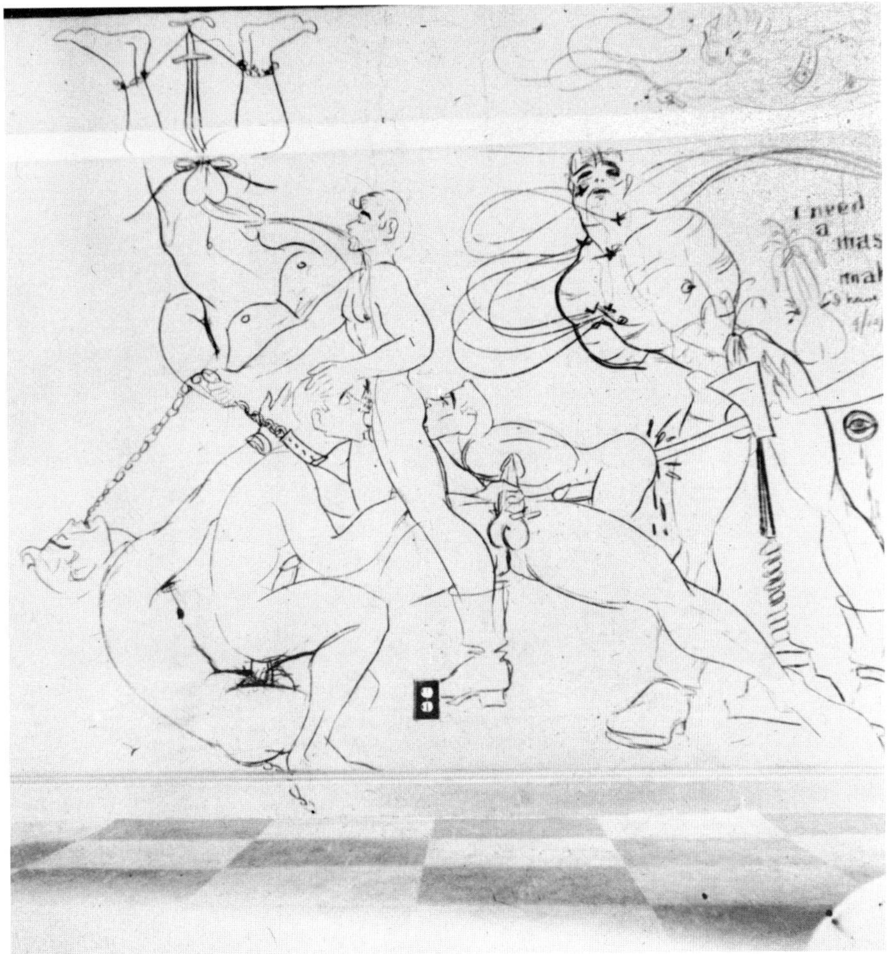

"Tonight, at the bar, / in the Members Only room, / the usual collection of aging 'cyclists'/ lounge / wearing painfully tight jeans / elaborately arranged to show maximum amount of cock and balls. / Even in summer a lot of them wear full leather." Ralph Pomeroy, "The Leather Bar" ([c. 1969] 1983, 344)

66

Fantasies:
phallic

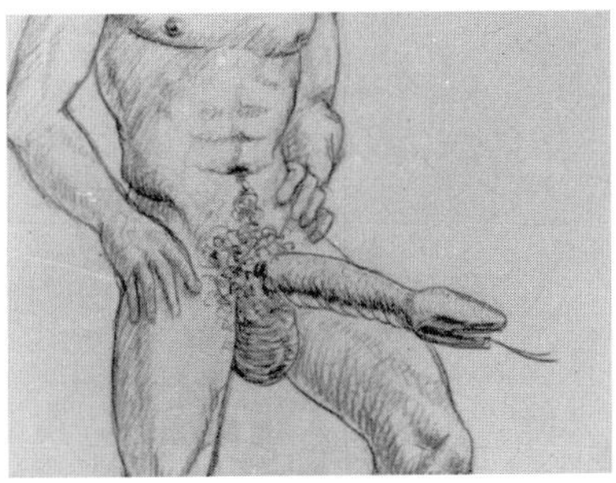

It wouldn't take rocket science to imagine that the penis is the core of this book's whole visual territory. Although there are unexpectedly only a few of the close-up meat and money shots that would, after Stonewall, come to dominate hardcore film and video porno (e.g., figs. 97, 127-128), the cock is nevertheless front and center throughout *Lust*. The organ that never

FANTASIES:
PHALLIC

sleeps is literally the compositional center of many images (look at figs. 11, 30, 80, 94, 100, 115, 118, 139, 145, 151, 152, 163, 169, 216, to mention only a few)—even when bursting out of its covering as in figures 24, 27, 58, and 63. Did the artist take a ruler to the blank page and decide precisely where it goes and work outwardly in concentric circles, adding the rest of the body and the scene? No subtle aesthetic shifts in composition; it's dead center, as if a religious icon, sometimes seeming appliquéed like a halo or the sacred heart, not done in gold leaf but usually with special graphic weight, lots of extra ink and texture added. Etienne's expertise in such special "emphasis" comes through in figure 63, and especially figures 191-192, where the organ has a life of its own, with everything else literally revolving round it. And then there's the odd symmetrical overhead effect in the "sixty-nine-in repose" cycle of figures 154-156, also icon-like, two for the price of one. As I said, no science needed to spot *this* rocket. (In contrast, the visual cult of the ass is comparatively subdued, cultivated by some of the S/M artists but most excessively by Spartacus [figs. 230-235].)

Size, as I've mentioned above, may be the national obsession of the American artists in *Lust Unearthed*, but most of the other artists also exaggerate a bit with this loaded object. So much so that when it's normal it stands out as a bizarre aberration, as in the following cluster's sixty-nine variation series (figs. 74-77), or in Paul Smara's otherwise highly stylized vignettes of his not especially monstrous "monsters" in heat (figs. 133-136).

Basically all of *Lust Unearthed* is one big phallic fantasy, but what I've assembled in this section in particular are two charming series that play outright with the penile obsession, self-reflexively tinkering with the Toy and perhaps even forgetting the primary objective of arousing the reader's own in the process. Their dates and provenance are unknown, but either could easily be pre-World War II. In the first, the organ eerily assumes new shapes, functions, and dimensions, sometimes detached like a one-eyed monster in a 1950s sci-fi film, or transmogrifying into a sacred altar or a tower for Lilliputian mountain-climbers and wankers, or a warped cello or a serpentine organ straight out of the Garden of Eden. I've included only four from the second series since this anonymous artist's fixation on tender sixty-niners under a dream-like tent full of bizarre phallic chandeliers and other kitsch bric-a-brac becomes repetitious. His penises are also detached but far less threatening, like a chorus of decorative little curlicues in this temple to Priapus lite.

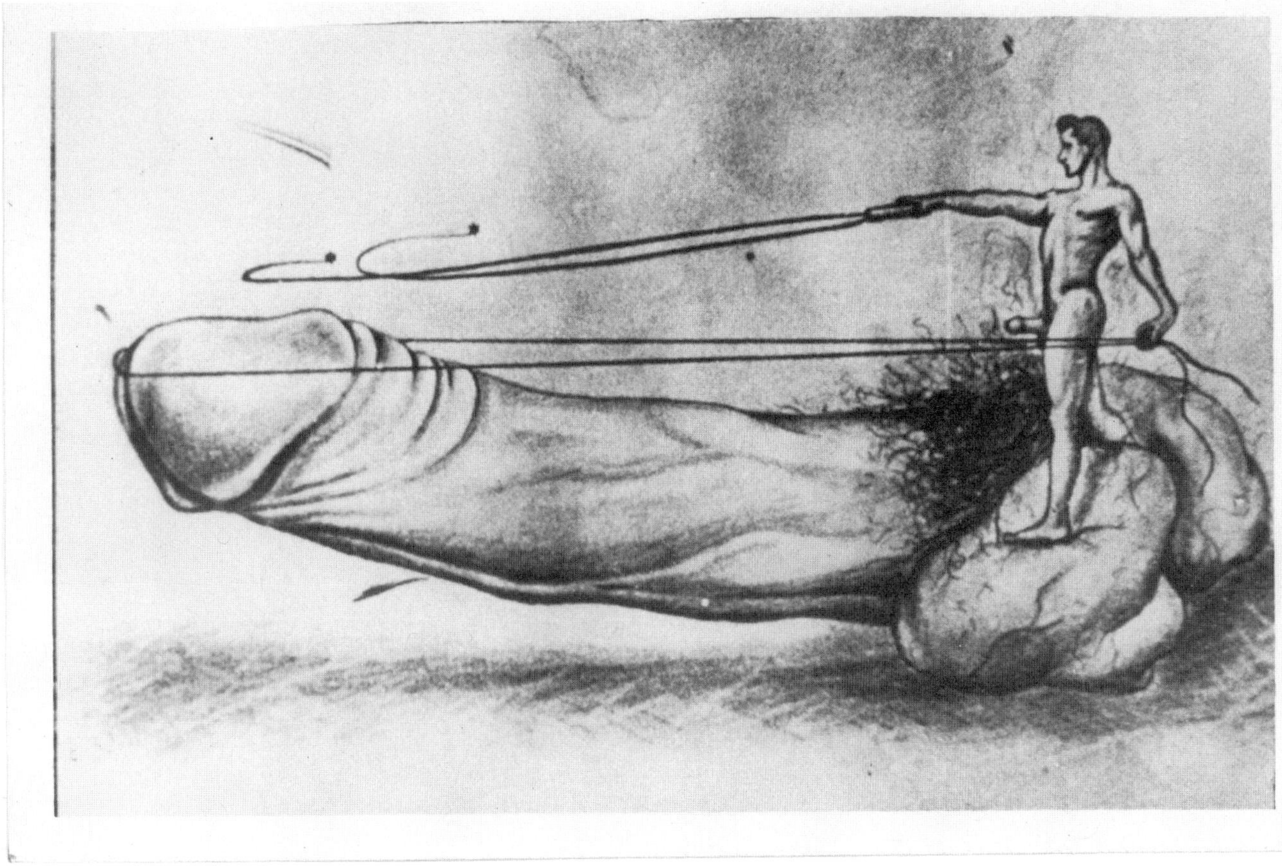

I am not sure whether the unknown author of this and the following six variations on the giant omnipresent phallus was actually interested in arousal, or in riffing, wryly, excessively, hauntedly, on the organ that obsessed him—and our society—everywhere. Judging from this one, the artist may have just seen *Ben-Hur* (1959), but I think these drawings are earlier, based on the hairstyles. Otherwise there is no sense of provenance or date.

67

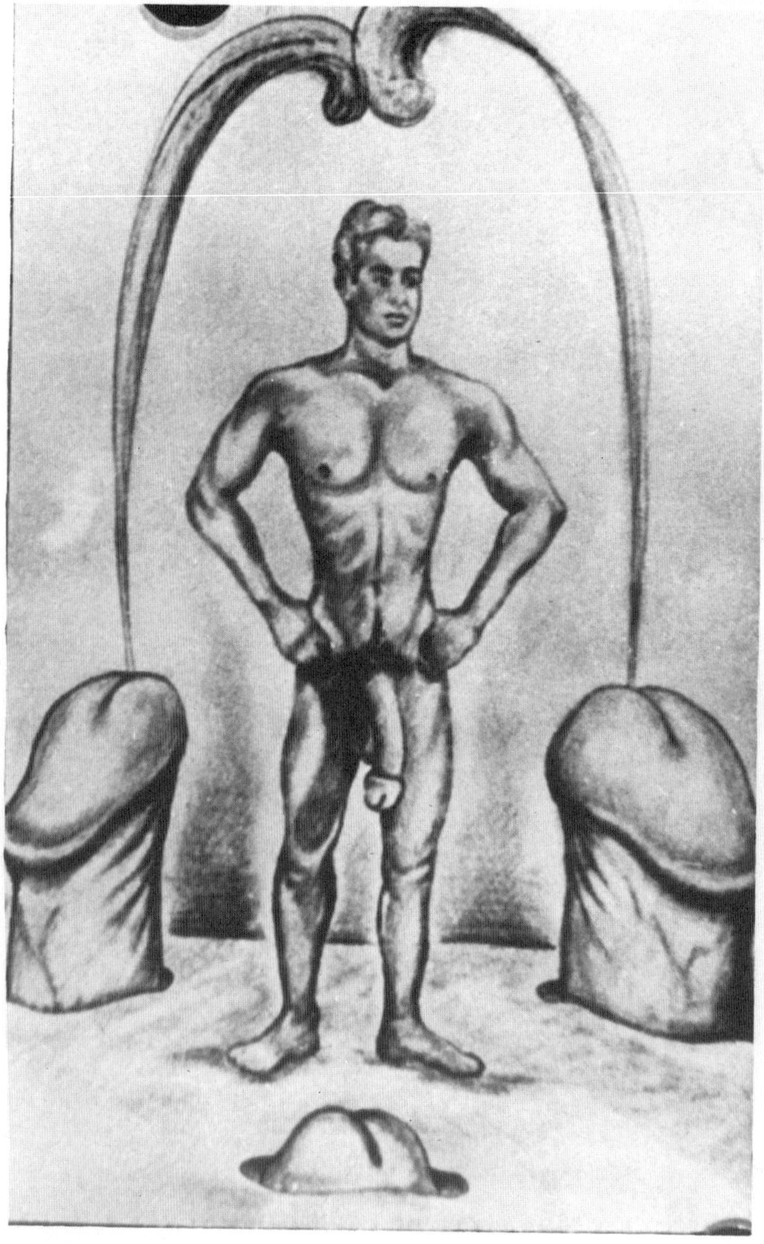

". . . o symphysis pubis! Tunica albuginea! Vasa efferentia! corpus cavernosum et spongiosum! o ampulla of vas! . . .

68

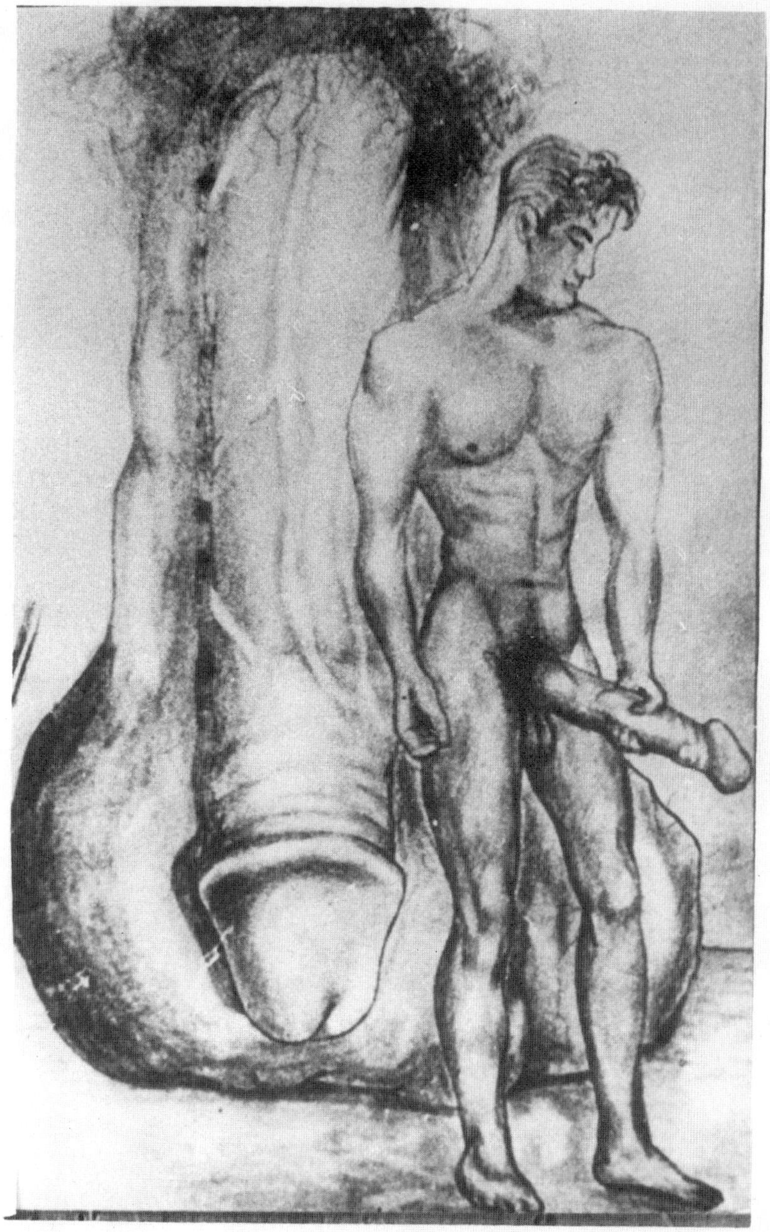

. . . o meatus and bulb! o cutaneous dorsal vein! o lobulous membranous convoluted pouch!" James Mitchell, "Gay Epiphany" ([c. 1969] 1983, 331)

69

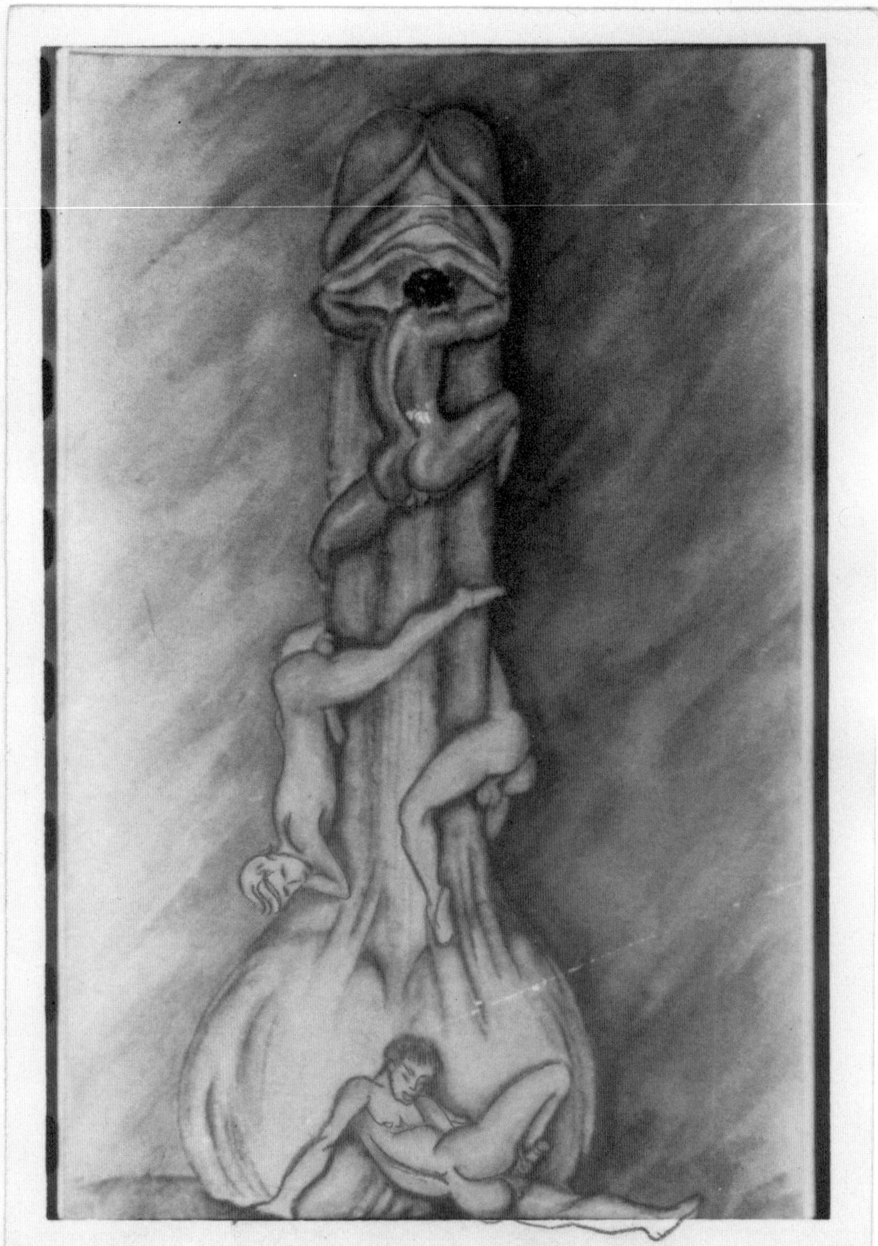

"His sexual organ, the symbol of this silly pilgrimage, and also the cause of my severe self-consciousness and unromantic sense of humor, really was a fantastic object. No matter what infantile prejudice you might be· swayed by, or pagan superstition, or pornographic habit of mind, you could not call it beautiful; it was just a desperate thickness, a useless length of vague awkward muscle . . .

70

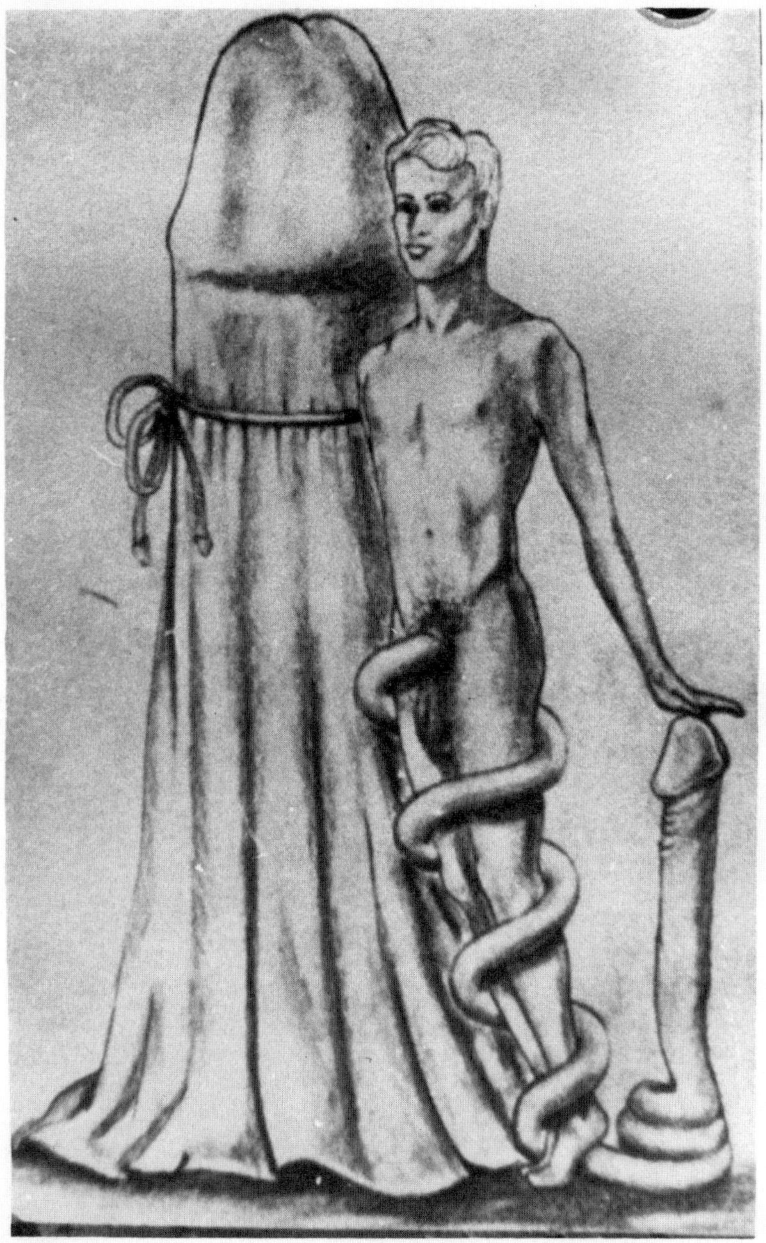

. . . An unusual amount of foreskin covered it, protruded from the end of it, thickly pursed like a rose. In the other dimension also, around the somewhat flattened shaft, the skin was very coarse and copious. . . . A thing to frighten maidens with, and to frighten pillagers out of an orchard; a thing to be wreathed with roses, then forgotten. . . ." Glenway Wescott, *A Visit to Priapus* ([1938] 1995, 15-16)

71

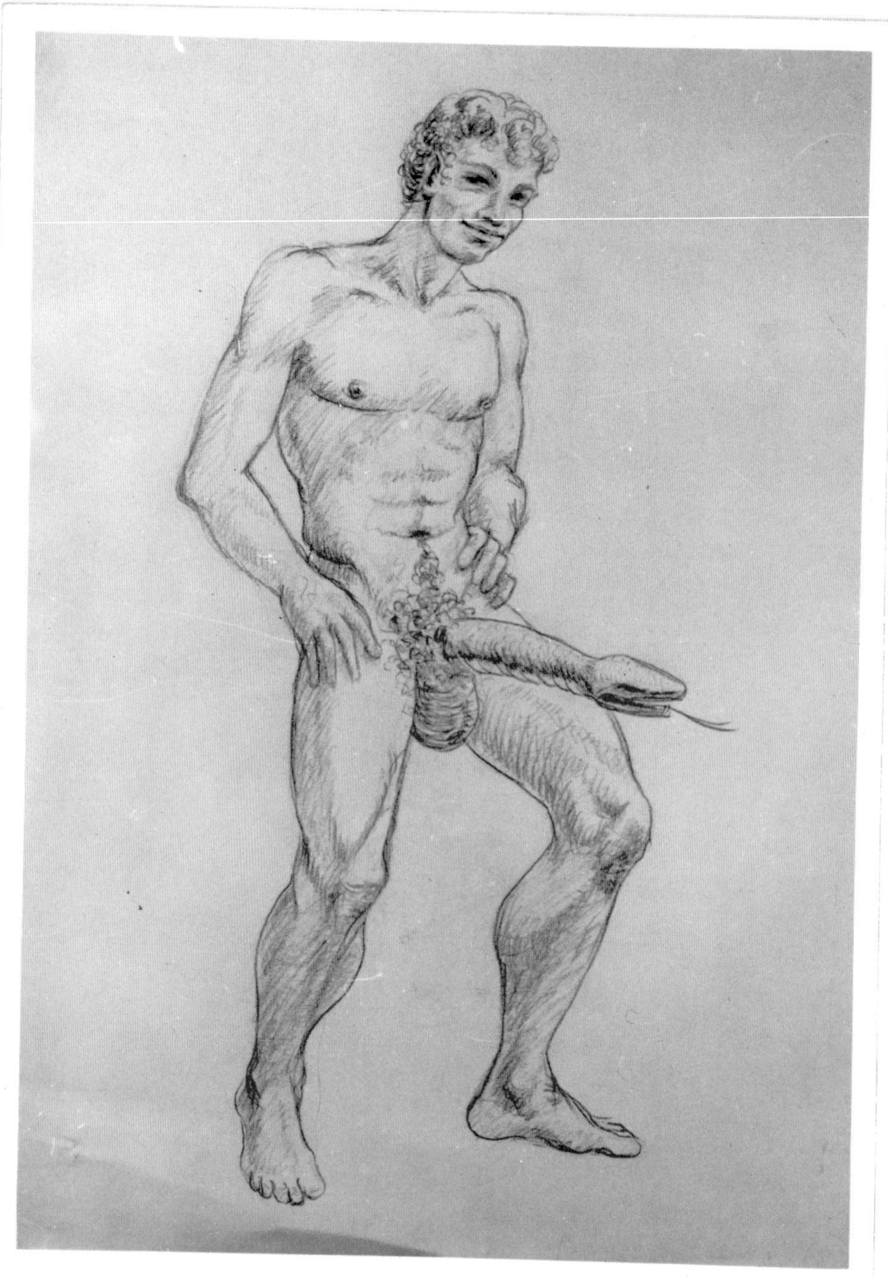

"Happening to wear that ostentatious organ, that heavy heraldry of sex, that sacred-looking simulacrum, he more or less consciously would have it serve him as a means to an end, a pretext, an allurement; . . . and as a substitute for what it symbolized, which was what he partially lacked. The entire night was booby-trap; and sex was the bait; and I was the booby." Glenway Wescott, A *Visit to Priapus* ([1938] 1995, 26)

72

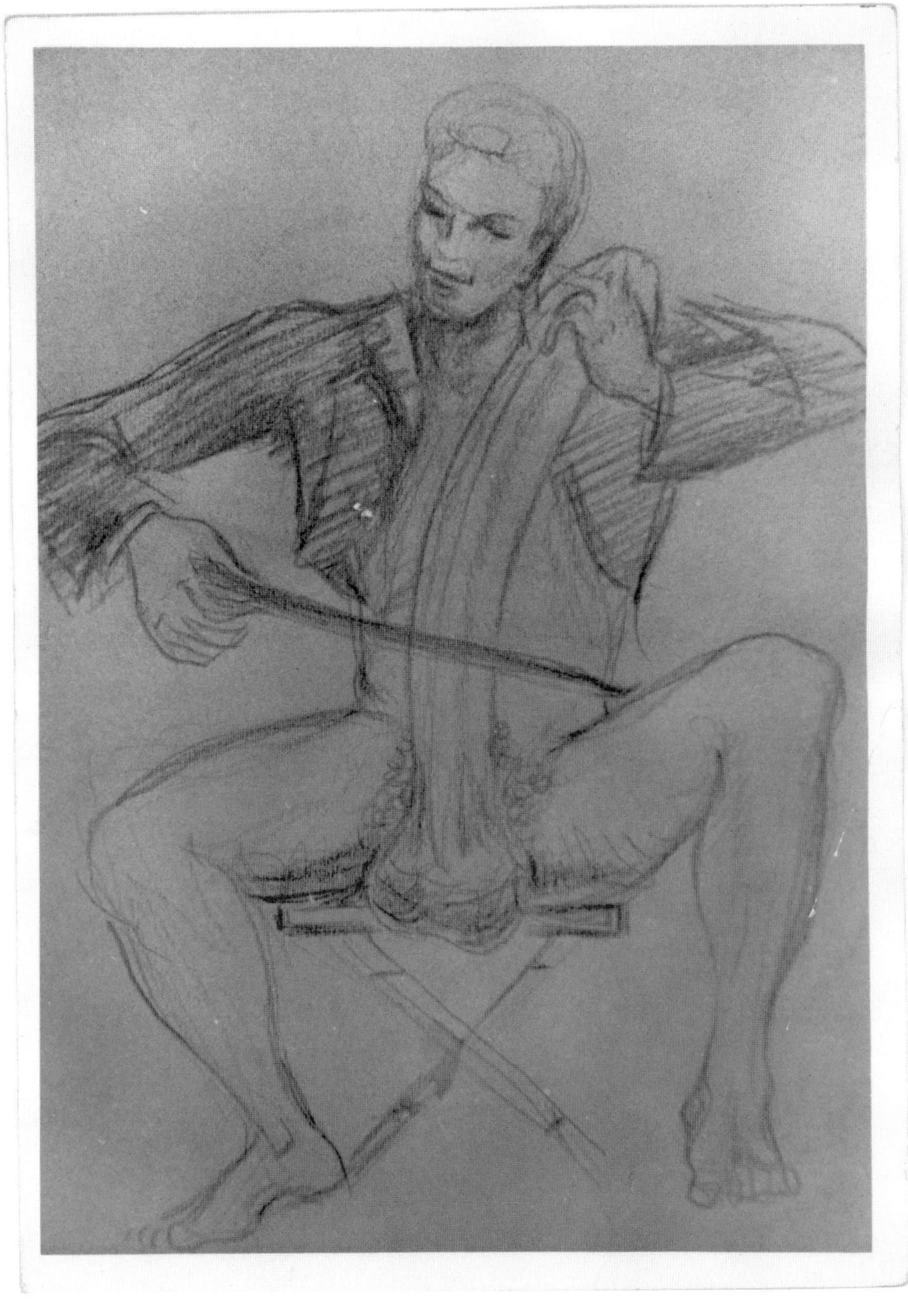

“Slipping my lips round the Byzantine dome of the head, / with the tips of my tongue I caressed the sensitive groove, / Lovingly bowed on his G-String. ‘Go on,’ he said. / ‘Quick. Suck me!’ Very slowly I started to move.” “The Platonic Blow,” attrib. W. H. Auden (c. 1930s)

73

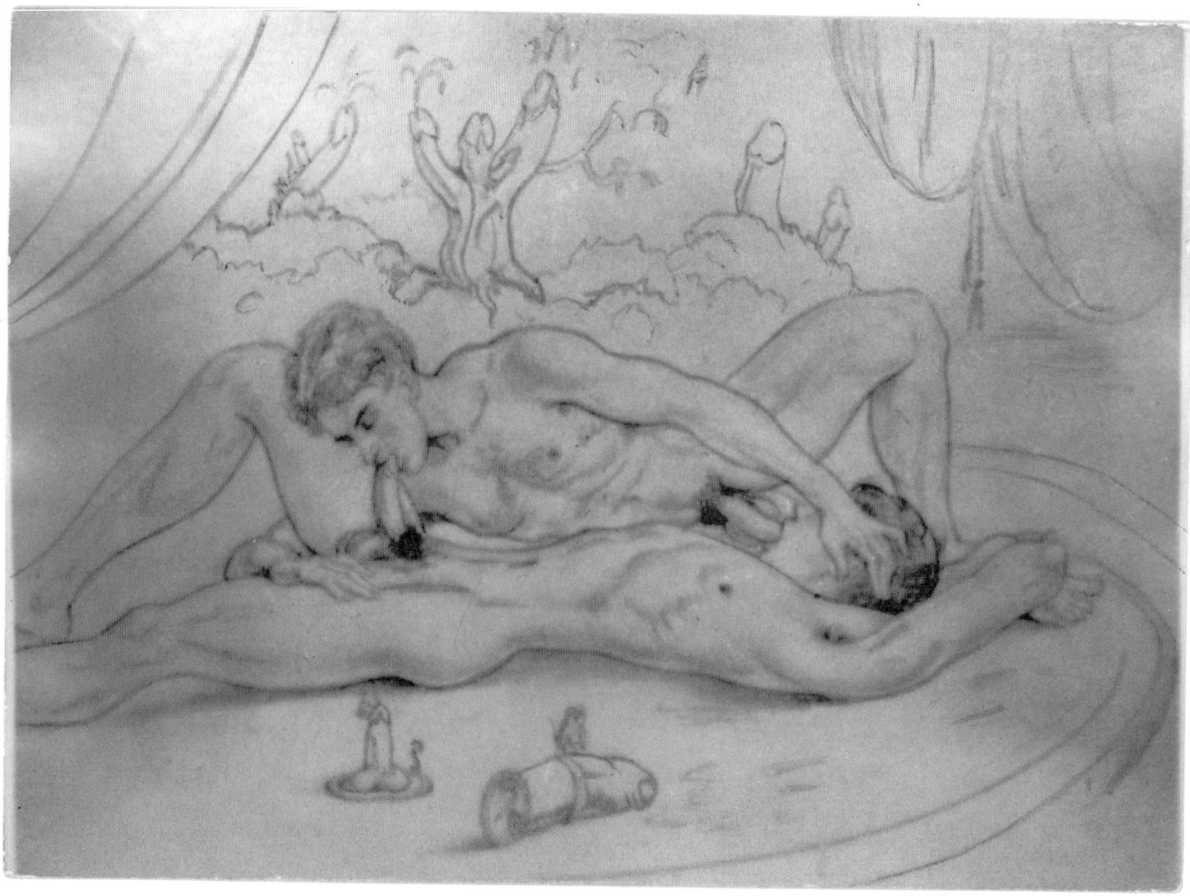

Another unknown artist obsessed with the phallus, but not as an irrepressible monster, rather as a decorative embroidery for his favorite act. His fixation on sixty-nine contradicts the basic rule of pornography: variation, or "diff'rent strokes for diff'rent folks." But then the underground allowed, even encouraged, personal fixations, without regard to audience diversity.

74

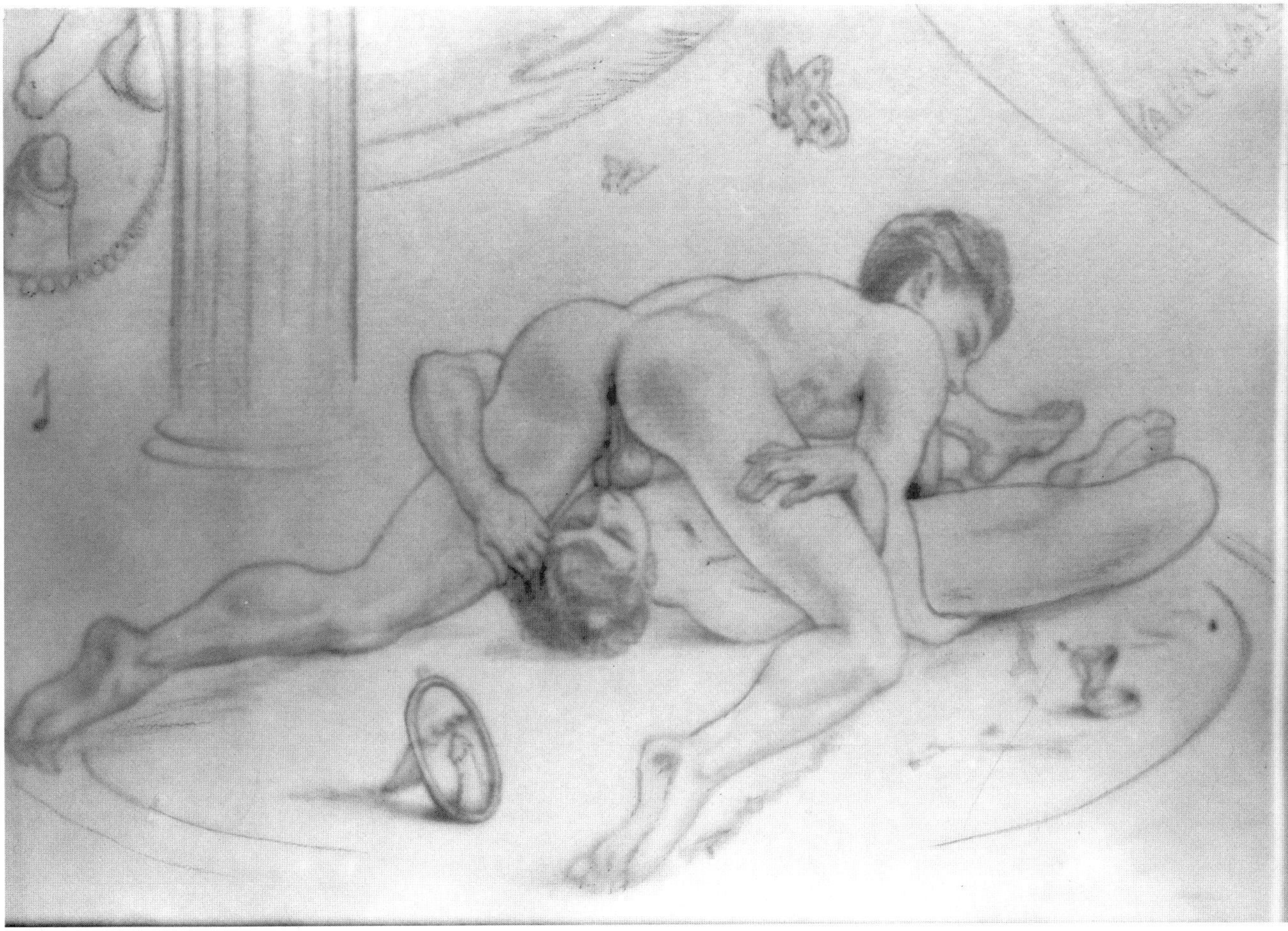

"His cock is big and red when I am there / and his persistent lips are like sweet wine." Paul Goodman, "Lines" ([c. 1968] 1983, 325)

75

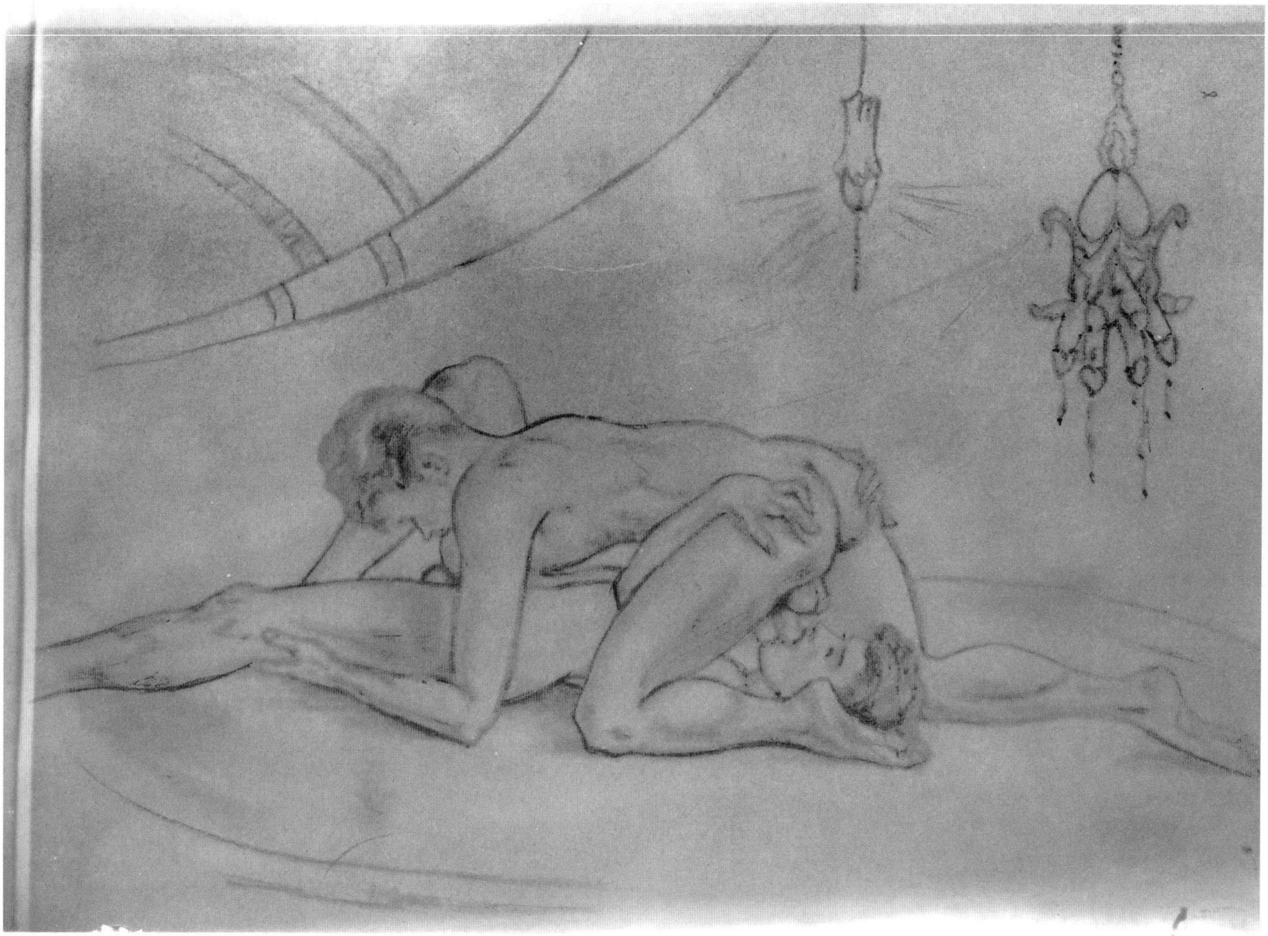

According to the classic post-Stonewall sex guide *The Joy of Gay Sex*, "A quip used to circulate that sixty-nining is what Princeton boys like to do since it's so *fair*. And the fairness, the equality, is what most people complain about; how difficult it is to concentrate either on the pleasure of sucking cock or on being sucked when both delights are offered simultaneously. The problem is an embarrassment of riches . . .

76

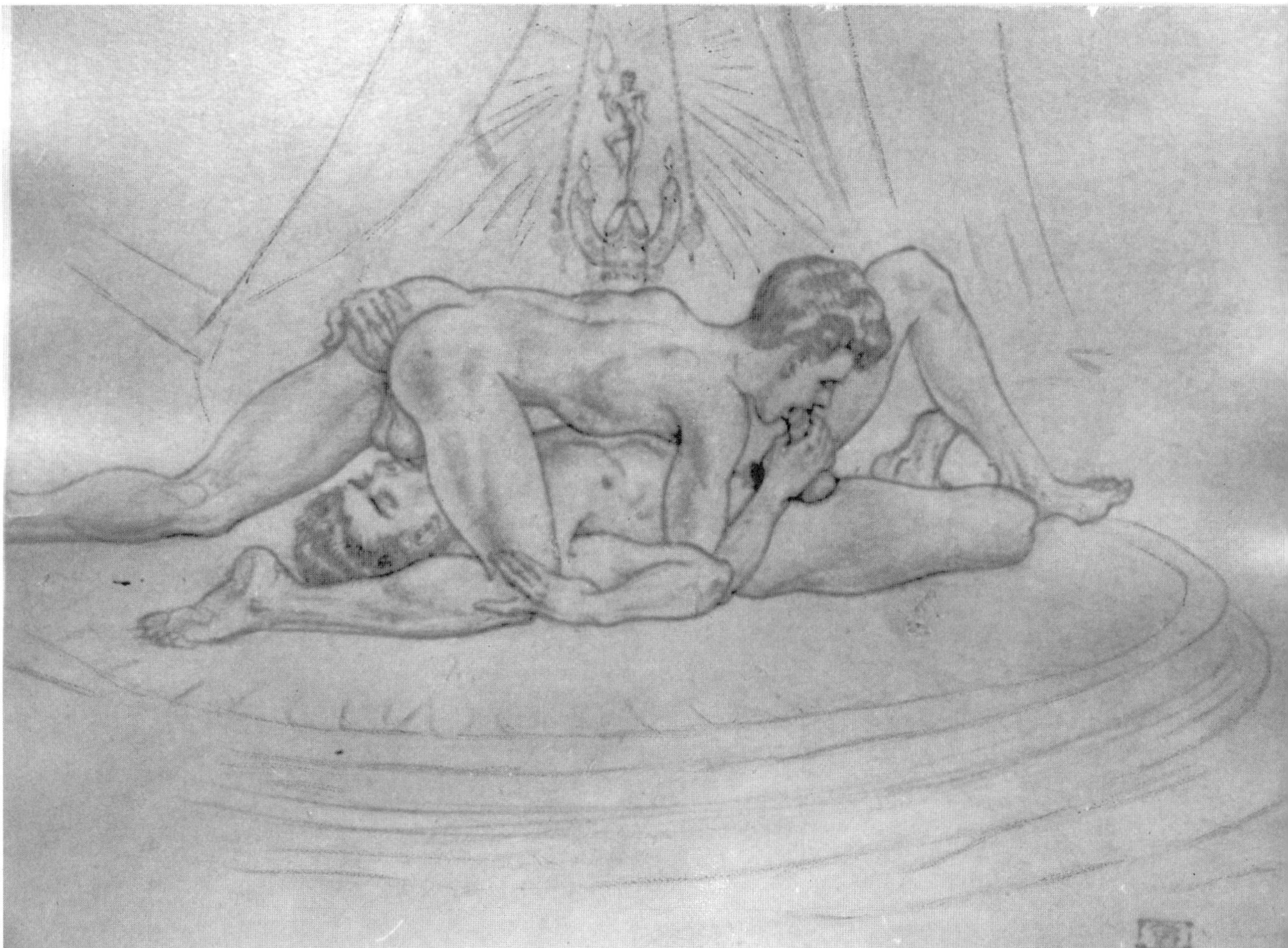

. . . Sixty-nining does, however, have its own distinct charms. If someone's doing you, occasionally you become so carried away with ecstasy that you long for more—and more is his cock. From what he does while sucking you, you can tell what he wants you to do to his cock. There is total reciprocity." (Silverstein and White, 1977, 201) Reciprocity does not explain the act's relative scarcity in the visual repertory, due I think to the lack of visual access and to the lack of difference and drama inherent in this very reciprocity. **77**

Fantasies:
Thebans and Thracians

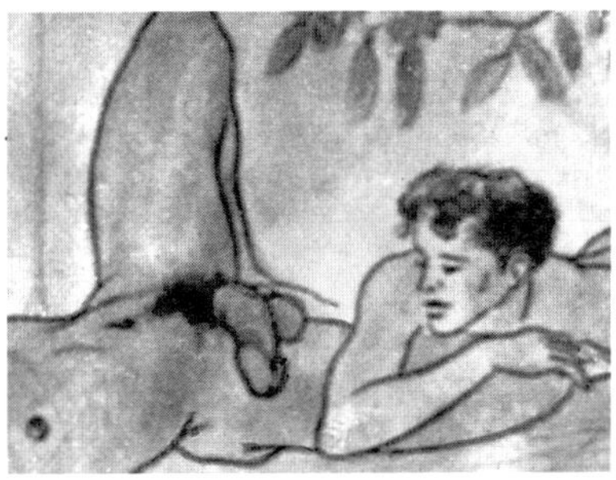

"The unspeakable vice of the Greeks" (to quote E.M. Forster's *Maurice* [1914 (1981) 51]) has been invoked as an alibi or an ideal—or both—by Euro-American queers and proto-queers since at least the Renaissance. When the "mainstay of Athenian society" came up in the novel, *Maurice*, and by extension his entire generation of early-twentieth-century young questioners,

Fantasies:
Thebans and Thracians

were "touched" by "a breath of liberty." But they were also turned on.

The following two narrative series, Jean Vincent's "Alexander the Great," produced in German-speaking Europe in the interwar years, and the anonymous "The Captive" (American, probably around 1960), offer rich testimony to the way pop histories kindle erotic fantasy, even in homosocial military societies based on erotic mentorship and martial friendship, and on "rape-and-plunder" conquest.

The characters in "The Captive" are Romans and their prisoner Thracian, but all the better since centurion outfits were the staple of fantasy life for generations brought up on Cecil B. DeMille, *Ben-Hur*, and the dozens of cheap sword-and-sandals epics shot in the Mediterranean throughout the postwar era. Musclebound gay heartthrob Steve Reeves appeared in many of them, from *Goliath and the Barbarians* to *Hercules and the Queen of Sheba* (both 1959). Not that the peplum movies ever mentioned the unspeakable vice of the Greeks, but they hardly needed to with all those gleaming pecs. Alongside, the mail-order physique studios of the same period cashed in on the genre with a homo twist. Interestingly, Richard Fontaine's high camp short *The Captives* (U.S.A., c. 1959) also involved a barbarian prisoner and his horny captors, but with very lite torture and a happy-ever-after conjugal ending. Which spinoff came first, softcore 8mm poser or hardcore graphics strip? Hollywood's *Gladiator* made a killing in 2000 and now that it has spawned *Troy* and two Alexander biopics waiting in the wings as of this writing, we're in for a whole new generation of the thighs-and-tunic stuff in the current decade—both homo and crypto-homo (for there's no other kind).

Meanwhile, both "Alexander the Great" and "The Captive" show how amenable and versatile classical narratives are for absorbing the erotic and political agendas of artists and their periods. Witness how easily "Alexander the Great" fits into an epic that even Ernst Röhm and the S.A. might have liked, and how integrated "The Captive" is, with its masochist dream of multiple ravishment and fisting, into the emerging leather sexual imagination of the 1950s: this minority within a minority, visible not only on the obscene graphics underground and physique movies about bikers and hoods, but also in consolidating urban geographies (figs. 65-66).

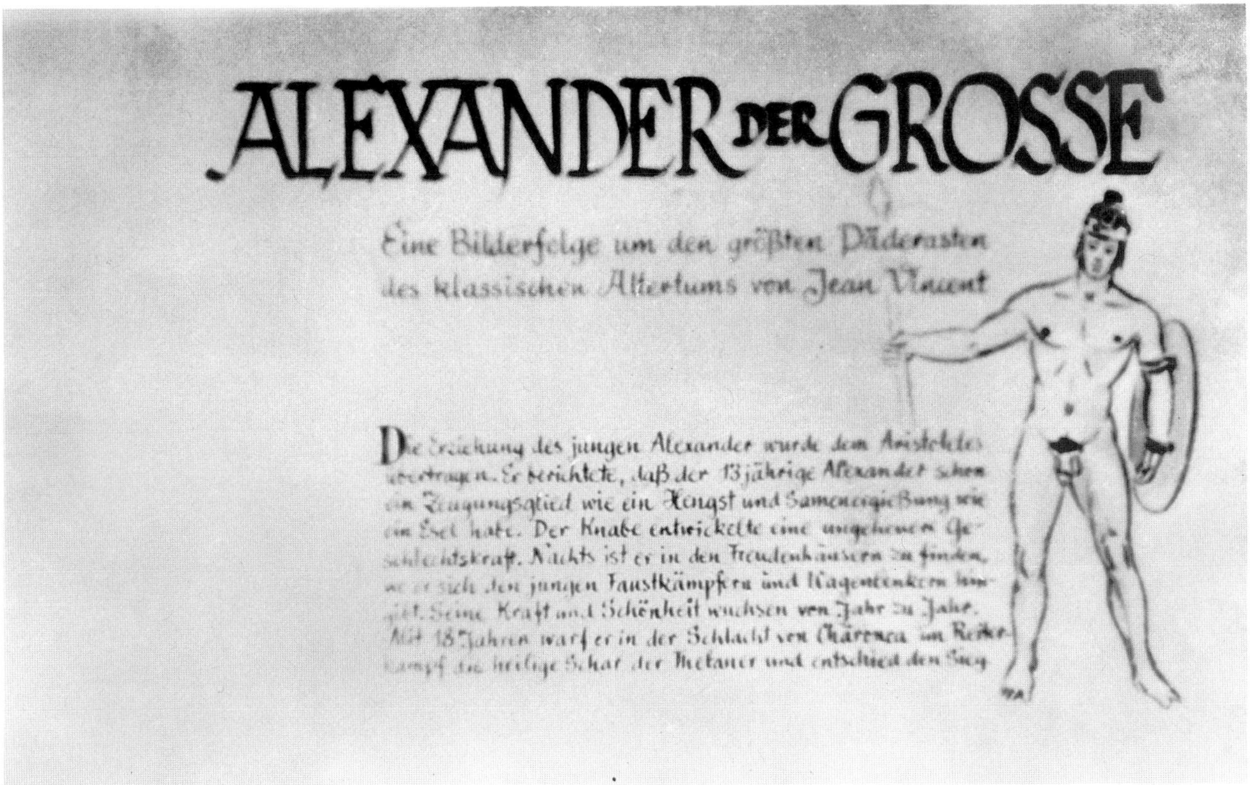

"A Picture Series on the Greatest Homosexual of Classical Times, by Jean Vincent. The upbringing of the boy Alexander was assigned to Aristotle. He reported that the 13-year-old Alexander already had an organ as fertile as a colt's and his seed poured forth like a donkey's. The boy developed an immense sexual power. At night you could find him at the brothels, where he abandoned himself to young pugilists and charioteers. His power and beauty grew from year to year. At the age of eighteen, he threw himself into the cavalry battle of Chaeronea 78
against the holy band of Thebans and won the victory."

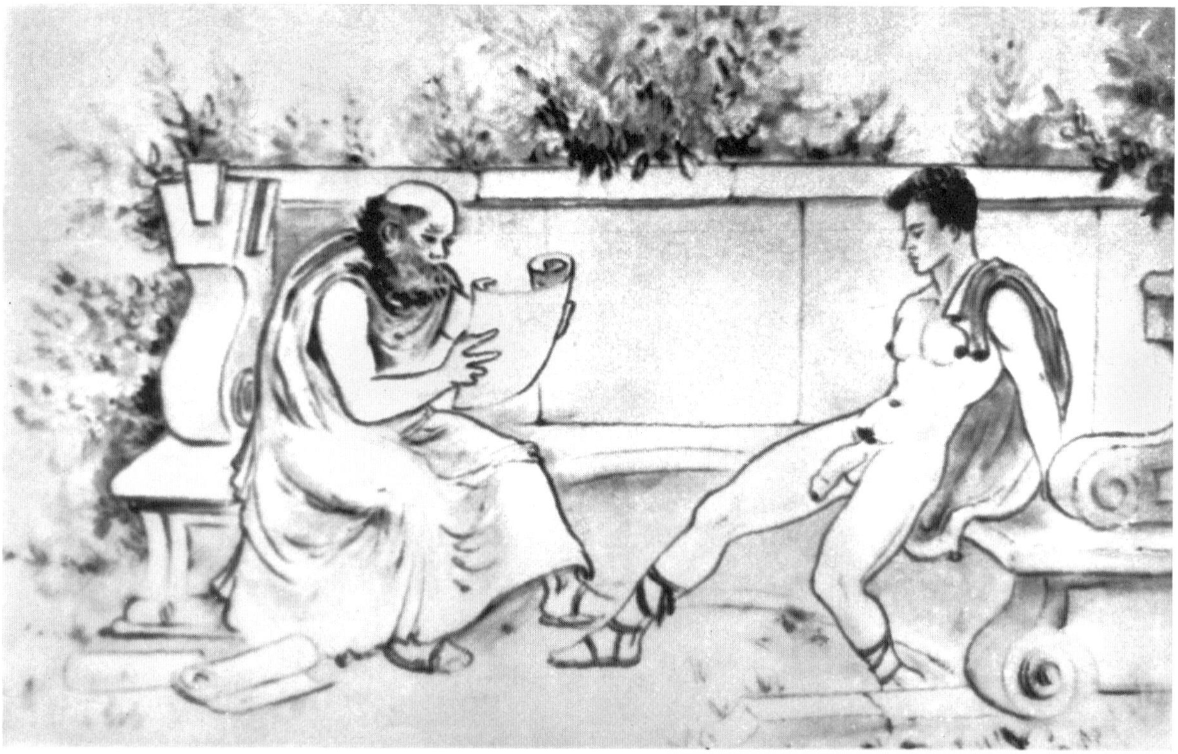

Needless to say, Jean Vincent's series on Alexander put less stress on military strategy than on amorous initiation, and echoed all of the longing that modern Europeans had invested in their classical ancestors, nude tutorials and high-laced sandals and all.

79

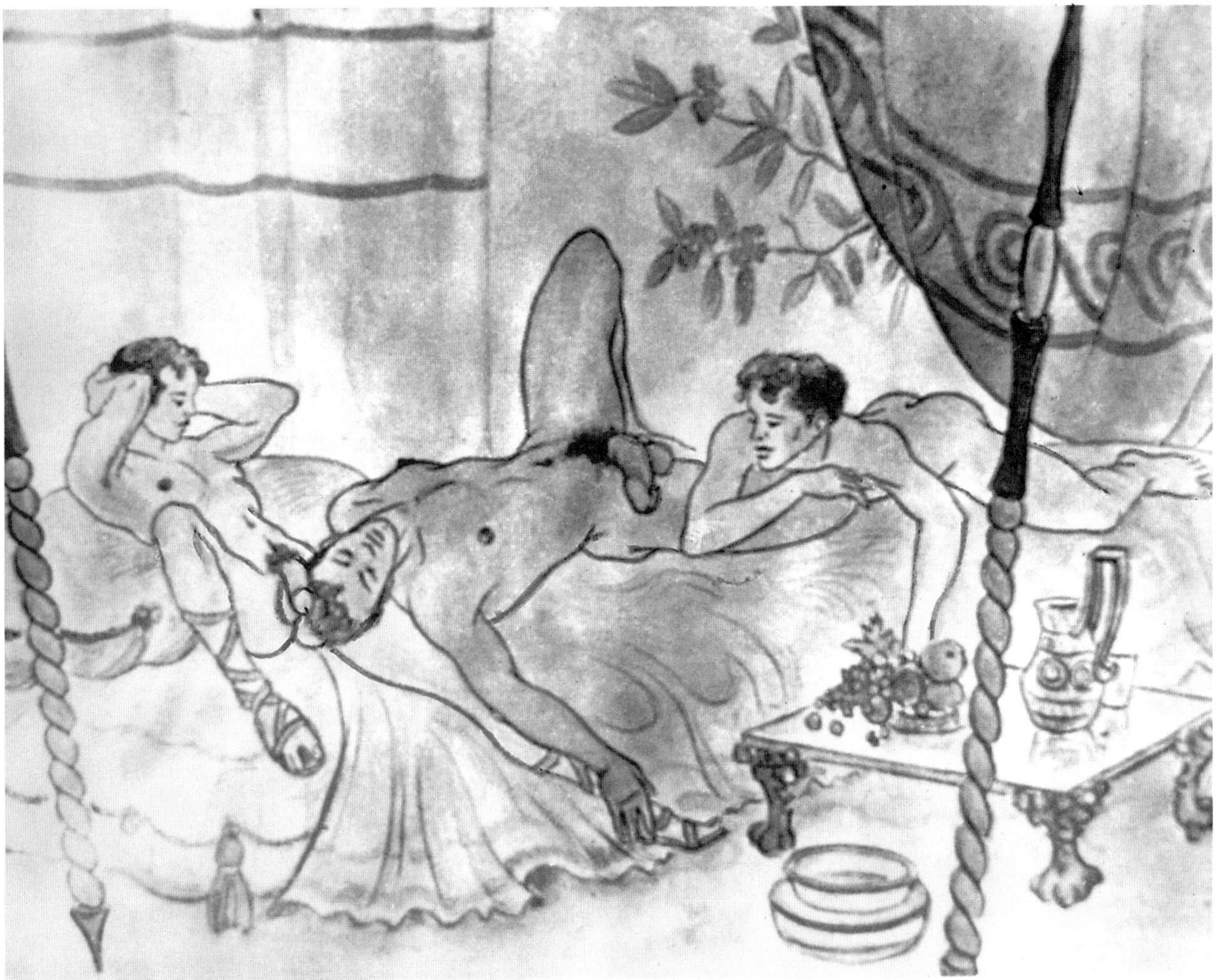

"Durham, I love you . . . I do—I have always— . . . I tell you, I do—I came to say it—in your very own way—I have always been like the Greeks and didn't know." E.M. Forster, *Maurice* ([1914] 1981, 65)

80

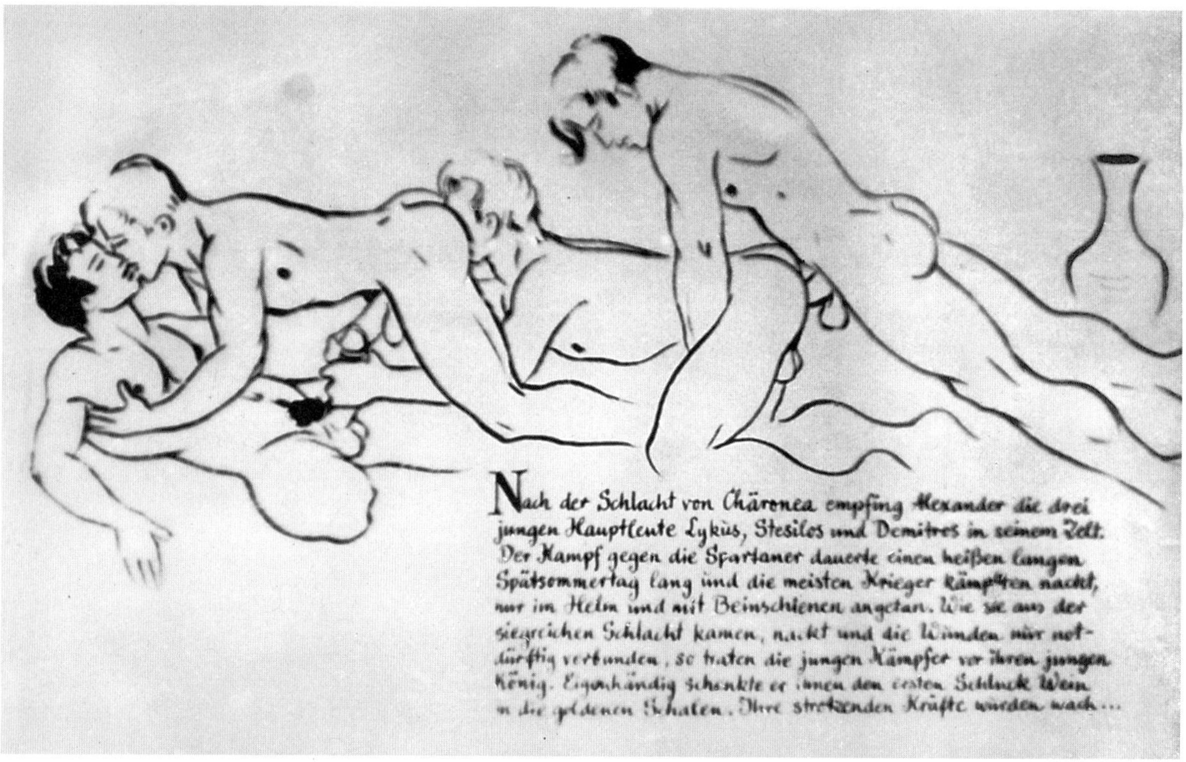

"After the Battle of Chaeronea, Alexander received three young nobles Lykos, Stesilos and Demitros in his tent. The struggle against the Spartans lasted a hot long late summer's day, and most of the warriors fought naked, only clad in helmets and shinpads. As they came out of the victorious battle, naked with their wounds only meagrely bound, the young warriors stepped forward towards their young king. He himself bestowed upon
81 them the first gulp of wine in the golden bowl. Their bursting strength was roused up."

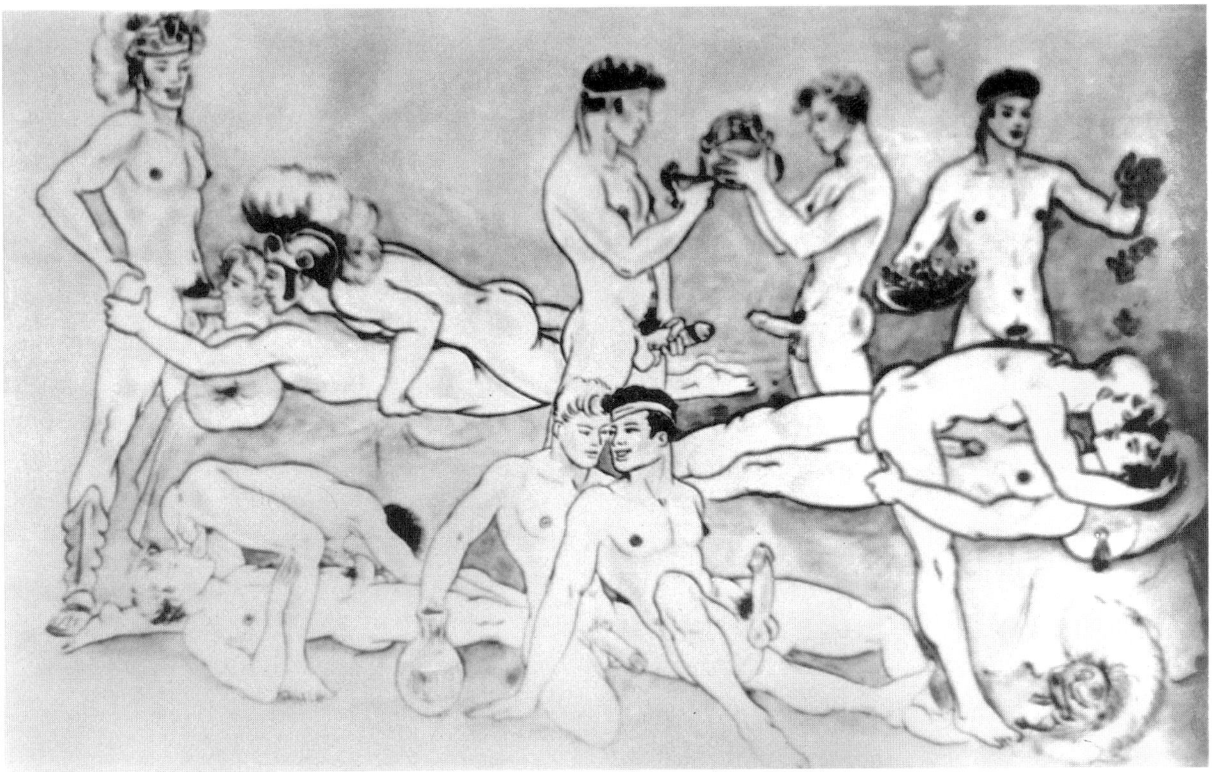

Within the context of interwar German culture, the classical epic "Alexander" was clearly not addressed to Magnus Hirschfeld's progressive, "third-sex" constituency of sexual liberation, rather to its lesser-known gay ideological tendency that pushed all-male institutions, nudism, and Socratic mentorship, and didn't exactly challenge the growing militarism in Germany. This tendency's magazine *Der Eigene* even had a handsome helmeted soldier from the *Wehrmacht* on its cover.

82

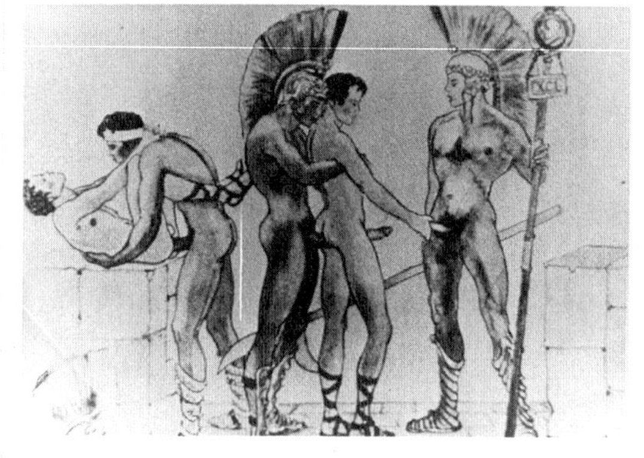

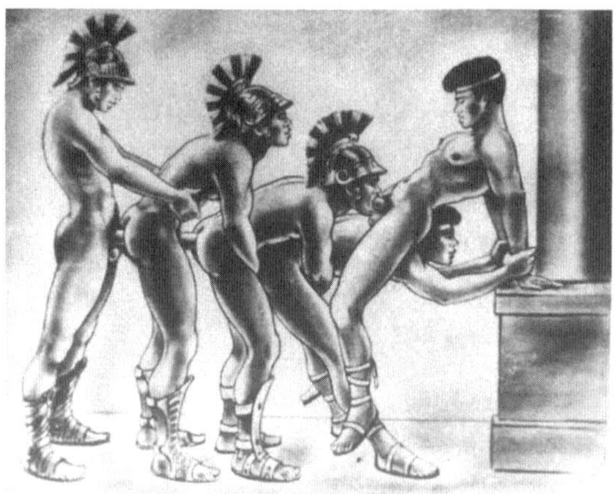

Other classical orgies from the Alexander series that appeared in *Out/Lines*. Jean Vincent ever-so-slightly mixed up ancient history—but then so did Hollywood's Oliver Stone and Colin Farrell in 2004.

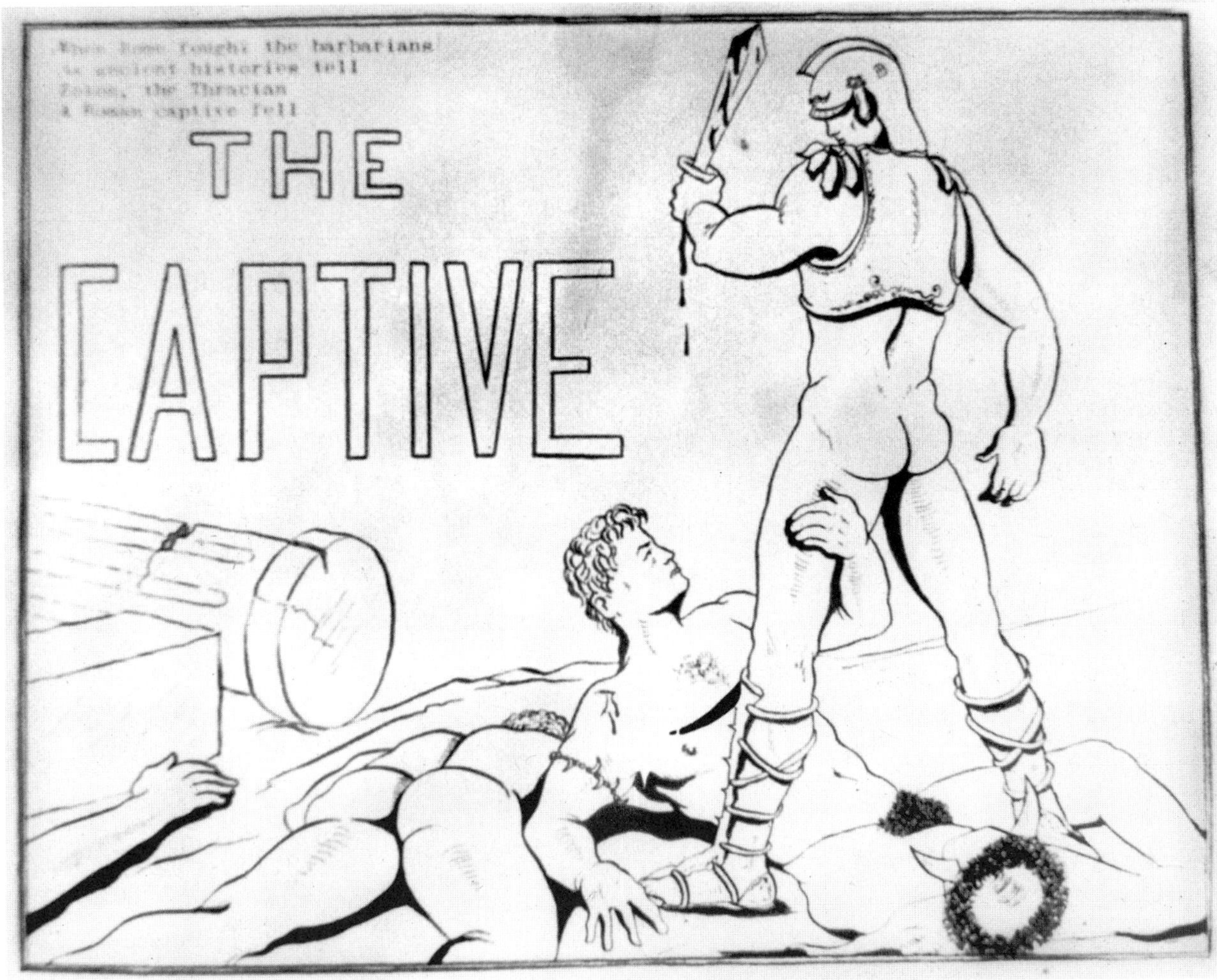

Another classical epic fantasy is probably American, perhaps from the 1950s, and has the distinction of being told in rhyming quatrains: "When Rome fought the barbarians / The ancient histories tell, / Zoton the Thracian / A Roman captive fell." "The Captive" has the centurions following the Greek custom of wearing only helmets and shinpads, but otherwise went considerably further than the campy sword-and-sandals fantasies of the period, whether graphic or cinematic. **84**

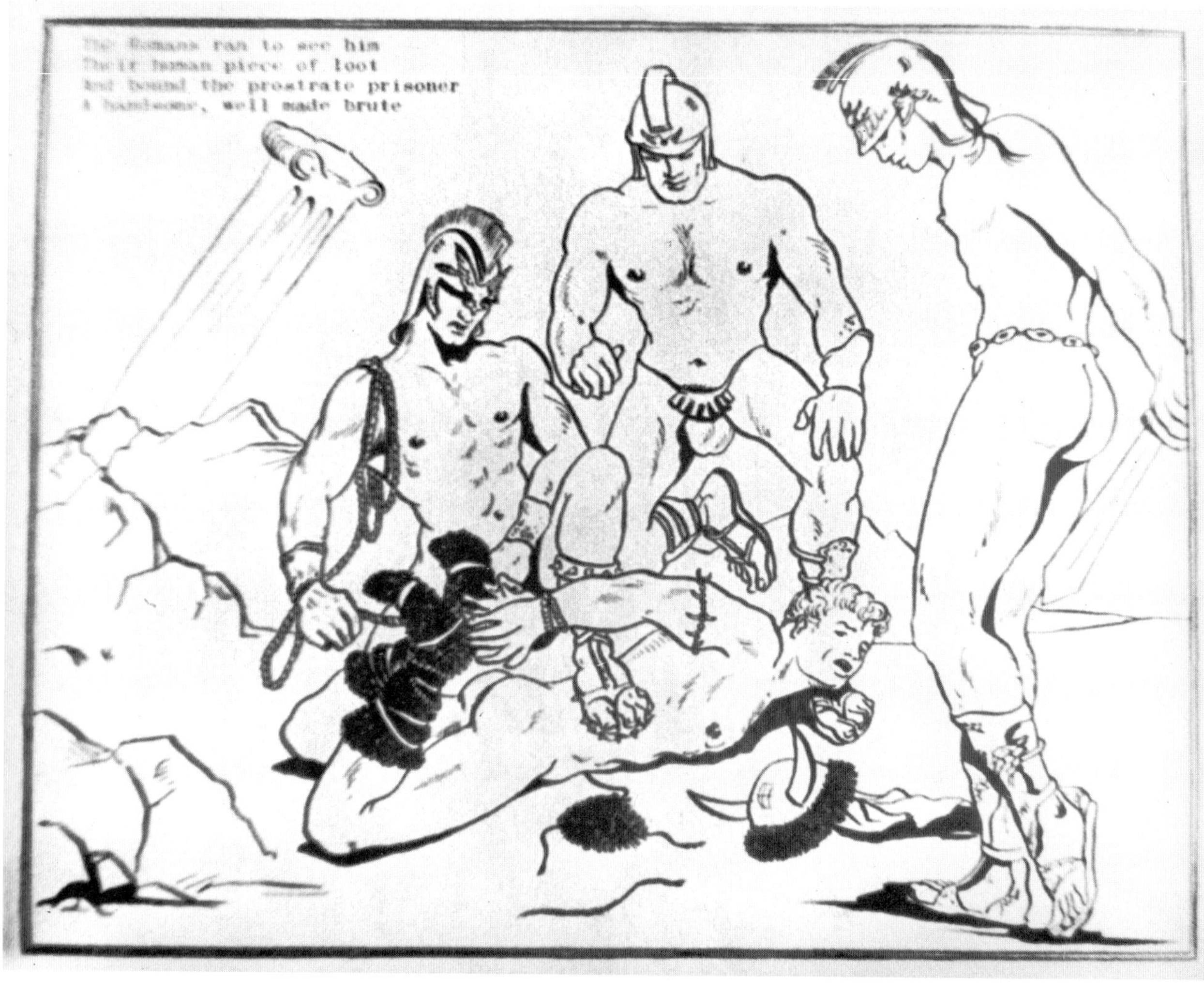

"The Romans ran to see him, / Their human piece of loot, / And bound the prostrate prisoner, / A handsome, sturdy brute." What I mistook to be a pubic wig in the previous frame is now revealed to be a fur jockstrap. Those Thracians! Quatrains on the next two panels, absent from the DuBek selection: "Now stripped of all his armor, / They led him from the field, / His body all but naked, / His manhood all revealed." "They set the torture for him:/ The branding irons hot. / Caius spied his asshole— / The torture they forgot."

85

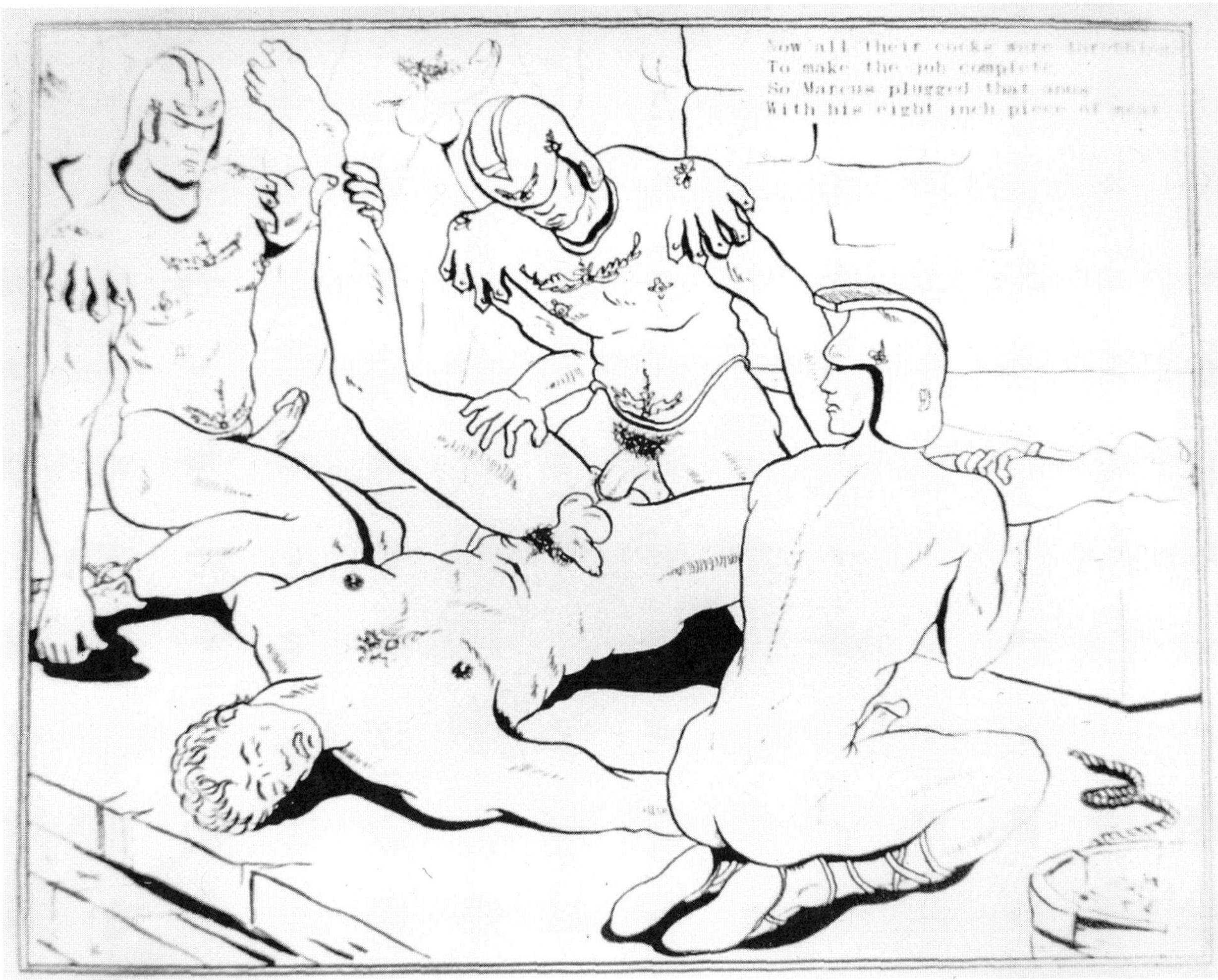

"Now all their cocks were [throbbing?] / To make the job complete / So Marcus plugged that anus / With his eight inch piece of meat." One detail that strikes me as surprisingly realistic for such an over-the-top gang bang narrative is that Zoton remains unstimulated throughout—all the more so since the fantasy can be entered from the point of view of either the ravished or ravishers or both.

86

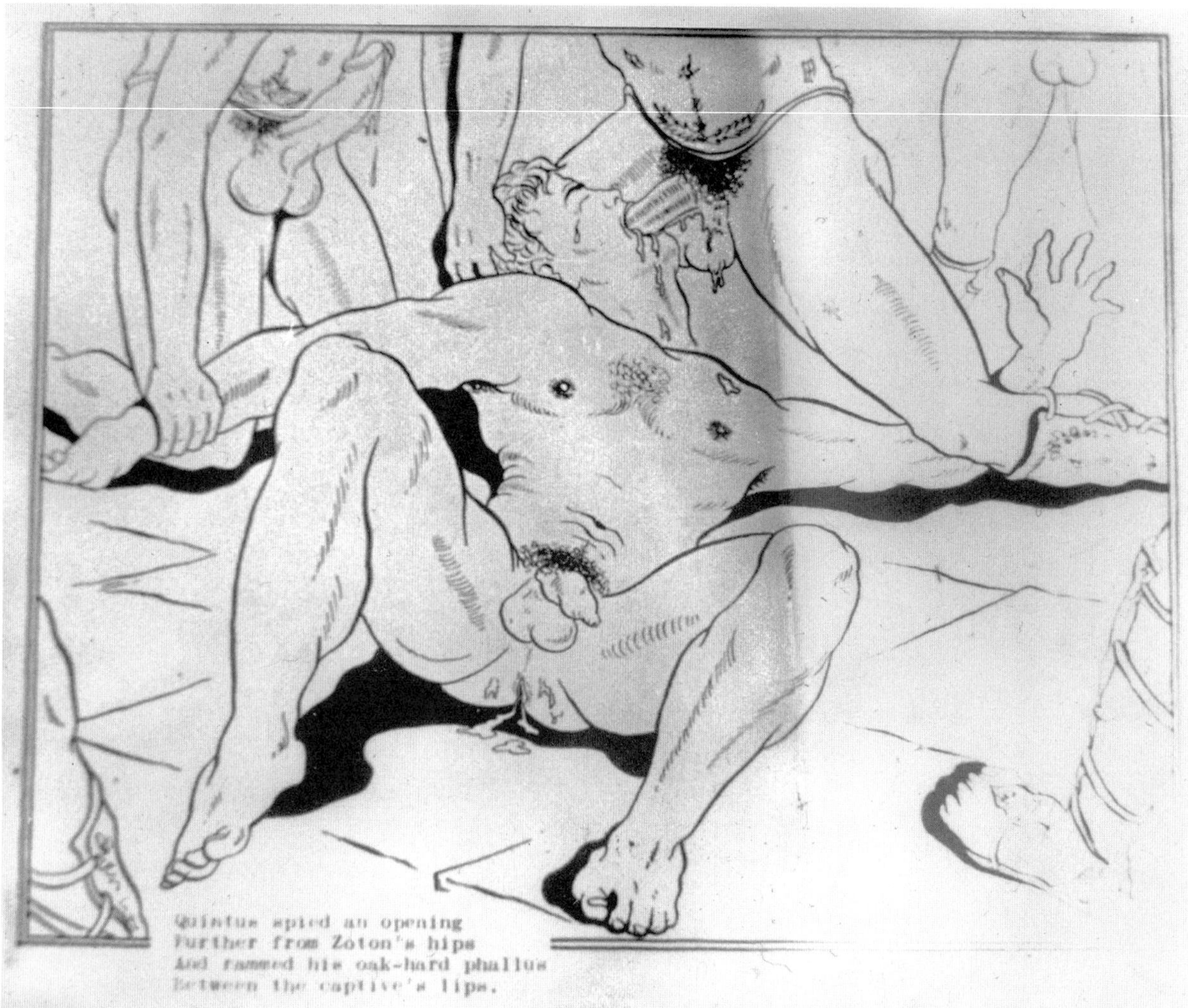

"Quintus spied an opening / Further from Zoton's hips / And rammed his oak-hard phallus / Between the captive's lips."

87

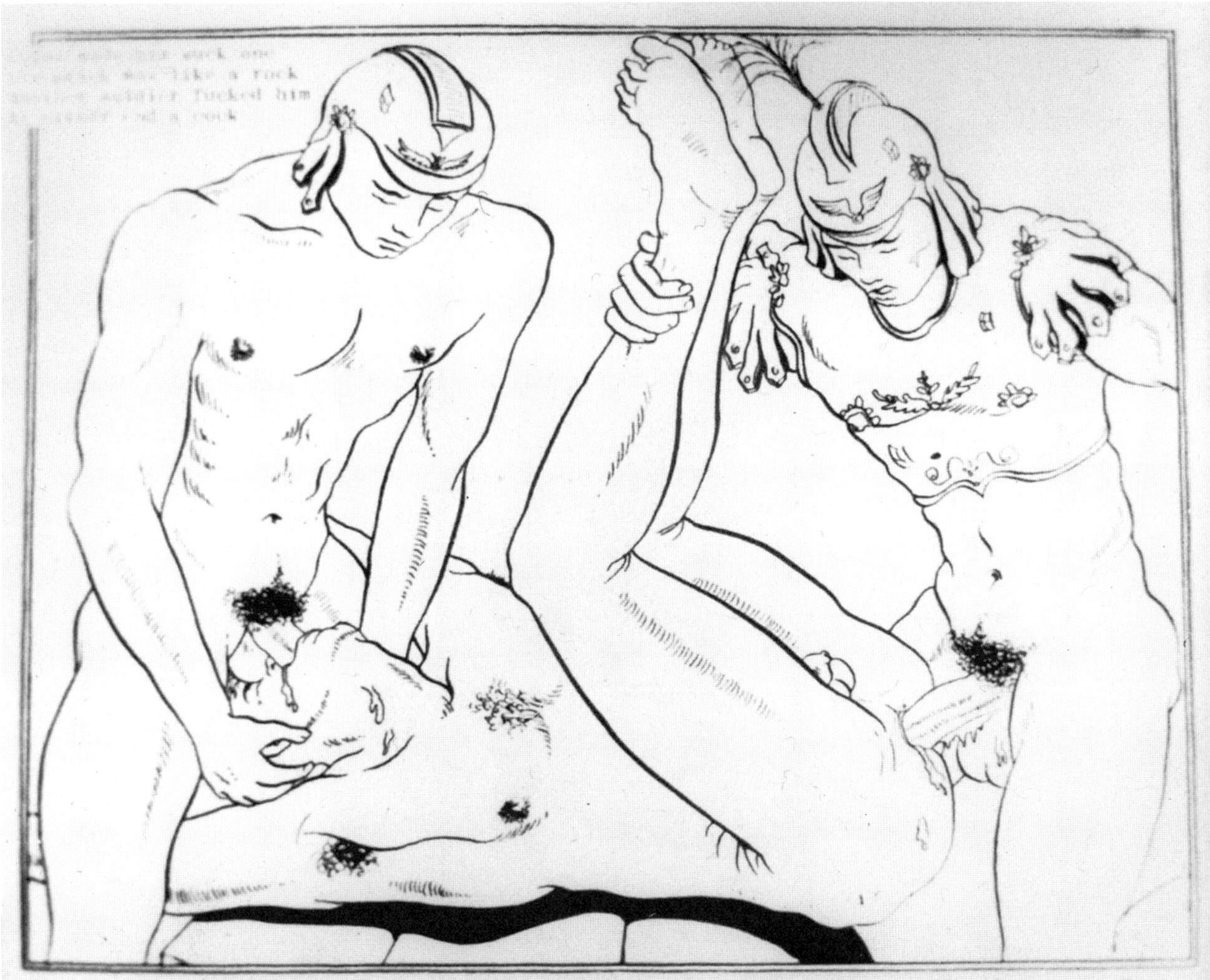

Such a three-way chain is relatively common in DuBek's selection, as well as contemporary porn, a fantasy sometimes of coercion, more often of satiation. The poetic gloss is unfortunately illegible, something about rock rhyming with cock. What else is new?

88

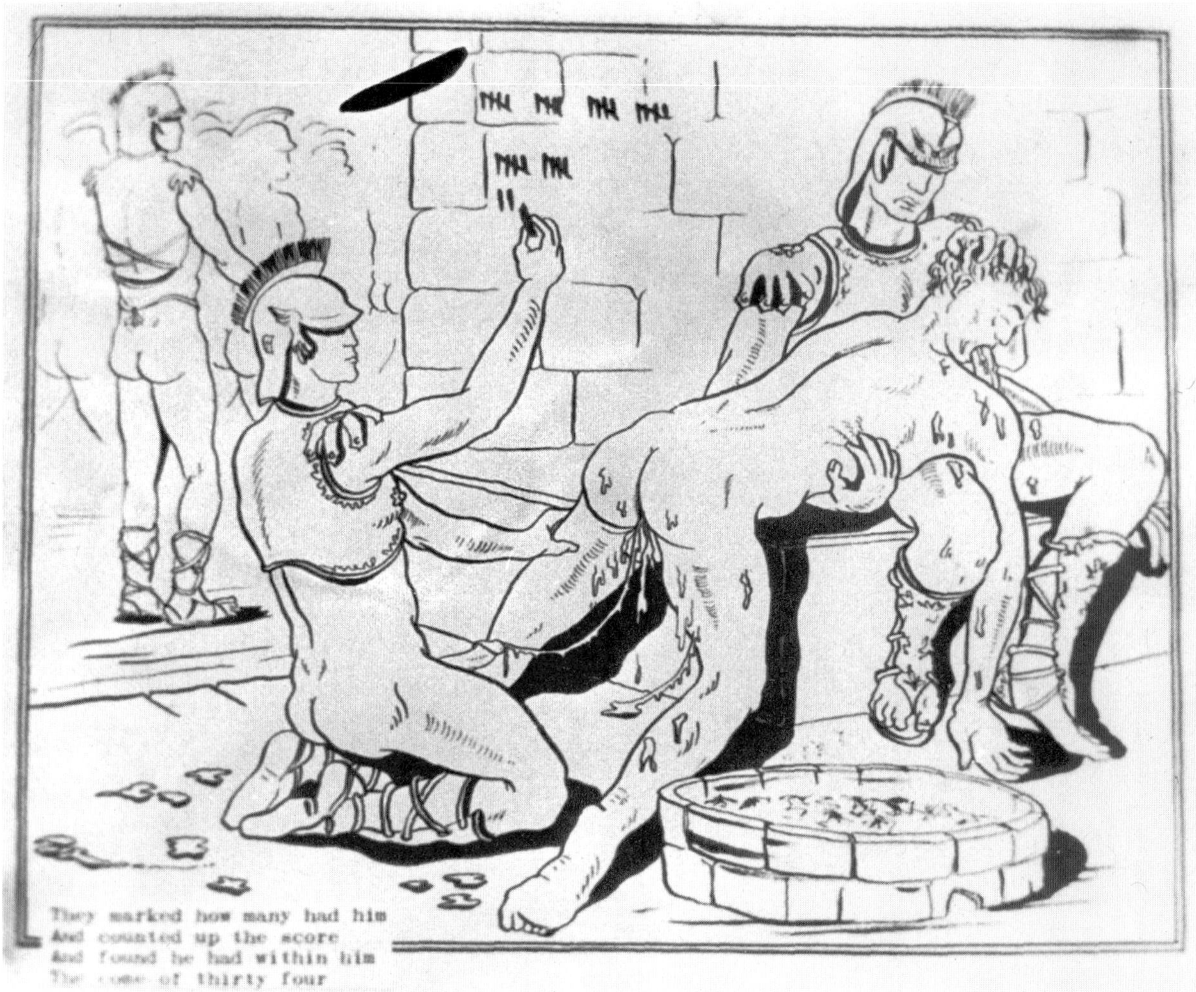

89 “They marked how many had him / And counted up the score / And found he had within him / The come of thirty-four.” The *Captive* artist is clearly a comic book professional. Does the surfacing of bits of the series in different collections confirm its wide circulation in the pre-Stonewall underground, when classical fantasies were no less popular above ground as well, both secular and religious, from Steve Reeves to Charlton Heston and Kirk Douglas?

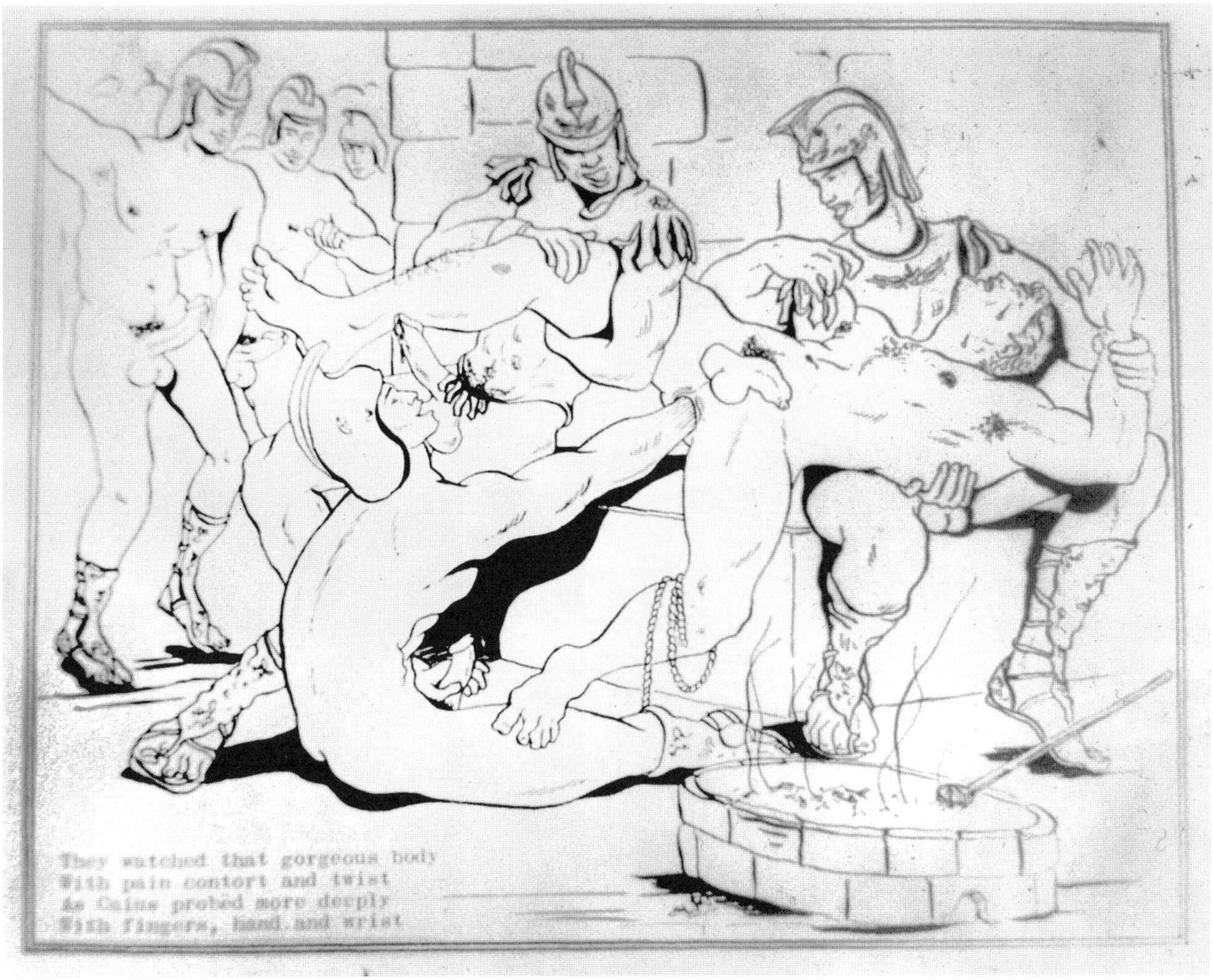

"They watched that gorgeous body / With pain contort and twist / As Caius probed more deeply / With fingers, hand and wrist." The caption of the previous omitted panel: "He reached with probing fingers / An entrance quick to gain / He shoved them in—not quickly— / And Zoton cried with pain."

90

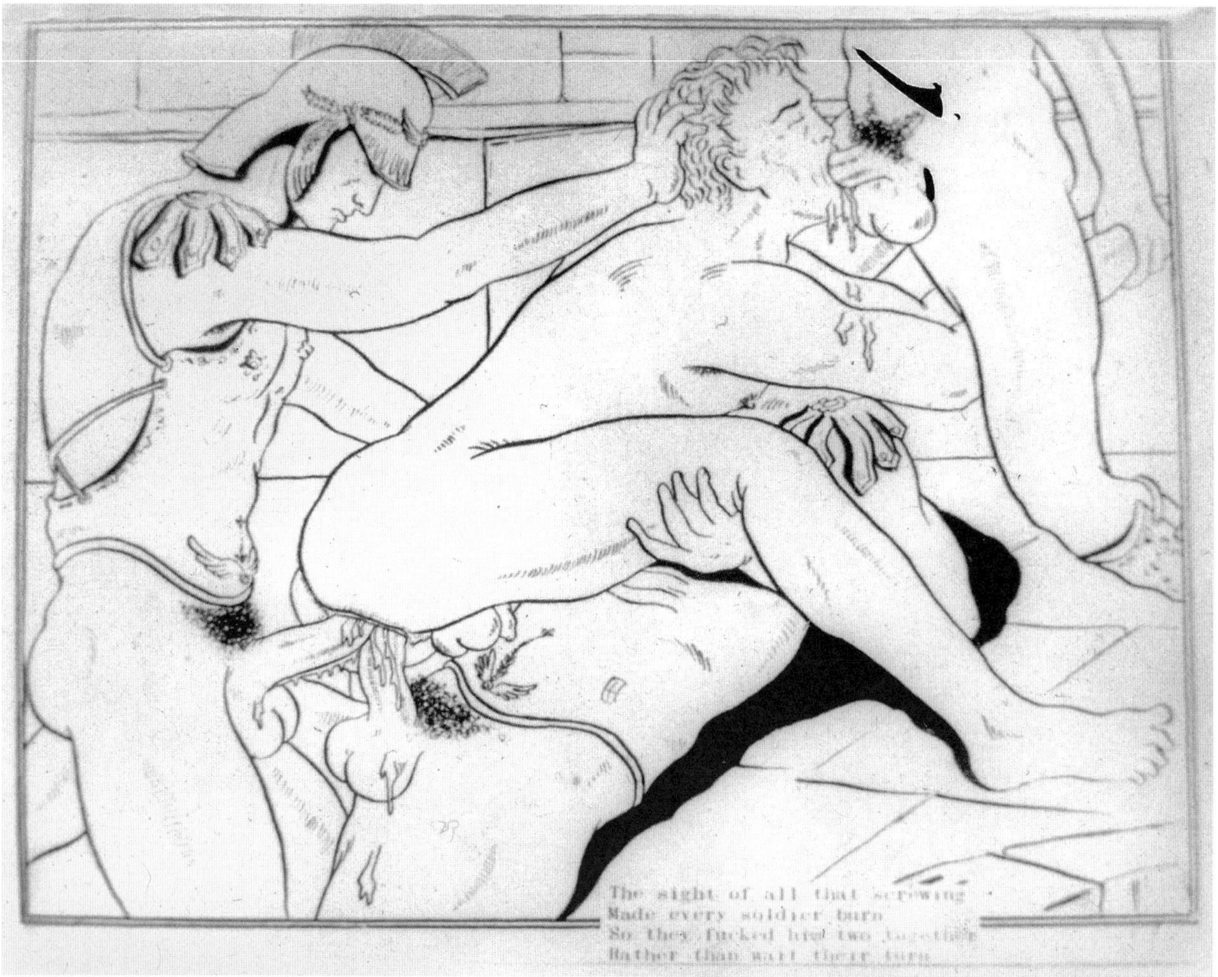

"The sight of all that screwing / Made every soldier burn. / So they fucked him two together / Rather than wait
their turn." Disabused more than twenty years ago of my innocence and ignorance about the historical S/M
underground in pre-Stonewall gay culture (when I saw Dr. Kinsey's movies shot in that underground at the
start of the 1950s, and discovered London's fetish-flavored physique studio "Royale" from the same decade), I
91 never cease to be amazed by its fervor, diversity, and organization as evidenced by a document like this.

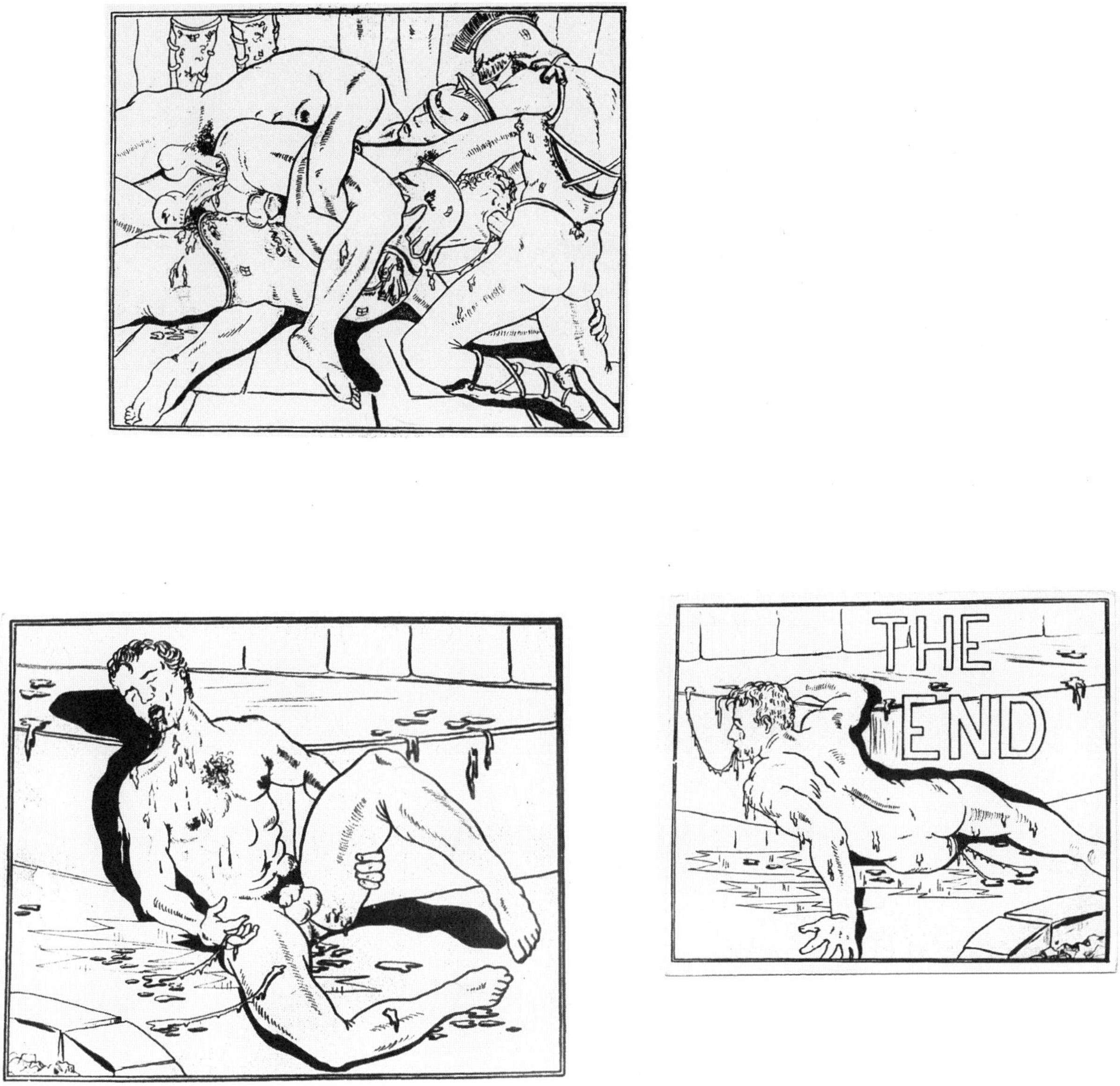

These three panels alone were available for *Out/Lines* (Figures 136-137), but had no captions. The missing one for the top image here is: "Three by three they rammed him / And so the tally grew, / His mouth stretched wide by one cock / His bleeding ass by two." Thus concludes "The Captive." Does Zoton's domination of the final frames amid his puddles of bodily fluid suggest the artist's ultimately masochistic identification with the fantasy of extreme ravishment by those helmeted soldiers? **92**

Fantasies: uniforms

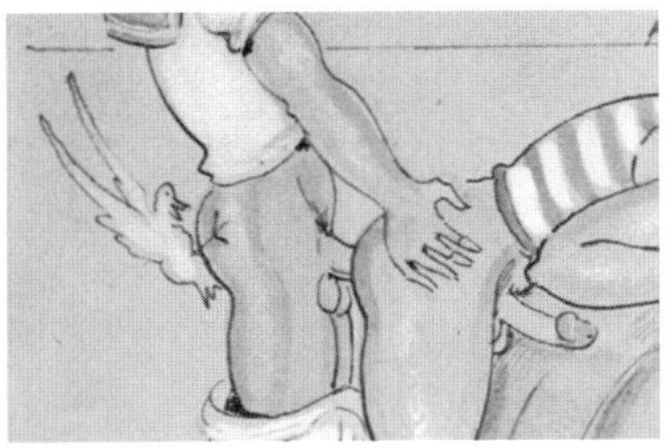

Uniforms are already shorthand for nationality, rank, affiliation, both conformism and individuation, plus raw gender identity. So they fit just fine into the hardcore graphics underground, also dependent on visual shorthand. What men wear and how they wear it or take it off are this book's most popular visual motifs. Almost two-thirds of the images evoke the pleasure of the uniform, both military and civilian, textile and epidermal (see figs. 96 and 108-09 for perspectives on sailors' tattoos and scars as uniforms).

FANTASIES: UNIFORMS

I am a non-uniform kind of guy with a notoriously vanilla penchant for the jaybird innocence of figures 155 (is body hair a uniform?), 208, and 219. Making this book, however, has *almost* converted me to the sensory pleasure of the textural confrontation of skin, hair, membrane, and fluid with standard-issue cloth, leather, and metal.

The generations of men who valued these pictures lived in militarized societies, and many, like DuBek, were socialized within same-sex military organizations—not to mention scouts and *Wandervögels* and sports teams. No wonder that their fantasy life was often costumed in khaki and navy whites, and deeply imprinted with the fetishism of other accoutrements of masculinity in a gender-structured, hierarchical society. The bare nudity of Soungouroff's postcards (figs. 33-37) or Cadmus's sketchpages (figs. 217-218) lacks the punch of social reference, and even the minimal undershirt, lowered trousers and laceup civilian shoes of the latter's more finished drawing (fig. 163) add a nuance of fetish. It's interesting that French's sketch of not-a-stitch group bathing (fig. 237) got uniforms added later (plus an imposing whip!), in deference to its civil service sponsors, but perhaps also to add some spice (Spring 2002 16).

In the following assortment of twenty-seven images, most of the fastidiously textured uniforms are military, but the plain civilian boots of the last two (fig. 118-19) add variety. Notice also that those two well-shod toughies are both bareheaded, a very rare phenomenon in the uniform universe: everyone else (save one) wears serviceman caps or their civilian analogues, jauntily tilted or rammed down or tossed on the bed at the corner of the frame. It's as if headgear swells up the male object of desire, and the British police and guardsman helmets in particular add much to the charisma of our erectile hunks. They also surely get in the way. But we are in a fantasyland after all, so functionality doesn't really matter, does it?

In fact, uniforms start out as functional equipment, as the abundance of civilian workplace uniforms eroticized elsewhere in this collection demonstrate, from miner's helmets (fig. 49) to climbers' leather shorts (figs. 9-10, 237, 230-31). In losing their primary use-value, as in visual erotica and real-life sexual scripts, uniforms acquire a new functionality of fetishism, whether that has to do with sex-role powerplay or simple aesthetic embroidery, or else with a documentary impulse to enrich our fantasy with real-world context, texture . . . and textile.

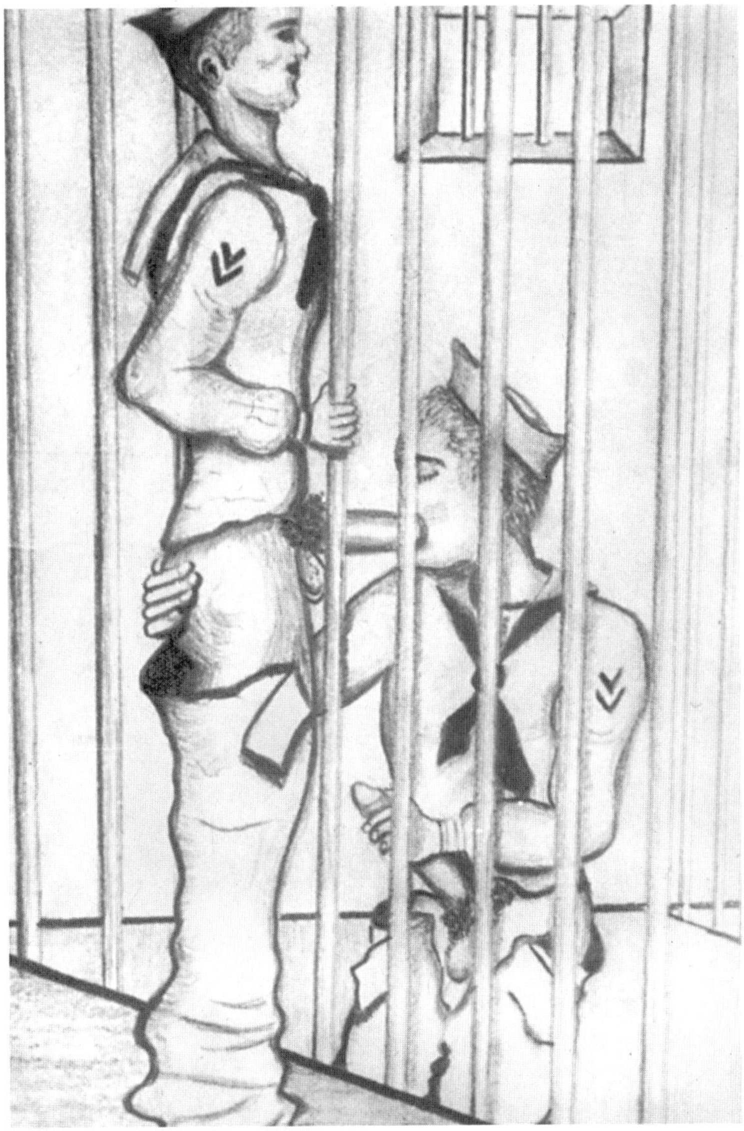

This amateur drawing (of unknown date, probably American) concisely sums up all of the fetishism for uniforms that has animated gay male erotic culture since at least the nineteenth century. It also begs the question of what these poor young sailors, with their immaculate whites, did to end up in the stir in conveniently adjoining cells. Or is only the sailor on the right there, with his angel on the left on a surreptitious mission of mercy to his hungry buddy? 93

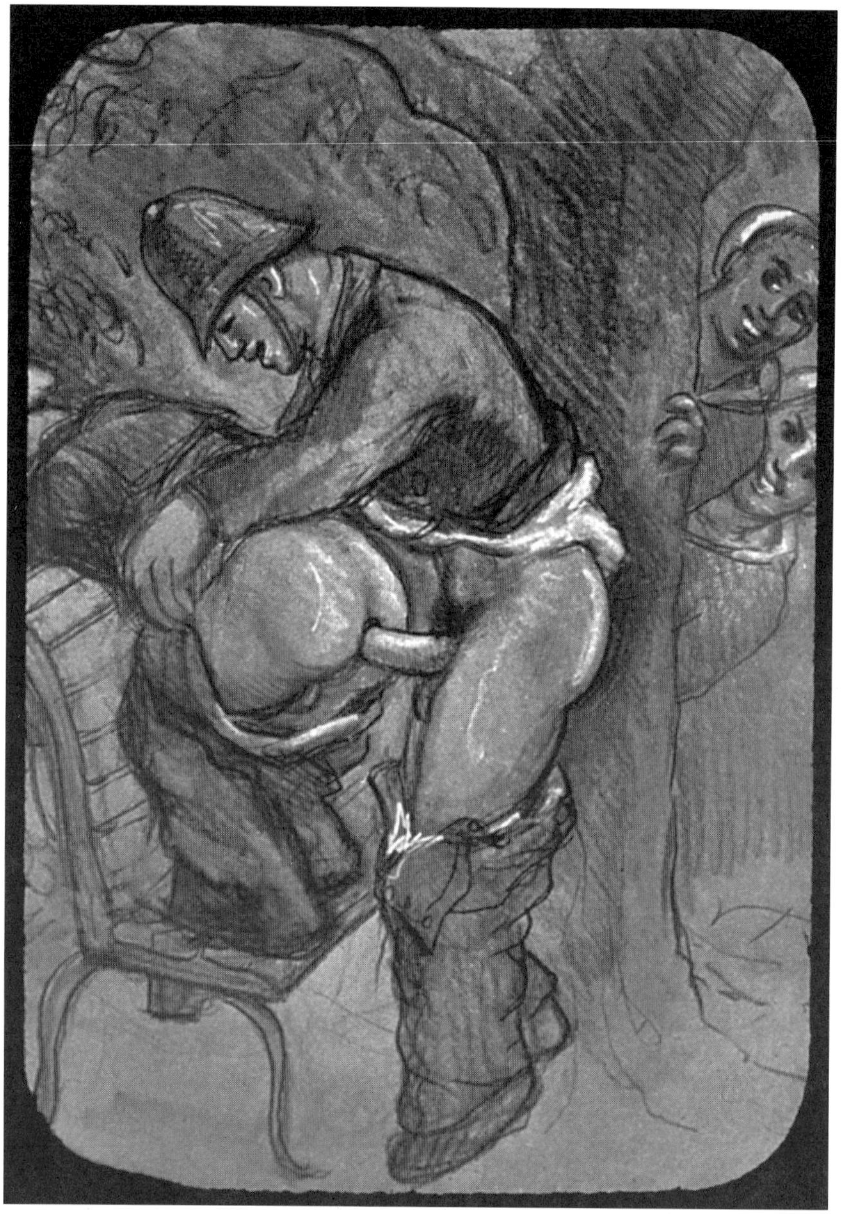

94

Happyface feels differently from Genet about getting fucked by a uniformed cop: "Querelle was overwhelmed by such a strong feeling of abandonment that he let Mario do what he wanted. The train disappeared into the night, with desperate speed. It was rushing to some unknown destination [. . .]—unlike any place the sailor had known for a long time. Only the sleeping passengers might have been witnessees to his making love to a cop: but they just left him and the cop behind like two lepers or beggars on a river bank." Jean Genet, *Querelle de Brest* ([1947; 1953] 1974, 206)

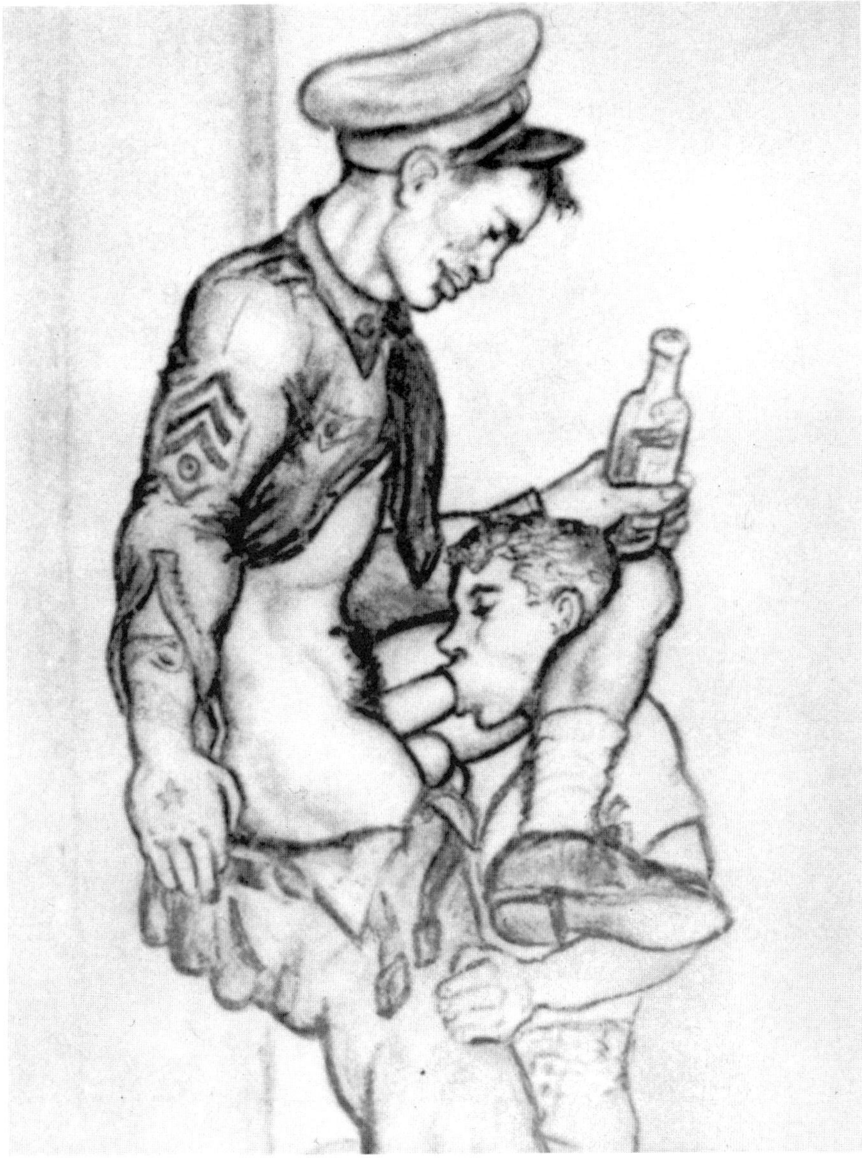

This anonymous American, whom we are calling Red Riding Wolf, is also responsible for Figures 55 and 171-174. Uniforms are the essence of his script of Experience hitting on Innocence, and this U.S. Army staff sergeant knows it so much that he can't even loosen his tie for a blowjob.

95

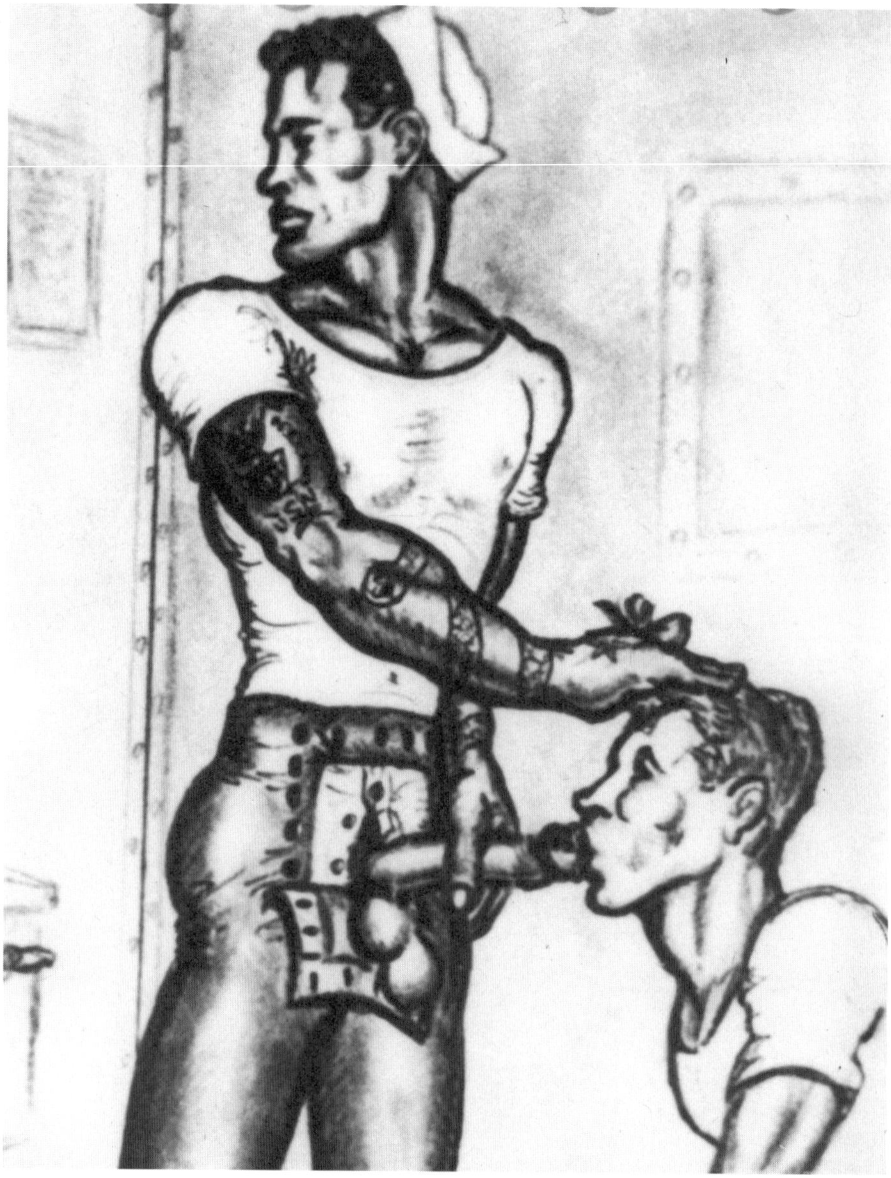

“This was a thing I had never done before, reluctantly since and out of politeness if requested. [. . .] I have noticed that those normal young men who request for themselves this form of amusement never offer it in return. [. . .] it may produce quicker results for them than masturbation, but they are not quick, and to be practically choked for ten minutes or so after one’s own orgasm has passed is something I have never enjoyed . . .

96

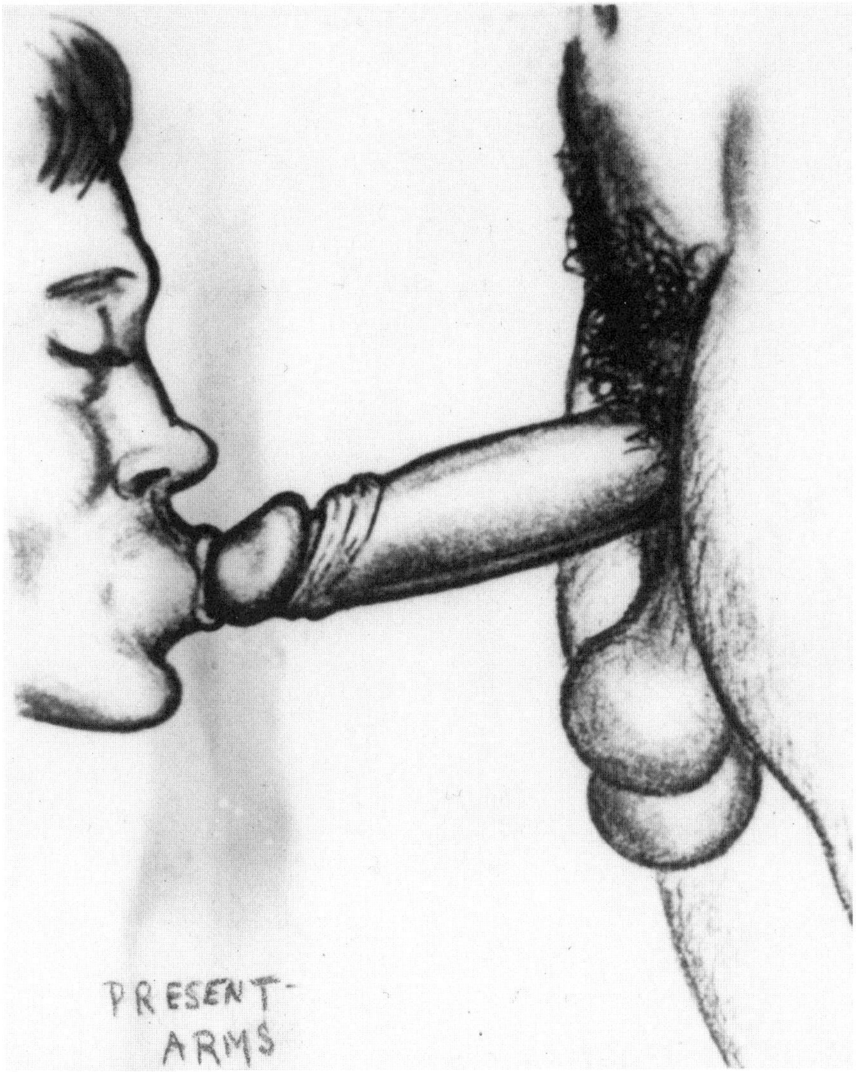

. . . I suppose I acted towards my sailor thus because his body was so beautiful and desirable that I simply wanted to eat it." J.R. Ackerley, *My Father & Myself* (1968, 130)

97

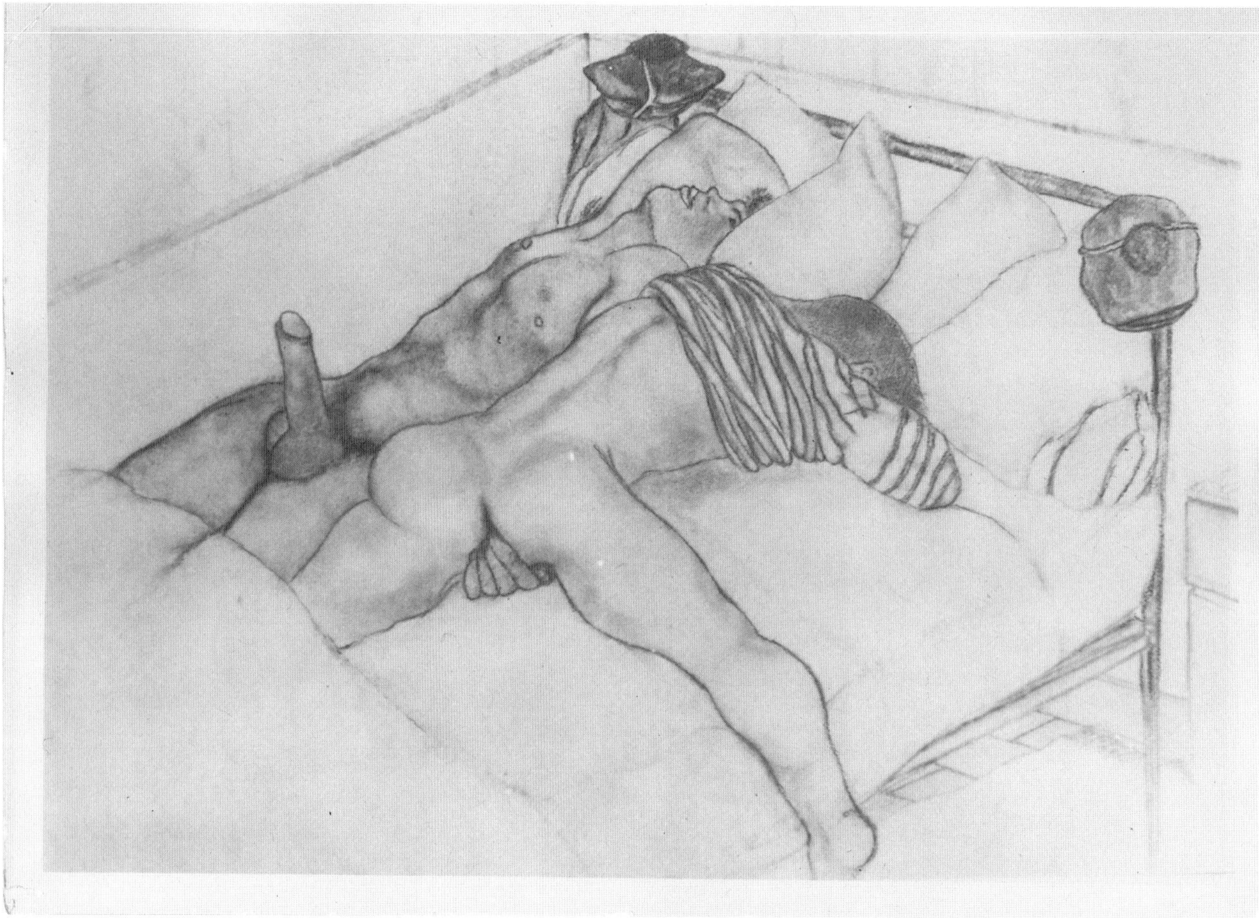

This series amplifies the great mystery surrounding the only non-Euro-American image included in *Out/Lines*
(Fig. 154), a scene of intercultural military sucking and fucking in what seemed to be a Japanese prison. That
image, reportedly circulating in the port of Yokohama in the postwar period, sparked much questioning on my
part not only about its provenance, but also about Japanese traditions in general: as with Japanese erotic art, it
98 is the *clothed* body that was eroticized there rather than the nude.

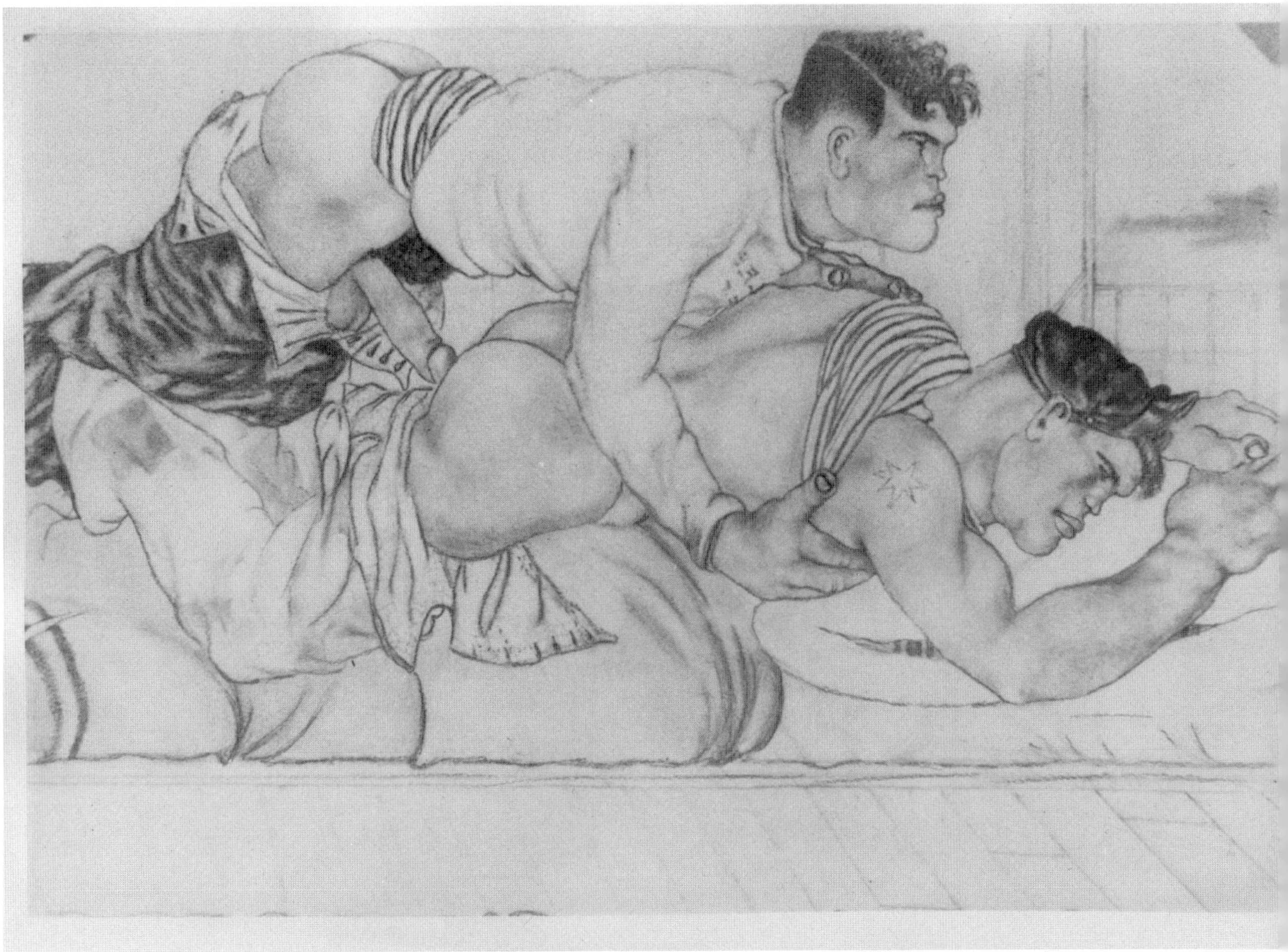

DuBek had a entire set of these pictures, which are deliriously delectable, but didn't answer any of my questions. All the more so since as a group they seemed to resemble stylistically another set of deliriously delectable military-themed images from the same period, attributed to the Frenchman Paul Smara (Figures 104-110), and not only in eroticization of uniforms and fabrics. It now seems clear that Frenchman was indeed the culprit, but what was his connection to Japan?

99

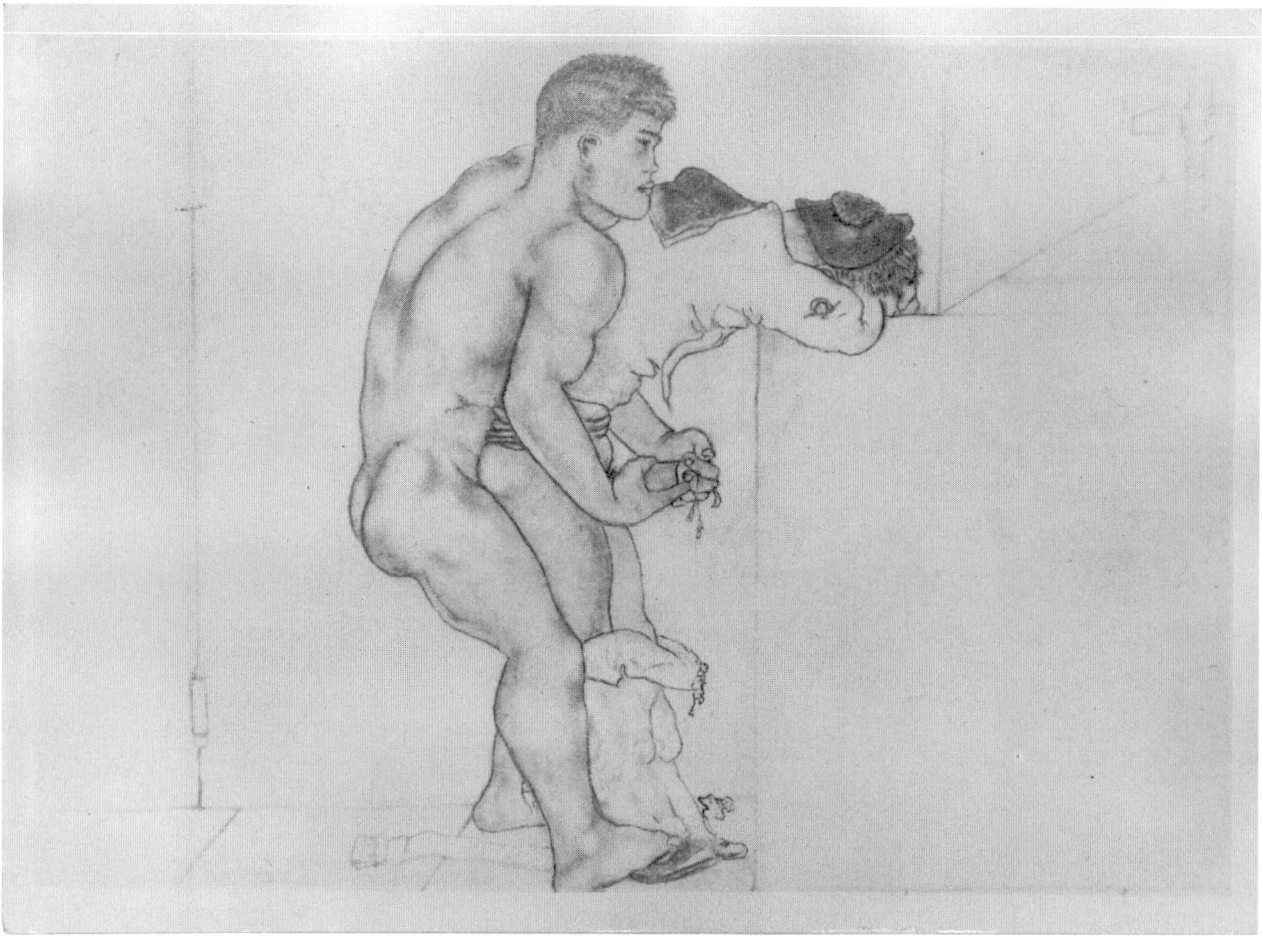

"... But what gestures of affection were appropriate? What caresses? His muscles did not know which way to bend to obtain a curve. Norbert was crushing him. Slowly he penetrated him up to the point where his belly touched Querelle, whom he was holding close, with sudden, fearsome intensity, his hands clasped round the sailor's belly.

100

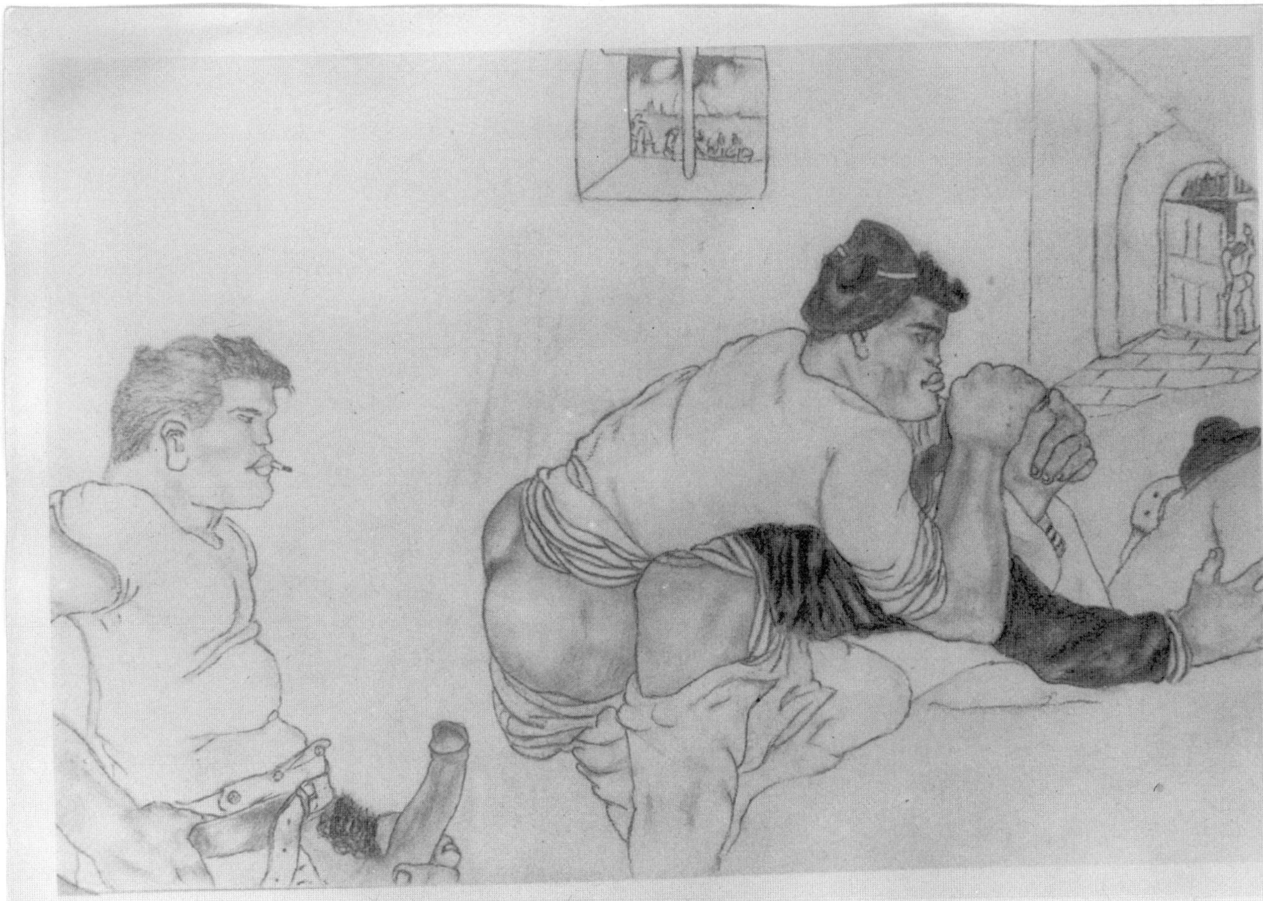

. . . He was surprised how warm it was inside of Querelle. He pushed in farther, very carefully, the better to savor his pleasure and his strength. Querelle was astonished at suffering so little pain. . . ." Jean Genet, *Querelle de Brest* ([1947; 1953] 1974, 74)

101

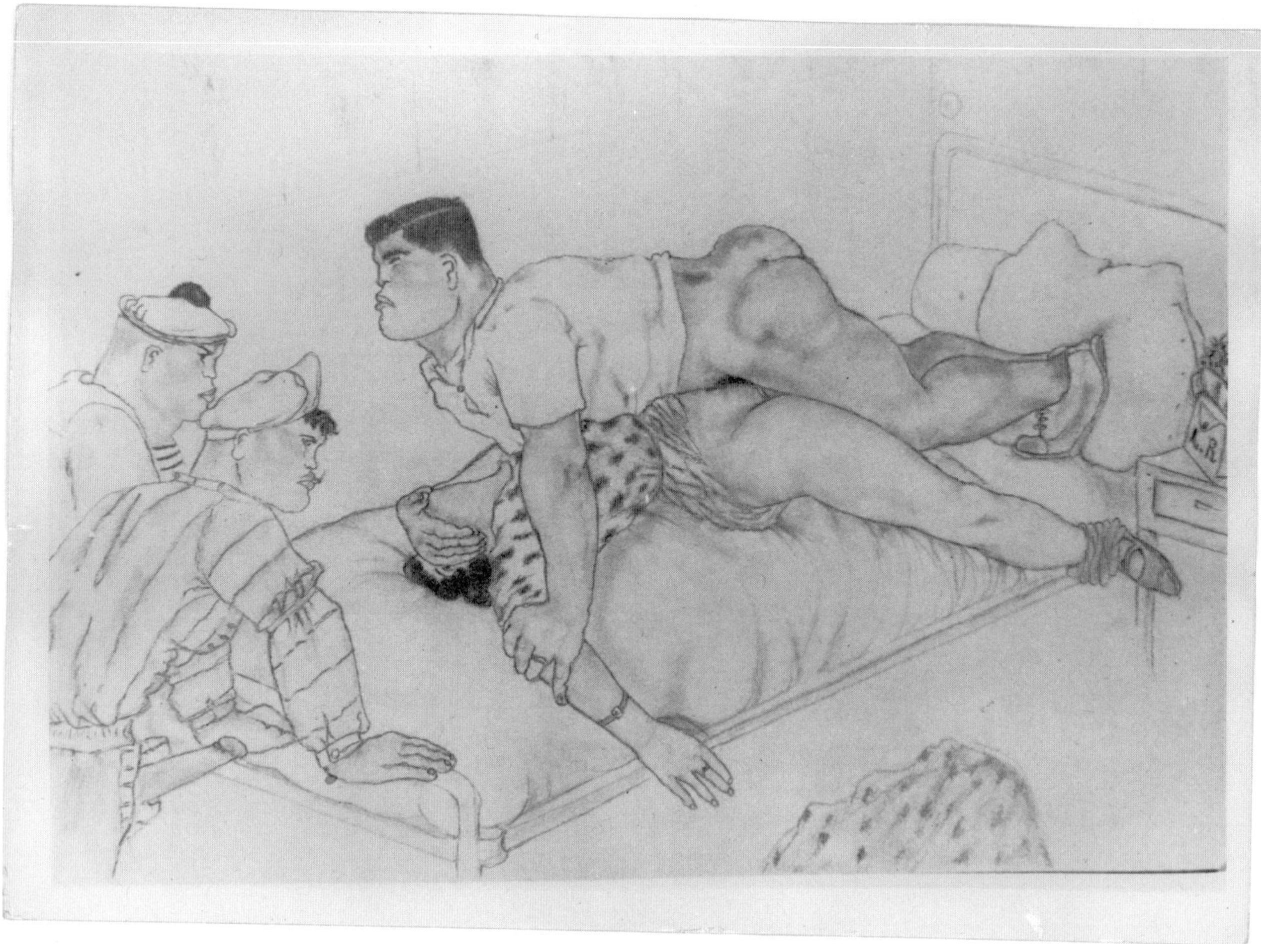

The motionless female partner in this anecdote is so incidental, if not antithetical, to its homosocial dynamic of oblique erotic charge, that she looks like a blowup doll, struggling to breathe with her face covered (although the details of her nylons, purse, and jewelry are fascinating). Not that her partner's face, uncovered and raised to the light, is any more expressive than her hidden face. . . . Other than the sailor on the upper left, are the
102 other two men civilians, perhaps sportsmen?

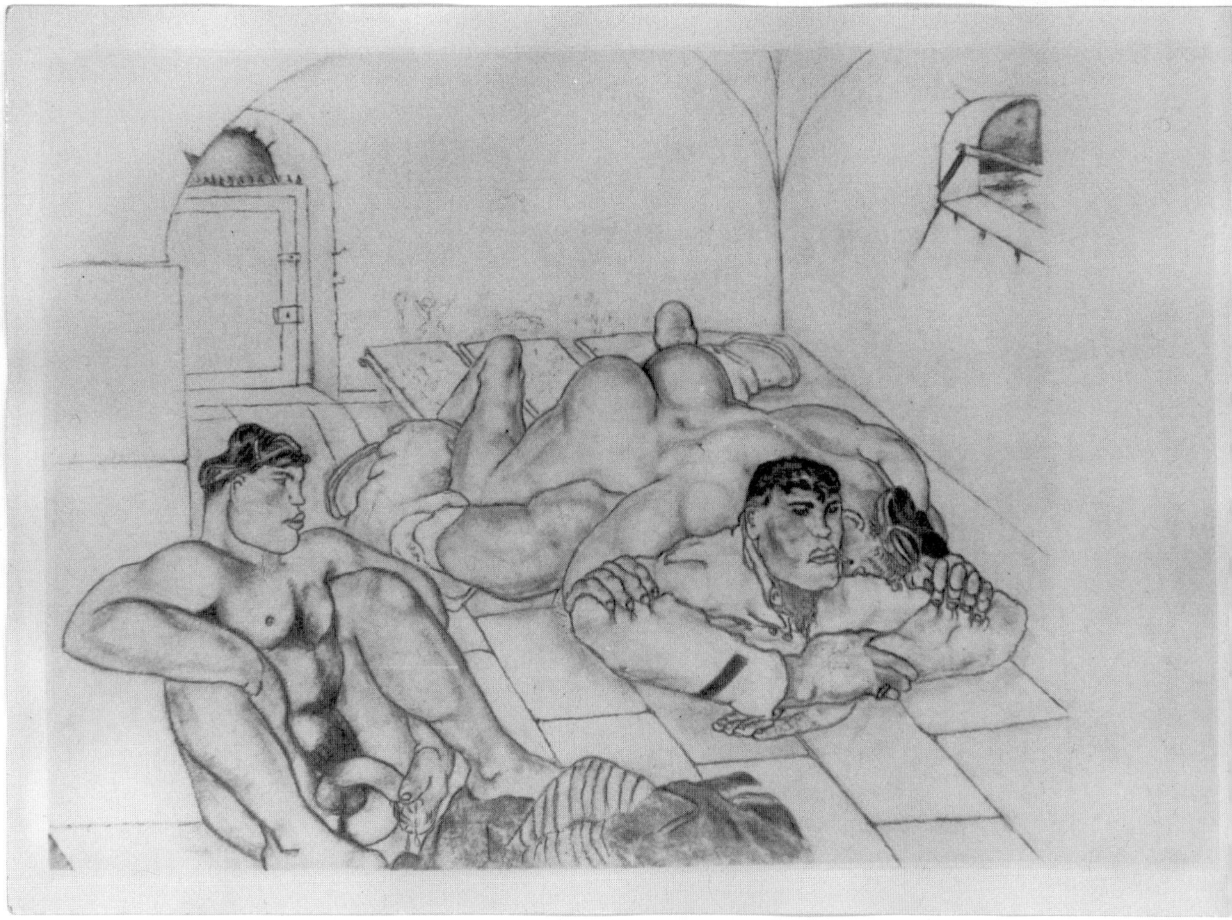

"...What he felt was a new *nature* entering into him and establishing himself there, and he was exquisitely aware of his being changed into a catamite." Jean Genet, *Querelle de Brest* ([1947; 1953] 1974, 75). I know that the fuckee's expression is as impassive as all the others in this series of soulless fornication, but that doesn't stop me from reading into it Genet's moment of existential recognition.

103

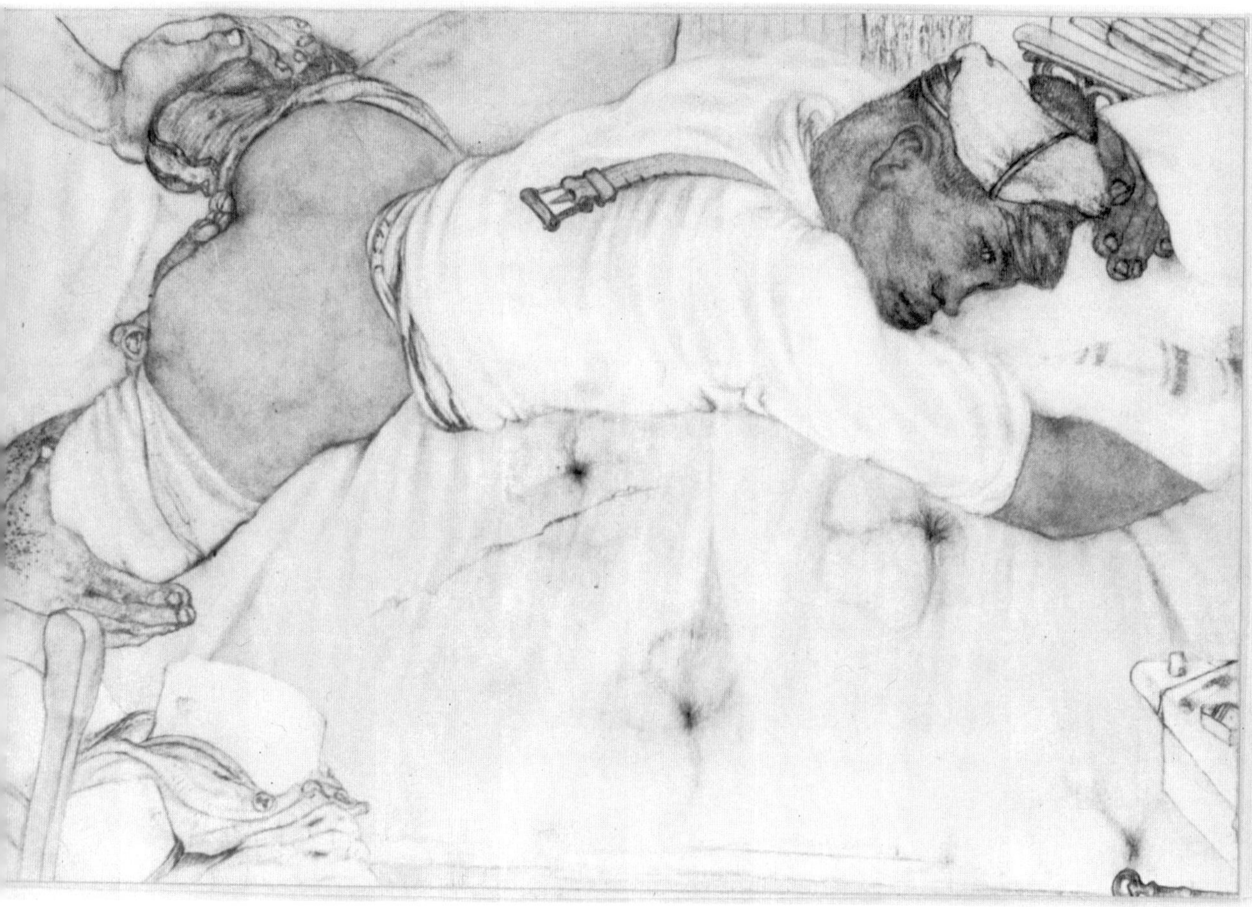

"Querelle was waiting, head bowed, blood mounting to his face; Nono looked at the sailor's buttocks: they were small and hard, round, dry, and covered with a thick brown fleece which continued on to the thighs and—but there, more sparsely—up to the small of the back, where the striped undershirt just peeped out from under the raised jersey. [. . .] The monstrousness of male love affairs appears in the uncovering of that part of the body,
104 framed by undershift and dropped pants. 'That's the way I like you.' Querelle did not reply. . . ." Jean Genet, *Querelle de Brest* ([1947; 1953] 1974, 74)

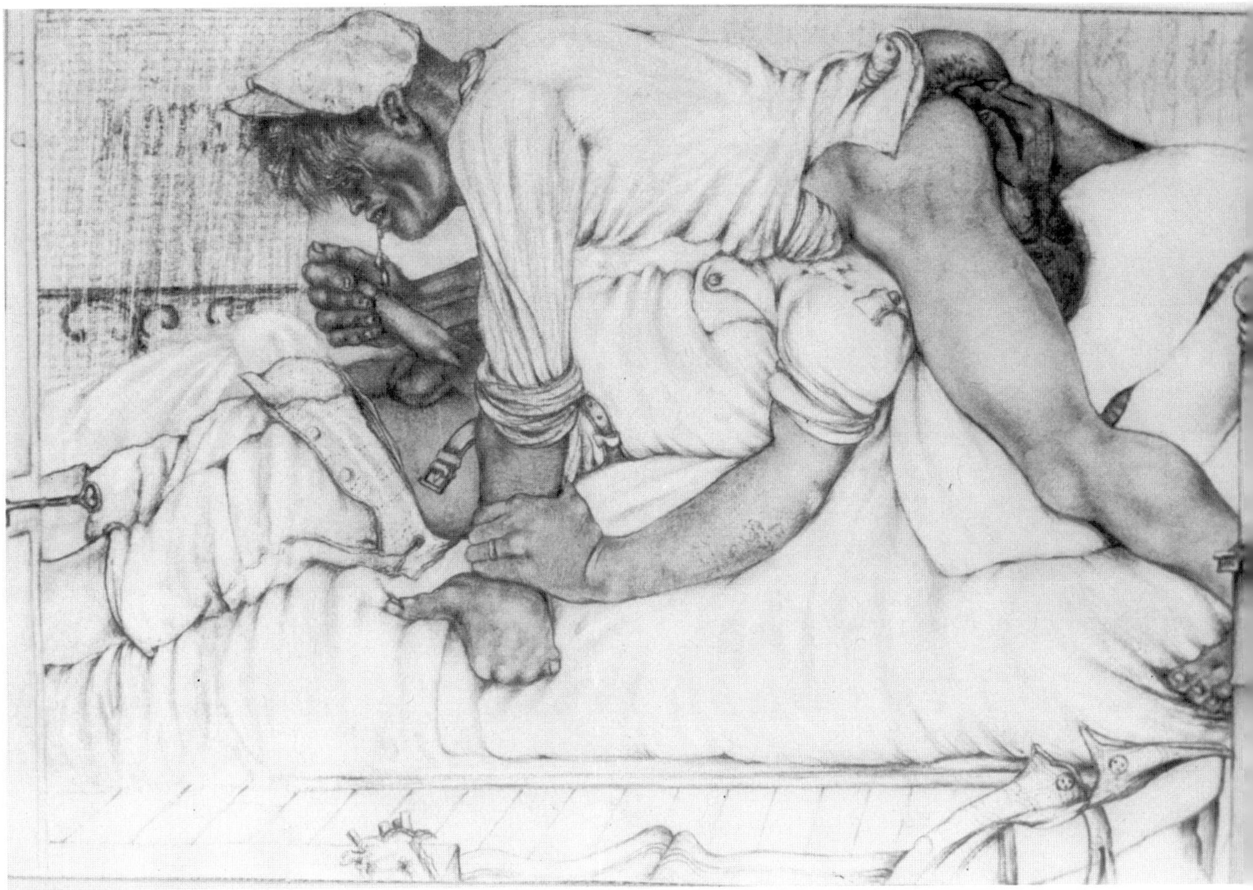

Starting opposite, this cycle of seven uniform-themed vignettes are attributed to Paul Smara (E. Paul Dubois), and date from the 1940s. Little is known about Smara: he was a friend of Genet, who asked him to illustrate his *Thief's Journal* (1948) but was turned down (Oberlé 2001). His compositions in charcoal and pencil and various highlights have circulated on the gay collectors' market in France.

105

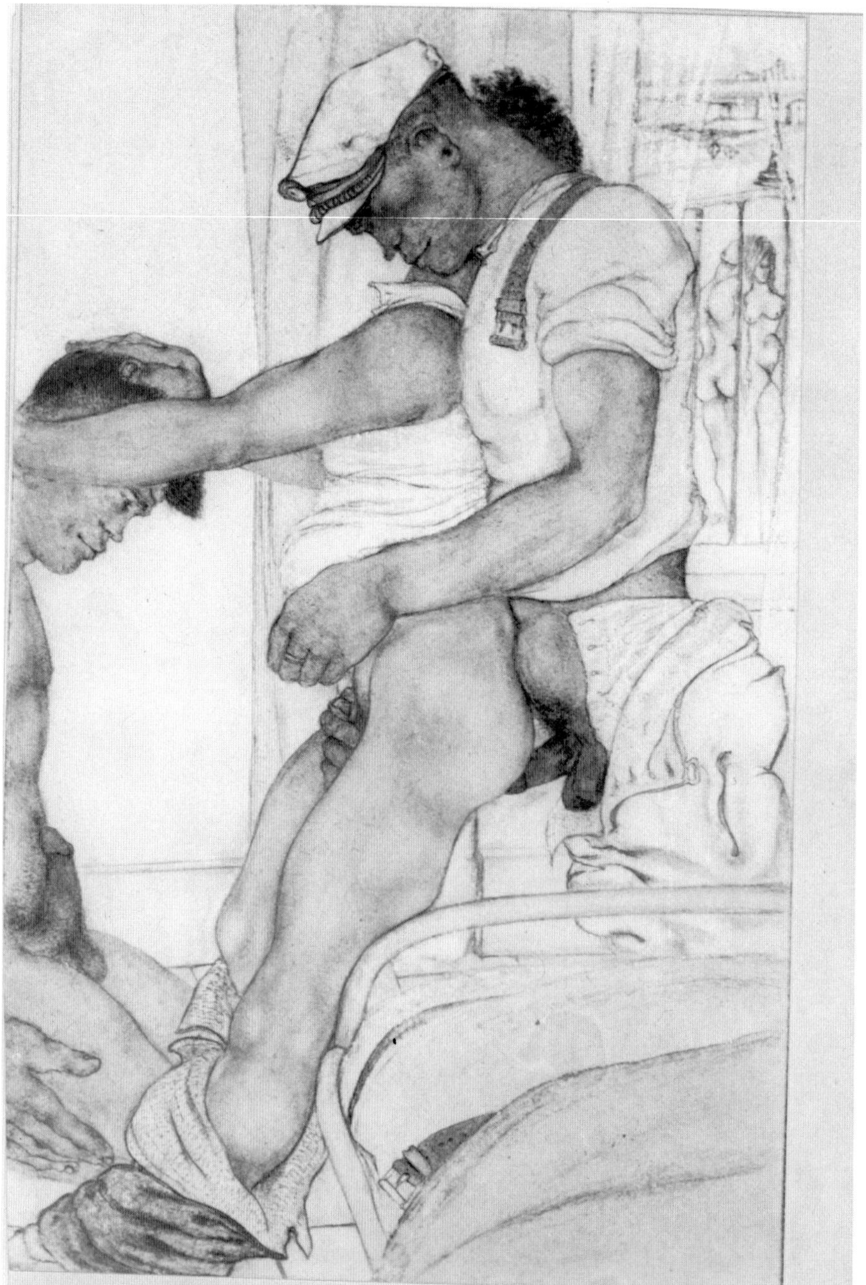

In this business, hasty attributions of anonymous homoerotic works are risky, and I now repent of my Smara attributions in *Out/Lines* (Figures 145-146, 188-189). Of those two sets, the first and perhaps the second are by "Cheekbones," the same sadly still anonymous artist reproduced (or traced) in Figures 38-42 in the present volume. All have the usual thing for sailors, uniforms, and well-sculpted faces.

106

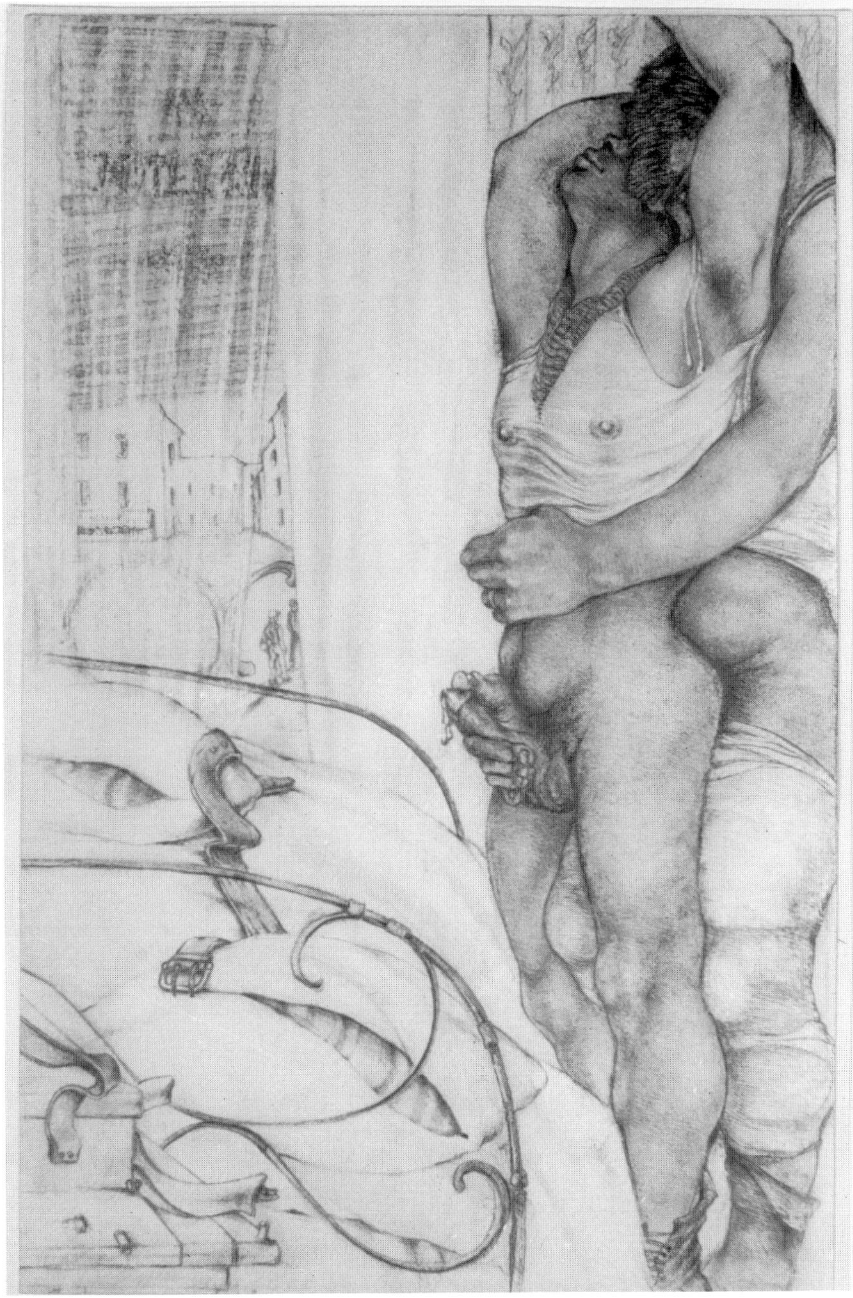

Some of Smara's correspondence is also known, wherein he refers to his horny hulking brutes as "my monsters." He also wrote a never-published long poem celebrating "sailors, mechanics and other surly comrades, furnished rooms, 'intimate half-heartedness, the stuff of solid guys putting out. . . sly wildlife . . . the school of Uranian vice. . . bestial spasms. . . .' " (Oberlé 2001). Smara lived until the early 1970s. 107

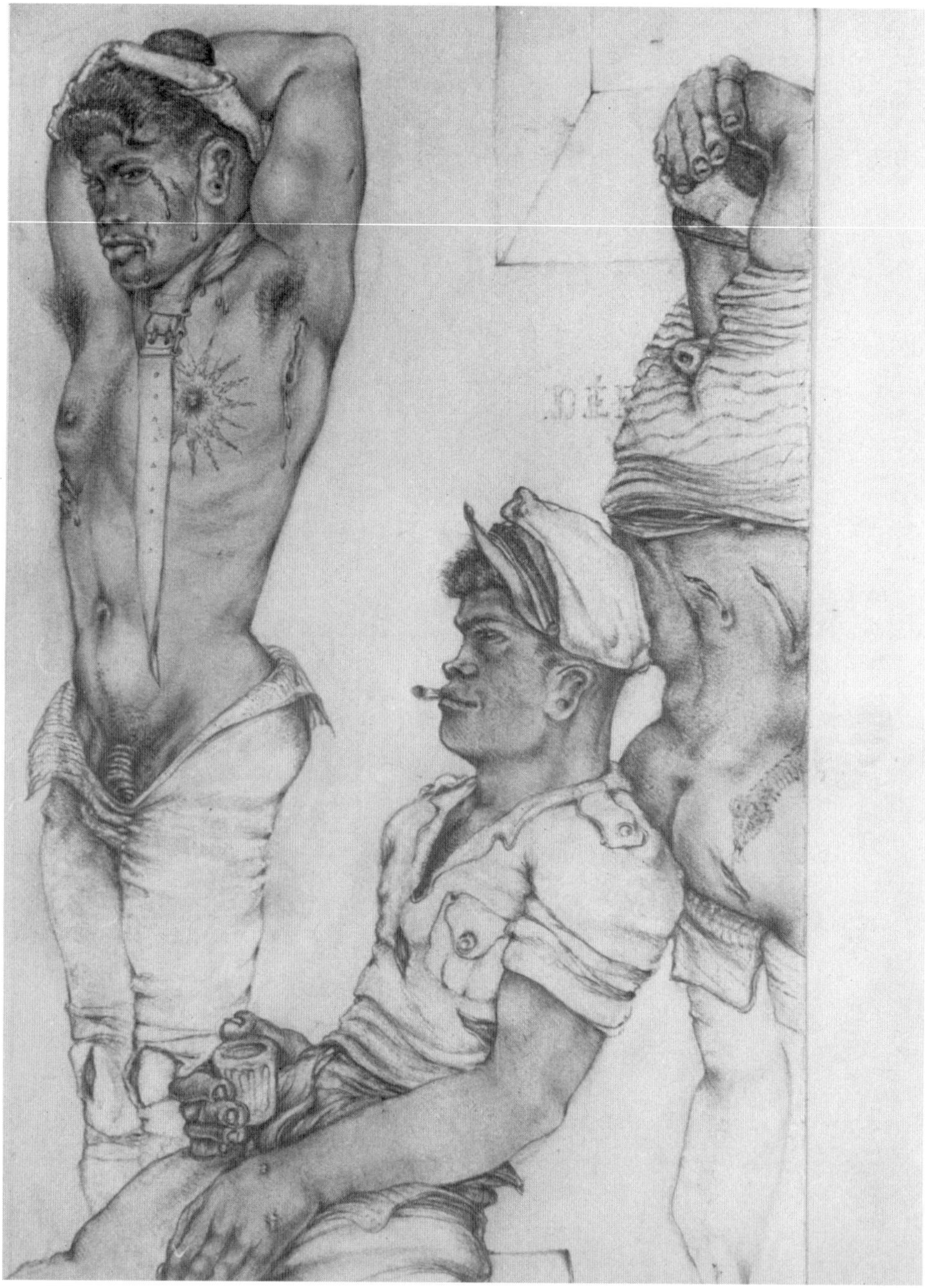

108 "Ever since becoming obsessed with the picture of St. Sebastian, I had acquired the unconscious habit of crossing my hands over my head whenever I happened to be undressed. Mine was a frail body, without so much as a pale shadow of Sebastian's abundant beauty. But now once more I spontaneously fell into the pose. As I did so my eyes went to my armpits. And a mysterious sexual desire boiled up within me. . . ." Yukio Mishima, *Confessions of a Mask* ([1949] 1958, 88)

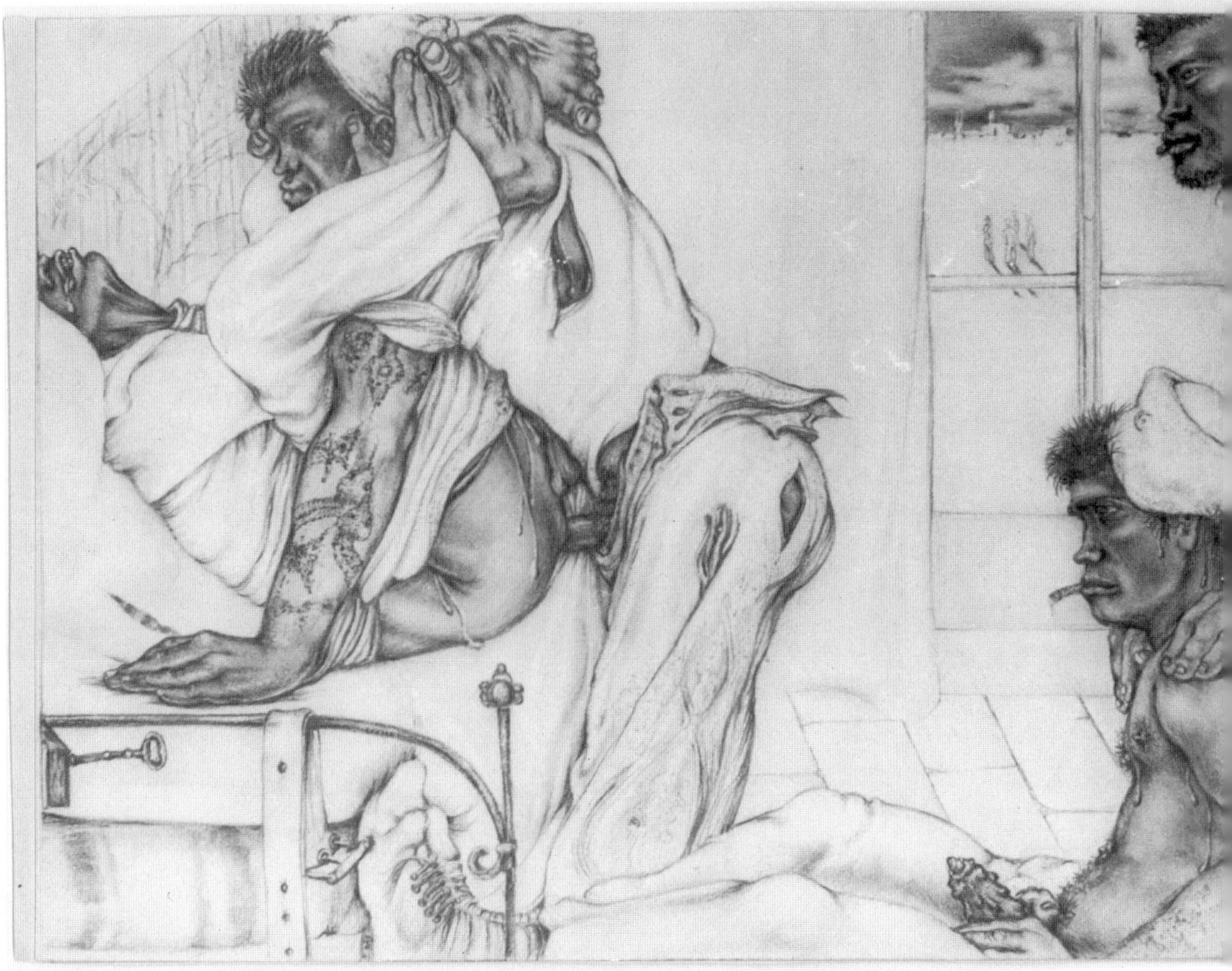

What is going on? Have these brutes been trying to kill the thing they love again? And would someone please tell me what St. Sebastian (on the left in 108) has wound around his dick and why? In any case, more Genet moments: if there's something that's sexier than freshly laundered whites, it's apparently whites (and the skin underneath) that have been gashed in a knife fight.

109

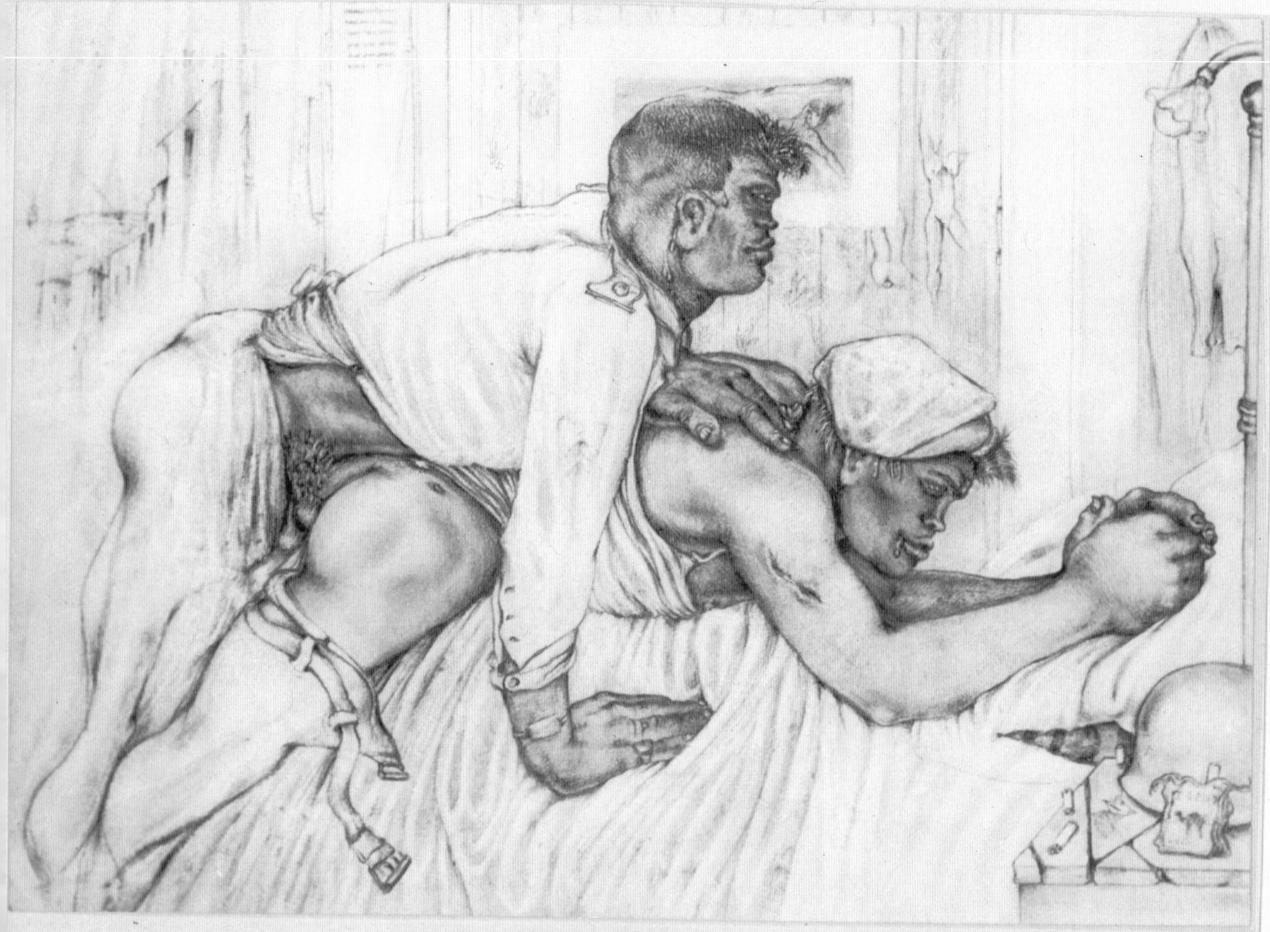

110 "... He pulled the curtains which seemed unnecessary because the windows were so dirty. He had a white body. Not in good condition. Going to fat. Very good sex, though, surprisingly. The bed had springs which creaked. First time I've experienced that. He sucked my cock. Afterwards I fucked him. It was difficult to get in. He had a very tight arse. A Catholic upbringing, I expect. He wanted to fuck me when I'd finished. It seemed unfair to refuse after I'd fucked him. So I let him. We lay in bed and talked for a while. He showed me a photograph of his fiancée." Joe Orton, *The Orton Diaries* ([1967] 1986, 45)

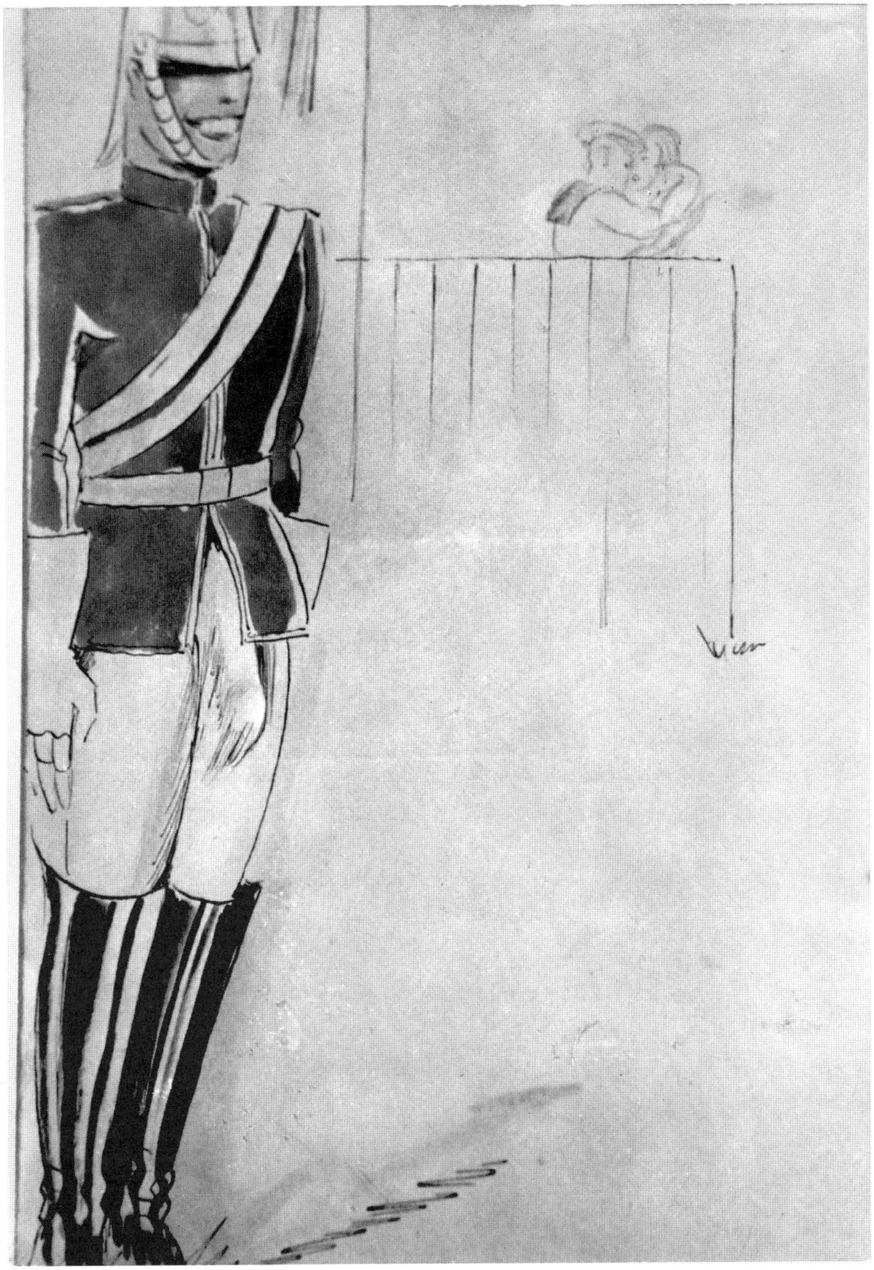

"His Majesty's Brigade of Guards had a long history in homosexual prostitution. Perpetually short of cash, beer, and leisure occupation, they were easily to be found of an evening in their red tunics standing about in the various pubs they frequented. [. . .] some kind gentleman might appear and stand them a few pints, in return for which and the subsequent traditional tip—a pound was the recognized tariff for the Foot Guards then, the
Horse Guards cost rather more—they were perfectly agreeable to, indeed often eager for, a 'bit of fun.'" J.R. 111
Ackerley, *My Father & Myself* (1968, 135)

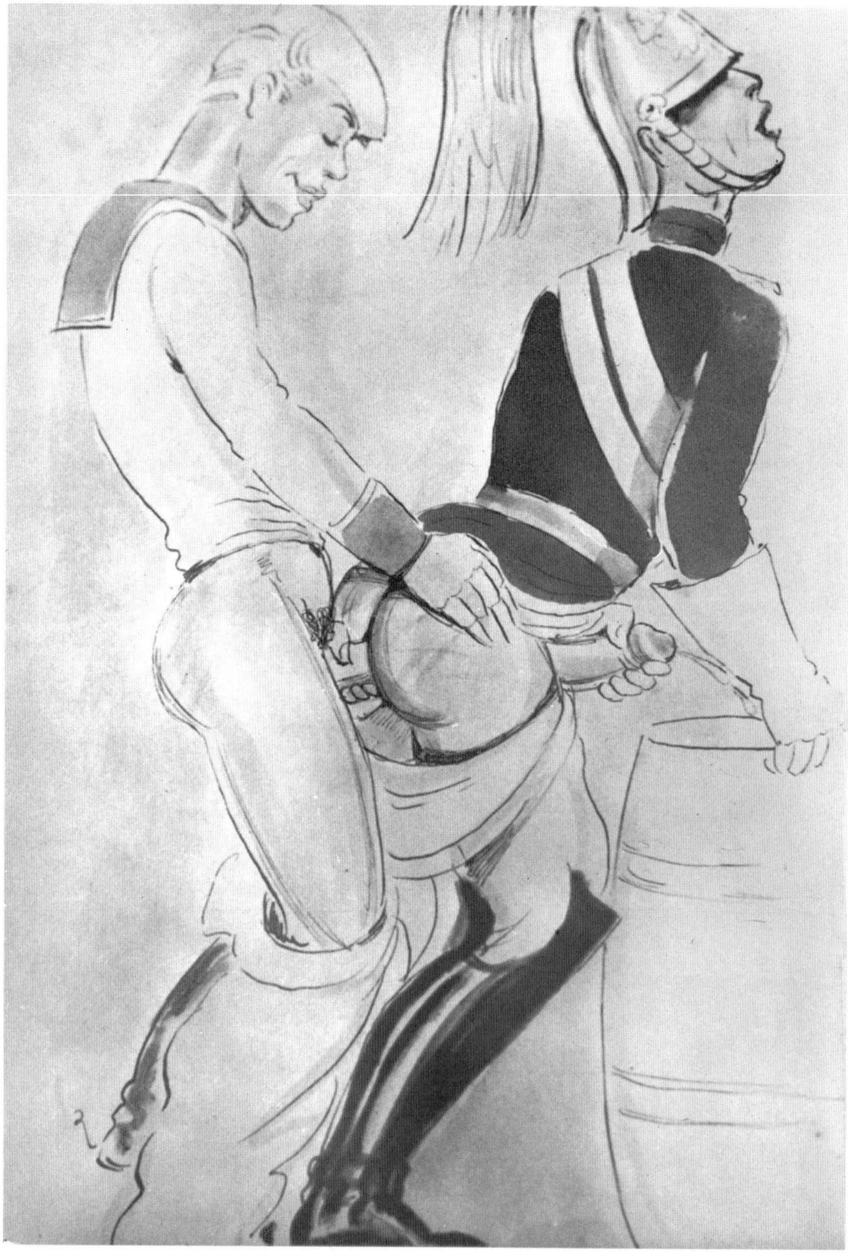

112 Across the Channel from Smara, different uniforms and tone. This series is by the anonymous Briton who crafted my fey, porno-loving bellhops in *Out/Lines* and whom we can thus call "Bellhops." (See also the two-somes of Figures 157-170 [and the *Lust Unearthed* cover], the threesomes of 200-205, and the foursomes of 213-215.) For "Bellhops," uniforms are not badges of machismo attitude, rather a decorative layer of charm, a complement to a gentlemanly choreography that has very little to do with pecking order or down-to-earth forbidden desire.

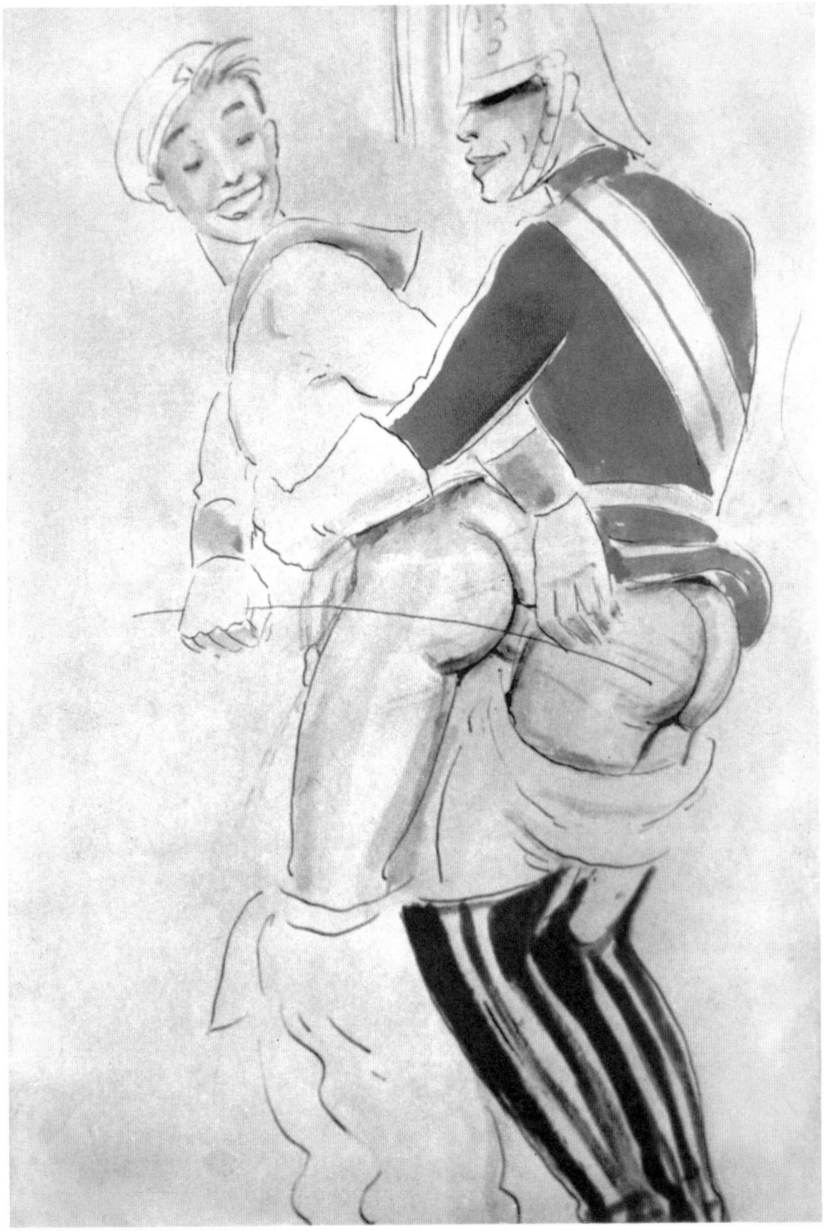

"The Household Cavalry are a fine body of men, much admired for their magnificent physique and the splendour of their accoutrements, but it will hardly be claimed for them that they are—or at any rate were—refined in their tastes and habits. . . . Sex and beer and the constant problem of how to obtain these two luxuries [. . .] represented the main leisure preoccupation of many guardsmen and troopers . . . 113

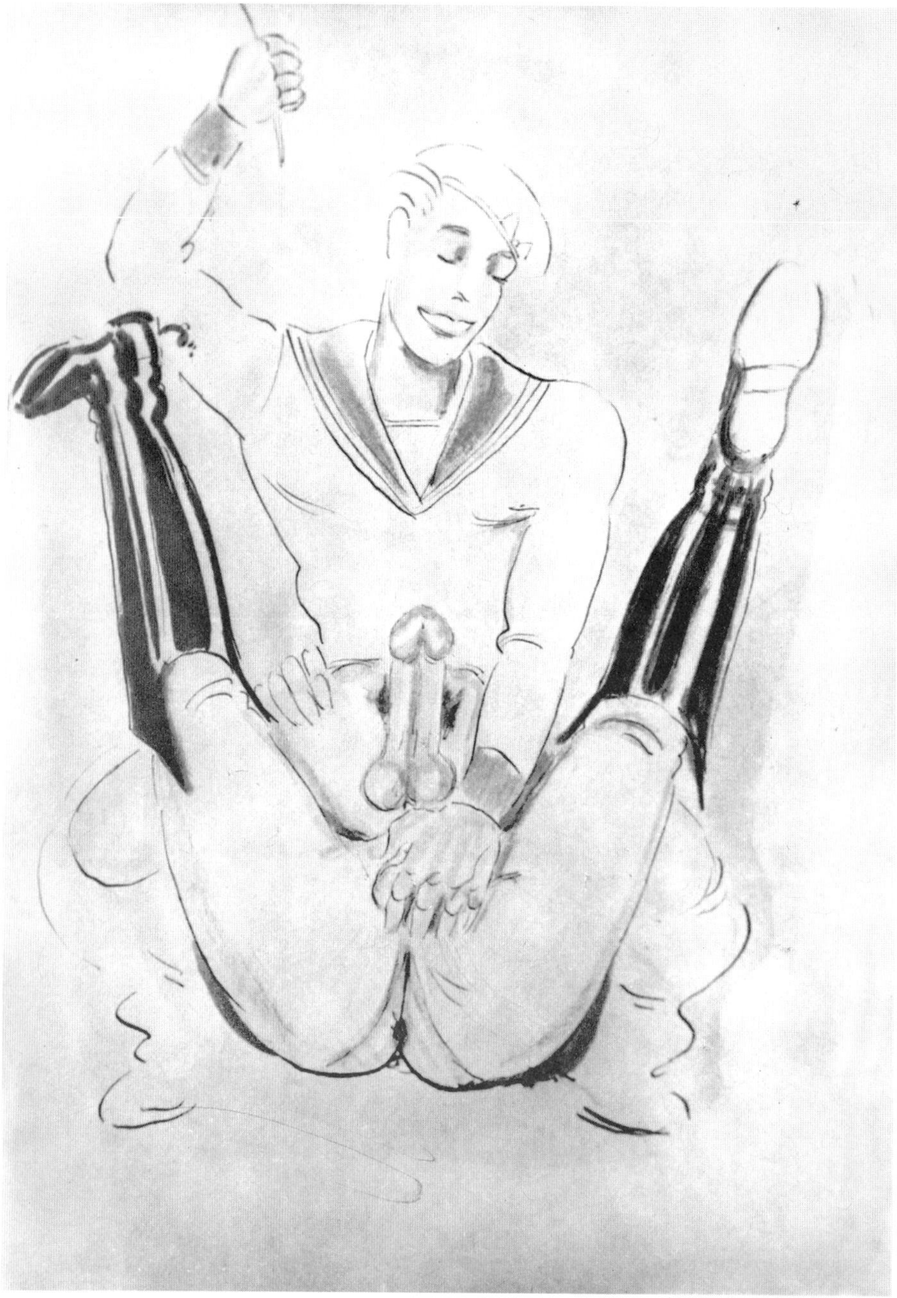

. . . Nor is this surprising. Healthy and vigorous young men, like my father, the merest boys, suddenly transplanted from a comparatively humdrum provincial or country life into a London barrack-room, exercised and trained all day to the bursting point of physical fitness, and let loose in the evening, with little money and large appetites . . .

114

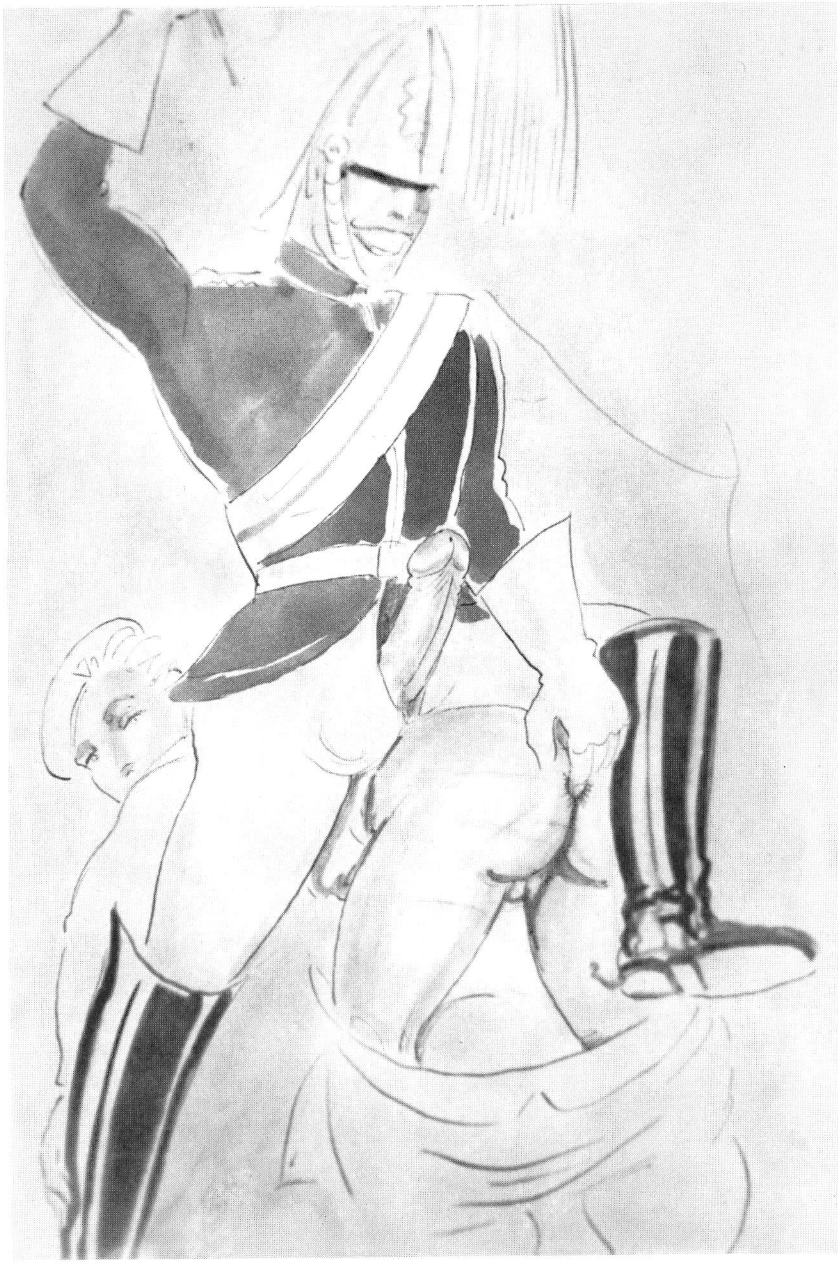

. . . to prowl about the Monkey Walk in Hyde Park, the pubs, or West End streets, in uniforms of the most conspicuous and sometimes provocative design—it is hardly surprising that their education in the seductions and pleasures of the world should take rapid strides." J.R. Ackerley, *My Father & Myself* (1968, 23)

15

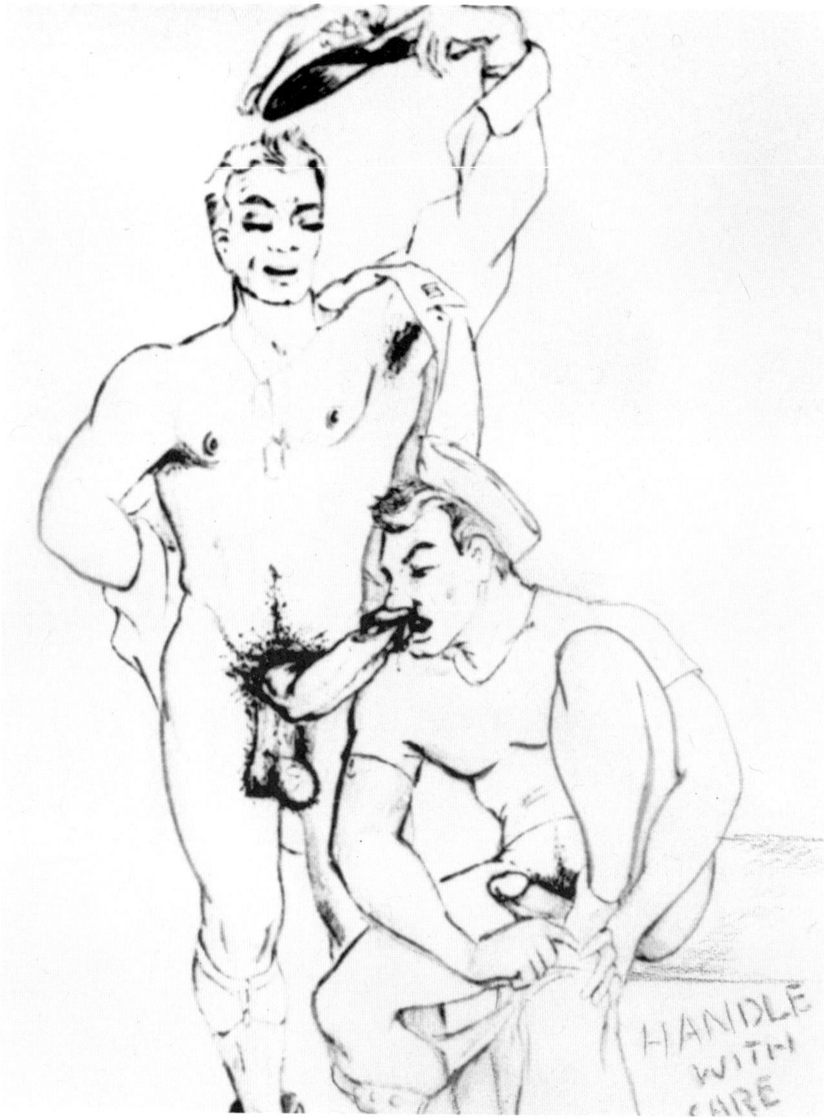

A smattering of images by an anonymous American, labelled "World War II era" in fountain pen by the voracious collector who had turned a fey twenty-five years old the same year as Pearl Harbor. Genet, six years DuBek's elder, spent most of the war in jail or fantasizing about Germans, not GI's.

116

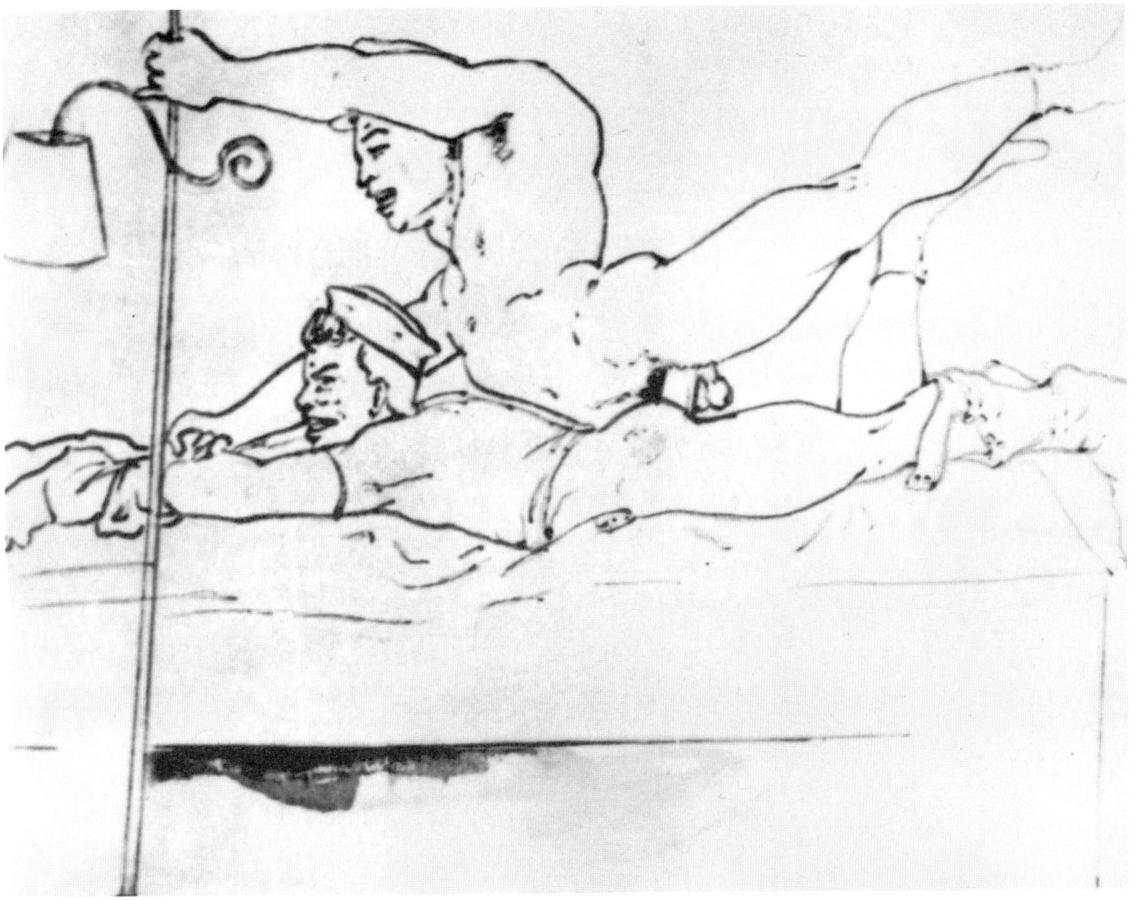

". . . The two men heard nothing but the sound of each other's breathing. Querelle felt like weeping over the skin he had sloughed and abandoned—where? at the foot of the city wall of Brest?—but his eyes, open in one of the deep folds of the velvet bedcover, remained dry. "Here it comes." At the first thrust, so strong it almost killed him, Querelle whimpered quietly, then more loudly, until he was moaning without restraint or shame. [. . .] 'Is that what it's like, being a real fairy?' he thought." Jean Genet, *Querelle de Brest* ([1947; 1953] 1974, 75-76) **117**

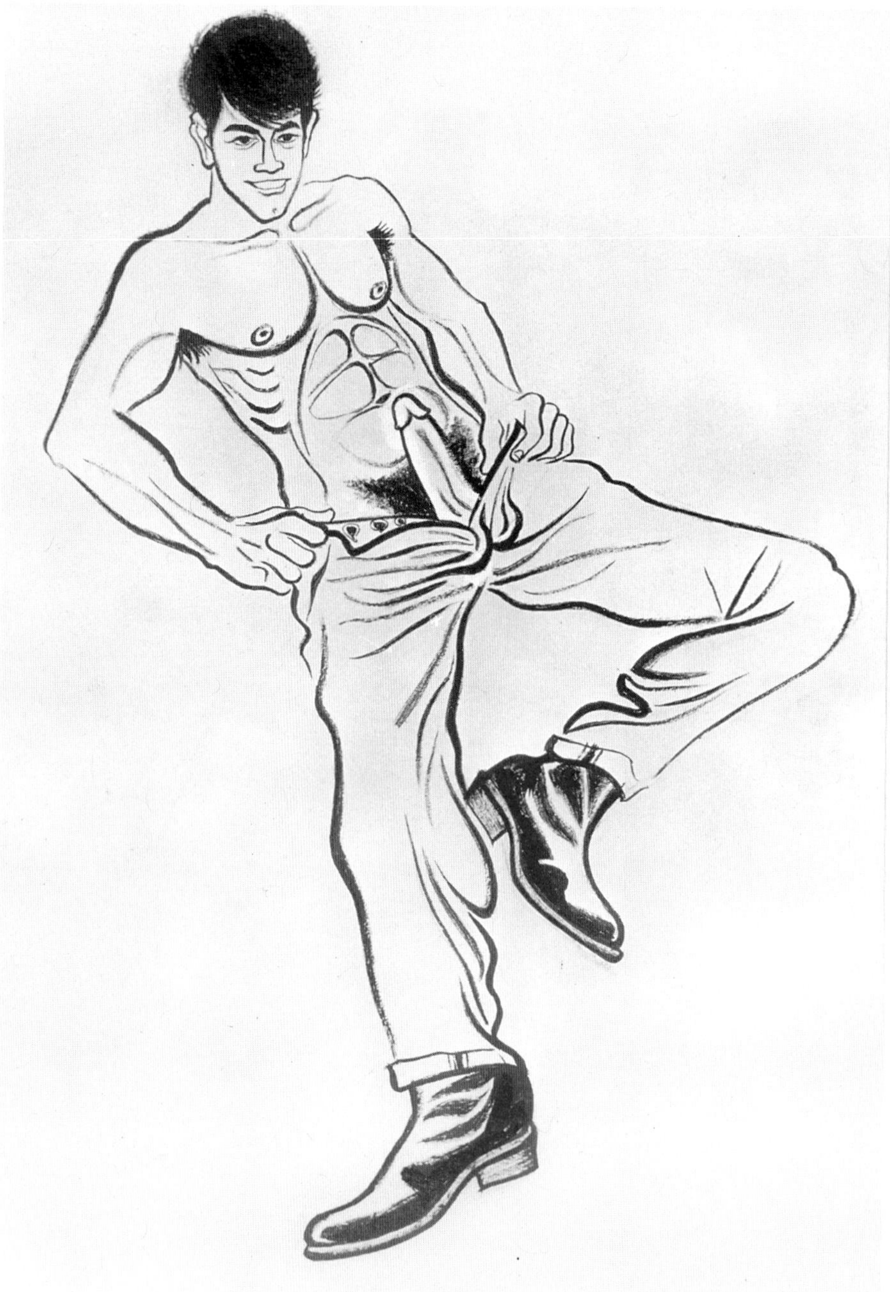

"Clayton loved those boots, and they had a certain attraction for me, too. Funny how someone else's boots are always sexier than your own. After he took them off, he would peel his very tight trousers down those magnificent thighs. And they he would feel himself lovingly, through his jockey shorts. Then, with a grunt, off would come his undershirt." Phil Andros [Sam Steward], "The Poison Tree," *$tud* ([1966] 1982, 24)

118

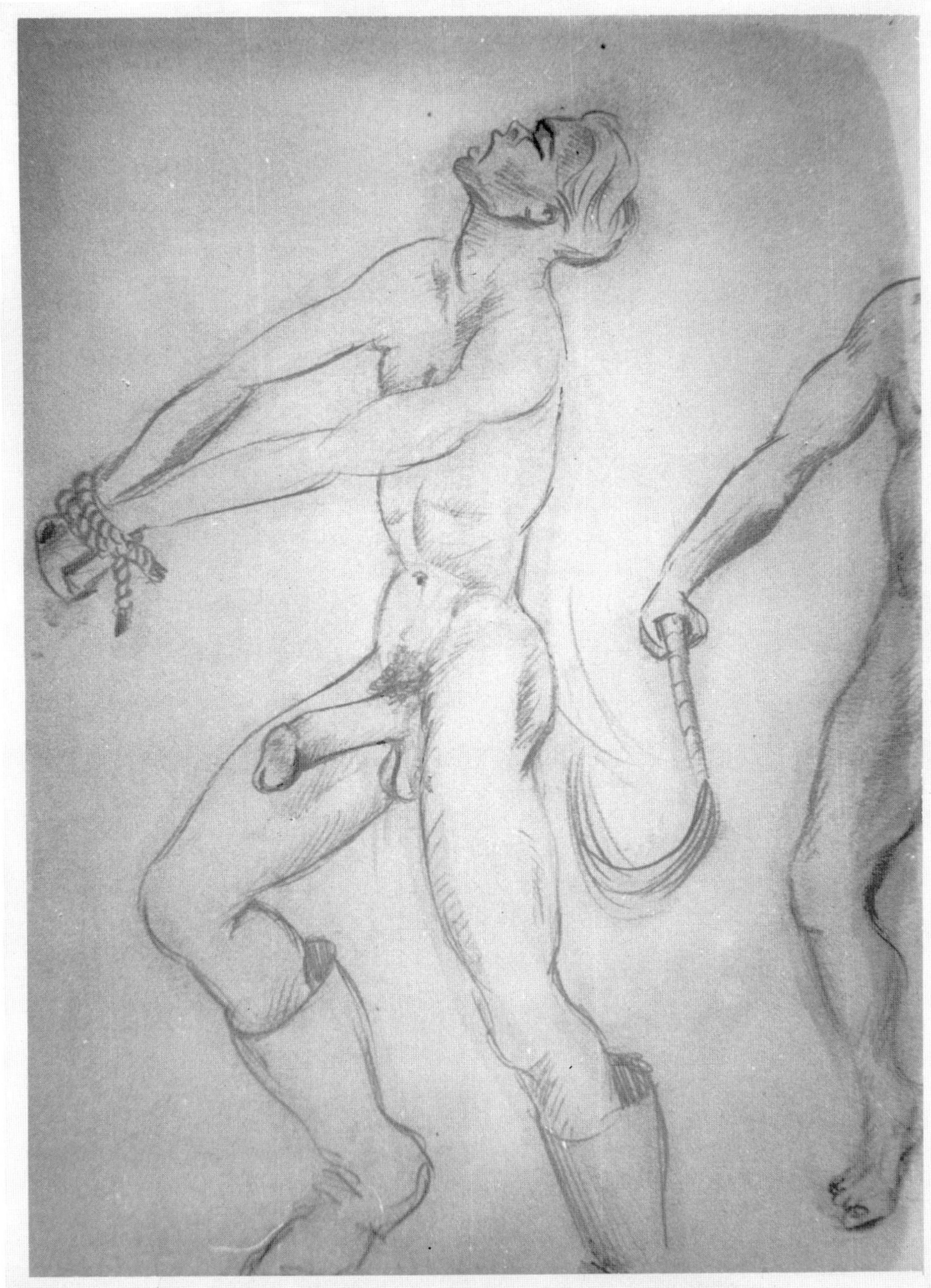

In these two pictures (see also Figures 144-145, 175-176, 208), boots are the key link in the vestimentary enactment of power play. Boots often constitute a uniform in and of themselves. S/M is only a minor interest on the part of "El Greco" (on this page, see also Figures 27-32 and 120), whose interest in boots and uniforms is more about social theatre rather than interpersonal power play.

119

Beachiness:
boys in the sand

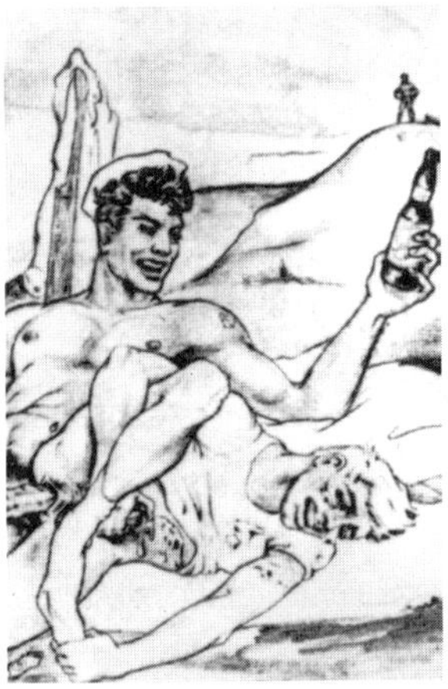

Beachiness: boys in the sand

The beach, the shore, the waterfront, the harbor: the liminal zone between land and water allows the baring of bodies and solitude for the primal act, the site of desire. An archetypal, edenic space, beaches have also evolved as gay male social and political spaces as well, a "heterotopia," to use Michel Foucault's expression (1986, eruditely using the Greek for "other" and "place"), to accommodate the social, psychic, and erotic need of queer society for another "other place" away. Away from our "Villages," ghettos, and metropolitan pavement, beaches are "other spaces" to get away to, spaces to dream about. Remember not only DuBek's beloved Fire Island, but also the legendary "other" spaces of Provincetown, Key West, Land's End, Muscle Beach. . . . Or north of the border, the queer spaces of our three metropoles, Vancouver's Wreck Beach, Toronto's Hanlan's Point, Montreal's quadrant plenitude of Ste-Marguerite, Oka, Île des fesses and Île Notre-dame. . . . Is it any wonder that that Fire-Island-set porno film *Boys in the Sand* (Wakefield Poole, 1971), the pioneering hardcore theatrical feature, the epitome of all beachiness, is still, some say, unsurpassed?

These nineteen images come in small clusters and isolated freeze frames of bodies meeting water, plus one large nine-panel narrative encompassing the simple formula of boy sees boy, boy fucks boy, boy says seeya. The setting of a bit of dune grass and palm foliage plus the elemental emptiness of the shoreline transforms this encounter into the most elegant and timeless of erotic dreams. Visually it is also organized like a film, complete with establishing shots and close-ups, and as such reflects the compulsive itch in 1960s gay male culture towards big-screen audio-visual narratives that would finally be assuaged in the 1970s.

Unlike the uniform motif which has to do with bodies and their coverings, the beach and water motifs are elemental, often sacramental as well. Beachiness is also spatial and social, regardless of its frequent abstraction: the haunting beach scene with two African men, opposite, by a presumed white Frenchman whom we have called "El Greco," suggests and *demands*—no matter how sparse the data of costume and passing steamer—a historical canvas of the intersection of colonialism and desire beyond the frame.

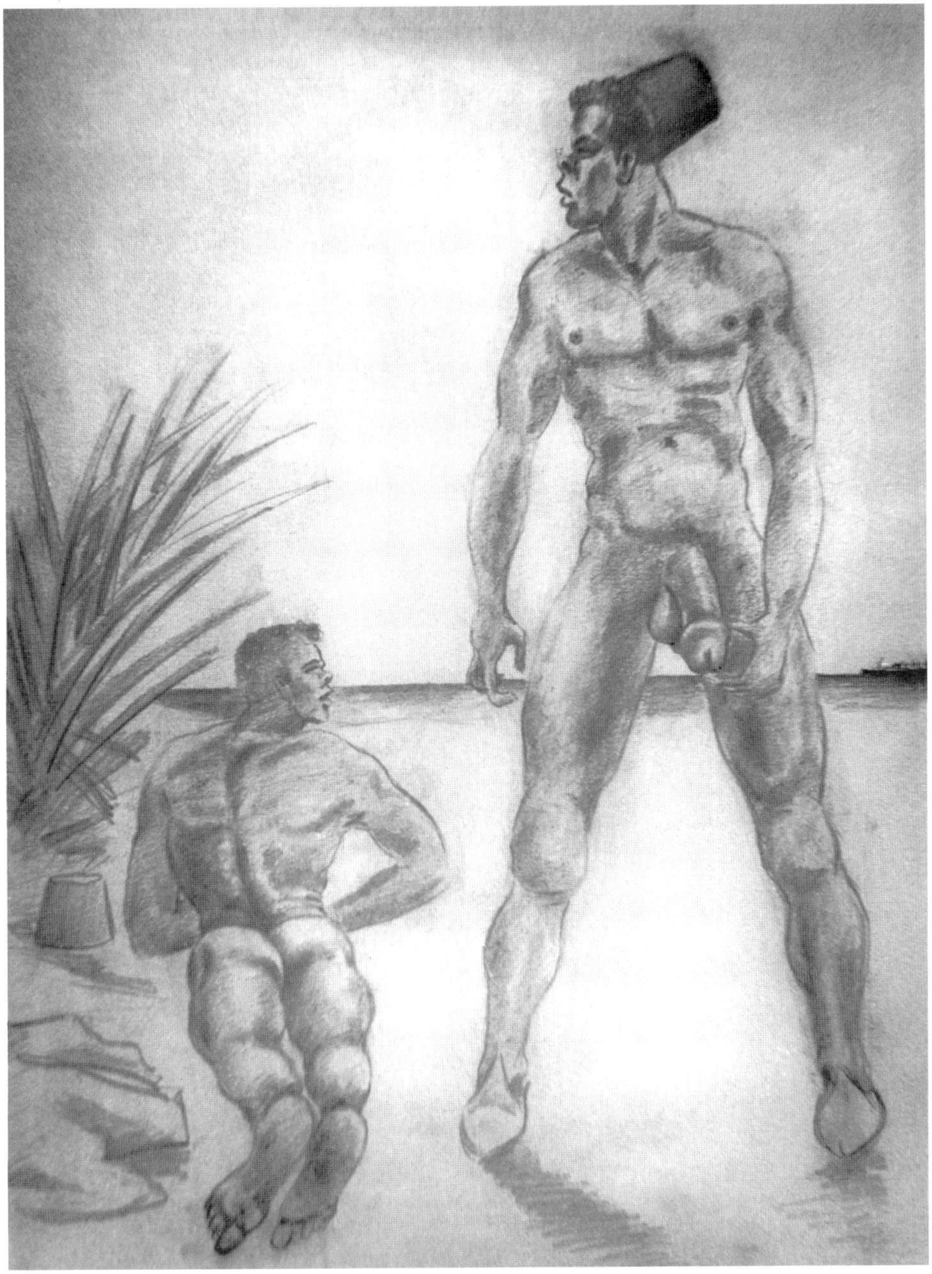

"The sun shone out of a clear blue sky all day. Got very sunburnt today. Mohammed Khomsi arrived at The Windmill. He's full of the fact that he's starting life as a page-boy at a hotel in Gibraltar. [. . .] small, happy-looking and nineteen. He has a good body, not over-developed, not underdeveloped. [. . .] I invited him back to the flat for tea. [. . .] 'Please I must fuck you,' he said, 'I've had no *l'amour* for many weeks.'" Joe Orton, *The Orton Diaries* ([1967] 1986, 163). "El Greco," France, c. 1950. **120**

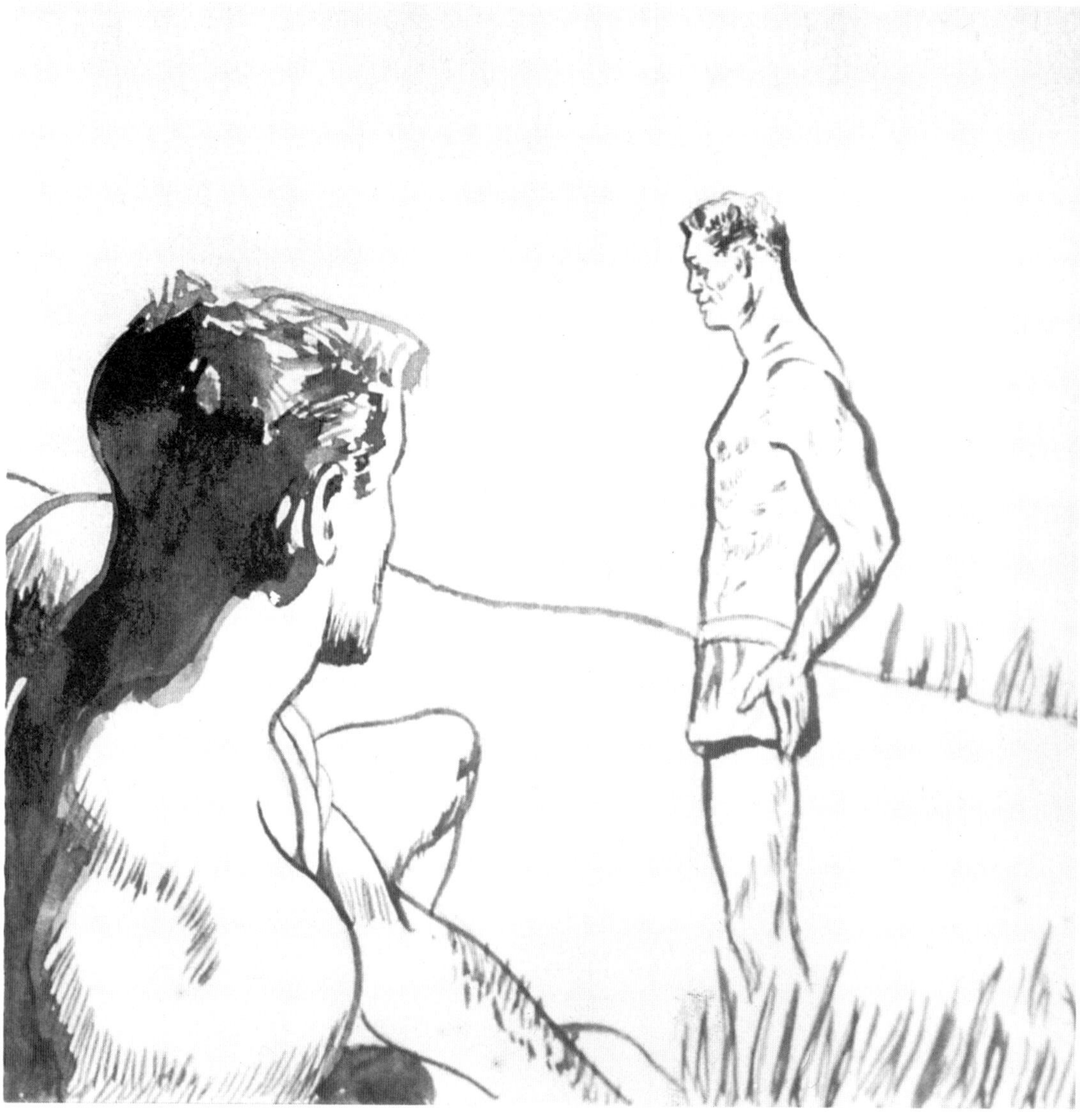

This minimalist but dream-like narrative on a tropical beach captures both the archetypal and the epidermal excess of *Boys in the Sand*, which it anticipates by a decade or more. U.S.A., c. 1960.

121

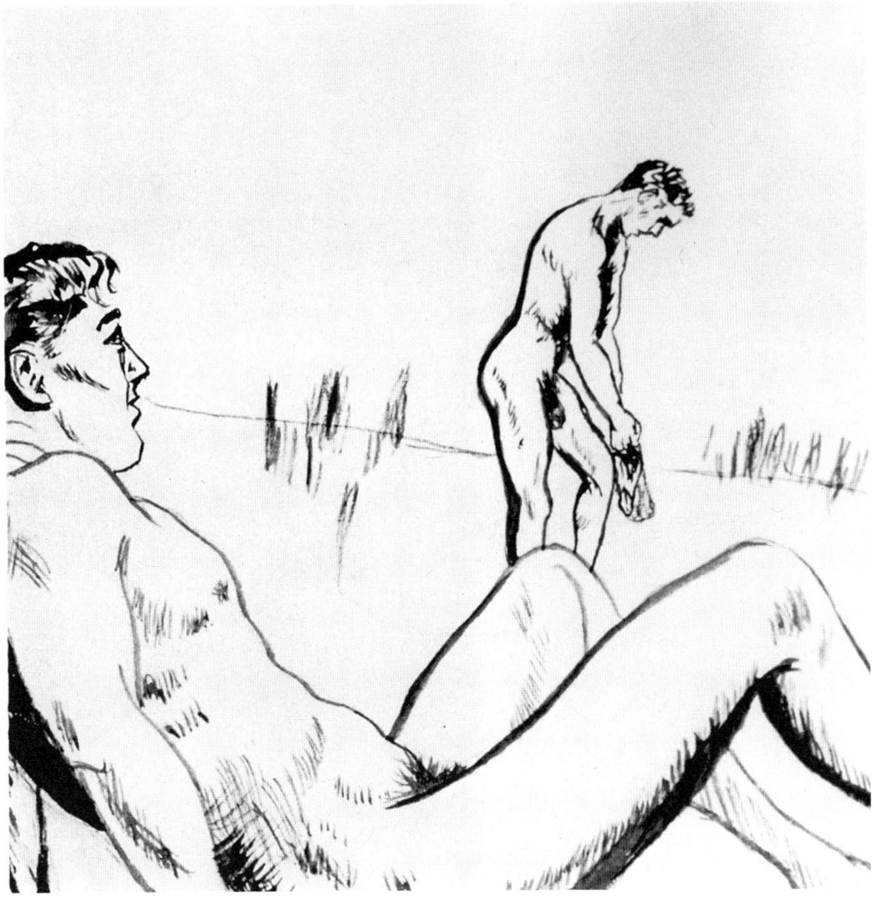

"I found him down by the water, cavorting alone on the springboard; for the first time he had discarded his trunks without my suggesting it. All day we stayed together around the terrace and on the rocks, talking, swimming, reading, and just lying flat in the hot sun. Nor did he return to his room when night came. . . ." Paul Bowles, "Pages from Cold Point," *Collected Stories* ([1947] 1980, 98)

122

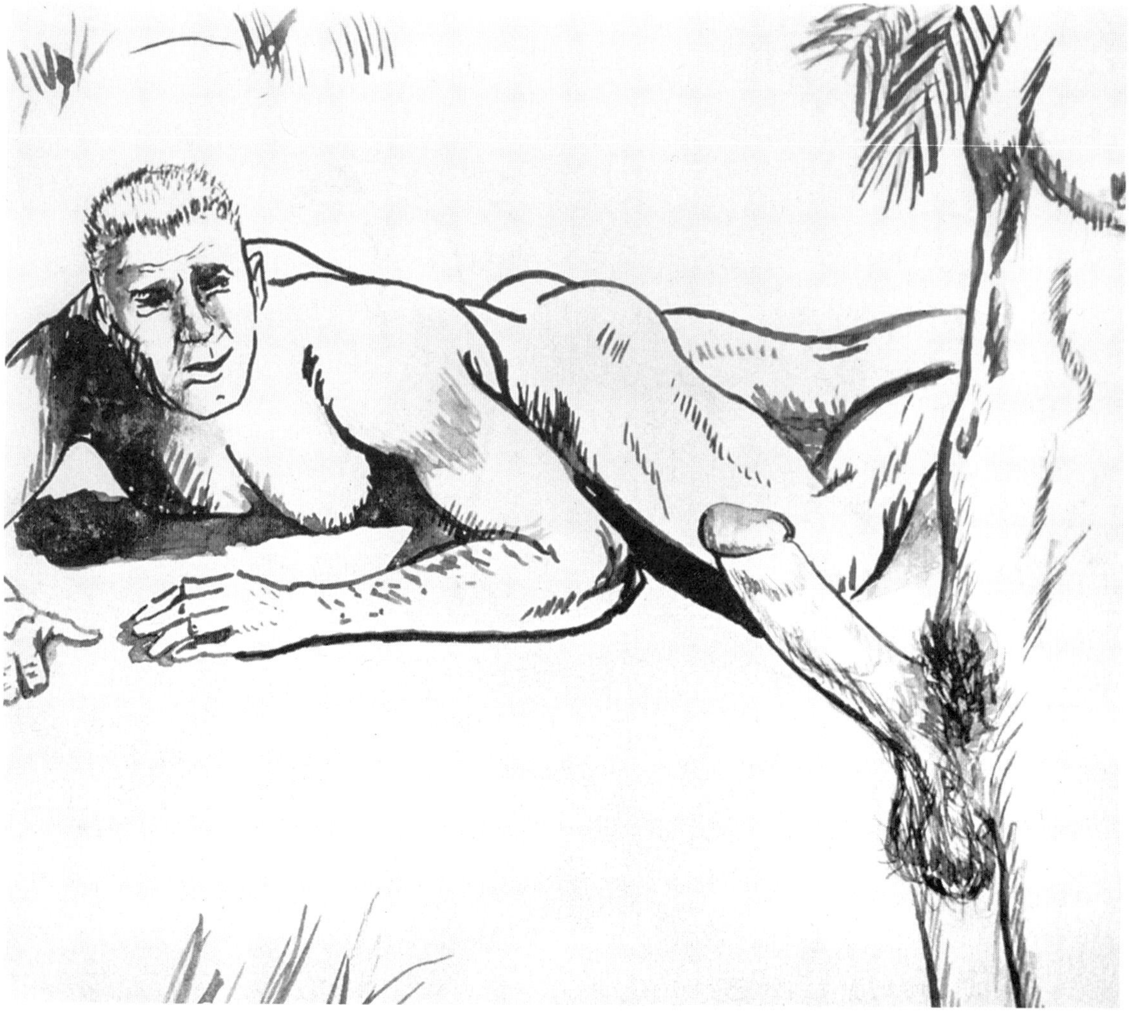

"Then a ripple appeared out in the middle of the ocean. A delicate, white splashing like an advancing wave developed. The ripple advanced rapidly in the direction of this part of the shore. As it reached the shallows and seemed about to break, suddenly in the middle of the wave a swimmer stood out. Quickly his body seemed to erase the wave . . .

123

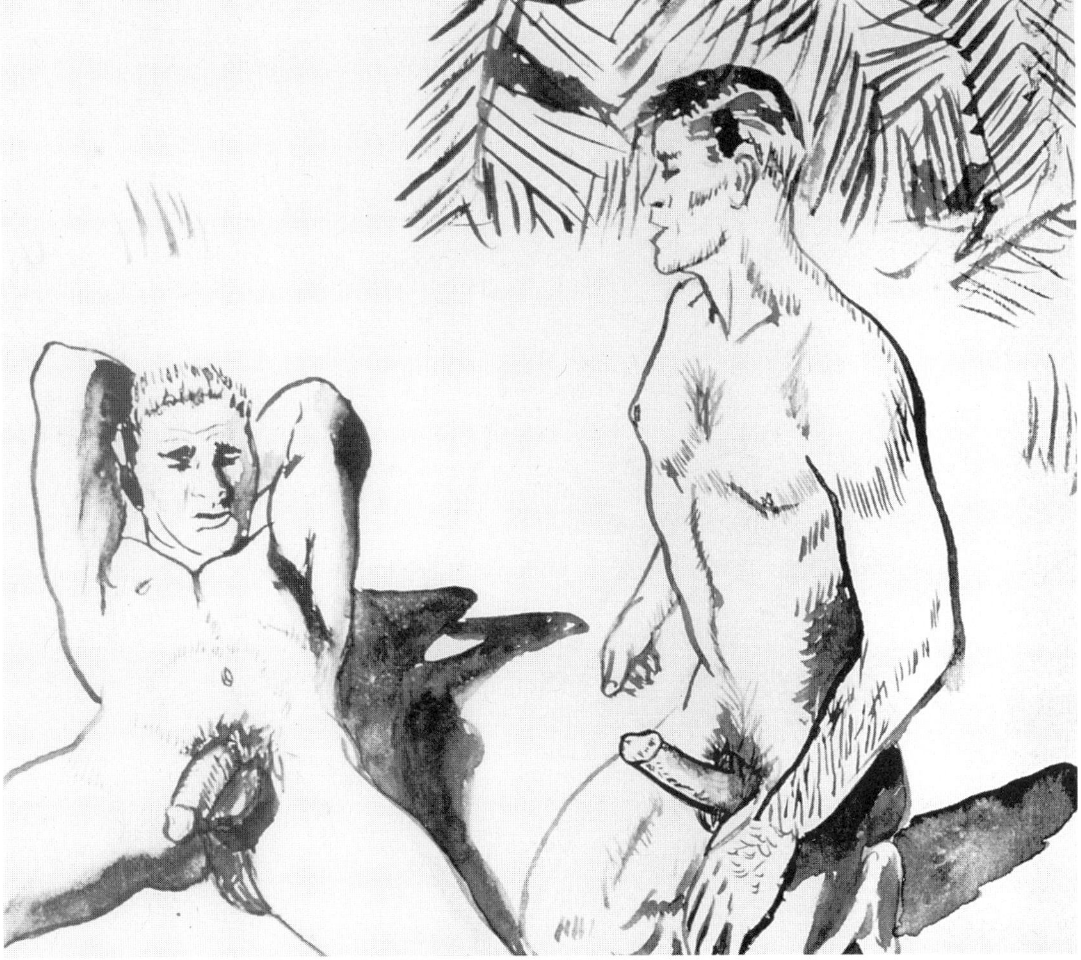

. . . Then he stood up. His sturdy legs kicked the ocean shallows as he walked forward. It was an amazingly beautiful young man. His body surpassed the sculptures of ancient Greece. . . . It overflowed with gentle beauty and carried such a noble column of a neck, such gently sloping shoulders, such a softly broad chest, such elegantly rounded wrists, such a rapidly tapering tightly filled trunk, such legs, stoutly filled out like a heroic sword. . . ." Yukio Mishima, *Forbidden Colors* ([1951] 1974, 25) **124**

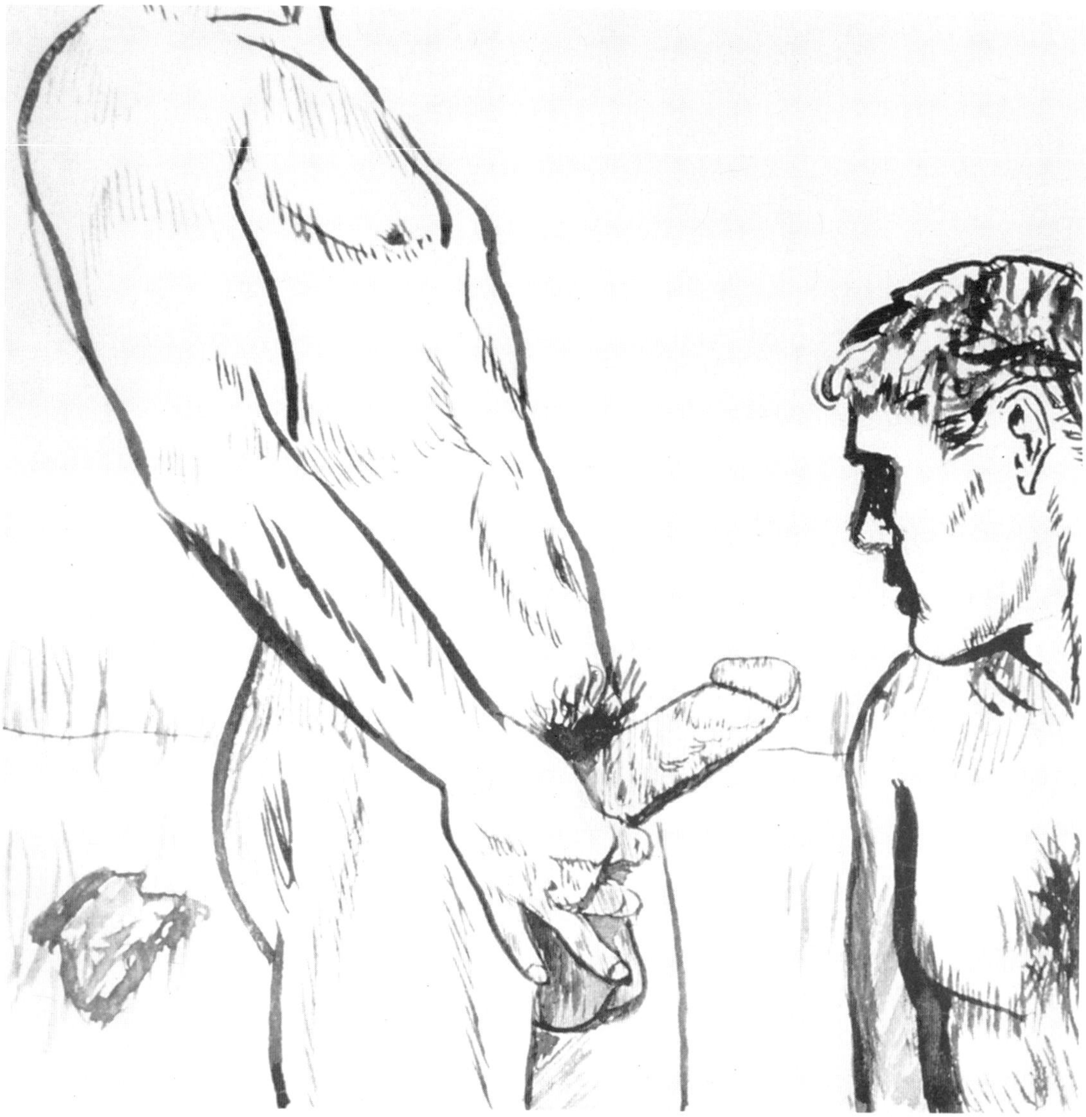

“‘. . . And from the time I saw you naked in the river—beautifully naked, white and perfect as an ancient god, strong, graceful—’ His hand was on Ephraim’s belly, almost spanning it. ‘I want to see you again as you were in the river—see you and adore you—’ [. . .] ‘It is yours to do with as you wish,’ Cyrus whispered . . .

125

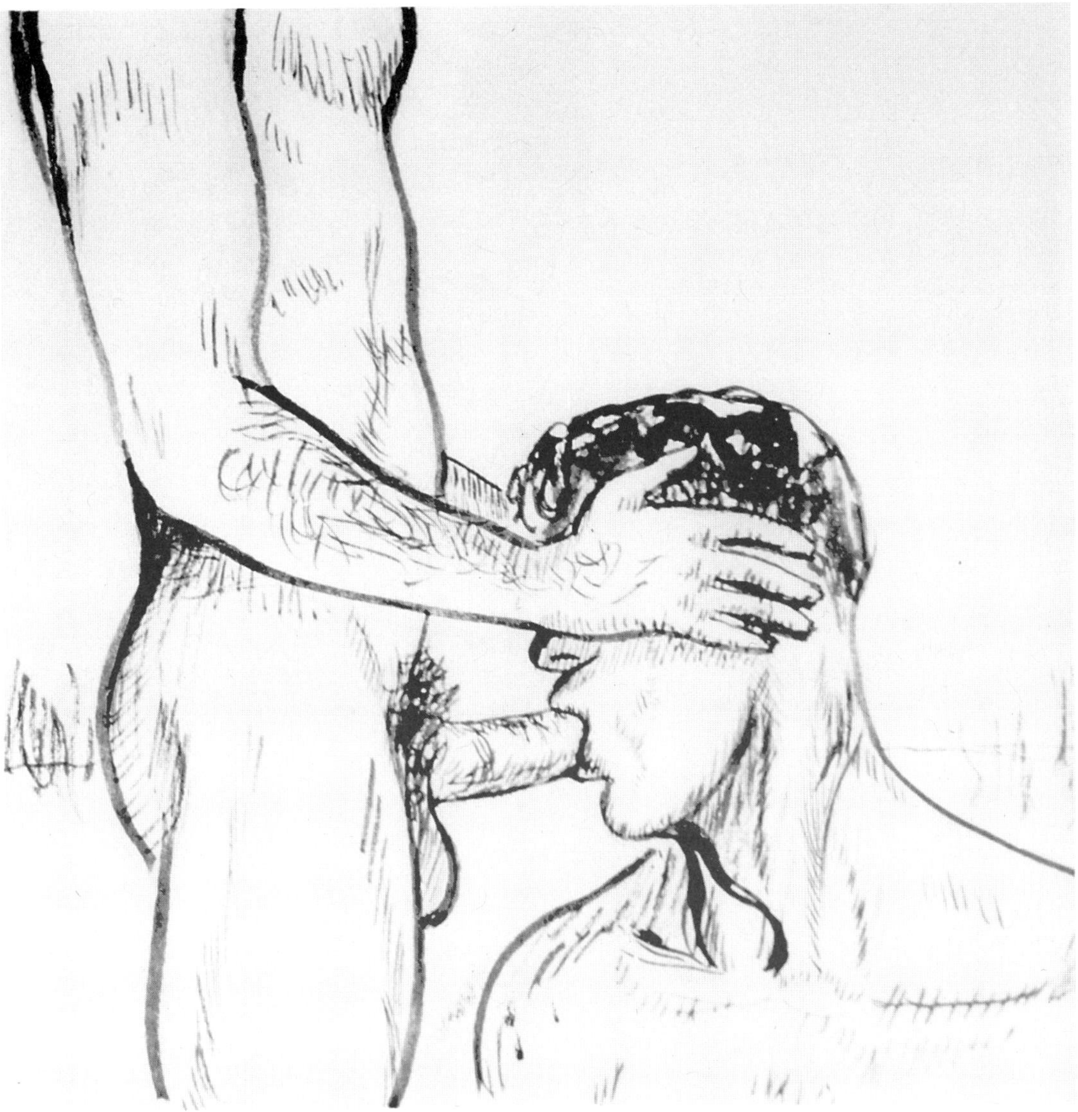

. . . Staring at Ephraim, he continued, ‘I am glad that I excite you, for I wish to make love to you, kiss you wherever I wish, take your penis in my mouth and drain your love from you, because you are beautiful and handsome.’ Ephraim answered slowly, ‘I want you to do that—and now I want to look at you, to enjoy the sight of you—’” Richard Amory, *Song of the Loon* (1966, 44-45) Out of print since the early seventies, *Song of the Loon* will be published by Arsenal Pulp Press in 2005 with an introduction by Michael Bronski. **126**

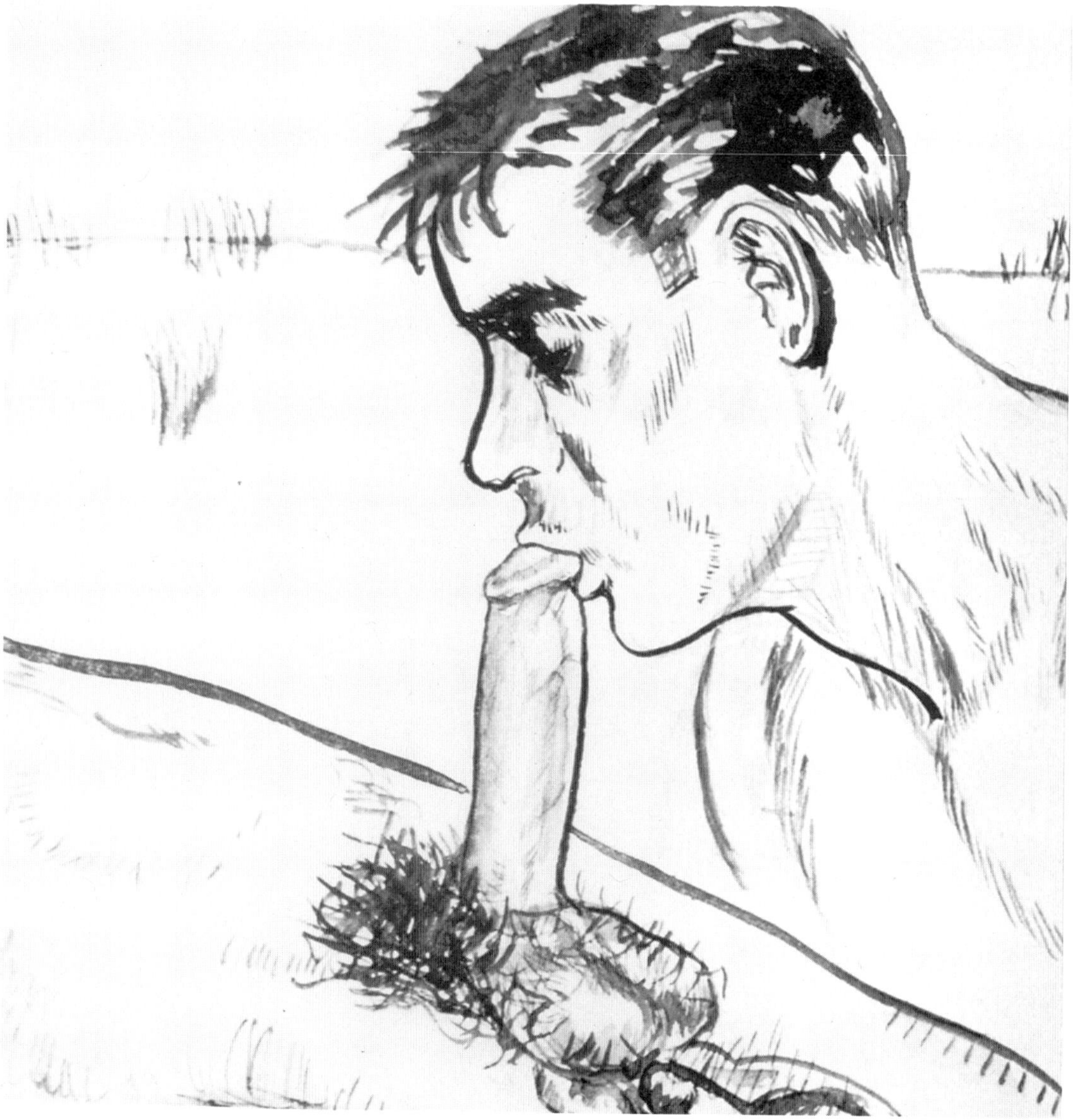

"André's phallicity was understandably tired. But it responded to his lips. . . . Hugh balked as he mouthed it. Was it really necessary to do this? And then he knew again it was . . .

127

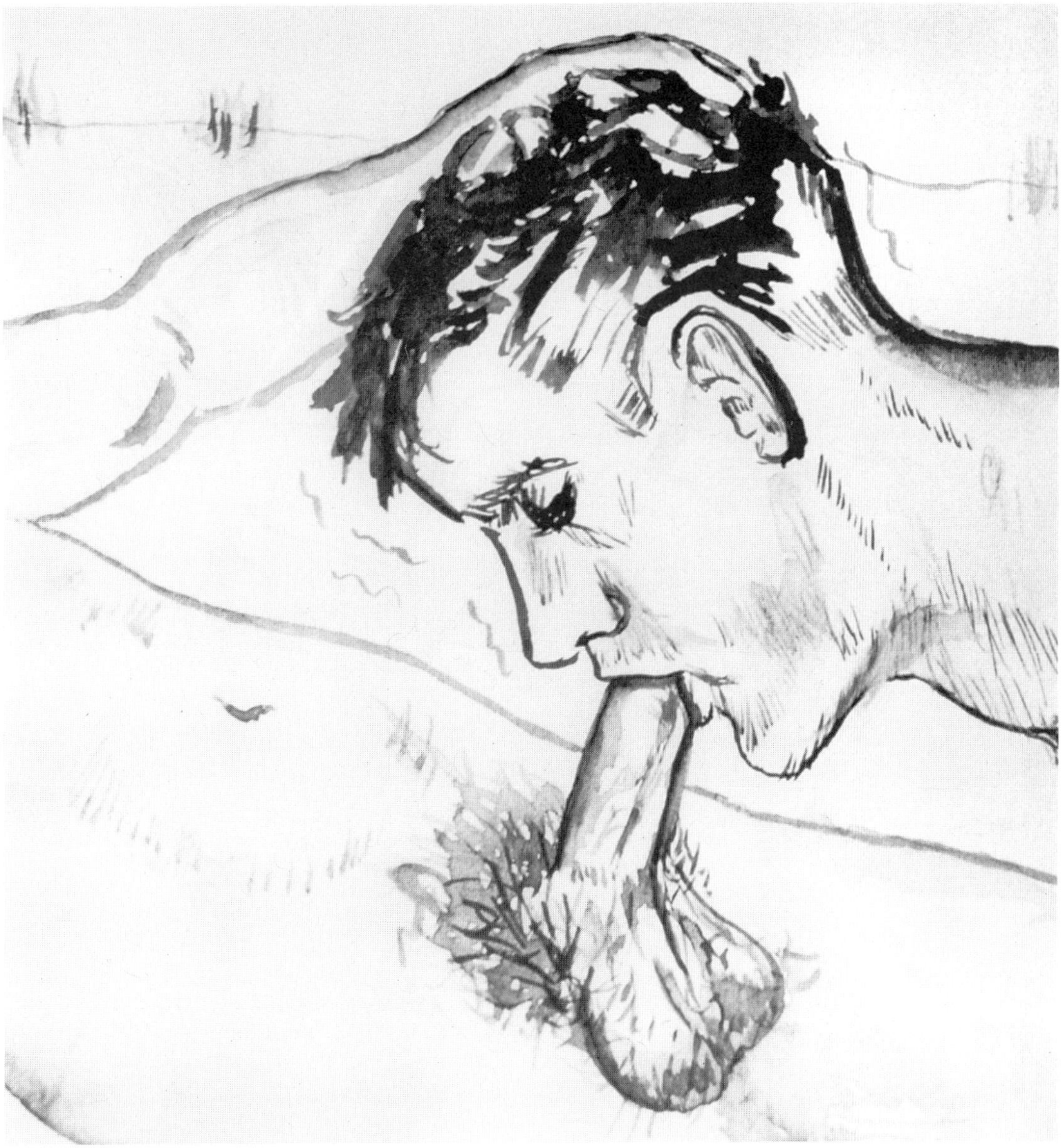

. . . and thrust himself wholehog onto the cock, foreskin unravelled to flower the cocktree till André was risen and the rood deep into Hugh's high humiliation. It was life, a life, given and taken. Carnivoracious charity. Till André took Hugh's head like a buttock and thrust steep onto him his life haemorrhaging against Hugh's gullet like the rich farewell of a Côte de Nuits. . . ." Scott Symons, *Place d'Armes* ([1967] 1978, 217)

128

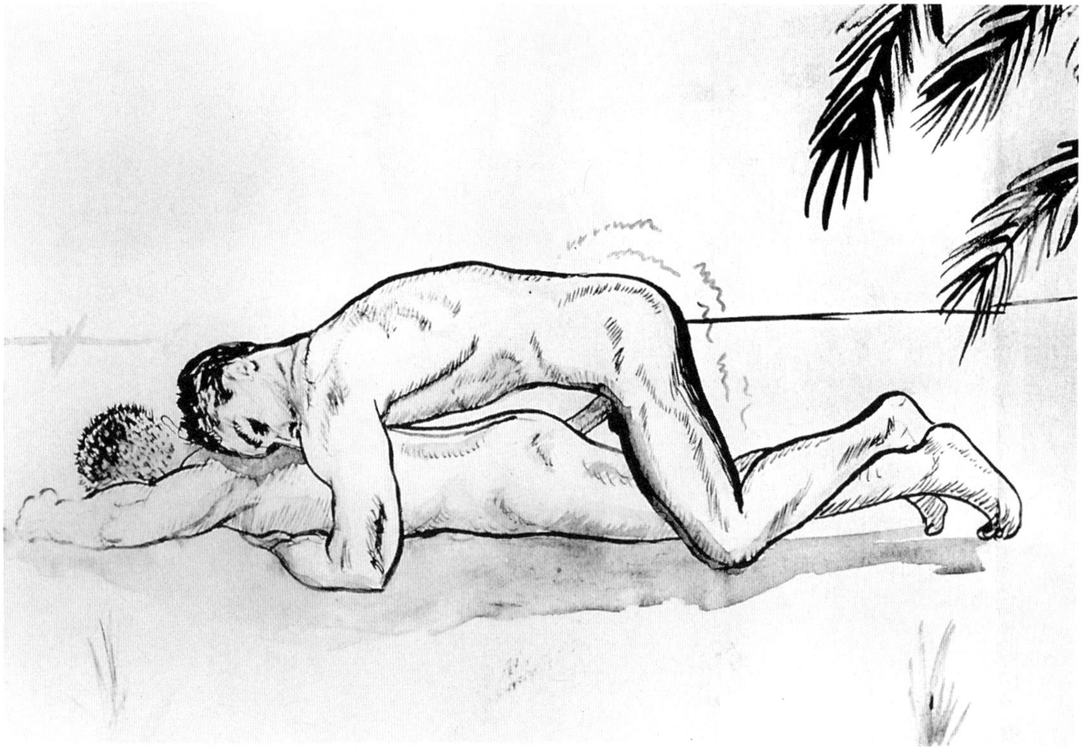

Looking at this series one final time, I realized I'd projected an entire ocean onto it and imagined the sound of the surf throughout. Although several frames include horizons that could imply the sea on the other side . . .

129

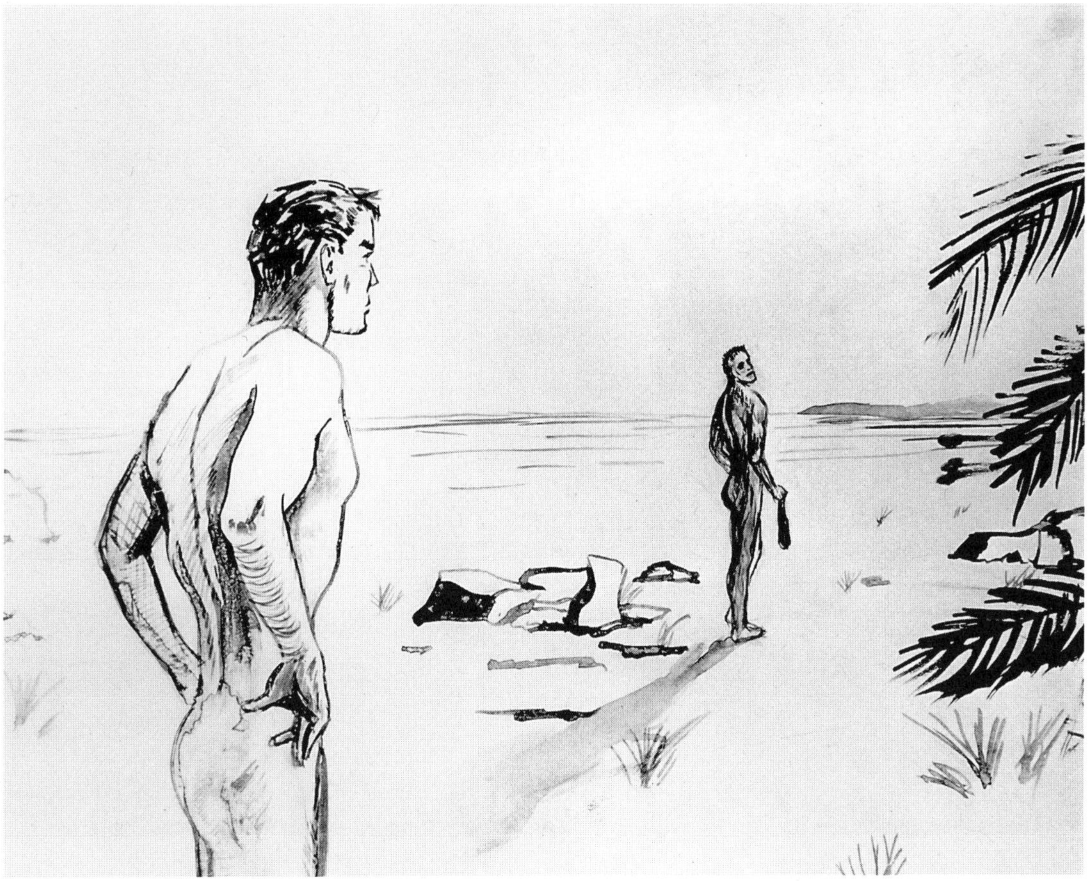

. . . it's really only in this final image, as the sexy stranger recedes into the vanishing point and a distant promontory, looking back just once, that the water is even hinted at . . .

130

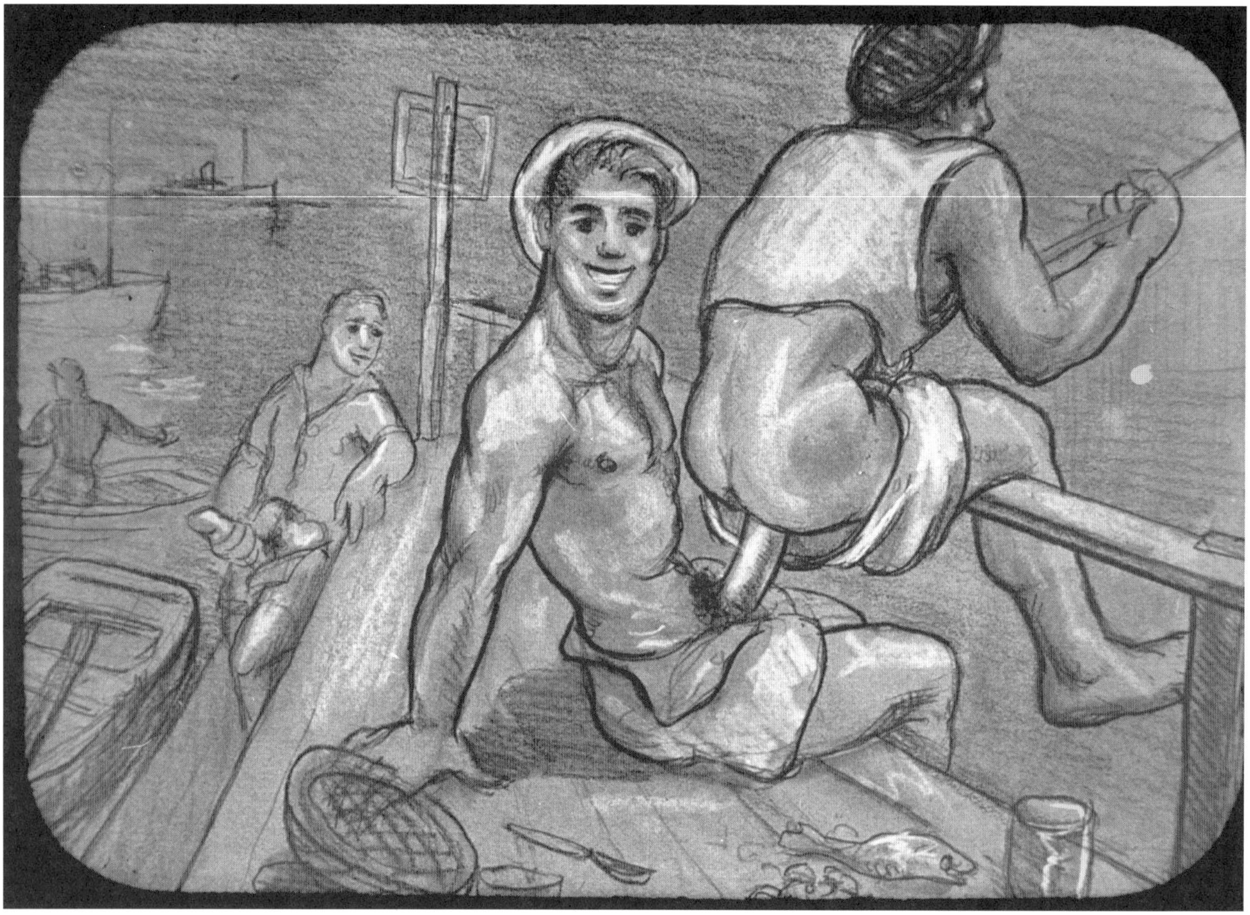

Happyface did lots of beach scenes, who knows whether they're supposed to be Brighton or some anonymous naval R&R site somewhere in the Empire. These two waterfront scripts, wharf and rowboat respectively, add variety to the beach formula. If this wharf scene defies the law of gravity, not to mention public-private decorum, and is unique in Happyface's work, he often revisited the boating fantasy, always complete with one or
131 more of those pesky skinny-dipper voyeurs—this time with a interracial dynamic.

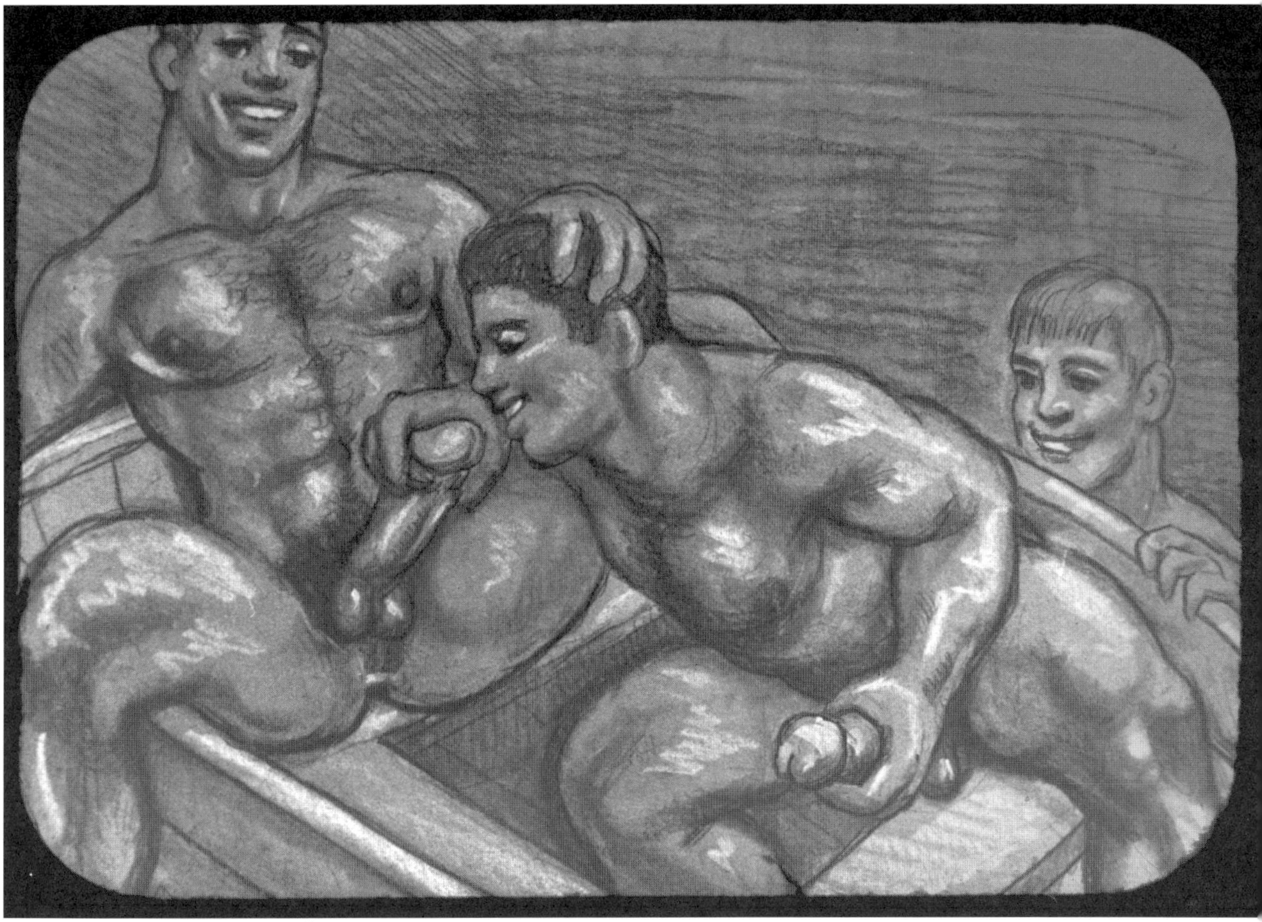

"... to hear human voices presently, or to feel the craft seized by the hands of someone splashing in the
water alongside. Only when several people had climbed in and crouched chattering around him did he
move his arm and squint up at them. Five young men, all whom looked remarkably alike, surrounded
him. Water dripped down upon him from their naked bodies. [. . .] During this time one of them dived
overboard, [. . .] and returned with a green coconut whose top he had sliced off. He began to let the water **132**
dribble into the photographer's face. . . ." Paul Bowles, "Tapiama," *Collected Stories* ([1957] 1980, 289)

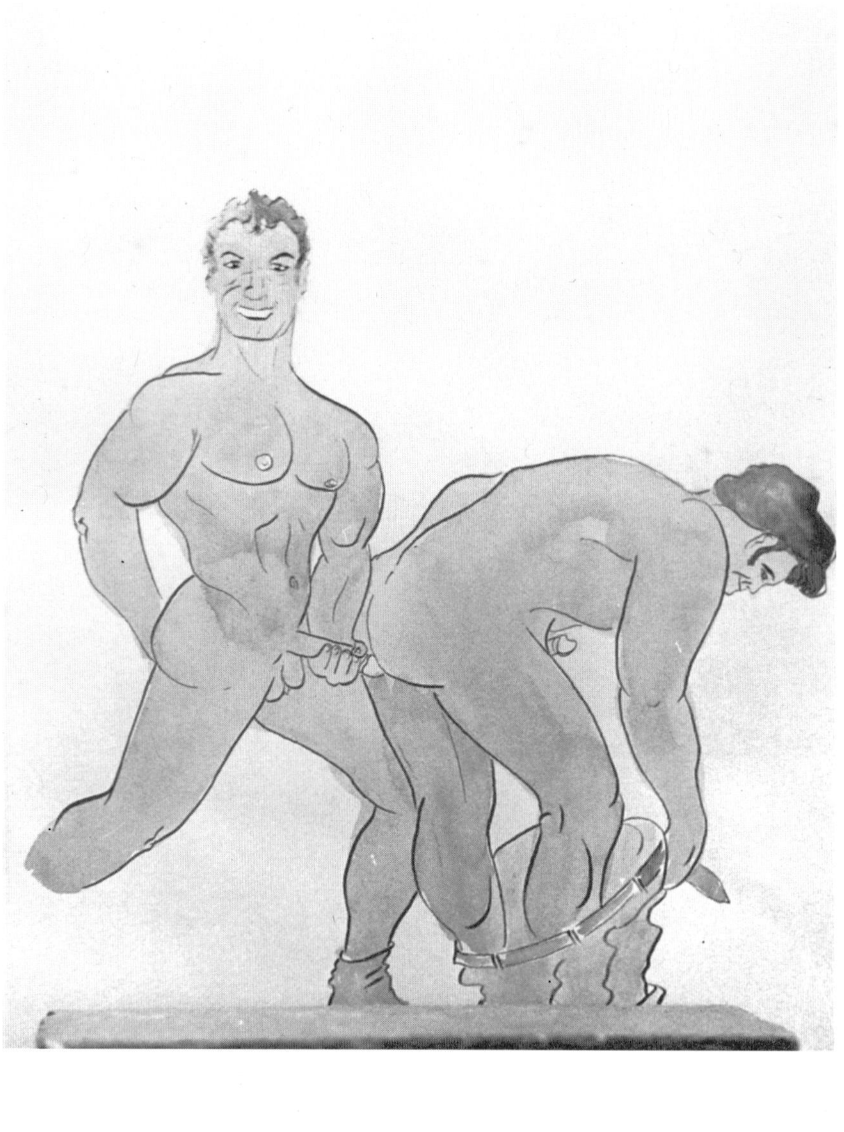

Faces were not this beach scriptwriter's strong point, but his real-world dicks, Elvis hairdos, and overall freshness of incident save the day. U.S.A., c. mid-1950s.

133

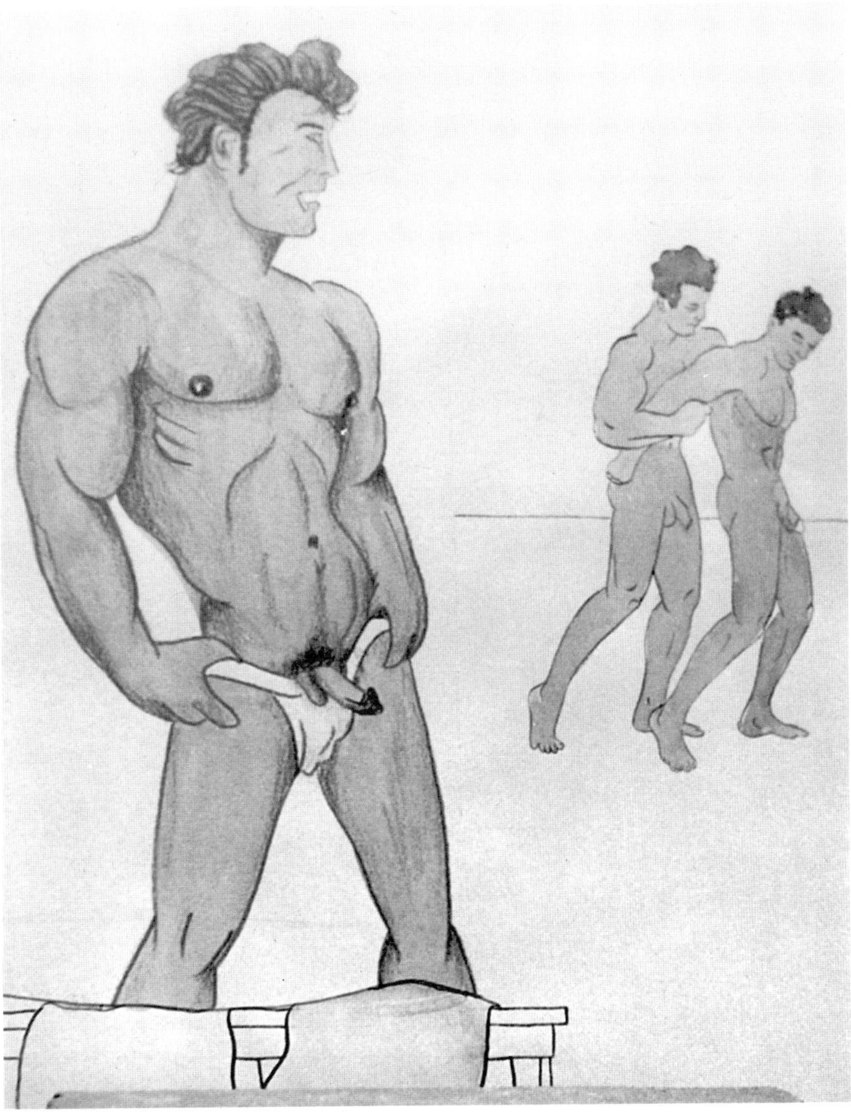

“‘Ah,’ said Joe, sitting down. ‘Wrestlers!’ We all looked at the two young sailors wrestling on the beach, their white bodies streaked with red where the sand had burned them. ‘Do you like to wrestle?’ asked Joe turning to me. I said no, and Mr. Royal, impervious to malice, repeated that I was a football player. ‘I can see that,’ said Joe, playing with two straws. . . .” Gore Vidal, “Three Strategems” *A Thirsty Evil* ([1950] 1981, 19) **134**

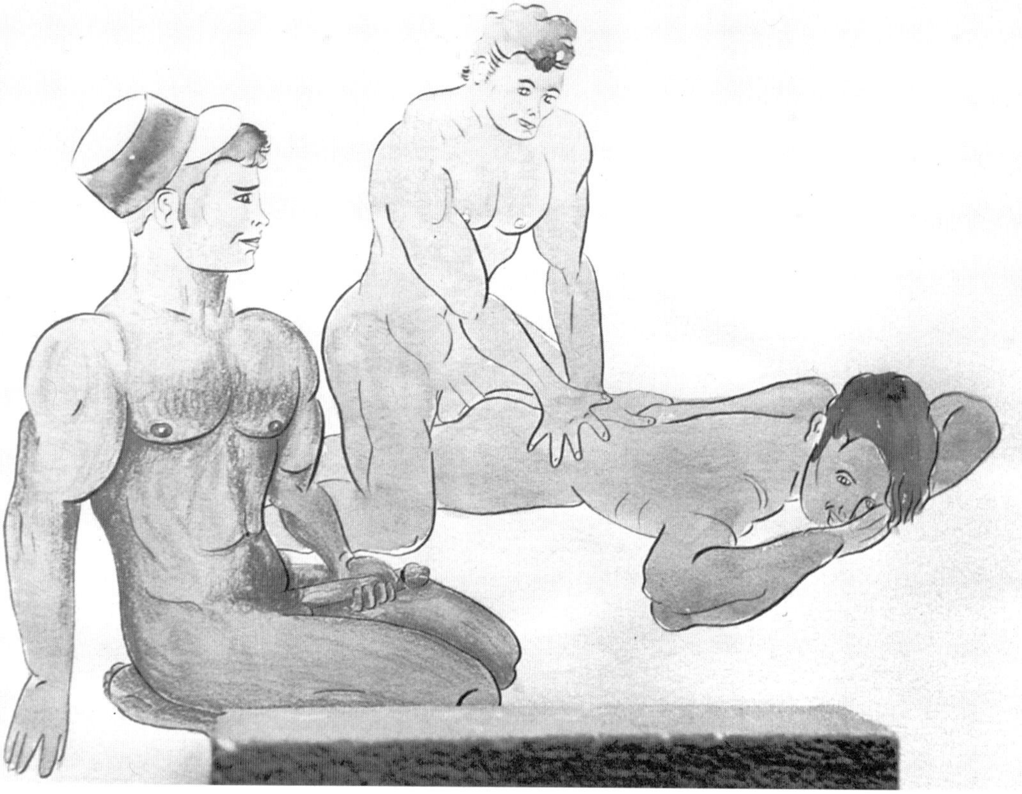

135

This image is apparently inspired by a softcore riff on artificial respiration by *Physique Pictorial's* in-house graphic artist Art Bob (Vol. 5, No. 4 [Winter 1955], 17). In the original, the foreground figure holds a lifesaving book rather than his penis, and instructs his pals on lung compression, not anal penetration. Our anonymous underground artist was in fact merely making explicit what the magazine was really winking and thinking about.

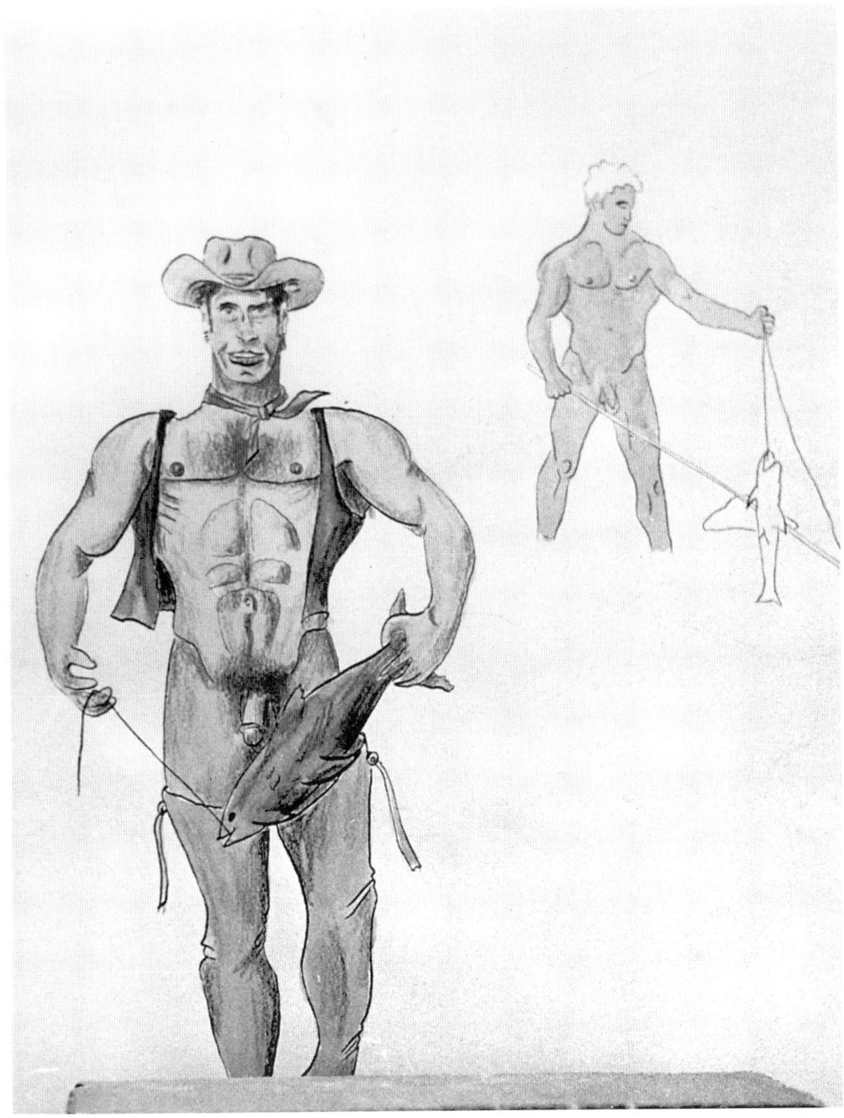

Why is this gym queen wearing his cowboy hat and leather vest while deep sea casting? Note the eraser or wooden edge that held down this four-image series when being re-photographed by some anonymous philanthropist . . . maybe even DuBek.

136

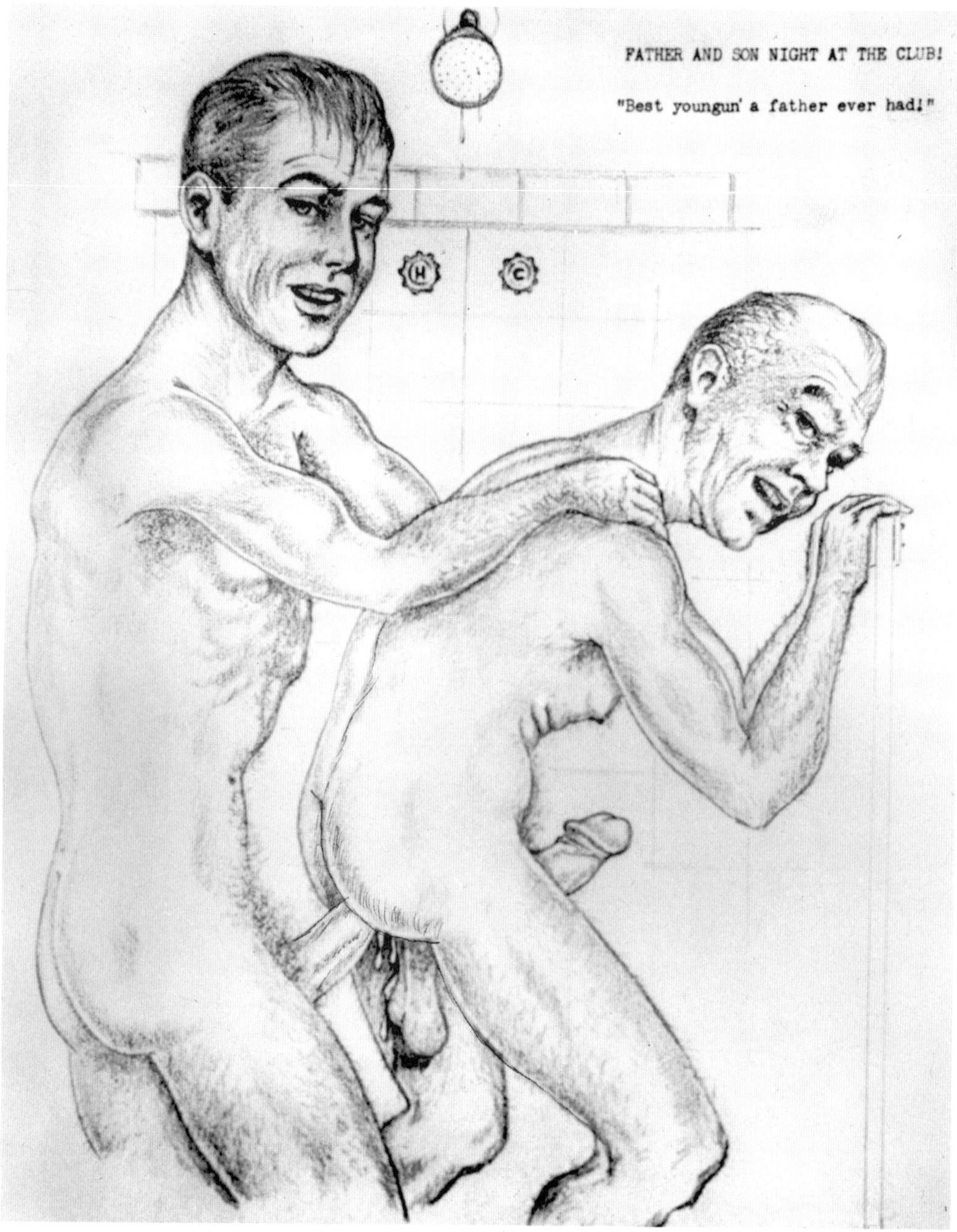

137 Showers are not beaches, but are the sites of primal aquatic scenarios all the same. I know this anonymous American artist, whom I call "Underwood," for several iconoclastic scenes of the 1960s, all commented on by acerbic typewritten dialogue. Possibly self-taught and dependent on photographs, Underwood's two images in *Out/Lines* dealt with race and with the military (Figures 184-185), and here he tackles another serious taboo. I am referring not to father-son incest, although that one certainly frightens the horses, but rather to *age*: is there another man over forty anywhere in this selection of erotic fantasies?

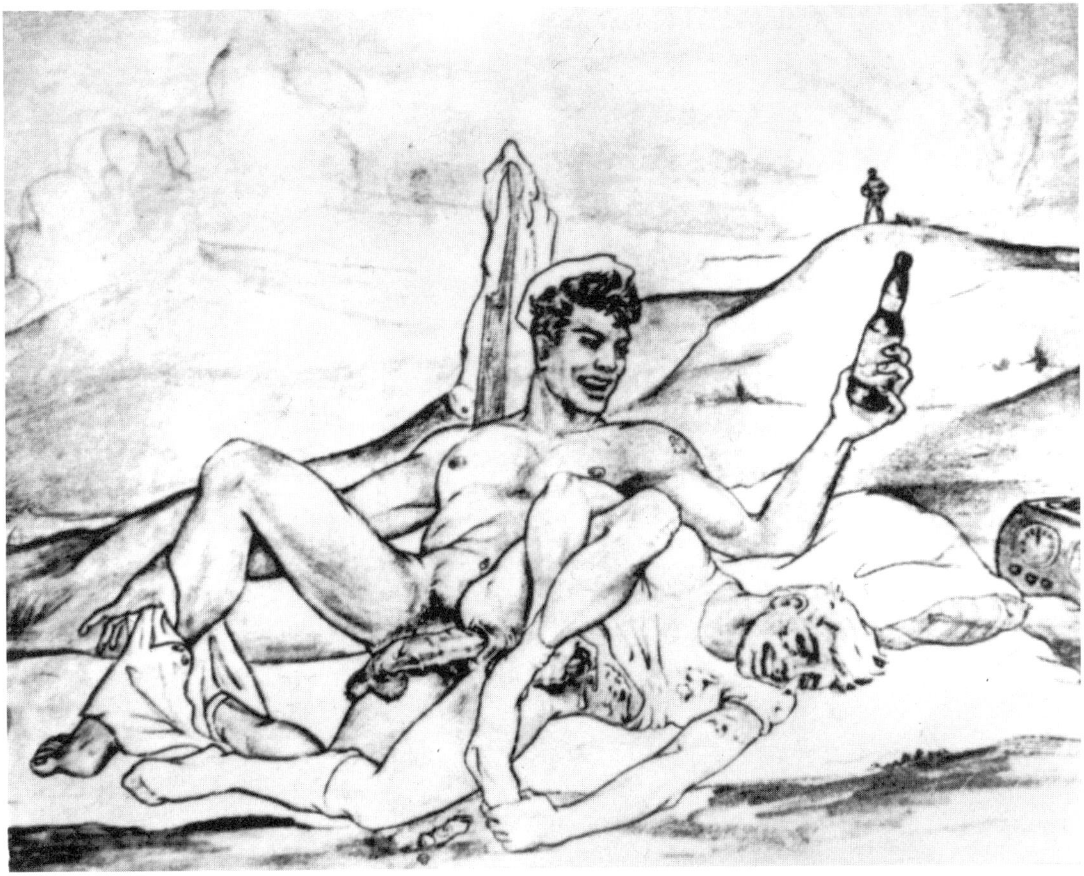

This idyl of military R&R from our WWII artist (see also Figures 116-17, 211), no doubt taking place after the battle of Iwo Jima or something, hoists its beer like product placement. Does the portable radio imply that DuBek should not have been dating this series to the forties, but rather the late fifties? Never mind, the anonymous artist was rather skilled at managing eight limbs not yet fully liberated from their standard issue boxers.

138

Please Master . . . : S/M

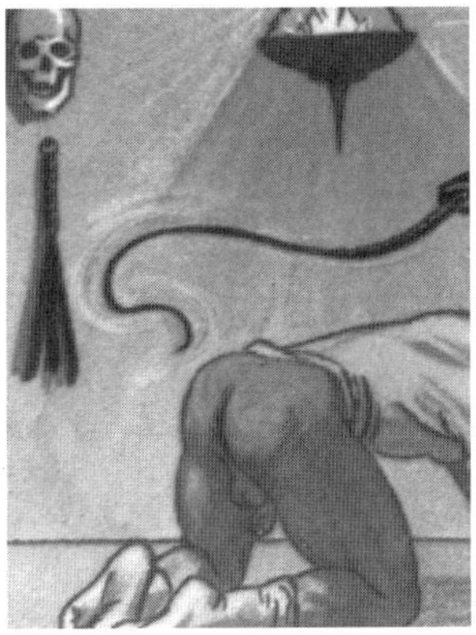

DuBek was not into S/M, but had a curious mind and commitment to exploring the gamut of human desire. His S/M collection is rich and bold. Myself, with no personal stake in the universe of ritualized interpersonal power play—other than an absolutely unequivocal intellectual and political commitment to diversity—my job too is to tell it like it is.

Please Master . . . : S/M

Perhaps my outsider status allows a slightly more objective assessment of the four or five S/M artists gathered together in this cluster of fifteen images, as well as those represented elsewhere in the book, whether fetish, kinky or leather-flavored or fully hardcore. (Elsewhere in *Lust,* see especially "The Captive" [fig. 84-92], but also entries by Caillaux [fig. 22] and Spartacus [fig. 234-235], and the anonymous whips/boots/toilet mural of 65-66. This is not to mention one self-censored image from the Frenchman "Cheekbones" described in the introduction.) Outsider "objectivity" is familiar as well in the commercial porn production sector, where producers often cater to the whole spectrum of turn-ons, regardless of whether it's their thing or not, in order to make a profit. I'm sure their insider customers can tell the difference.

My immediate observation about this corpus is that the bottom's pleasure is concretely visible in the form of erection or ejaculation in only two images. As in motion picture porno, it is a real challenge to show male sexual pleasure otherwise. To add to the complexity, only two of the fifteen pictures portray submission *without* bondage, as do two others elsewhere in the book, namely Bellhops' you-do-me-I-do-you switching tandem (114-115), in which the naughty, smiling reciprocity doesn't exactly capture the essence of power play. Is this duo an example of the un-implicated outsider production mentioned above? Otherwise, in the absence of the explicit denotation of consent in almost all of DuBek's S/M images, it is by no means clear to an outsider whether they are rape fantasies or submission/domination fantasies. The consent protocols of real-life interpersonal theatre are hard to spell out visually without recourse to dialogue or narrative sequence. I noticed a similar dynamic in more contemporary S/M visual narrative materials, the *Meatmen* comics that were the object of the Vancouver litigation (Leyland, 2000). However, in these more sophisticated and more intricate narratives, there is more play with the ambiguities around consent than in DuBek's simple vignettes from within an earlier, perhaps less self-conscious time and constituency.

It must be clear that I am personally attracted more to the camp theatricality of these scenes than to their fantasy world. While I can respect the icy fetish artistry of the three-way bondage scene (fig. 151), I respond more instinctively to spooky shadows (fig. 140), melodramatic post-coital headaches (fig. 141), or demonically cross and cross-eyed daddies (fig. 146), the end of a whip tenderly wound around the mother of all erections with fulgent flares flaming out. But maybe my outsider irreverence can yield an insight: do these eruptions of theatricality in S/M offer better raw material to the graphic eroticist than the time-based stasis around endurance, isolation, or total surrender, or the dark silence of the gag or the hood?

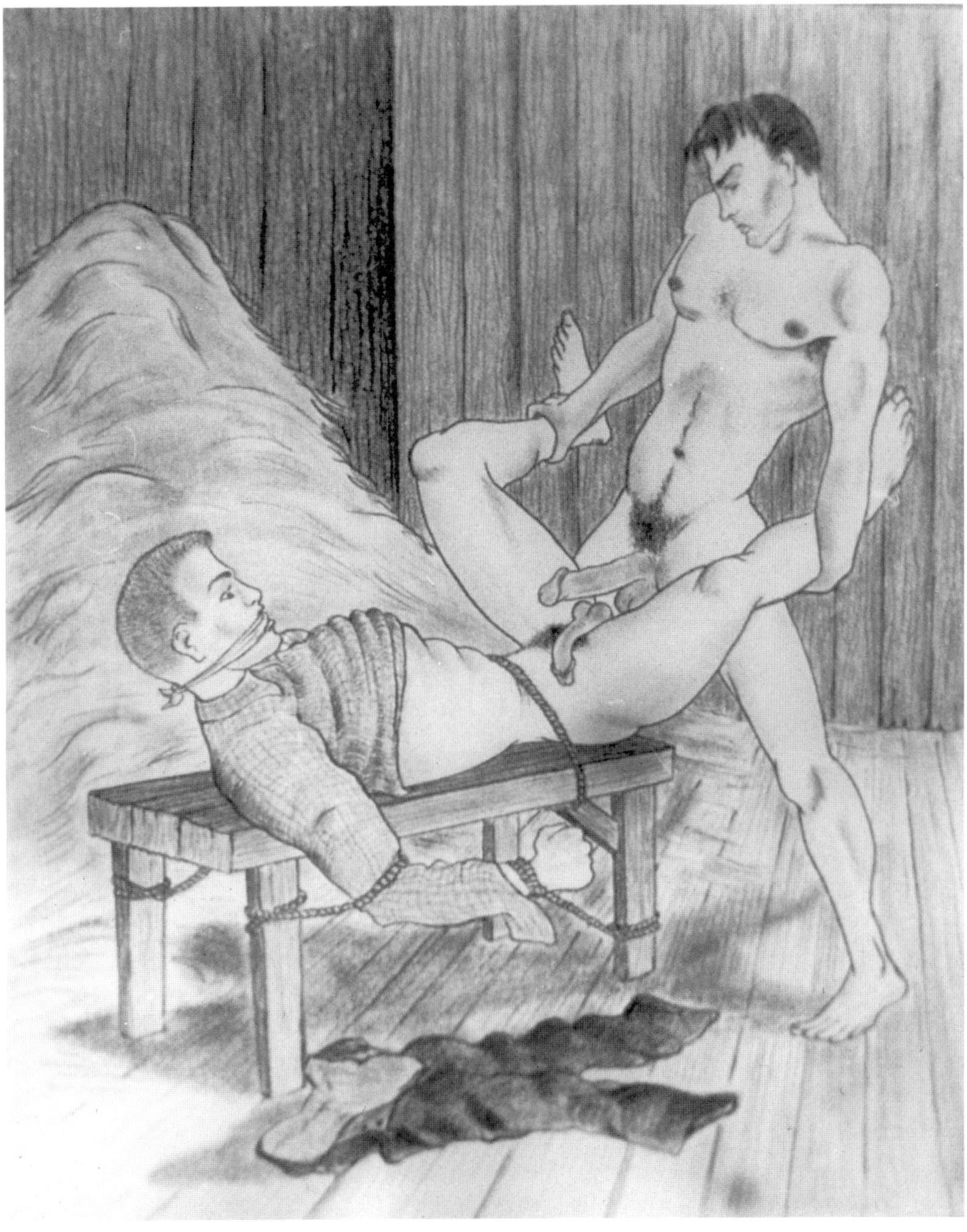

This five-image bondage series has icy precision, and unfolds in the archetypal settings of American boyhood, from the barn to the high school gym. As is common in S/M erotic fantasy, the consent protocols in these fifteen vignettes can be inferred but are not explicit.

139

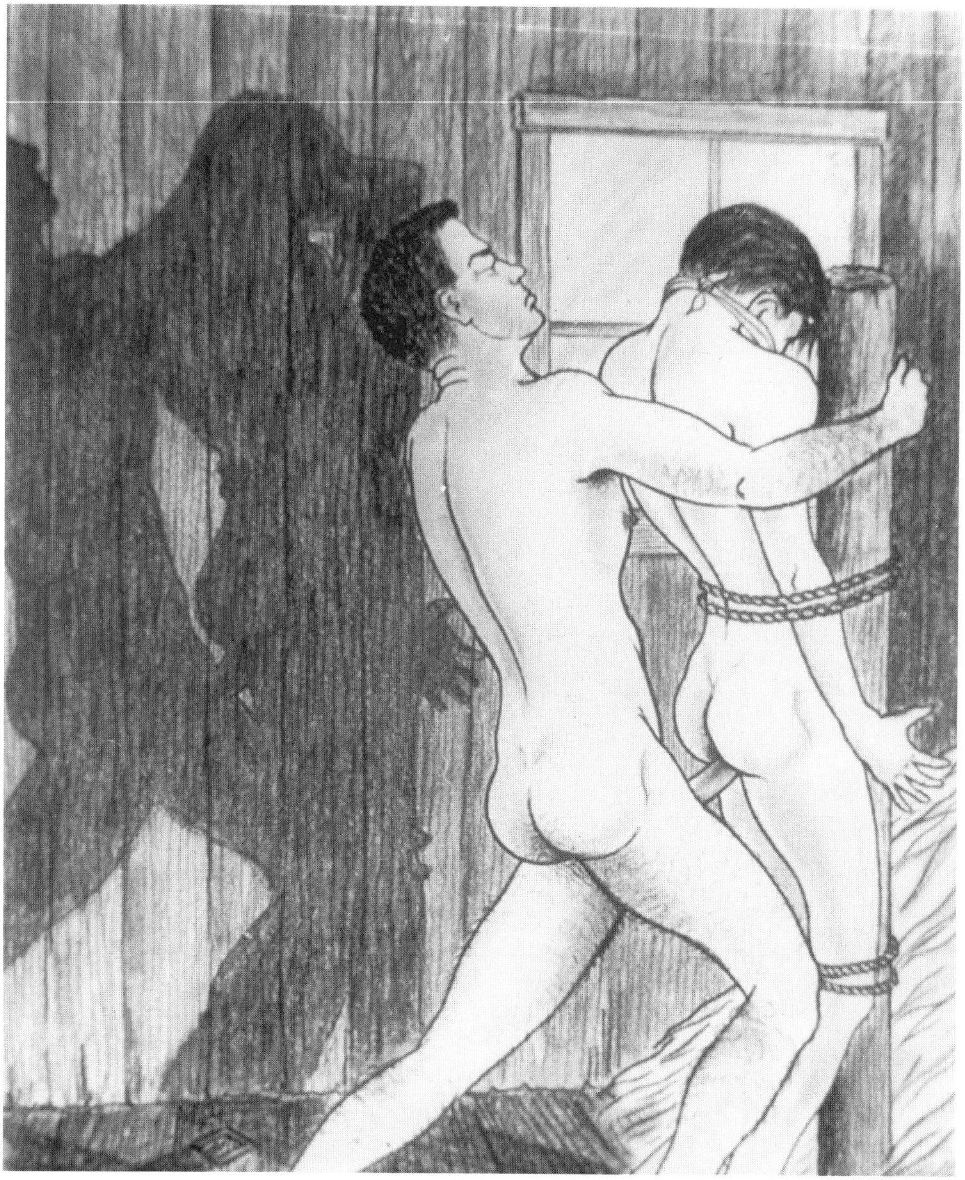

"Suddenly, overwhelmed equally by rage and desire, Jim threw himself at Bob. They grappled. They fell across the bed. Bob was strong but Jim was stronger. Grunting and gasping, they twisted and turned, struck out with arms, legs, but Bob was no match for Jim and, at the end, he lay facedown on the bed, arm bent behind him, sweating and groaning. Jim looked down at the helpless body, wanting to do murder. Deliberately he twisted
140 the arm he held. Bob cried out . . .

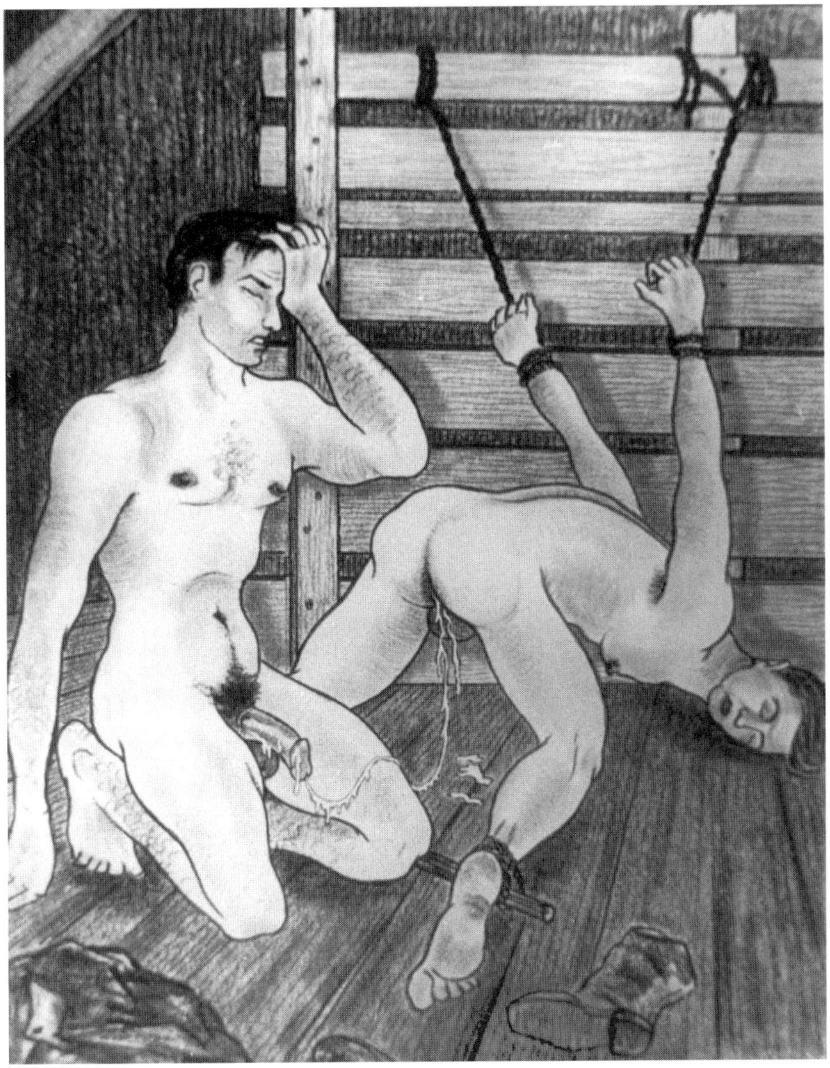

. . . Jim was excited at the other's pain. What do do? Jim frowned. Drink made concentration difficult. He looked at the heaving body beneath him, the broad back, ripped shorts, long muscled legs. One final humiliation: with his free hand, Jim pulled down the shorts, revealing white, hard, hairless buttocks. 'Jesus,' Bob whispered. 'Don't. Don't.'

Finished, Jim lay on the still body, breathing hard, drained of emotion, conscious that the 141
thing was done, the circle was completed, and finished."Gore Vidal, *The City and the Pillar* ([1948; 1965] 2003, 203)

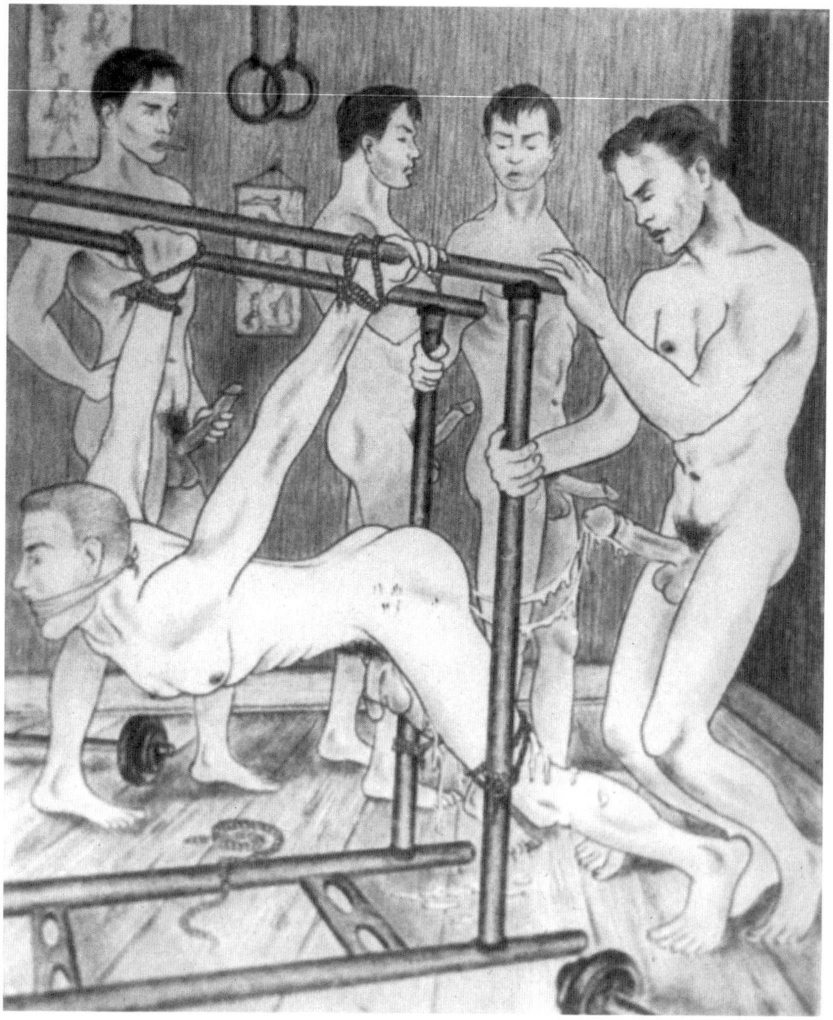

"Long shot of Mick and the four Whips confronting each other...Rowntree: *Take off your coat.* Mick takes off his coat deliberately, holding it with one hand. *Go to the bars.* [. . .] He turns to face the Whips at the far end of the gym, leaning indolently against the bar. Rowntree: *Bend over.* [. . .] he bends over. Rowntree . . . runs forward, giving him a tremendous swipe with his cane. He returns to his place, walking, pauses, then runs back and
142 beats Mick again. . . ." Lindsay Anderson and David Sherwin, *If. . .* ([film, 1968] 1969)

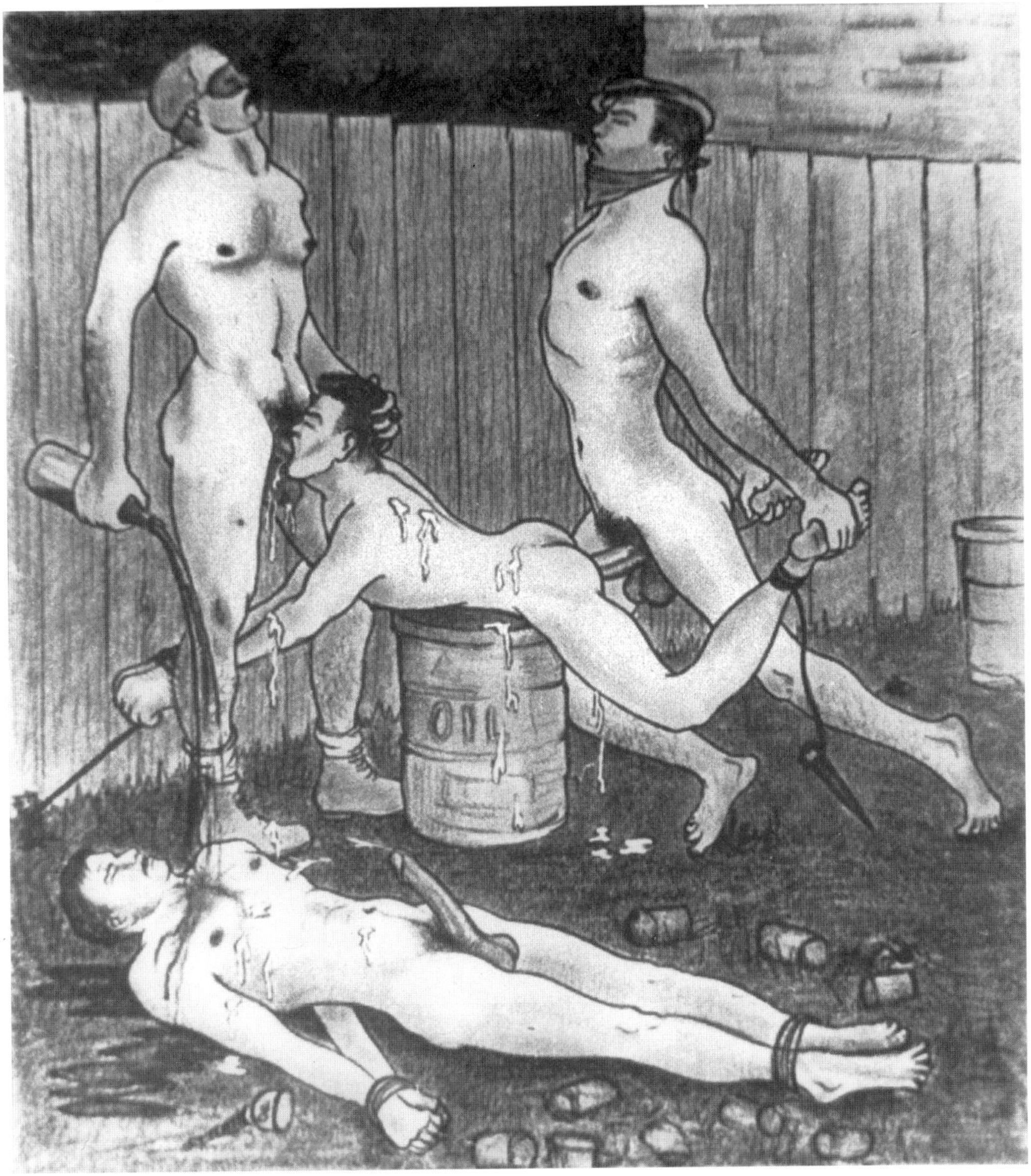

There's something about these ropes of cum here and opposite that recall "The Captive" (84-92, especially 88). Different media, different narrative structure, bulkier bodies . . . but same cum, similar graphic style, same scene . . . tentatively same artist, no? This final complex orgy, located in a back alley behind the garage or bikers' clubhouse (beer cans strewn over the ground), suggests other questions as well: why the masks? what's
the additional liquid? why a different visual quality from the rest of the series? and why is everyone seemingly 143
floating just off the ground?

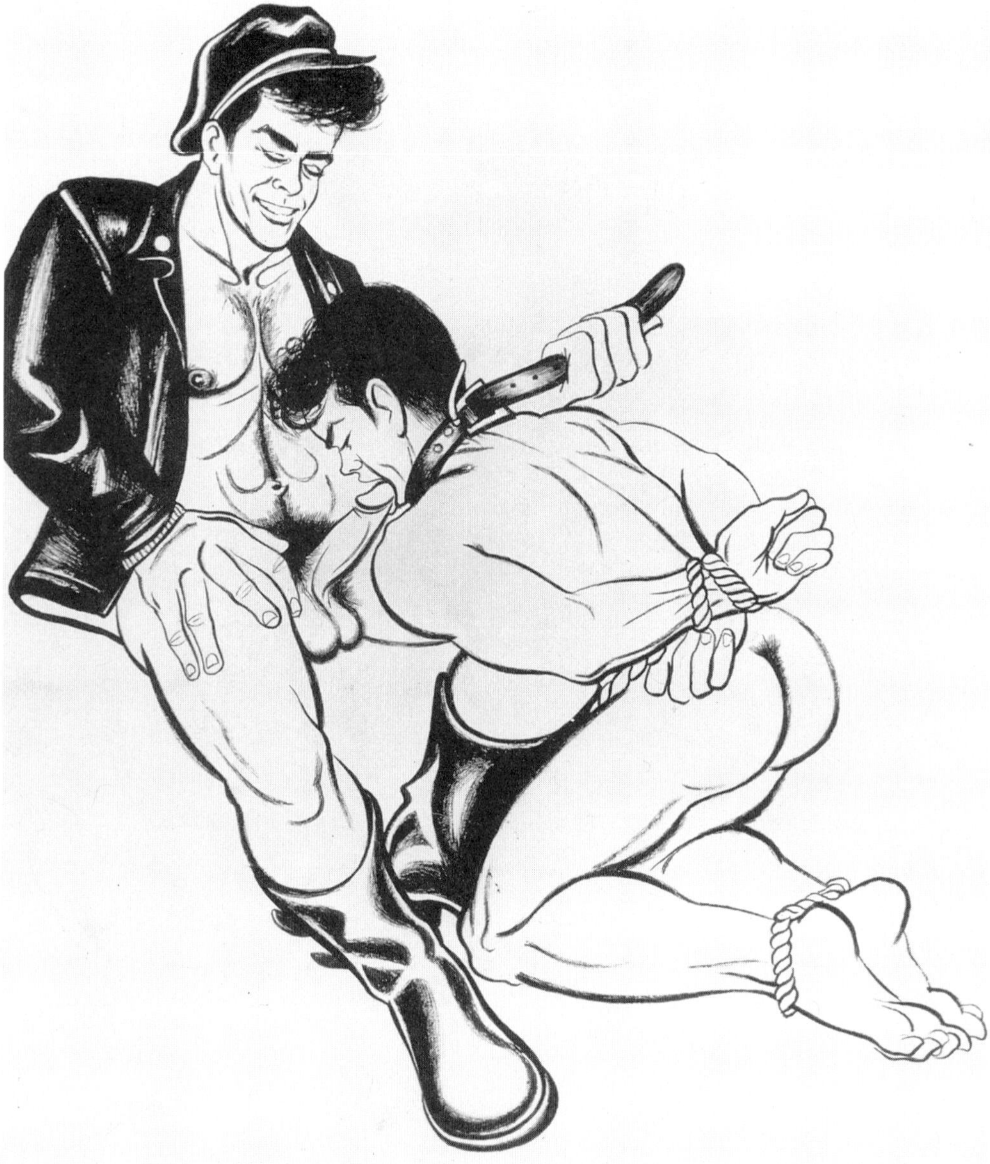

More serious boots from the sure-handed crafter of the smiling toughie of Figure 117 (see also 174-175, 207), not to mention the other lovingly delineated accessories. Obviously a confident commercial artist—perhaps in the comic book sector? U.S., c. 1965.

144

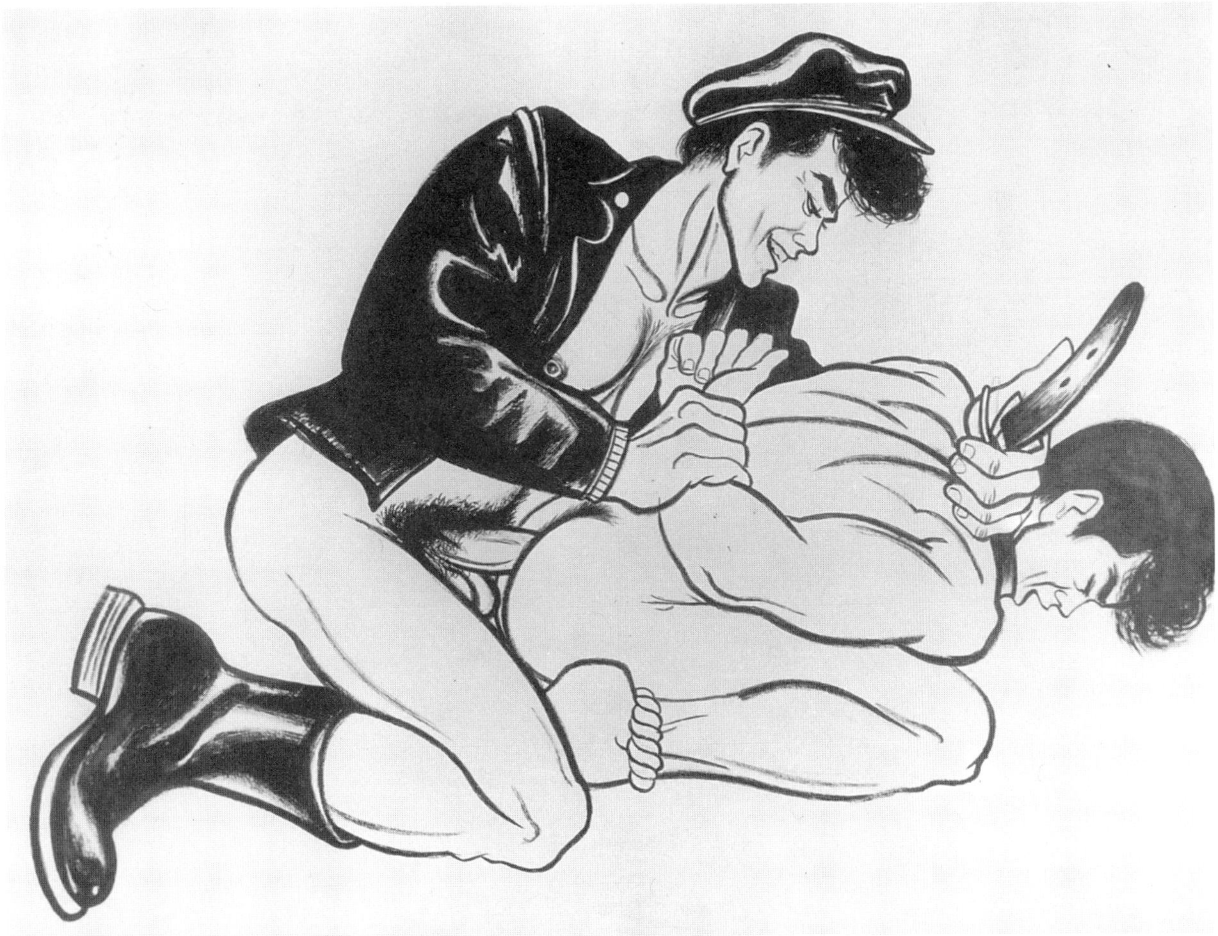

"I had a presentiment then that there is in this world a kind of desire like stinging pain. Looking up at that dirty youth, I was choked by desire, thinking, 'I want to change into him,' thinking, 'I want to be him.' Yukio Mishima, *Confessions of a Mask* ([1949] 1958, 8)

145

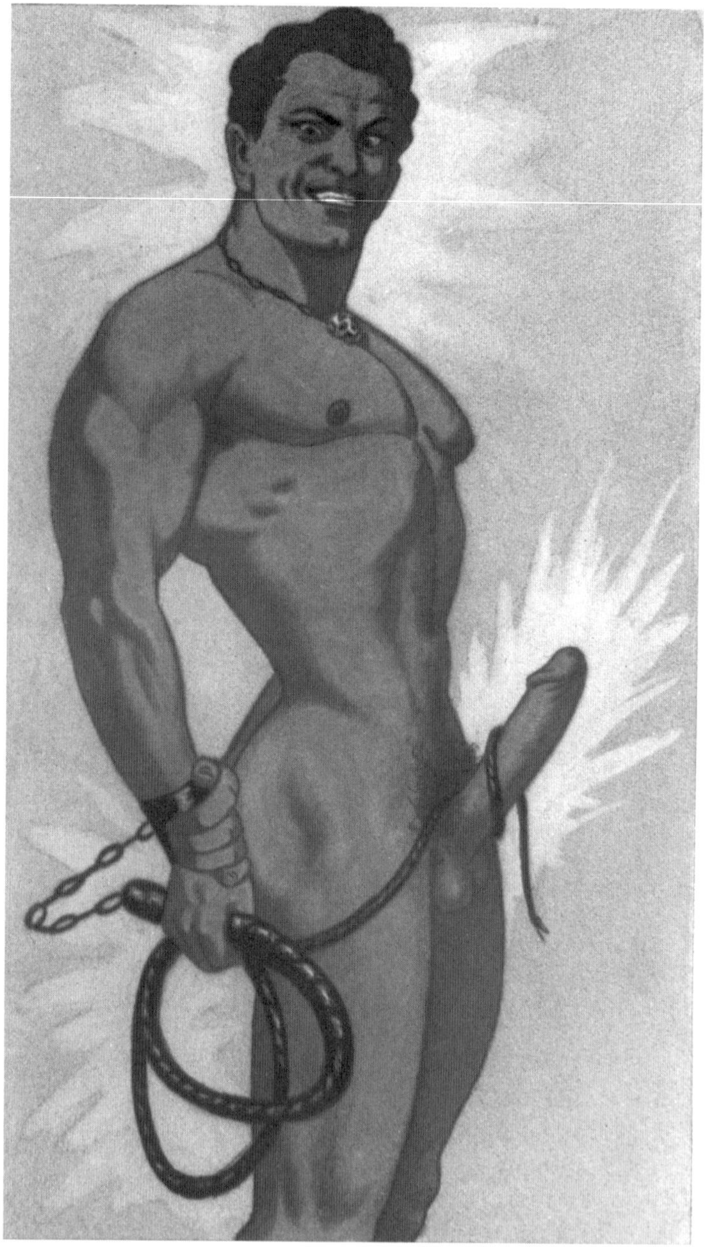

146 "please master, please look into my eyes, / please master order me down on the floor." Allen Ginsberg, "Please Master" ([1968] 1983, 338). Another comic book artist on sabbatical from drawing super villains? This over-the-top stylist is at his best when he injects an edge of high camp, as here or in Figure 64. No decor here. A pity, for sometimes the decor of satanic dungeons—and attics—is a little more exciting than the activities that take place therein, as opposite.

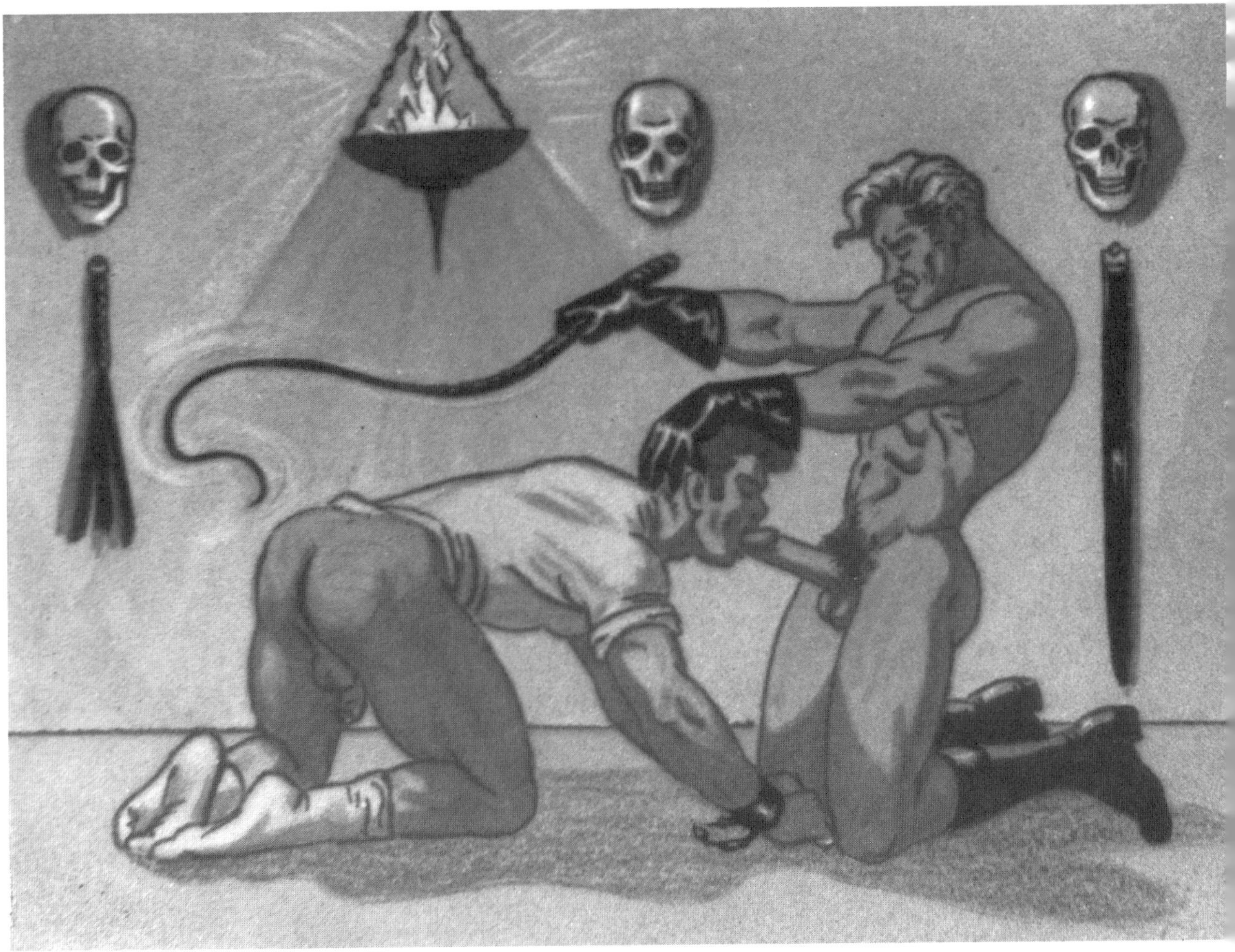

"The walls were completely draped with some blood-red bunting [. . .] purloined from one of the store-rooms [. . .] In the front part of the room stood some low boxes, covered with material, which served as seats; at the back, in the acute angle formed by the sloping ceiling and the floor, a sort of bed had been made, large enough for three or four people, and this part could be darkened by the drawing of a curtain [. . .] .

On the wall by the door hung a loaded revolver. Törless did not like this room." Robert Musil, *Young Törless* ([1906] 1971, 52) 147

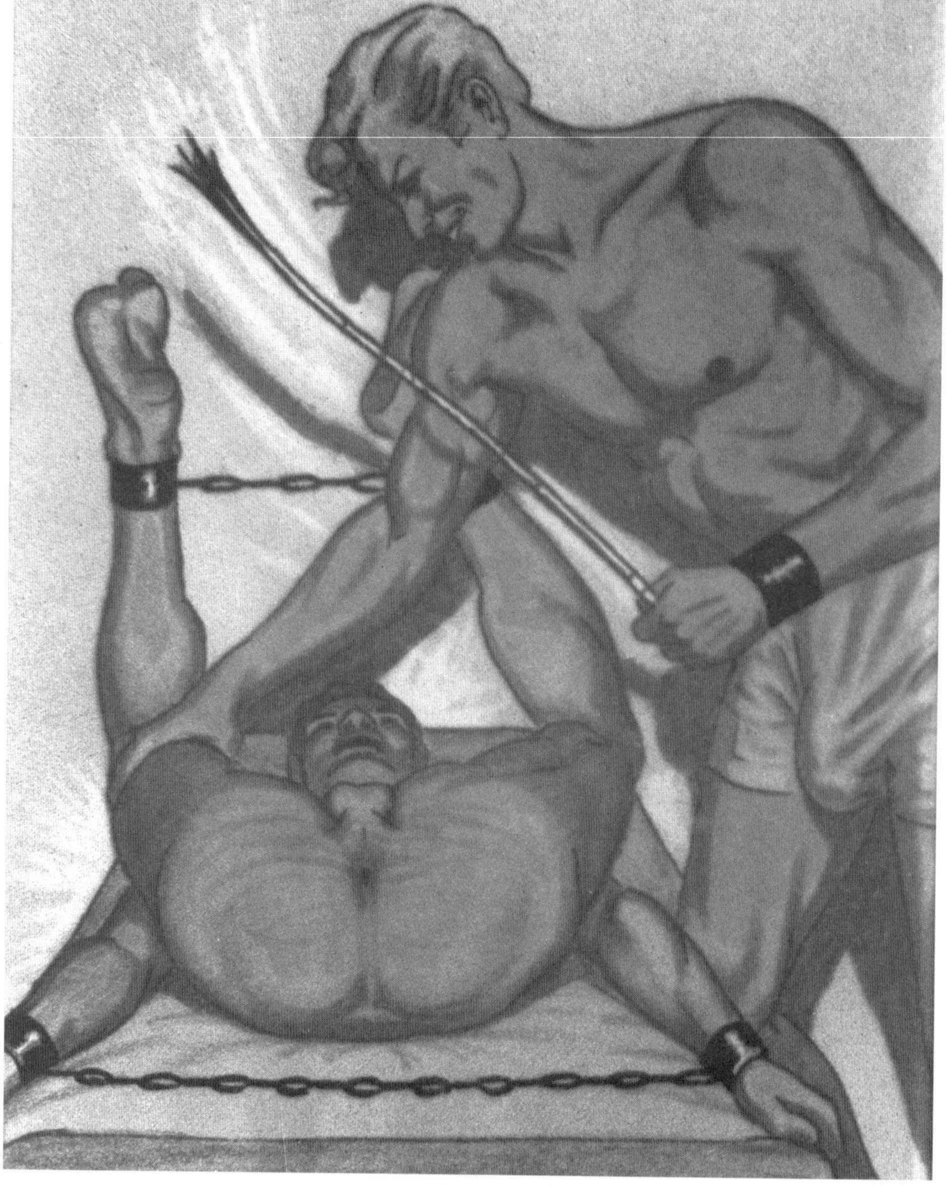

"But the hot proximity of the soft skin, this other person's skin, haunted him, enclosing him, suffocating him. And Basini kept on whispering: 'Oh yes . . . oh yes . . . please . . . oh, I should so gladly do whatever you want!'

Törless could find nothing to say to this. While Basini went on whispering and he himself was lost in doubt and consideration, something had sunk over his senses again like a deep green sea. Only Basini's flicker-
148 ing words shone out in it like the glint of little silvery fishes . . .

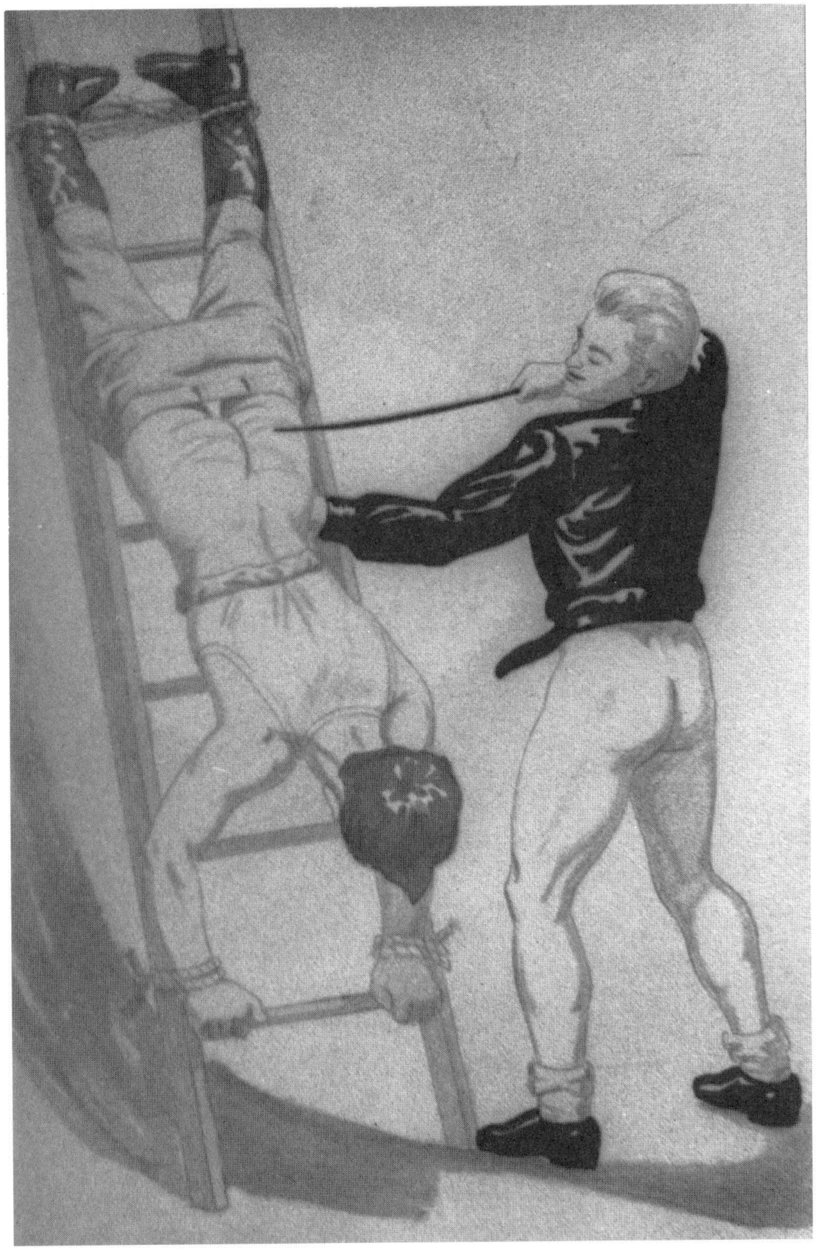

. . . He was still holding Basini off with his arms. But something made them heavy, like a moist tepid warmth; the muscles in them were slackening . . . he forgot them. . . . Only when another of those daring words touched him did he start awakening again, all at once feeling—like something fearful and incomprehensible—that this very instant, as in a dream, his hand had drawn Basini closer." Robert Musil, *Young Törless* ([1906] 1971,143) **149**

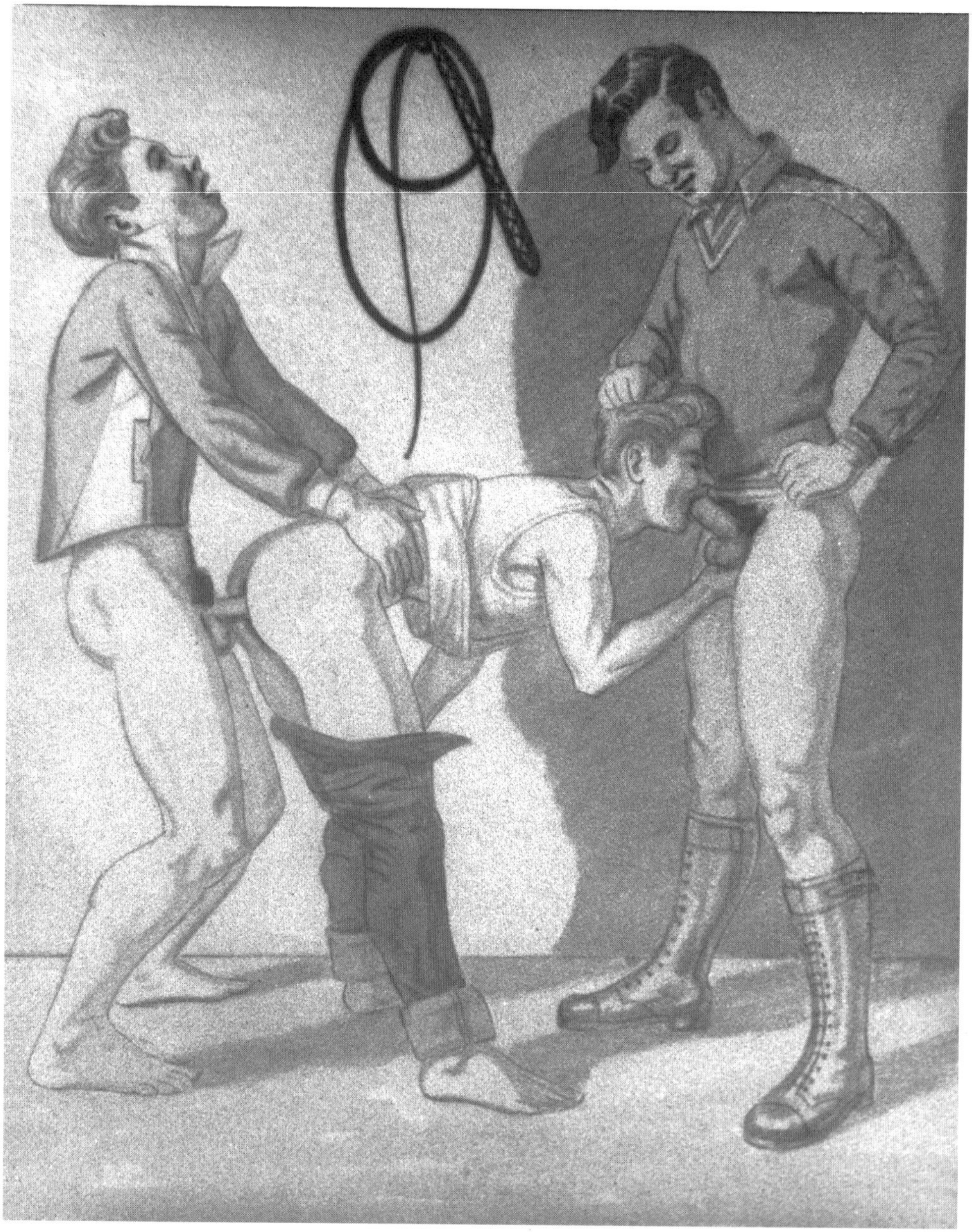

"A gurgling in his throat—and he rises on his knees, face pressed against the wide belt, which he unbuckled urgently with his teeth. Like a dog retrieving a stick and bringing it back to its master, with his teeth clutching the buckle [. . .] crouched on all fours brandishing the belt before me, dangling it from his mouth extended beggingly toward me. 'Use it, use it!' he insisted." John Rechy, *City of Night* (1963, 266)

150

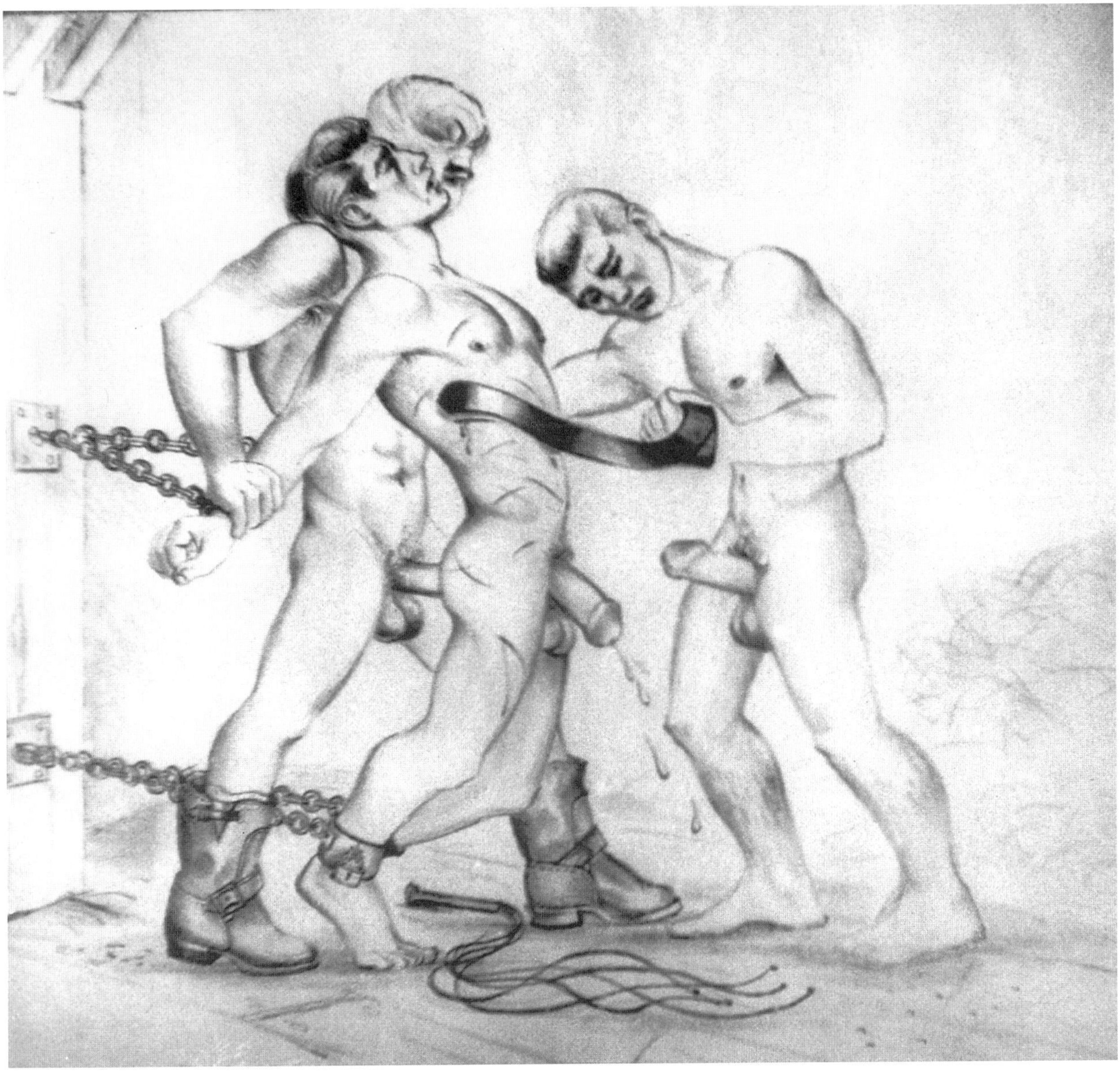

This unique dungeon scene, probably U.S. c. 1960, was not apparently part of any of DuBek's series or clusters, but was clearly Mel Gibson's inspiration for *The Passion of the Christ* (2004). I suspect it's by an insider with a hard-on (to use Tom of Finland's famous test for inspiration). Who else would have devoted such precise attention to the boots, strap, restraints, and cat-o'-nine-tails? **151**

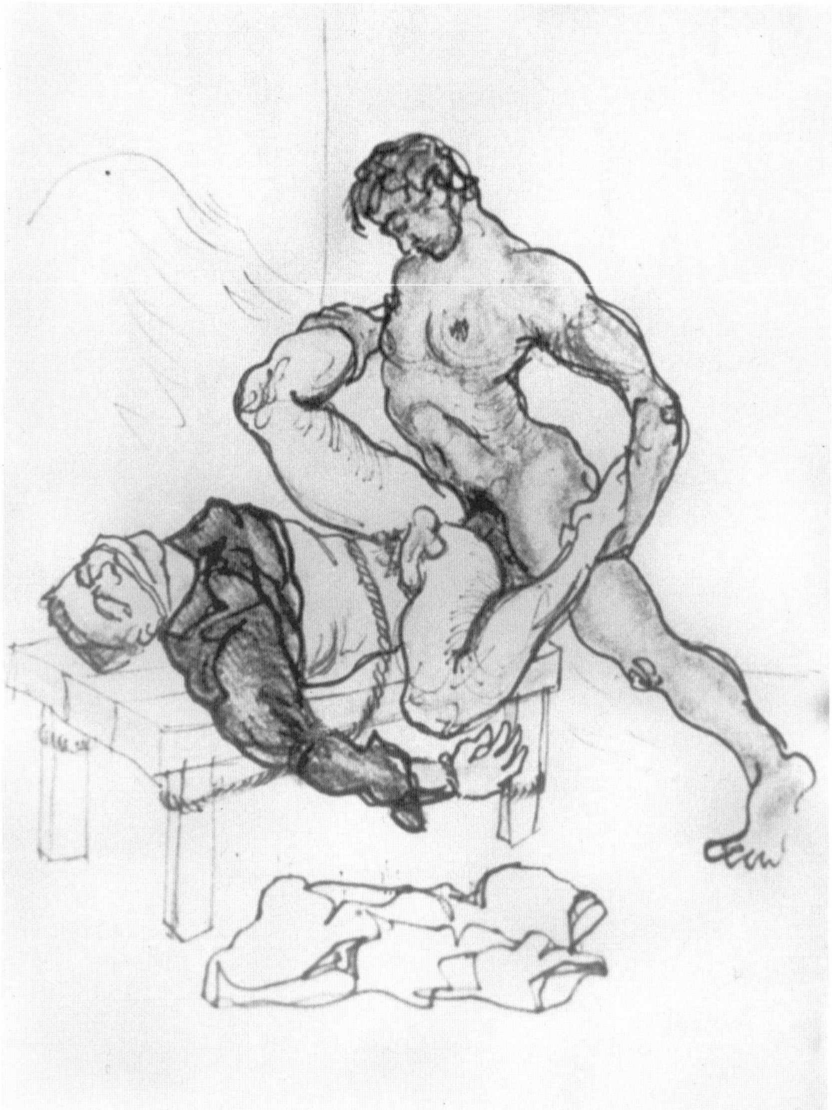

This pair of bondage fuck pictures has a wonderful sense of movement, echoing Etienne, but is clearly by a trained artist who knew what he was doing. Notice uncanny resemblance to Figure 139: who was "inspired" by whom?

152

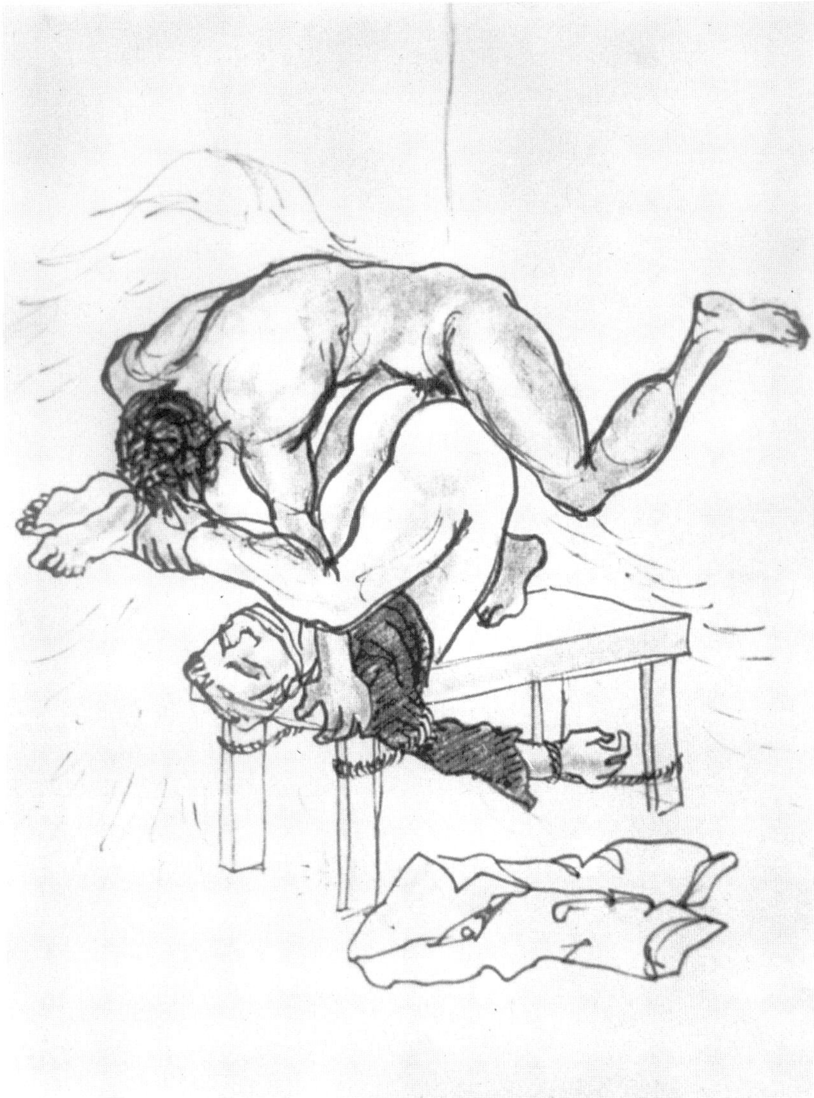

"Please master call me a dog, an ass beast, a wet asshole,
& fuck me more violent, my eyes hid with your palms round my skull
& plunge down in a brutal hard lash thru soft drip-flesh
& throb thru five seconds to spurt out your semen heat
over & over, bamming it in while I cry out your name I do love you."
Allen Ginsberg, "Please Master" ([1968] 1983, 340). **153**

Couples

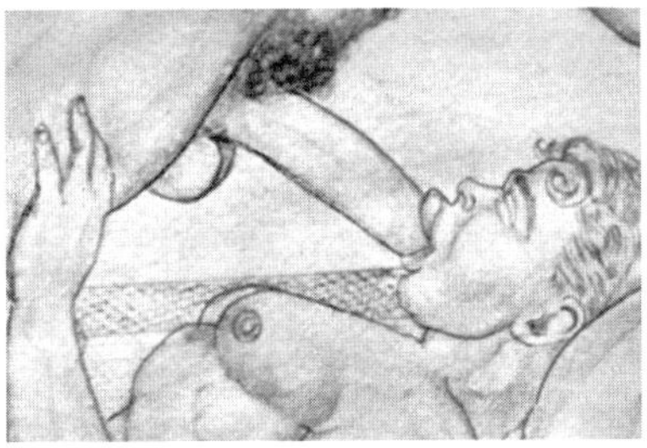

In *Out/Lines,* I innocently reflected on the "ideological and emotional weight" of the duo (writing in early 2000s). I could not have predicted how much more weight would accumulate in the coming years, how the same-sex couple would become a defining political issue of the decade. However, if you look closely at the twosomes here—twenty-three in the following section and almost half of the pictures in this book—the weight was already clear before Stonewall, from the intense spiritual communion that is evident in Caillaux's eyelock (fig. 18) to the everyday tenderness of the symmetrical sleepers (in the following three images). The weight is there paradoxically as well in the flippancy of the carefree sailors who have just met, swiving their silly brains out in public, and who will probably never see each other ever again (figs. 157-160). This irrepressible romanticism about the couple is certainly culturally constructed, but it's our culture and there's not much we can do about it.

Couples

I have just implied that waking up together in a bed implies a committed relationship while outdoors sex in broad daylight implies ephemerality, but it ain't necessarily so. As in *Out/Lines,* the couple scenes show the underground artists torn between sanctioned vanilla sex in a real bed and the transgressive "outer limit" variety, standing up, on the sly, or out of doors. The former outnumbers the latter by not quite two to one. Furthermore, DuBek's couples, at least those followed over a couple of images or more, are not restricted to top-and-bottom role-playing: the brunette curly-haired French sailor on the promenade is doing both French passive and Greek active, and the other two couples in this section follow suit (opposite, and figs. 161-162) as does the tropical beach couple (figs. 121-130). Except in the specialized scenes of S/M, couples usually connote ideals of symmetry, reciprocality, and even sameness (especially those softcore couples, figures 222 and 226-227, idealized as mirror images to the point of high camp absurdity). Meanwhile, the gently airbrushed couple-in-bed portrait (fig. 166), trying out the gentle scissors position for anal relations, enacts what I called in *Out/Lines* an overstated affirmation-wistful, "positive images" exaltation (Waugh 2002, 38).

In the Hollywood "Production Code" era, heterosexual kissing stood in for the cultural baggage around the couple, and in *Out/Lines* I called kissing the "special sacrament of the melodrama genre" (however rare kissing was in that selection, with only six examples; Waugh 2002, 38). But kissing is even more on the back burner here, snuck in only five times as background action (figs. 32, 81-82, 199, 214), as well as the intense boys in figure 207 who are on the verge. Many of these couples are so masculinist à la Genet that they don't even fuck ventral-ventral (see fig. 109 for one of the few exceptions), let alone kiss. It's dual fucking, sixty-nine (figs. 74-77), or suck-then-fuck that invokes the sentimentality here. Fortunately, the sugar is cut occasionally—thanks to the versatility of the drawing as opposed to the photo—for example, the "Home Sweet Home" parody (fig. 64) where ideal coupledom gets a few smart smacks on its ass.

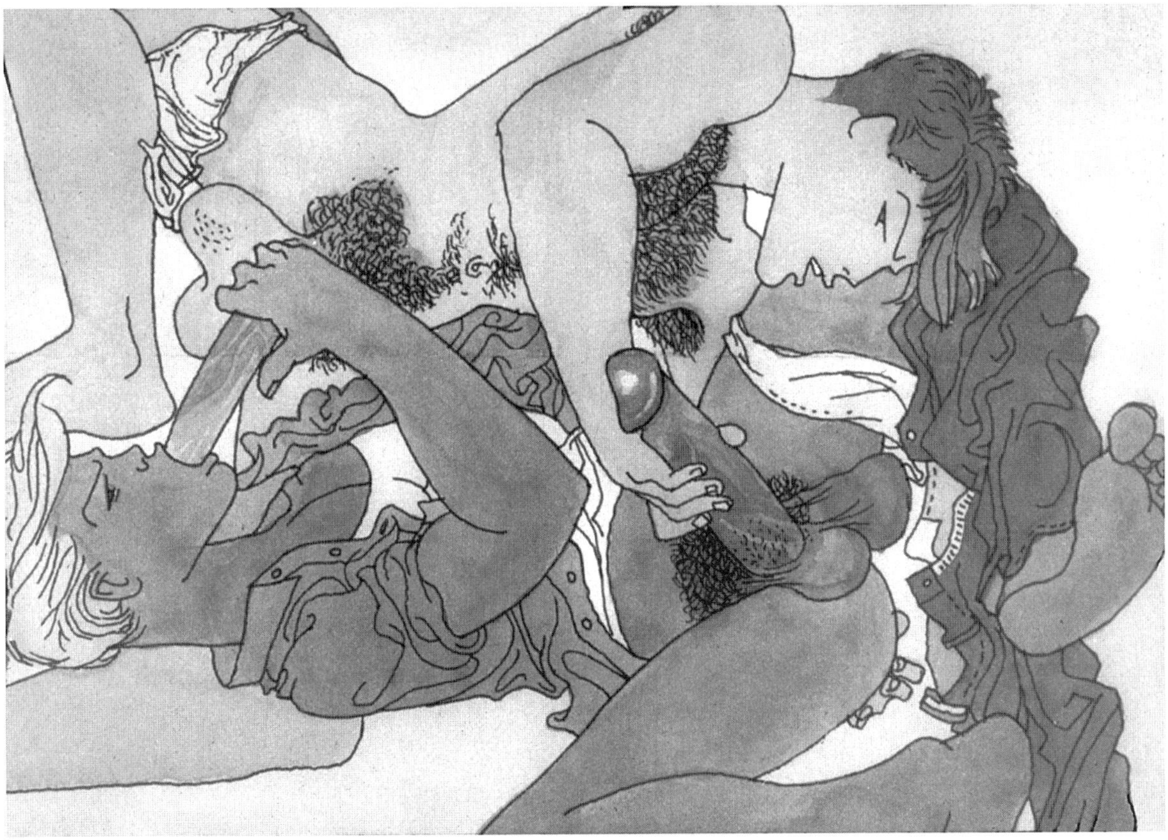

This group of a half dozen or so images of sharp-chinned young men getting it on were part of DuBek's slide stash. These three sixty-nine compositions (sex on this page; the following are two tender sleeping set-ups) epitomize the overwhelming romanticism that the couple motif brings out in any artist with his guard down. (See Figures 206-207 for this artist's stab at triangle and group scenes, considerably less charged.)

154

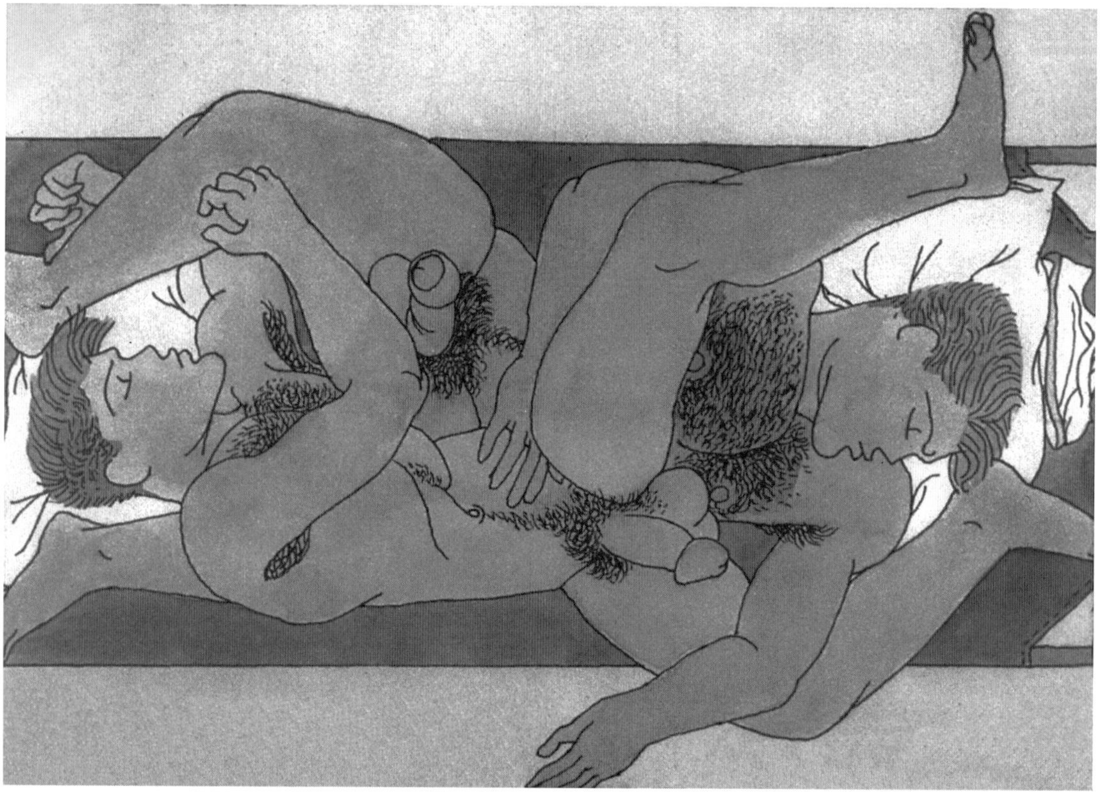

"The next day was Saturday and I had the afternoon off, so I got up early in the morning. Claytie was still asleep, his mouth half open, his black hair unruly. The covers were pulled down below his belly. His torso was something Greek and wonderful. I looked at him a moment and then put on my boots and jeans and jacket. . . ."
Phil Andros [Sam Steward], "The Poison Tree," *$tud* ([1966] 1982, 27)

155

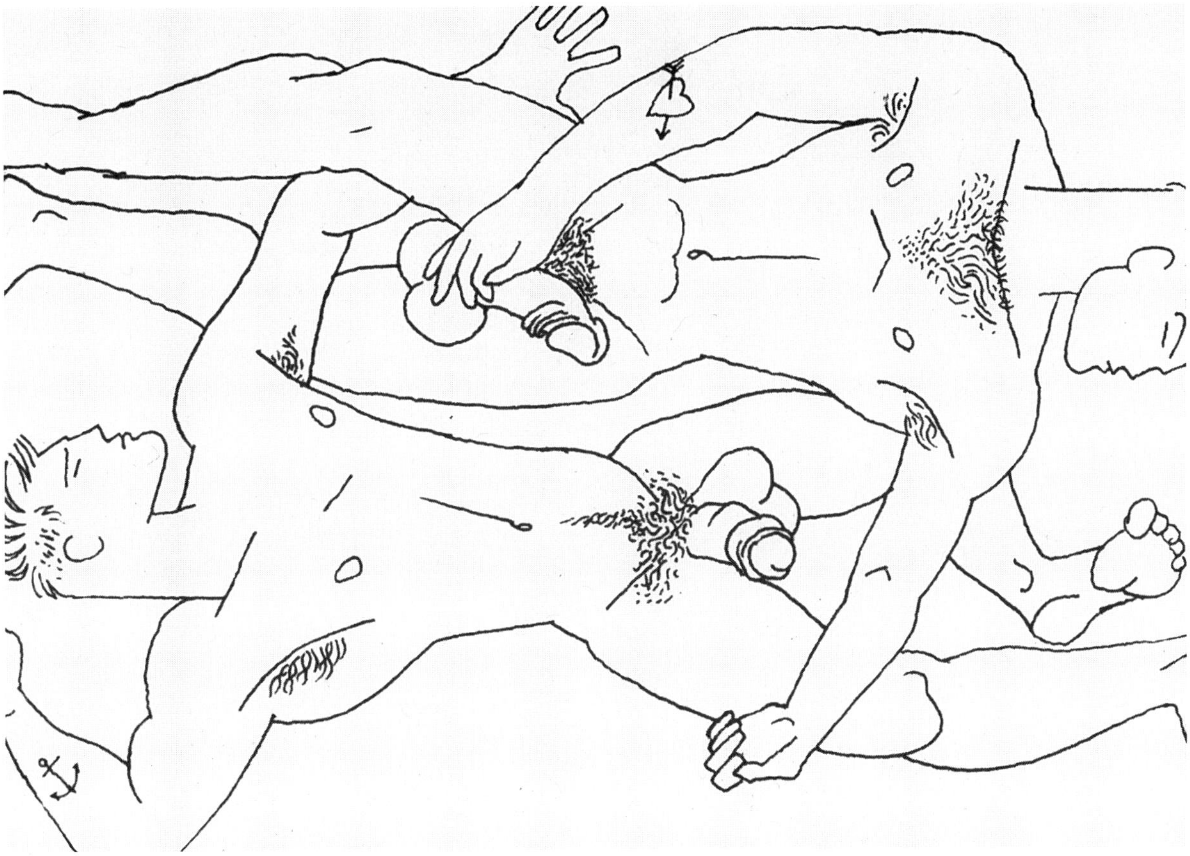

"Jim woke before dawn. The sky was gray and the stars were fading. The fire was almost out. He touched Bob's arm and watched him wake up. They looked at one another. Then Bob grinned and Jim said, 'You're still going Monday?'" Gore Vidal, *The City and the Pillar* ([1948; 1965] 2003, 31)

156

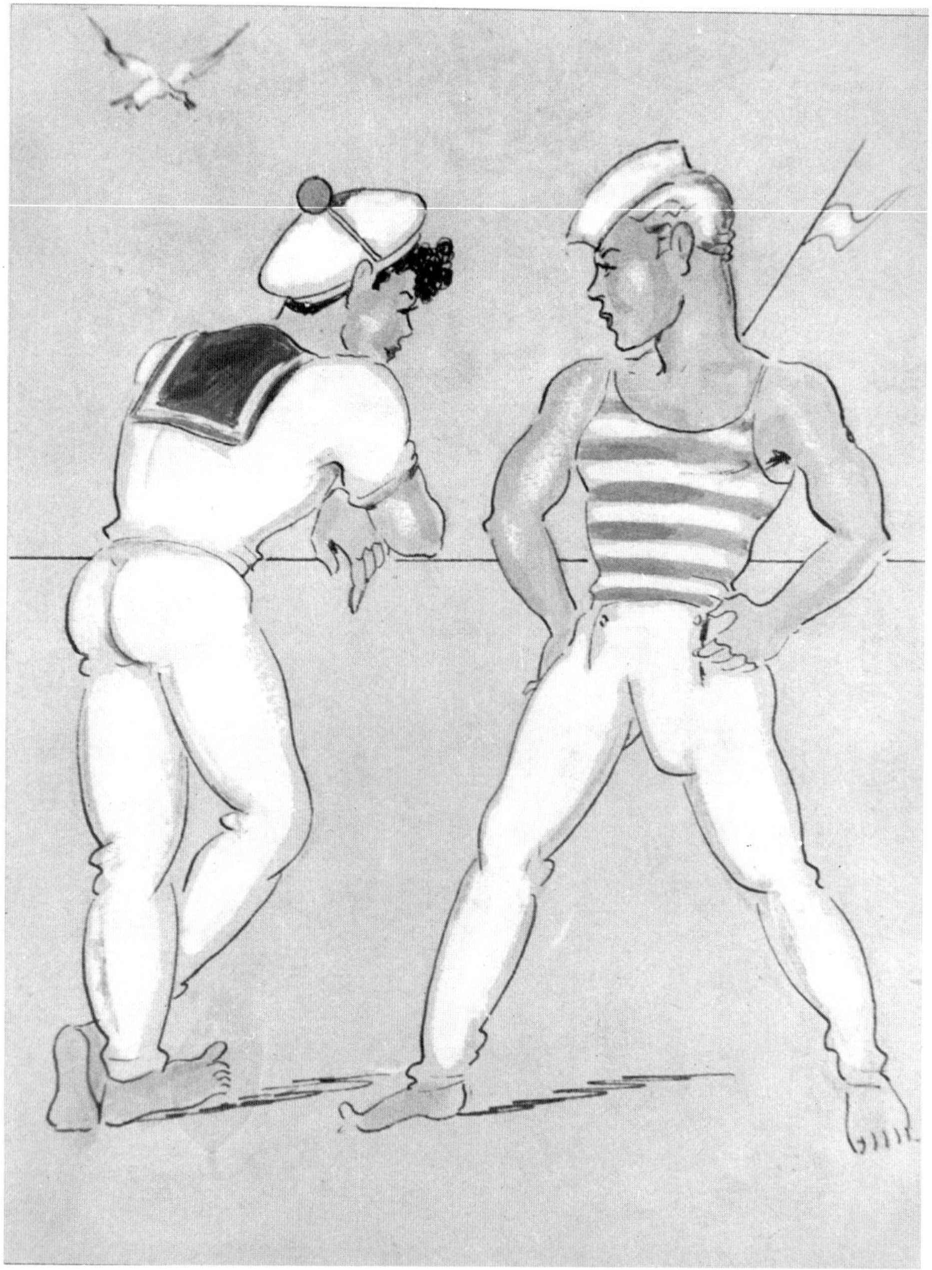

The Bellhops artist was an exciting discovery in *Out/Lines*, with his image of glamorous bellhops driven to lust by pornography, but only a few examples were available.

157

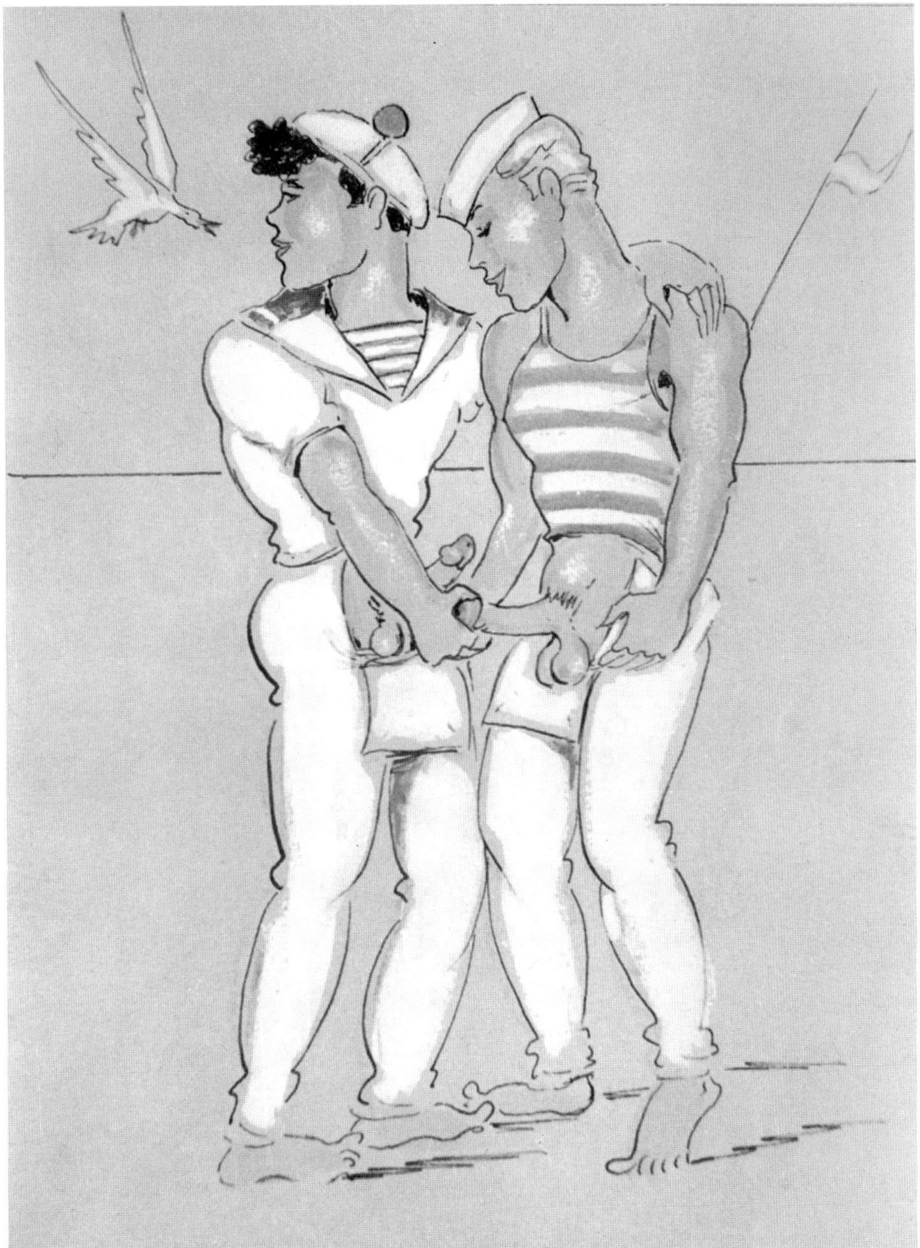

DuBek struck it rich. In this 1930s series of nautical love at first sight and the seagull who wants to get in on the act, the range and richness of Bellhops's work, frothy but not deep, confirm him as a major subject for research, an ingenious and naughty ancestor of all perverts, and the patron saint of all fairies.

158

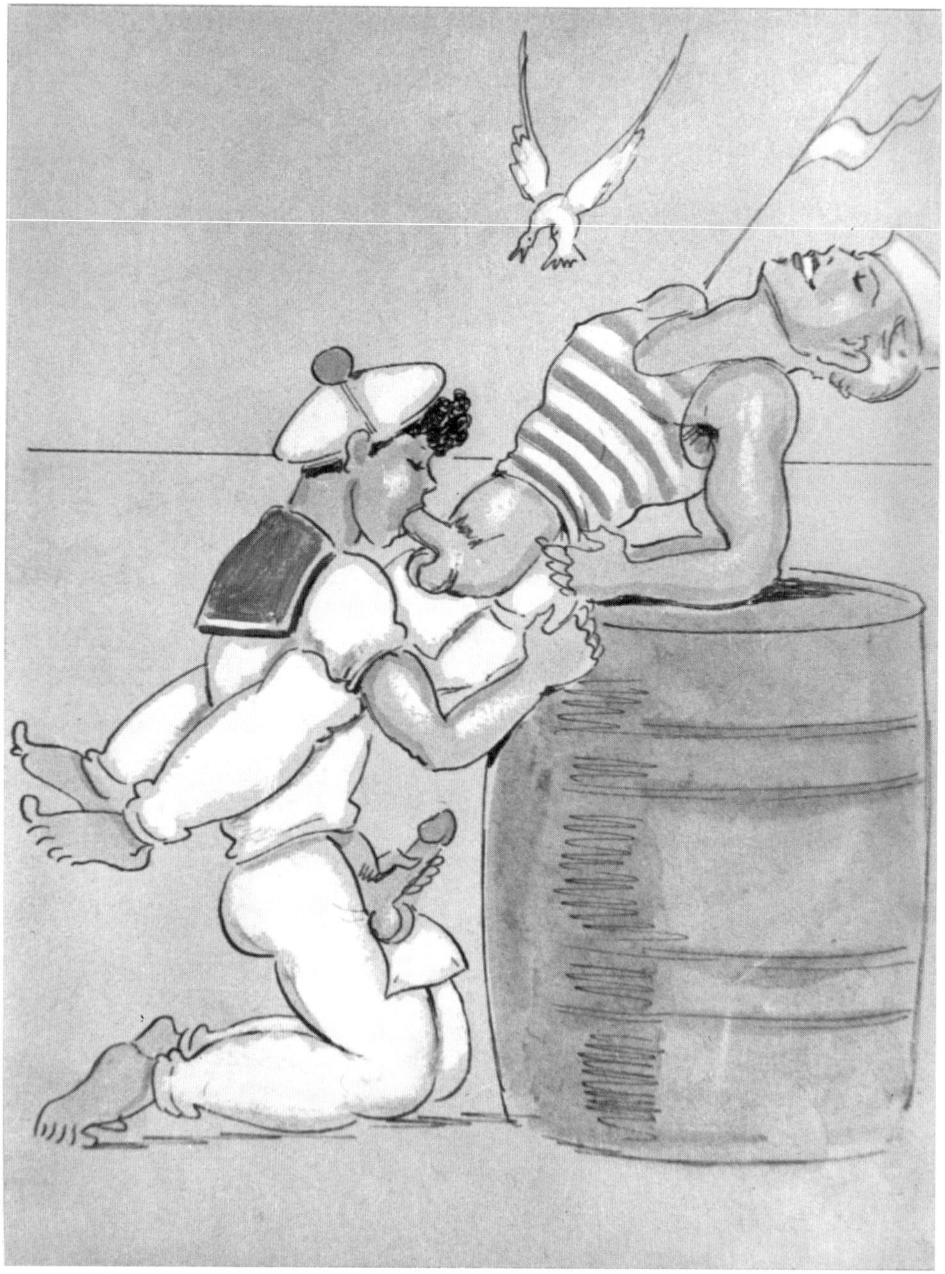

This suck-then-fuck combo articulates—over a barrel, on a hyberbolically lyrical beachfront promenade—the raunch of the moment and . . .

159

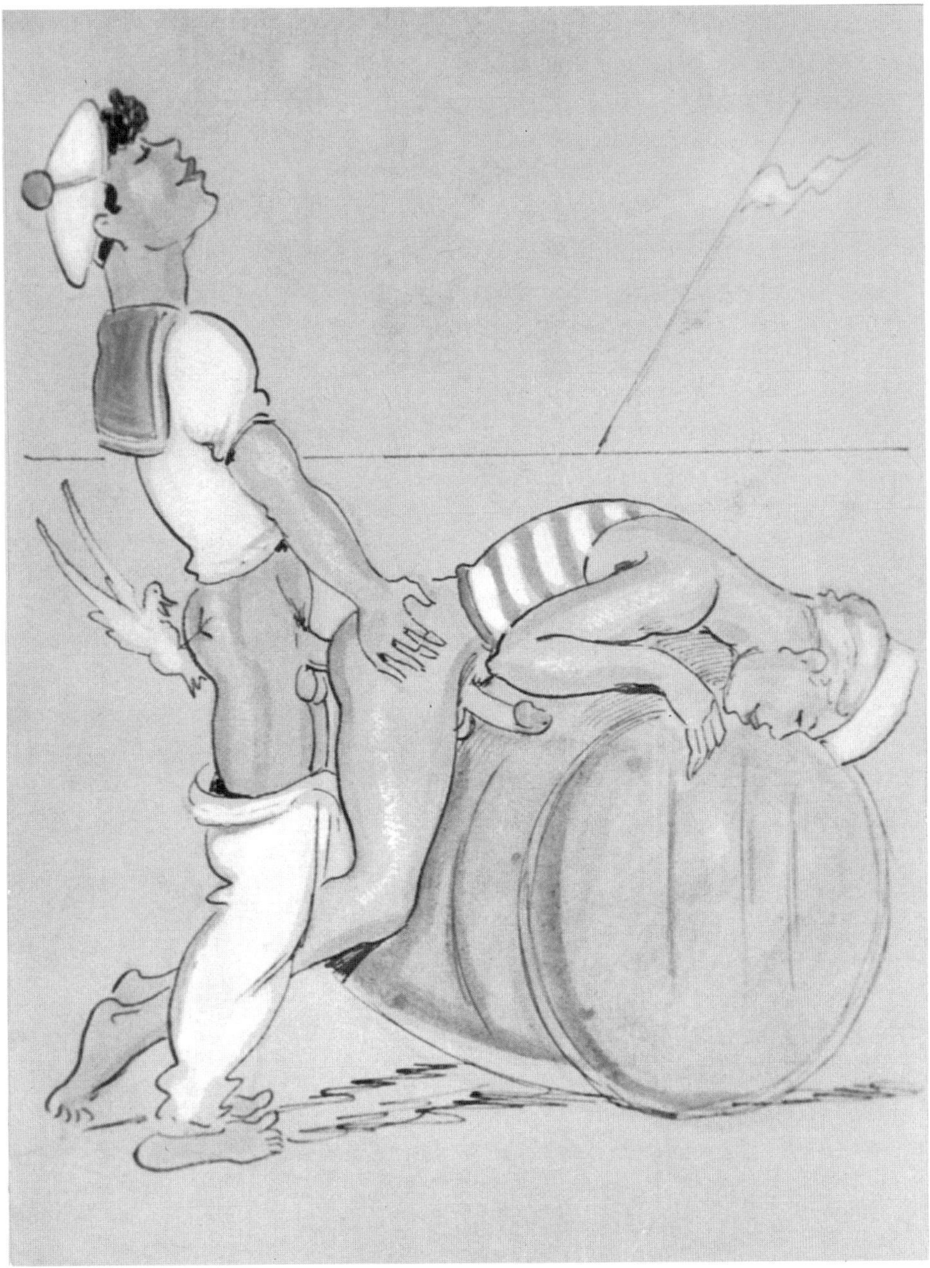

. . . all the happily-ever-after, many-splendored thing that birds (seagulls, especially), bees, educated fleas, and two men do, even if they will probably never see each other ever again.

160

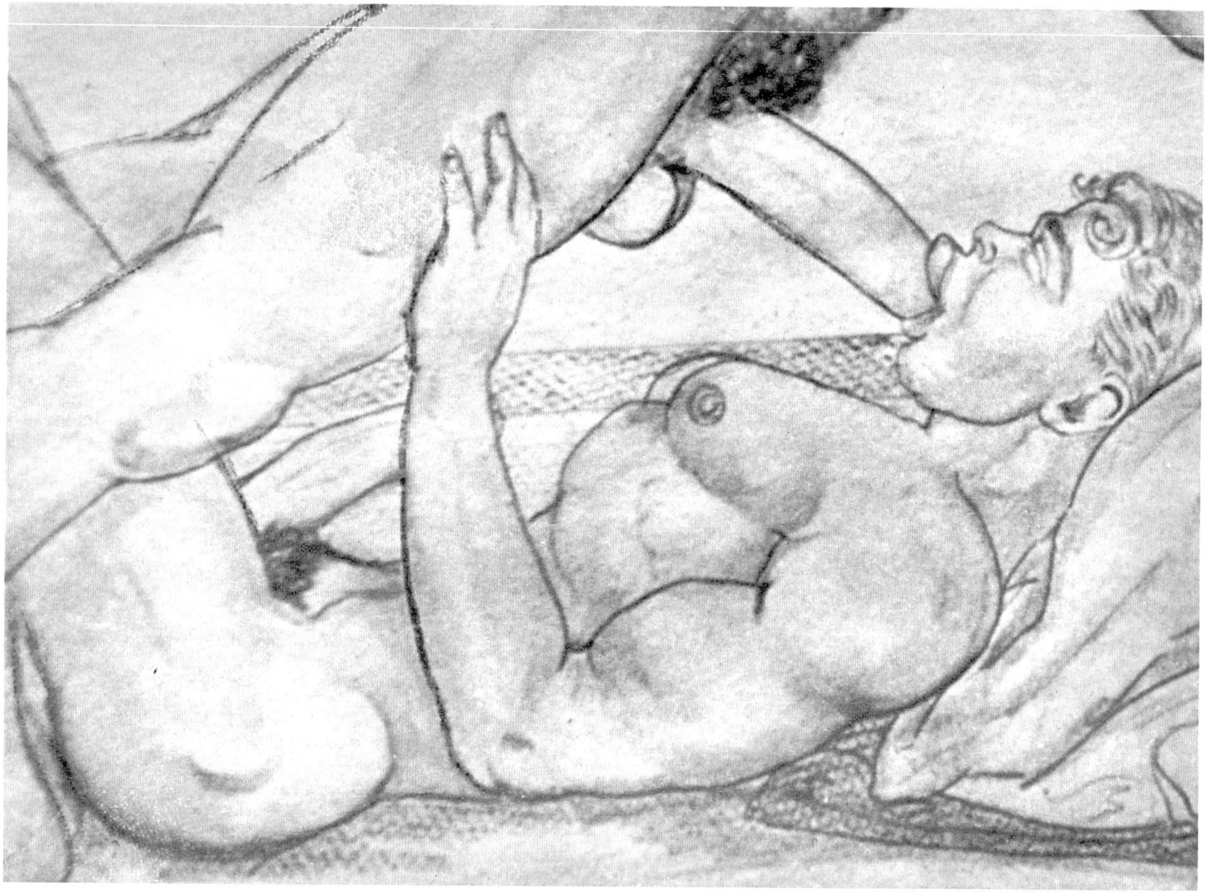

The aesthetic style of another suck-and-fuck diptych, likely amateur-drawn, is comparatively underwhelming . . .

161

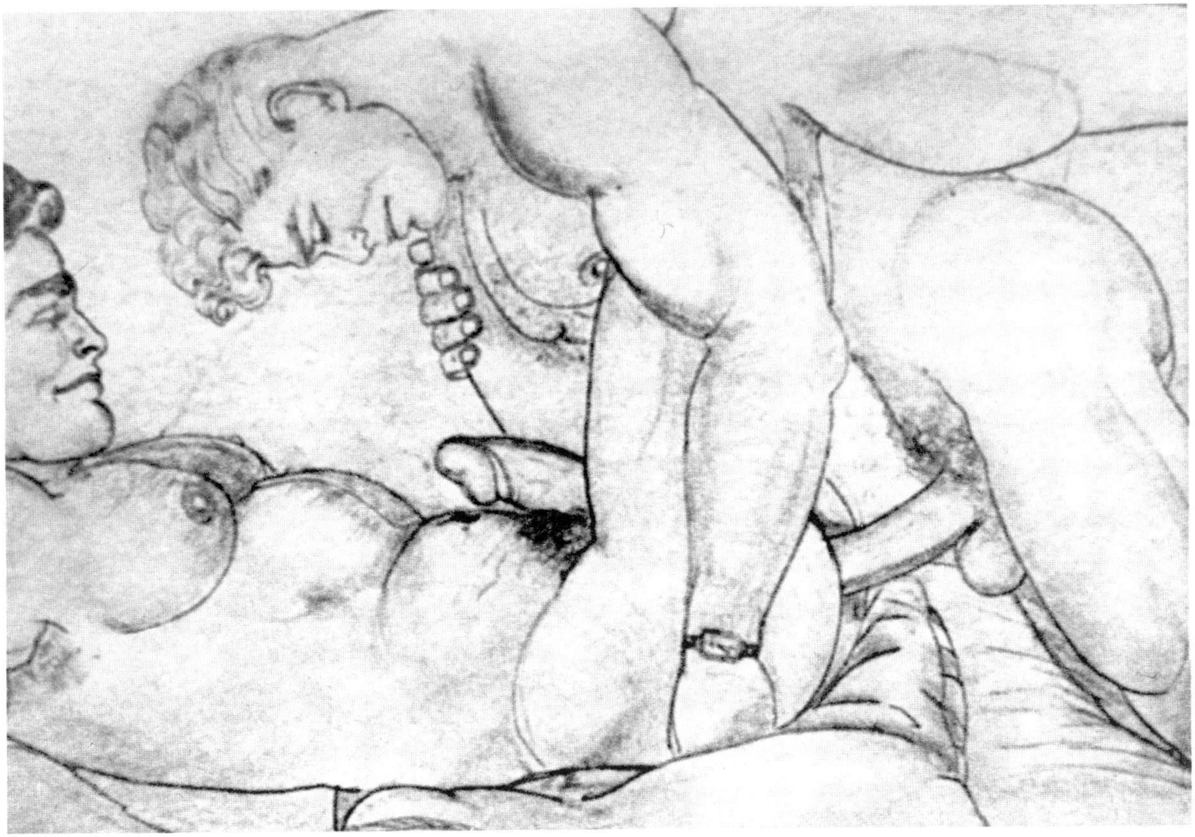

. . . but compensated for by over-the-top gusto and down-to-business wham bam. Probably U.S.A., c. 1950s.

162

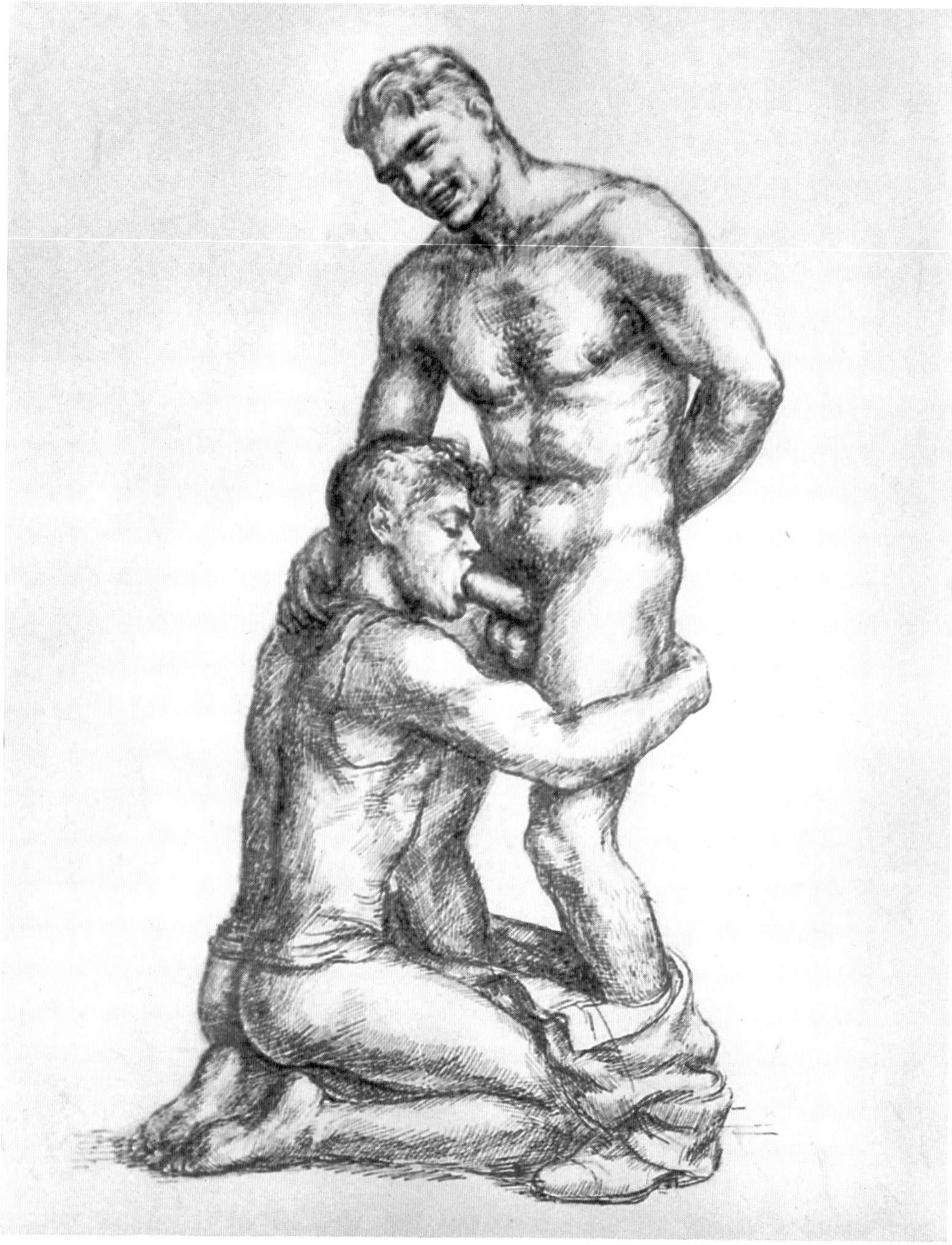

When a sample of this series showed up in *Out/Lines* (Figure 172), art historian friends pooh-poohed my hope that this might be by Paul Cadmus, the dean of American homoerotic artists (1904-1999). A newly constituted e-mail jury (Jonathan Weinberg and Justin Spring) now says yes, that DuBek was probably right in his notations attributing them to his friend Cadmus. They are in all likelihood photos of drawings by the famous rebel
163 whose rare "hardcore" experiments ended up deposited with his famous collaborator Dr. Kinsey in the 1940s or 1950s.

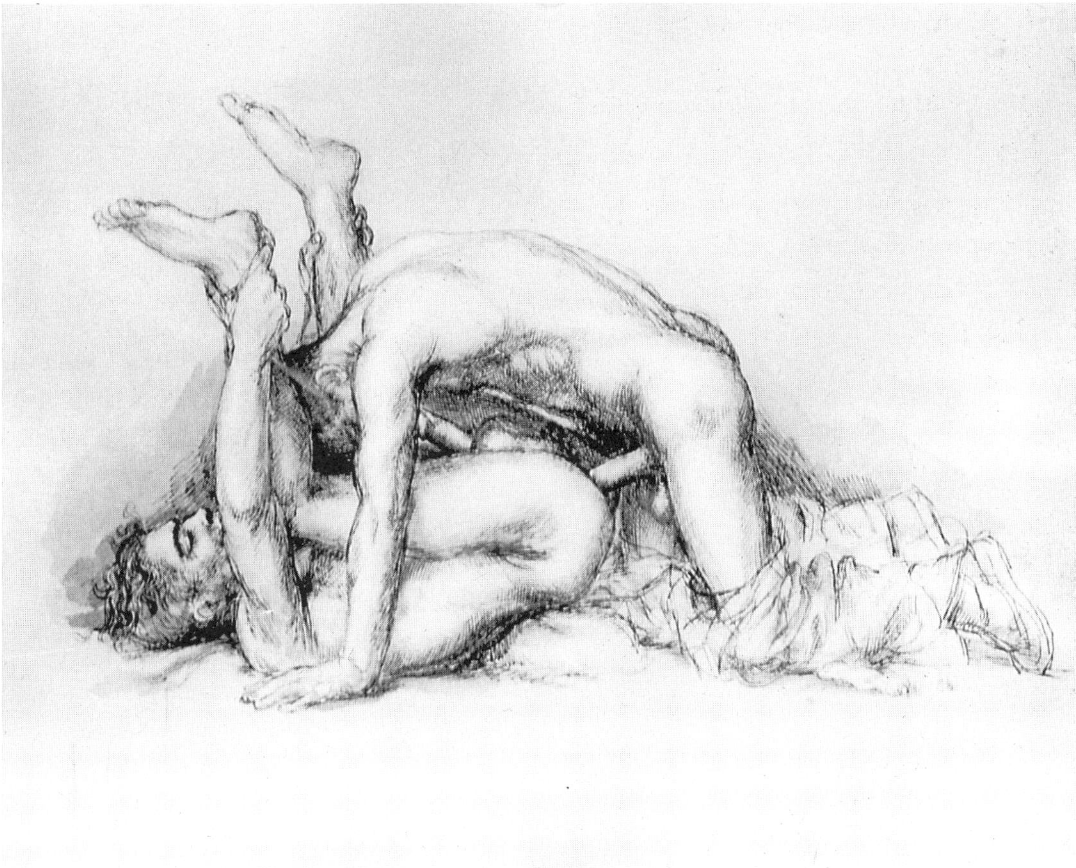

Perhaps DuBek got his photos of Cadmus drawings from the artist himself. In any case, they were certainly circulating on the underground graphics network, as *Out/Lines* demonstrated. No doubt there were just a few too many indiscreet friends of the artist or Kinsey Institute confidants with photo stands to keep a good thing under wraps. See the sketch page in a different style on the next page, as well as Figures 218-219.

164

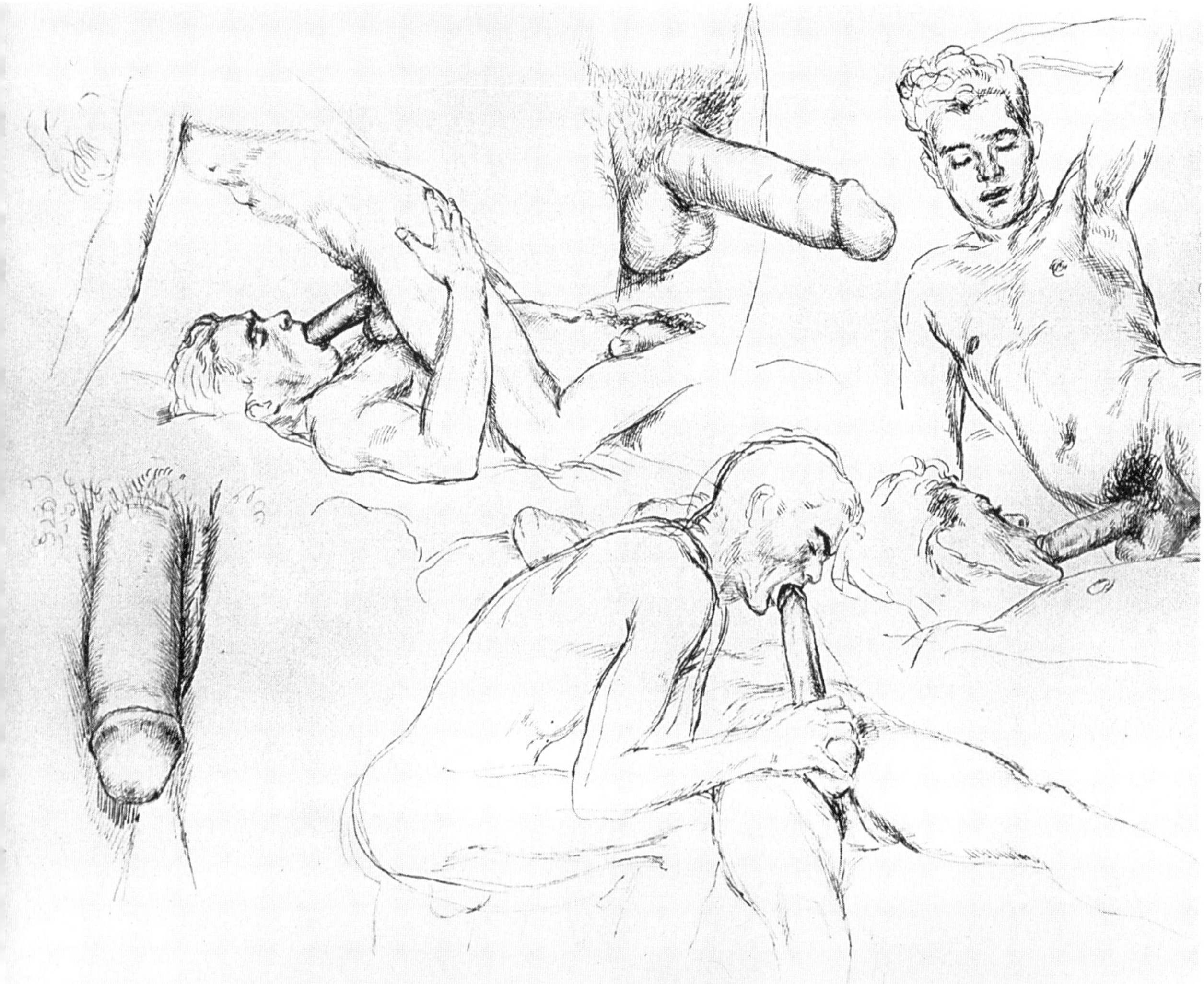

165 My first impression of the Cadmus drawings and sketch pages like this one were that they must have been based on live model sessions. However, Cadmus told Justin Spring that such work was based on photos supplied around 1937 by a Museum of Modern Art "accomplice" named Allen Porter (Spring 2002, 32-33). To me, they do not look like hardcore beefcake from the underground marketplace of the period. Perhaps vintage pictorialist work, or else specially commissioned or private photos?

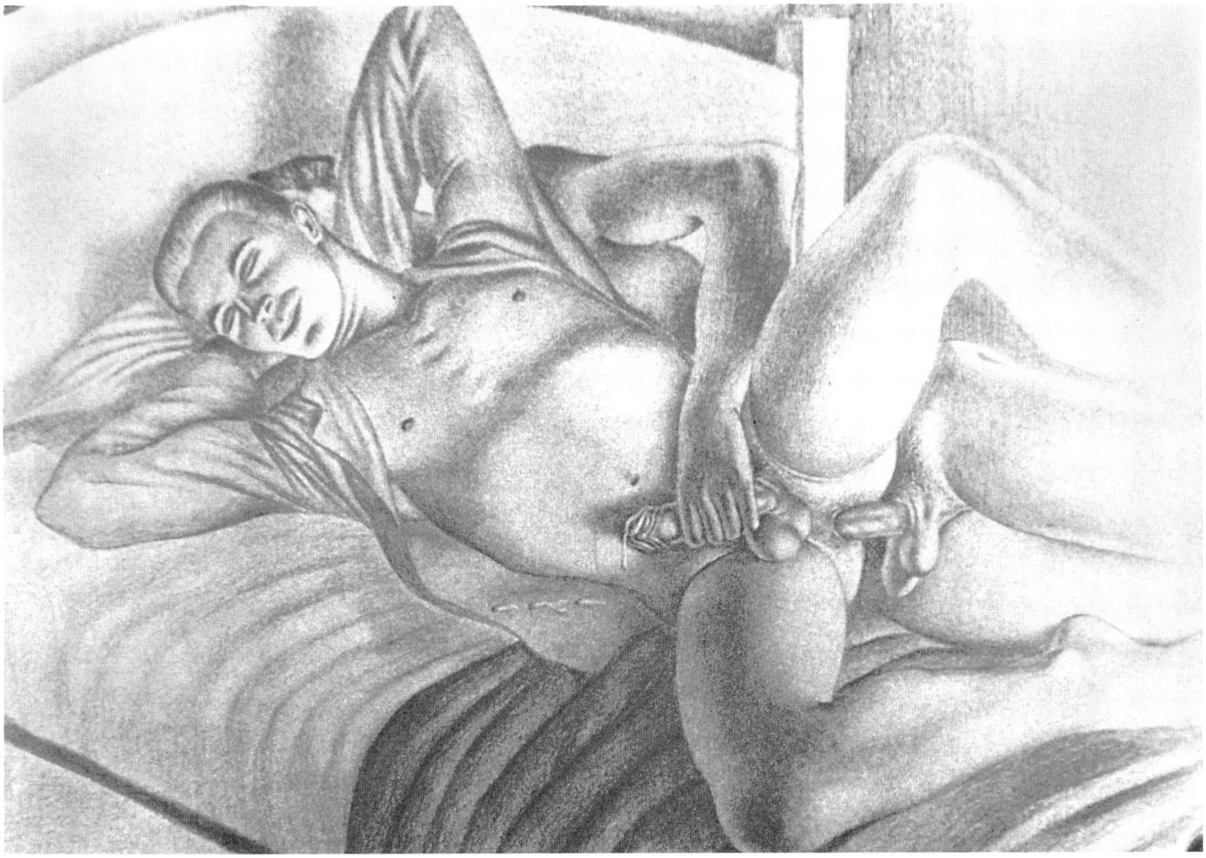

This decorous chiaroscuro image of a scissors position was probably a commercial one from the emerging porno marketplace of the 1960s, probably also based on a photo. Apparently DuBek's only example of this artist's work—no doubt American with all that airbrush effect.

166

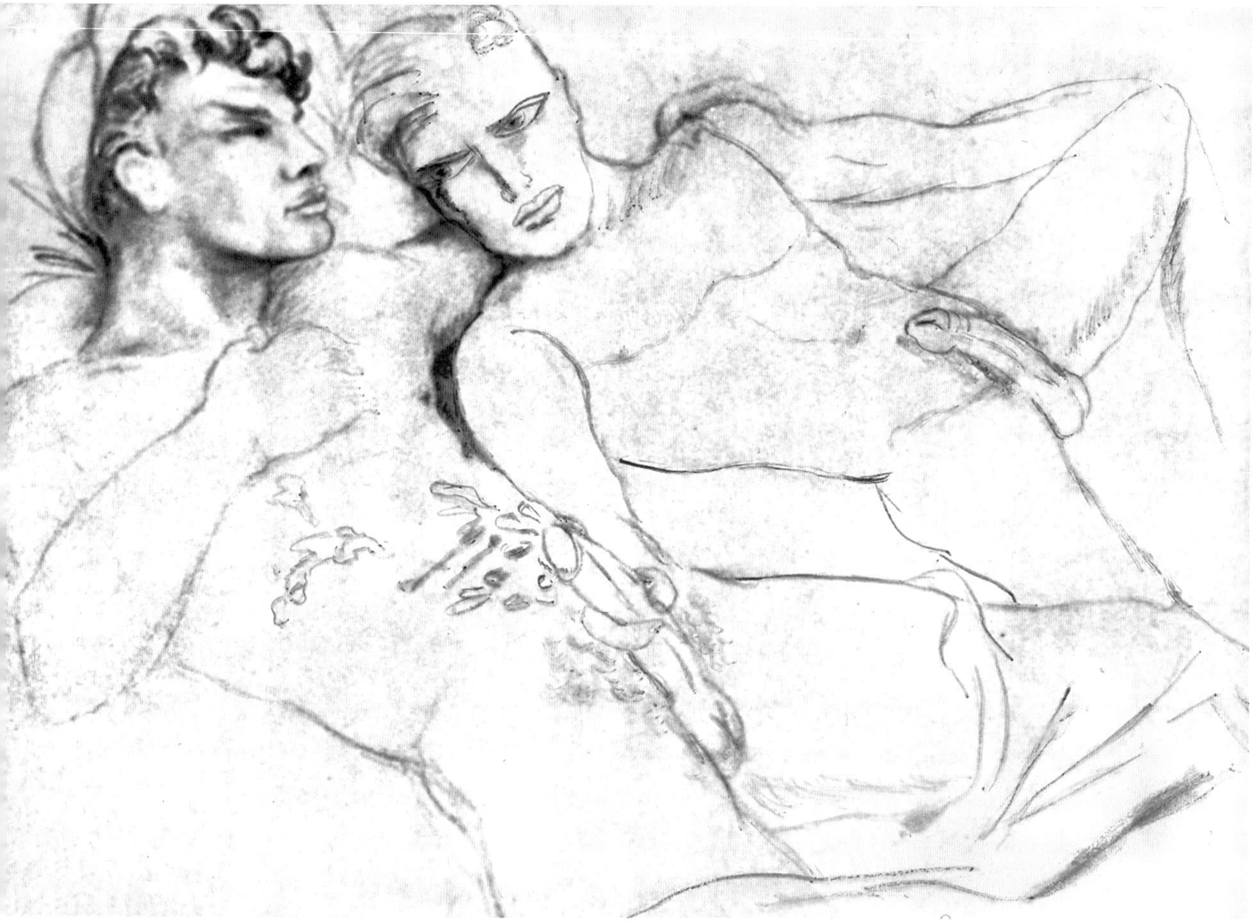

". . . The skin was as smooth as he remembered. Lightly he touched the stray coppery hairs which grew below
the deep-set navel. Then, carefully, like a surgeon performing a delicate operation, he unbuttoned Bob's shorts.
Bob stirred, but did not wake, as Jim opened wide the shorts to reveal thick blond pubic hair from which
sprouted the pale quarry. Slowly his hand closed around Bob's sex. He held him for what seemed a long time.
167 Held him, until he looked up to find that the other was awake and watching him. . . ." Gore Vidal, *The City
and the Pillar* ([1948; 1965] 2003, 202)

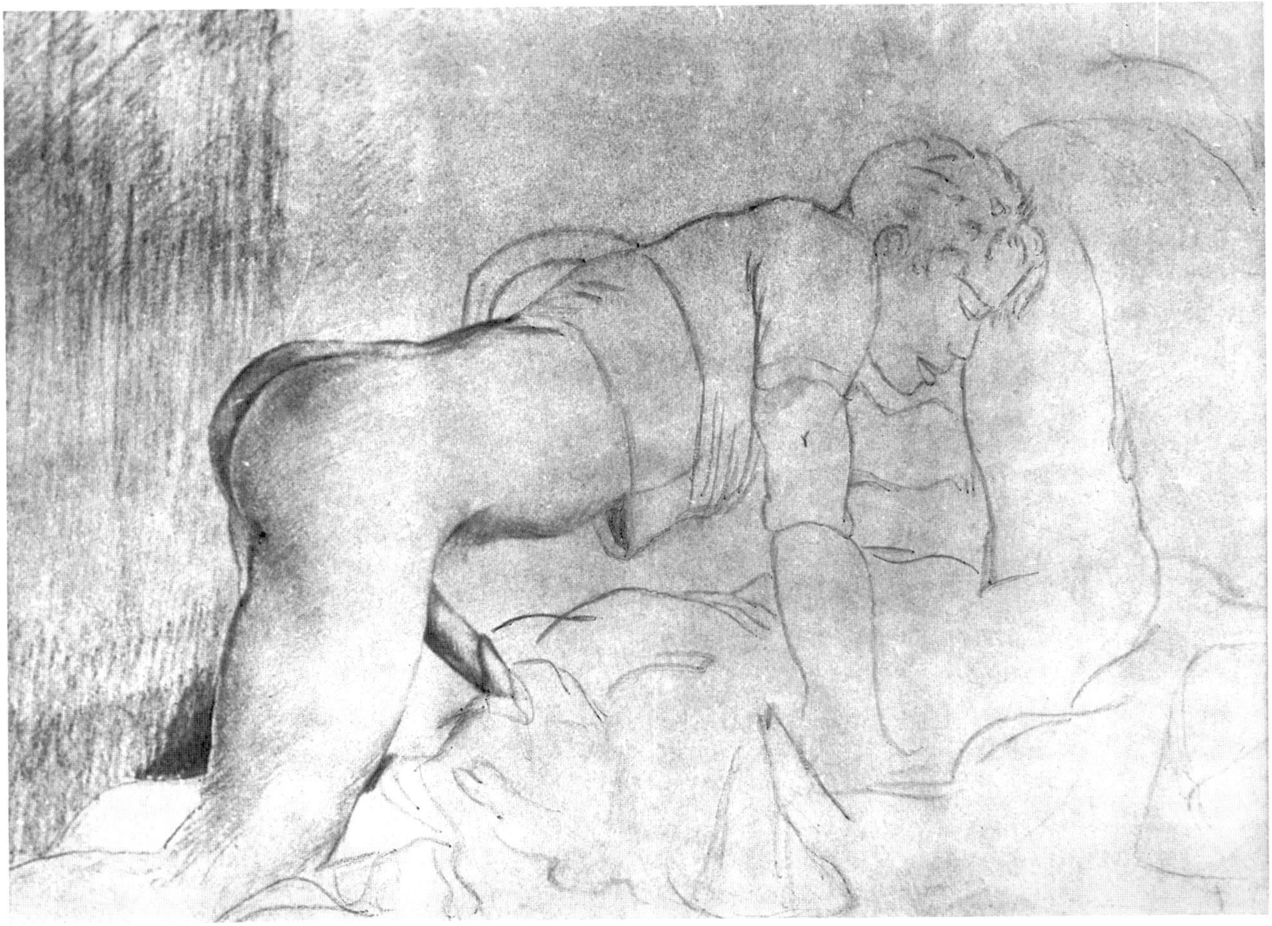

DuBek had grouped this image with his Cadmus stash, perhaps by mistake, for I am more inclined to the French connection, perhaps Caillaux (see also Figure 23).

168

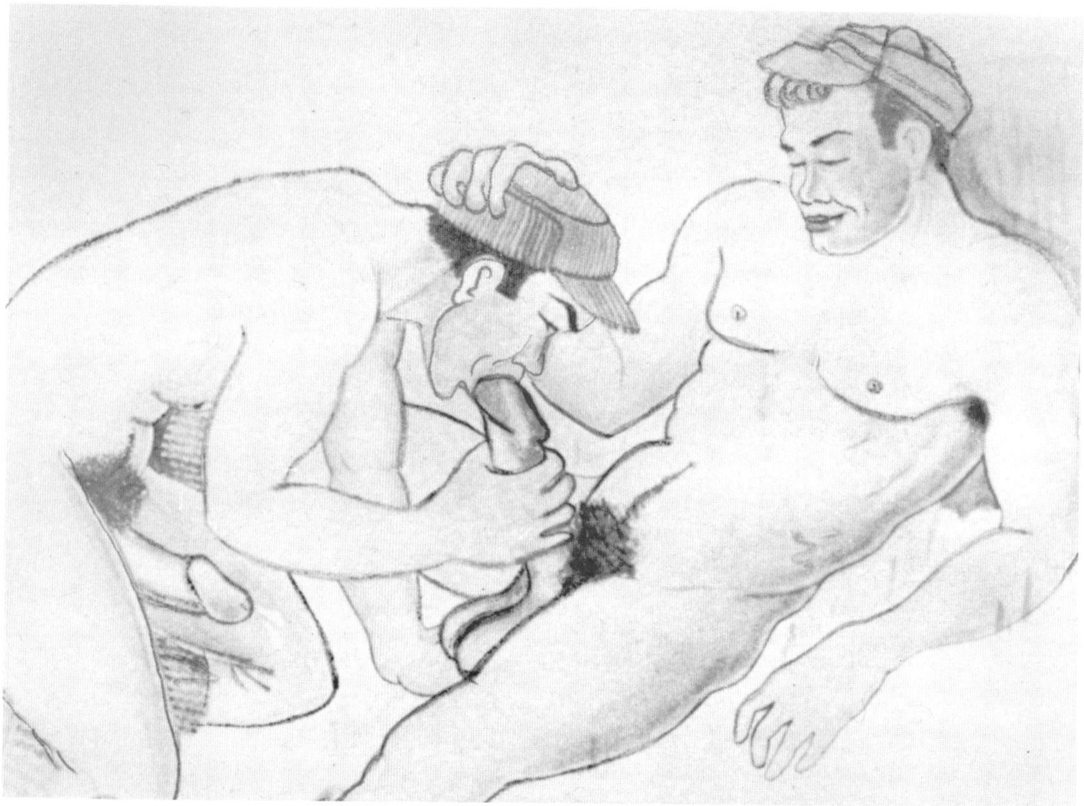

"Querelle turned around, abruptly, and squatted down on the ground. As if ordained by fate, the detective's prick plunged into his mouth, just as the train plunged into the tunnel leading to the station." Jean Genet,
169 *Querelle de Brest* ([1947; 1953] 1974, 206)

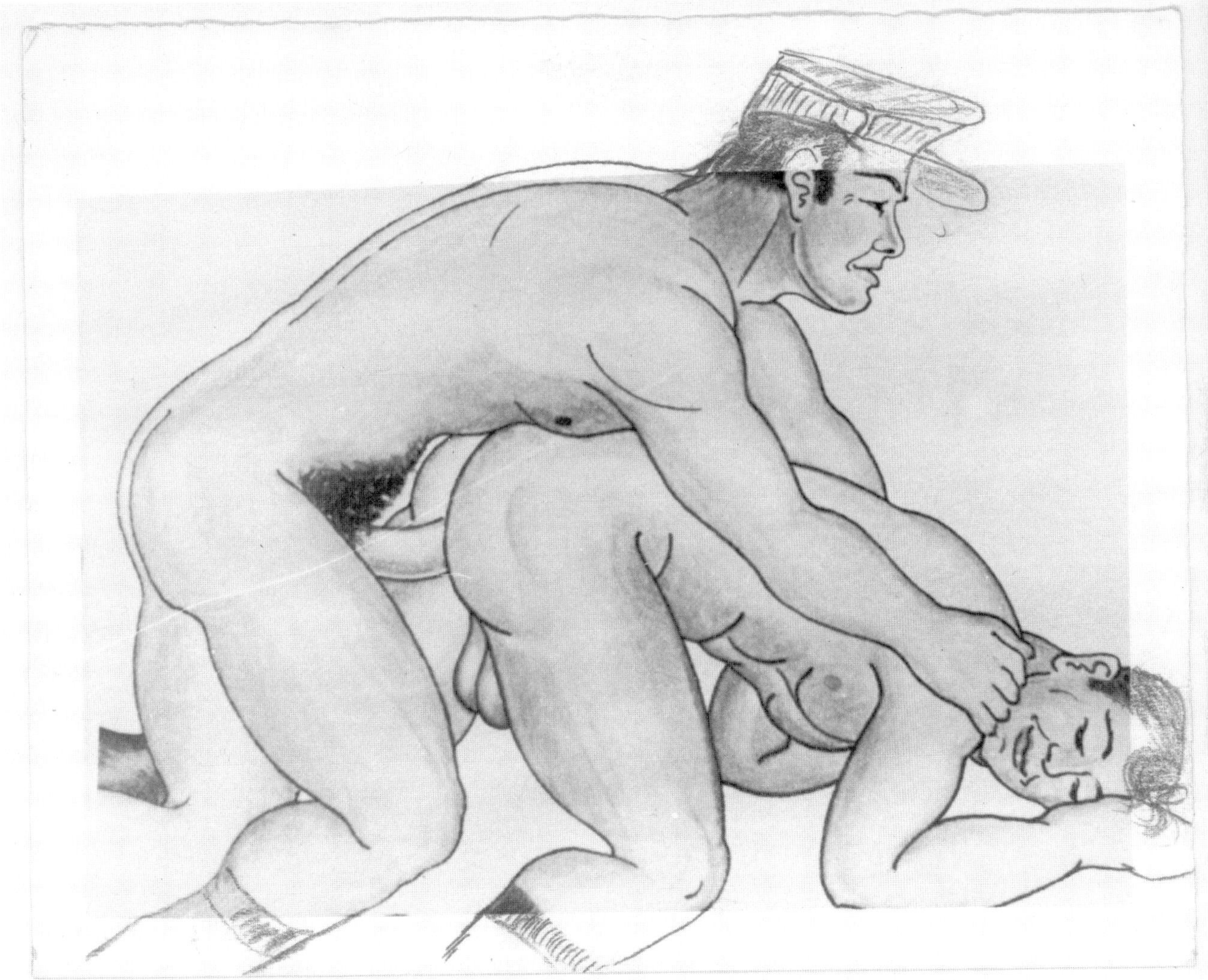

Not exactly standard fetish headgear on this enthusiastic couple, but obviously meaningful to someone. If not sailors or cops, are they ranchers? lumberjacks? truckers? railroad engineers?

170

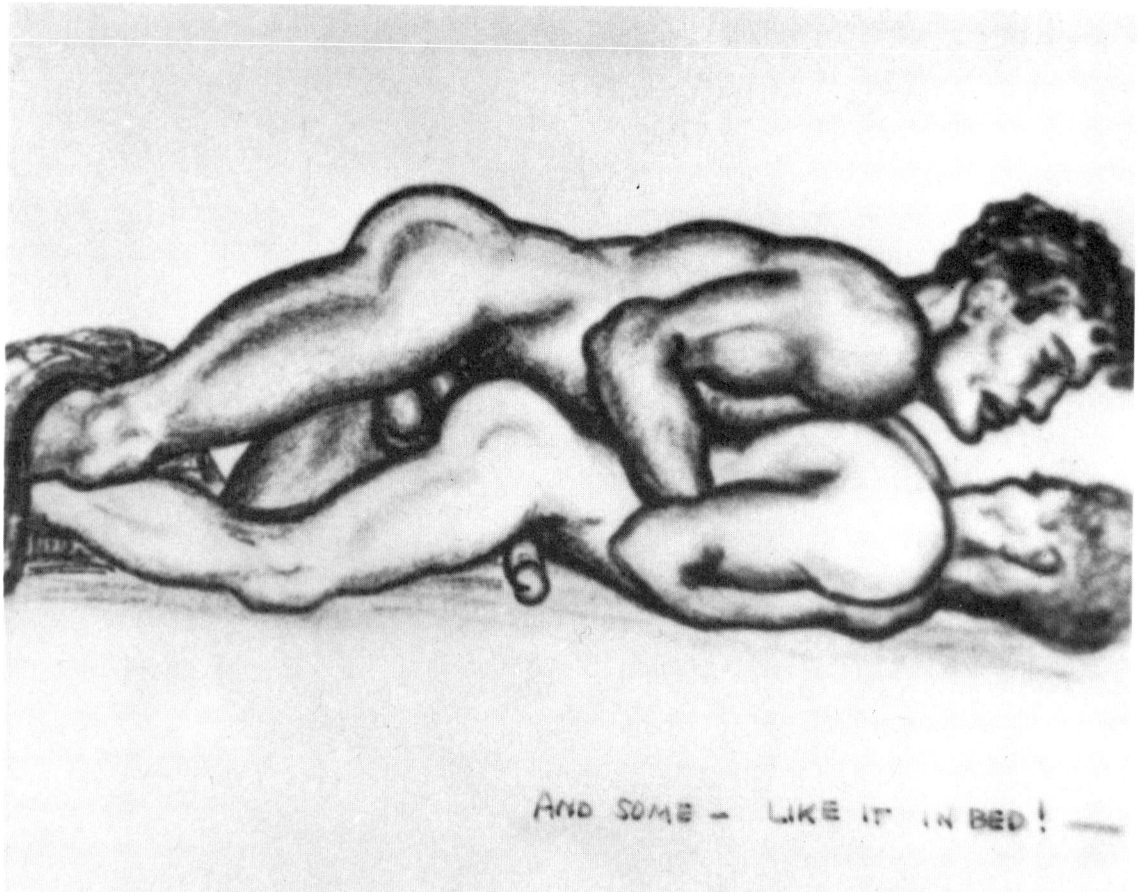

Red Riding Wolf (see Figures 55, 95-97) is known not only for his hard-edged couples but also for his fondness for overripe captions.

171

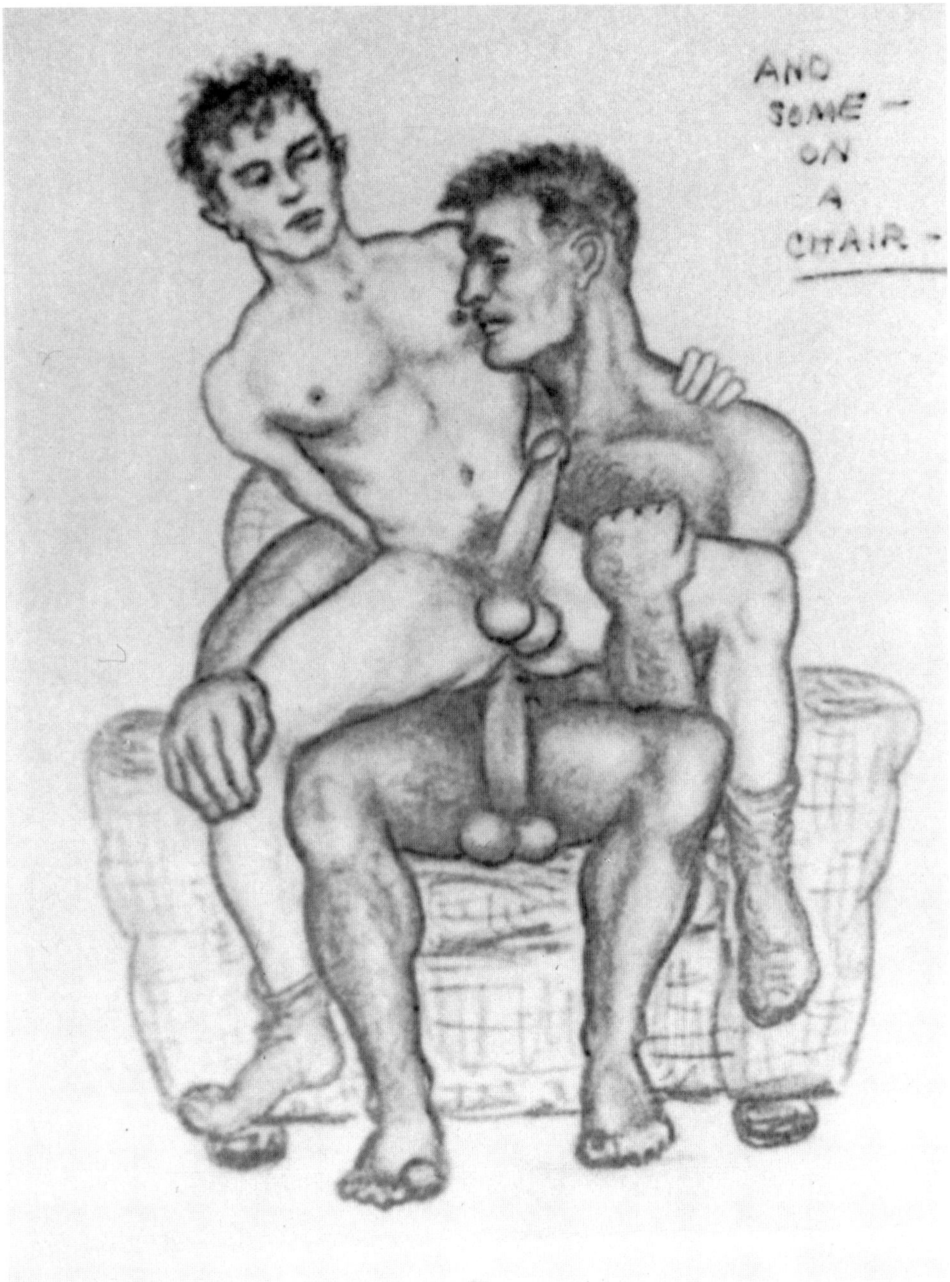

"'Oh, you've a grand cock,' he said, stroking it. I realized how much of sex was missed in Morocco by not being able to talk the language." Joe Orton, *The Orton Diaries* ([1967] 1986, 204)

172

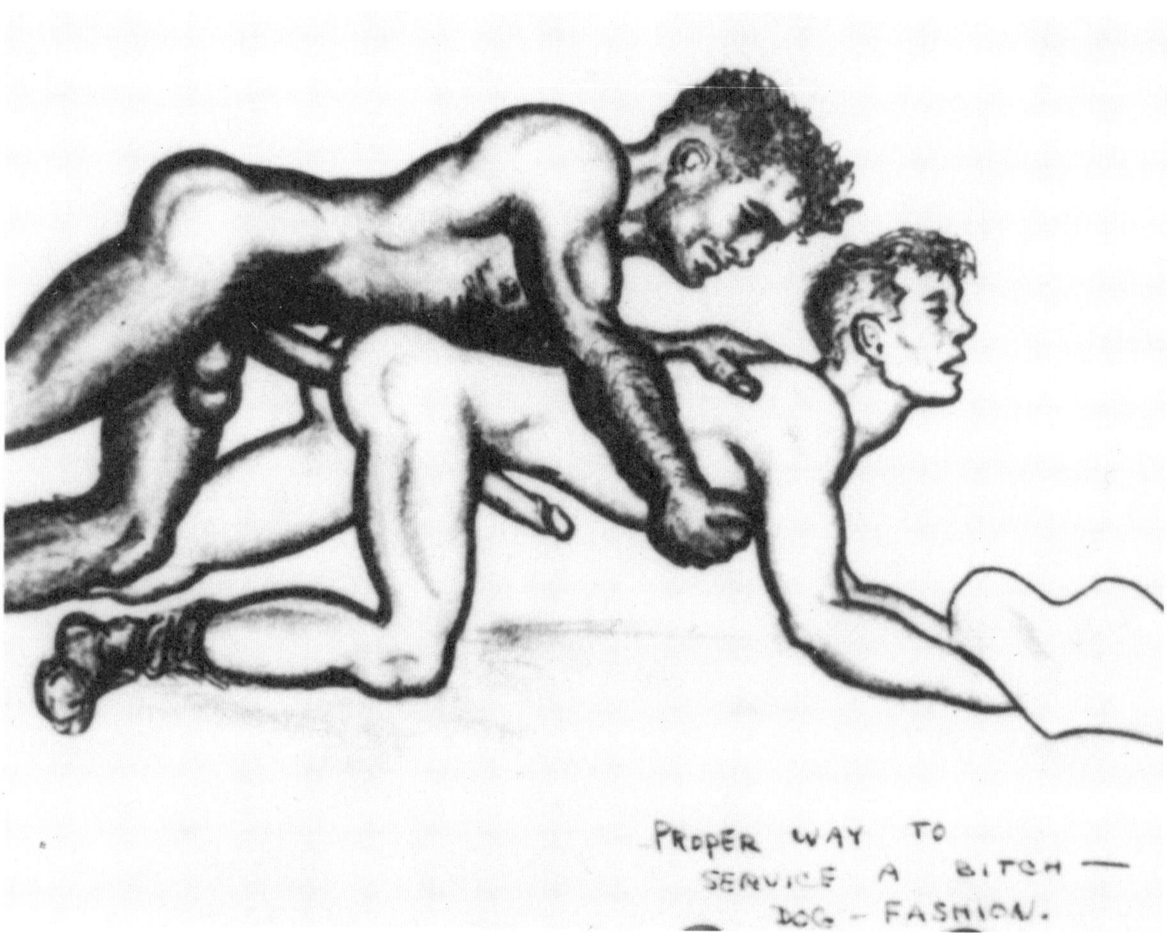

Red Riding Wolf's sense of fucking is not very politically correct, now or in the context of the sixties when he produced his work . . .

173

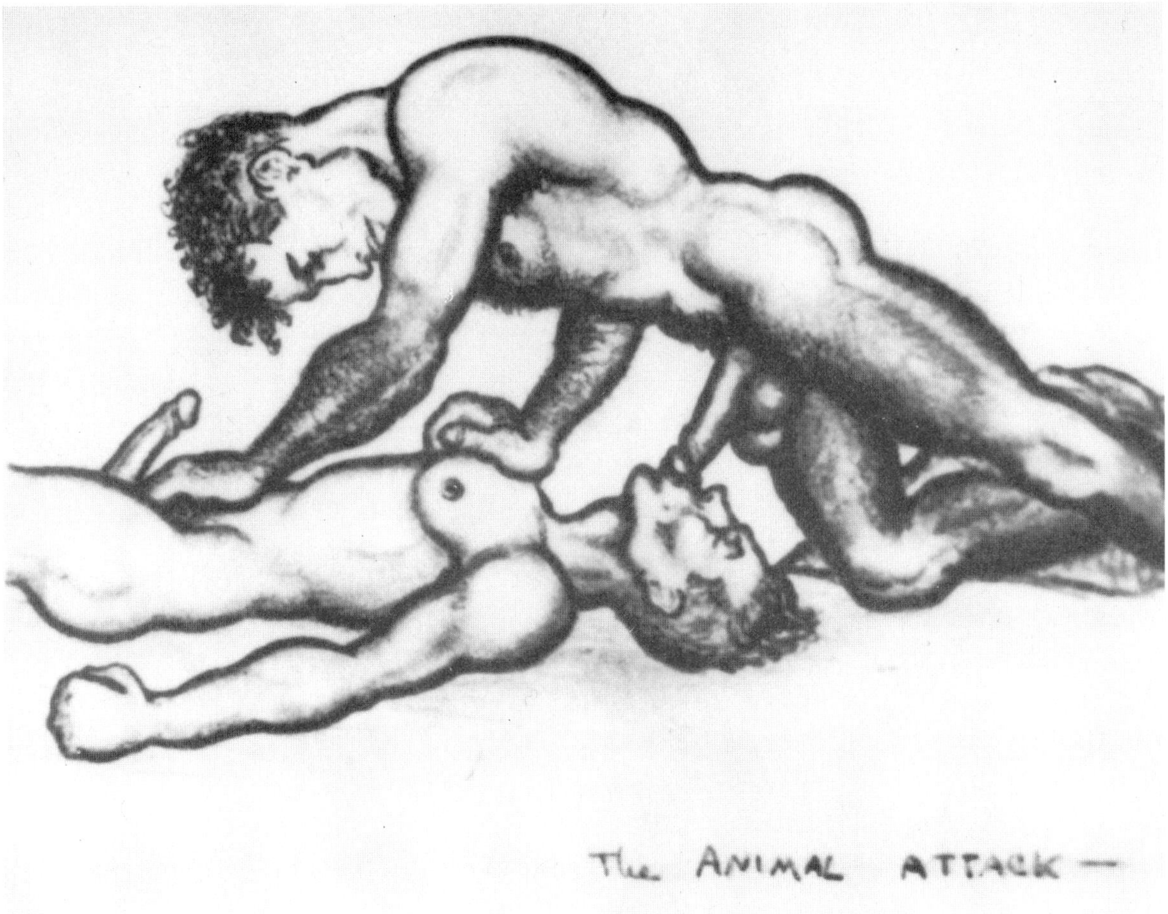

. . . In fact, this punitive and/or animalistic connotation of anal sexuality is prevalent everywhere in pre-Stonewall culture, whether in heterosexual folklore or in stag movies (Waugh [2001] 2004) or in queer sexual fantasy.

174

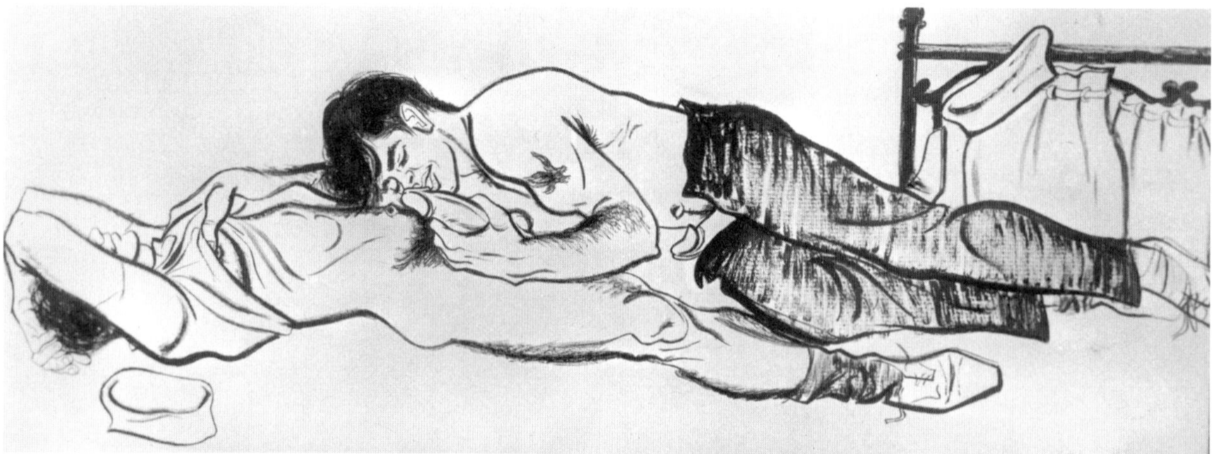

For all of this artist's fixation on jeans, sailor caps, and tattoos, not to mention serious footwear (especially in Figures 118 and 144-145), he's clearly a vanilla romantic couple kind of guy at heart (notice the "twin jets" couple opposite with heart-shaped cumwads). This tender one of two sailors, one shy and the other obviously not, is one of my my favorites, and not only because it offers virtually the only nipple action in the collection.

175

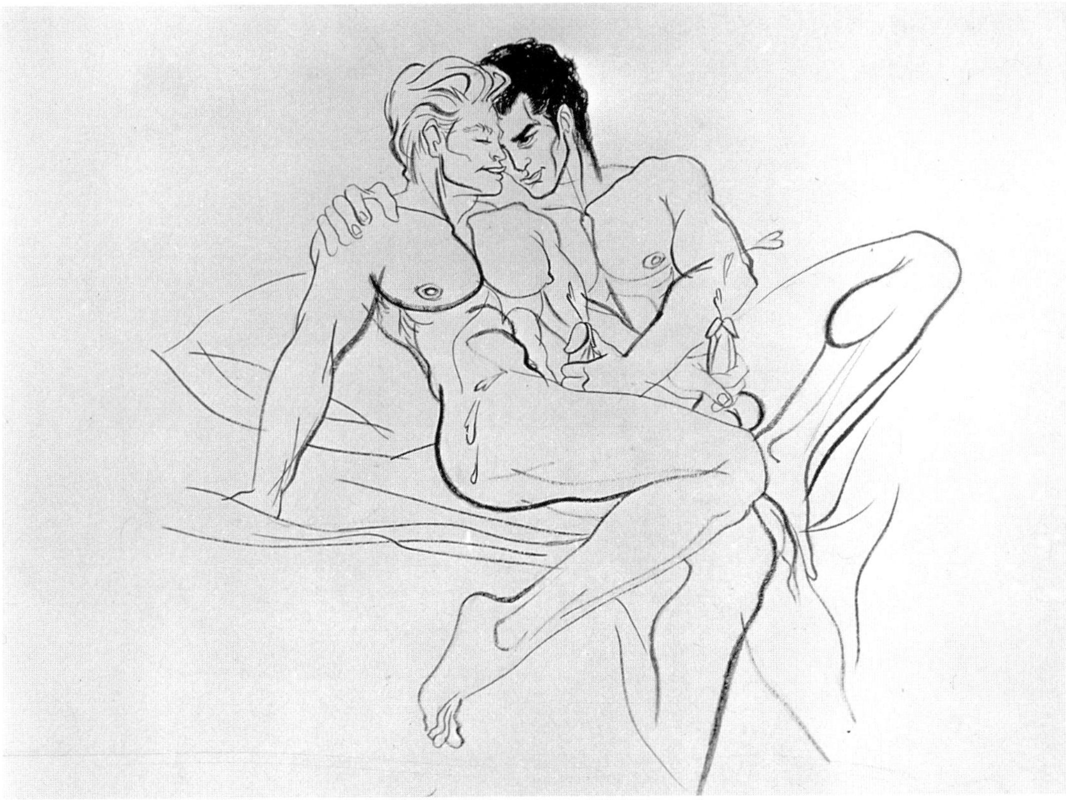

"'You mean I should do it for you and you do it for me?'
'Yeah, or else we can do it to ourselves.'
'Okay,' said Rudolf and moved over to the bed. I noticed at the moment he agreed, he began to get excited. So did I. [. . .] I put one arm under his head so that my hand came down on his nipple, which I pinched a little. Not to be outdone, he did the same thing to me. And then we each reached across with the other hand and began." Phil Andros (Sam Steward), *$tud* ([1966] 1982, 173) **176**

Trios

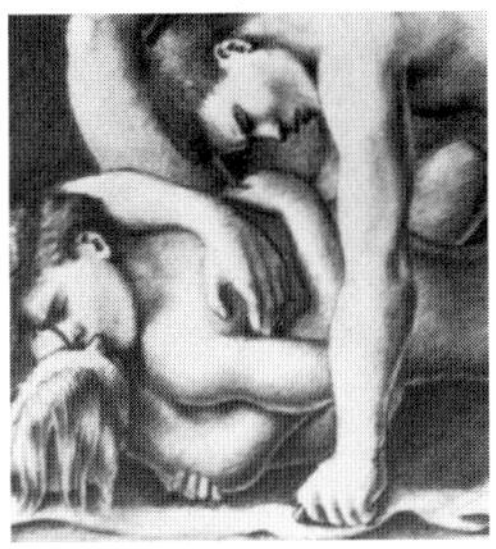

If couples carry all the ideological weight of romantic idealization and current political struggles, trios are trouble. This section gathers thirty-one of the collection's more interesting threesomes (well, the last one is a "double date"), about half the total number in the book. Trios then were popular with the underground graphics eroticists, but, unsurprisingly, only in half the measure that traditional couples fired their imaginations and lust.

Trios

The Joy of Gay Sex was encouraging but ultimately cautionary:

> **Three's company**. A threesome is a way for lovers to add spice to home cooking. It can also be very satisfying even when the participants have just met [. . .]
>
> Threesomes don't always work; it is not unusual for one of the participants to become jealous or feel left out. Sometimes lovers think a threesome would be a nifty idea, but in execution one or both of them turns possessive and broods. Or if three strangers are involved, two of them may hit it off so well that they want to be alone and the third is left high and dry. Sometimes a third who goes home with a pair of lovers feels he's simply being used as a sexual convenience (Silverstein and White, 1977, 211).

Both the satisfactions and the tensions come out in this selection, especially in the "bisexual" triangles (Tom, Dick, and Cherry) that were popular in the pre-Stonewall imagination. In this regard also, White and Silverstein advise caution: "If [married couples] ask you to join them in bed, do so if you want to, but in most cases you will find that he will shy away from extensive physical contact with you and most of your attentions will be going to her." Writing before the current theories of homosociality and of men desiring each other through women, the authors don't get into such underlying complexities. But Etienne seems wry and observant about them in his series included here (figs. 180-198), of which an extensive sampling is provided to give a full sense of its unfolding, vigor and charm. In comparison with this nasty treat, the bisexual sandwiches and triangles of Figures 178-179 (solidarity sisters!), 200-205, and 206-207 are all anodine and good-natured Pollyanna.

As for the *same-sex* triangles here as well as elsewhere in *Lust Unearthed*, they often bring in relations of voyeurism on the part of the third partner and are thus off-centre in a not unsexy way, especially with Happyface (figs. 48-51), and the Yokohama-artist-who-may-be-Smara (figs. 101 and 103). (Not that I'm making any implied judgment about voyeurism being unbalanced . . . moi?) A few other images are enraptured with the possibilities of a greater equilaterality, if that's a word, and are close to what Silverstein and White, in step with 1970s liberationist ideology, call "exhilarating-and surprisingly intimate": Happyface's spouting trinity (fig. 47), Jean Vincent's post-coital tenderness (fig. 80), Smara's ambiguous trios (figs. 106 and 108), or Caillaux's three thugs on a rug (fig. 199).

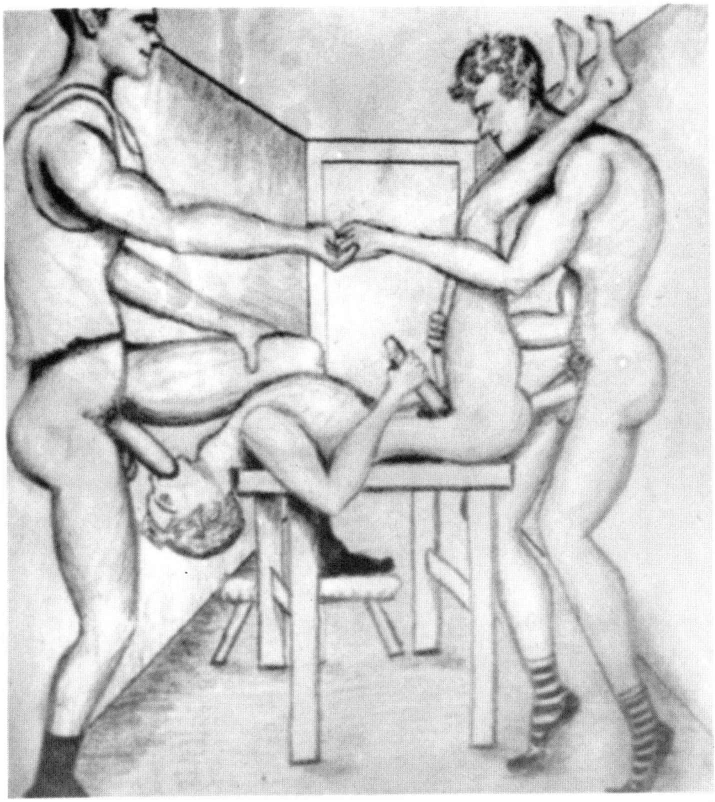

This amateur drawing of an ideal triangle, so delicately consummated, is perfect in every way, from the careful furniture arrangement to the inserters' tasteful socks and graceful tiptoes. Beware, however, for the foreshortening makes the room very claustrophobic and bodes ill for a relationship that is notoriously precarious.

177

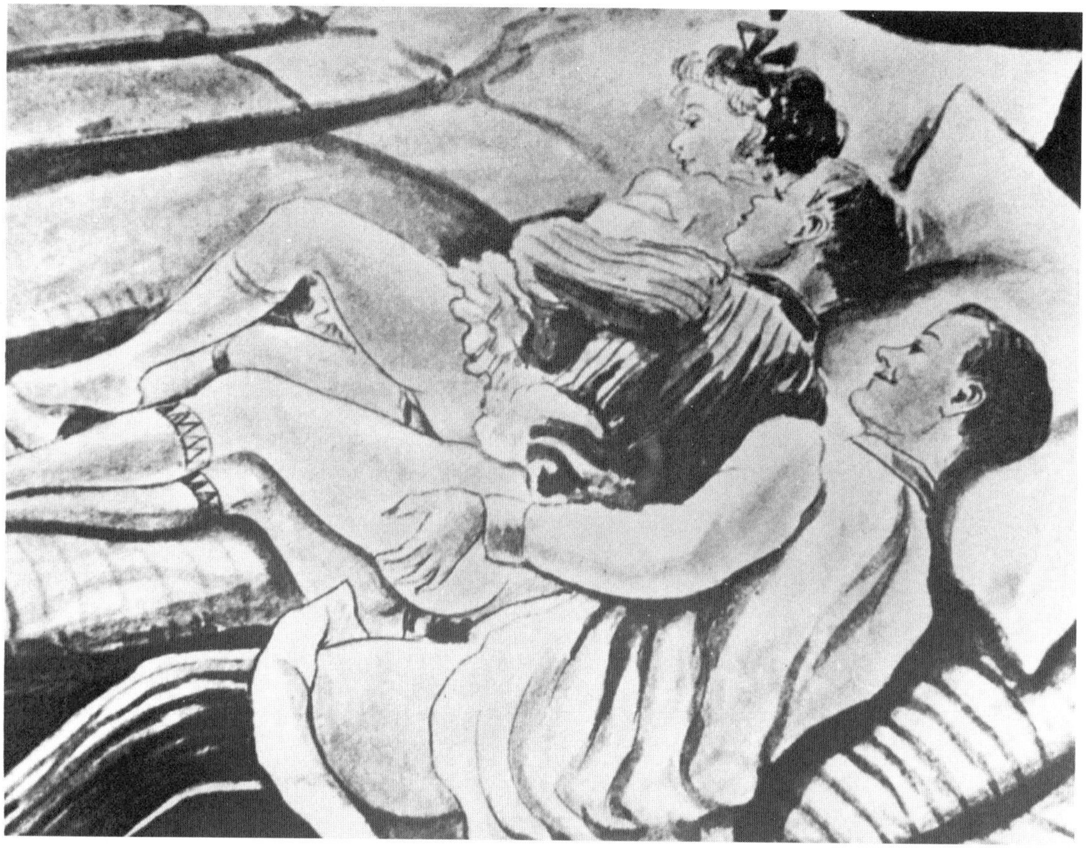

Bisexual triangles are another kettle of fish, as it were, but this rare idyllic view of two fairies (notice the hands) and their gal pal seems hunky-dory. Turns are taken at being the sandwich filling, and there seems little of the insidious potential for misogyny when men share a woman. Anonymous, probably 1930s.

178

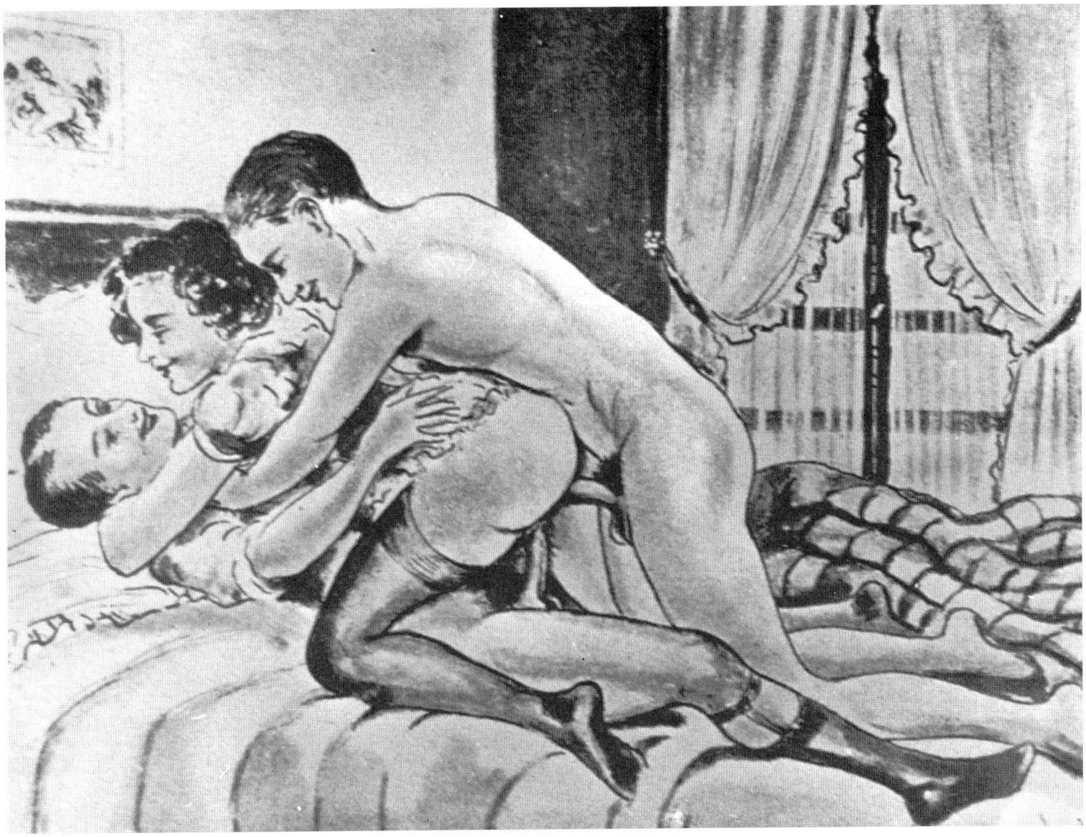

"Alfred returned my caresses. He confessed to me that he was not Rose's brother. He was her pimp. Rose continued to play her part and we ours. Alfred would wink, dig me in the ribs and sometimes start to giggle. Rose looked at him with surprise, not suspecting that we were in league and that there existed between us links that were strengthened by deceit. One day the hotel bell-boy came in and found us lying together, with Rose between us. 'You see, Jules,' she cried, indicating both of us, 'my brother and my fancy-man! Everything I love.'" Jean Cocteau, *Le Livre blanc* ([1928] 1990, 39) **179**

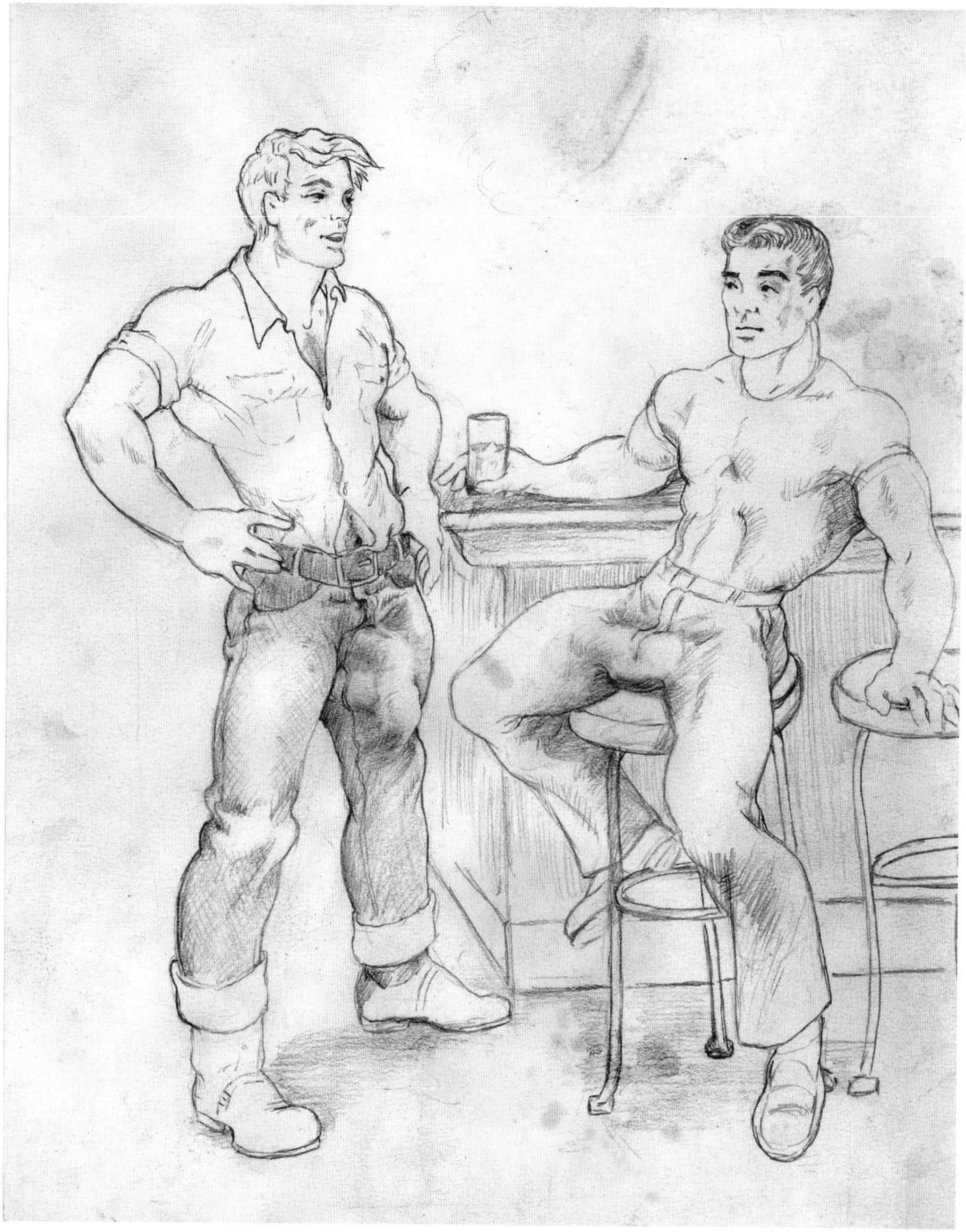

Etienne produced many versions of the bisexual triangle, and with his cynical bottom's view of human nature pushed Cocteau's undercurrent of mistrust all the way. This long series is one of several that DuBek had apparently got firsthand from his Chicago friend. See also Figure 63, which together with 180-198 are reproduced courtesy of Etienne's surviving partner Charles Renslow.

180

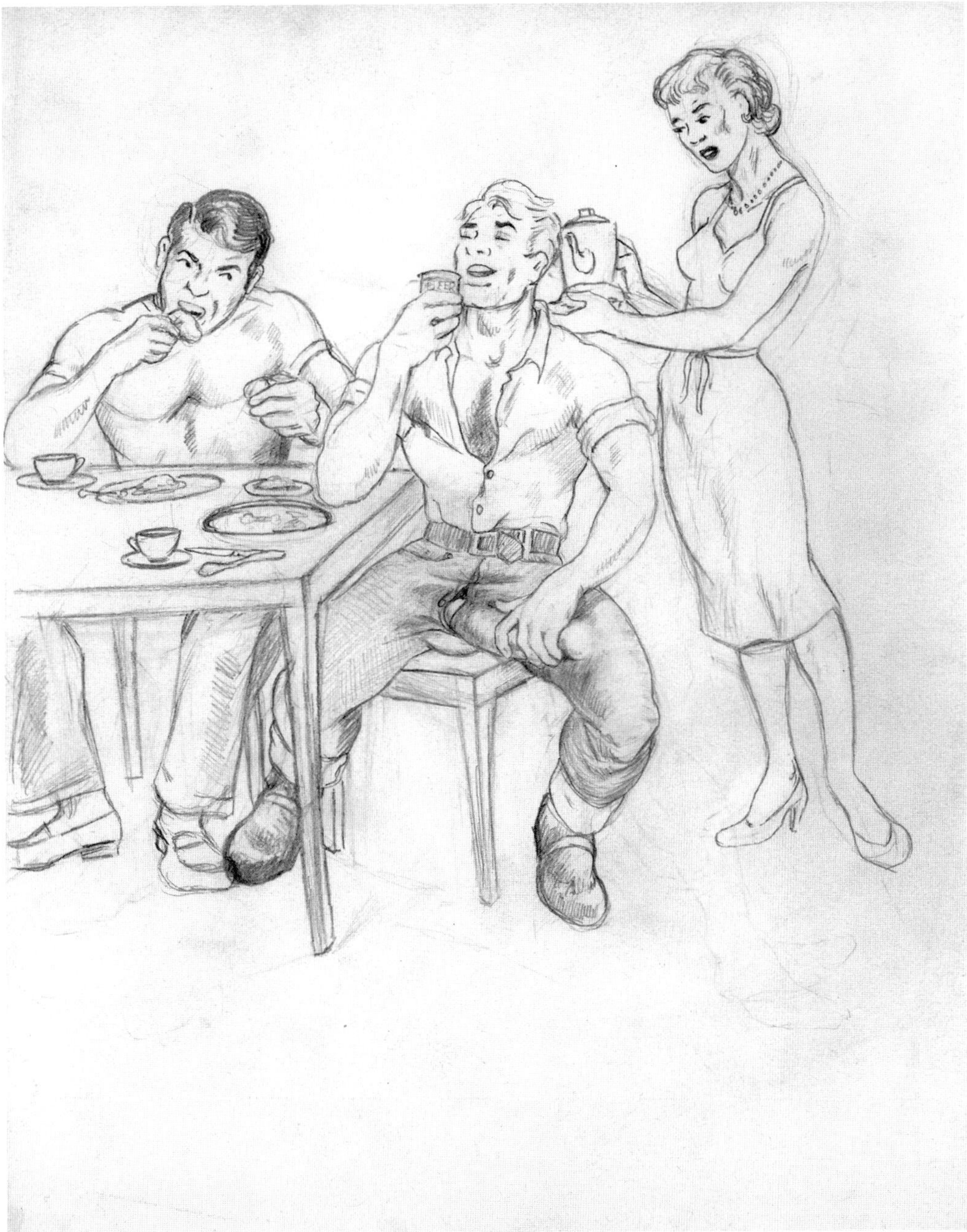

In *Out/Lines*, I described in this way the triangle interest: "Etienne's fascination with straight men enabled him to bring together the tropes of difference and domination with the tropes of whitebread sameness: the innocent blond wide-eyed hunk is inevitably confronted with the smirking and manipulative brunette top, working class or otherwise Other, who will steal him from his girlfriend or corner him into submissive pleasures that he had never anticipated." (Waugh 2002, 82). Here, hair color is switched but otherwise the pattern holds. **181**

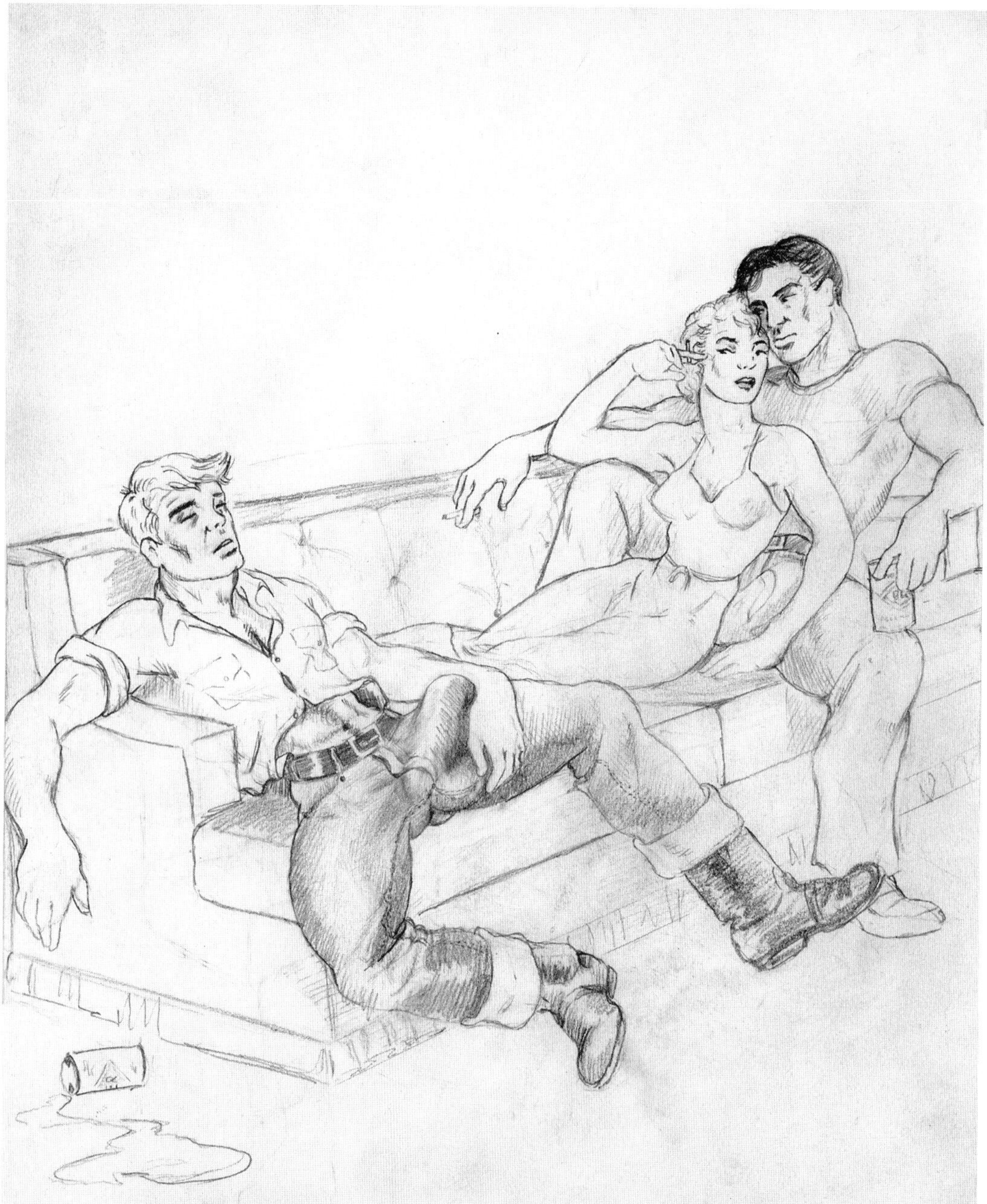

Blondy's motorcycle boots tell all. In comparison, Brunette's wimpy penny-loafers telegraph immediately that he's about to lose his wife, if not his cherry. I was asleep at the switch in *Out/Lines* when I didn't make anything of the fact that fourteen out of fifteen of his frames offered detailed and precise foreground renditions of shoes, boots, socks or or naked feet, and another anonymous series, "Toilet Pickup" (figures 116-127, since tentatively attibuted to Etienne), did much the same.

182

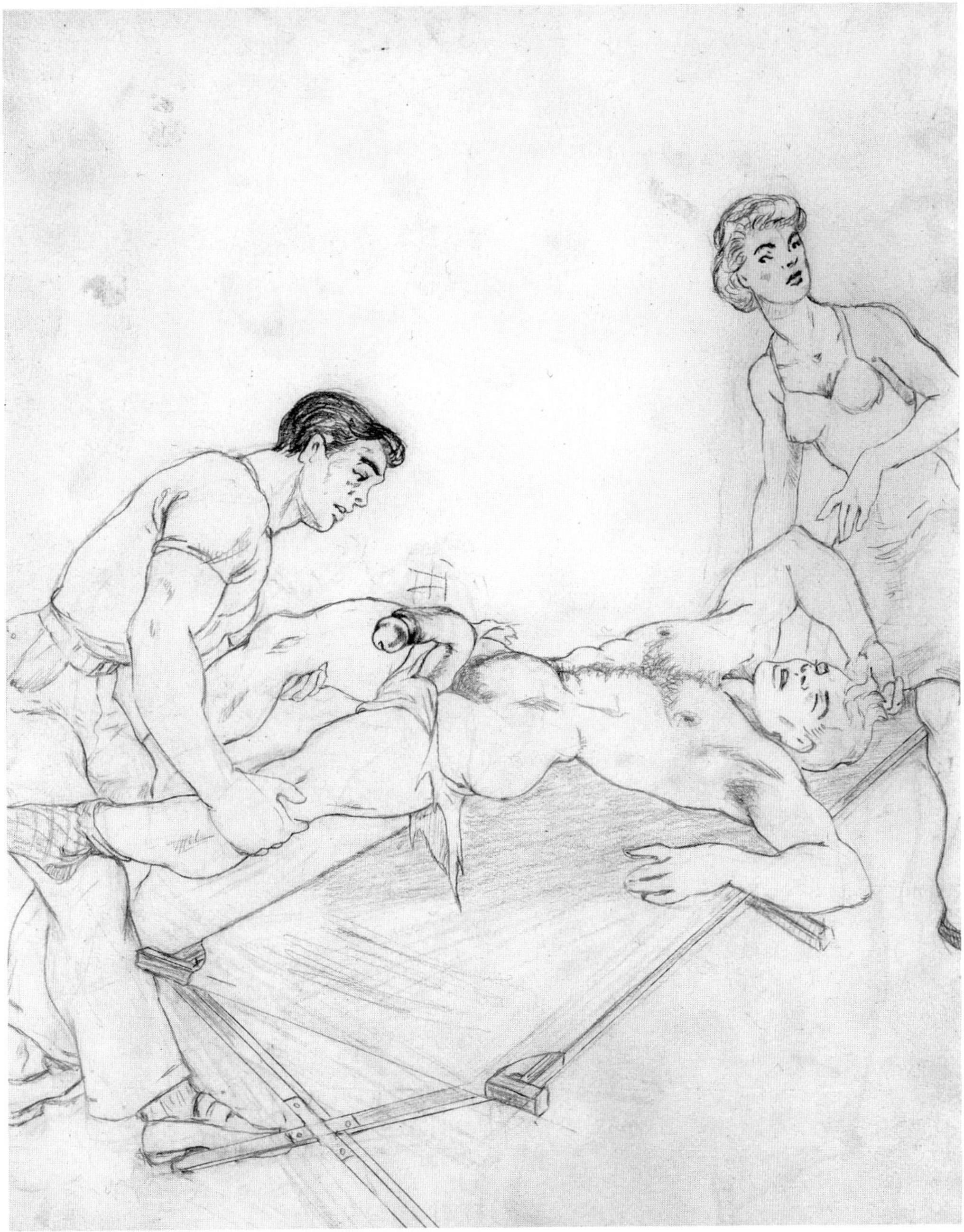

Blondy has passed out drunk on the sofa so the kindly couple undress their guest and move him onto the camp cot and Penny-loafers gets a glimpse of Blondy's dick. Foot fetish update: at this point Blondy's argyle socks, with those sexy holes at the toes, lovingly sustained in every frame, take over the role of the Wellingtons in embroidering the narrative with erotic energy.

183

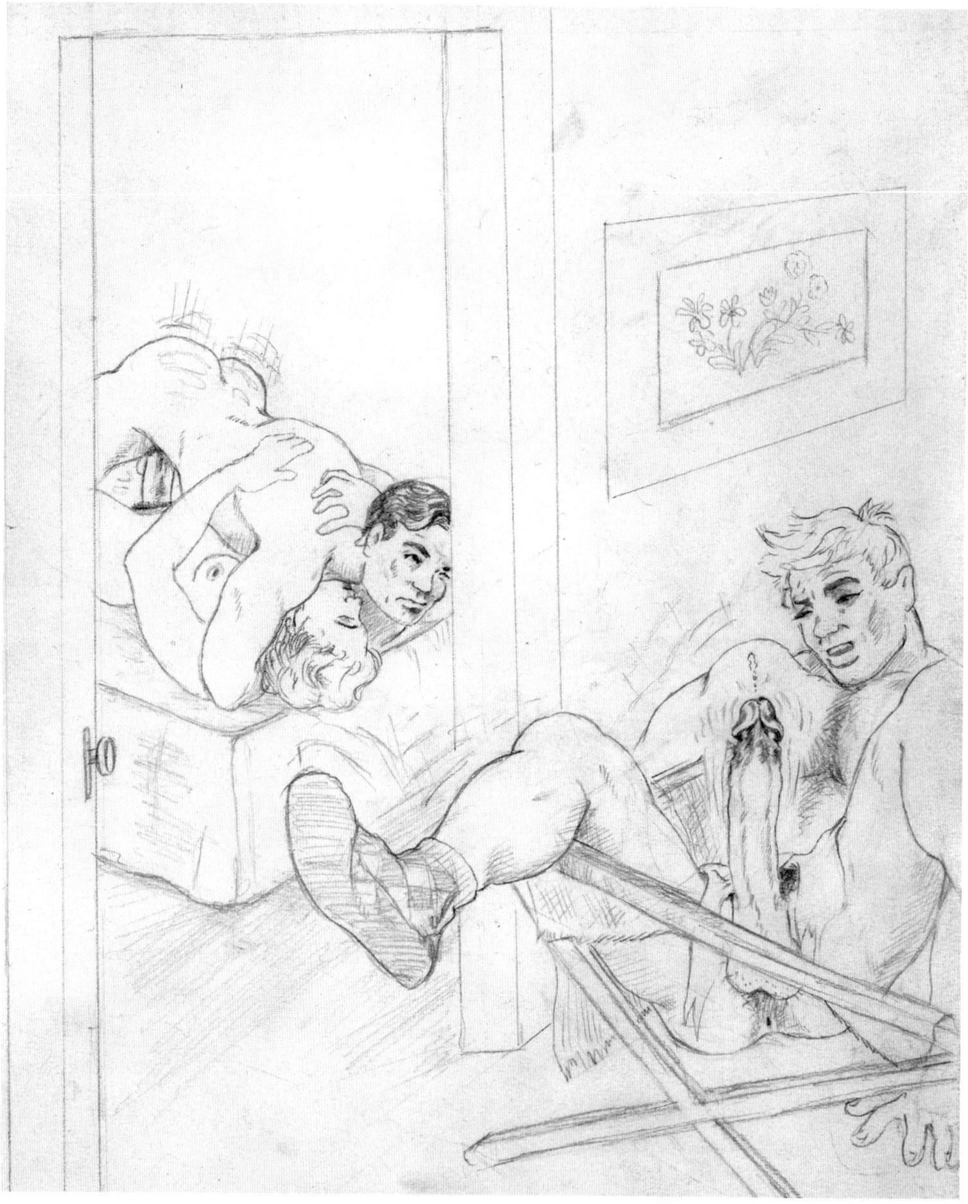

Penny-loafers is ploughing his wife with the bedroom door open but can't concentrate because he can't get that blond dick out of his mind; meanwhile, Blondy can't sleep on such a flimsy bed and with all that pre-cum in the air and the breeze teasing his perfect gem-like anus.

184

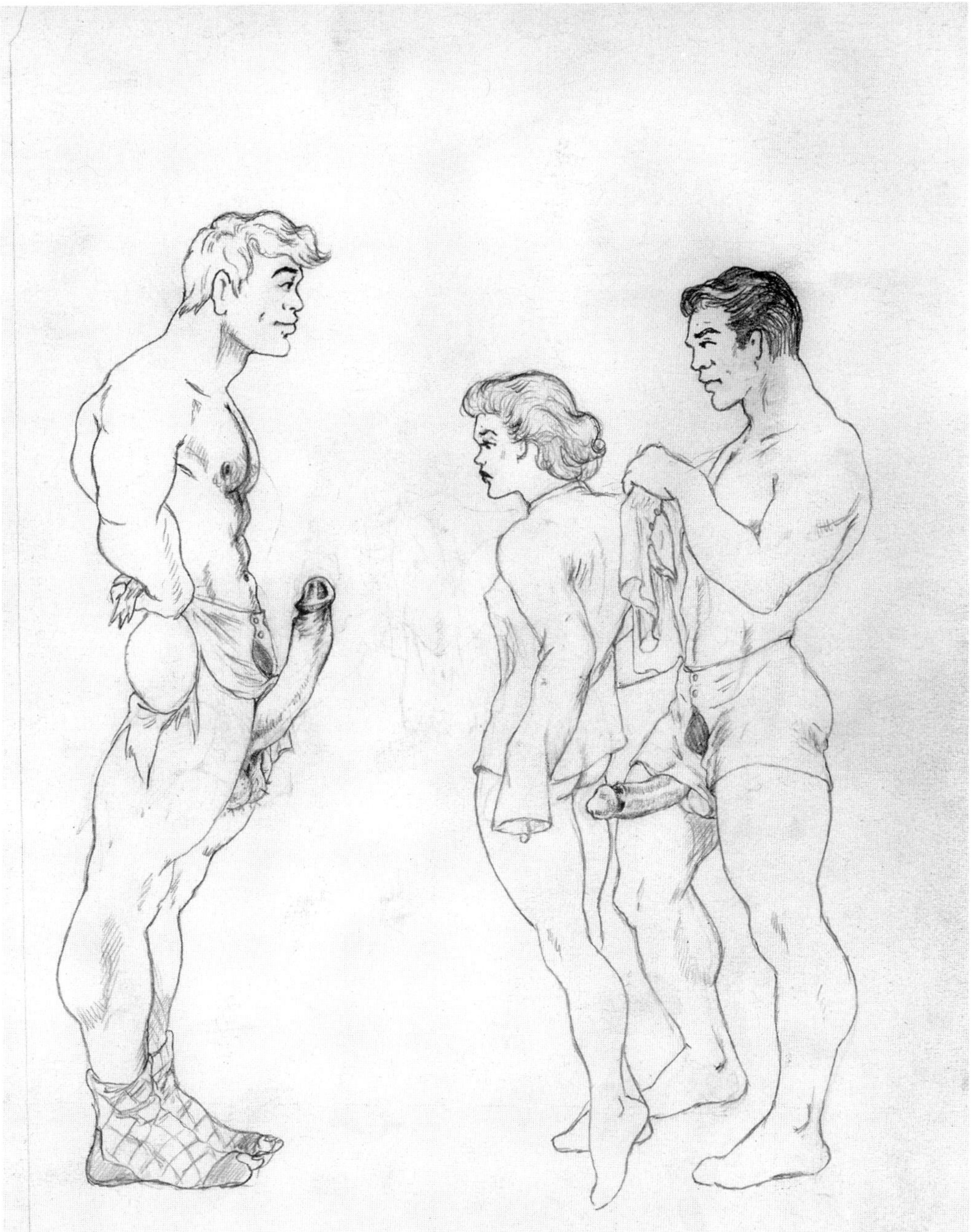

The order gets a little murky over the next five or so frames, not that it matters how drunken, horny Blondy ends up in the armchair when his concerned hosts have dumped him on the camp cot. . . . But I believe this one shows Penny-loafer helping his wife into the modesty of her pyjama top while wondering what to do with their guest, who suddenly seems wide awake.

185

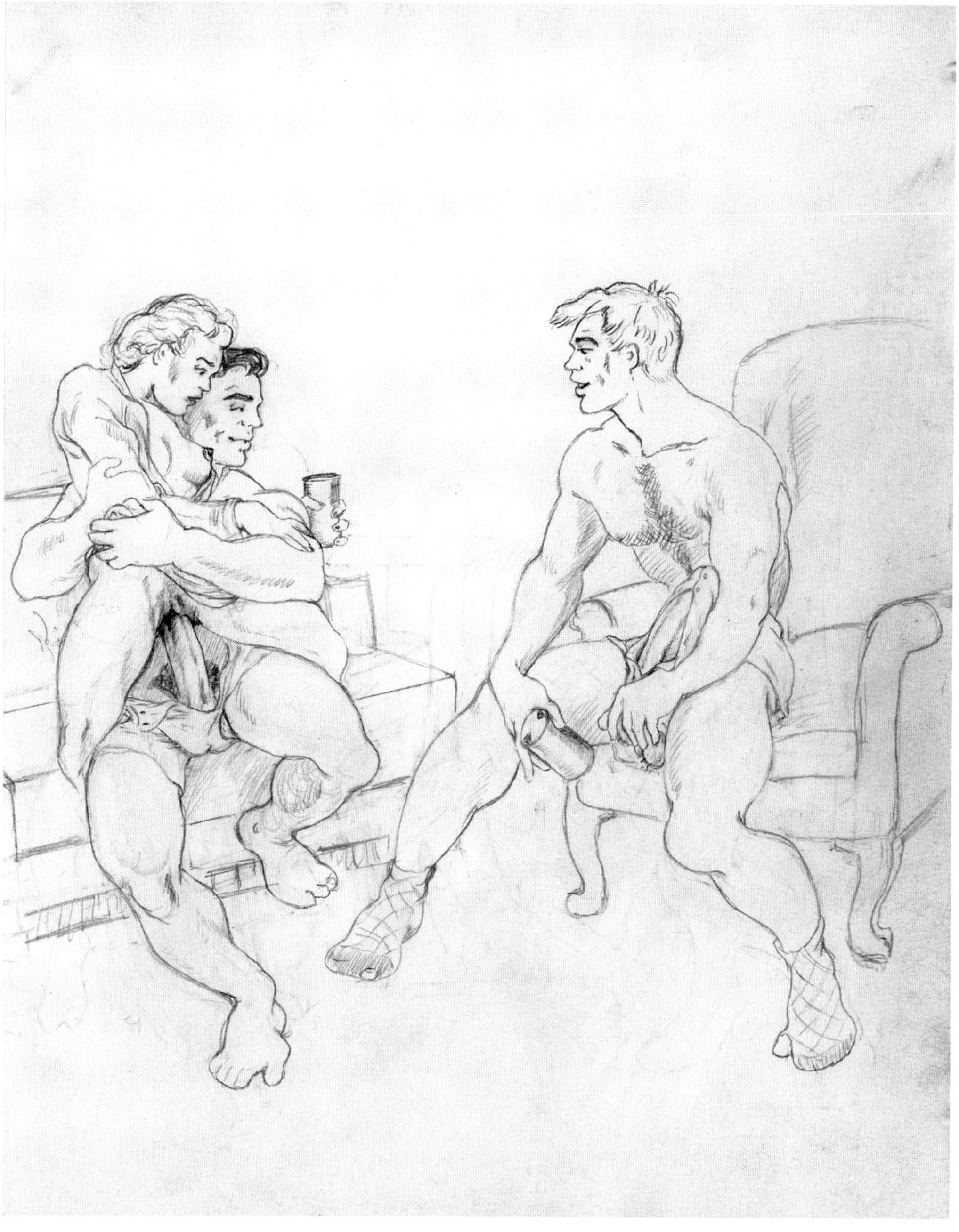

So let's have another beer, but Penny-Loafer seems to want to show off how he possesses the Missus to his buddy. She is less than happy about this.

186

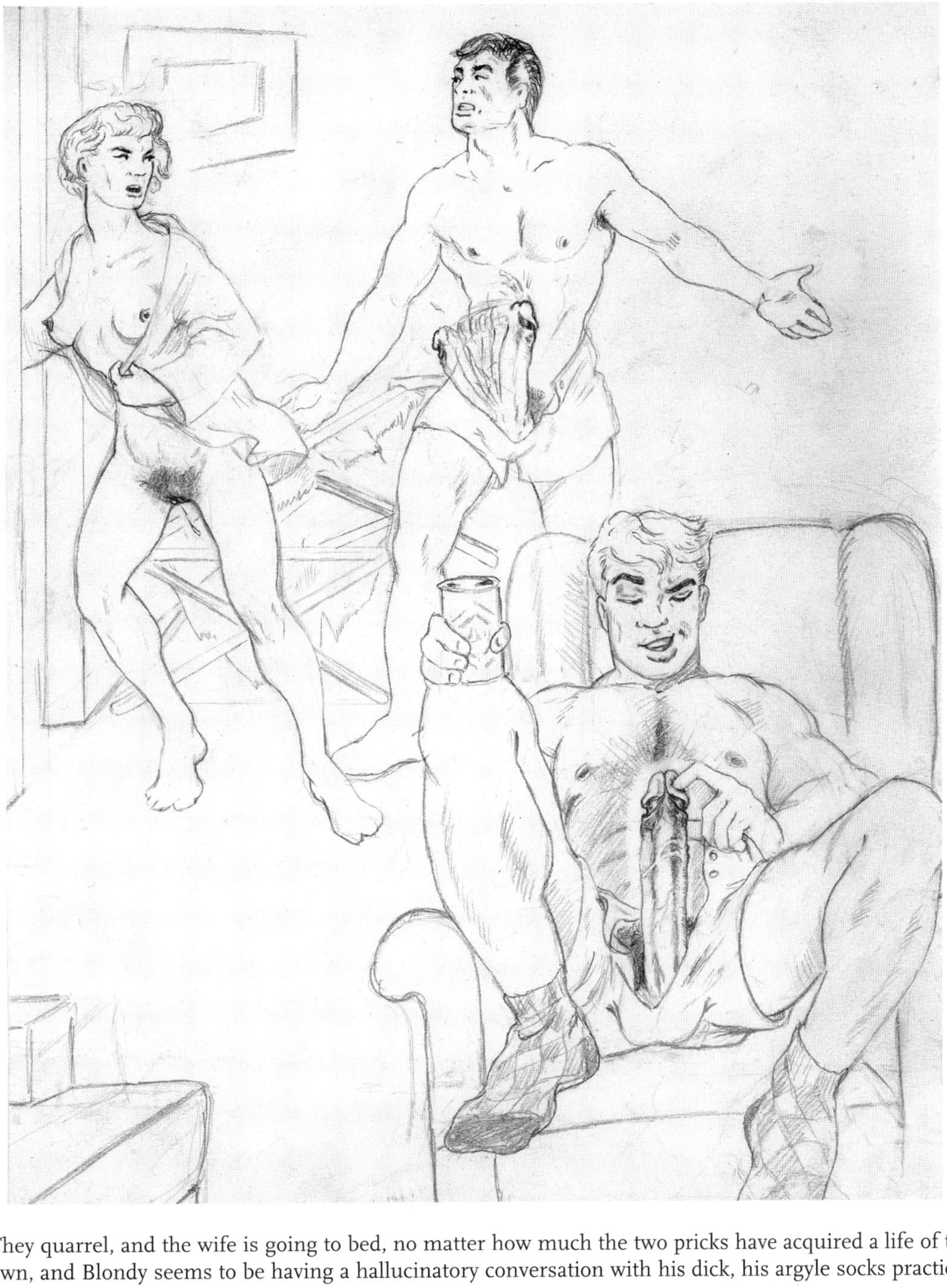

They quarrel, and the wife is going to bed, no matter how much the two pricks have acquired a life of their own, and Blondy seems to be having a hallucinatory conversation with his dick, his argyle socks practically filling half the frame.

187

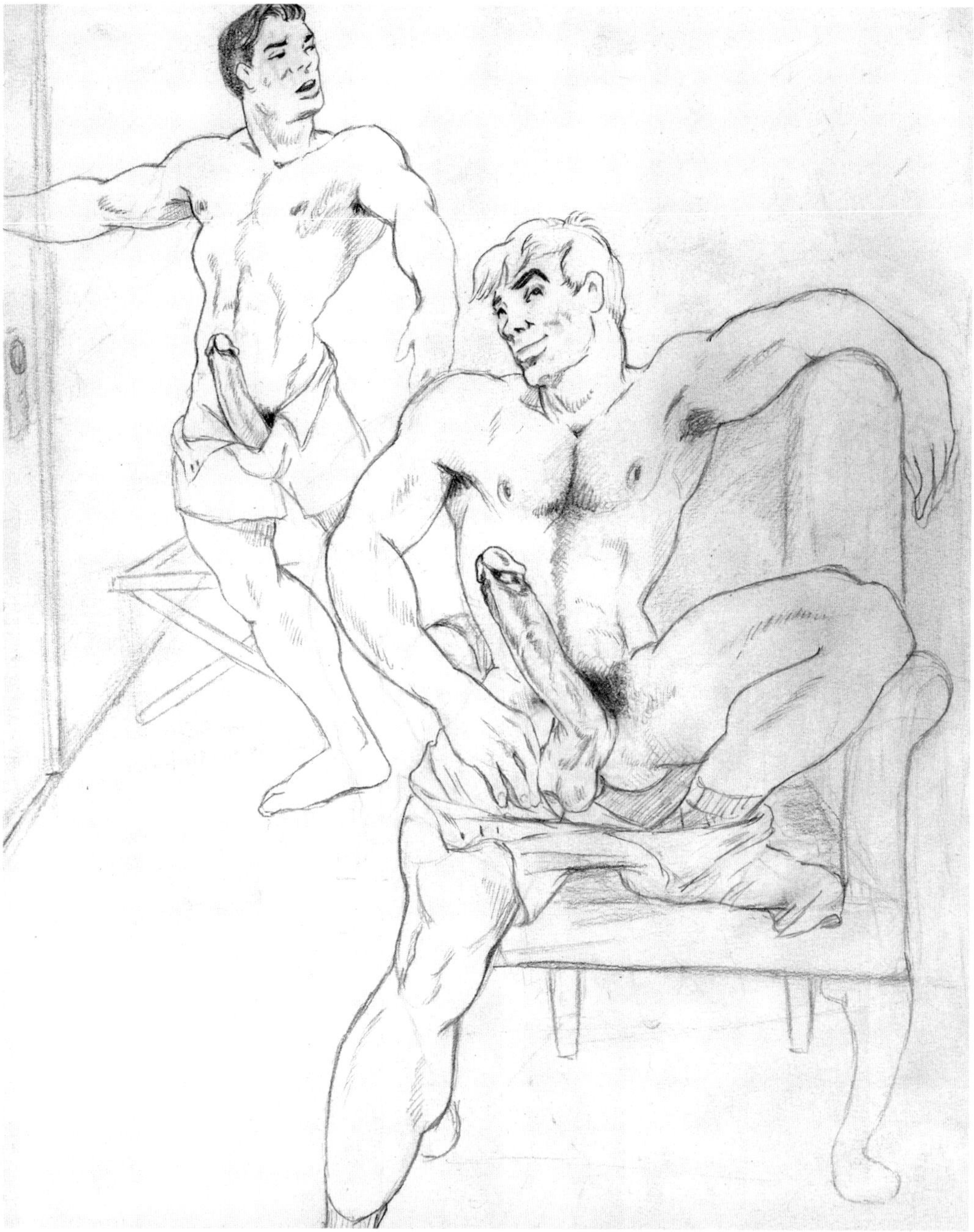

"... Mohammed had wanted to have a threesome with a girl. 'You me and girls,' he said. 'But where?' I said, not going to go in for that kind of thing in the apartment. 'Along the beach,' he said. I said 'perhaps.'" Joe Orton, *The Orton Diaries* ([1967] 1986, 163-164)

188

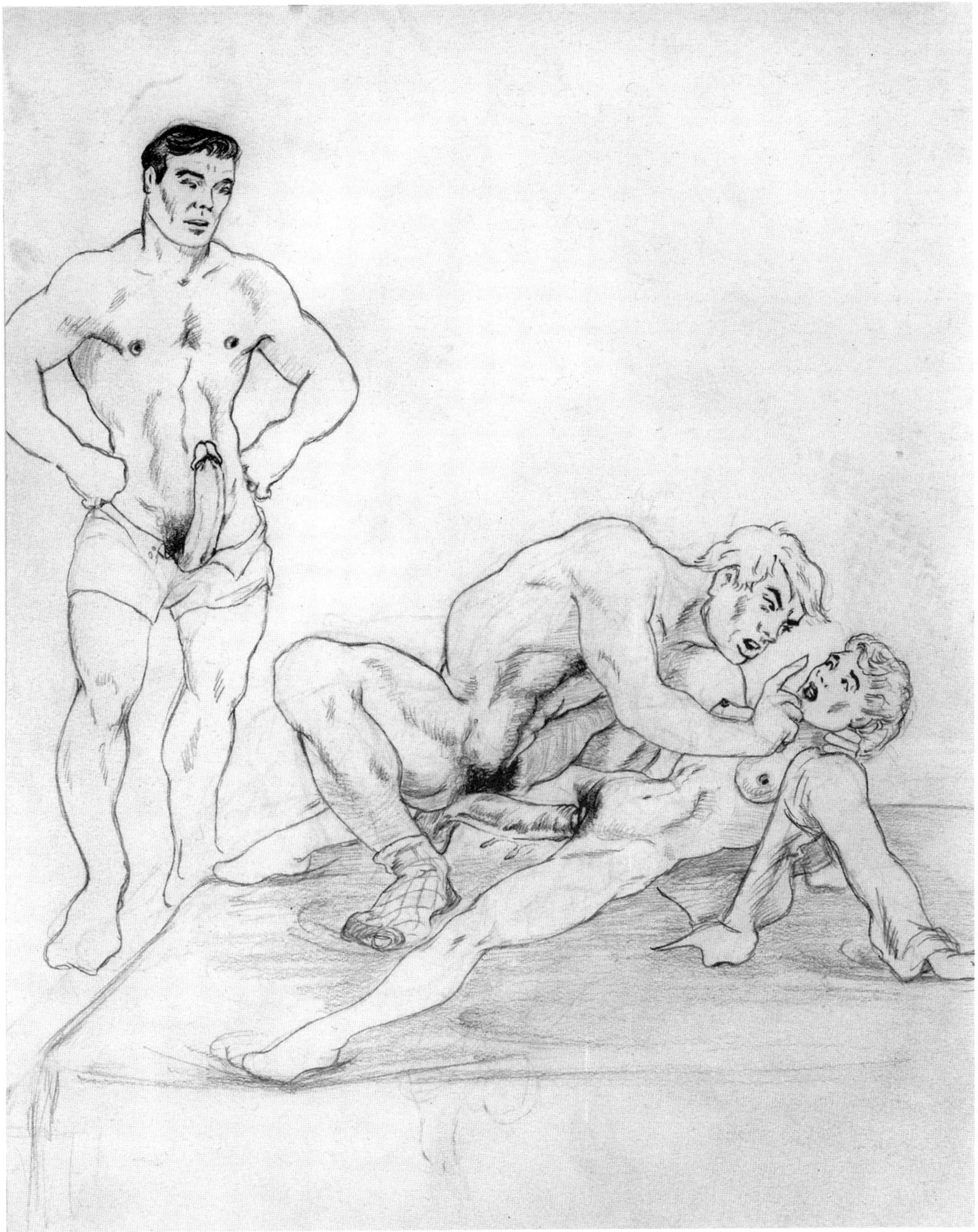

The solution is for Penny-loafers to ask Blondy to come and reason with his wife (opposite). A serious mistake, but Blondy gives it a try. His boxers somehow get lost in the trek to the bedroom but he gives her a talking to about conjugal duty anyway. Meanwhile, the hooded warrior has taken on a life of its own and is already knocking at heaven's door.

189

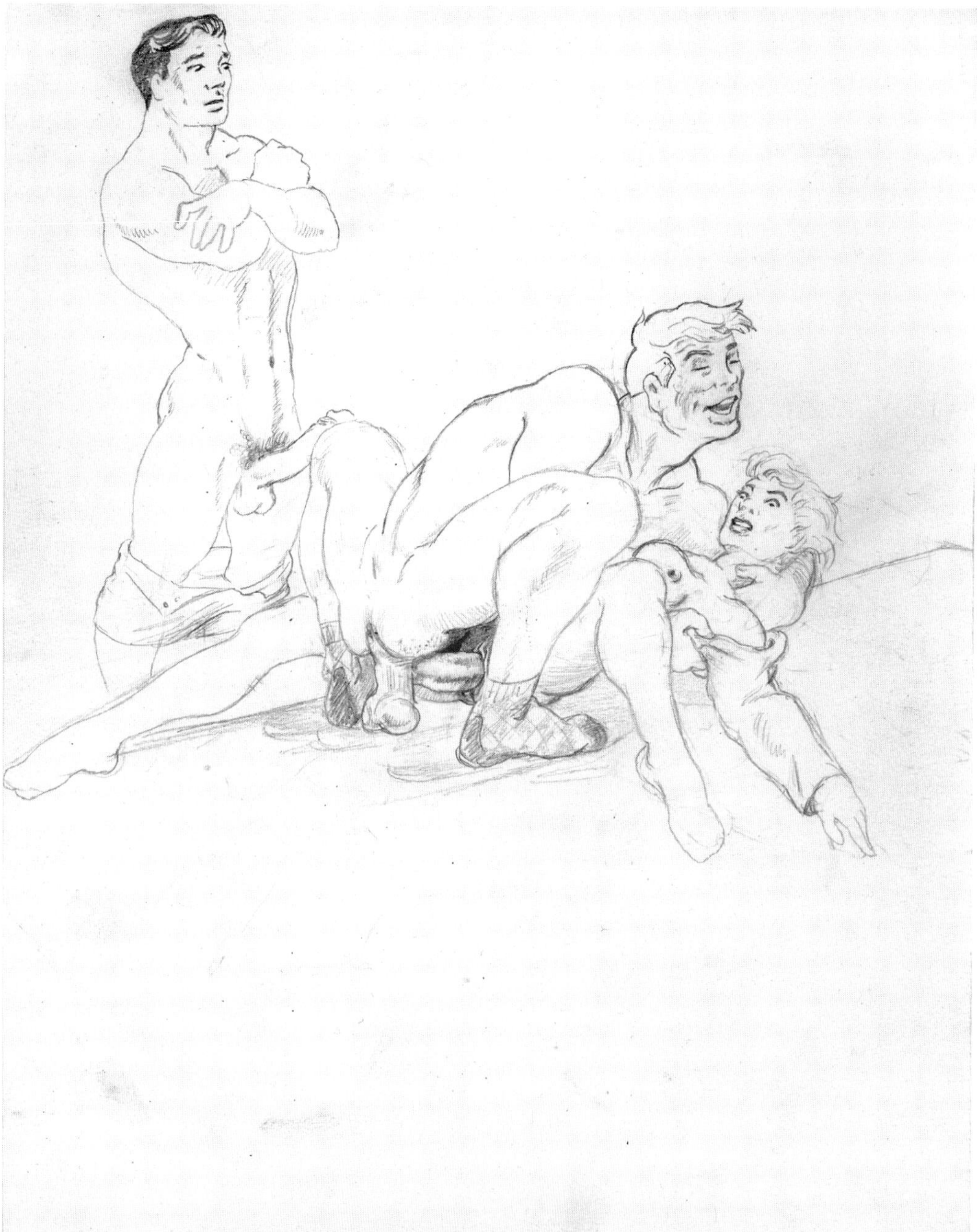

There's a breakthrough; the wife looks a little startled and Penny-loafer a bit consternated though no less aroused with his cock resting on Blondy's knee. Blondy is feeling fine.

190

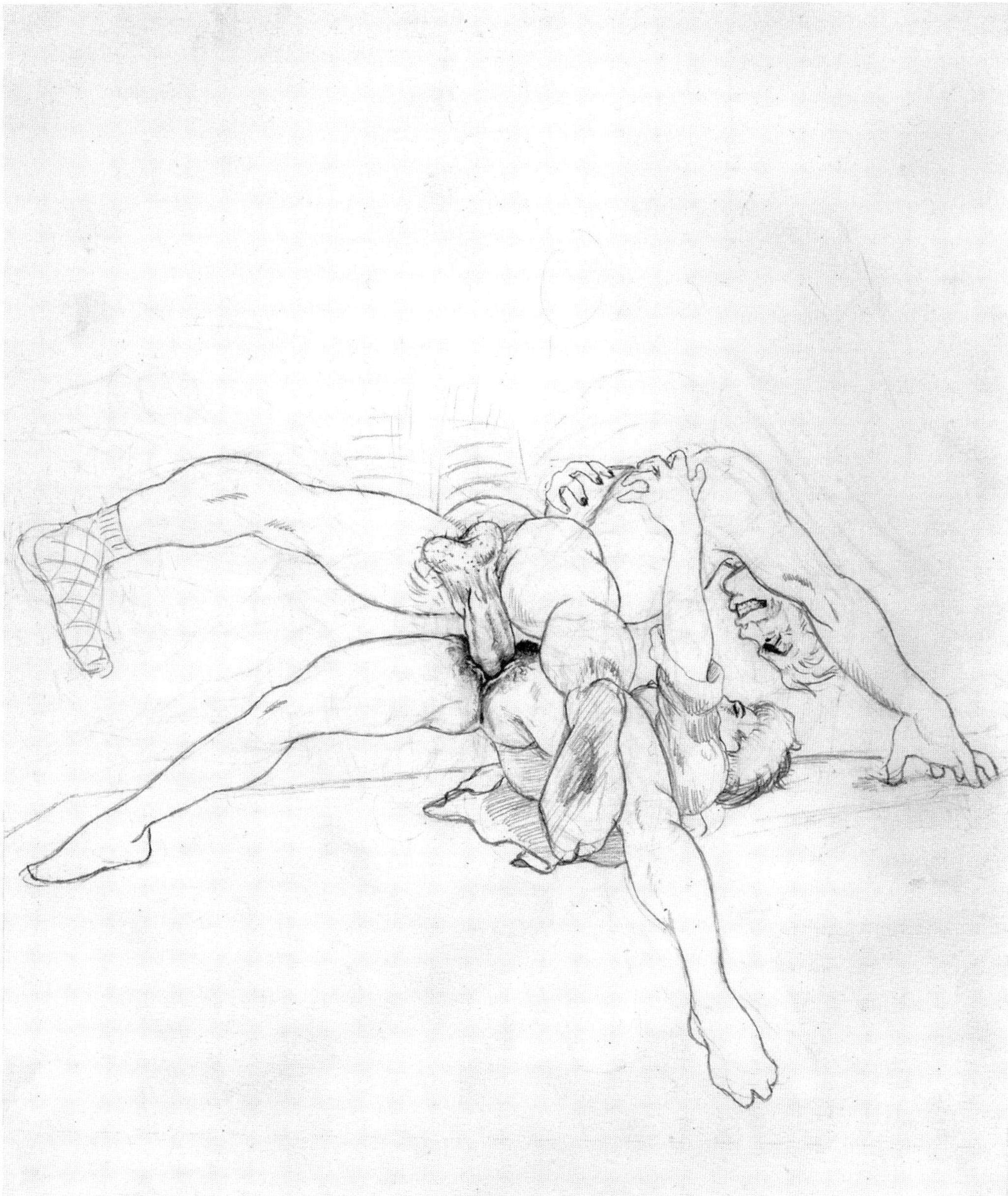

Penny-loafers temporary disappears from the scene, and as vigorous fucking ensues, Blondy's face acquires a diabolical intensity, his legs aloft in the acrobatic frenzy that only Etienne knows how to depict, and his dark meeting ground of yin and yang at the very center of the frame.

191

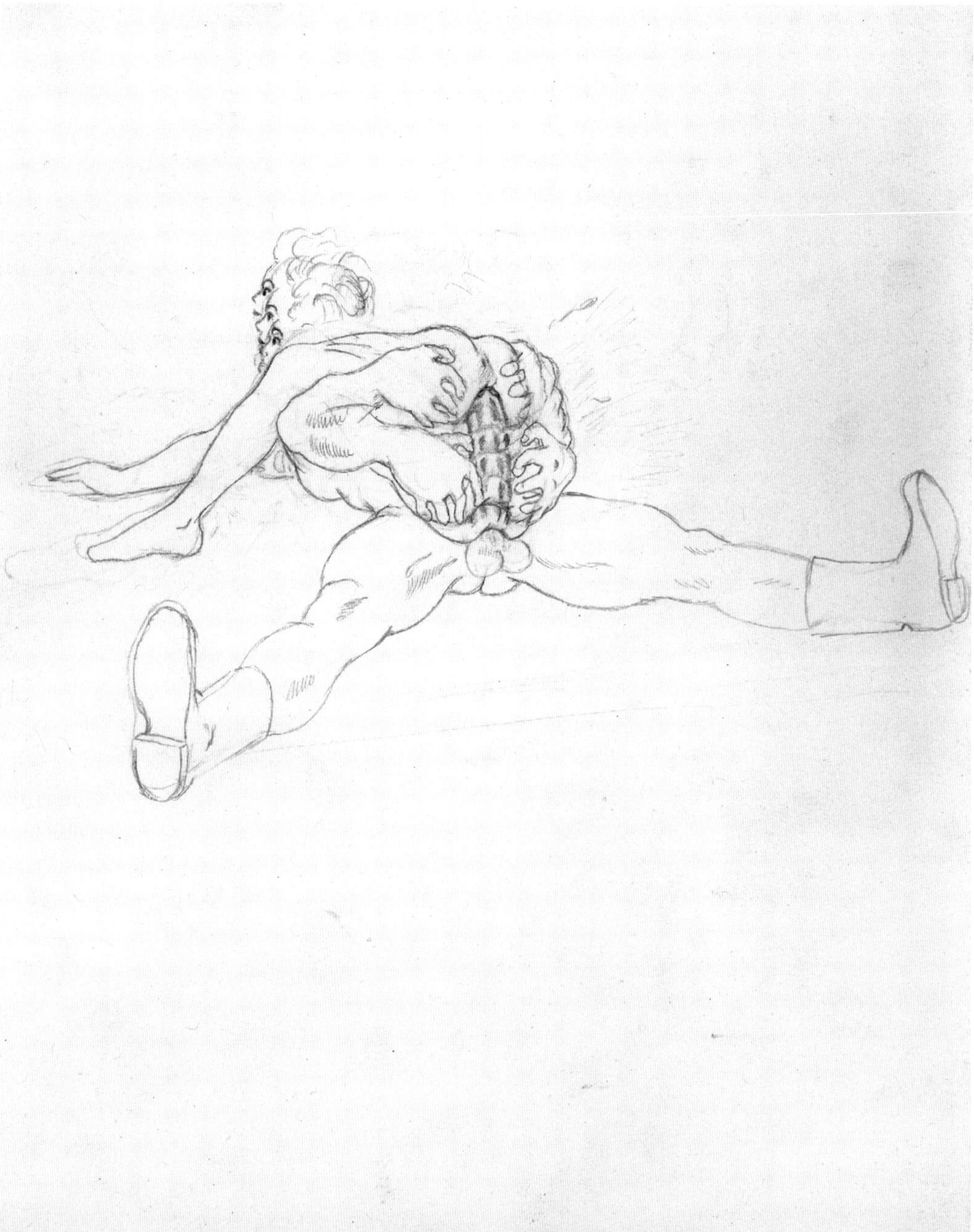

192

Here, dear reader, we insert four frames from Version B, with the best scholarly intentions, in which Blondy deflowers Penny-loafers, as he has obviously wanted from the start, but which does not happen in Version A (perhaps DuBek flushed the missing frames when the electrician rang the doorbell). First, however, Blondy continues his vigorous fucking with Mrs. Penny-loafer, and Etienne experiments with an ingenious technique for portraying vigorous motion.

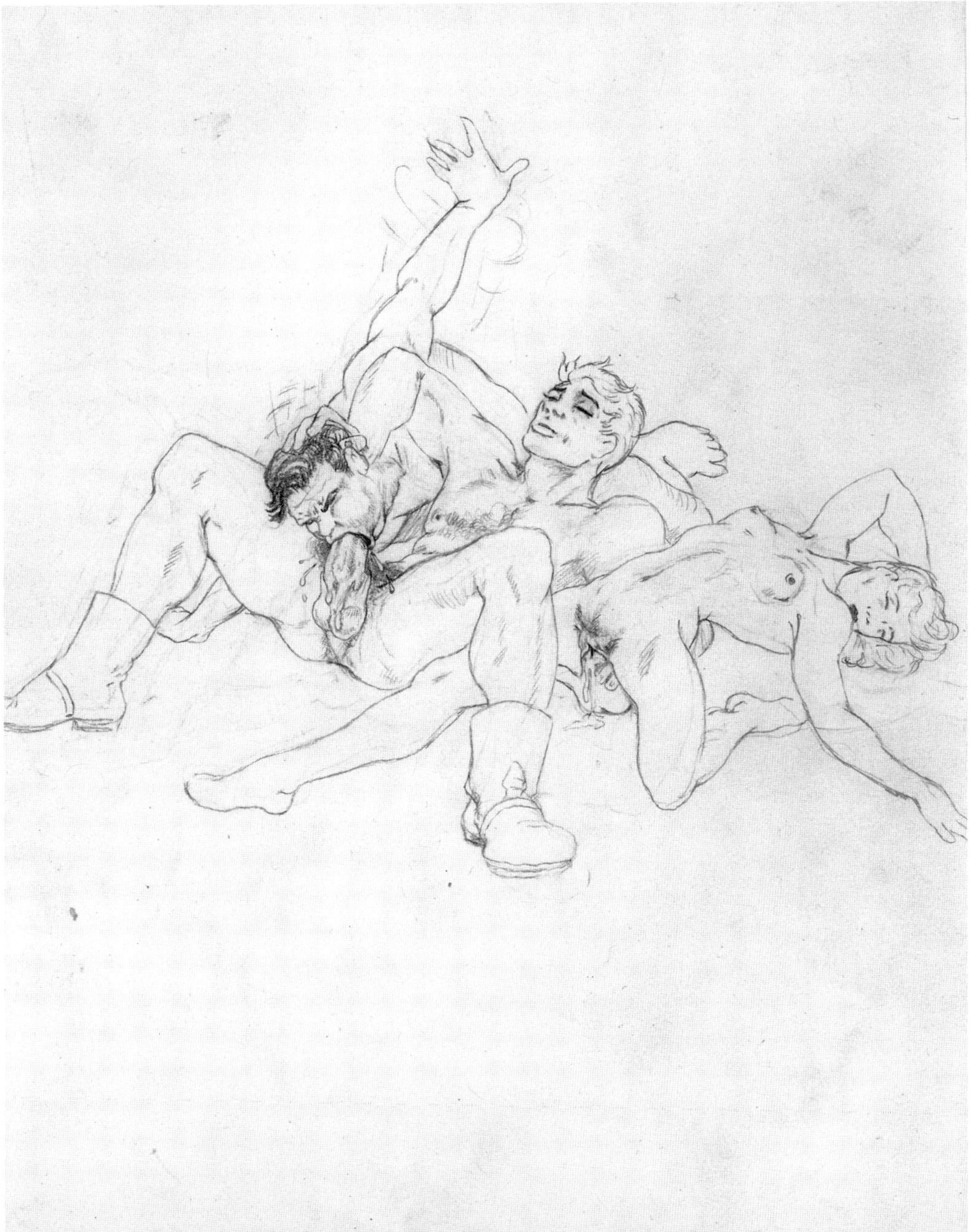

Note that, in Version B, Blondy has suddenly re-donned his Wellingtons, and having exhausted the lady of the house but with his fingers still active, gently invites Penny-loafers for a taste.

193

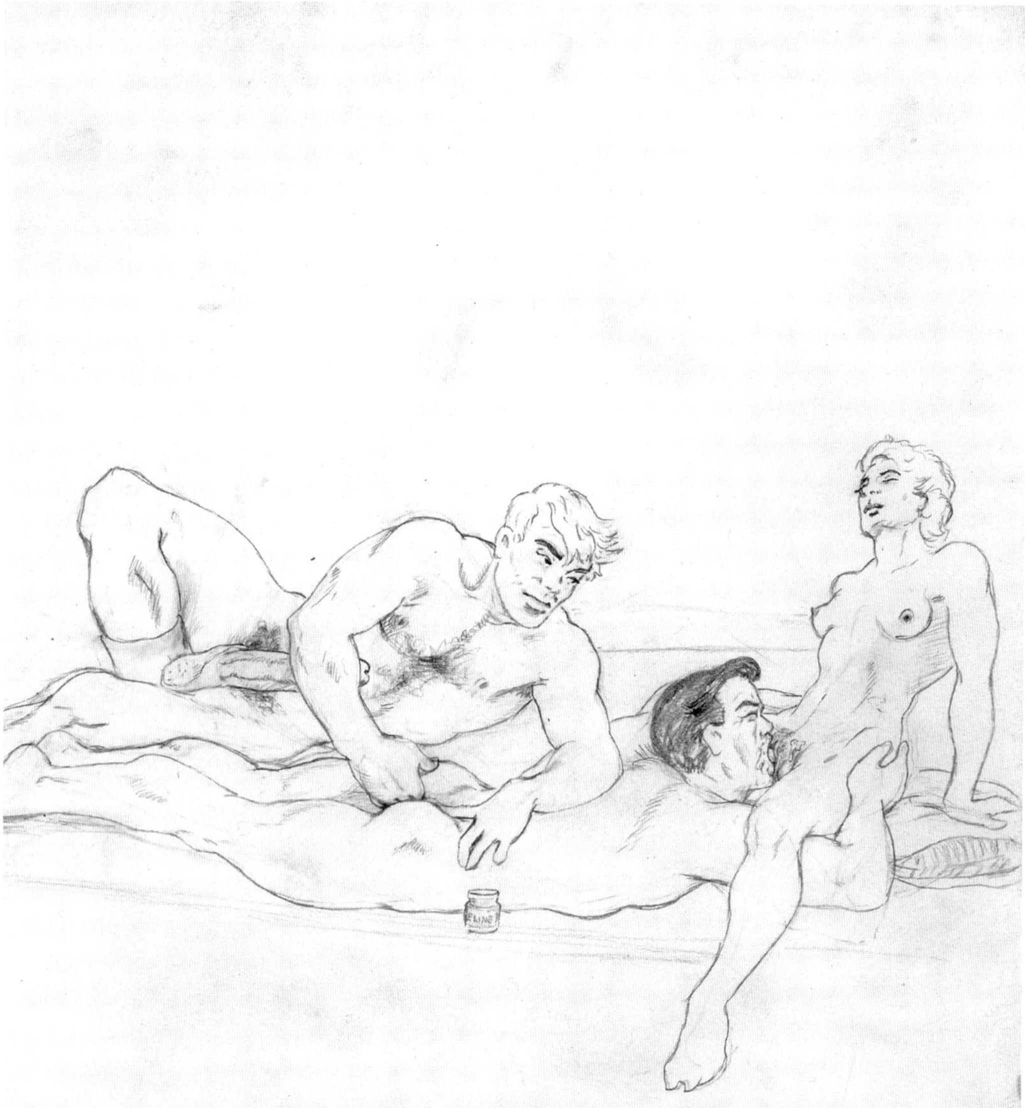

Penny-loafers also tries a taste of his buddy and his wife simultaneously, feigning unawareness of Blondy's further lubricious designs. As for Mrs. Penny-loafers—or should I say Genet's Madame Lysiane?—". . . her love for Robert—or for Querelle? For a second she became confused [. . .] Now she was sure the brothers loved each other so greatly that they had deemed it necessary to find a third person to disengage them and to provide a
194 diversion . . .

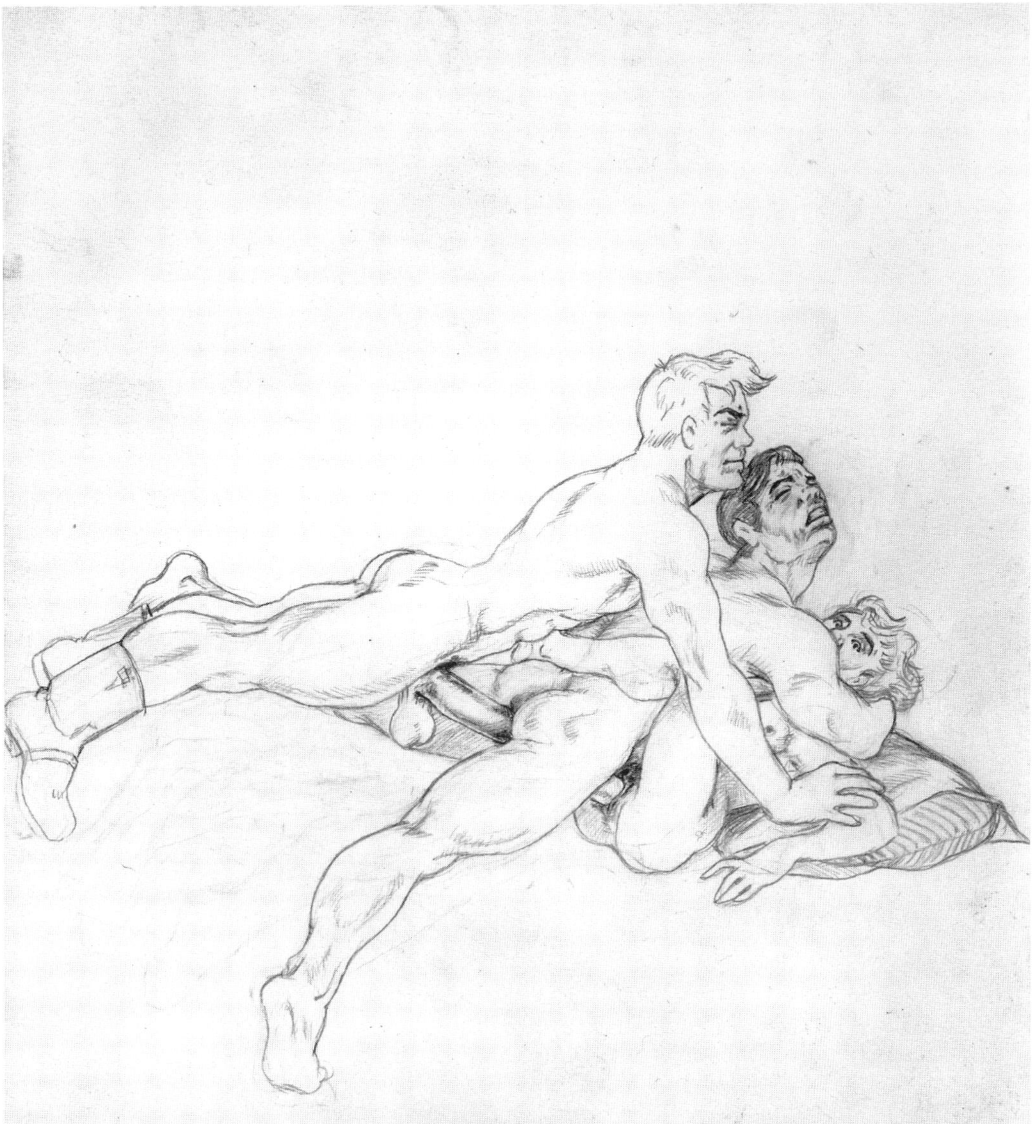

. . . She was overcome by shame at seeing herself as this person, although she did not believe it for a second. [. . .] 'You only have eyes for one another. I don't exist any more. I just don't exist! What does that make me, tell me? And how could I ever get between you two?'" Jean Genet, *Querelle de Brest* ([1947; 1953] 1974, 185)

195

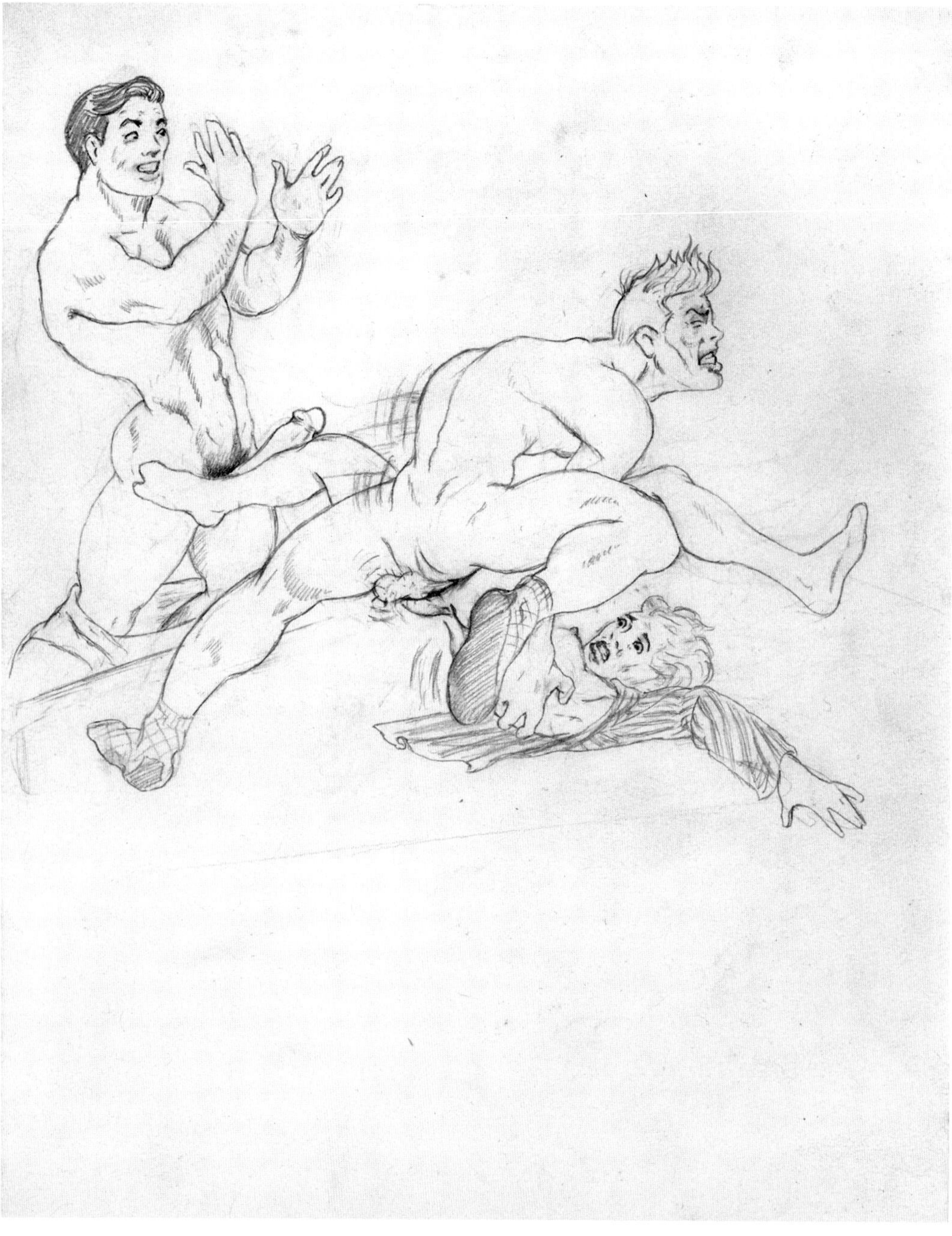

Coming back to Version A, is Penny-loafer momentarily forgetting himself and applauding the show or trying to attraction Blondy's attention and bring the conjugal workshop to an end?

196

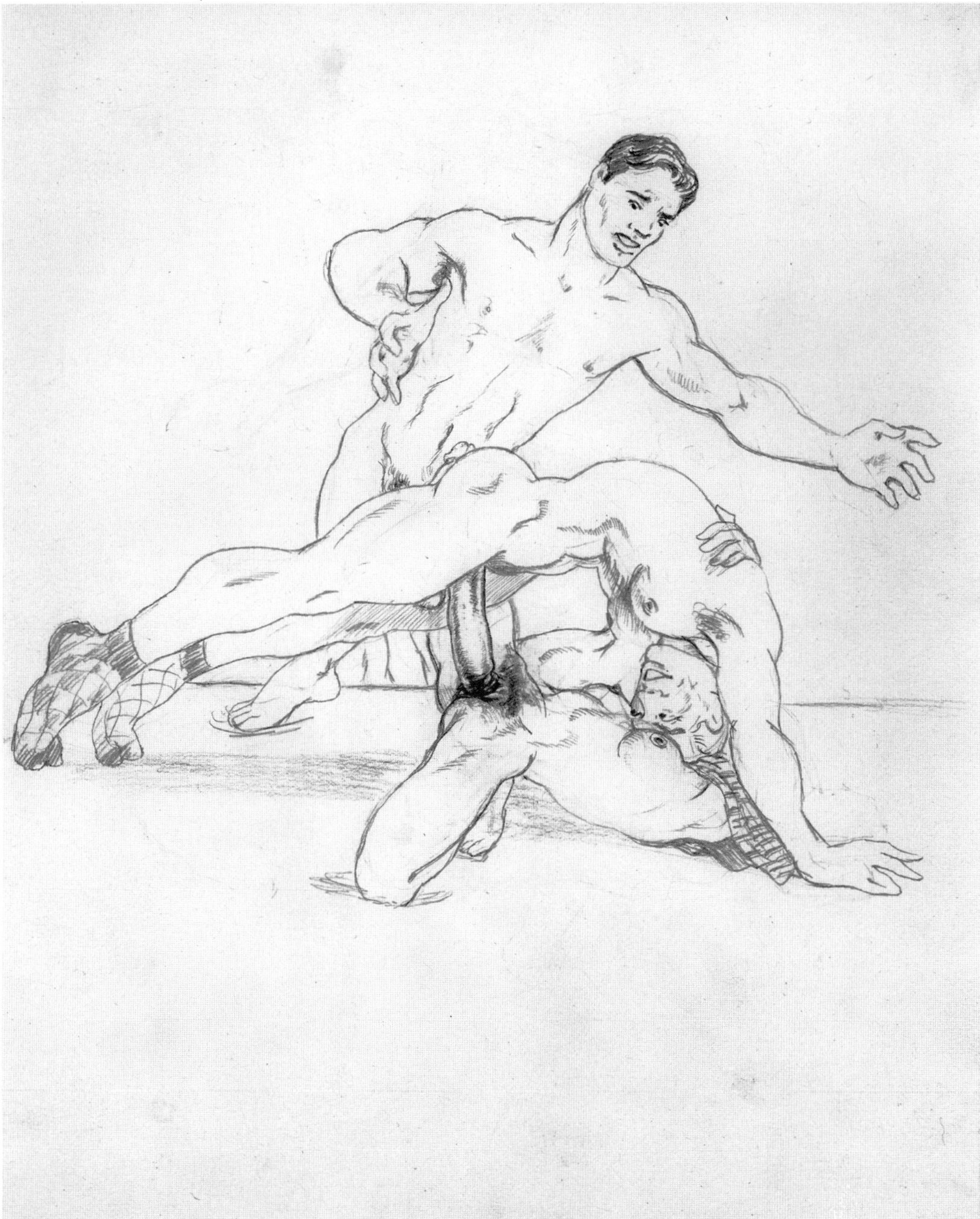

This has gone far enough, but it's too late, for Blondy is pulling out, wondering what that big warm round thing on his ass is and feeling a bit cross-eyed after all that effort. The wife has lost her head, and basically disappears from the narrative.

197

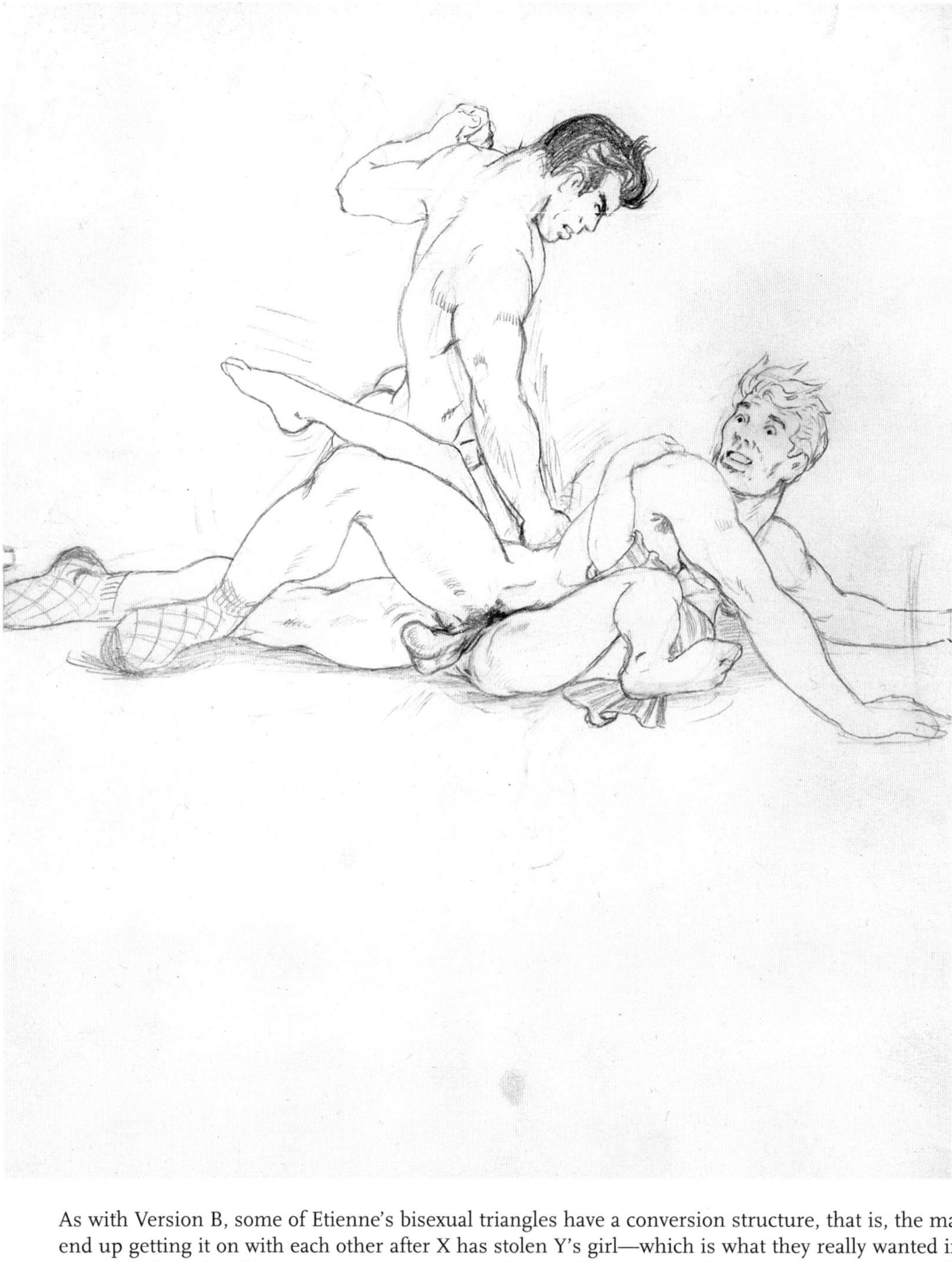

As with Version B, some of Etienne's bisexual triangles have a conversion structure, that is, the male buddies end up getting it on with each other after X has stolen Y's girl—which is what they really wanted in the first place. Ye olde tale of the grocery delivery boy, the housewife, and the sailor husband was apparently another DuBek favorite. In Version A, for some reason, the men come together, as is often the case, only within Mrs.
198 Penny-loafer's vagina, and in the encounter of fists, and the woman is reduced to a pair of legs and an orifice.

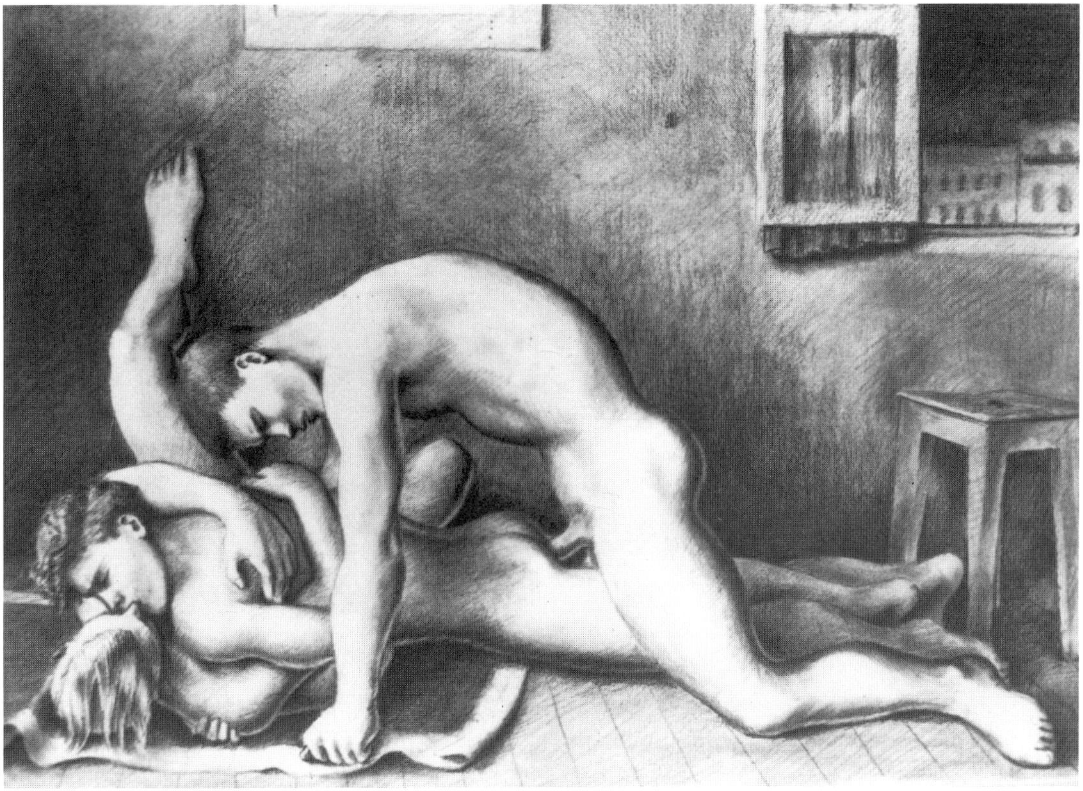

Caillaux's same-sex triangle is a glimpse of Paris at night and a front-and-center kiss slightly softer than Genet's: "It was the first time Querelle kissed a man on the mouth. [. . .] as it was an act of love, and of forbidden love, he knew that he was committing evil. His erection hardened. Their mouths remained soldered together, their tongues lolling round each other or pricking each other with their tips; neither one of them dared to move on to the rough cheeks, where a kiss would have been a sign of tenderness. . . ." Jean Genet, *Querelle de Brest* ([1947; 1953] 1974, 206) 199

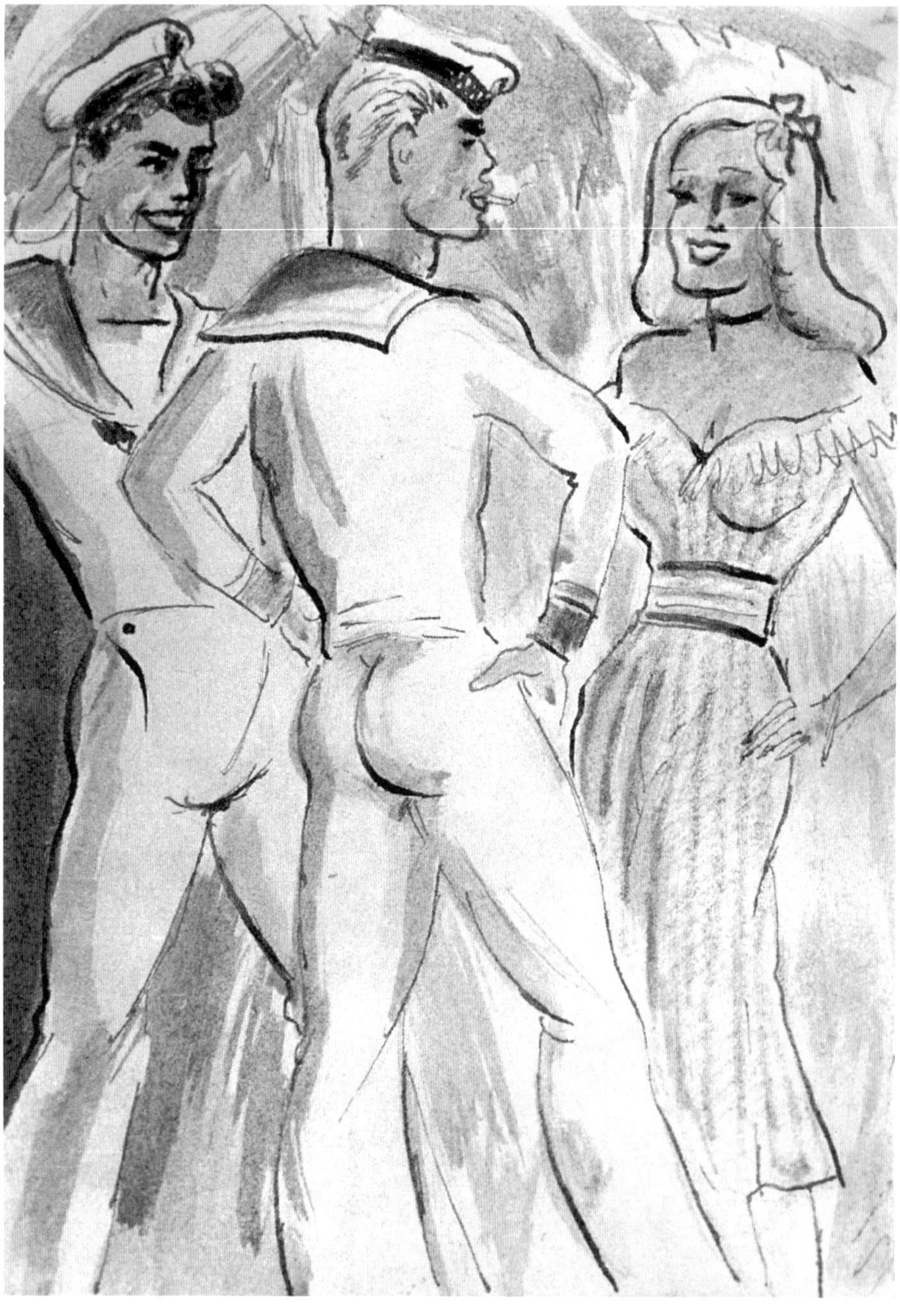

Triangle trauma is barely visible underneath this charming fluff from the Bellhops artist (see Figures 111-115), perhaps a little later in his career than the other work in *Lust,* since her hairdo is very forties and the men are less nelly than they used to be.

200

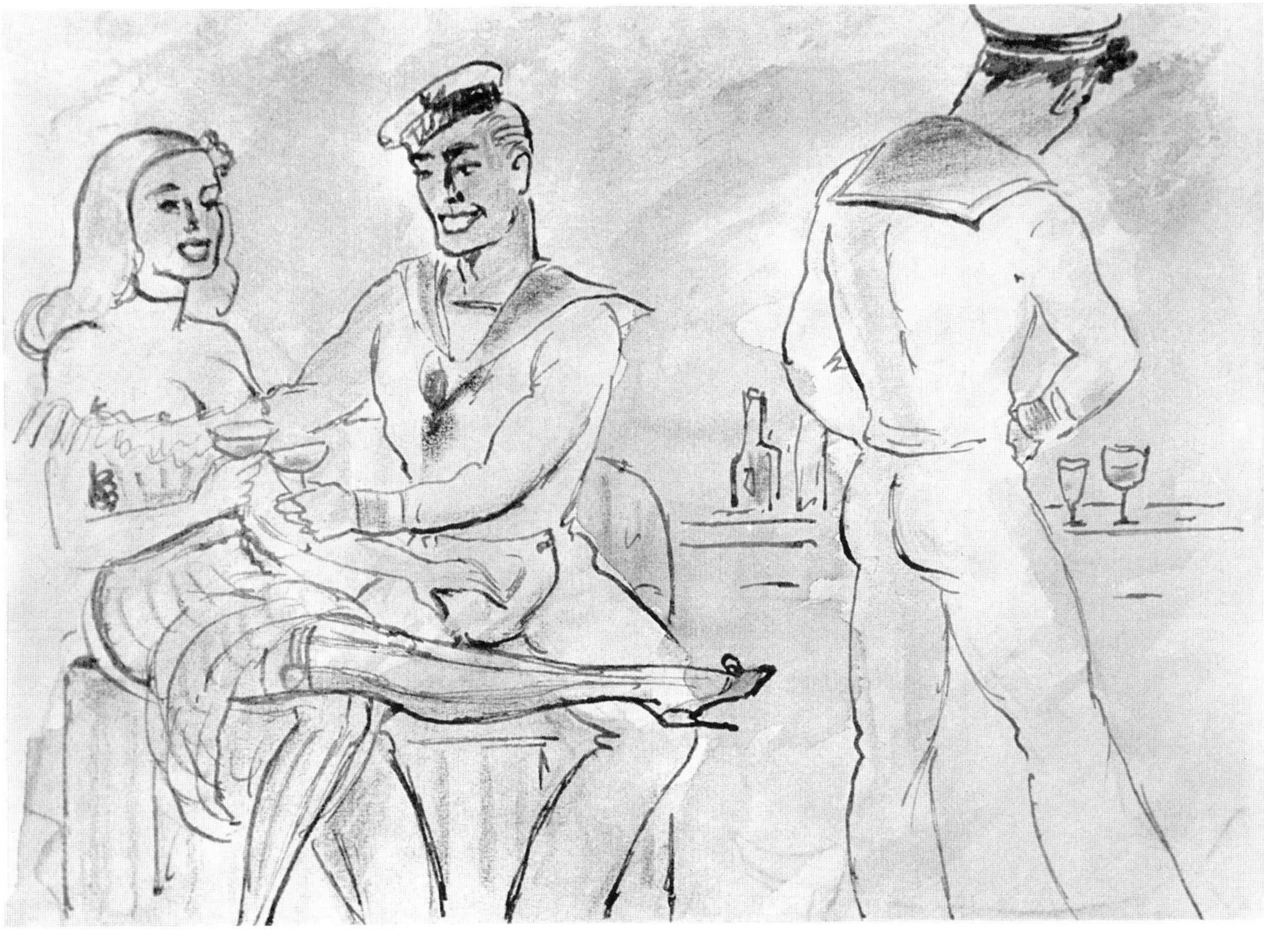

"When Giovanni spoke, his voice was thick with fury and relief and unshed tears. 'Where have you been?' he cried. 'I thought you were dead! [. . .] or thrown into the river—what have you been doing all these days?' I was able, oddly enough, to smile. And I was astonished at my calm. 'Giovanni,' I said, 'I want you to meet my fiancée.'" James Baldwin, *Giovanni's Room* ([1956] 1988, 170-171)

201

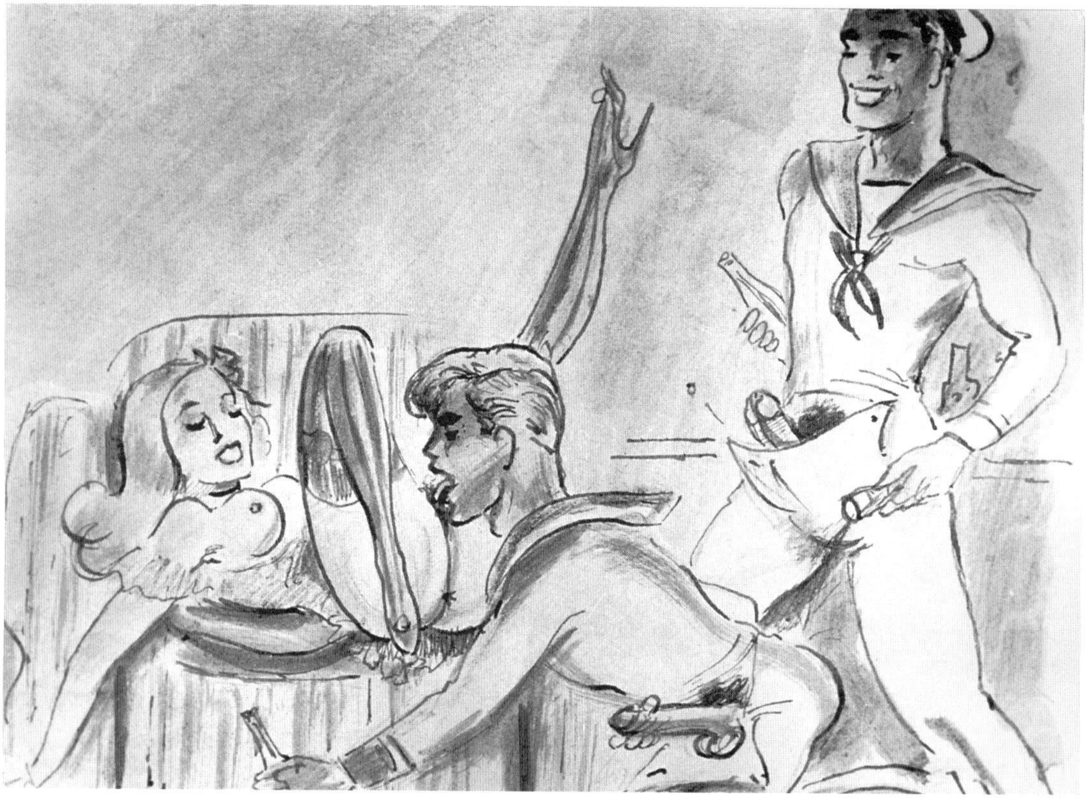

"'In the bed everything went remarkably well. I necked with A. Tills more to show willing than anything else since I'd much rather have begun on Dave. It was like having to eat bread before touching the jelly at school parties. After a decent interval I turned and necked the blue-eyed Dave who had a very sexual body. A. Tills sucked my cock . . .

202

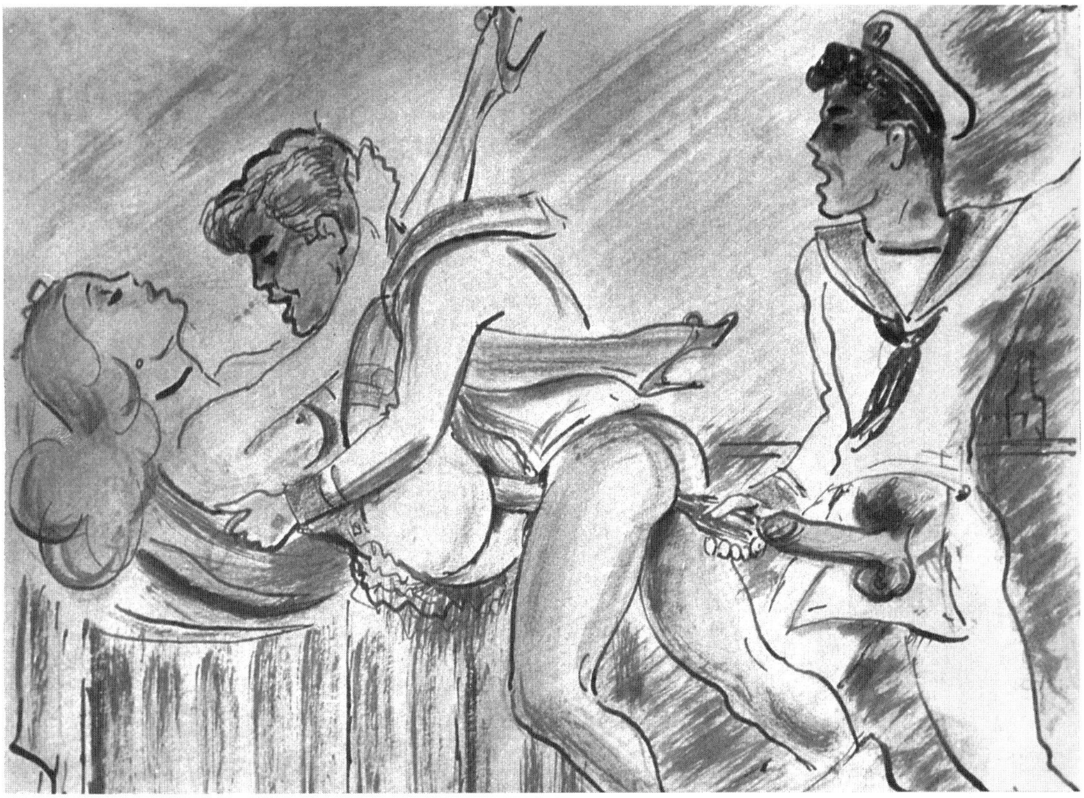

. . . After a while I turned Dave over and shoved my cock up his arse. He gave a yelp and I took it down. A. Tills produced vaseline and I put it on my cock. A. Tills put some up the blue-eyed Dave's bum and I began again. It went up like a treat." Joe Orton, *The Orton Diaries* ([1967] 1986, 105-06)

203

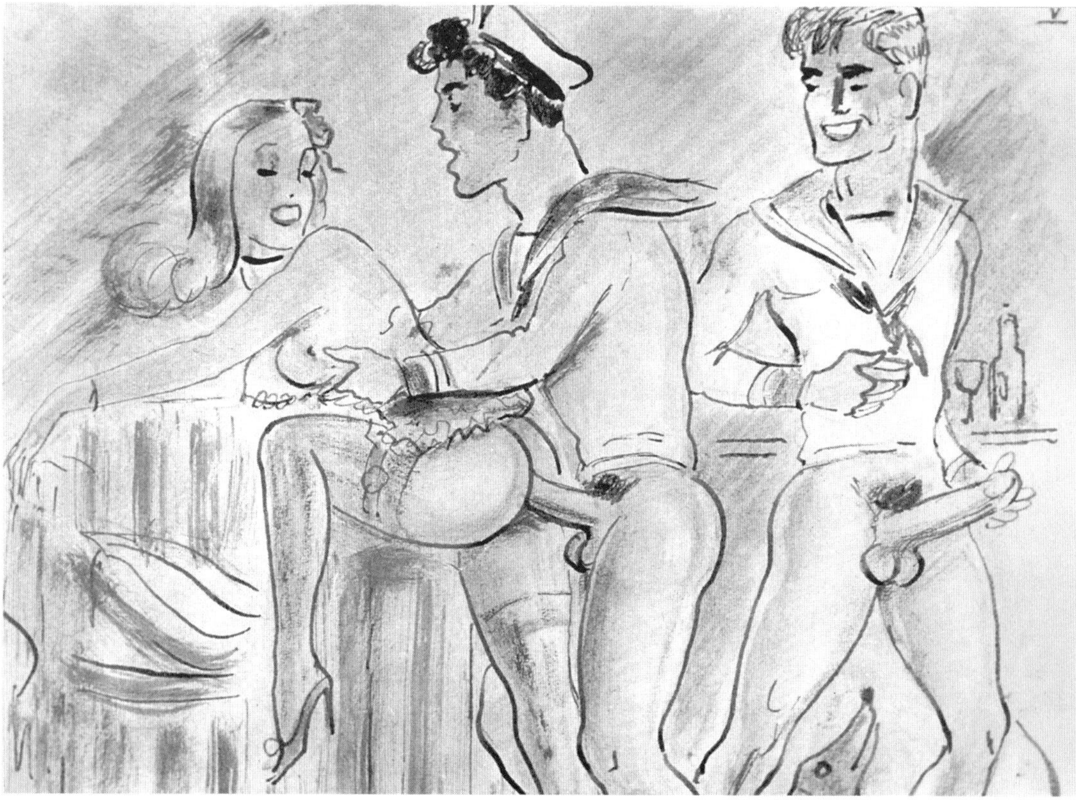

204 "I had to fuck on spit because the vaseline was in the other bedroom. [. . .] seeing the red underpants still round his ankles, I pulled them up over the boy's knees so that if lifted myself I could see my cock going in and out. I suddenly wanted to piss. I went into the bathroom. 'I demand that vaseline,' I said. [. . .] The door suddenly opened and Kenneth appeared. He said, 'You've been in there for an hour, and you're just asking for vaseline.'" Joe Orton, *The Orton Diaries* ([1967] 1986, 213). The graphic artists are also devoted to details of the lubricant.

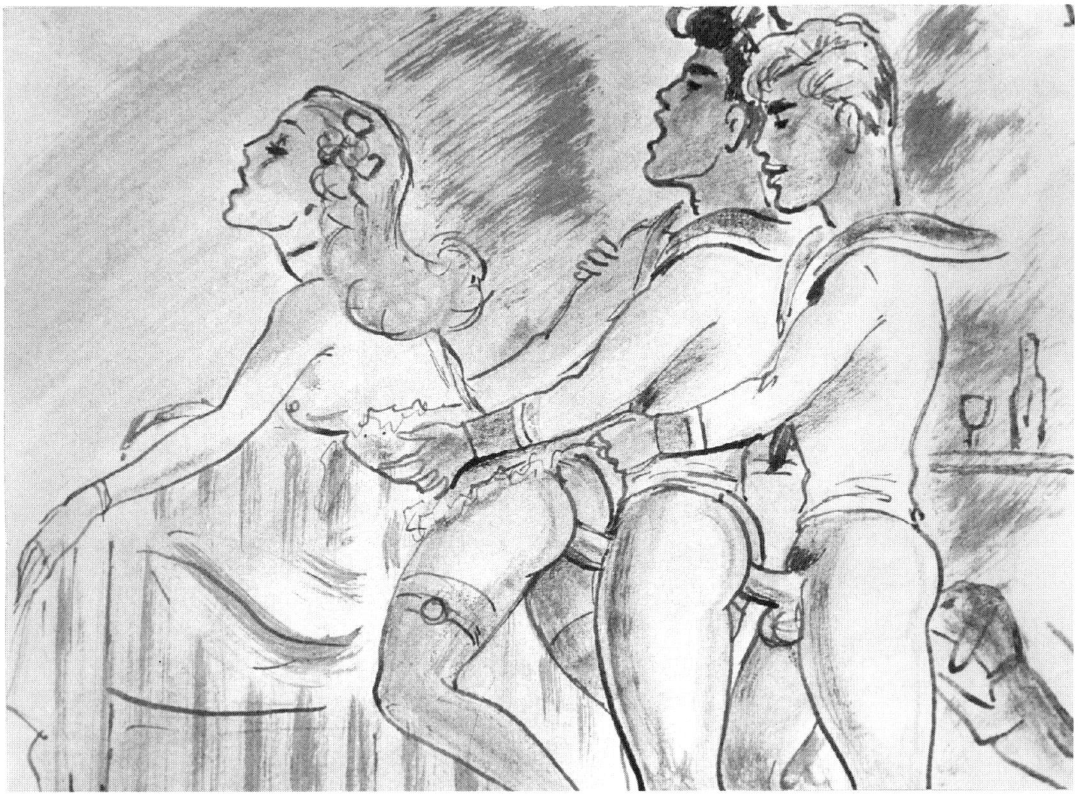

Note the toy dachshund who, like the same artist's queer seagull of Figure 157, does not accept human-animal boundaries and makes it a four-item doggie-style daisy chain.

205

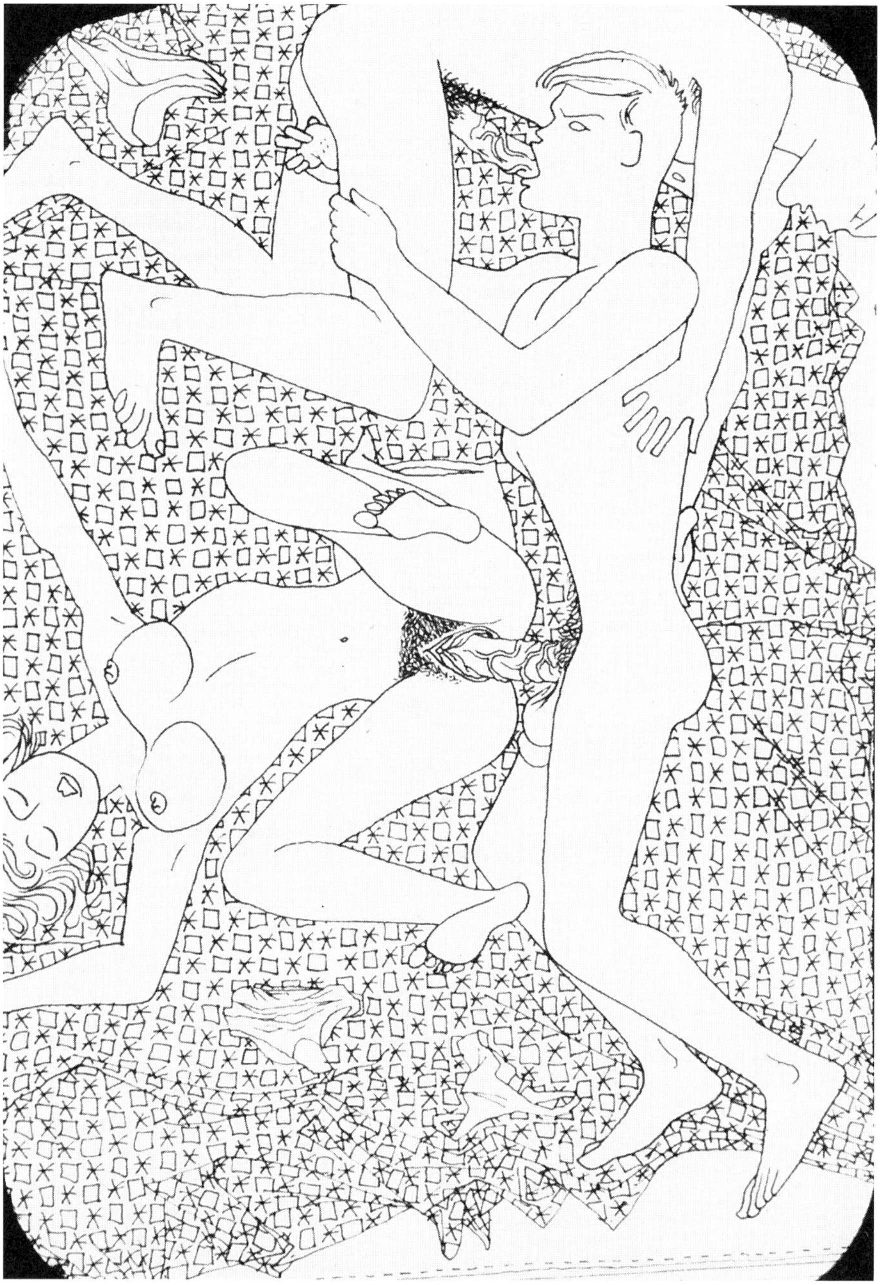

206 An overhead view of a *broken* triangle by the sharp-chin slide purveyor, who is fascinated by the textures of the bedspread and the veins of the pricks. Observant reader Bruce Eves speculates that the anonymous author of this wonderful drawing, along with plates 154, 155, 156, 207, and our parting image on page 319, is none other than the young Andy Warhol (see pages 16-17). Certainly plausible, based on stylistic similarities to the early drawings, as well as biographical overlaps between the collector and the artist. . . . A subject for further research!

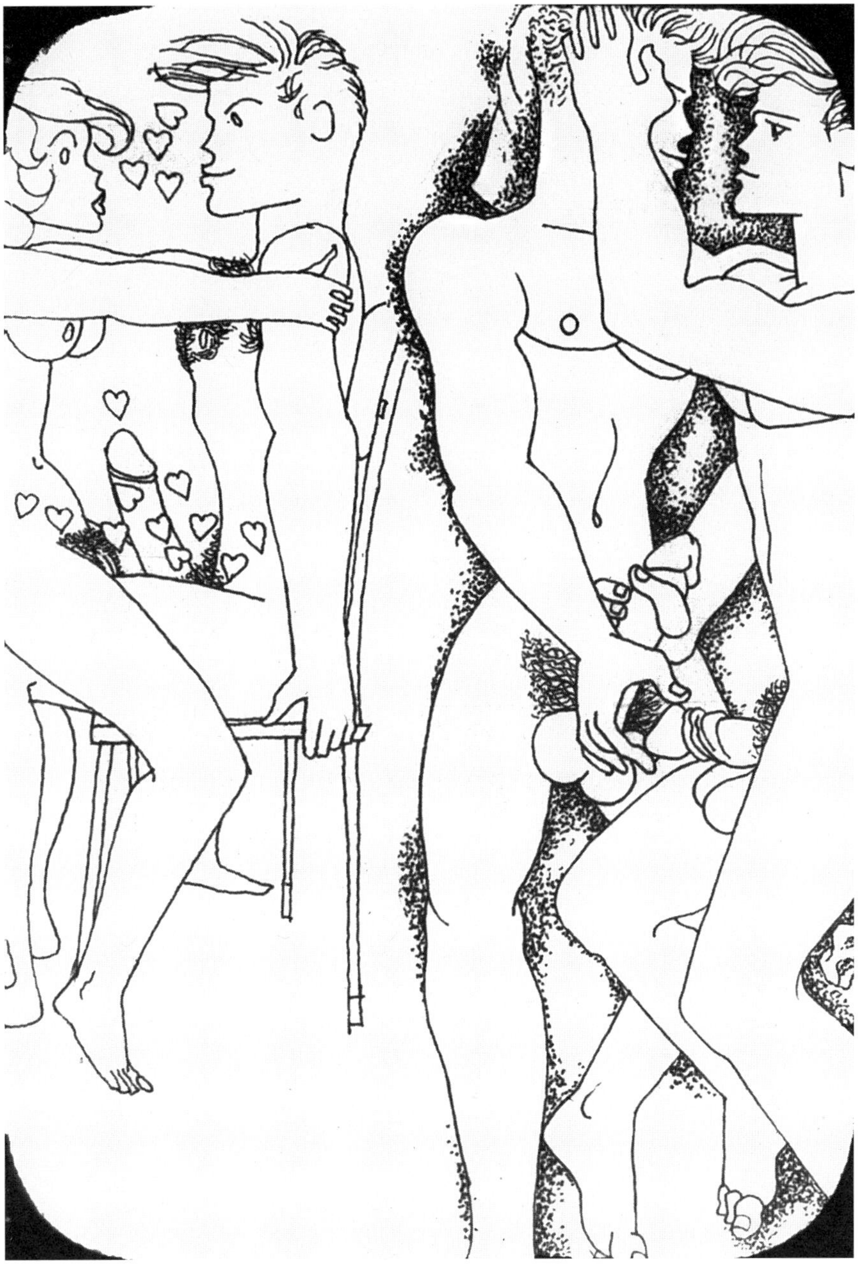

Not very symmetrical as far as double dates go. I'm not sure why the same-sex couple is disproportionately larger and more detailed than the hetero couple, nor why it is the latter who gets all the heart-shaped bubbles in the erogenous zone.

207

GROUP DYNAMICS

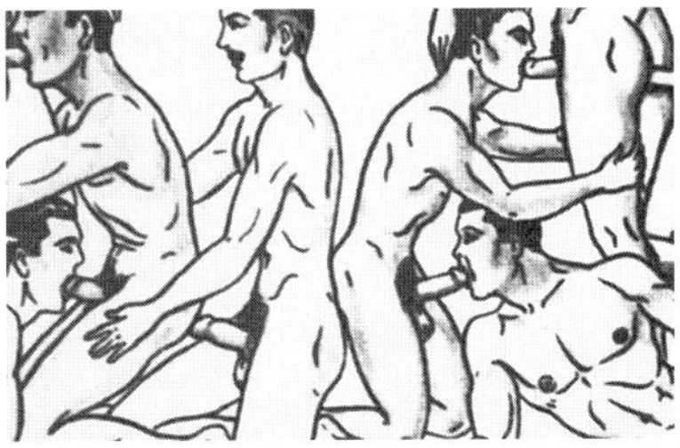

Orgy or group fantasies are a small coherent group within this selection, with a very specific mandate that is difficult to pull off—in real life as on the page. There are thirteen in this cluster but about thirty-five in total throughout *Lust Unearthed*, only half the number of trio scenes which is in turn half again the number of couple fantasies. (Interestingly, pinups or solo figures constitute the smallest group—fewer than twenty—but some of the participants in the orgies look lonely and might as well be solos . . .).

Group Dynamics

Styles vary, but most orgy fantasies end up overwhelmed by the graphic challenge of assembling all the participants in a credible-looking configuration. In Figure 143, all the participants seem to be floating an inch or so above the nice perspectival back alley setting: small wonder that some of the best group scenes dispense with gravity entirely, as in Figure 208 (or Happyface's wonderful aerial acrobatics in *Out/Lines*, fig. 77). Other orgy pictures end up looking somewhat like abstract and non-sexual choreographies, and in one of Jean Vincent's several efforts, one of his yachtsmen has even donned ballet slippers (fig. 14)! Some group pictures have the hieratic quality of religious art, like Bellhops's foursome efforts (figs. 214-215), which with a few details changed could serve as sketches for stained glass windows.

Otherwise, the attempts at circularity or linearity, circle jerks or daisy chains, endow the image with an aura of abstraction, often as an intellectualized catalogue of permutations, more about the graphic challenge than the inspiration of lust. One can imagine the artist's hard-on slacking as he tries to remember whose leg that is. . . . Muscle cramps abound! Gang bangs make it easier for the artist with their processional dynamic (figs. 89, 142, and possibly 219), and the same is true of S/M crowd scenes in general because of the highly ritualized element. Then there are the faux orgies, basically theater performances of traditional couples with spectators lined up rather than other participants (fig. 102).

My ultimate favorites are figure 15, which hardly looks like an orgy at all, but rather a nude cocktail party with erections and a couple of passed-out partiers, and Spartacus's 234-235 set, saved by its softcore market niche from having to look like anything other than a typical slow afternoon at the Montreal YMCA locker room.

The upshot of all of this is that orgy shots simply aren't very hot, and the relative scarcity of them may simply be a response to the market: novelty items that leave consumers wondering where the meat is.

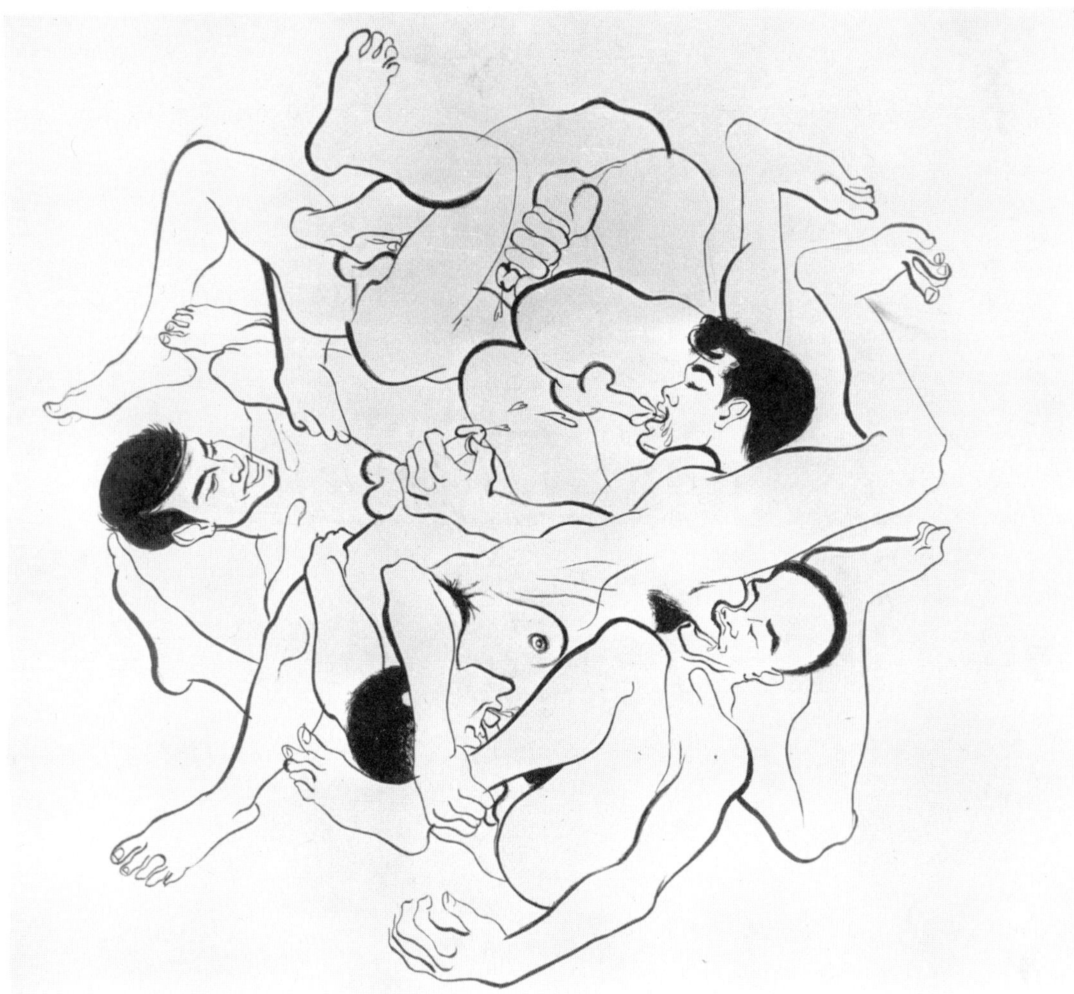

Perfect for a rose window skylight in a priapic cathedral, this composition is the zenith of group complementarity with three simultaneous ejaculations, four happy heads, five sets of legs, and six cocks. Orgies are a favorite fodder for the graphic imagination, but much less inspiring in real life (I am told). Readers already know this unwavering pen through the blissful couples of Figures 118, 144-145, and 175-176.

208

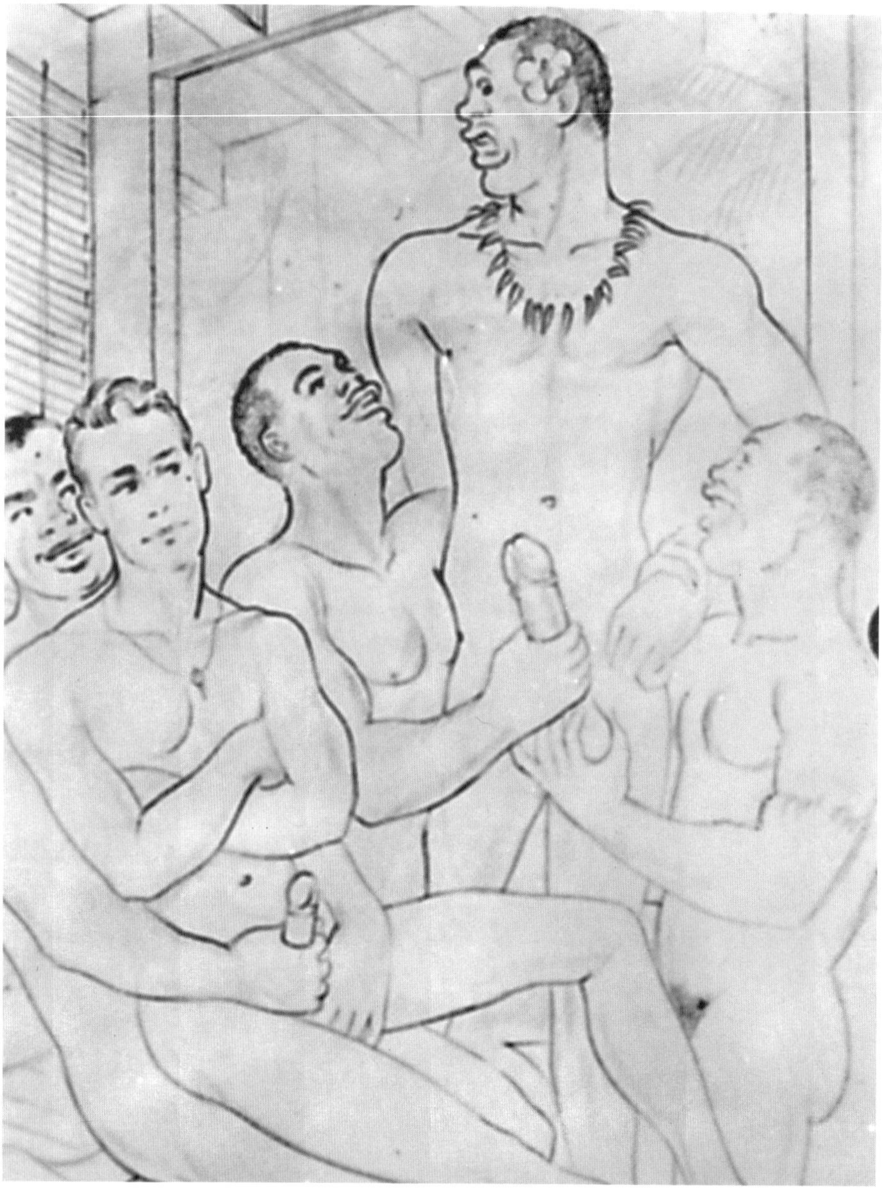

Racial difference is not a major preoccupation of this selection that is largely white-centric, even more so than in *Out/Lines* for some reason. But there's an interesting contrast between these two group scenes where difference is at the center, by an unknown artist on the left (provenance and date unknown) and the mature Jean Vincent on the right.

209

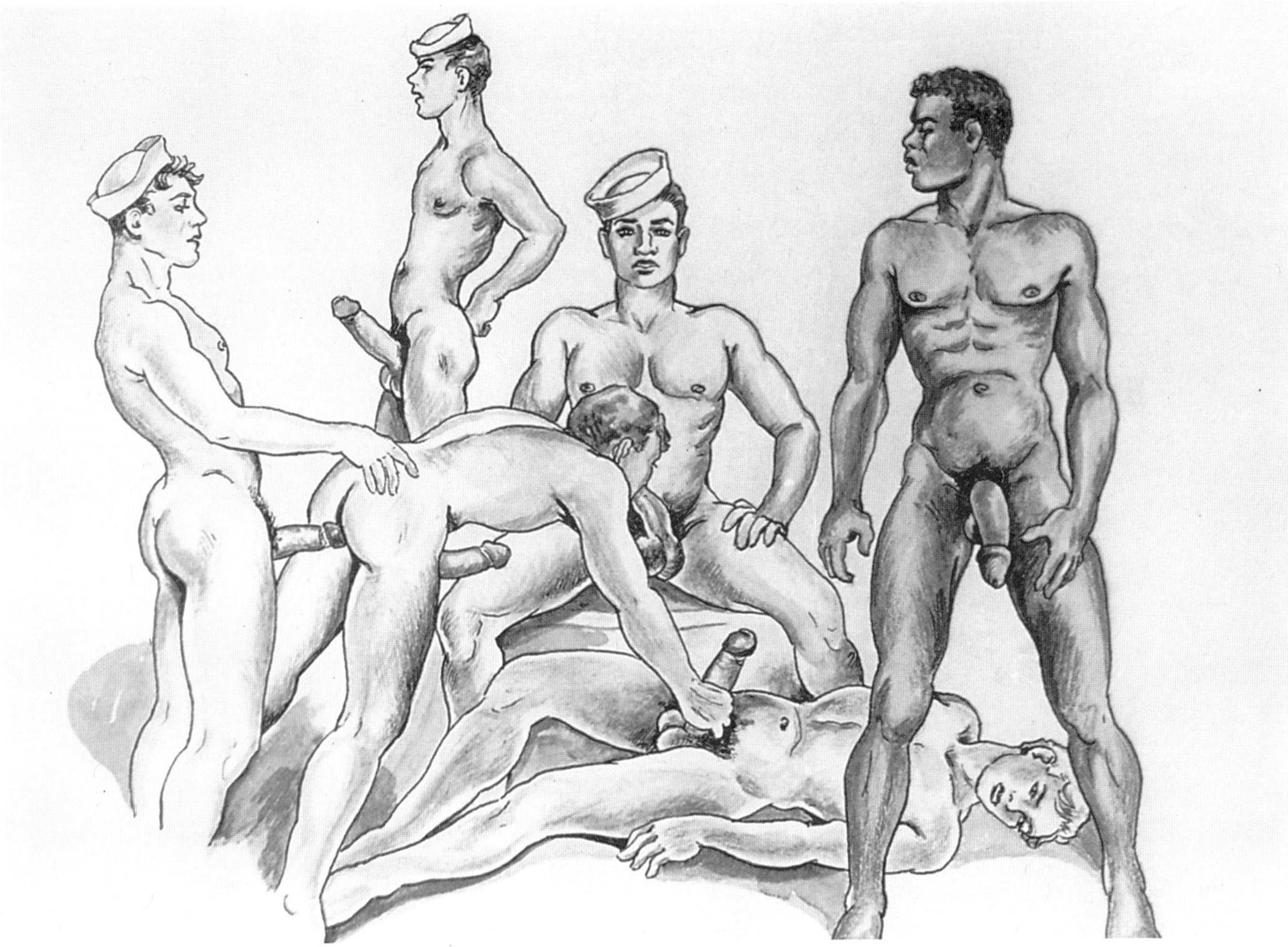

Opposite, a complacent white man is the center of attention in a stereotyped tropical scene, whereas here the black man is aloof and troubled (as well as flaccid). Curiously in both, the black characters are "othered," whether majority or minority.

210

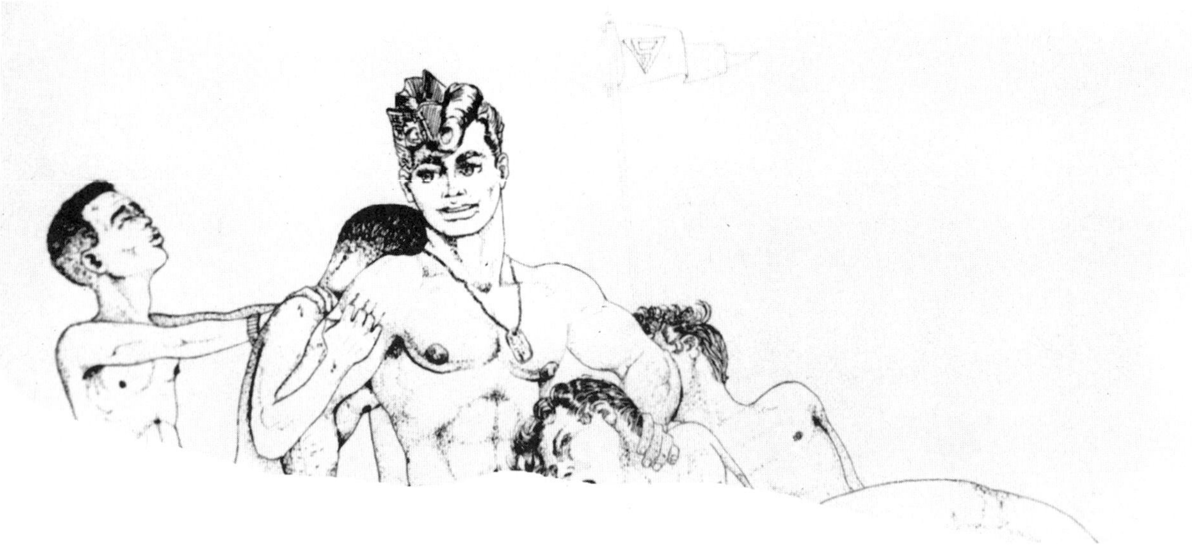

Scouts are less common than might be expected in this erotically charged homosocial universe. This image of
a gentle scoutmaster swarmed by his teenaged charges (prob. U.S.A., c. 1960) has been cropped in deference
to the dangers of doing historical research in an atmosphere of contradictory, anti-erotic and anti-child para-
noia, both legal and commercial. Ephebophilia has been accepted in other cultures, and the erotic dimensions
211 of mentorship have been forthrightly explored by scholars within earlier, more open-minded regimes, from
Weimar Germany to the pre-1975 U.S. (Angelides 2004).

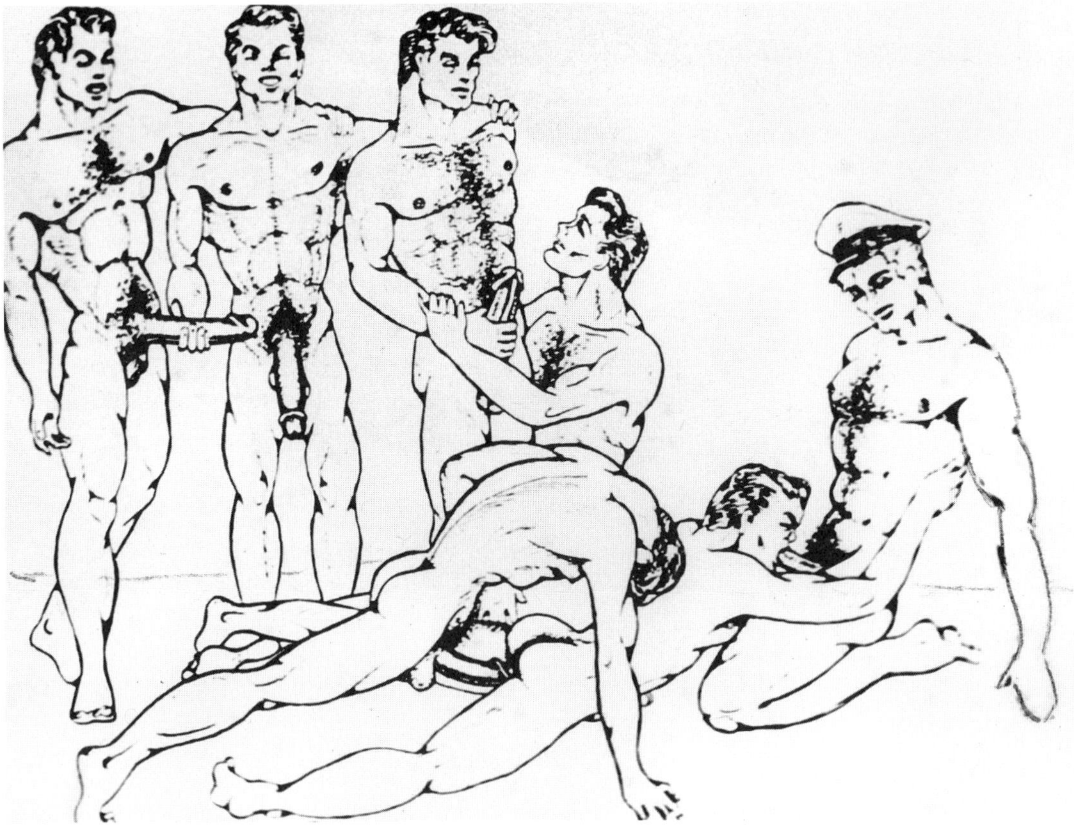

"I'd never seen anything like it. They were all over Rex. He lay there on his back on the floor, his right forearm across his eyes, his long perfect body stretched out full length, the legs spread wide. . . . And the fourteen lips and hands at work—all over him, every inch—feet, toes, arms, ears, torso, legs—and the main lucky one, of course. I was so fascinated I could hardly take my eyes off the spectacle. . . ." Phil Andros, "Mirror, Mirror on the Wall," *$tud* ([1966] 1982, 41). DuBek's "World War II era" artist at work again, cf. Figures 138, 116-117. **212**

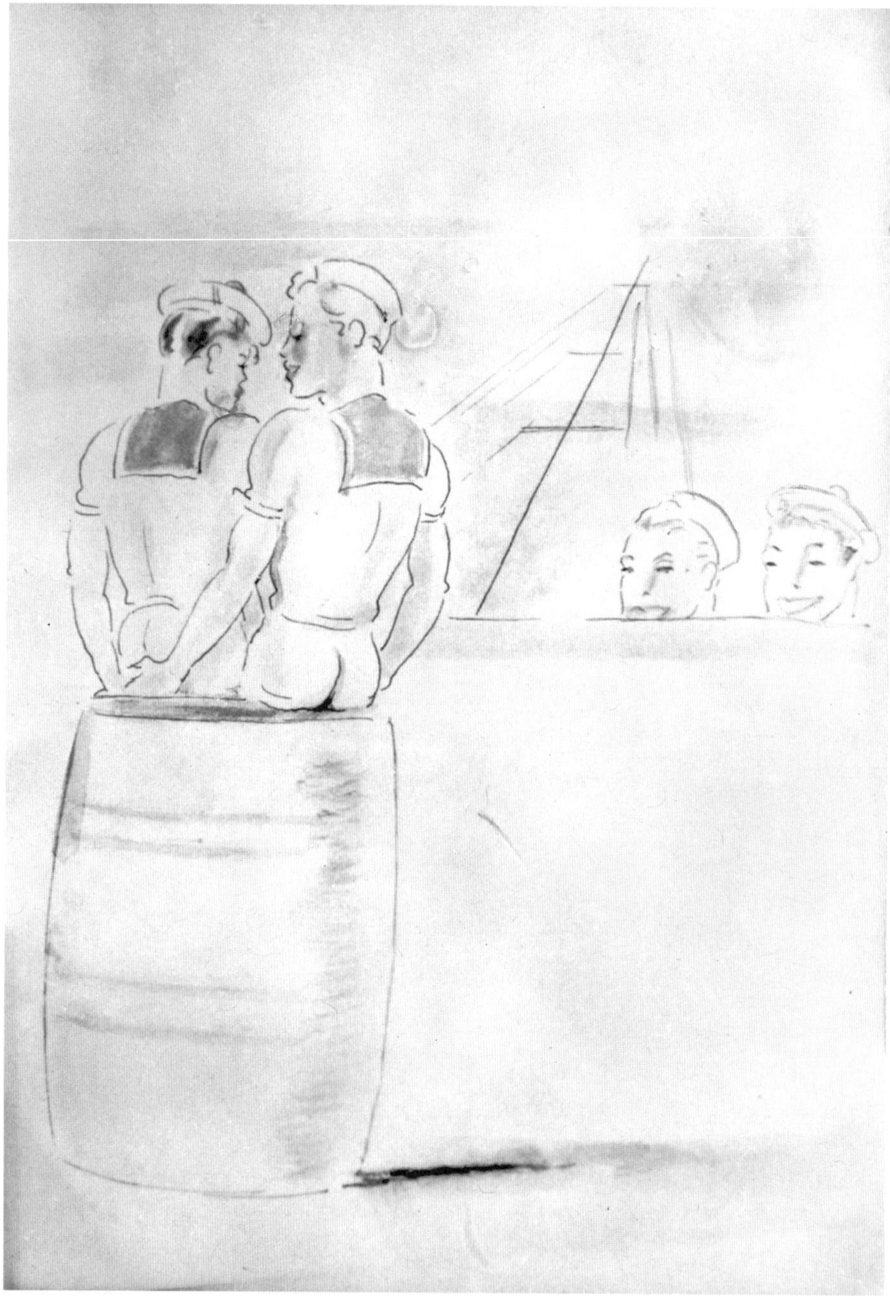

The Bellhops artist at it again (see Figures 111-115, 157-160, 200-205). Intergenerational group relations are not his forte, and the only way he can seem to connote the younger age of the initiate bottom couple is by making them smaller in scale than the sailor fairy tops.

213

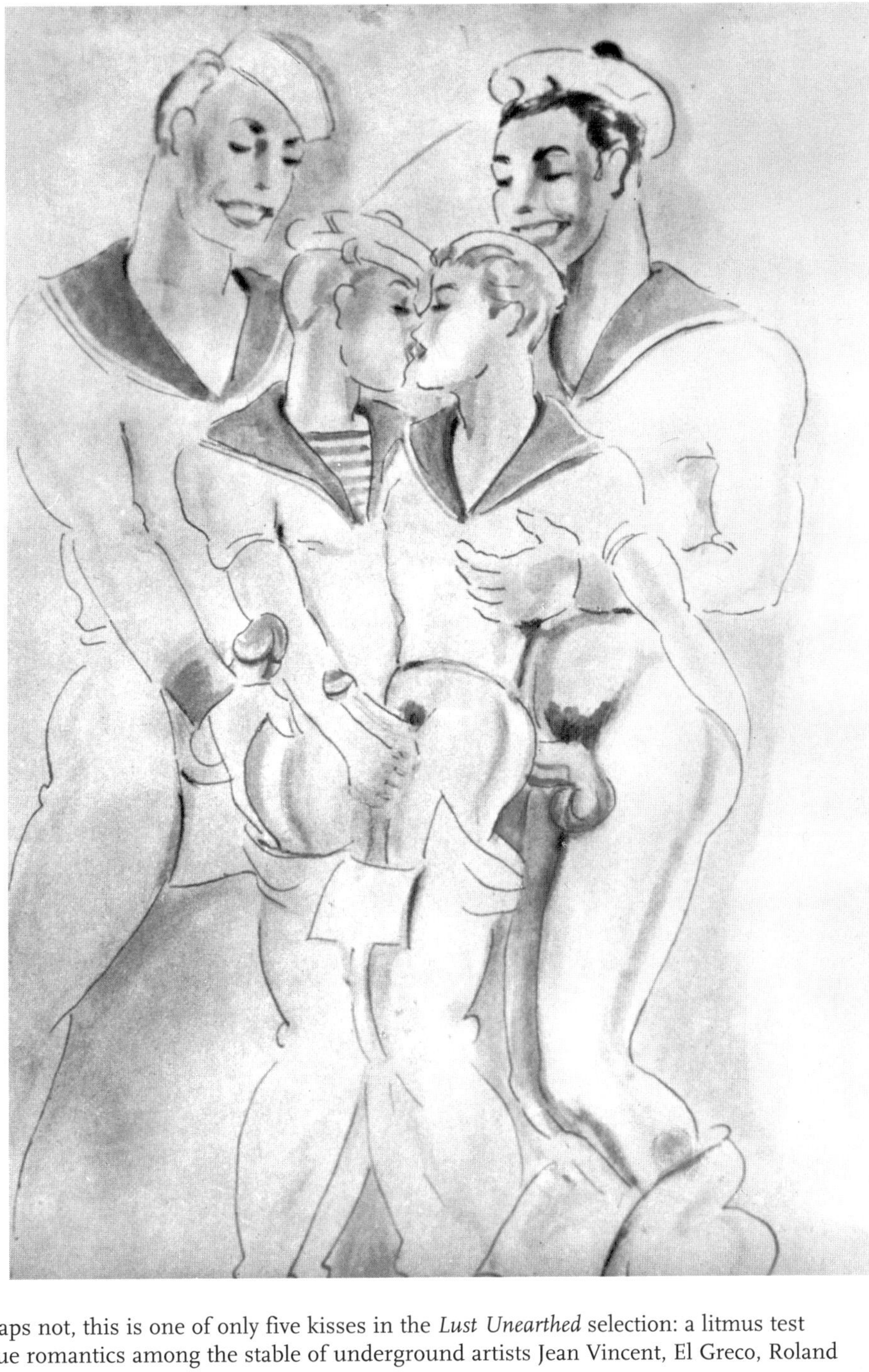

Surprisingly, or perhaps not, this is one of only five kisses in the *Lust Unearthed* selection: a litmus test for identifying the true romantics among the stable of underground artists Jean Vincent, El Greco, Roland Caillaux, and Bellhops.

214

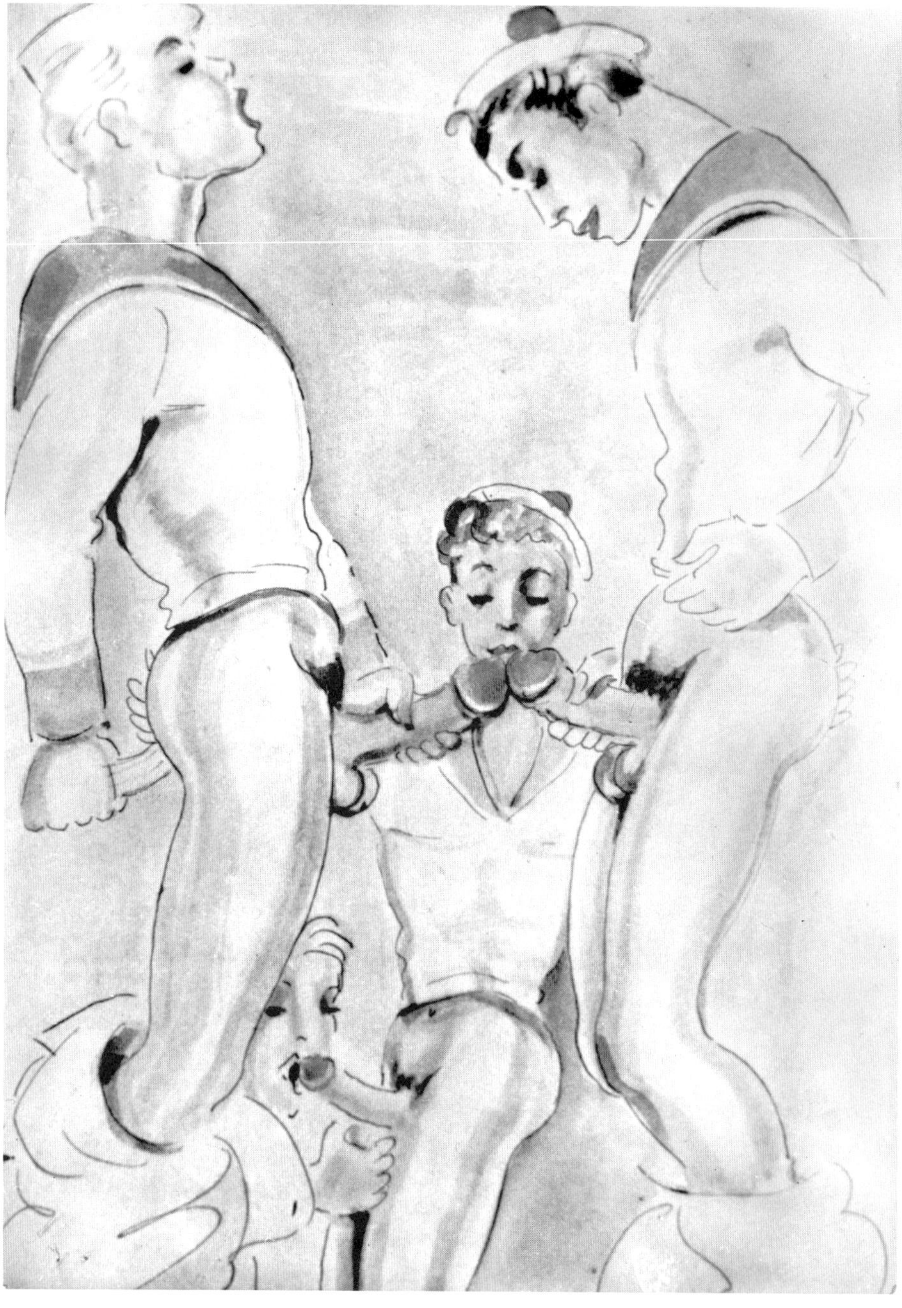

"The men stood in the shadows of the trees or walked along the sidewalk. This company—this choosing, crav-
ing, pursuing, joyfully seeking, sighing, dreaming, loitering company—this company with sentiments whetted
by the narcotic of custom [. . .] In the night many, many, wide-open, thirsty glances met and melted into each
other. At the bend of the path, hand in hand, shoulder against shoulder, eyes over shoulders, while the night
215 breeze softly rustled the branches; now coming, now going again, the appraising looks sharply cast crossed in
the same place [. . .] . . .

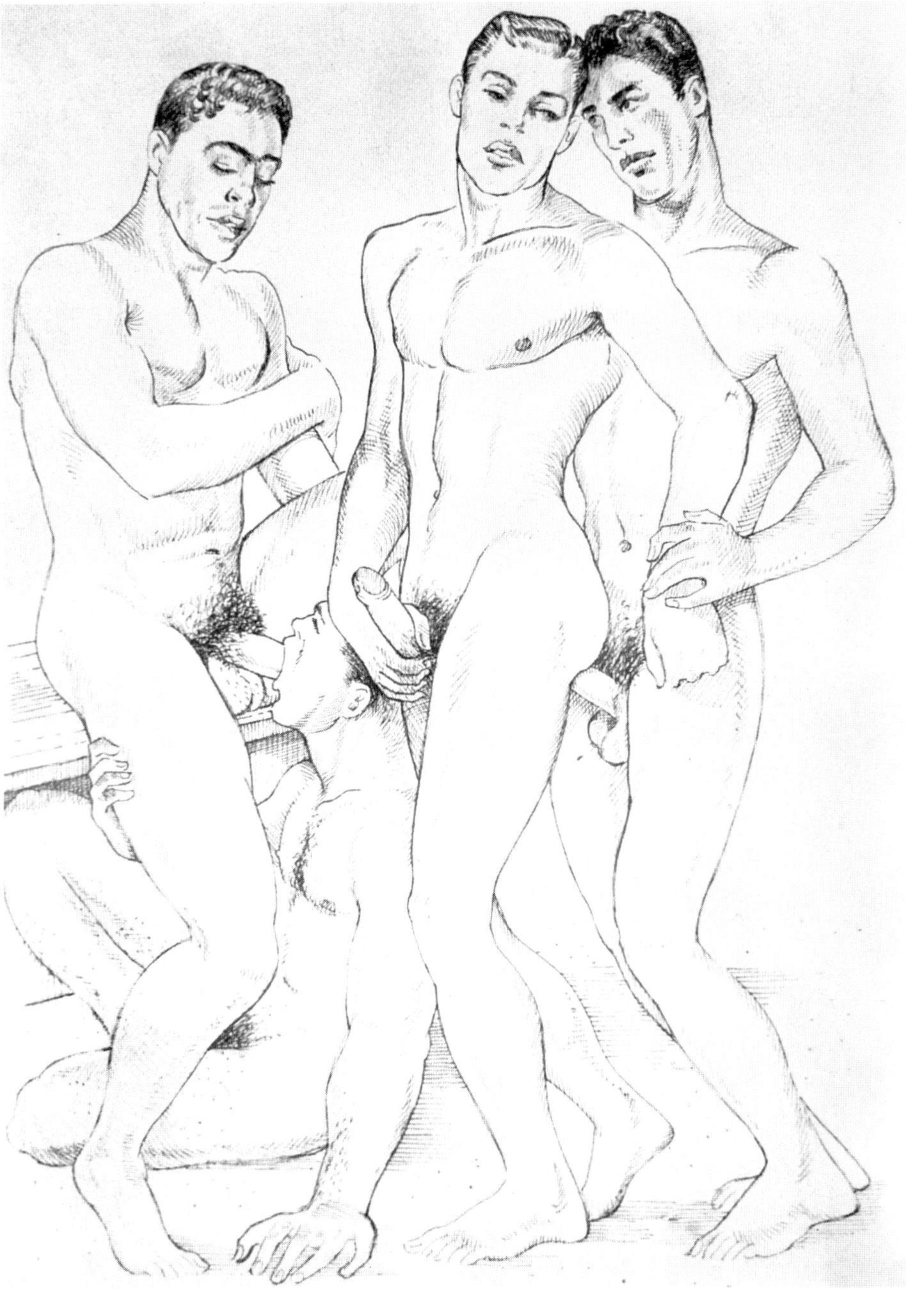

. . . They are all my comrades, Yuichi thought as he walked. Rank, occupation, age, beauty notwithstanding,
they are a fellowship welded by the same emotion—by their private parts, let us say. What a bond! These men
do not have to sleep together. *From the day we were born we have slept together.* In hatred, in jealousy, in scorn,
coming together for a short moment of love just to keep warm." Yukio Mishima, *Forbidden Colors* ([1951] 1974,
61). The above expert ink draftsman was represented in *Out/Lines* with his "Green Door" sequence, Figures **216**
132-134. This sauna foursome is equally graceful.

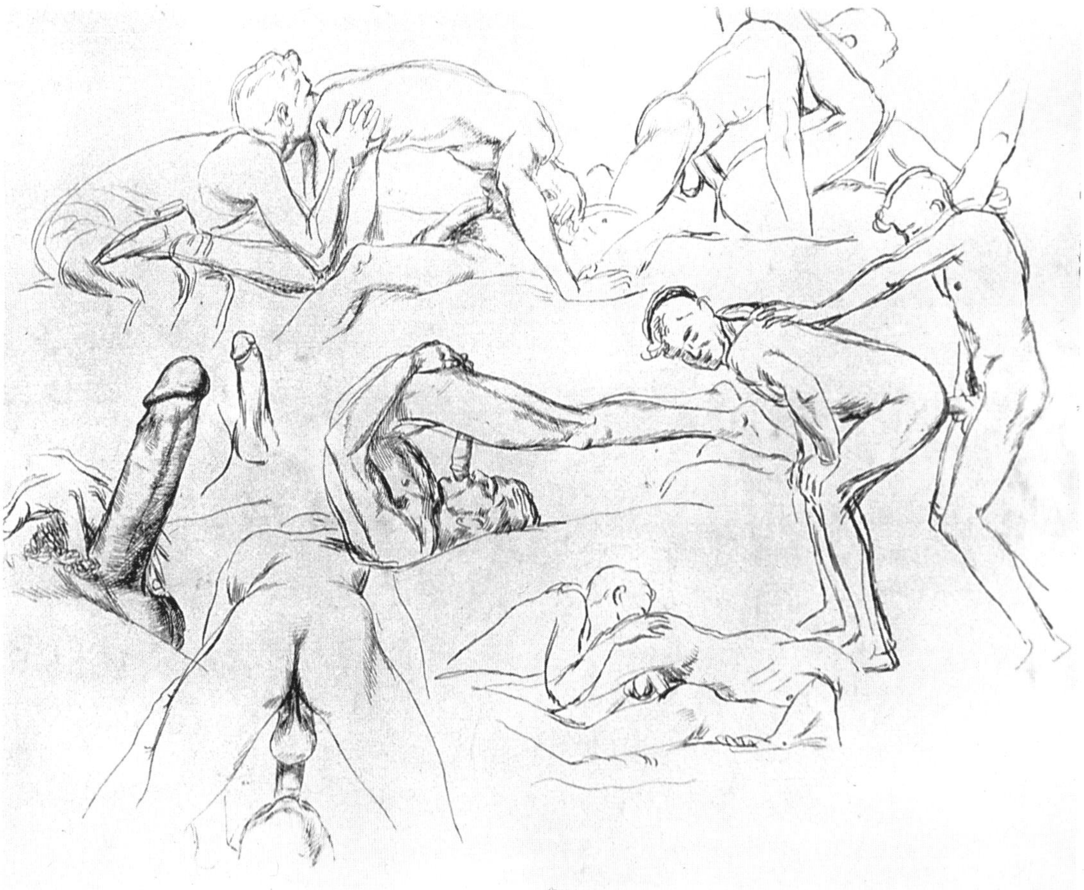

Two further works probably by Cadmus show an inspired session extrapolating from the photos he remembered using in the late thirties and in all likelihood deposited with his later friend Dr. Kinsey (see also Figures 163-165). He clearly loved the exercise in contrasting angles and scales, in improvisation and sandwich-making, but Spring may be right that such work does not work as either art or eroticism.

217

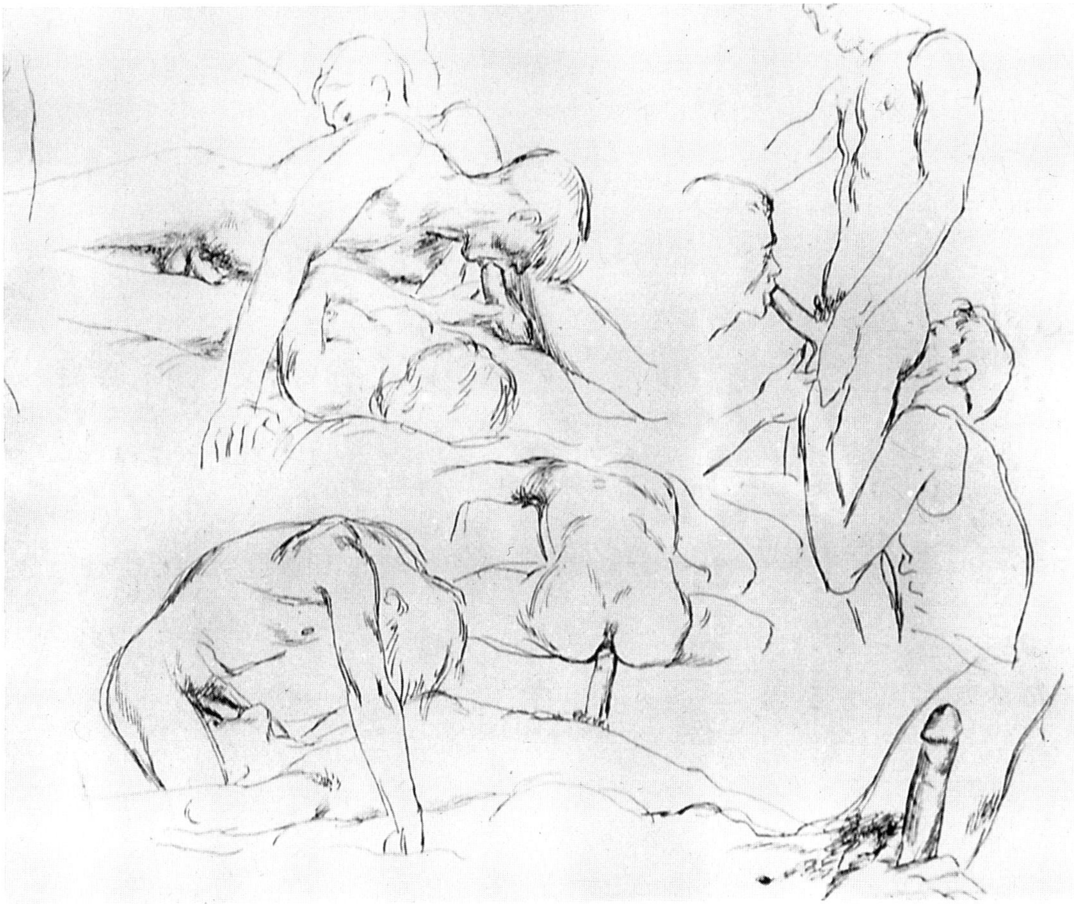

Note the bisexual threesome, upper left, and the cumulative orgy effect achieved by the casual collage approach. Explicit work by Cadmus, such as DuBek's three sketch pages, these plus Figure 165, as well as the more completed drawings of Figures 163-164, were experiments he would not build on for lack of interest (but also because of risk?) and have only recently been acknowledged in the Cadmus literature. (Spring 2002, 32-33)

218

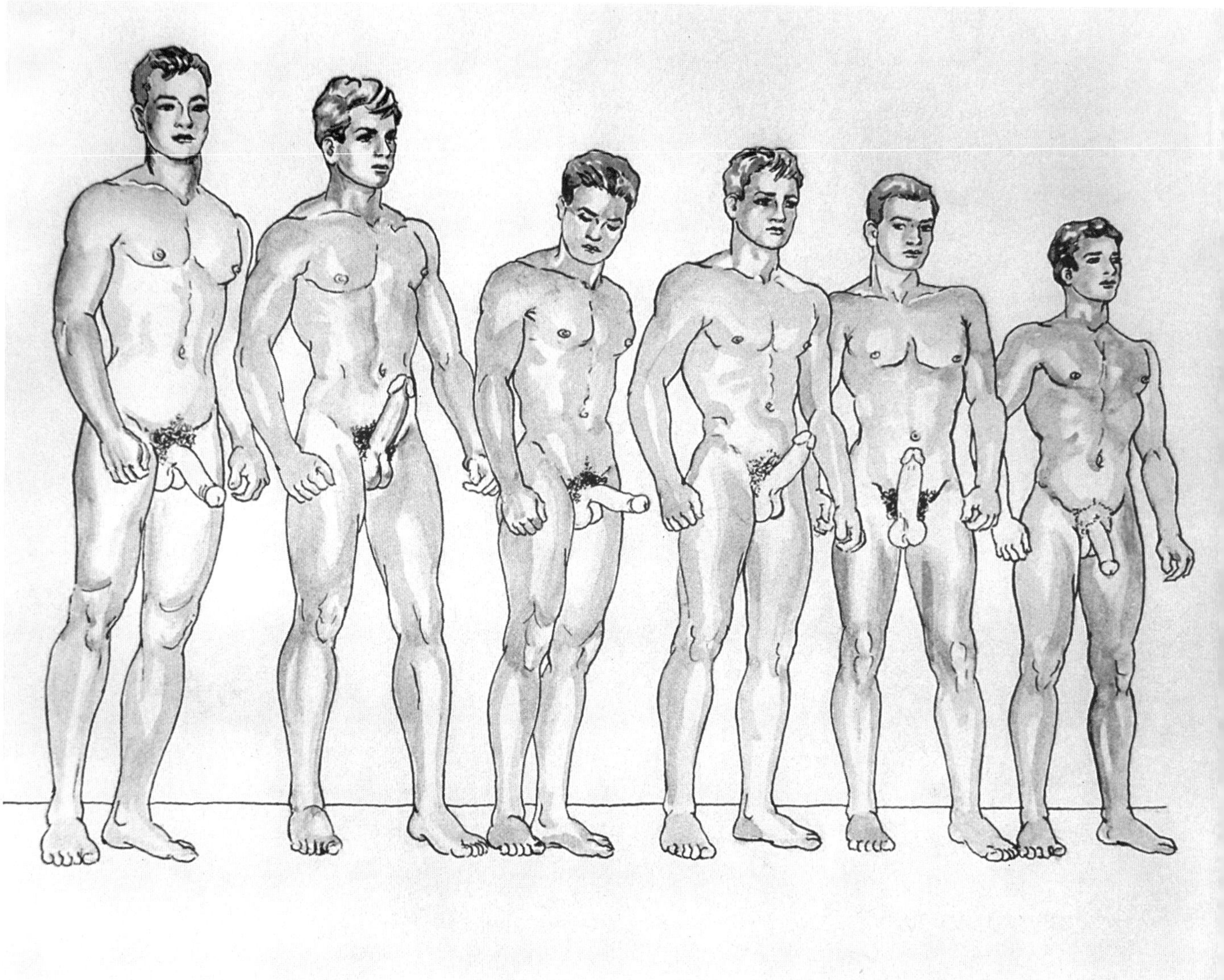

I can't decide whether this lineup resembles more an antechamber for a porno audition, a police lineup, or a procession of apostles in a Byzantine mural. Another contribution by the prolific Jean Vincent, its simplicity is deceptive: I love the way two of the men are subtly checking out the competition—which, I am told, is what orgies are all about anyway. My student and proofreader Marcus Greatheart says it reminds him of *seancody.com*
219 but I don't know what he's talking about.

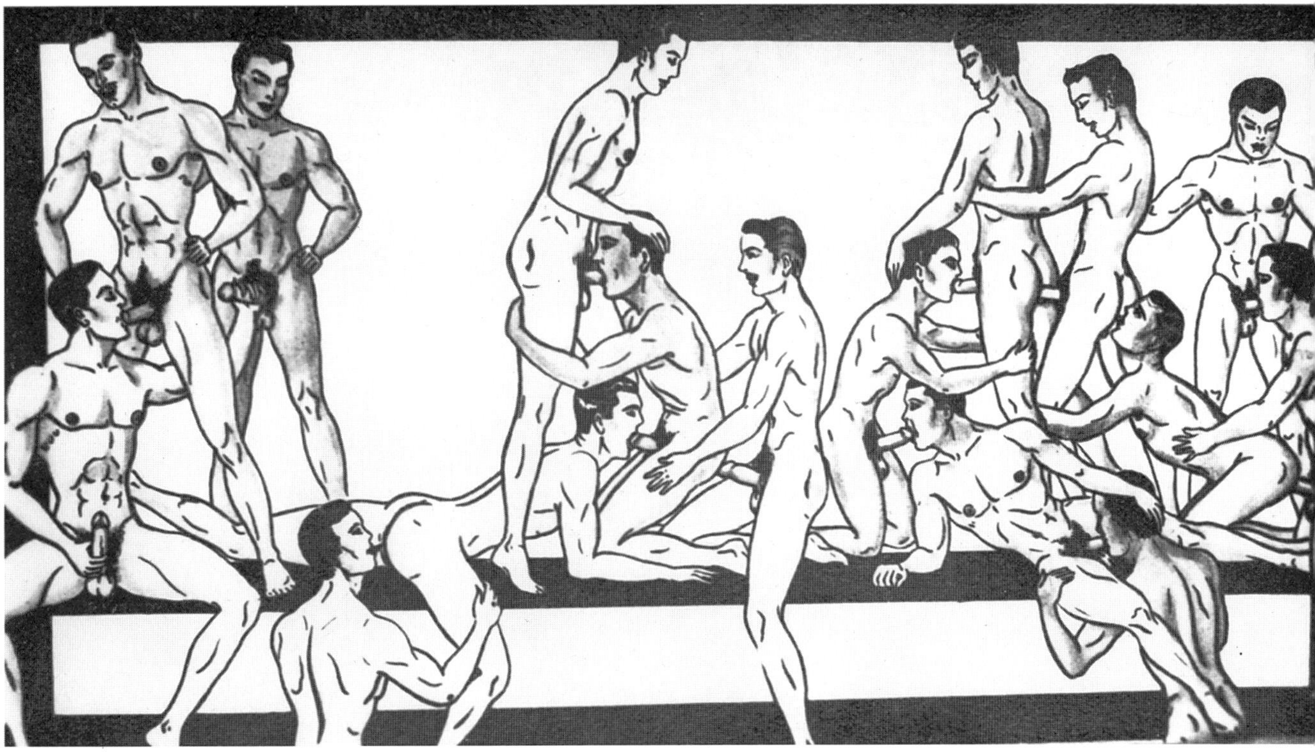

Somewhat clumsier, apparently a tracing of the three-tiered original and superior drawing, printed by Falkon (1972 Fig. 105). Falkon attributed the original to "Andy," a professional anthropological and scientific illustrator who died in his seventies around 1960. DuBek's ink tracing removed the racial diversity from Andy's cast, praised by Falkon, who also commended his skill at creating an unprecedented nine-man chain.

220

Softcore

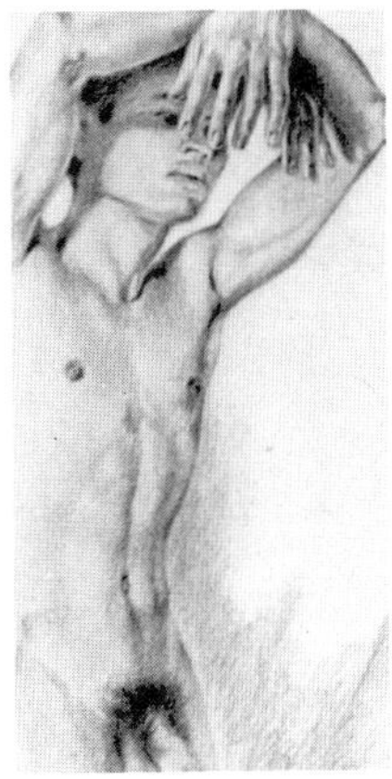

Softcore images are aboveground and "licit" by definition and do not belong in this collection of illicit underground hardcore. This genre of soft, sly subterfuge was at its peak in the 1950s and 1960s, trying to proclaim the legitimacy of gay desire while jumping through the hoops of official and unofficial censorship. I have included a small taste within this otherwise coherent selection for two reasons: to testify to DuBek's voracious, undiscriminating impulse to accumulate erotic images without dwelling on distinctions between the licit and illicit, implicit and explicit, commercial and underground, high art and low low low (display is another matter, and I am told that the images decorating the walls of his apartment were "high" and "soft" only) ; and secondly to set off the distinctiveness of the hardcore graphics underground that more or less lurched to a halt shortly after Stonewall and *Boys in the Sand* made it (or most of it) legal.

Softcore

Interestingly certain recent censorship cases have focused on vintage softcore (for example, the Paul Reubens, a.k.a. Pee-wee Herman, persecution of 2002 [Hudson & Graham 2004]), as if the forces of reaction were discovering fifty years too late how clever the "physique" photographers and artists had been at circumventing the codes and alibis of heterosexual propriety.

As I demonstrated in *Out/Lines,* the worlds of hardcore and softcore sometimes intersected, with "explicit" artists such as Tom of Finland, "Lowenhaupt," and Art Bob working on both sides of the line. Another kind of intersection is evident here in figure 135, a naughty variation on a coyly softcore image that had been published in one of the physique magazines in the mid-fifties. No doubt many others of these drawings were based on softcore photographic physique models, with appropriate organs and activities added and stirred.

Some artists behind this modest sampling of seventeen softcore images had clearly not yet recovered from the shock of the sudden legitimation of the undraped (though still flaccid) penis in the late 1960s (fig. 221, and well as the loopily kinky Spartacus figs. 230-33). As for Conrad (figs. 221-222) and Carl Corley (figs. 224-226), they are in fact celebrating the necessary subterfuges of an earlier sensibility—the genre I've often called "childlike bachelors at play"—whether through earnest longing, or through pull-out-all-the-stops metaphorical shenanigans, respectively. If, as repeatedly stated in *Out/Lines,* the underground was for a brave minority as opposed to the emerging softcore mainstream, there was no lack of creative ingenuity and sexy fantasy in that world aboveground all the same—as DuBek recognized in his collecting habits.

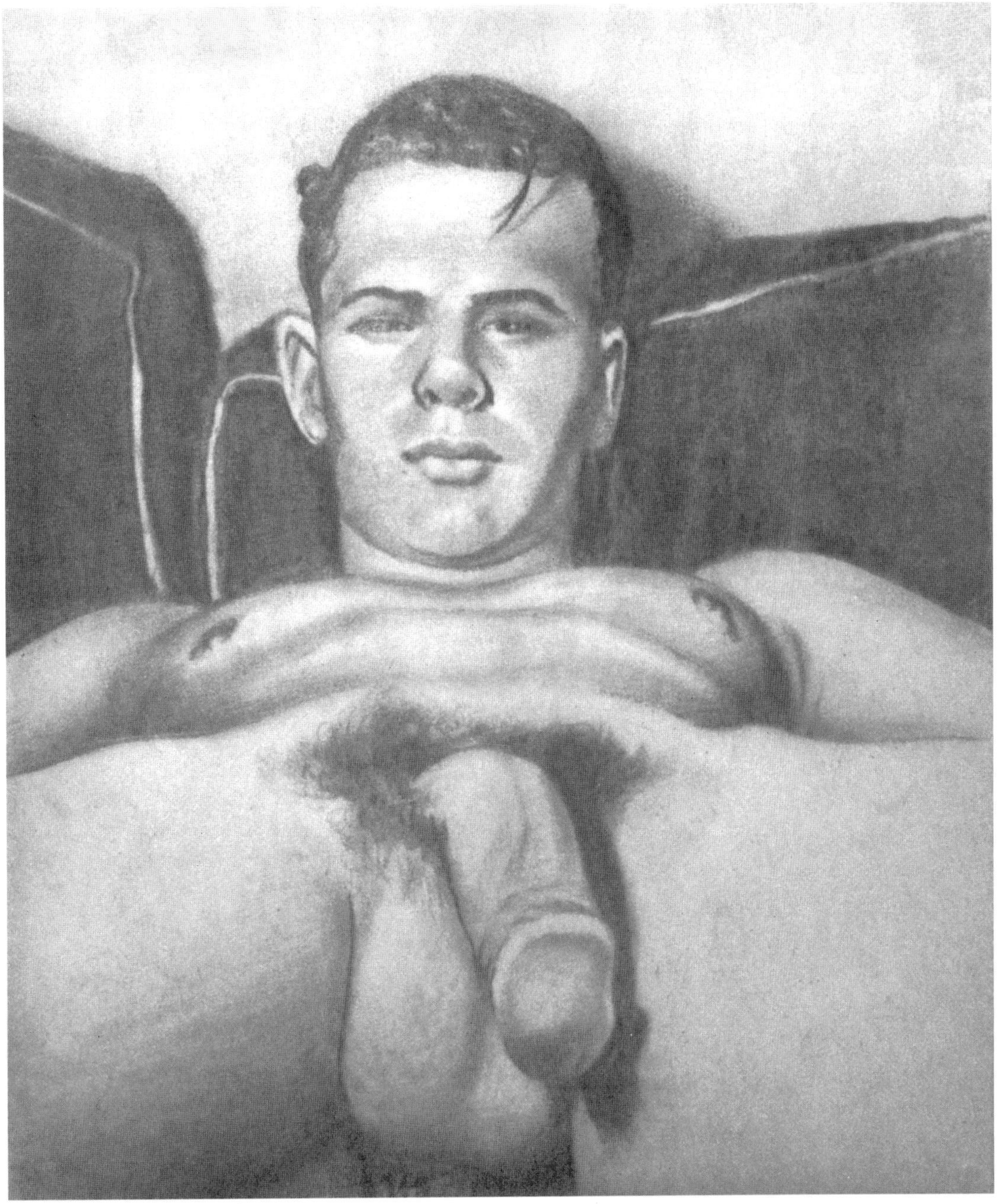

Typical of the sixties for its push towards realism, this lushly romanticized airbrushed crotch shot portrait, apparently inspired by a photo, anticipates the centerfolds of post-Stonewall skin mags in its commodified blandness, but also epitomizes the obsessiveness of licit gay representations at the moment when the penile breakthrough happened. U.S.A., c. mid-1960s.

221

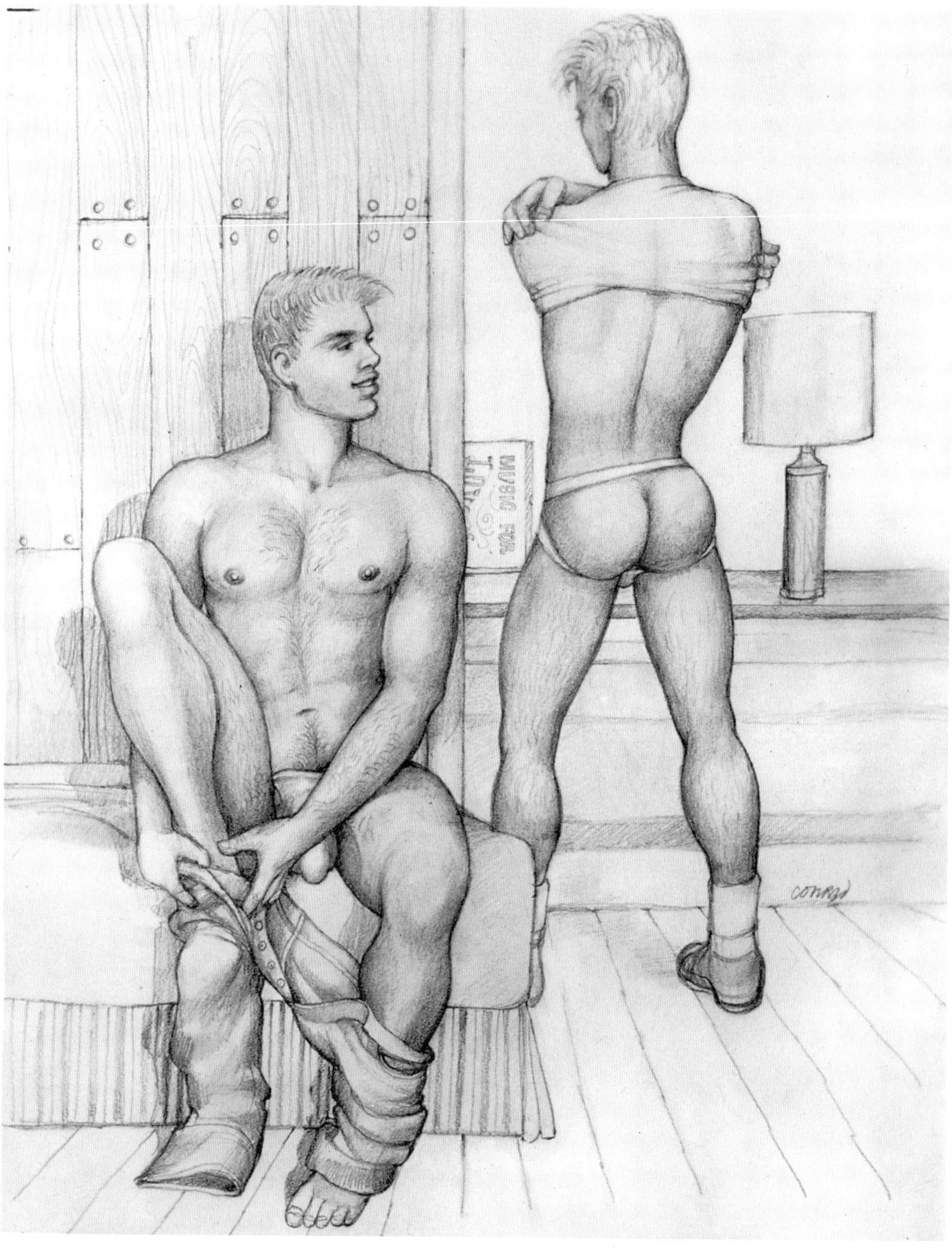

Structured by the coyness of the early 1960s physique marketplace, these images were marketed in sets through the mail by the studio of the British physique photographer Neil Edwards in New York City. Softcore imposed not only a coyness on homoerotic fantasy, but an intense sense of romantic longing, especially around couple images and private shared space. Of course, the album cover, “Music for Lovers”, makes it all explicit, at
222 least in words if not in visual details. Conrad, U.S.A., 1964.

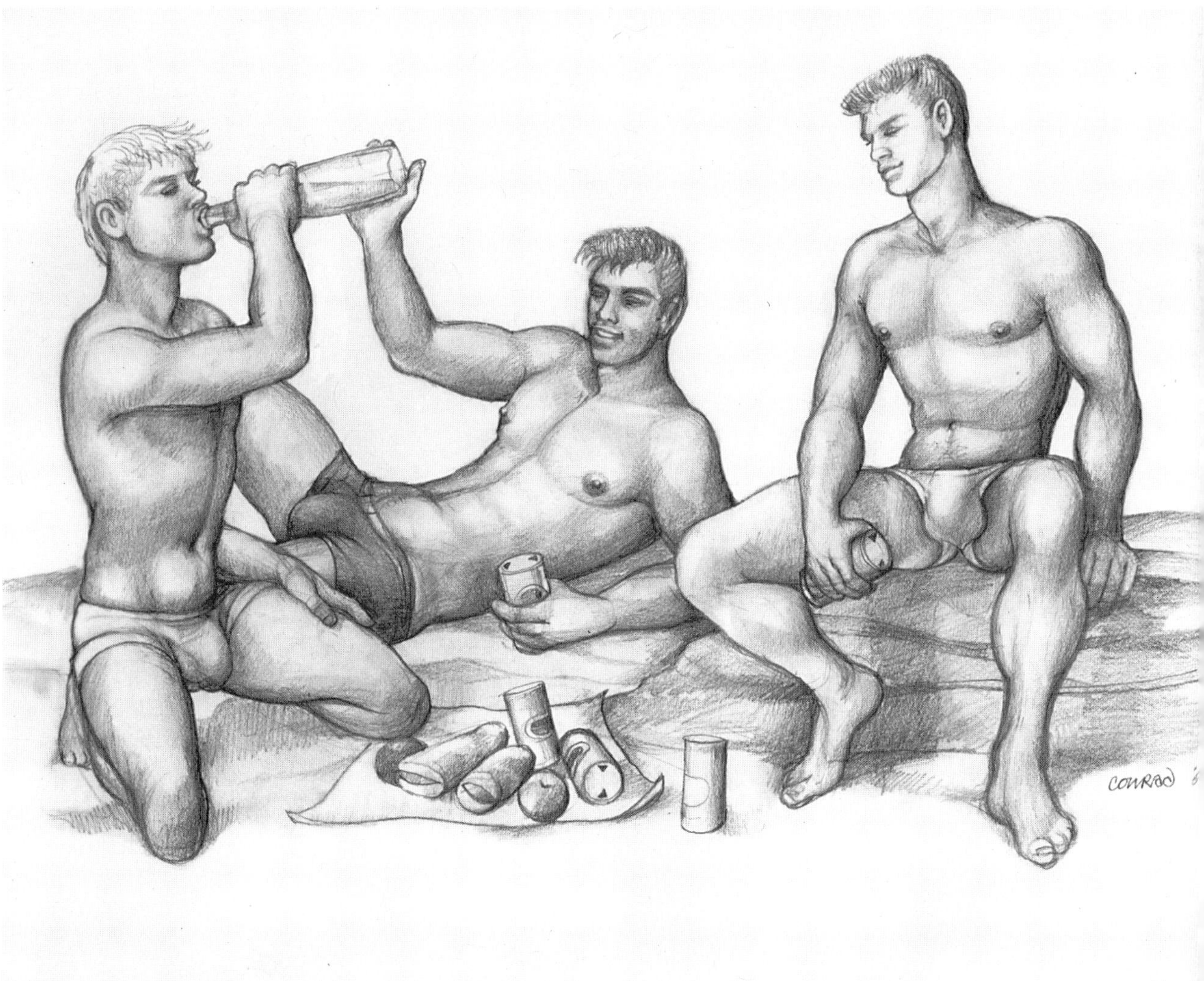

Heartfelt fantasies of comradeship and male bonding, the bulging jockstraps say as much as the phallic sandwiches. Utopian photorealism. This 1964 commercial product is the only work in the entire collection that is dated on the image.

223

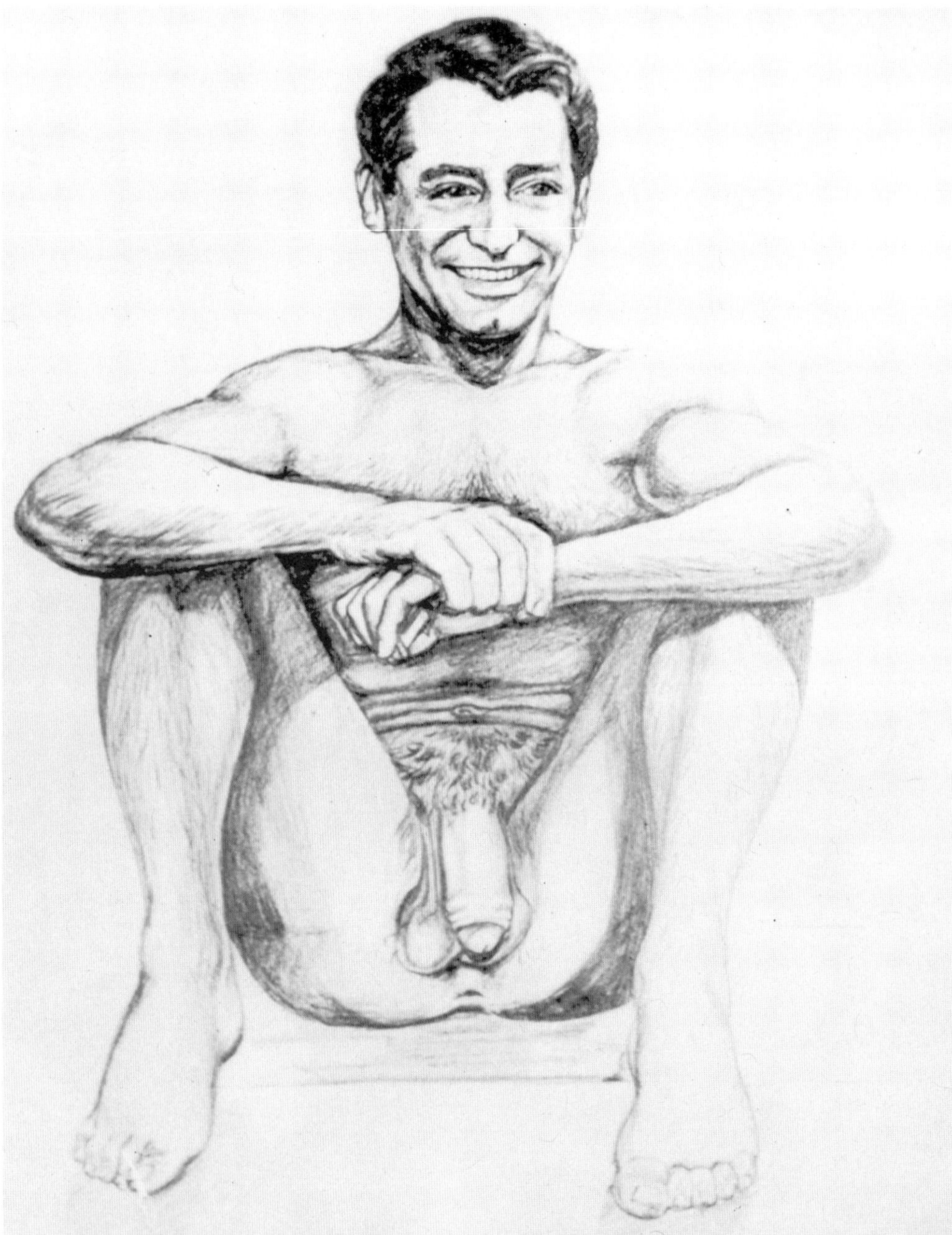

224 Another kind of realism: this well-rendered likeness of Cary Grant's head grafted onto a generic crotch shot nude body was captioned in DuBek's fountain pen, taking note not only of Grant's real name but also implying his real sexual identity. The slight archness, if not bitchiness, of the effect, echoing Grant's well-known tuxedoed squat publicity shot of the 1950s, connotes the collector's familiarity with the sexual hypocrisy of the Hollywood star system and the entertainment world in general. Anon., U.S.A., c. 1960.

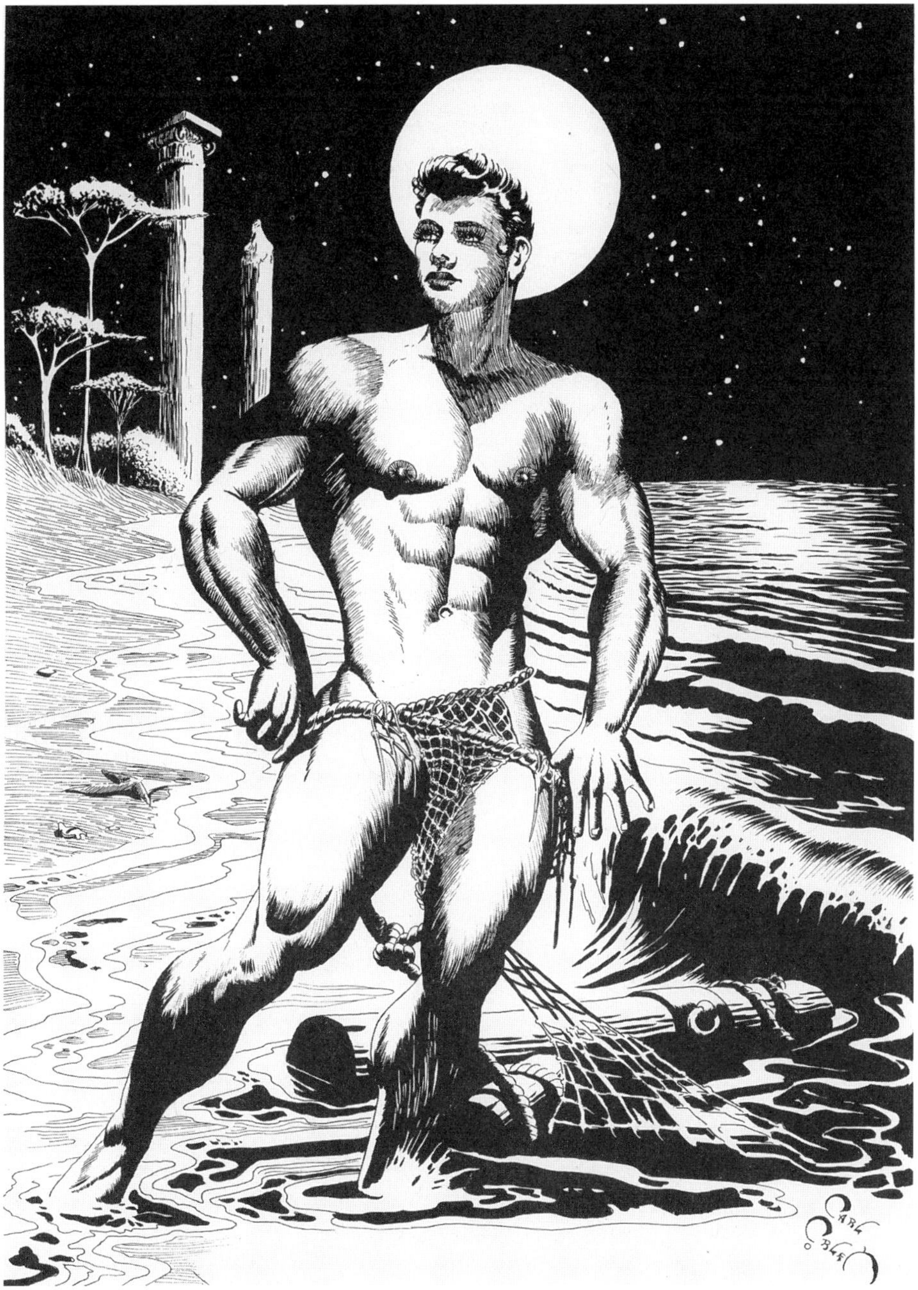

Carl Corley (b. 1921) is the softcore artist whose over-the-top romanticism is one of my discoveries of the
DuBek collection (having momentarily forgotten Falkon's single example [1972, Fig. 21]). Bred in the southern
U.S., the artist behind this hunky hero emerging from his shipwreck with his fetching fishnet posing strap
intact and the moonlit illumination perfect, was according to Falkon a physique artist in the 1950s (Falkon
1972, 47) and became known also in the late 1960s for his gay pulp erotic novels, often cowboy-Indian-themed, 225
with titles like *Sky Eyes* (1967) and *The Purple Ring* (1968), all adorned with his lavish covers. U.S.A., c. 1960.

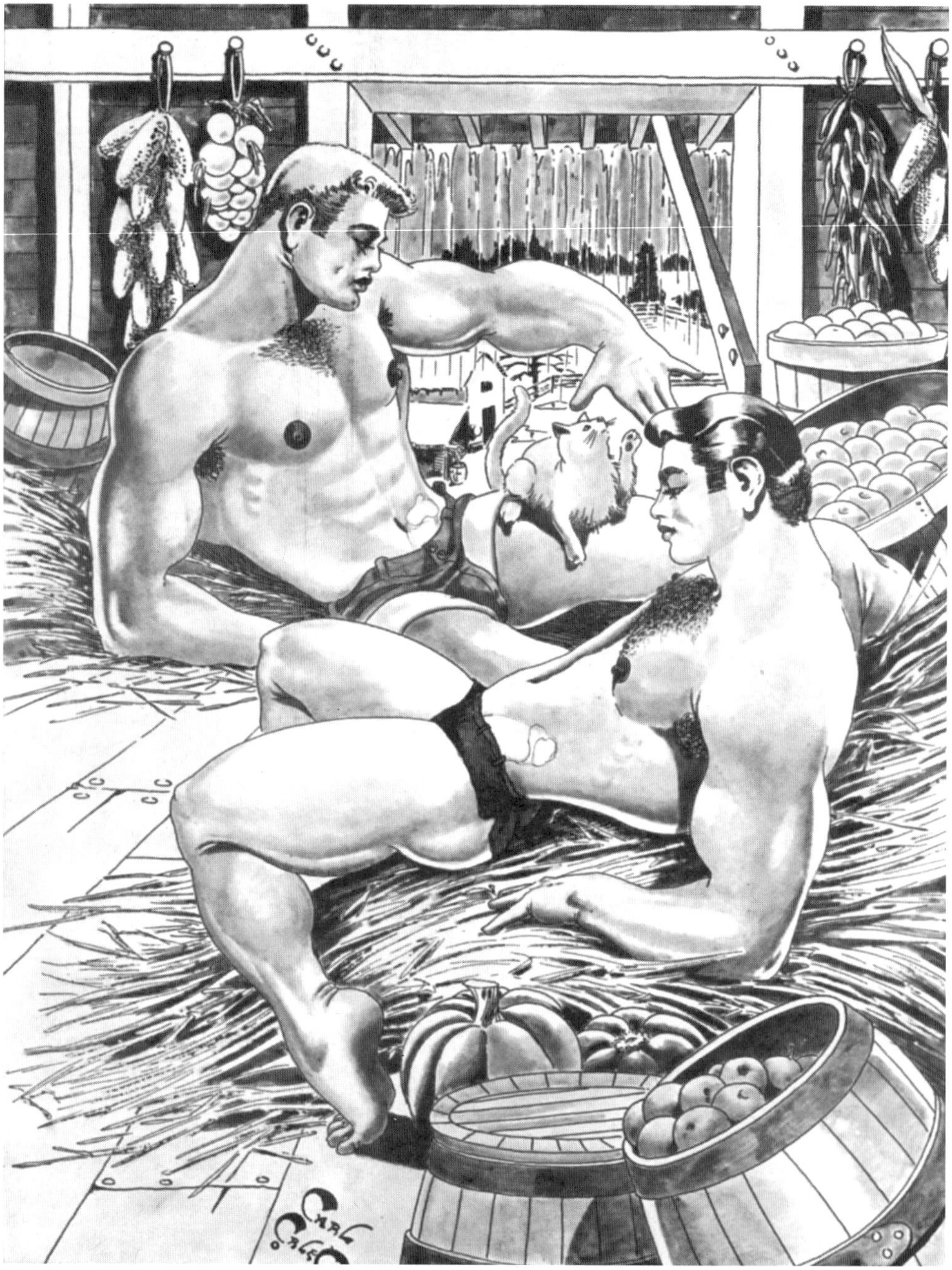

Corley's kitsch-rich frame is bursting with detail as well as with southern pastoral sentimentality. What better way for a rustic couple to while away a rainy September afternoon than to play with kittens in the hayloft? Corley was clearly a gifted pro, obsessive in the perfectionism in his details of water and foliage. DuBek may have acquired his Corley graphics through a Chicago mail order service "Sir Prise Publishers." The artist is
226 profiled and interviewed at length in Howard 1999 and his fiction is excerpted in Bronski 2002.

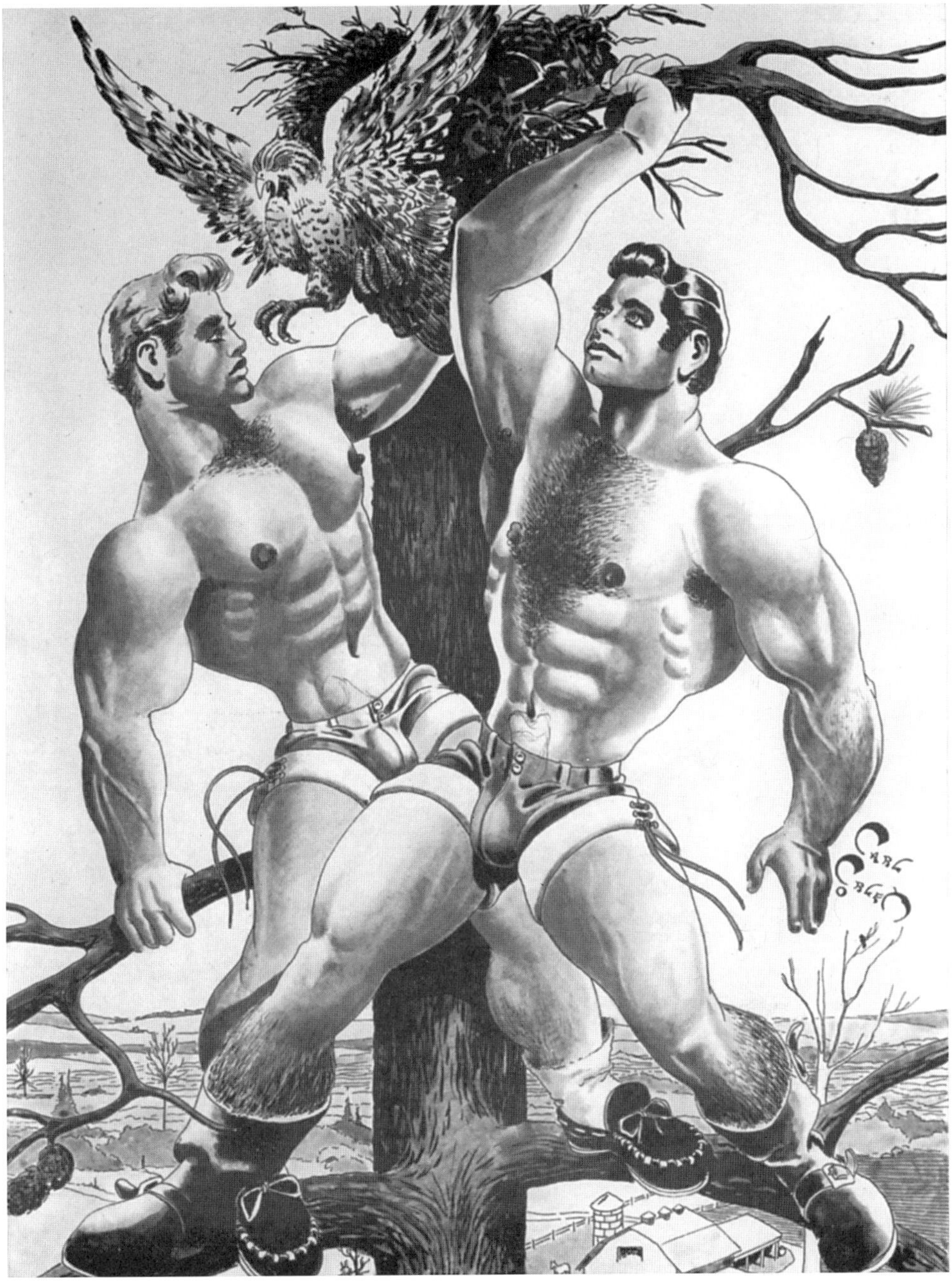

The pumped-up prettyboys, no doubt modelled after physique posing photos, are a little more heroic than in the image opposite, though not overly smart. I don't know how this unique fantasy of treeclimbers attacked by a castrating mother eagle, with the bucolic open farmland down below, fits in with manifest destiny, but I know it does. Who defaced these two images with the protuding penises? Certainly not me: it was hardly necessary
with all the bursting corncobs and pine cones. **227**

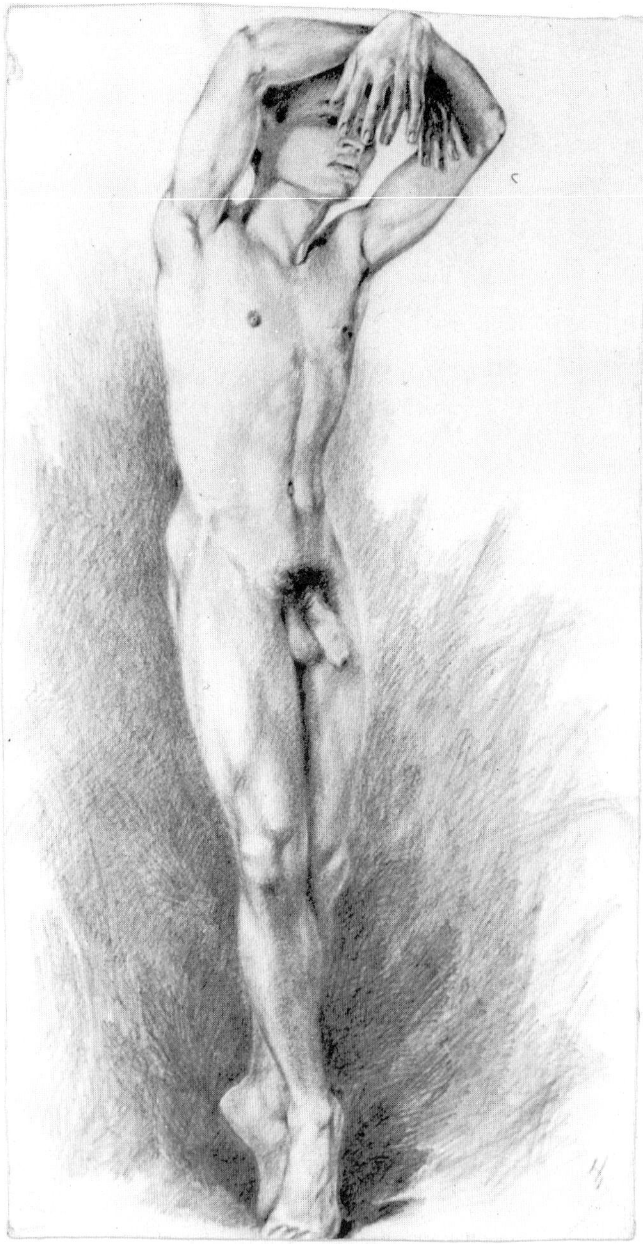

A pair of nudes by Andrey Avinoff, 1884-1948, a wealthy Czarist diplomat who ended up director of Pittsburgh's Carnegie Museum of Natural History for two decades before his death. Better know for his watercolors of wildflowers and orchids, Avinoff evidently excelled also in the tony and idealist soft eroticism that DuBek's friends say was on display in his apartment, putting a respectable face on the thousands of discreetly
228 stowed skin magazines and suck-and-fuck pictures.

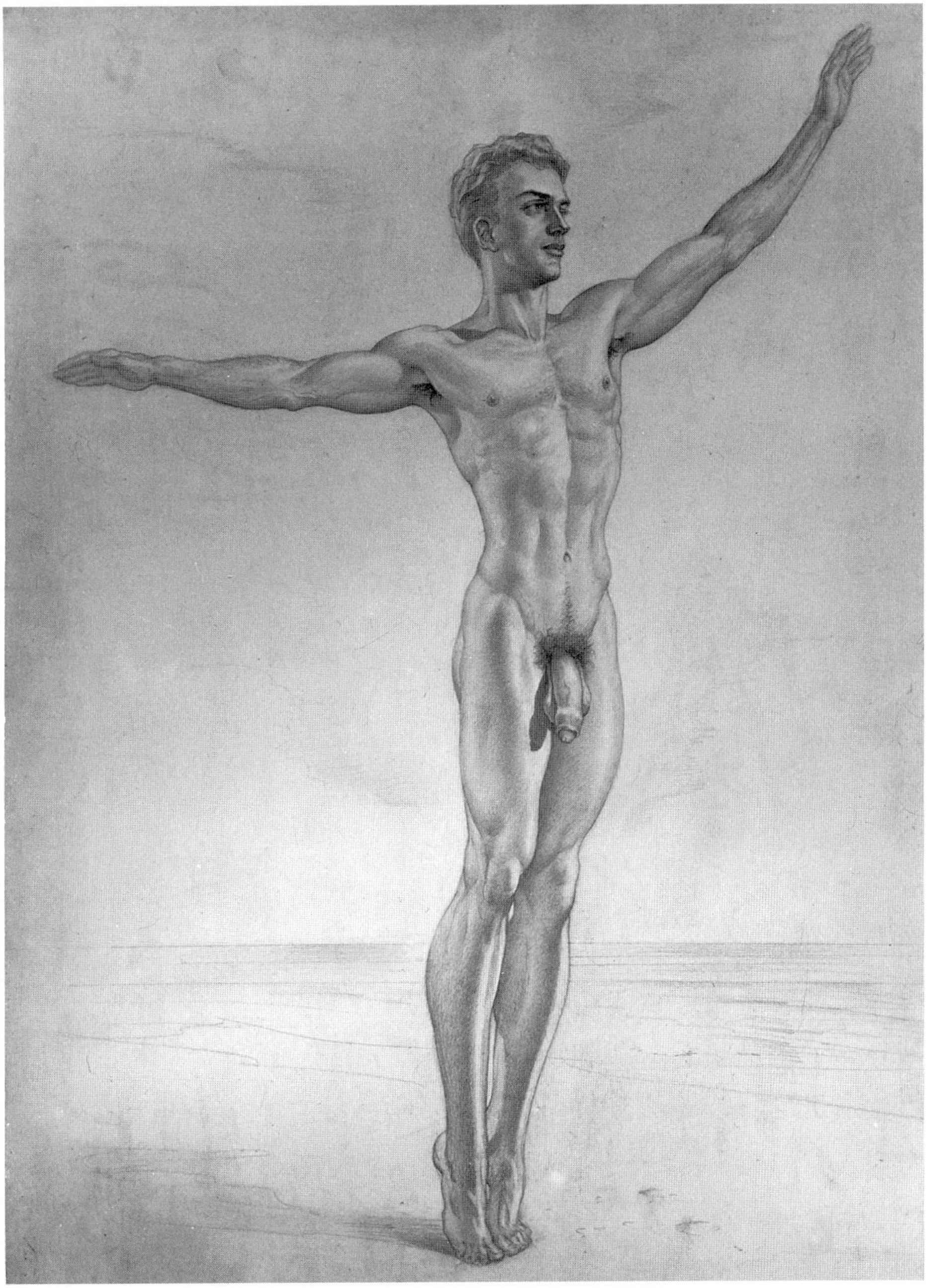

Slim and slightly fey, but still respectably hung, this dancer offers an alternative body type and model of masculinity to the musclebound giants elsewhere in this softcore universe.

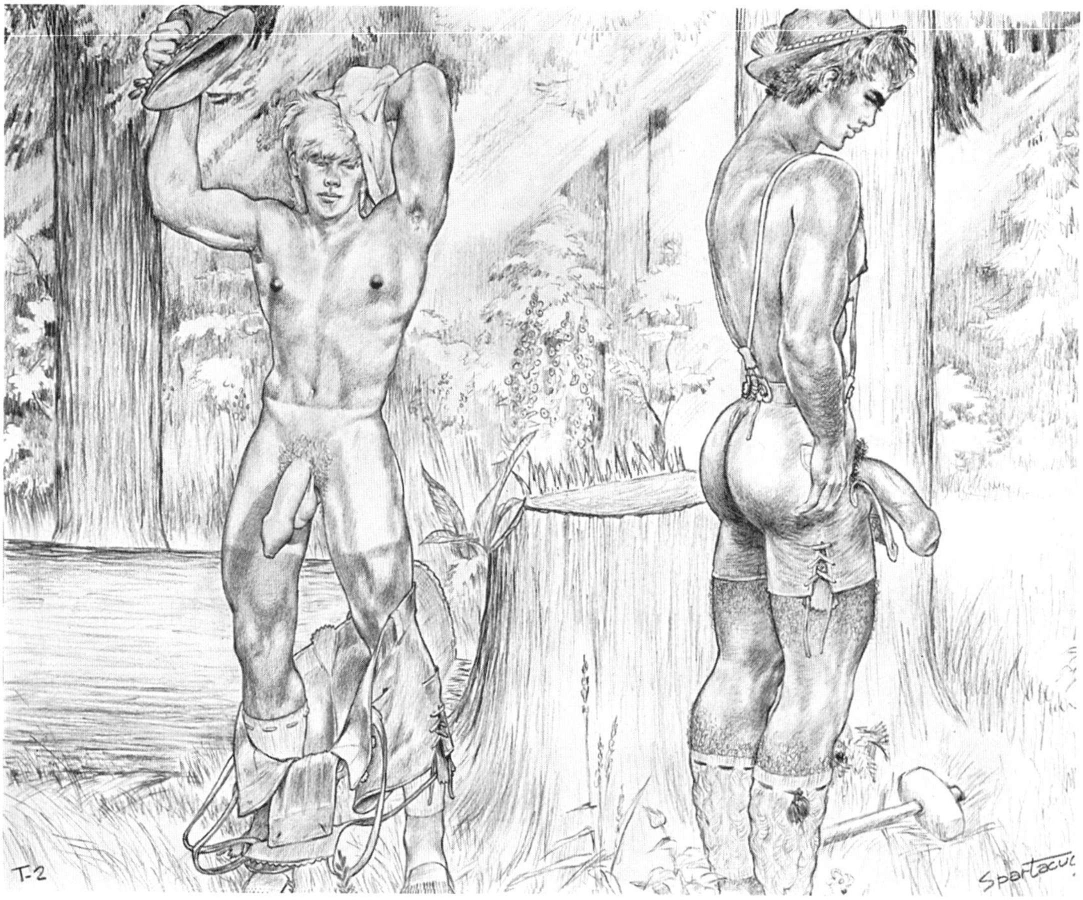

"Tyrolean Mountaineers," 1977. Part of the stable at Athletic Model Guild's *Physique Pictorial* magazine
(Hollywood), Spartacus had been a popular contributor to the softcore magazine's pages and mail order line
since 1958, when he was based in Oregon. When AMG and the whole physique world went full frontal a
decade later, following favorable court decisions, Spartacus followed, making contributions like these to the
230 short-lived "danglie" genre. As photographers and artists from AMG's Bob Mizer to Tom of Finland got used to
their unexpected legitimacy and anatomical freedom, they may have gone ever-so-slightly overboard in the cock
department.

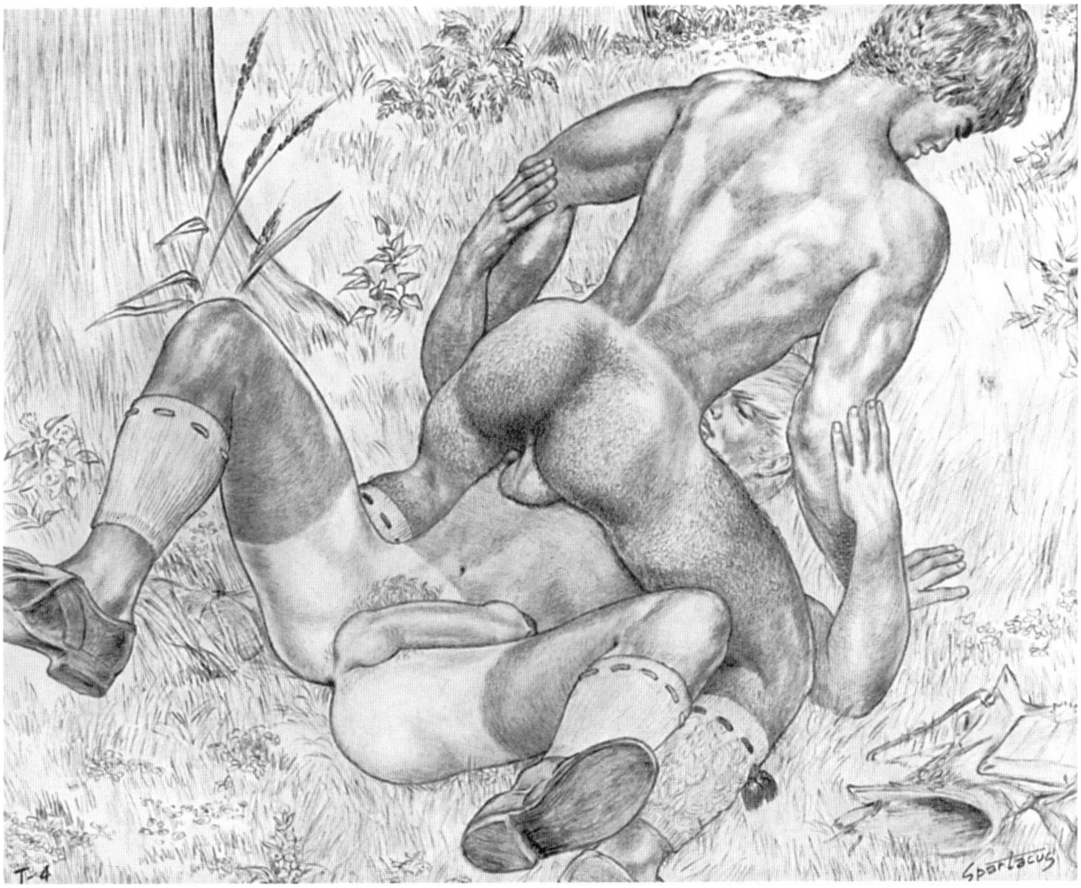

This pair of sylvan fantasies are part of a larger series in which rather infantile but hyperbolically endowed young men, sporting shaggy 1971 haircuts, chop, gambol, undress, bathe, and wrestle in the alpine woods. These six items from the 1970s do not belong to the pre-Stonewall period, strictly speaking, but DuBek apparently relished this fanatical but flaccid silliness that by the mid-seventies was increasingly anachronistic.

231

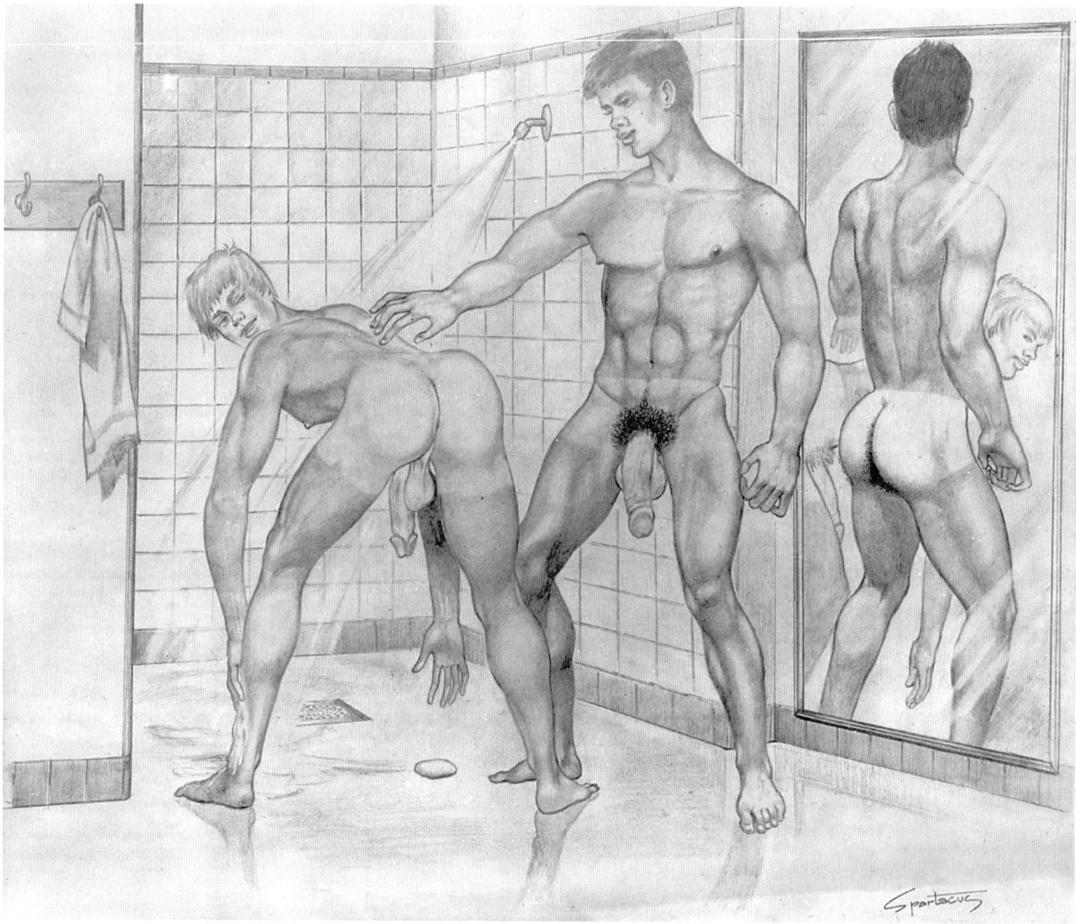

An inspired interpreter of institutions of male bonding, Spartacus's favorite site may have been the athlete's
locker room. Penises had been set free, but Spartacus's fetish body part seems to have been buttocks, complete
with the perfect assholes and fastidious perineums that Mizer was overwhelming his readers with in photog-
raphy at the same time (since he was still not able to use erections). The mirror device in this riff on the hoary
232 old "dropped soap" formula allowed Spartacus to give the golden globes an additional fetishistic frisson.

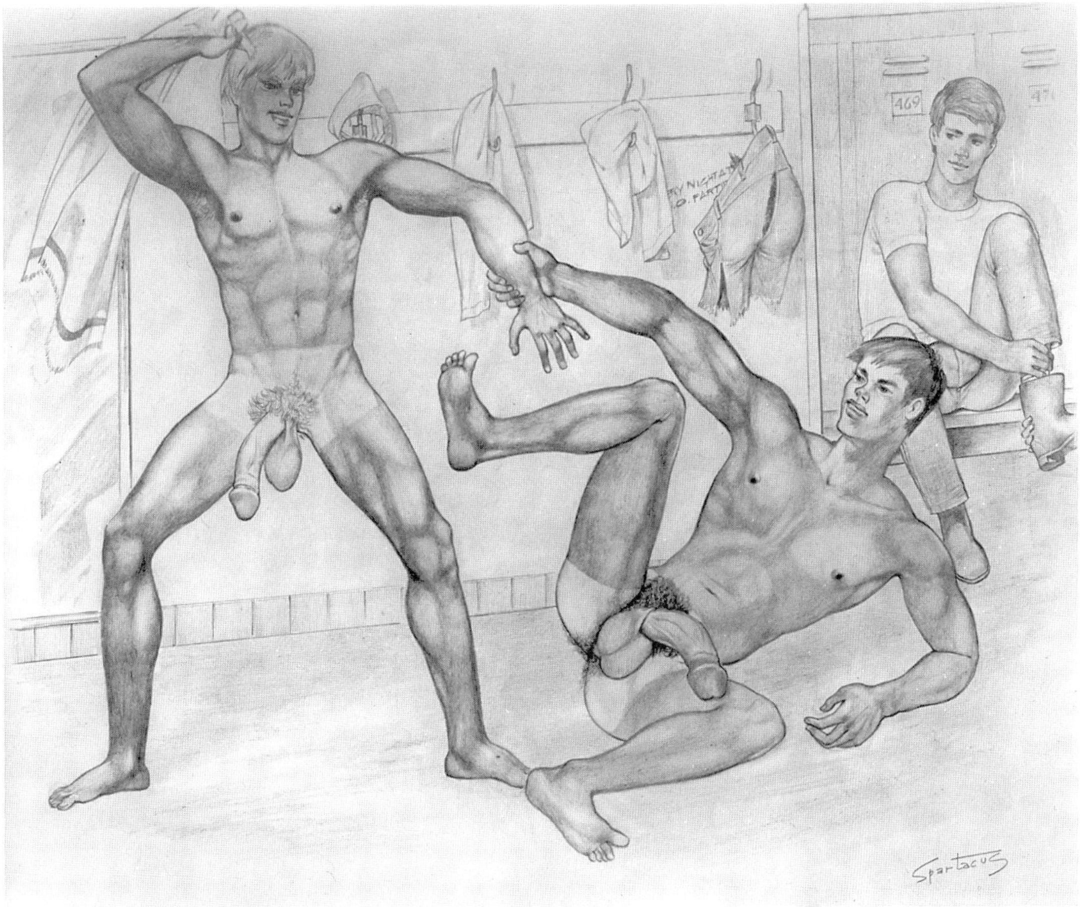

Of course, the soap joke is exactly what the whole series is really about, however strictly it observes the self-censorship codes of the last pre-Stonewall years. Formulaic combat ensues, designed for maximum frontality and visibility.

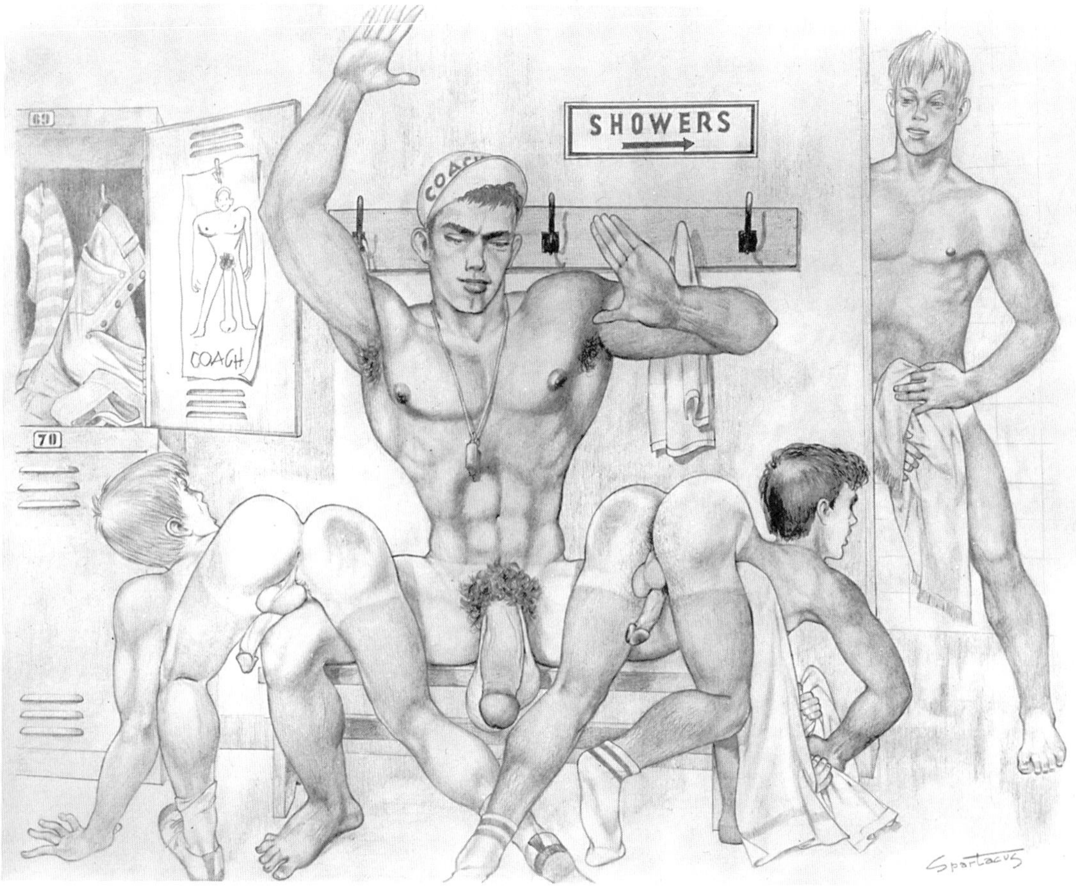

All of this in turn leads to punishment from the father-figure/coach, administered heartily to his fully-grown but child-like charges. These drawings are a product of the imagination, previously published twice (Stanley [1974] 1997). Nevertheless fantasies may become legally equivalent to acts by the time you read this, and the proof of age of these characters, all eighteen of age or older, is held on file at Pleasantville High.

234

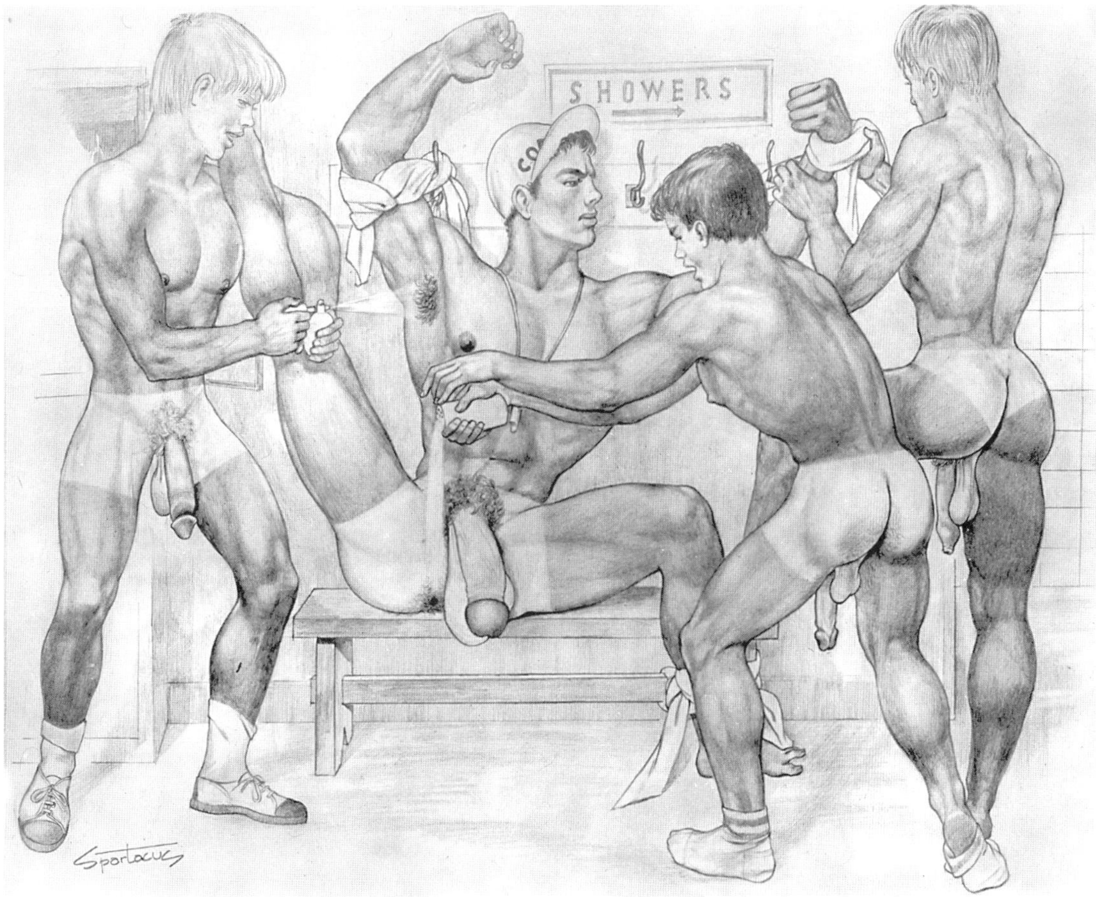

But they revolt, and administer their own kind of punishment, whether perfuming the coach's becoming armpit or tying him up in preparation for a kind of group revenge that is strongly implied but left undepicted.

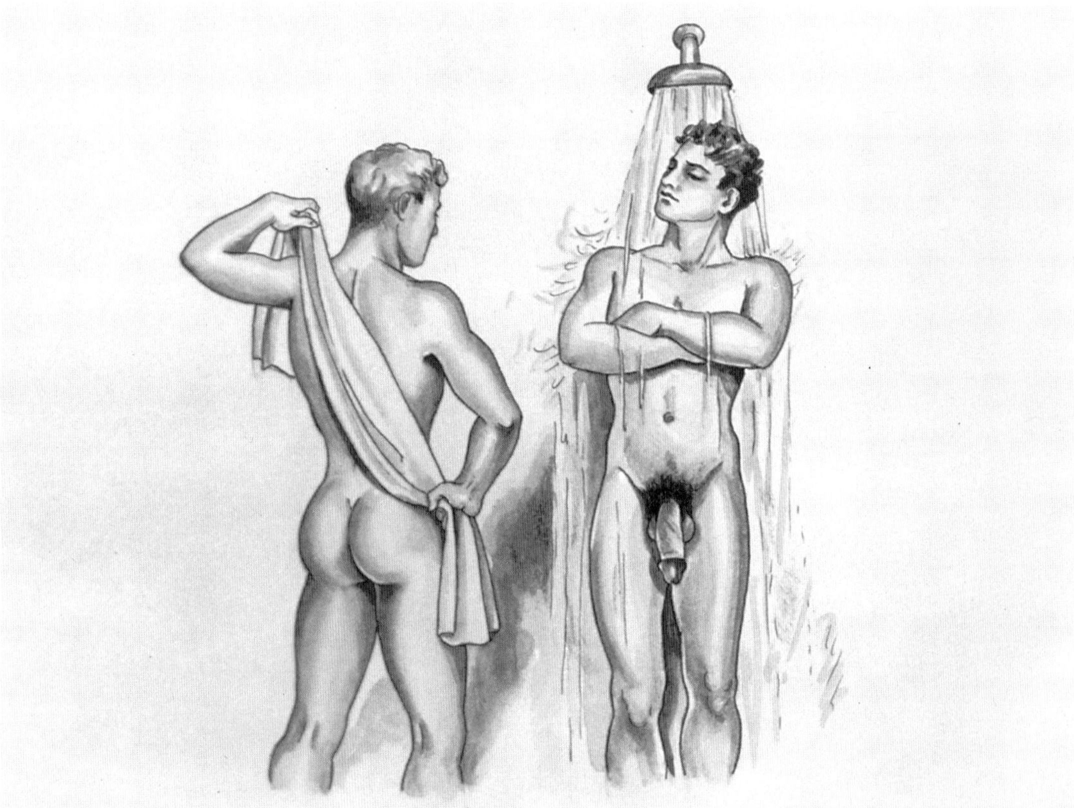

236 The mature Jean Vincent's tame but potent ritualization of voyeurism and exhibitionism through bathing. "Then he got undressed and got into the bath. He has a nice body. Not over-developed. Heavy shoulders, narrow hips. A beautiful little arse. Not hairy. His shoulders are slightly pock-marked with the remains of adolescent spots. As he finished bathing and I thought to myself, 'I'm going to fuck this before we go to the theatre,' the phone rang." Joe Orton, *The Orton Diaries* ([1967] 1986, 149)

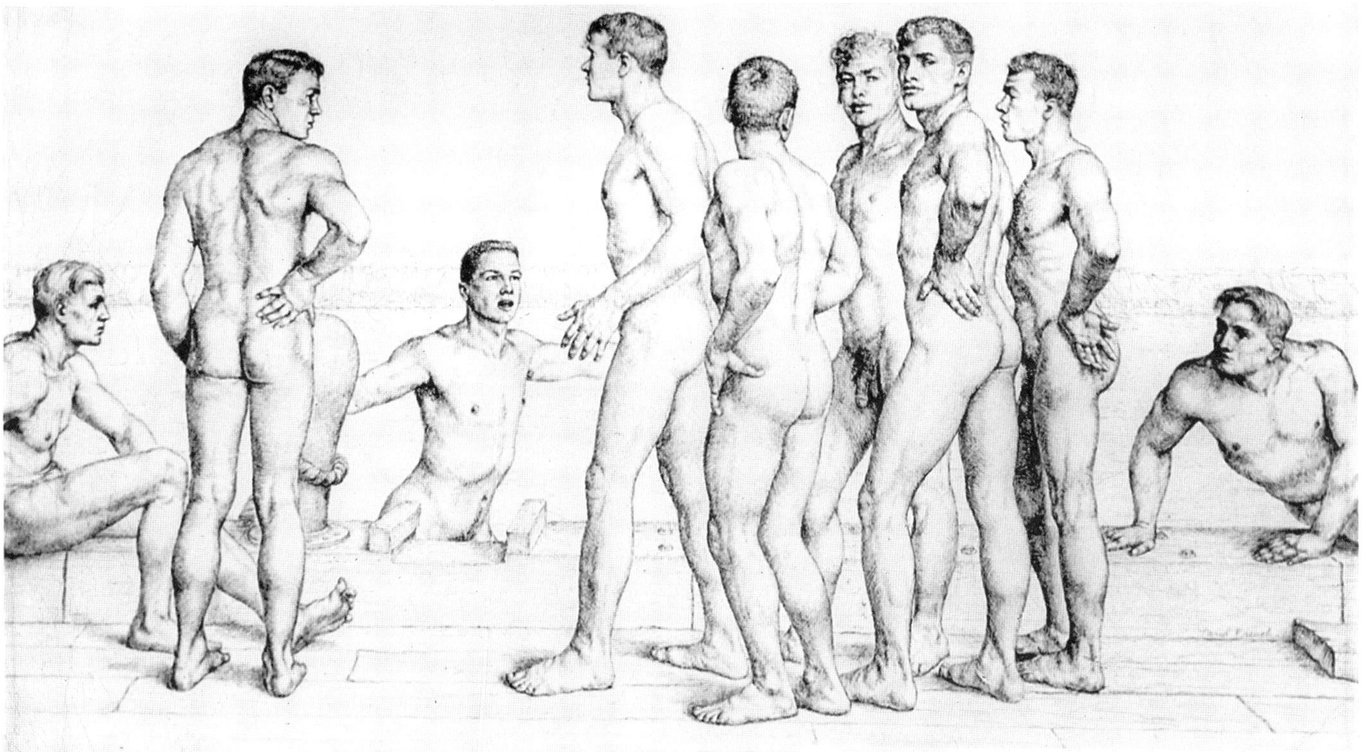

With pictures like this, DuBek took full advantage of the high art alibi. These nine perfect bodies bathing were a sketch for bisexual painter Jared French's 1939 mural about Confederate "Cavalrymen Crossing a River," commissioned for a Virginia post office. (Spring 2002, 16). Inspired, according to Weinberg and Spring, by Michelangelo's study of soldiers at the Battle of Cascina interrupted while bathing (16th century), I think French's mural also nods to an American queer inspiration: "Swimming Hole" (1884) by Thomas Eakins incor- **237**
porates a self-portrait of the artist as nude onlooker as his young friends skinny-dip—a mirror image of the aloof voyeur on the right.

WORKS CITED IN CAPTIONS

Ackerley, J.R. *My Father and Myself.* New York: Coward-McCann, 1968.
Amory, Richard. *Song of the Loon: A Gay Pastoral in Five Books and an Interlude.* San Diego: Greenleaf Classics, 1966.
Anderson, Lindsay and David Sherwin (film, 1968). *If....* New York: Simon and Schuster, 1969.
Andros, Phil (Sam Steward, 1966). *$tud.* Boston: Alyson Publications, 1982.
Auden, W. H. (attrib., c. 1930s). "The Platonic Blow." Unpublished.
Baldwin, James. *Giovanni's Room.* New York: Laurel, 1956.
Bowles, Paul. *Collected Stories, 1939-1976.* Santa Barbara: Black Sparrow Press, 1980.
Cocteau, Jean (1928). *Le livre blanc.* Trans. Margaret Crosland. London: Peter Owen, 1990.
Forster, E. M. (1914). *Maurice.* New York and London: W. W. Norton and Company, 1981.
Genet, Jean (1947; 1953). *Querelle.* Trans. Anselm Hollo. New York: Grove Press, 1974.
Ginsberg, Allen (1968). "Please Master." *The Penguin Book of Homosexual Verse,* ed. Stephen Coote. New York: Penguin, 1983: 338-340.
Goodman, Paul (c. 1968). "Lines." *The Penguin Book of Homosexual Verse,* ed. Stephen Coote. New York: Penguin, 1983: 325-326.
Lorca, Federica Garcia (1934). "Ode to Walt Whitman." *The Penguin Book of Homosexual Verse,* ed. Stephen Coote. New York: Penguin, 1983: 308-312.
Mishima, Yukio (1951). *Forbidden Colors.* Trans. Alfred H. Marks. New York: Berkeley Medallion Books, 1974.
— (1947). *Confessions of a Mask.* Trans. Meredith Weatherby. Norfolk: New Directions, 1958.
Mitchell, James (c. 1969). "Gay Epiphany." *The Penguin Book of Homosexual Verse,* ed. Stephen Coote. New York: Penguin, 1983: 330-331.
Musil, Robert (1906). *Young Törless.* Trans. Eithne Wilkins. New York: Penguin, 1971.
Orton, Joe (1966-67). *The Orton Diaries.* Ed. John Lahr. London: Methuen, 1986.
Pomeroy, Ralph (c. 1969). "The Leather Bar." *The Penguin Book of Homosexual Verse.* Ed. Stephen Coote. New York: Penguin, 1983: 344-345.
Rechy, John. *City of Night.* New York: Ballantine, 1963.
Symons, Scott (1967). *Combat Journal for Place d'Armes.* Toronto: McClelland and Stewart, 1978.
Wescott, Glenway (1938). *A Visit to Priapus.* New York: private printing, Jerry Rosco, 1995.
Vidal, Gore (1950). "Three Strategems." *A Thirsty Evil.* San Francisco: Gay Sunshine Press, 1981: 9-28.
— (1948; 1965). *The City and the Pillar.* New York: Vintage International, 2003.

OTHER SELECT BIBLIOGRAPHY

Angelides, Steven. "Feminism, Child Sexual Abuse, and the Erasure of Child Sexuality." *GLQ: A Journal of Lesbian and Gay Studies,* 10.2 (2004): 141-78.
Bate, Neel ("Blade") (1940s). *The Barn and More Dirty Pictures by Blade.* New York: Stompers/Leslie-Lohman Gallery, 1980.
Benjamin, Walter (1934). "The Author as Producer." *Understanding Brecht.* Ed. Stanley Mitchell. London: New Left Books, 1973.
Beurdeley, Cécile. *L'Amour Bleu.* New York: Rizzoli, 1978.
Bronski, Michael. *Pulp Friction: Uncovering the Golden Age of Gay Male Pulps.* New York: St. Martin's, 2002.

Bruhm, Steven and Natasha Hurley. *Curiouser: On the Queerness of Children.* Minneapolis: University of Minnesota Press, 2004.

(Caillaux, Roland) Cardon, Patrick., ed. (1945). *Vingt lithographies pour un livre que j'ai lu.* Lille: Gai-Kitsch-Camp, 1996.

Cocteau, Jean. *Erotic Drawings.* Ed. Annie Guédras. Cologne: Taschen, 1999.

D'Emilio, John and Estelle B. Freedman. *Intimate Matters: A History of Sexuality In America.* New York: Harper and Row, 1988.

Dyer, Richard. "Coming out as going in: the image of the homosexual as sad young man." *The Matter of Images.* New York and London: Routledge, 1993: 73-92.

Falkon, Felix Lance. *A Historic Collection of Gay Art.* San Diego: Greenleaf Classics, 1972.

Foucault, Michel. "Text/Context of Other Space." *Diacritics* 16.1 (1986): 22-27.

Hohmann, Joachim S. *Der Kreis: Erzählungen und Fotos.* Ed. Erich Lifka. Frankfurt and Berlin: Foerster Verlag, 1980.

Hooven, F. Valentine III. *Beefcake: The Muscle Magazines of America 1950-1970.* Cologne: Taschen, 1995.

—. *Tom of Finland: His Life and Times.* New York: St. Martin's Press, 1993.

Howard, John. *Men Like That: A Southern Queer History.* Chicago: University of Chicago Press. 1999.

Hudson, Mike and Chad Graham. "Censorship: The Big Chill." *The Advocate,* 11 May 2004: 48-53.

Kanfer, Stefan. *A Journal of the Plague Years.* New York: Atheneum, 1973.

Koestenbaum, Wayne. *The Queen's Throat: Opera, Homosexuality, and the Mystery of Desire.* New York: Poseidon Press, 1993: 62.

Leyland, Winston., ed. *Meatmen, Special S&M Comics Edition. Vols. 18 and 24.* San Francisco: Leyland Publications, 1996; 2000.

Lobel, Michael. "Warhol's Closet." *Art Journal.* 55.4 (Winter 1996): 42-50.

Meyer, Richard. *Outlaw Representation: Censorship and Homosexuality in Twentieth-Century American Art.* New York: Oxford University Press, 2002.

Oberlé, Gérard. "Les Frangins et les frégates. -L'Univers de Paul Smara, un artiste à découvrir." (Of brothers and frigates: the universe of Paul Smara, an artist to discover) Sales catalogue, *L'Étude Poulain et le Fur.* Hôtel des ventes du Palais, Palais des congrés de Paris, January 2001.

Silverstein, Dr. Charles and Edmund White. *The Joy of Gay Sex: An Intimate Guide for Gay Men to the Pleasures of Gay Lifestyle.* New York: Crown Publishers, 1977.

Smith, John W., ed. *Possession Obsession: Andy Warhol and Collecting.* Pittsburgh: The Andy Warhol Museum, 2002.

Spring, Justin. *Paul Cadmus: The Male Nude.* New York: Universe, 2002.

Stanley, Wayne., compiler. *The Complete Reprint of Physique Pictorial.* Vols. I (1951-1960); II (1960-67); III (1968-1990). Cologne: Taschen, 1997.

Tagame, Gengoroh. *Gay Erotic Art in Japan: Vol. 1: Artists from the Time of the Birth of Gay Magazines.* Trans. Yuji Kitajima. Tokyo: Pot Publishing Co., 2003.

Thompson, Rachel. "'An Adult Thing'? Young People's Perspectives on the Heterosexual Age of Consent." Special Issue, *Sexualities,* 7.2 (May 2004): 133-149.

Waugh, Thomas. *Hard to Imagine: Gay Male Eroticism in Photography and Film from Their Beginnings to Stonewall.* New York: Columbia University Press, 1996.

—. *The Fruit Machine: Twenty Years of Writings on Queer Cinema.* Durham, N.C.: Duke University Press, 2000.

—. *Out/Lines: Underground Gay Graphics From Before Stonewall.* Vancouver: Arsenal Pulp Press, 2002.

— (2001). "Homosociality in the Classical American Stag Film: Off-Screen, On-Screen." *Porn Studies.* Ed. Linda Williams. Durham and London: Duke University Press, 2004.

INDEX

THE GLBT HISTORICAL SOCIETY

Telling our stories . . .

Preserving our past . . .

Celebrating our 20th anniversary in 2005, the GLBT Historical Society in San Francisco is an internationally renowned center for interpretation and documentation of queer history and culture. We sponsor a lively mix of programs designed to increase public appreciation of gay, lesbian, bisexual, transgender and other sexual minority communities.

Galleries. Two galleries offer exhibits telling the diverse stories of queer life over the past century—tales of finding love and forming families, of surviving tragedies and savoring triumphs, of creating cultures and organizing for rights and visibility.

Archives. An exceptional collection brings together manuscripts, periodicals, photographs, erotica, ephemera and works of art. Scholars, filmmakers, journalists, students and the simply curious use materials to discover the queer history of the Bay Area and beyond.

Talks & Tours. A year-round program of talks by authors, historians and culture-makers brings the exhibits and historical collections to life. And guided tours take visitors into the archives for a behind-the-scenes look at the primary sources of GLBT history.

Website. An award-winning website at www.glbthistory.org features virtual exhibits, historical resources and access to the catalogs of the society's collections.

Making it happen . . .

Located in a city that ranks as a top tourist destination, the GLBT Historical Society reaches out to visitors to enlighten, entertain and create social change by telling the stories of our lives. Our dream is to build the first full-scale museum of queer history and culture in North America—an institution that will rank in every guidebook as a must-see for tourists and locals alike.

As a nonprofit with deep roots in the community, we look to GLBT people and their friends across the U.S. and around the world to help us make this dream a reality. You can make it happen by visiting our current galleries, attending our programs, using our archives—and above all, by supporting the GLBT Historical Society as a volunteer, member and donor.

You're invited . . .

To learn more about the GLBT Historical Society and to become a member, visit our website at *www.glbthistory.org* or call (415) 777-5455. Or visit our galleries and archives at 973 Mission St., Suite 300, San Francisco, CA 91405.

Thomas Waugh, born in 1948 in Ontario, received his PhD in Film Studies from Columbia University and since 1976 has taught film studies at Concordia University, Montreal, where he also developed curriculum on HIV/AIDS and a program in sexuality studies. A programmer and lecturer, his other books are *Comin' At Ya!: The Homoerotic 3-D Photographs of Denny Denfield* (Vancouver: Arsenal Pulp Press, 2007), *Gay Art: A Historic Collection* (Vancouver: Arsenal Pulp Press, 2006); *The Romance of Transgression in Canada: Queering Sexualities, Nations, Cinemas* (McGill Queen's Unversity Press, 2006); *Out/Lines: Gay Underground Graphics from before Stonewall* (Vancouver: Arsenal Pulp Press, 2002); *The Fruit Machine: Twenty Years of Writings on Queer Cinema* (Duke University Press, 2000); *Hard to Imagine: Gay Male Eroticism in Photography and Film from their Beginnings to Stonewall* (Columbia University Press, 1996); and "*Show Us Life*": *Towards a History and Aesthetics of the Committed Documentary* (New Jersey: Scarecrow Press, 1984, 1988).

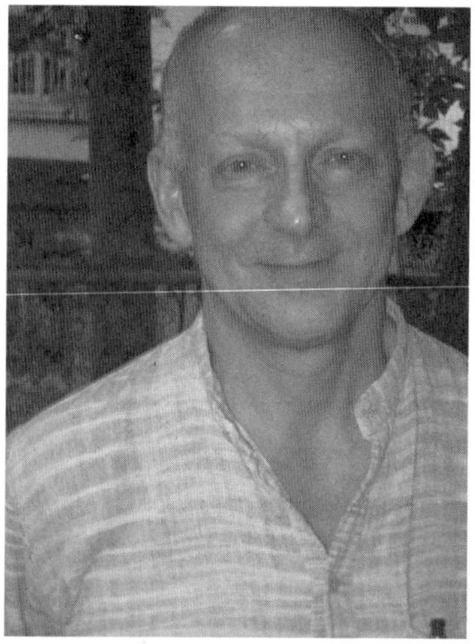

Photo: Babak Salari

Willie Walker (1949-2004) was born in Texas but later moved to Montana where he was trained in the health care field. In 1981, he heard the call from San Francisco, where he continued working in health care and developed an interest in queer community history and began collecting its artifacts. In 1986, he was one of the founding members of the Lesbian Gay Bisexual Transgender Historical Society, one of the leading queer community archives in the world. He continued as a self-taught archivist and pillar of the organization until he withdrew for health reasons in the early 2000s. One of his final responsibilities was the processing and cataloguing of the Ambrose DuBek collection, completed in 2003.

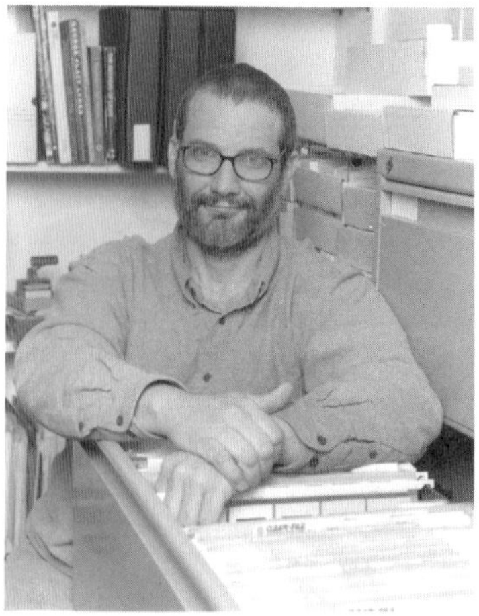

Photo: Daniel Nicoletta

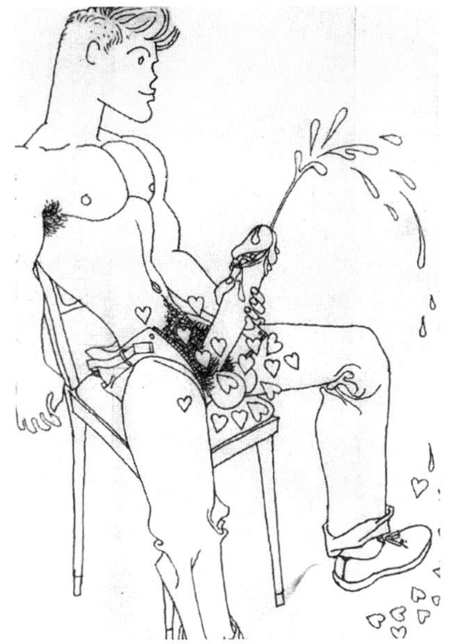